iDentities

PAT CHAPPELL

1

Richmond

TEACHER'S BOOK

Contents

Language Map

		Speaking / Topic	Grammar	Vocabulary / Strategies	Writing
1	1.1	What's the story behind your name?		Family: compound words and phrasal verbs	
	1.2	Do / Did you get along with your parents?	Using *-ing* forms: subjects, verbs, and expressions	Common uses of *get*	
	1.3	How many pets have you lived with?		Suffixes for nouns and adjectives	
	1.4	What difficult people do you know?	Using the infinitive with adjectives: active and passive sentences		
	1.5	Do you still make voice calls?		Developing an argument (1)	An effective paragraph: topic sentences; using connectors
2	2.1	What's most on your mind right now?		Noun modifiers: nouns and adjectives; expressing surprise	
	2.2	Do you worry about your diet?	Using noun, verb, and sentence complements	Expressions for food habits	
	2.3	Who's the smartest person you know?		Describing ability; reference words	
	2.4	Do you enjoy science fiction?	Degrees of certainty: *may, might, must, can,* and *could*		
	2.5	What was the last test you took?		Expressing advantages and disadvantages; agreeing and disagreeing	A for-and-against essay: listing pros and cons, contrasting, and reaching a conclusion
Review 1 *p.26*					
3	3.1	Do you get embarrassed easily?	Narrative style	Physical actions; creating suspense	
	3.2	How often do you take selfies?	Past narration: simple, continuous, and perfect tenses; spoken grammar	Longer numbers	
	3.3	What invention can't you live without?		Words to describe inventions; binomials: repeated words, opposites, and related words	
	3.4	What was your favorite activity as a child?	Describing past habits and states: simple past, *used to*, and *would*		
	3.5	What makes you really happy?			Telling a story (1): linking words to sequence events
4	4.1	Are you ever deceived by ads?		False advertising: phrasal verbs; developing an argument (2)	
	4.2	Are teachers important in the digital age?	Conjunctions to compare and contrast ideas: *although, (even) though, despite, in spite of, unlike, while,* and *whereas*		
	4.3	What was the last rumor you heard?		Time expressions; similes	
	4.4	How would you describe yourself?	Reflexive pronouns with *-self / -selves*; reciprocal actions with *each other / one another*	Avoiding repetition	
	4.5	How many pairs of glasses do you own?		Figurative expressions	A product review: making generalizations
Review 2 *p.48*					

Language Map

	Speaking / Topic	Grammar	Vocabulary / Strategies	Writing
5 5.1	What's your biggest life decision so far?		Collocations with verbs to discuss adversity; building a narrative	
5.2	What would you love to be able to do?	Imaginary situations (1): *wish* and *if only*	Expressing encouragement	
5.3	How important is a college degree?		Expressing negative ideas; prefixes: *over-*, *under-*, and *inter-*	
5.4	Did you make any mistakes today?	Imaginary situations (2): mixed conditionals		
5.5	How lucky are you?			Telling a story (2): using a good range of adjectives
6 6.1	Have you ever Googled yourself?		Verbs and expressions for online privacy	
6.2	Do you worry about privacy?	Using passive structures: *be*, modal verbs, and *have*	Responding to an argument	
6.3	What makes you suspicious?		More privacy words and expressions	
6.4	Are you into social media?	Question words with *-ever*: *who, what, which, when,* and *where*		
6.5	Who do you share your secrets with?			A *how to* ... guide: giving specific directions
Review 3 *p.70*				
7 7.1	How important is music to you?		Success expressions; talking about changing tastes	
7.2	What was your most recent disappointment?	Conjunctions to express purpose and reason: *(in order) to, so (that), as, since, because (of)*, and *due to*	Uses of *so*	
7.3	What's the best movie you've seen?		Failure expressions; words that are nouns, verbs, or both	
7.4	When was the last time you went to a museum?	Modifying nouns: *another, some other* and *the others*		
7.5	Which musician do you listen to the most?			Writing a review: using adverbs effectively
8 8.1	Has fear ever held you back?		Expressing fears; physical symptoms of fear	
8.2	Are you good at improvising?	Describing past ability: *could* and *was / were able to*		
8.3	How much attention do you pay to the news?		Common verb + noun collocations	
8.4	What prevents you from traveling more?	Expressing obligation, permission, and advice: *must / have (got) to, had better, be allowed to, be supposed to*, and *should / ought to*		
8.5	Who do you usually turn to for advice?			A message of advice: using friendly comments for naturalness
Review 4 *p.92*				

Language Map

	Speaking / Topic	Grammar	Vocabulary / Strategies	Writing
9				
9.1	How much time do you spend on your own?	Word order for objects and phrasal verbs	Verbs and expressions for interacting with people	
9.2	What behavior is rude in your culture?	Uses of *which* in non-restrictive clauses		
9.3	What does your age group worry about the most?		Describing attitudes	
9.4	Would you be a good detective?	Reduced relative clauses: active and passive		
9.5	What do you spend the most money on?		Developing an argument (3)	A problem-solution essay: conjunctions to express purpose, to compare, to concede, and to express reason
10				
10.1	How do you like to get around town?		Phrasal verbs; talking about unexpected events	
10.2	What's your idea of a perfect vacation?	Negative questions; indirect questions: *Wh-* and *yes-no*	Forming nouns from phrasal verbs	
10.3	Which foreign country would you most like to live in?		Words with literal and figurative meanings	
10.4	Has your daily routine changed over time?	Talking about acquired habits: *be* and *get used to*		
10.5	Which are your two favorite cities and why?			A travel report: using synonyms and figurative expressions in descriptions
Review 5 *p.114*				
11				
11.1	What recent news has caught your eye?		Words and expressions for talking about the news	
11.2	Have you ever laughed at the wrong moment?	Reporting what people say (1): reported statements and questions		
11.3	What was the last video you shared?		Expressions for emotional reactions	
11.4	What's your definition of gossip?	Reporting what people say (2): reporting patterns with the infinitive and base form	Expressions for gossiping	
11.5	Would you enjoy being world famous?			A letter of complaint: writing a formal email
12				
12.1	How optimistic are you?		Expressing optimism and pessimism	
12.2	Will the world be better in 100 years?	Talking about the future (1): predictions with *going to*, *will*, future perfect and future continuous	Uses of *by*; other ways to make predictions	
12.3	What's the coldest place you've been to?		Expressions for discussing innovation	
12.4	What was the last excuse you made?	Talking about the future (2): expressing plans and intentions, decisions, and scheduled events; time clauses		
12.5	What will your life be like 10 years from now?		Expressions for degrees of certainty	An email to your future self: using adverbs for emphasis
Review 6 *p.136*				

Introduction

iDentities 1 is the first in a ground-breaking, two-level course for adults, younger and older, at Upper-Intermediate (B2) and Advanced (C1). With an eye-catching design, lots of interesting topics and opportunities for personalization in both levels, iDentities, like the English ID series, will help your students progress faster and be able to express their identity in English.

iDentities works either as a free-standing course, or as a natural follow-on from English ID 0-3.

Unique features of iDentities

iDentities offers many familiar features from English ID and adds new ones specifically designed for students at a higher level. These include:

- Two extra units for a total of twelve, with skills development and writing fully integrated into the unit.
- Contemporary, highly original topics that cater to adult learners, both younger and older. iDentities' topics offer truly interesting twists and new angles.
- Challenging listening skills, such as notetaking and making inferences. Listening always leading to speaking on the same topic.
- More challenging **Make it personal** activities that include students' own ideas on a range of topics, enabling them to express their identity more fully in English.
- Pronunciation fully integrated with speaking.
- An increased emphasis on inductive grammar and more focus on the subtleties of language. Students will be able to express themselves with more precision in many different contexts, both formal and informal.
- A new and expanded **Grammar expansion** section with new aspects of structures taught and accompanying activities, as well as unique activities on the grammar of song lines.
- A rich vocabulary syllabus with an expanded focus on phrasal verbs, collocations, idioms, discourse markers, word formation and dictionary definitions.
- New **How to say it** sections that present conversation strategies, formulaic language, and higher level, natural ways of performing functions.
- Increased focus on register contrasts, where relevant.
- More systematic attention to writing with a full page per unit.
- A brand new **Keep talking** section that not only leads into writing, but is preceded by listening, for a rich integrated skills lesson.
- A two-page review unit after every two units for a total of six.

At the same time, the key features of English ID are retained:

- Question titles to open the units, which now serve as schema builders for higher level topics.
- Song lines in every lesson offering relevance to help English come alive.
- **Common mistakes** continued at a higher level.
- A **Make it personal** speaking activity to end every page.
- Visual pronunciation, highlighting stress on syllables, as well as pronunciation activities throughout the book.
- The **World of English** concept, now with specific names for boxes to capture the language points covered.
- Plus the light, humorous style, student-friendly, and teacher-friendly approach, now with a fully interleaved Teacher's Book for easy classroom management.

Like English ID, iDentities will enable your students to be able to express their own identity in English more fluently and with greater accuracy.

If English ID was all about learning to be yourself in English, iDentities is about pushing, developing and polishing your English-speaking self, in order to feel 'at home' in English.

What do upper-intermediate and advanced-level adults expect from an English course?

You might want to note down your own answers before you read on.

Our research suggests that, above all, learners at any level expect:

- to become fluent listeners and speakers as quickly as possible;
- confidence building, quick results, and a strong sense of progress;

- contemporary, interesting content, i.e., real-life, adult relevance with lots of personalization;
- overt teaching of grammar and vocabulary, a systematic approach to pronunciation, plenty of skills practice, and useful study tips;
- an appropriate, adult teaching style combined with strong self-study elements, including autonomous learning tools to speed up their learning;
- value—both for the time they invest and the money they spend.

As students progress in level, they have additional expectations:

- tangible progress—to feel the time they invest in studying continues to reward them with clear results;
- increased focus on accuracy, as well as fluency to give them the necessary self-confidence to express more complex arguments;
- the ability to express themselves with more precision, using a wider range of words, expressions and grammatical structures, leading to fluency and spontaneity in English;
- recycling of familiar structures with new and more subtle distinctions (e.g., perfect tenses, modal verbs, future forms)

Methodology

Like English ID, iDentities is in every sense a communicative course, teaching learners to speak in as short a time as possible and focusing on both fluency and accuracy. You will note, for example, the large number of speech bubbles and the **Common mistakes** (with anticipated errors that should be avoided) presented in most lessons.

Learners need to be given opportunities to express their own ideas and opinions. English ID and iDentities progressively adapt as the series evolves to reflect the best learning practices at each of the learner's advancing levels. By the upper-intermediate and advanced levels, there is an increased focus on levels of formality, as a student's need to master various registers gradually increases.

The same goes for the lexis—where the initial simple task of matching vocabulary to pictures in the early levels of English ID becomes more abstract and contextualized in iDentities—and grammar, where spoon-feeding is reduced and inductive learning increased, as learners' confidence and foreign language learning experience grow.

iDentities provides the tools to allow you, the teacher, to incorporate your own pedagogical identity into the course, as well as to emphasize what you think will be more relevant for your learners.

Flexi-lessons

iDentities follows on from English ID to offer a unique flexi-lesson structure because one lesson is never enough to practice and consolidate all of its content. iDentities, therefore, gives students more opportunities than most books to revisit, consolidate or extend what they first learned in the previous lessons.

Constant and consistent recycling of language is essential for memorization, making learning much more likely. iDentities regularly builds bridges between lessons rather than packaging lessons in 'artificially tidy' units just to fit a notional design. Besides, every lesson / institution / teacher is different, with its own identity. A lesson structure where there is little or no connection between lessons is unlikely to foster efficient or optimum learning—hence our flexi-lessons. As students are now at a higher level, you will also notice that topics are pursued in more depth, with sub-themes of broader topics developed through the unit.

Key concepts

English promotes the three friendlies: it is language-friendly, learner-friendly and teacher-friendly.

1. Language-friendly

iDentities, like English ID is not just another international series. It is a language-friendly series, which embraces students' existing language knowledge and background, to help them better understand how English works.

2. Learner-friendly

iDentities respects the learner's need to be spoken to as an adult, so students explore a full range of topics requiring critical thinking. iDentities also helps students to negotiate and build their own new identity in English.

In addition, iDentities:

- supports students, helping them avoid obvious errors in form, word order and pronunciation;
- motivates students, as they discover they can recognize a lot of English, which they already have 'inside themselves';

- offers a vast range of activities, resources and recycling in order to ensure students have enough practice to finally learn to speak English.

3. Teacher-friendly

iDentities respects each teacher's need to teach as he or she wants to. Some wish to teach off the page with minimal preparation, others dip in and out, while others largely follow the Teacher's Book. All these options have been built into iDentities from the start.

The flexi-lesson structure helps teachers to individualize, personalize and vary classes, as well as focus on what is important for them.

The Teacher's Book has a teaching-friendly visual code, providing a straightforward 'quick route' or a substantially longer one. Everything that is essential is clearly separated from all the optional extras.

Key features

1. A 60-question syllabus

Every lesson begins with a question as the title, which serves as a natural warm-up activity to introduce and later review each lesson topic. At the high-intermediate and advanced levels, these questions serve the very important role of schema building, as topics logically become more complex, varied, and include more real-world information.

Therefore, these questions offer:

- an introduction to the lesson topic, an essential component for a good lesson, as, in some cases, topics may be new to students;
- a short lead-in to create interest, paving the way for the integration of skills, grammar, and content;
- an opportunity for students to get to know and feel comfortable with each other before the lesson begins, facilitating pair and group work.

2. A balanced approach to grammar

Our rich grammar syllabus offers an eclectic approach to meet the needs of all students. It offers an innovative combination of:

- inductive grammar, with students discovering patterns and completing rules for themselves in and around the lesson-page grammar boxes;
- deductive grammar, through interesting facts about language and regular reminders of key rules, in addition to important usage notes;
- a discrete degree of proactive, contrastive grammar analysis, by showing what not to say via **Common mistakes**;
- a wide variety of extra grammar practice in review units, the Workbook, on the Richmond Learning Platform, as well as suggestions for extra contextualized writing in the Teacher's Book.
- a new **Grammar expansion** feature at this level, containing 24 pages of explanation and exercises (two per unit) focusing on more advanced language points. This section can be done in class, or assigned as homework. The corresponding core lesson is indicated in each case.

3. It has to be personal

Each phase of every lesson (and most Workbook lessons) ends with **Make it personal** activities: real, extended personalization—the key stage in any language practice activity. Students expand all topics and main language items into their own lives, opinions, contexts, and experiences. This is how students continue to construct and consolidate their English identity. Successfully 'making it personal' is what makes students believe that they can be themselves in English.

4. Avoid common mistakes to speak better, more quickly

Most lessons include **Common mistakes**, a flexible resource to foster accuracy. We highlight what to avoid before, during and / or after any lesson. **Common mistakes** helps maximize self- and peer-correction too. Students are enabled to help and teach themselves, by anticipating and therefore more quickly avoiding, reviewing and remembering typical learner errors. At the high-intermediate and advanced levels, these sections help reinforce language as it is taught, thereby avoiding L1 transfer and fossilization.

If short of time, as teachers so often are, **Common mistakes** can help you cut through a longer, more inductive presentation and get to the practice activity more quickly.

5. Integrated skills

The fifth lesson in each unit is an integrated skills page, which gives students the opportunity to immerse themselves in a highly-engaging, contemporary topic and practice all four skills in real-world activities.

6. Useful language boxes

Teachers who have used English ID will be familiar with **World of English** boxes throughout the book that highlight interesting and useful language points. In iDentities, these boxes have been made more specific. They now have exact names like *Common uses of* get, *Types of noun modifiers*, or *More about* can *and* could, which immediately focus student and teacher attention on the point covered, enabling classes to use their time more efficiently.

7. Classic song lines to 'hook' language

iDentities continues on from English ID with its use of music in exercises, cultural references, images, and, most obviously, the authentic song lines in each lesson. In addition, music as a theme features prominently in several lessons.

Why music? Songs are often the most popular source of authentic listening practice in and out of class. Most students have picked up a lot of English words through songs, theme tunes to TV programs, etc. But often they don't realize they know them or the exact meaning of what they're singing.

The song lines empower both teachers and students by offering useful language references and pronunciation models; and an authentic source of student-friendly input to elicit, present, practice, personalize, extend and 'hook' almost anything.

Unique to English ID and iDentities, the song lines have a direct link to each lesson, whether to illustrate grammar, lexis or the lesson topic, and are designed to provide an authentic hook to help students remember the lesson and the language studied. Students may also enjoy the fun, **Language in song** bonus activities in the **Grammar expansion** section.

iDentities Teacher's Book offers a useful **Song activities** bank of cultural, background and procedural notes for every song line, including the artist's name, suggestions on exactly where and how to exploit it, and optional activities. You can find this useful resource on pages 334-348.

Tip

We don't suggest you use these songs in full. Many aren't actually appropriate when you look at the complete lyrics, but the lines we've chosen are globally famous and should be easy to identify, find on the internet and be sung by at least some students. Obviously, with your own classes you can exploit the song lines in a variety of ways.

Some ways to use song lines in iDentities:

- Play / show (part of) the song as students come into class
- Sing / hum the song line and / or look for links to the song at an appropriate time during the class to help students remember the lesson later
- Read and guess the artist's gender, message, etc.
- Analyze the song for pronunciation: rhyme, repeated sounds, alliteration
- Expand. *What comes before / after this line? What's the whole song about?*
- Change the tense and see how it sounds. *Why did the artist choose this tense?*
- Provoke discussion around a theme / issue
- *What do you associate the song with?* E.g., a moment, vacation, dance, movie
- Search online for other songs that connect to the lesson in some way
- Use sections of the song as a class warm-up, review, listening for pleasure, an end of the lesson sing-along, etc.

Course structure and components

Nowadays, English courses may be too long or inflexible, meaning teachers have either to rush to get through them—denying students the practice they need to achieve an adequate degree of fluency—or start omitting sections, often leaving students feeling frustrated. iDentities was designed to be flexible, so you can tailor it to fit your timetable. It provides 80-100 class hours of teaching.

iDentities has...

- twelve core units, each comprised of five approximately one-hour lessons. That's 60 lessons containing listening, grammar, vocabulary, speaking, reading, and writing
- authentic video in selected lessons
- twelve one-page Writing lessons, to be done in class and / or at home
- six two-page Review lessons, for use in class and / or at home
- 20 pages of Grammar expansion + corresponding exercises
- selected audio scripts that encourage students to focus on specific listening points
- a comprehensive list of separable and inseparable phrasal verbs and their meanings
- Workbook: one page of review and extra practice material per lesson

- Richmond Learning Platform for iDentities, which can be accessed using the code on the inside front cover of the Student's Book
- Digital Book for Teachers: IWB version of the Student's Book

Vocabulary

iDentities focuses on high-frequency words and expressions in context, and provides a variety of word-building tools, including a 3-page **Phrasal verb list** on page 165 of the Student's Book. This summarizes the most common phrasal verbs used in English and is a great resource for cover-and-test-yourself memorization, as well as a 'mini dictionary' for reading and listening. If time permits, encourage students to write what are often the more formal Latinate equivalents alongside them in pencil and learn both.

By limiting new vocabulary sets to only seven items per section, iDentities ensures that students are never overloaded and will transfer to their productive use the new words and expressions presented.

Skills

Speaking

iDentities teaches spoken English and prioritizes oral fluency.

In order to learn both quickly and well, students should be given every opportunity to try to express their ideas and opinions in comprehensible English at every stage of every lesson. In iDentities every lesson , be it a listening, vocabulary, grammar, reading or writing focus, is full of controlled oral practice and personalized speaking opportunities, clearly marked and modeled by multiple speech bubbles on every page.

iDentities offers fluency, accuracy and pronunciation practice at every opportunity. **Keep talking** sections consolidate and put into practice the language learned and lead directly into **Writing** on the facing page, where students can choose from among topics they've already discussed. This significant unique feature not only encourages the integration of skills, but develops the very important skill of distinguishing levels of formality and registers. The presentation of more formal language and register contrasts is expanded further in iDentities 2.

Finally, at the upper-intermediate and advanced levels, the importance of language strategies and speech acts increases, as anyone who has to function in a foreign language begins to realize. 'Fluent' English consists of far more than grammatical sentences. For that reason, iDentities offers a new **How to say it** section, which highlights expressions and responses especially useful for managing conversations successfully.

Listening

iDentities has more listening than most other high-intermediate and advanced courses: frequently 13 to 16 activities per unit that include scripts of increasing length, more challenging activities focusing on inference, as well as gist and detail listening, and numerous 'Listen to check' activities that provide additional language information for students.

Listening homework should be set as often as possible as what students most need is to spend the maximum time in the company of English in order to become truly confident when expressing themselves in English. These days this is relatively easy—they can listen whilst doing other things, at home, traveling, at the gym, etc.

In addition to the material included in the course itself, teachers may find some of the following suggestions helpful, either in or out of class:

- have students create their own listening practice at this level—listening to music or podcasts, watching TV or movies, using bi-lingual websites to work out what words mean, etc.
- dictogloss short sections of any listening activity—listen and remember (or write down) all you can, then compare in pairs.
- pause mid-listening to check comprehension

If time permits ...

- sensitize students to how words blur and have a variety of sound shapes in connected speech
- explain how pronunciation changes
- expose students to 'the difficult', e.g., phoneme variations in connected speech; dictate multiple examples of weak forms
- model processes used by L1 listeners: decoding sounds into words / clauses and building larger scale meaning
- transcribe elision as they hear it: old people = *ole people*, a blind man = *a bly man*, etc.
- study and interpret, e.g. pairs: *He said he called* vs *He said he'd call*

The following are some ideas for listening homework that you could set your students:

- Listening to recordings of the class itself (flipped)—instructions, stories, pair work, roleplay, etc.

- Web-based listening: songs, podcasts, YouTube, radio, audio books, TV (with subtitles in L1 & L2)
- Homework partners—call / record messages, check answers with partner, dub favorite movie scene, etc.

Reading

In iDentities, reading texts become longer and in iDentities 2 will consist almost exclusively of authentic material. To prepare students to read such material, both levels include a wider range of reading skills. Activities focus on such areas as pronoun reference; new lexical sets where students can see words and expressions in context; predicting; capturing the essence of a section and the author's intention; and perhaps most importantly, interacting with the content of the text. **Make it personal** activities in **Reading** lessons allow students to react to and evaluate the author's ideas by presenting their own.

Writing

The fifth and final lesson in each unit is different from the others. The first page leads to a substantial **Keep talking** activity; the second is dedicated to process writing.

Our writing syllabus is primarily covered by these twelve activities, with twelve different genres and additional attention to writing in the Review units and Workbook. Here students are given a clear written model, a variety of tasks to analyze it, specific writing tips and a structured model to draft, check, then share with a classmate, before finally submitting it to you or posting on the class learning platform / wiki. The intention is to protect you, the busy teacher, from having to dedicate time to excessive marking of avoidable mistakes, as well as to help students be more in control of their own writing.

The left-hand page of each lesson introduces the topic through listening, via genres such as radio shows, lectures, or dialogues. Additional development of listening skills then moves into open-ended speaking, the **Keep talking** section that synthesizes the unit through discussion, personalized role-playing, surveys, or problem-solving situations. This section frequently presents **How to say it** expressions to facilitate the activity.

Each lesson then ends with a process writing activity, twelve in total. While it's harder and harder to get students writing meaningfully these days, it remains a critical activity and a key component of most communicative exams. It's also a skill that students may need in the future if they ever use English for personal or work-related communication. Therefore, a unique feature of iDentities is to include only authentic genres in the twelve units.

- Tasks simulate 'real-life' writing as closely as possible, and in every case, a full model is provided.
- A clear step-by-step guide as to how to create a similar writing is given.
- **Write it right** sections and the *Before, While, After* format continues from English ID.

Pronunciation

To the extent that you choose to work on pronunciation, any of the following ideas may be helpful:

- Emphasize the relevance of the pronunciation tasks to improve listening comprehension and increasingly natural sounding English.
- Make sure students understand that their pronunciation does not need to be 'perfect' or 'near native', but it does need to be clear and facilitate communication.
- Explore what students already know, e.g., from song lines, TV, their travels, etc.
- Model new words in context rather than in isolation. E.g., give nouns + article, i.e., *'a bird'*, *'an old elephant'* not just *'bird'* or *'elephant'*. Model and teach words in pairs: *shoes and socks; men and women; the sun and the moon*, etc. so they get used to stressing and reducing. In this way, the focus on intonation, phrase or sentence stress, word boundaries, etc. increases.
- Respond naturally to incorrect models or effects of 'wrong' intonation and encourage repetition to say it better, e.g., say *Excuse me?* in response to incorrect pronunciation or flat intonation.
- Highlight linking (a line between words: *an_orange*), pauses (/ = short pause, // = longer pause) and sentence stress shift (eliciting different meanings according to which words are stressed).
- Work on transcripts, e.g., shadow read text and sub-vocalize to self; notice and underline most stressed words / pauses / links. Turn any audioscript into a proper listening / pronunciation teaching vehicle.
- Spot the music, e.g., help them hear changes of pitch
- Track, shadow, rehearse, imitate, repeat and record themselves

Systematic visual pronunciation activities give real help in many lessons. Pink syllables have been retained in iDentities to show you how to stress new, poly-syllabic words when they first appear.

Therefore, iDentities offers real help with all aspects of pronunciation.

Review lessons

There is ample opportunity for revision and recycling throughout the book via the six review lessons. These include many additional activities focusing on speaking, grammar, listening, reading, writing, self-test (error-correction), and point of view (debate). Some skills alternate across the review units, but all are thoroughly covered.

Learner autonomy

iDentities offers a clear layout, lessons that progress transparently, and many language explanations. While these features greatly facilitate classroom teaching, they also allow for easy review and autonomous learning. Depending on the classroom hours available, many activities in the course (e.g., selected vocabulary, grammar, reading, and writing tasks) could be assigned for homework. The student-friendly grammar boxes, with additional explanation in **Grammar expansion**, also allow for easy review. The actual review units can be assigned for homework also.

Another way to encourage learner autonomy is with the brand new **search tasks** included in iDentities. These days, we all depend more and more on online search tasks, seeking information or translations, purchasing items, etc. The classroom should be no different, so students are invited individually or in groups to look online for their own texts and authentic information to bring greater personalization, individualization and localization, to many activities. These can be done before, during or after class, depending on your needs and the availability of technology (and time!). Students are also encouraged to search for additional information they may need to develop their arguments for **Keep talking** activities or writing tasks.

If it seems feasible, you may wish to consider 'flipping' more of your classes, too. Before any major presentation or review activity, have students search online for material to support the next lesson. This is especially useful for weaker students, who might be struggling to keep up, but also works for stronger students, who might even be able to lead the next class themselves.

A key element in the thinking behind both iDentities and English iD has been to produce textbooks which are not too long. iDentities 1 is made up of twelve five-page units, which leaves teachers more time to do whatever is most needed, including searching online and, of course, customizing lessons with local names, places, and references.

Richmond Learning Platform for iDentities

Welcome to Richmond Learning Platform for iDentities. This extremely useful and user-friendly blended learning tool has been developed in parallel with the series and combines the best of formal and informal learning to extend, review and test core lesson content. The full range of resources is available to teachers and students who adopt either of the iDentities levels. The Richmond Learning Platform will be regularly updated with new features and content, and we believe both students and teachers will enjoy and benefit from its content. The Richmond Learning Platform for iDentities includes:

- interactive activities to cover all language points in iDentities Student's Books
- Skills Boost: extra reading and listening practice available in interactive format
- Tests: Unit Tests and Revision Tests
- Resources for teachers
- Downloadable audio
- Access to authentic video material

To access the platform, go to richmondlp.com and use the access code on the inside front cover of the Student's Book.

Workbook

In the Workbook, a single page corresponds to each Student's Book lesson, designed to consolidate and reinforce all the main language. Exercises can be used in class, e.g., for fast finishers, or extra practice of specific areas.

The Workbook includes:

- a variety of exercises, texts and puzzles to scaffold, continue practicing and extend the main grammar and vocabulary of each lesson;
- Skills Practice: several listening activities per unit to continue practicing the most important skill outside class, plus plenty of short, enjoyable reading texts
- Song lines: students are asked to look back at the five song lines in the unit and find the link to the lesson—a fun way of reviewing each unit

Interleaved Teacher's Book

iDentities offers a rich, complete, teacher-friendly, lesson plan for every left and right hand page of each lesson. It provides a complete step-by-step lesson plan from beginning to end, offering:

- lesson overviews and aims
- an optional books-closed warm-up for every lesson
- an alternative books-open warm-up based around the question title
- step-by-step notes and suggestions for each on-page activity, including background information and language notes where appropriate
- help with identifying the focus of each activity and any new language being presented; additional help (where relevant) on presenting increasingly complicated grammar
- teaching tips to vary and hone your teaching skills
- suggestions for multi-level classes (ideas for both stronger and weaker students)
- extra writing options for every lesson
- a complete answer key and audioscript
- background information and step-by-step, teaching notes for the song lines

Digital Book for Teachers / IWB

The Digital Book for Teachers is a separate medium containing all the pages of the Student's Book. Teachers can use this resource to promote variety in their classes, so that students can see the images on the IWB instead of looking at the book.

On the next pages you will find detailed information about all the features of iDentities.

»iDentities

STUDENT'S BOOK 1

Contemporary, original topics

Challenging listening skills, followed by speaking on the same topic

Expanded focus on high-frequency phrasal verbs, collocations, idioms and discourse markers

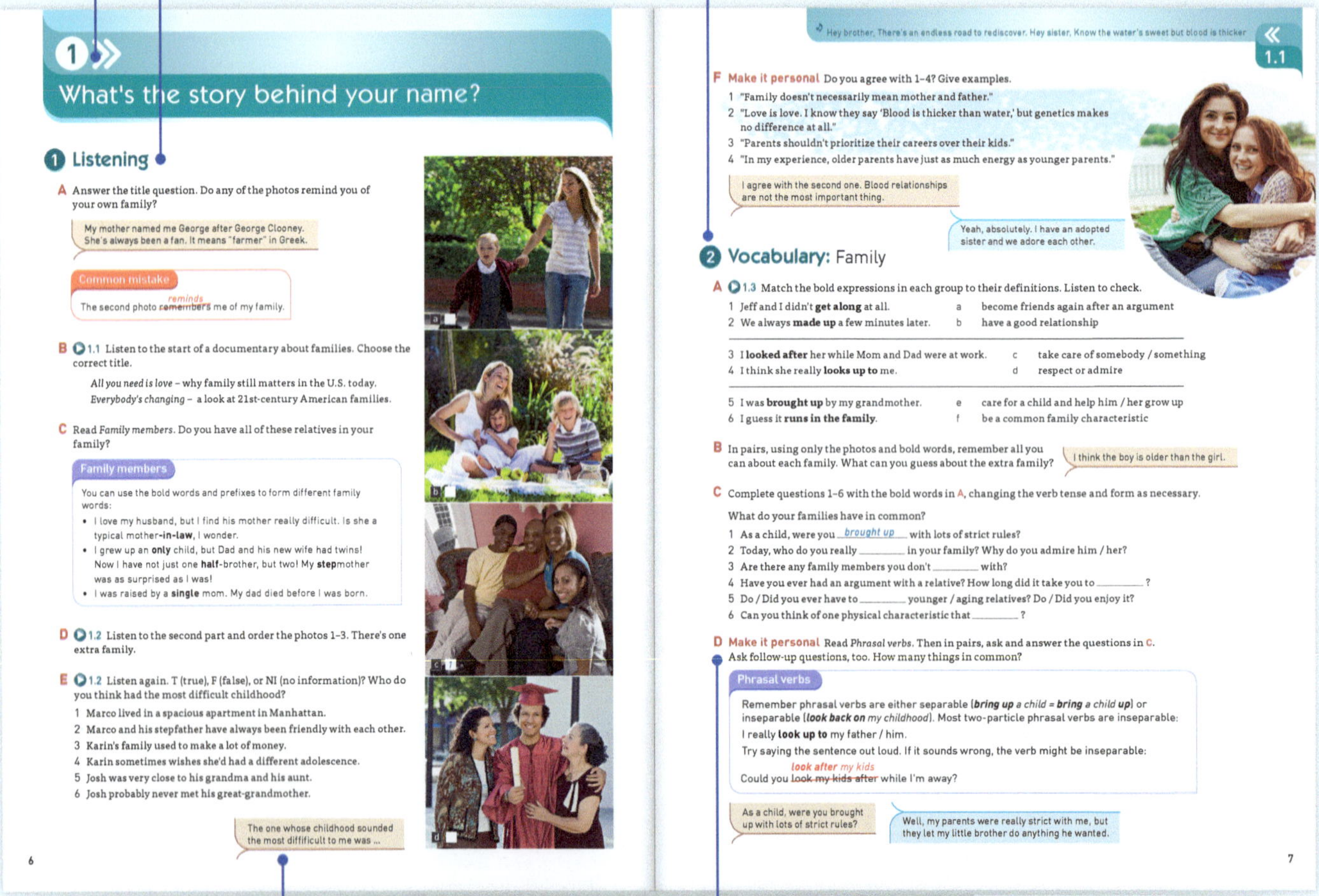

1 »

What's the story behind your name?

1 Listening

A Answer the title question. Do any of the photos remind you of your own family?

> My mother named me George after George Clooney. She's always been a fan. It means "farmer" in Greek.

Common mistake

The second photo ~~remembers~~ reminds me of my family.

B 1.1 Listen to the start of a documentary about families. Choose the correct title.

All you need is love – why family still matters in the U.S. today.
Everybody's changing – a look at 21st-century American families.

C Read *Family members*. Do you have all of these relatives in your family?

Family members

You can use the bold words and prefixes to form different family words:

- I love my husband, but I find his mother really difficult. Is she a typical mother-**in-law**, I wonder.
- I grew up an **only** child, but Dad and his new wife had twins! Now I have not just one **half**-brother, but two! My **step**mother was as surprised as I was!
- I was raised by a **single** mom. My dad died before I was born.

D 1.2 Listen to the second part and order the photos 1–3. There's one extra family.

E 1.2 Listen again. T (true), F (false), or NI (no information)? Who do you think had the most difficult childhood?

1 Marco lived in a spacious apartment in Manhattan.
2 Marco and his stepfather have always been friendly with each other.
3 Karin's family used to make a lot of money.
4 Karin sometimes wishes she'd had a different adolescence.
5 Josh was very close to his grandma and his aunt.
6 Josh probably never met his great-grandmother.

> The one whose childhood sounded the most difficult to me was ...

a b c 1 d

6

Hey brother, There's an endless road to rediscover. Hey sister, Know the water's sweet but blood is thicker

« 1.1

F Make it personal Do you agree with 1–4? Give examples.

1 "Family doesn't necessarily mean mother and father."
2 "Love is love. I know they say 'Blood is thicker than water,' but genetics makes no difference at all."
3 "Parents shouldn't prioritize their careers over their kids."
4 "In my experience, older parents have just as much energy as younger parents."

> I agree with the second one. Blood relationships are not the most important thing.

> Yeah, absolutely. I have an adopted sister and we adore each other.

2 Vocabulary: Family

A 1.3 Match the bold expressions in each group to their definitions. Listen to check.

1 Jeff and I didn't **get along** at all. — a become friends again after an argument
2 We always **made up** a few minutes later. — b have a good relationship

3 I **looked after** her while Mom and Dad were at work. — c take care of somebody / something
4 I think she really **looks up to** me. — d respect or admire

5 I was **brought up** by my grandmother. — e care for a child and help him / her grow up
6 I guess it **runs in the family**. — f be a common family characteristic

B In pairs, using only the photos and bold words, remember all you can about each family. What can you guess about the extra family?

> I think the boy is older than the girl.

C Complete questions 1–6 with the bold words in A, changing the verb tense and form as necessary.

What do your families have in common?

1 As a child, were you _brought up_ with lots of strict rules?
2 Today, who do you really ______ in your family? Why do you admire him / her?
3 Are there any family members you don't ______ with?
4 Have you ever had an argument with a relative? How long did it take you to ______ ?
5 Do / Did you ever have to ______ younger / aging relatives? Do / Did you enjoy it?
6 Can you think of one physical characteristic that ______ ?

D Make it personal Read *Phrasal verbs*. Then in pairs, ask and answer the questions in C. Ask follow-up questions, too. How many things in common?

Phrasal verbs

Remember phrasal verbs are either separable (***bring up** a child* = ***bring** a child **up***) or inseparable (***look back on** my childhood*). Most two-particle phrasal verbs are inseparable:

I really **look up to** my father / him.

Try saying the sentence out loud. If it sounds wrong, the verb might be inseparable:

Could you ~~look my kids after~~ *look after my kids* while I'm away?

> As a child, were you brought up with lots of strict rules?

> Well, my parents were really strict with me, but they let my little brother do anything he wanted.

7

Speech bubbles contain models for speaking tasks

Students personalize what they have learned so as to consolidate their English identity

Lesson titles are questions which can be used as schema builders and help students identify with the language

Emphasis on inductive grammar and focus on the subtleties of language

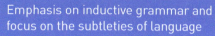

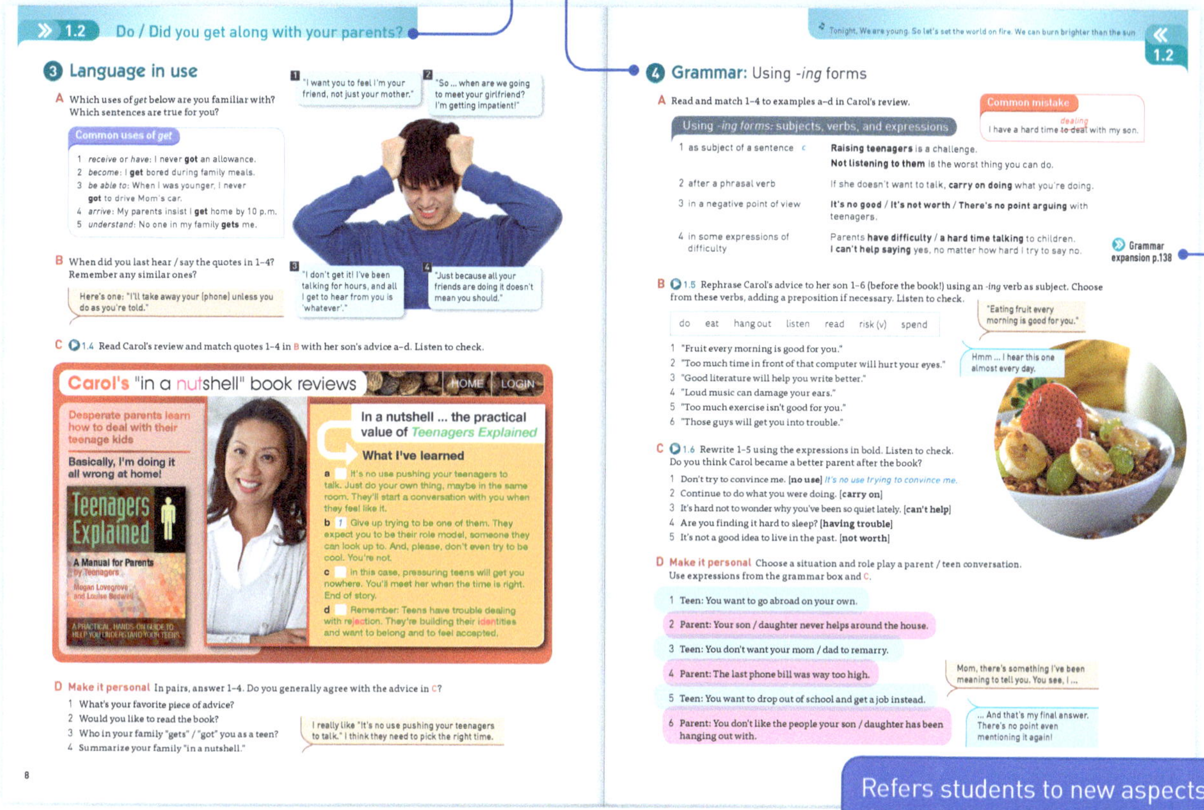
1.2 Do / Did you get along with your parents?

3 Language in use

A Which uses of *get* below are you familiar with? Which sentences are true for you?

Common uses of *get*
1 *receive or have:* I never **got** an allowance.
2 *become:* I **get** bored during family meals.
3 *be able to:* When I was younger, I never **got** to drive Mom's car.
4 *arrive:* My parents insist I **get** home by 10 p.m.
5 *understand:* No one in my family **gets** me.

1 "I want you to feel I'm your friend, not just your mother."
2 "So ... when are we going to meet your girlfriend? I'm getting impatient!"
3 "I don't get it! I've been talking for hours, and all I get to hear from you is 'whatever'."
4 "Just because all your friends are doing it doesn't mean you should."

B When did you last hear / say the quotes in 1–4? Remember any similar ones?

Here's one: "I'll take away your (phone) unless you do as you're told."

C 1.4 Read Carol's review and match quotes 1–4 in B with her son's advice a–d. Listen to check.

Carol's "in a nutshell" book reviews — HOME | LOGIN

Desperate parents learn how to deal with their teenage kids

Basically, I'm doing it all wrong at home!

Teenagers Explained — A Manual for Parents by Teenagers

In a nutshell ... the practical value of *Teenagers Explained*

What I've learned

a It's no use pushing your teenagers to talk. Just do your own thing, maybe in the same room. They'll start a conversation with you when they feel like it.

b Give up trying to be one of them. They expect you to be their role model, someone they can look up to. And, please, don't even try to be cool. You're not.

c In this case, pressuring teens will get you nowhere. You'll meet her when the time is right. End of story.

d Remember: Teens have trouble dealing with rejection. They're building their identities and want to belong and to feel accepted.

D Make it personal In pairs, answer 1–4. Do you generally agree with the advice in C?
1 What's your favorite piece of advice?
2 Would you like to read the book?
3 Who in your family "gets" / "got" you as a teen?
4 Summarize your family "in a nutshell."

I really like "It's no use pushing your teenagers to talk." I think they need to pick the right time.

8

Tonight, We are young. So let's set the world on fire. We can burn brighter than the sun — 1.2

4 Grammar: Using *-ing* forms

A Read and match 1–4 to examples a–d in Carol's review.

Common mistake: I have a hard time ~~to deal~~ *dealing* with my son.

Using *-ing forms*: subjects, verbs, and expressions

1 as subject of a sentence	**Raising teenagers** is a challenge. **Not listening to them** is the worst thing you can do.
2 after a phrasal verb	If she doesn't want to talk, **carry on doing** what you're doing.
3 in a negative point of view	**It's no good / It's not worth / There's no point arguing** with teenagers.
4 in some expressions of difficulty	Parents **have difficulty / a hard time talking** to children. **I can't help saying** yes, no matter how hard I try to say no.

Grammar expansion p.138

B 1.5 Rephrase Carol's advice to her son 1–6 (before the book!) using an *-ing* verb as subject. Choose from these verbs, adding a preposition if necessary. Listen to check.

do eat hang out listen read risk (v) spend

1 "Fruit every morning is good for you."
2 "Too much time in front of that computer will hurt your eyes."
3 "Good literature will help you write better."
4 "Loud music can damage your ears."
5 "Too much exercise isn't good for you."
6 "Those guys will get you into trouble."

"Eating fruit every morning is good for you."
Hmm ... I hear this one almost every day.

C 1.6 Rewrite 1–5 using the expressions in bold. Listen to check. Do you think Carol became a better parent after the book?
1 Don't try to convince me. [no use] *It's no use trying to convince me.*
2 Continue to do what you were doing. [carry on]
3 It's hard not to wonder why you've been so quiet lately. [can't help]
4 Are you finding it hard to sleep? [having trouble]
5 It's not a good idea to live in the past. [not worth]

D Make it personal Choose a situation and role play a parent / teen conversation. Use expressions from the grammar box and C.
1 Teen: You want to go abroad on your own.
2 Parent: Your son / daughter never helps around the house.
3 Teen: You don't want your mom / dad to remarry.
4 Parent: The last phone bill was way too high.
5 Teen: You want to drop out of school and get a job instead.
6 Parent: You don't like the people your son / daughter has been hanging out with.

Mom, there's something I've been meaning to tell you. You see, I ...
... And that's my final answer. There's no point even mentioning it again!

Refers students to new aspects of the structure and extra activities

A wide range of reading skills encourage students to interact with the texts

Interesting and useful language points

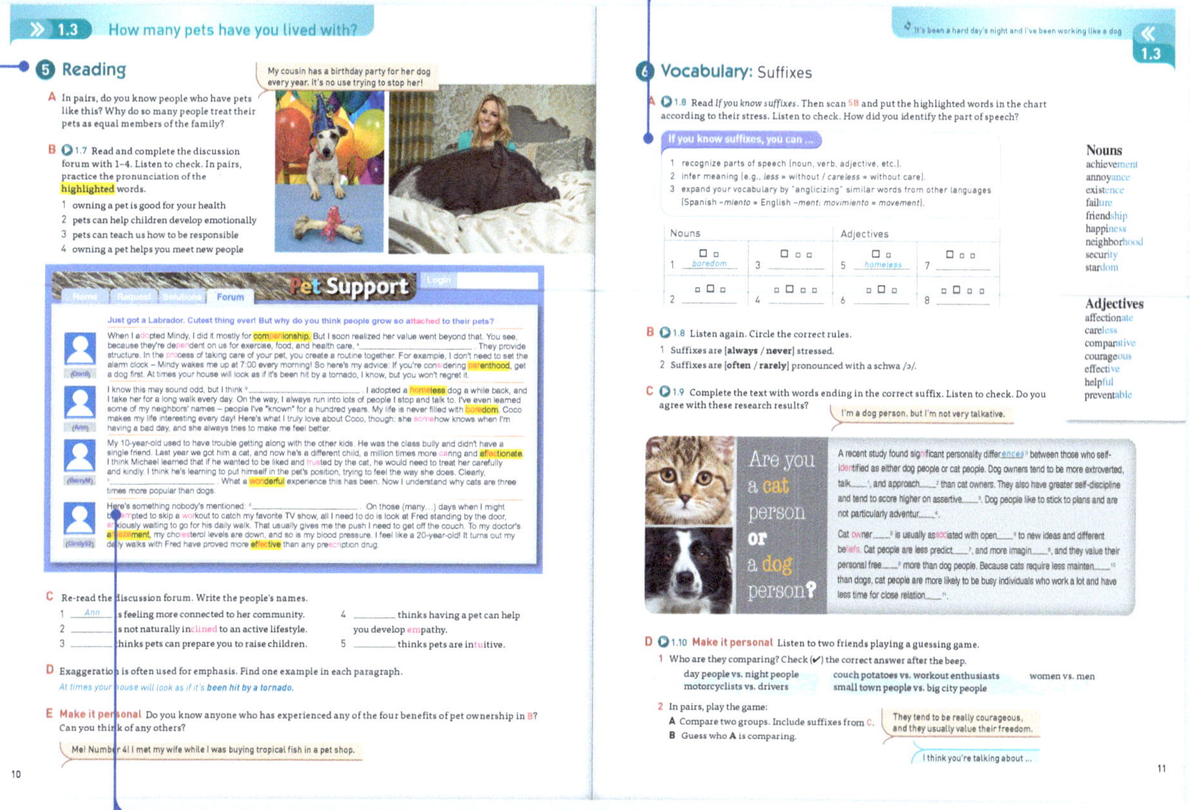
1.3 How many pets have you lived with?

5 Reading

A In pairs, do you know people who have pets like this? Why do so many people treat their pets as equal members of the family?

My cousin has a birthday party for her dog every year. It's no use trying to stop her!

B 1.7 Read and complete the discussion forum with 1–4. Listen to check. In pairs, practice the pronunciation of the highlighted words.
1 owning a pet is good for your health
2 pets can help children develop emotionally
3 pets can teach us how to be responsible
4 owning a pet helps you meet new people

Pet Support — Home | Request | Solutions | Forum | Login

Just got a Labrador. Cutest thing ever! But why do you think people grow so attached to their pets?

When I adopted Mindy, I did it mostly for companionship. But I soon realized her value went beyond that. You see, because they're dependent on us for exercise, food, and health care, ¹______. They provide structure. In the process of taking care of your pet, you create a routine together. For example, I don't need to set the alarm clock – Mindy wakes me up at 7:00 every morning! So here's my advice: If you're considering parenthood, get a dog first. At times your house will look as if it's been hit by a tornado, I know, but you won't regret it. (Doris)

I know this may sound odd, but I think ²______. I adopted a homeless dog a while back, and I take her for a long walk every day. On the way, I always run into lots of people I stop and talk to. I've even learned some of my neighbors' names – people I've "known" for a hundred years. My life is never filled with boredom. Coco makes my life interesting every day! Here's what I truly love about Coco, though: she somehow knows when I'm having a bad day, and she always tries to make me feel better. (Ann)

My 10-year-old used to have trouble getting along with the other kids. He was the class bully and didn't have a single friend. Last year we got him a cat, and now he's a different child, a million times more caring and affectionate. I think Michael learned that if he wanted to be liked and trusted by the cat, he would need to treat her carefully and kindly. I think he's learning to put himself in the pet's position, trying to feel the way she does. Clearly, ³______. What a wonderful experience this has been. Now I understand why cats are three times more popular than dogs. (BennyM)

Here's something nobody's mentioned: ⁴______. On those (many...) days when I might be tempted to skip a workout to catch my favorite TV show, all I need to do is look at Fred standing by the door, anxiously waiting to go for his daily walk. That usually gives me the push I need to get off the couch. To my doctor's amazement, my cholesterol levels are down, and so is my blood pressure. I feel like a 20-year-old! It turns out my daily walks with Fred have proved more effective than any prescription drug. (Cindy92)

C Re-read the discussion forum. Write the people's names.
1 *Ann*'s feeling more connected to her community.
2 ______'s not naturally inclined to an active lifestyle.
3 ______ thinks pets can prepare you to raise children.
4 ______ thinks having a pet can help you develop empathy.
5 ______ thinks pets are intuitive.

D Exaggeration is often used for emphasis. Find one example in each paragraph.
At times your house will look as if it's been hit by a tornado.

E Make it personal Do you know anyone who has experienced any of the four benefits of pet ownership in B? Can you think of any others?

Me! Number 4! I met my wife while I was buying tropical fish in a pet shop.

10

It's been a hard day's night and I've been working like a dog — 1.3

6 Vocabulary: Suffixes

A 1.8 Read *If you know suffixes*. Then scan 5B and put the highlighted words in the chart according to their stress. Listen to check. How did you identify the part of speech?

If you know suffixes, you can ...
1 recognize parts of speech (noun, verb, adjective, etc.).
2 infer meaning (e.g., *-less* = without / *careless* = without care).
3 expand your vocabulary by "anglicizing" similar words from other languages (Spanish *-miento* = English *-ment: movimiento* = *movement*).

Nouns		Adjectives	
1 *boredom*	3	5 *homeless*	7
2	4	6	8

Nouns: achievement, annoyance, existence, failure, friendship, happiness, neighborhood, security, stardom

Adjectives: affectionate, careless, competitive, courageous, effective, helpful, preventable

B 1.8 Listen again. Circle the correct rules.
1 Suffixes are [always / never] stressed.
2 Suffixes are [often / rarely] pronounced with a schwa /ə/.

C 1.9 Complete the text with words ending in the correct suffix. Listen to check. Do you agree with these research results?

I'm a dog person, but I'm not very talkative.

Are you a cat person or a dog person?

A recent study found significant personality differ*ences*¹ between those who self-identified as either dog people or cat people. Dog owners tend to be more extroverted, talk___², and approach___³ than cat owners. They also have greater self-discipline and tend to score higher on assertive___⁴. Dog people like to stick to plans and are not particularly adventur___⁵.

Cat owner___⁶ is usually associated with open___⁷ to new ideas and different beliefs. Cat people are less predict___⁸, and more imagin___⁹, and they value their personal free___¹⁰ more than dog people. Because cats require less mainten___¹¹ than dogs, cat people are more likely to be busy individuals who work a lot and have less time for close relation___¹².

D 1.10 Make it personal Listen to two friends playing a guessing game.
1 Who are they comparing? Check (✔) the correct answer after the beep.
day people vs. night people — couch potatoes vs. workout enthusiasts — women vs. men
motorcyclists vs. drivers — small town people vs. big city people
2 In pairs, play the game:
A Compare two groups. Include suffixes from C.
B Guess who A is comparing.

They tend to be really courageous, and they usually value their freedom.
I think you're talking about ...

11

Word stress highlighted in pink in reading texts

Introduction

Authentic videos present topics in real contexts

Song lines help English come alive!

1.4 What difficult people do you know?

7 Listening

A In pairs, what characteristics do difficult people have in common?

Difficult people don't listen. They just talk.

B 1.11 Listen to / Watch (0.00–2.46) Mary Bolster discuss difficult people and choose the correct answers.

1 Mary Bolster is ...
   a psychologist.
   the editor of a health magazine.
   a doctor.
2 She talks about all of these difficult people except ...
   salespeople.
   parents.
   bosses.
   coworkers.

C 1.11 Listen / Watch again. True (T) or False (F)? Which of the speaker's reasons do you remember?

The best way to deal with difficult people is to ...

1 try to change how you react to them.
2 just state the facts as neutrally as possible.
3 act hurt so they feel guilty.
4 make sure they know you're angry.

D Make it personal Have you ever followed the advice in the video? Did it work?

Well, I once had a teacher who was very unreasonable, and I felt totally stressed out. I decided to ...

8 Language in use

A 1.12 Read and complete the webpage with 1–4. Listen to check. Did you learn any new ways of dealing with difficult people?

1 It's important for you to put yourself in other people's positions
2 It's useful to give yourself time to think
3 These guidelines will make it easier for you to be understood
4 It feels good to be heard

THIS WEEK'S SURVIVAL TIPS

Topic of the week Dealing with difficult people

Coming up soon:
- Meeting your in-laws for the first time
- New Year's Eve with the whole family
- Your first day at school / work
- Your first job interview
- Passing your driver's test
- An oral test in English
- Saying "no" to people you love

Five easy ways to help you talk to difficult people:

a Pause and take a deep breath. Count to ten, if necessary. ________ and assess the situation. The less you react, the better.
b Think like them. ________ so you can see the situation from another perspective. Listen carefully. If you were in their situation, what would it feel like?
c Concede a little. Even if you agree with only one percent of what they are saying, let them know. Remember: ________ and have your opinion valued.
d Watch your body language. Look the other person in the eye, smile if you can, and don't cross your arms. ________. Remember: Successful communication is less than ten percent verbal.
e Above all, be patient.

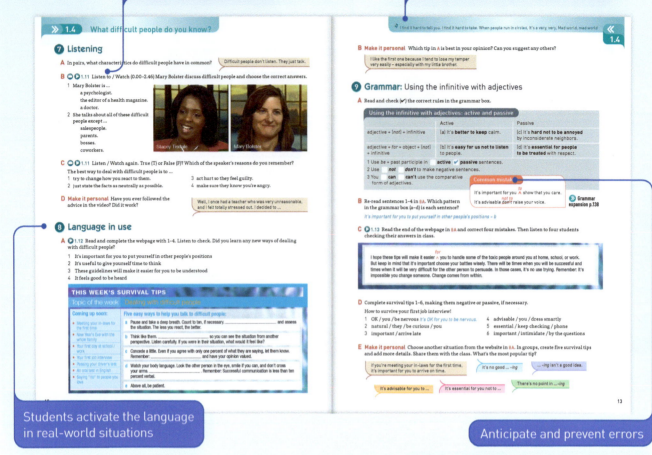

Students activate the language in real-world situations

I find it hard to tell you. I find it hard to take. When people run in circles, it's a very, very, Mad world, mad world

1.4

B Make it personal Which tip in A is best in your opinion? Can you suggest any others?

I like the first one because I tend to lose my temper very easily – especially with my little brother.

9 Grammar: Using the infinitive with adjectives

A Read and check (✔) the correct rules in the grammar box.

Using the infinitive with adjectives: active and passive

	Active	Passive
adjective + (*not*) + infinitive	(a) It's **better to keep** calm.	(c) It's **hard not to be annoyed** by inconsiderate neighbors.
adjective + *for* + object + (*not*) + infinitive	(b) It's **easy for us not to listen** to people.	(d) It's **essential for people to be treated** with respect.

1 Use *be* + past participle in ☐ **active** ✔ **passive** sentences.
2 Use ☐ ***not*** ☐ ***don't*** to make negative sentences.
3 You ☐ **can** ☐ **can't** use the comparative form of adjectives.

Common mistakes

It's important for you ^to show that you care.
It's advisable ~~don't~~ *not to* raise your voice.

Grammar expansion p.138

B Re-read sentences 1–4 in 8A. Which pattern in the grammar box (a–d) is each sentence?

It's important for you to put yourself in other people's positions – b

C 1.13 Read the end of the webpage in 8A and correct four mistakes. Then listen to four students checking their answers in class.

I hope these tips will make it easier ^*for* you to handle some of the toxic people around you at home, school, or work. But keep in mind that it's important choose your battles wisely. There will be times when you will be successful and times when it will be very difficult for the other person to persuade. In those cases, it's no use trying. Remember: It's impossible you change someone. Change comes from within.

D Complete survival tips 1–6, making them negative or passive, if necessary.

How to survive your first job interview!

1 OK / you / be nervous *It's OK for you to be nervous.*
2 natural / they / be curious / you
3 important / arrive late
4 advisable / you / dress smartly
5 essential / keep checking / phone
6 important / intimidate / by the questions

E Make it personal Choose another situation from the website in 8A. In groups, create five survival tips and add more details. Share them with the class. What's the most popular tip?

If you're meeting your in-laws for the first time, it's important for you to arrive on time.

It's no good ... -*ing*

... -*ing* isn't a good idea.

It's advisable for you to ...

It's essential for you not to ...

There's no point in ...-*ing*

13

Anticipate and prevent errors

Preceded by listening and leads into writing

Rich, integrated skills page

1.5 Do you still make voice calls?

10 Listening

A 1.14 What do you think Steve Jobs' opinion on technology was? Listen to the beginning of a radio program to check.

We should limit how much technology our kids use at home.
We should encourage our kids to be as digitally connected as possible.

Steve Jobs, co-founder, chairman and CEO of Apple Inc. (1955–2011)

B 1.15 In pairs, list three possible arguments for Jobs' opinion. Listen to the rest of the interview. Were any of your ideas mentioned?

C 1.15 Listen again and fill in the missing words.

According to Dave Jackson, the guest on the radio program, ...

1 online *bullying* is a real problem, but there are others.
2 too much texting can stop teens from developing ________.
3 texting can affect students' ________ progress.
4 electronic devices are making people ________.
5 it's ________ to chat every day by text with people you haven't met face to face.

D Which statement in C do you agree with most? In pairs, explain your choice. Any big differences?

I believe online bullying is a terrible problem, but I agree, too much texting is, too.

11 Keep talking

A 1.16 **How to say it** Complete sentences 1–4. Listen to check. Then repeat, sounding as convincing as you can.

Developing an argument (1)

1 For one *thing*, I believe digital technology is making people crueler.
2 What's ________, texting is making teens lazy.
3 Not to ________ the fact that we're unlearning how to communicate in the real world.
4 On ________ of that, our digital relationships are becoming too superficial.

B Read Dave Jackson's survey results and choose a statement you strongly agree with. List three arguments to support it.

Summary of results of survey on parenting skills

It's important for children to receive a weekly allowance.	agree 53%	disagree 47%
Children should grow up as slowly as possible.	agree 82%	disagree 18%
It is also the parents' job – not only the school's – to educate children.	agree 37%	disagree 63%
It's no use choosing your children's careers for them.	agree 64%	disagree 36%
It's essential for parents to be strict with their children.	agree 51%	disagree 49%

C In groups, present your ideas using *How to say it* expressions. Your classmates will take notes on 1–3.

1 Were there any long pauses?
2 How many expressions were used?
3 Were there any important mistakes?

It's important for children to get a weekly allowance to begin to appreciate money. For one thing ...

14

Waiting for your call, Baby, night and day. I'm fed up, I'm tired of waiting on you.

1.5

12 Writing: An effective paragraph

A Read this paragraph from a student exam. Answer 1–3.

1 How many arguments does the writer use?
2 Which ones do you agree with?
3 Which words / expressions does the writer use to introduce each argument?

Name: ....
Date: ....

IT'S ESSENTIAL FOR SCHOOLS TO HAVE PHONE RULES

If you've ever had to look up a word online, need a quick calculator, or need to check the weather or a fact quickly, you know your phone can be a useful learning resource. However, I believe technology should be restricted in class for three reasons. First, playing games, posting Facebook® updates, and watching videos while the teacher and other students are talking is rude and disrespectful. If cell phones have to be turned off in movie theaters, libraries, during exams, at border controls, and on planes, why are classrooms any different? In addition, texting back and forth in class might generate unnecessary gossip and make everybody uncomfortable. People don't want to think they're being talked about behind their backs. Finally, it's important for students to get used to not going online whenever they want to. Self-discipline and the ability to focus are critically important in today's hyper-connected world. For all of these reasons, I strongly believe that schools should implement stricter phone rules.

B Read *Write it right!* Then underline the topic sentence in A.

Write it right!

A topic sentence is the most important sentence in any paragraph because it summarizes the rest of the paragraph for the reader. The topic sentence is sometimes, but not always, the first sentence.

When building your argument, use connectors to add each new idea:

First,
To begin with,
↓
In addition,
Besides that,
Moreover, (more formal)
↓
Finally,
Lastly,

C Read the Common mistakes. Then punctuate the beginning of the paragraph below.

Common mistakes

Hyper-connected kids get bored ~~easily,~~ *easily.*
~~in addition they~~ *In addition, they* find it hard to focus.

There are several advantages to texting over voice calls, ~~to~~ *To* begin with it allows shy people to say things they wouldn't otherwise besides that when you text someone you can think carefully about the message before hitting send.

D Your turn! Write a 100-word paragraph arguing in favor of the statement you chose in 11B.

Before
Order your arguments clearly and logically. Write a topic sentence expressing the main idea of your paragraph.

While
Use a variety of connectors to link your ideas.

After
Proofread your paragraph carefully and check punctuation. Email it to a classmate before sending it to your teacher.

15

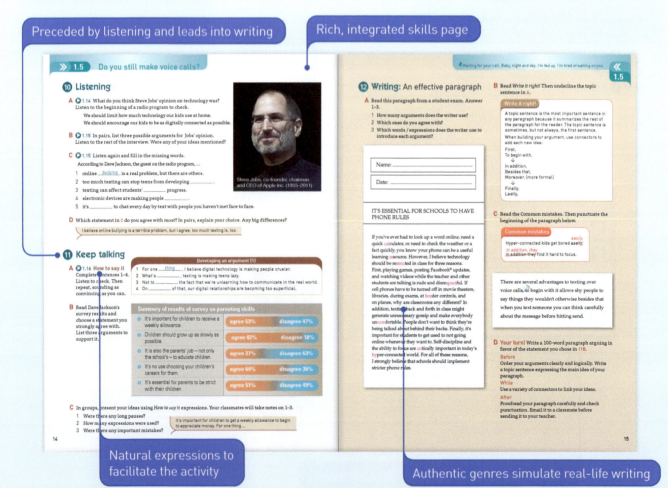

Natural expressions to facilitate the activity

Authentic genres simulate real-life writing

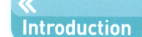

Reviews systematically recycle language

Review 1
Units 1–2

1 Listening

R1.1 Listen to Joe and Amy and choose the best inferences A–D. What did they say that supports your answers? Check in AS R1.1 on p.162.

1 When he was a teenager, Joe probably did something ...
A embarrassing but not serious.
B dangerous and illegal.
C motivating and exciting.
D cool and fun.

2 Joe uses the expression "Need I say more?" because ...
A he doesn't want to go into details.
B he's already told the whole story.
C he might have forgotten what happened.
D he'd like to continue with his story.

3 Amy keeps the conversation going by ...
A talking about herself.
B showing interest.
C being overly curious.
D changing the subject.

4 Joe and Amy are probably ...
A close friends.
B brother and sister.
C just getting to know each other.
D teacher and student.

2 Grammar

A In pairs, rewrite 1–6 about Joe. Begin with the underlined words and use modal verbs.

1 Maybe Joe was arrested when he was 16.
2 I doubt he has a criminal record. He seems like such a nice guy.
3 I'm pretty sure they moved because of something more minor.
4 Maybe his grandparents liked change in general.
5 I'm pretty sure his grandparents had an interesting life.
6 I doubt they made much money, though.

B Role play the conversation between Joe and Amy, changing the details to those of a story you've heard or read about. Act out your conversation for the class. Whose is the most creative?

C Make it personal Write sentences with your opinion. Share in groups. Any disagreements?

1 The best thing about moving to a new city is ...
2 A problem with our school is ...
3 One advantage of this city (town) is ...
4 The most difficult thing about getting up in the morning is ...
5 A disadvantage of having a part-time job is ...
6 A good thing about having older parents is ...

3 Reading

Read the title. What do you think the article is about? Skim the article quickly. Were you right?

Science fiction may soon be fact!

Do great new developments in science start as science fiction? And does the creative process of science fiction encourage breakthroughs in science? According to the Center for Science and the Imagination (CSI) at Arizona State University, founded in 2012 to foster cooperation between writers, artists, and scientists, the answer to both questions may be yes.

Science fiction authors have a long history of imagining life-changing technology. Rockets for space travel were popular in science fiction long before they became reality, culminating in the Apollo mission that put a man on the moon in 1969. During the most exciting periods of innovation, science has had many "dreamers."

While space travel is still too expensive, other elements of science fiction stories have become part of everyday life. The "picture phone" of the 1964 World's Fair was a failure initially. For one thing, service was only available in three cities, and customers had to schedule screen time in advance. Calls were prohibitively expensive, with a three-minute call between New York and Washington, D.C. costing $16, or the equivalent of $120 today. By 1968, the project had been judged a failure. Yet today, free video calls over WiFi are a fact of life around the world.

Of course, much scientific innovation happens without science fiction stories. Future computers may be a big theme in science fiction today, but the foundations of modern computing were established in the 1940s and 50s. The most imaginative ideas may lack funding, and surprising innovation may happen spontaneously. Nevertheless, according to CSI, even though failed ideas can be expensive, scientists should be encouraged to keep dreaming.

4 Writing

Using the ideas in the article and three of the words or expressions below, write a paragraph to support the following statement.

Ideas that sound like science fiction today may be real tomorrow, and companies should fund scientists' innovative ideas.

First, To begin with, →	In addition, Besides, Moreover, →	Finally, Lastly,

5 Point of view

Choose a topic. Then support your opinion in 100–150 words and record your answer. Ask a partner for feedback. How can you be more convincing?

a You see many advantages to owning a pet. OR
You think pets are a lot of unnecessary work.
b You feel there are far too many rude people using technology inappropriately. OR
You feel technology is a wonderful modern invention.
c You think there's no such thing as types of intelligence, and you can learn anything if you put your mind to it. OR
You think people have unique talents and should spend their time developing those.
d You don't believe what appears in science fiction will ever be real. OR
You think the world is a mysterious place, and it's impossible to know what's true.

A complete Grammar reference with exercises

Grammar expansion

1 *stop*, *remember*, *forget*, and *try* do after 1.2

I **stopped to buy** some meat for dinner. (= I stopped at the store in order to buy meat.)
I **stopped buying** meat when I became a vegetarian. (= I no longer buy meat.)

I **remembered to call** Dad on his birthday. (= I didn't forget to call Dad.)
I'm sure I talked to Dad last week, but I don't even **remember calling** him. (= I don't have a memory of the fact that I called Dad.)

I sometimes **forget to call** my parents to say I'll be late. (= I don't always remember to call my parents.)
I'll **never forget calling** my parents to say I was getting married. They were so thrilled! (= I remember clearly calling my parents.)

I'm **trying to concentrate**. Please be quiet. (= I'm attempting to concentrate.)
I **tried writing** down new words, but I still couldn't remember them. (= I experimented with writing down new words.)

More on *try* and *forget*

Only use *try* + *-ing* when the meaning is "to experiment with something." When the meaning is "to attempt," use an infinitive:
I've been **trying to be** nicer to my little sister.

Only use *forget* + *-ing* to remember the past. Otherwise, use the infinitive.
I sometimes **forget to set** the alarm, and then I'm late for school.

2 Using the infinitive with adjectives: More on negative sentences do after 1.4

Pay close attention to the position of the negative. Whether it goes with the verb or the adjective often depends on what's being emphasized.

It's important for you **not** to go. (= You shouldn't go.)
It's **not** important for you to go. (= You don't have to go.)

It's critical for my daughter **not** to fail her exam. (= She must pass.)
It's **not** critical for my daughter to pass her exam. (= It's OK if she fails.)

Sometimes if you move the negative, the sentence no longer makes sense. When in doubt, say the sentence aloud.

It's essential **not** to feel intimidated during an interview. (= Relax and don't feel intimidated.)
~~It's **not** essential to feel intimidated during an interview.~~ (= Meaning is unclear.)

Sometimes both choices are possible and have a very similar meaning.

It's **not** helpful to ... It's helpful **not** to ...	pressure your children. (= You shouldn't pressure them.)

1A Complete 1–8 with the infinitive or -*ing* form of the verbs.

1 I remember _______ (meet) Tim at a party last year. He was thinner then.
2 We stopped _______ (look) at the flowers. They were really beautiful.
3 I'm trying _______ (finish) as fast as I can! Be patient.
4 She stopped _______ (go) to dance class. She said it was really boring.
5 At the last minute, we remembered _______ (take) an umbrella. It's a good thing because it started pouring!
6 He forgot _______ (check) that the door was locked, and a robber walked in.
7 I tried _______ (take) French classes, but in the end, I realized I liked English better.
8 I just can't forget _______ (see) Tom again after all these years. I think I'm still in love!

1B Make it personal Write and share three facts about yourself. Use *remember*, *stop*, *try*, or *forget*.

2A Match the sentence beginnings with the most logical ending.

1 It's important not to — a ☐ agree with everything your teenager says.
2 It's not important to — b ☐ contradict your children in front of their friends. It could embarrass them.

3 It's not essential for you to — a ☐ understand your children at all times.
4 It's essential for you not to — b ☐ have rigid opinions.

5 It's not critical for older parents to — a ☐ be stuck in the past.
6 It's critical for older parents not to — b ☐ be up-to-date with technology.

2B Choose two sentences you agree with from A. Then give a reason for your opinion.

2C Circle the most logical options. When both seem possible, circle both.

1 [**It's important not to / It's not important to**] think all teenagers are alike. People mature at different rates, and 2 [**it's useful not to / it's not useful to**] make comparisons. If you want to have a good relationship with your teen, 3 [**it's essential not to / it's not essential to**] make unrealistic demands. In addition, things were very different when you were young, and it's 4 [**critical not to / not critical to**] be close-minded. Teens listen to their friends more than their parents, and it's 5 [**helpful not to / not helpful to**] begin sentences with "When I was your age ... "

Bonus! Language in song

♫ It's been a hard day's night, and I've been working like a dog.

- What do you think the expression "a hard day's night" means?
- Give the singer from 1.3 on page 11 some advice beginning with "It's important (not) to ..."

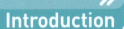

Workbook to practice and consolidate lessons.

1.2 Do / Did you get along with your parents?

A Read the online forum. Check (✓) the problems you had (or have) with your parents.

B Replace the bold *get* verbs with these verbs in the correct form. One is used twice.

arrive at	become	have an opportunity
receive	understand	

Q What annoys you about your parents?

When I'm in the bathroom for ten minutes or more, they **get** angry and start banging on the door. 1 ________

My parents are always criticizing my look. It's like, why are you wearing jeans and that T-shirt? They just don't **get** me. 2 ________

I never **get** to watch what I want on TV. My dad's always in the living room, watching sports programs. 3 ________

If I don't **get to** the table in time for meals, they start calling me on my phone. "Where are you?" It drives me crazy. 4 ________

When I was a kid, all my friends **got** an allowance, but did I? No! Never. I had to wash the car or look after my baby brother just to get $5. 5 ________

My mom **gets** really mad when I don't clean my room. But I don't see why. After all it's mine, not hers! 6 ________

C Order the words in 1–6 to make sentences.

1 asking / not / help / bad / idea / is / for / a
____
2 on / but / we / started / carried / tennis / raining / playing / it
____
3 it's / to / on / not / going / exhibit / Sunday / the / worth
____
4 baby / new / a / having / exhausting / is / totally
____
5 help / about / nervous / next week's / can't / feeling / I / exams
____
6 ideas / new / thinking / for / a / of / hard / time / have / I / work
____

D Make it personal Rewrite two sentences in **B** so they're true for you.

1 ________
2 ________
3 ________

4

How many pets have you lived with? 1.3

A Read the blog post and check (✓) its main purpose.

1 To offer advice for pet owners.
2 To make people laugh.
3 To complain about the author's pet.

B Re-read and match underlined phrases 1–3 with definitions a–e. There are two extra ones.

a	a lot	b	ever	c	mostly
d	in reality	e	anywhere		

IS YOUR CAT PLOTTING TO KILL YOU?

Don't get me wrong. I love pets. I wouldn't hurt an animal [1] in a million years. The thing is, would they say the same about us? When your kitty is lying in front of the radiator in a state of complete happiness, is she dreaming of being a tiger in the jungle, hunting wildlife … or hunting you?

How to tell if your cat is plotting to kill you? is the subject of a book and an online feed, and it is the funniest site [2] on earth. Owners take pictures of their pet when it clearly has murder in mind. Notice that look of annoyance on your cat's face? Oh yes, watch out!

The book is extremely funny, and I've started looking at my cat, Cloud, with new eyes. If she's plotting to kill me, what would she do if my hamster escaped in the living room? Cloud would be [3] a thousand times more dangerous to a little orange thing like that. One false move and my hamster would quickly see its Facebook® status change from "pet" to "snack." I'm starting to think that perhaps it's only our size that keeps us alive.

C 2 Complete what these pet owners said with a form of the word in CAPITALS. Listen to check.

1 Pet *ownership* isn't easy, but it's a wonderful experience. OWNER
2 I love cats because they're so ________ . AFFECTION
3 I think almost everyone in this ________ has a dog. NEIGHBOR
4 We didn't know anything about keeping a pet iguana, but the salesperson at the pet shop was very ________ and explained everything to us. HELP
5 The countryside is the best place to have a horse because you have the ________ to ride wherever you want. FREE
6 Ricky taught his parrot to speak, and now it's incredibly ________ . It doesn't shut up! TALK
7 We've lost the tortoise! It's Cathy's fault. She's always so ________ . This time, she left it alone in the garden, and now it's disappeared! CARE
8 Having a dog has brought us so much ________ . I can't imagine life without our furry friend. HAPPY

D Make it personal Complete this sentence so it's true for you.

In my opinion, ________ make perfect pets because ________
________ .

5

1.4 What difficult people do you know?

A 3 Listen and number Ki-Yeon's problems in the order you hear them, 1–4. One problem isn't mentioned.

Ki-Yeon's …

aunt is calling him a lot.
cousin can't come to the wedding.
family doesn't want to pay for the wedding.
fiancée can't find a wedding dress.
brother hasn't taken care of the invitations yet.

B 3 Listen again. T (true) or F (false)?

1 In Korea, it's traditional to give wooden ducks as a wedding present.
2 Ki-Yeon doesn't like his mother-in-law.
3 In Korea, the grandparents pay half the cost of the wedding.
4 The wedding ceremony is in February.
5 Ki-Yeon's cousin is expecting a baby.
6 Ki-Yeon talked to his aunt about the food for the wedding.

C Complete the wedding advice using the words in parentheses.

What are your tips for organizing a wedding?

1 *It's essential for you to tell* everyone what time the ceremony begins. (essential / you / tell)

2 ________ your guests the details over the phone. (better / not / give)

3 ________ each guest a map of how to get to the wedding. (advisable / send)

4 ________ stressed, but you should try not to panic. (hard / not / get)

5 ________ all your guests to respond to the wedding invitations. (good / idea / you / ask)

6 ________ the food before you know exactly how many people are coming. (no / point / choose)

D Make it personal What's your best piece of advice for a close friend who's getting married next week?

____
____

6

Do you still make voice calls? 1.5

Writing an effective paragraph

A Complete the paragraph with these connectors.

besides	it's important	lastly
on top of that	to begin with	

HONEY, COULD YOU TEXT THE KIDS AND TELL THEM THAT DINNER IS READY?

Smart phones: a curse for all generations?

Many parents give their kids a smartphone as a form of babysitter, even during family meals. However, (1) ________ for parents to think carefully before allowing their children to bring a smartphone to the dinner table. (2) ________ , this suggests that it's fine for children to use their gadgets on social occasions. (3) ________ , it prevents shy children from learning how to interact with other family members and makes it difficult for older relatives to begin a conversation with them. (4) ________ , many games on these devices are incredibly addictive, and children play them too much already. (5) ________ , dinner is a moment for a family to enjoy quality time together. Smartphones disrupt that happy atmosphere.

B Choose the best topic sentence (a–c) to complete three paragraphs from other student essays.

(1) ☐ Teenagers are so glued to their smartphones that they lose interest in talking to other family members. Sometimes they are so engaged with the screen that they don't even say hello to their parents when they get home from work.

a Teenagers spend too much time playing games online.
b Some parents are unable to communicate clearly with their kids.
c Using technology makes teenagers antisocial.

(2) ☐ People can receive work emails or messages at the dinner table, in the bathroom, or even as they are getting ready for bed. This can increase stress levels at home when they should be trying to relax.

a The biggest problem is the number of instant messages that people send and get about unimportant things.
b It is no use thinking that someone's job stops when he or she leaves the office.
c People spend too long on the computer in the office.

(3) ☐ Children and younger teens often stay glued to their devices late into the night. This makes them tired and even angry the next day, and that causes arguments. Some educators suggest that it is essential for parents to turn the house WiFi off at night. But is that a solution? Children can still access the Internet on their phones.

a Many problems come from not getting enough sleep.
b Parents are worried about the cost of all this technology.
c The problems are worse in the evening than the morning.

C Write a new topic sentence for a paragraph in **B**, using your own ideas.

____
____

D Look back at lessons 1.1–1.5 in the Student's Book. Find the connection between the song lines and the content of each lesson.

E 4 Listen to the five question titles from the unit, and record your answers to them. If possible, compare recordings with a classmate.

7

Richmond Learning Platform for Identities, includes:

- **Interactive activities** to cover all language points in Identities Student's Books
- **Skills Boost:** extra reading and listening practice available in both interactive and PDF format
- **Tests:** Unit Tests and Revision Tests delivered in separate A and B versions
- **Resources** for teachers
- Downloadable **audio**
- Access to **video**

Interactive grammar activities

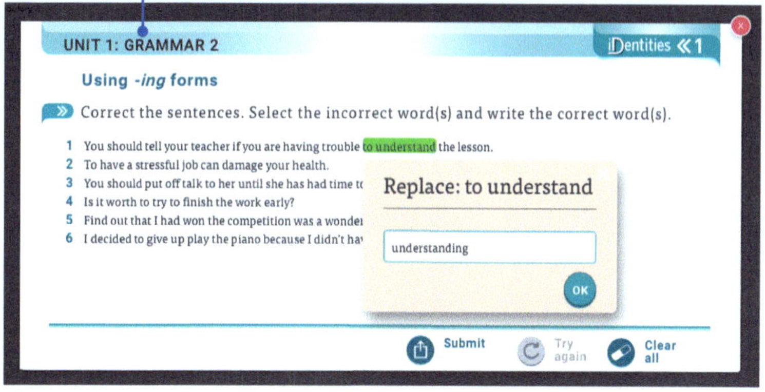

Interactive vocabulary activities

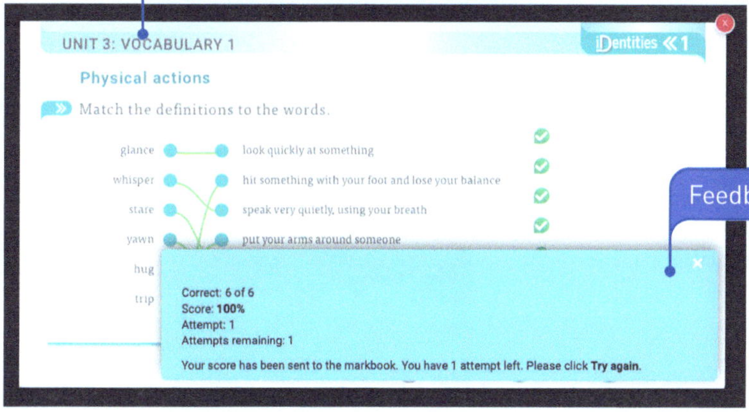

Feedback on scores for students

Skills Boost: Interactive reading and listening activities

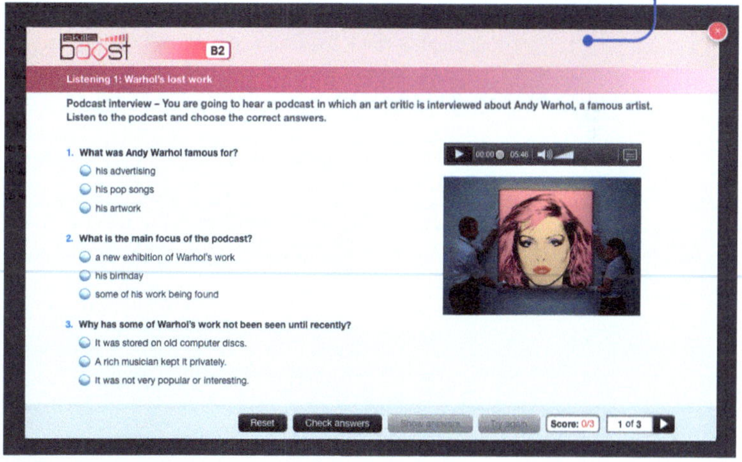

Scores visible for teachers in Markbook

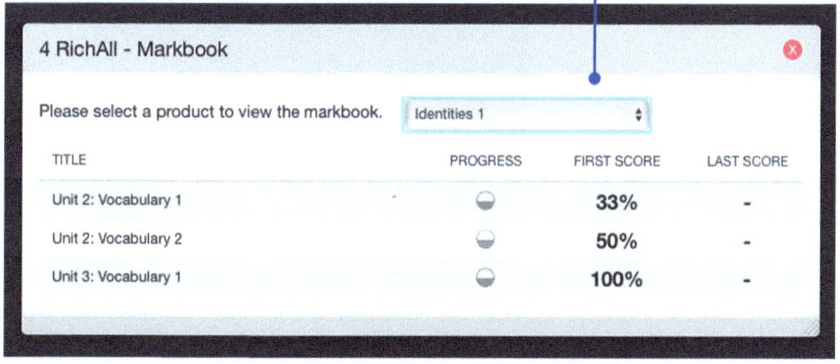

1 »
What's the story behind your name?

1 Listening

A Answer the title question. Do any of the photos remind you of your own family?

> My mother named me George after George Clooney. She's always been a fan. It means "farmer" in Greek.

Common mistake

The second photo ~~remembers~~ *reminds* me of my family.

B 1.1 Listen to the start of a documentary about families. Choose the correct title.

All you need is love – why family still matters in the U.S. today.

Everybody's changing – a look at 21st-century American families.

C Read *Family members*. Do you have all of these relatives in your family?

Family members

You can use the bold words and prefixes to form different family words:

- I love my husband, but I find his mother really difficult. Is she a typical mother-**in-law**, I wonder.
- I grew up an **only** child, but Dad and his new wife had twins! Now I have not just one **half**-brother, but two! My **step**mother was as surprised as I was!
- I was raised by a **single** mom. My dad died before I was born.

D 1.2 Listen to the second part and order the photos 1–3. There's one extra family.

E 1.2 Listen again. T (true), F (false), or NI (no information)? Who do you think had the most difficult childhood?

1 Marco lived in a spacious apartment in Manhattan.
2 Marco and his stepfather have always been friendly with each other.
3 Karin's family used to make a lot of money.
4 Karin sometimes wishes she'd had a different adolescence.
5 Josh was very close to his grandma and his aunt.
6 Josh probably never met his great-grandmother.

> The one whose childhood sounded the most difficult to me was ...

a

b

c 1

d

Lesson Aims: Sts review and learn family words (*in-law, half-, step-*) and phrasal verbs to talk about family.

Skills	Language	Vocabulary	Grammar review
Talking about names Describing family Asking and answering questions about your family	Talking about your family, e.g. *I have a half-brother. I was raised by a single mom. My brother looks up to me.*	*-in law, half-, step-, single* *bring up, get along, look after, make up, run in the family*	Lesson includes review of simple present, simple past, present perfect, some modal verbs, and some passives

Warm-up

Ask sts: *Do you have a big or small family? Which family members do you live with? Do you get along with them? Why / Why not?* In pairs, sts discuss the questions. Elicit and board names for family members, including *stepmother, stepsister* etc. Teach or elicit *single-parent family*.

1 Listening

A Note: The lesson title questions in IDentities are all intended as warm-up activities, a natural lead-in to the topic of the lesson itself. Ask sts to discuss the two questions in pairs. Set this up using your own names as an additional example.

Classcheck by having some sts report their partners' answers, e.g. *My partner is named after ... Photo c reminds her of her family because....* Ask: *What name would you give to your own son/daughter/grandchildren, and why?*

Refer sts to the **Common mistake**. Elicit new sentences using *to remind someone of something*. Point out that we also use *remind* with the *to* infinitive, e.g. *Remind your sister to buy some coffee.*

Optional activity

Weaker classes: To revise family vocabulary, ask sts to draw their family tree, using as many family words as they know, e.g. *cousin, uncle, aunt, mother, father*

B 1.1 Before sts listen, discuss the meanings of the titles with the class. Ask sts if they agree with them.

Play the audio for sts to choose the correct title. Peercheck, then classcheck.

Answer

Everybody's changing – a look at 21st century American families

See Teacher's Book p.311 for Audio script 1.1.

Tip

Remember to quickly paircheck after each listening phase, before plenary checking answers. When sts turn to face each other and share what they have understood, this will maximize your opportunity to see how much (or how little!) each individual has understood.

C Go through the **Family members** and check understanding. Highlight the difference in meaning between *half-brother* (one parent in common) and *stepbrother* (no parents in common).

In pairs, sts discuss which of the relatives they have. Class feedback and invite some sts to tell the class.

D 1.2 Focus on the photos. Ask: *What do you think the relationship between the people in each photo is?* Pre-teach or elicit *sibling*.

Play the audio. Sts listen and match the speakers to the photos. Peercheck, then classcheck. Ask: *How did you decide? How do you know it wasn't photo b?*

Answers

1 c 2 a 3 d

See Teacher's Book p.311 for Audio script 1.2.

E 1.2 Sts read through the statements. Discuss the meaning of *be close to* and try to agree on a class definition.

Re-play the audio for sts to mark the sentences T (true), F (false) or NI (no information). Classcheck, and get sts to correct the false statements.

Weaker classes: If necessary, play extracts again for parts they find hard, or use the audio script for a third listen and read stage.

Discuss with the class who they think had the most difficult childhood.

As a follow-up, in groups of three or four, sts discuss what they think are the ingredients which contribute to a happy childhood. Have them agree on a list of their top five.

Answers

1 F 2 F 3 NI 4 T 5 T 6 T

Optional activity

Stronger classes: Sts imagine they are one of the people in photo b and write a short paragraph about their family, including information about who they live with, whether they get on well together, where they live, and whether they have good memories of their childhood. Ask individual sts to read out their paragraphs to the class.

Song lyric: See Teacher's Book p.334 for notes about the song and an accompanying activity to do with the class.

F Make it personal Elicit the meaning of *Blood is thicker than water* (= family relationships are stronger than those you have with people not related to you). Ask if there is a similar expression in sts' language.

In pairs, sts discuss the quotes. Encourage them to give reasons for their opinions. Invite sts to share their opinions with the class.

Optional activity

Weaker classes: Elicit and board expressions for giving opinions and agreeing/disagreeing for sts to use in F, e.g. *I think that ..., In my opinion ..., I don't agree. I disagree. That's not true.*

2 Vocabulary: Family

A 1.3 Sts do the matching, then peercheck. You can play the audio for them to check their answers or check answers as a class.

As a follow-up, ask sts to write a sentence about themselves using one of the bold expressions. To make it more gamelike, tell sts their sentence can be true or false for their partner to guess. Have sts compare their sentences with a partner. Then ask sts to report their partners' sentences to the class.

Answers

1 b 2 a 3 c 4 d 5 e 6 f

See Teacher's Book p.311 for Audio script 1.3.

Optional activity

Stronger classes: Books closed. An alternative way of doing this activity is to board the sentences, leaving gaps where the bold expressions are. Write up the bold expressions separately in a random order. Sts match the expressions to the correct sentences.

B Elicit some example sentences about the photos on p.6 using the bold words, e.g. *Karin looked after her sister Amanda. Josh got along very well with his grandmother and Aunt Agatha.*

In pairs, sts think of as many sentences as they can about the photos using the bold words in A. Class feedback.

Suggested answers

Photo a: Karin had to **look after** her little sister, Amanda. Even now, Amanda **looks up to** her.
Photo b: At first, Marco **didn't get along** with his stepfather, Jeff, but after each fight, they always **made up** a few minutes later.
Photo c: Josh was **brought up** by his grandmother and aunt. She was a strong woman like his great grandmother. It **runs in the family**.

C Use the example to set this up. Sts complete the remaining questions. Peercheck, then classcheck. To speed up the process, only focus on any disagreements, rather than going through each sentence one by one each time.

Answers

1 brought up 2 look up to 3 get along 4 make up
5 look after 6 runs in your family

D Make it personal Go through **Phrasal verbs**. Elicit other examples of phrasal verbs and get sts to say whether they are separable or inseparable, e.g. separable: *pick up (He picked up his coat. / He picked his coat up.)*; inseparable: *go out (He went out with my sister.)*

In pairs, sts ask and answer the questions in C. If they need more practice, have them swap partners and ask their new partner the questions.

Classcheck by asking: *Did you find out anything interesting / surprising about your partner? Did you have anything in common?*

Tip

Phrasal verbs are very common in English. Point out to sts that there is no easy way to learn them, as they have no logical pattern. Sts simply need to learn the verb together with the preposition it comes with. Suggest they record them in a separate section in their vocabulary notebooks, headed 'Phrasal verbs', and highlight the preposition in some way to help them remember it. Note that there is a reference list of all the phrasal verbs in this course on pp.00-00 of the Student's Book.

Workbook p.3.

F Make it personal Do you agree with 1–4? Give examples.

1 "Family doesn't necessarily mean mother and father."
2 "Love is love. I know they say 'Blood is thicker than water,' but genetics makes no difference at all."
3 "Parents shouldn't prioritize their careers over their kids."
4 "In my experience, older parents have just as much energy as younger parents."

I agree with the second one. Blood relationships are not the most important thing.

Yeah, absolutely. I have an adopted sister and we adore each other.

2 Vocabulary: Family

A 1.3 Match the bold expressions in each group to their definitions. Listen to check.

1 Jeff and I didn't **get along** at all.
2 We always **made up** a few minutes later.

a ☐ become friends again after an argument
b ☐ have a good relationship

3 I **looked after** her while Mom and Dad were at work.
4 I think she really **looks up to** me.

c ☐ take care of somebody / something
d ☐ respect or admire

5 I was **brought up** by my grandmother.
6 I guess it **runs in the family**.

e ☐ care for a child and help him / her grow up
f ☐ be a common family characteristic

B In pairs, using only the photos and bold words, remember all you can about each family. What can you guess about the extra family?

I think the boy is older than the girl.

C Complete questions 1–6 with the bold words in A, changing the verb tense and form as necessary.

What do your families have in common?

1 As a child, were you _brought up_ with lots of strict rules?
2 Today, who do you really ______ in your family? Why do you admire him / her?
3 Are there any family members you don't ______ with?
4 Have you ever had an argument with a relative? How long did it take you to ______ ?
5 Do / Did you ever have to ______ younger / aging relatives? Do / Did you enjoy it?
6 Can you think of one physical characteristic that ______ ?

D Make it personal Read *Phrasal verbs*. Then in pairs, ask and answer the questions in C. Ask follow-up questions, too. How many things in common?

Phrasal verbs

Remember phrasal verbs are either separable (***bring up*** *a child* = ***bring*** *a child* ***up***) or inseparable (***look back on*** *my childhood*). Most two-particle phrasal verbs are inseparable:

I really **look up to** my father / him.

Try saying the sentence out loud. If it sounds wrong, the verb might be inseparable:

Could you ~~look my kids after~~ ***look after*** *my kids* while I'm away?

As a child, were you brought up with lots of strict rules?

Well, my parents were really strict with me, but they let my little brother do anything he wanted.

3 Language in use

A Which uses of *get* below are you familiar with? Which sentences are true for you?

Common uses of *get*

1 *receive* or *have*: I never **got** an allowance.
2 *become*: I **get** bored during family meals.
3 *be able to*: When I was younger, I never **got** to drive Mom's car.
4 *arrive*: My parents insist I **get** home by 10 p.m.
5 *understand*: No one in my family **gets** me.

1 "I want you to feel I'm your friend, not just your mother."

2 "So ... when are we going to meet your girlfriend? I'm getting impatient!"

3 "I don't get it! I've been talking for hours, and all I get to hear from you is 'whatever'."

4 "Just because all your friends are doing it doesn't mean you should."

B When did you last hear / say the quotes in 1–4? Remember any similar ones?

Here's one: "I'll take away your (phone) unless you do as you're told."

C 1.4 Read Carol's review and match quotes 1–4 in **B** with her son's advice a–d. Listen to check.

Carol's "in a nutshell" book reviews

HOME LOGIN

Desperate parents learn how to deal with their teenage kids

Basically, I'm doing it all wrong at home!

Teenagers Explained
A Manual for Parents
by Teenagers
Megan Lovegrove
and Louise Bedwell
A PRACTICAL, HANDS-ON GUIDE TO HELP YOU UNDERSTAND YOUR TEENS.

In a nutshell ... the practical value of *Teenagers Explained*

What I've learned

a ___ It's no use pushing your teenagers to talk. Just do your own thing, maybe in the same room. They'll start a conversation with you when they feel like it.

b *1* Give up trying to be one of them. They expect you to be their role model, someone they can look up to. And, please, don't even try to be cool. You're not.

c ___ In this case, pressuring teens will get you nowhere. You'll meet her when the time is right. End of story.

d ___ Remember: Teens have trouble dealing with rejection. They're building their identities and want to belong and to feel accepted.

D Make it personal In pairs, answer 1–4. Do you generally agree with the advice in **C**?

1 What's your favorite piece of advice?
2 Would you like to read the book?
3 Who in your family "gets" / "got" you as a teen?
4 Summarize your family "in a nutshell."

I really like "It's no use pushing your teenagers to talk." I think they need to pick the right time.

Lesson Aims: Sts talk about relationships between parents and teenagers and practice giving advice

Skills	Language	Vocabulary	Grammar review
Reading a book review Role playing a parent–teen conversation	Giving advice, e.g. *It's no use pushing your teenagers to talk.* Talking about relationships between parents and teenagers, e.g. *There's no point arguing with teenagers. No one in my family gets me.*	Phrases with *get* *bring up, get along, look after, make up, run in the family*	Using *-ing* forms, e.g. after phrasal verbs, as subject of a sentence, after specific phrases

Warm-up

Highlight the expression *get along with* in the lesson title question. Point out that it has the same meaning as *get on with*.

Ask: *Do / Did you get along with your parents? What things do / did you usually argue about?* In pairs, sts discuss the questions, then feedback to the class.

Get each pair to think up a list of topics they most frequently argue about, e.g. money, going out, girlfriends / boyfriends. Ask sts to share ideas with the class and agree on the five most frequent causes of arguments. Class feedback and board the topics.

3 Language in use

A Read through the sentences in **Common uses of *get*** and check understanding.

Sts turn the sentences into questions, then ask and answer questions in pairs, e.g. *Do you get an allowance? Do you get bored during family meals?*

Classcheck by asking sts to report back their partners' answers.

Optional activities

- **Stronger classes:** Books closed. Board the sentences from the **Common uses** box. Sts rewrite the sentences using a synonym for *get*. Then have them open their books and compare their synonyms with the definitions of *get*.
- Sts write five true sentences about themselves for each use of *get* in A, but using a new phrase, e.g. *I got an amazing new video game for my last birthday. I always get hungry at about 10 p.m.*

B Focus on the photo and the four speech bubbles. Discuss the meaning of *whatever* in speech bubble 3 (= I don't really care). Explain that this is a colloquial expression used a lot by teenagers.

Ask: *How old do you think the boy is? Who do you think is saying these things?* (His parents.) Ask sts if their parents say similar things. Elicit other things parents commonly say to their teenage children.

C 1.4 Focus on the review title and the photo of the author, Carol. Get them to guess the meaning of *in a nutshell* (= in the fewest possible words). Then have them quickly read through the review and find out what type of book is being reviewed (a guide for parents with teenage children).

Sts read the text in more detail and do the matching activity. Check the meanings of any unknown words in the review. Highlight the meaning of *It's no use ...* (= used for saying that something is unlikely to have a successful result).

Explain that what they are going to hear is a radio interview with Carol Zimmerman, the author of the book. Play the CD for sts to check their answers. Paircheck first to help you see where some might have had difficulty.

Answers

a 3 b 1 c 2 d 4

See Teacher's Book p.311 for Audio script 1.4.

Tip

Even if there are unknown words in the reading text, encourage sts to do the activities without pre-teaching them. This will develop their ability to guess meanings from context. You can go through the vocabulary with the class after they have had a go at the task, including the pronunciation of new words.

New words have the stressed syllables highlighted in pink. Encourage sts to try the pronunciation using the color code, e.g. reJECtion and iDENtities.

Song lyric: See Teacher's Book p.334 for notes about the song and an accompanying activity to do with the class.

D **Make it personal** Focus on the model in the speech bubble.

In pairs, sts answer the questions. When answering question 4, encourage sts to use the language from the lesson and talk about their family, e.g. *I get annoyed with my mom because ..., I really look up to my dad because ....*

Class feedback, and invite volunteers to tell the class something they learned about their classmates' family.

4 Grammar: Using *-ing* forms

A Go through the grammar box and check understanding of the example sentences. Point out that we sometimes use *in* after *There's no point* and *have difficulty*, e.g. *There's no point in arguing ..., Parents have difficulty in talking ...*

Refer sts back to the review in C and get them to make a list of all the *-ing* forms, then match them to 1–4 in the grammar box. Elicit that *They're building* in d is the present continuous form and does not fall into any of the categories 1–4.

Elicit examples of other phrasal verbs which are followed by the *-ing* form, e.g. *give up, worry about, look into, start off.*

Refer sts to **Common mistake**. Ask them which of the uses (1–4) this is. Personalize by asking if this sentence is one they have used themselves.

Answers

1 c (pressuring teens) 2 b (give up trying)
3 a (It's no use pushing) 4 d (Teens have trouble dealing)

Refer sts to the **Grammar expansion** on p.138.

Optional activities

- **Weaker classes:** Go through the basic spelling rules for the *-ing* form.
- In pairs, sts write a new sentence for each of the uses 1–4 in the grammar box. Monitor pairs, checking for accuracy. Invite several pairs to read their sentences to the class.
- Ask: *What annoys parents about their teenage children? What annoys teenagers about their parents?* Brainstorm ideas with the class, e.g. What annoys parents: being untidy, spending too much time on digital devices, spending too much money. What annoys teenagers: bugging them, asking them questions, giving them advice.

  In pairs, sts think of as many other ideas as they can. Encourage them to use the *-ing* form of the verb.

B 1.5 Read the speech bubble to the class and point out this is the answer to sentence 1. Sts rewrite sentences 2–6, adding prepositions as necessary. Point out that there is one extra verb in the box that they don't need.

Weaker classes: Before sts rewrite 2–6, go through the verbs in the box and elicit which of the verbs need prepositions (*listen to, hang out with*).

If you are short of time, check answers as a class. Otherwise play the audio for sts to check their answers. Explain that they are going to hear exchanges between Carol and her son, Phil.

Answers

1 Eating fruit every morning is good for you.
2 Spending too much time in front of that computer will hurt your eyes.
3 Reading good literature will help you write better.
4 Listening to loud music can damage your ears.
5 Doing too much exercise isn't good for you.
6 Hanging out with those guys will get you into trouble.

See Teacher's Book p.311 for Audio script 1.5.

C 1.6 Go through sentences 1–5. Check they know the meaning of the verbs in parentheses. Sts rewrite the sentences using the expressions in bold.

Again, if you are short of time, check answers as a class. Otherwise play the audio for sts to listen to Carol and Phil again to check their answers.

Answers

1 It's no use trying to convince me.
2 Carry on doing what you were doing.
3 I can't help wondering why you've been so quiet lately.
4 Are you having trouble sleeping?
5 It's not worth living in the past.

See Teacher's Book p.312 for Audio script 1.6.

Optional activity

Ask sts to think of other advice they might give to the parents of teenagers, using *no point, not worth, no use, e.g. There's no point trying to give teenagers advice!*

D Make it personal Go through the situations. Ask: *Have you ever been in any of these situations?* Ask them to tell the class what happened and how the situation was resolved (or not!)

Brainstorm and board phrases sts might use in the role plays, e.g. *Travelling on your own isn't safe. Hanging out with those friends will get you into trouble. There's no point leaving school if you don't know what you want to do.*

Role play one of the situations with yourself playing the teen, and a stronger st as your parent to set this up. Be sure to begin and end with the language in the speech bubbles. Then have two sts roleplay a second situation, before the whole class do it in pairs, using the situation of their choice.

Weaker classes: Have sts write out their roleplays first, then try and learn them. Get them to act them out from memory. If necessary, they can write down five or six prompt words to help them.

Workbook p.4.

4 Grammar: Using *-ing* forms

A Read and match 1–4 to examples a–d in Carol's review.

Common mistake

I have a hard time ~~to deal~~ *dealing* with my son.

Using *-ing forms:* subjects, verbs, and expressions	
1 as subject of a sentence *c*	**Raising teenagers** is a challenge. **Not listening to them** is the worst thing you can do.
2 after a phrasal verb ☐	If she doesn't want to talk, **carry on doing** what you're doing.
3 in a negative point of view ☐	**It's no good / It's not worth / There's no point arguing** with teenagers.
4 in some expressions of difficulty ☐	Parents **have difficulty / a hard time talking** to children. **I can't help saying** yes, no matter how hard I try to say no.

» Grammar expansion p.138

B ▶ 1.5 Rephrase Carol's advice to her son 1–6 (before the book!) using an *-ing* verb as subject. Choose from these verbs, adding a preposition if necessary. Listen to check.

do eat hang out listen read risk (v) spend

1 "Fruit every morning is good for you."
2 "Too much time in front of that computer will hurt your eyes."
3 "Good literature will help you write better."
4 "Loud music can damage your ears."
5 "Too much exercise isn't good for you."
6 "Those guys will get you into trouble."

"Eating fruit every morning is good for you."

Hmm … I hear this one almost every day.

C ▶ 1.6 Rewrite 1–5 using the expressions in bold. Listen to check. Do you think Carol became a better parent after the book?

1 Don't try to convince me. [**no use**] *It's no use trying to convince me.*
2 Continue to do what you were doing. [**carry on**]
3 It's hard not to wonder why you've been so quiet lately. [**can't help**]
4 Are you finding it hard to sleep? [**having trouble**]
5 It's not a good idea to live in the past. [**not worth**]

D **Make it personal** Choose a situation and role play a parent / teen conversation. Use expressions from the grammar box and C.

1 Teen: You want to go abroad on your own.
2 Parent: Your son / daughter never helps around the house.
3 Teen: You don't want your mom / dad to remarry.
4 Parent: The last phone bill was way too high.
5 Teen: You want to drop out of school and get a job instead.
6 Parent: You don't like the people your son / daughter has been hanging out with.

Mom, there's something I've been meaning to tell you. You see, I …

… And that's my final answer. There's no point even mentioning it again!

5 Reading

A In pairs, do you know people who have pets like this? Why do so many people treat their pets as equal members of the family?

My cousin has a birthday party for her dog every year. It's no use trying to stop her!

B 1.7 Read and complete the discussion forum with 1–4. Listen to check. In pairs, practice the pronunciation of the highlighted words.

1 owning a pet is good for your health
2 pets can help children develop emotionally
3 pets can teach us how to be responsible
4 owning a pet helps you meet new people

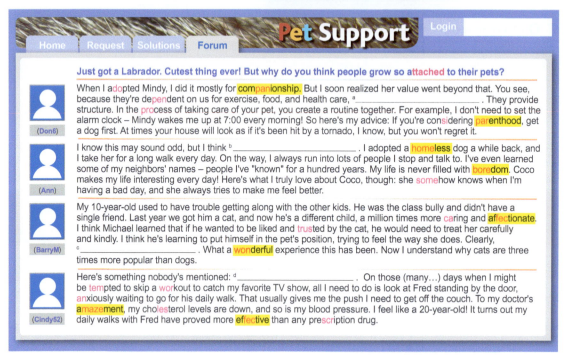

Pet Support Login

Home | Request | Solutions | Forum

Just got a Labrador. Cutest thing ever! But why do you think people grow so attached to their pets?

(Don6) When I adopted Mindy, I did it mostly for **companionship**. But I soon realized her value went beyond that. You see, because they're dependent on us for exercise, food, and health care, [a] ______________________. They provide structure. In the process of taking care of your pet, you create a routine together. For example, I don't need to set the alarm clock – Mindy wakes me up at 7:00 every morning! So here's my advice: If you're considering **parenthood**, get a dog first. At times your house will look as if it's been hit by a tornado, I know, but you won't regret it.

(Ann) I know this may sound odd, but I think [b] ______________________. I adopted a **homeless** dog a while back, and I take her for a long walk every day. On the way, I always run into lots of people I stop and talk to. I've even learned some of my neighbors' names – people I've "known" for a hundred years. My life is never filled with **boredom**. Coco makes my life interesting every day! Here's what I truly love about Coco, though: she somehow knows when I'm having a bad day, and she always tries to make me feel better.

(BarryM) My 10-year-old used to have trouble getting along with the other kids. He was the class bully and didn't have a single friend. Last year we got him a cat, and now he's a different child, a million times more caring and **affectionate**. I think Michael learned that if he wanted to be liked and trusted by the cat, he would need to treat her carefully and kindly. I think he's learning to put himself in the pet's position, trying to feel the way she does. Clearly, [c] ______________________. What a **wonderful** experience this has been. Now I understand why cats are three times more popular than dogs.

(Cindy52) Here's something nobody's mentioned: [d] ______________________. On those (many…) days when I might be tempted to skip a workout to catch my favorite TV show, all I need to do is look at Fred standing by the door, anxiously waiting to go for his daily walk. That usually gives me the push I need to get off the couch. To my doctor's **amazement**, my cholesterol levels are down, and so is my blood pressure. I feel like a 20-year-old! It turns out my daily walks with Fred have proved more **effective** than any prescription drug.

C Re-read the discussion forum. Write the people's names.

1 *Ann* is feeling more connected to her community.
2 ________ is not naturally inclined to an active lifestyle.
3 ________ thinks pets can prepare you to raise children.
4 ________ thinks having a pet can help you develop empathy.
5 ________ thinks pets are intuitive.

D Exaggeration is often used for emphasis. Find one example in each paragraph.

*At times your house will look as if it's **been hit by a tornado.***

E **Make it personal** Do you know anyone who has experienced any of the four benefits of pet ownership in B? Can you think of any others?

Me! Number 4! I met my wife while I was buying tropical fish in a pet shop.

Lesson Aims: Sts learn vocabulary to talk about pet ownership, and read about and discuss the advantages of owning a pet.

Skills	Language	Vocabulary	Grammar
Reading a discussion forum about pets Playing a guessing game	Using exaggeration for emphasis, e.g. *At times your house will look as if it's been hit by a tornado.* Comparing groups of people, e.g. *Dog owners tend to be more extroverted than cat owners.*	Suffixes for adjectives and nouns, e.g. *-ment, -ship, -ness, -less (affectionate, amazement, boredom, companionship, effective, homeless, parenthood, wonderful)*	Review of comparative adjectives

Warm-up

Have sts, in pairs, think of as many other pets as they can in one minute. Class feedback and board the animals.

Ask the lesson title question: *How many pets have you lived with? What pets do you have now? Do you know anyone who has an unusual pet? Do you know anyone who treats their pet like a person? In what way?* In pairs, sts discuss the questions. Classcheck any interesting answers.

5 Reading

A Focus on the photos. Ask them to describe what they can see and if it reminds them of anyone. In pairs, sts discuss the questions. Monitor for any particularly good stories to share with class.

B 1.7 Have sts read through statements 1–4 and ask: *Do you agree with them all? Why / why not?* Focus on the forum title and headline question. Elicit / Tell sts that *labrador* is a breed of dog.

Set a time limit (one minute) to encourage sts to read it quickly for gist and to do the completion task.

Paircheck, then classcheck. The completed text is available on audio for sts to listen and check their answers.

Answers

a 3 b 4 c 2 d 1

See Student's Book p.10 for Audio script 1.7.

C Sts read sentences 1–5. Check they understand *intuitive* in 5 (= having the ability to understand or know something without any direct evidence).

Give sts a little longer this time to read the text so they can read for detail. Peercheck, then classcheck.

Answers

2 Ann 3 Cindy52 4 Don6 5 Ann

Optional activity

Board these definitions and ask sts to find words and expressions in the text which have a similar meaning:

1 *to rely on* (to be dependent on)
2 *to think about* (consider)
3 *meet* (run into)
4 *to imagine how someone else feels* (to put yourself in someone else's position)
5 *motivation* (push)

D Elicit or give examples to explain *to exaggerate* (= to make something seem larger, more important, better, or worse than it really is), e.g. *Oscar eats more than an elephant!* Have sts individually find examples in each paragraph. Peercheck, then classcheck. Ask: *Did you enjoy that text?* to get some feedback on their reading experience.

Answers

Para 1: At times your house will look as if it's been hit by a tornado.
Para 2: people I've "known" for a hundred years
Para 3: a million times more caring and affectionate
Para 4: I feel like a 20-year-old!

E **Make it personal** Use the example to encourage them to come up with more humorous options. Then invite volunteers to share their examples with the rest of the class. Can they think of any other benefits?

Optional activities

- **Stronger classes:** Sts write a short paragraph for about someone they know or someone they heard about in E.
- Have a class debate. Board this motion: *People who live in apartments should not be allowed to keep pets. Those that do, should have to pay tax.* Divide the class into four groups. Tell two of the groups they are going to argue 'For' and two of the groups they are going to argue 'Against'.

  In their groups, sts brainstorm ideas. If the groups need help, you can prompt them with a few ideas.

  Sts present their ideas to the class. Make sure each member of the group speaks. Encourage them to explain their points of view. Give each group a time limit to present their arguments.

  When all groups have spoken, have sts vote for the most convincing group (not their own!).

6 Vocabulary: Suffixes

A 1.8 Before reading **If you know suffixes**, ask: *What's a suffix?* (= a letter or group of letters added to the end of a word or root, forming a new word). *Why do you think it is useful to recognize patterns of suffixes?* (It helps you to guess the meaning of unknown words.)

Go through the suffix box together with the class. Focus on the list of nouns and adjectives, and elicit others which have similar suffixes, e.g. *loneliness, boyhood.*

Sts complete the chart, then play the audio for them to check their answers. Ask sts how they identified the parts of speech in each word.

Answers

1 boredom 2 amazement 3 parenthood
4 companionship 5 homeless 6 effective
7 wonderful 8 affectionate

B 1.8 After sts have circled the correct rules, drill pronunciation of the words in the completed chart in A and the pink box, checking that sts stress the correct syllable. If there's time, they can text each other in pairs too, A saying the root and B the suffix, e.g. A: *achieve* B: *ment*. Then they swap.

Answers

1 never 2 often

Optional activity

Choose a word from the chart and clap out the syllables, emphasizing the stressed one. Ask sts to guess which word it is. Have sts do this themselves in pairs, taking turns to clap out the syllables.

C 1.9 Sts read the text ignoring the gaps to get the general meaning. In pairs, sts do the gap-filling activity. Allow them to use a dictionary, if necessary.

Weaker classes: Write the suffixes in a random order on the board and then ask sts to match them to the words in the text.

Check answers as a class or play the audio for sts to listen to a conversation between Claire and Donald about the text, in order to check their answers.

Ask which of the people in the audio, the man or the woman, is not a dog lover (the man).

Discuss with the class whether they agree with the research results, getting them to justify their opinions by giving examples of dog/cat owners they know.

Model pronunciation of the highlighted words with their suffixes, reminding them of the rules in B.

Answers

differences, talkative, approachable, assertiveness, adventurous, ownership, openness, predictable, imaginative, freedom, maintenance, relationships

Optional activity

In small groups, sts write all the suffixes (e.g. *-ment, -ance, -ure*) that they have learned on individual cards. They take turns to turn over a card and read out the suffix. The other sts in the group have to write as many words as they can think of with that suffix in a given time (e.g. one minute).

D 1.8 **Make it personal** Play the audio for sts to listen to two friends playing a guessing game.

1 After sts have listened and guessed correctly, ask them to listen again and make a list of the adjectives they hear (*talkative, approachable, sociable, friendlier, predictable*).

2 In pairs, sts play the game. Perhaps add a couple more fun examples yourself if you think it will help them get going.

See Teacher's Book p.312 for Audio script 1.10.

Tip

Weaker classes: Sts will probably benefit from more modeling, so you can choose one or two pairs to model the guessing game for the whole class first.

Optional activity

For extra practice, put sts with a new partner and have them repeat the game. Choose a few pairs to play the game in front of the class while the others listen and make a note of the adjectives they hear.

Song lyric: See Teacher's Book p.334 for notes about the song and an accompanying activity to do with the class.

Workbook p.5.

6 Vocabulary: Suffixes

A 1.8 Read *If you know suffixes*. Then scan 5B and put the highlighted words in the chart according to their stress. Listen to check. How did you identify the part of speech?

If you know suffixes, you can ...

1 recognize parts of speech (noun, verb, adjective, etc.).
2 infer meaning (e.g., *less* = without / *careless* = without care).
3 expand your vocabulary by "anglicizing" similar words from other languages (Spanish *-miento* = English *-ment: movimiento* = *movement*).

Nouns		Adjectives	
■ ▫ 1 *boredom*	■ ▫ ▫ 3 ______	■ ▫ 5 *homeless*	■ ▫ ▫ 7 ______
▫ ■ ▫ 2 ______	▫ ■ ▫ ▫ 4 ______	▫ ■ ▫ 6 ______	▫ ■ ▫ ▫ 8 ______

Nouns
achievement
annoyance
existence
failure
friendship
happiness
neighborhood
security
stardom

Adjectives
affectionate
careless
comparative
courageous
effective
helpful
preventable

B 1.8 Listen again. Circle the correct rules.

1 Suffixes are [**always** / **never**] stressed.
2 Suffixes are [**often** / **rarely**] pronounced with a schwa /ə/.

C 1.9 Complete the text with words ending in the correct suffix. Listen to check. Do you agree with these research results?

I'm a dog person, but I'm not very talkative.

Are you a **cat** person **or** a **dog** person?

A recent study found significant personality differ*ences*[0] between those who self-identified as either dog people or cat people. Dog owners tend to be more extroverted, talk___[1], and approach___[2] than cat owners. They also have greater self-discipline and tend to score higher on assertive___[3]. Dog people like to stick to plans and are not particularly adventur___[4].

Cat owner___[5] is usually associated with open___[6] to new ideas and different beliefs. Cat people are less predict___[7], and more imagin___[8], and they value their personal free___[9] more than dog people. Because cats require less mainten___[10] than dogs, cat people are more likely to be busy individuals who work a lot and have less time for close relation___[11].

D 1.10 **Make it personal** Listen to two friends playing a guessing game.

1 Who are they comparing? Check (✔) the correct answer after the beep.

☐ day people vs. night people ☐ couch potatoes vs. workout enthusiasts ☐ women vs. men
☐ motorcyclists vs. drivers ☐ small town people vs. big city people

2 In pairs, play the game:

A Compare two groups. Include suffixes from C.
B Guess who **A** is comparing.

They tend to be really courageous, and they usually value their freedom.

I think you're talking about ...

7 Listening

A In pairs, what characteristics do difficult people have in common?

> Difficult people don't listen. They just talk.

B 1.11 Listen to / Watch (0.00–2.46) Mary Bolster discuss difficult people and choose the correct answers.

1 Mary Bolster is ...
- [ ] a psychologist.
- [ ] the editor of a health magazine.
- [ ] a doctor.

2 She talks about all of these difficult people except ...
- [ ] salespeople.
- [ ] parents.
- [ ] bosses.
- [ ] coworkers.

C 1.11 Listen / Watch again. True (T) or False (F)? Which of the speaker's reasons do you remember?

The best way to deal with difficult people is to ...

1 try to change how you react to them.
2 just state the facts as neutrally as possible.
3 act hurt so they feel guilty.
4 make sure they know you're angry.

D Make it personal Have you ever followed the advice in the video? Did it work?

> Well, I once had a teacher who was very unreasonable, and I felt totally stressed out. I decided to ...

8 Language in use

A 1.12 Read and complete the webpage with 1–4. Listen to check. Did you learn any new ways of dealing with difficult people?

1 It's important for you to put yourself in other people's positions
2 It's useful to give yourself time to think
3 These guidelines will make it easier for you to be understood
4 It feels good to be heard

THIS WEEK'S SURVIVAL TIPS

Topic of the week | Dealing with difficult people

Coming up soon:
- Meeting your in-laws for the first time
- New Year's Eve with the whole family
- Your first day at school / work
- Your first job interview
- Passing your driver's test
- An oral test in English
- Saying "no" to people you love

Five easy ways to help you talk to difficult people:

a Pause and take a deep breath. Count to ten, if necessary. ______ and assess the situation. The less you react, the better.

b Think like them. ______ so you can see the situation from another perspective. Listen carefully. If you were in their situation, what would it feel like?

c Concede a little. Even if you agree with only one percent of what they are saying, let them know. Remember: ______ and have your opinion valued.

d Watch your body language. Look the other person in the eye, smile if you can, and don't cross your arms. ______ . Remember: Successful communication is less than ten percent verbal.

e Above all, be patient.

12

Lesson Aims: Sts learn vocabulary to talk about dealing with difficult people and situations and listen to an expert giving advice.

Skills	Language	Vocabulary	Grammar review
Watching a video of an expert talking about dealing with difficult people Discussing survival tips for difficult situations, e.g. meeting your in-laws for the first time	Giving tips, using the imperative, e.g. *Pause and take a deep breath.*	Personality adjectives, e.g. *aggressive, annoying, assertive, demanding, inconsiderate, obnoxious, strident, unreasonable*	Using the infinitive with adjectives, e.g. *It's better to keep calm.*

Warm-up

Board the following adjectives and elicit the stress: *unreasonable, bossy, inconsiderate, selfish, controlling, opinionated, childish, arrogant, temperamental, rude*. Ask: *Can you think of anyone who has these personality traits?* Invite sts to add any other personality adjectives they know. If there's time, get them to think of opposite adjectives for each one.

Ask the lesson title question: *What difficult people do you know? What makes them difficult?* In pairs, sts discuss the questions.

7 Listening

A Ask: *What type of people do you commonly come into contact with on a daily basis?* Prompt sts if necessary, e.g. sales assistants, teachers / employers, friends, family members, work colleagues, classmates, neighbors.

Ask sts to think of someone they have come into contact with recently who they consider to be 'difficult', and tell their partner about them. Encourage them to use some of the adjectives from the warm-up. Ask them to agree on which personality traits difficult people tend to have in common.

B 1.11 Explain that sts are going to listen to / watch Stacey Tisdale, a presenter on a Howdini video interviewing Mary Bolster, who gives advice about dealing with difficult people. Ask them to try and guess what they might say. Don't confirm or deny their guesses at this stage.

Play the video for them to watch and choose the correct answers. Peercheck, then classcheck.

Answers

1 the editor of a health magazine 2 parents

See Teacher's Book p.311 for Video script 1.11.

Background information

Howdini, mentioned on the video, is a source of how-to videos and blogs by experts in various fields such as health, beauty, food, entertaining, pets, travel.

C 1.11 Go through statements 1–4 and check sts understand them. Re-play the video and have sts say which of the statements is true. Classcheck, then in pairs, see how many statements they can remember.

Weaker classes: You might want to play it a third time for them to check.

Answers

1 T 2 T 3 F 4 F

D **Make it personal** Ask: *What did you think of the interview? Do you think Mary Bolster's advice is good or bad? Why?* Invite sts to tell the class about situations where they have had to deal with difficult people and how they did it. Ask: *What other strategies could you use, apart from those advised by Mary Bolster? Can you think of any more difficult questions the interviewer could have asked?*

8 Language in use

A 1.12 Ask sts to read statements 1–4. Discuss the meaning of *to put yourself in other people's positions* (= to imagine how someone else feels in a difficult situation). Tell them we can also say *to put yourself in someone else's shoes*. Ask if there is a similar expression in their language.

Sts read through the webpage and match the statements with the gaps. Ignore the *Coming up soon* topics for now, they are dealt with in 9E.

Either play the audio for sts to check their answers or check answers as a class.

Answers

a 2 b 1 c 4 d 3

See Teacher's Book p.312 for Audio script 1.12.

Optional activity

Ask sts to underline and, for fun, in pairs mime the instructions on the webpage (*pause, take a deep breath, count to ten, assess the situation, think like them, listen carefully, concede a little, watch your body language, look the other person in the eye, smile, don't cross your arms, be patient*). They can quickly test each other in pairs, A: miming, B: saying the instruction. Remind them we use the imperative – (Don't +) base form – when we give advice or warnings.

B Make it personal Refer sts to the example in the speech bubble. Discuss the meaning of *to lose your temper* (= to get angry suddenly). Have sts discuss the questions in pairs, then open up to a class discussion. If there's time, have a class vote on the one they think is the most useful. Personalize further by asking: *Are you ever 'difficult' yourself?* or even *'Am I ever difficult as a teacher?'!*

9 Grammar: Using the infinitive

A Go through examples a–d in the grammar box . Highlight the forms in column 1 and check they understand the meanings. Highlight the position of *not* in the sentences (directly before the *to* infinitive). Refer sts to **Common mistakes**.

Sts check the correct rules. Peercheck, then classcheck. Elicit another example of each structure to ensure they have the patterns clear.

Answers

1 passive 2 not 3 can

Refer sts to the **Grammar expansion** on p.138.

B Sts re-read the sentences in 8A and match them to the patterns a–d in the grammar box. Classcheck.

Weaker classes: Ask sts which of the sentences 1–4 includes the passive form (3 and 4) before they do the task.

Answers

1 It's important for you to put yourself in other people's positions – b
2 It's useful to give yourself time to think – a
3 These guidelines will make it easier for you to be understood – d
4 It feels good to be heard – c

Song lyric: See Teacher's Book p.134 for notes about the song and an accompanying activity to do with the class.

C 1.13 Have sts do this individually. Invite volunteers to read out their corrected sentences, getting other sts to listen and correct them, if necessary. Then play the audio for them to listen to a class checking the answers to the task. Ask: *Do these sts on the audio sound similar to them? If not, how are they different?* Personalize further by asking: *Which of these mistakes might you have made before this lesson?*

Answers

I hope these tips will make it easier <u>for</u> you to handle some of the toxic people around you at home, school, or work. But keep in mind that it's important <u>to</u> (or <u>for you to</u>) choose your battles wisely. There will be times when you will be successful and times when it will be very difficult for the other person to <u>be</u> persuade<u>d</u>. In those cases, it's no use trying. Remember: It's impossible <u>to</u> change (or <u>for</u> you <u>to</u> change) someone. Change comes from within.

See Teacher's Book p.312 for Audio script 1.13.

D Before sts do the task, check any unknown vocabulary in the prompts, and elicit the stress on *advisable* and *intimidate*.

Have sts do the task individually. Paircheck, then classcheck. If there's time, sts can brainstorm more interview advice as this is a very generative situation many sts often face.

Answers

1 It's OK for you to be nervous.
2 It's natural for them to be curious about you.
3 It's important (for you) not to arrive late.
4 It's advisable for you to dress smartly.
5 It is not essential (for you) to keep checking your phone.
6 It's important (for you) not to be intimidated by the questions.

Optional activity

Board the following phrases: *It's not a good idea to ... , It's important not to ... .*

In pairs, sts think of as many ways to complete the phrases as they can.

E Make it personal Ask sts to look at the situations in the *Coming up soon* section of the webpage in 8A. Ask: *Which situation do you think you would find most difficult / awkward?* In pairs, sts rank them in order from 1–7 (1 = most difficult).

Put sts into groups. Encourage each group to choose a different situation and write survival tips for a webpage. Remind sts to use the *-ing* form in the grammar section on p.9, as well as the phrases in the grammar table in 9A.

Optional activity

Ask sts to make a poster entitled *How to be a successful English student*.

In pairs, have them brainstorm advice, e.g. *It's vital to listen carefully in class!* Tell them to choose the five best pieces of advice and create a poster. You can display the best ones on the classroom wall.

Workbook p.6.

B Make it personal Which tip in A is best in your opinion? Can you suggest any others?

I like the first one because I tend to lose my temper very easily – especially with my little brother.

9 Grammar: Using the infinitive with adjectives

A Read and check (✔) the correct rules in the grammar box.

Using the infinitive with adjectives: active and passive

	Active	Passive
adjective + (*not*) + infinitive	(a) It's **better to keep** calm.	(c) It's **hard not to be annoyed** by inconsiderate neighbors.
adjective + *for* + object + (*not*) + infinitive	(b) It's **easy for us not to listen** to people.	(d) It's **essential for people to be treated** with respect.

1 Use *be* + past participle in ☐ **active** ✔ **passive** sentences.
2 Use ☐ ***not*** ☐ ***don't*** to make negative sentences.
3 You ☐ **can** ☐ **can't** use the comparative form of adjectives.

Common mistakes

It's important for you ^*to* show that you care.

It's advisable ~~don't~~ *not to* raise your voice.

» Grammar expansion p.138

B Re-read sentences 1–4 in 8A. Which pattern in the grammar box (a–d) is each sentence?

It's important for you to put yourself in other people's positions – b

C ▶ 1.13 Read the end of the webpage in 8A and correct four mistakes. Then listen to four students checking their answers in class.

I hope these tips will make it easier ^*for* you to handle some of the toxic people around you at home, school, or work. But keep in mind that it's important choose your battles wisely. There will be times when you will be successful and times when it will be very difficult for the other person to persuade. In those cases, it's no use trying. Remember: It's impossible you change someone. Change comes from within.

D Complete survival tips 1–6, making them negative or passive, if necessary.

How to survive your first job interview!

1 OK / you / be nervous *It's OK for you to be nervous.*
2 natural / they / be curious / you
3 important / arrive late
4 advisable / you / dress smartly
5 essential / keep checking / phone
6 important / intimidate / by the questions

E Make it personal Choose another situation from the website in 8A. In groups, create five survival tips and add more details. Share them with the class. What's the most popular tip?

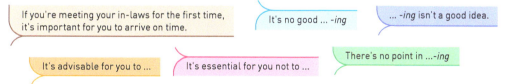

If you're meeting your in-laws for the first time, it's important for you to arrive on time.

It's no good … -*ing*

… -*ing* isn't a good idea.

It's advisable for you to …

It's essential for you not to …

There's no point in …-*ing*

10 Listening

A 1.14 What do you think Steve Jobs' opinion on technology was? Listen to the beginning of a radio program to check.

- [ ] We should limit how much technology our kids use at home.
- [ ] We should encourage our kids to be as digitally connected as possible.

Steve Jobs, co-founder, chairman and CEO of Apple Inc. (1955–2011)

B 1.15 In pairs, list three possible arguments for Jobs' opinion. Listen to the rest of the interview. Were any of your ideas mentioned?

C 1.15 Listen again and fill in the missing words.

According to Dave Jackson, the guest on the radio program, ...

1 online *bullying* is a real problem, but there are others.
2 too much texting can stop teens from developing ________ .
3 texting can affect students' ________ progress.
4 electronic devices are making people ________ .
5 it's ________ to chat every day by text with people you haven't met face to face.

D Which statement in **C** do you agree with most? In pairs, explain your choice. Any big differences?

I believe online bullying is a terrible problem, but I agree, too much texting is, too.

11 Keep talking

A 1.16 **How to say it** Complete sentences 1–4. Listen to check. Then repeat, sounding as convincing as you can.

Developing an argument (1)

1 For one *thing*, I believe digital technology is making people crueler.
2 What's ________, texting is making teens lazy.
3 Not to ________ the fact that we're unlearning how to communicate in the real world.
4 On ________ of that, our digital relationships are becoming too superficial.

B Read Dave Jackson's survey results and choose a statement you strongly agree with. List three arguments to support it.

Summary of results of survey on parenting skills

Statement	Agree	Disagree
It's important for children to receive a weekly allowance.	agree 53%	disagree 47%
Children should grow up as slowly as possible.	agree 82%	disagree 18%
It is also the parents' job – not only the school's – to educate children.	agree 37%	disagree 63%
It's no use choosing your children's careers for them.	agree 64%	disagree 36%
It's essential for parents to be strict with their children.	agree 51%	disagree 49%

C In groups, present your ideas using *How to say it* expressions. Your classmates will take notes on 1–3.

1 Were there any long pauses?
2 How many expressions were used?
3 Were there any important mistakes?

It's important for children to get a weekly allowance to begin to appreciate money. For one thing ...

Lesson Aims: Sts listen to a radio discussion about digital technology and learn language for developing a verbal and written argument.

Skills
Listening to a radio program about raising children in a digital age
Writing an effective paragraph, ordering arguments clearly and logically and using connectors

Language
Phrases for structuring and developing an argument, e.g. *First, To begin with, In addition, Besides that, Moreover, For one thing, On top of that, Not to mention the fact that, What's more, Finally, Lastly*

Warm-up

Board the lesson title question: *Do you still make voice calls?* and follow-up questions: *to who, how often, using an app?*, etc. Have sts discuss in pairs, then board other interesting questions about how they use their phones for them to add to their discussion: *Are there many differences between you? What are your favorite apps? What are the three most common things you do on your phone? How do you think phones/phone use will evolve in the future?*

Focus on the photo on page 14. Ask: *What do you know about Steve Jobs? When did he die?* Ask sts if they saw the Steve Jobs movie. Ask: *Who played Steve Jobs?* (Michael Fassbender). *Was he a 'difficult' man in any way? Would you like to have met him?*

Background information

Steve Jobs (1955–2011) was an American information technology entrepreneur. He was the co-founder, chairman and chief executive officer of Apple Inc. He revolutionized modern technology, changing people's attitudes to style and packaging. He met Apple co-founder Steve Wozniak, computer scientist, when he was 13. Wozniak was 18 at the time. They formed Apple Computer on April 1, 1976.

10 Listening

A 1.14 Encourage sts to guess what Steve Jobs' opinion on technology was. If they need prompting, ask: *Do you think he was in favor of children using technology?*

Ask sts to choose between the two statements, then play the audio for them to check. Classcheck. Ask: *Are you surprised by this?*

Answer

We should limit how much technology our kids use at home.

See Teacher's Book p.313 for Audio script 1.14.

B 1.15 In pairs, sts think of three possible arguments for Jobs' opinion. Encourage them to make as many guesses as possible, e.g. *because looking at screens is bad for children's eyes.*

Weaker classes: You could brainstorm possible arguments with the class.

Play the audio for sts to check if the guest on the radio show mentions any of their ideas. Class feedback.

See Teacher's Book p.313 for Audio script 1.15.

C 1.15 Sts can fill in the missing words from memory before they listen. Re-play the audio for sts to check their answers. Classcheck.

Answers

1 bullying 2 empathy 3 academic 4 antisocial
5 strange

D Sts discuss the statements in C with a partner and decide which they most agree with.

Check answers by asking sts to report back to the class which statements they and their partner agree / disagree with using these expressions: *We both agree that … . My partner thinks … but I disagree. I think … .*

As a follow-up, ask: *Do you think it's a good idea for restaurants and bars not to offer Wi-Fi to encourage people to interact more?*

11 Keep talking

A 1.16 **How to say it** Sts complete the sentences, then play the audio for them to check.

In pairs, sts practice the sentences. Monitor round the class checking pronunciation and stress.

Answers

1 thing 2 more 3 mention 4 top

B Go through the results of the survey. Ask: *Which do you agree / disagree with?*

Have sts work individually to choose a statement they strongly agree with and then list three arguments.

C In groups of four or five, sts take turns to present their ideas. Monitor round the class and give help where necessary. When all have finished, ask one or two sts to present their ideas to the whole class, and allow others to respond where they disagree.

Song lyric: See Teacher's Book p.335 for notes about the song and an accompanying activity to do with the class.

Warm-up

Ask: *Are you allowed to use cell phones in the classroom? What are the rules regarding cell phones? Do you agree with them?*

Ask sts to think of things they can do on a smartphone, e.g. *alarm clock, set reminders (e.g. homework!), flashlight, record pairwork, text/dictate messages, take photos, play games, take notes, send emails, add language learning apps*. Have them write a list.

Classcheck and board sts' ideas. Go through them one by one and ask whether each one is a useful function for the classroom.

12 Writing: An effective paragraph

A Focus on the essay title. Sts read through the essay quickly and underline all the different phone functions mentioned, e.g. checking the weather, calculator, looking up a word online.

Sts answer the questions. Peercheck, then classcheck. Ask them which of the functions they had in the list from the warm-up.

Answers

1. Three: using your cell phone is rude and disrespectful to teachers; texting in the classroom might result in gossip and make sts uncomfortable; sts need to learn self-discipline and get used to not being able to go online whenever they want to
2. Sts' own answers
3. First, In addition, Finally

B Go through **Write it right!** with the class. Elicit the topic sentence. Focus on the building argument phrases and ask which ones sts already use.

Answer

I believe technology should be restricted in class for three reasons.

C Go through **Common mistakes**, highlighting the punctuation errors. Ask: *Have you ever made these mistakes? What do you find hardest about English punctuation?*

Sts complete the the task. Paircheck, then classcheck.

Answer

There are several advantages to texting over voice calls**. To** begin with**,** it allows shy people to say things they wouldn't otherwise**. Besides** that**,** when you text someone**,** you can think carefully about the message before hitting send.

Tip

With exercises where sts are spotting errors, it's usually a good idea to give them a target number to aim for (in this case 5, including the example) so they don't spend too long on it nor start inventing all sorts of unlikely additional mistakes!

D Your turn! As this is the first writing activity, it's a good idea to set this up. If time, perhaps begin writing in class, although they could obviously do it all for homework.

Highlight the three-phase formula used throughout: Before, While and After, emphasizing the importance of all three.

Weaker classes: You could put sts in groups and have them choose one of the statements in 11B. Then they can brainstorm ideas together and plan their paragraphs before writing them up individually.

Sts could do this for homework. Assign each st a partner to email their essay to for peer correction.

Tip

When correcting sts' writing, use a correction code leaving them to correct their own mistakes, rather than making the corrections for them, e.g.

G = grammar mistake	WO = word order
Sp = spelling	M = missing word
P = punctuation	? = not clear
T = tense	! = silly mistake

Display the correction code on the classroom wall and use it consistently so that sts instantly recognize the correction.

Optional activity

Write the following common texting abbreviations on the board (without the meanings):

LOL (laughing out loud)	TTYL (talk to you later)
L8R (later)	BRB (be right back)
2moro (tomorrow)	THX (thanks)
CU (see you)	TQ (thank you)
IDK (I don't know)	NOYB (none of your business)
IDC (I don't care)	BTW (by the way)

In pairs, give sts one minute to guess what they stand for. Find out which pair got the most correct answers. Ask: *What abbreviations do you use in your language? Do you know any more abbreviations in English?*

Workbook p.7.

12 Writing: An effective paragraph

A Read this paragraph from a student exam. Answer 1–3.

1 How many arguments does the writer use?
2 Which ones do you agree with?
3 Which words / expressions does the writer use to introduce each argument?

Name: ....

Date: ....

IT'S ESSENTIAL FOR SCHOOLS TO HAVE PHONE RULES

If you've ever had to look up a word online, need a quick calculator, or need to check the weather or a fact quickly, you know your phone can be a useful learning resource. However, I believe technology should be restricted in class for three reasons. First, playing games, posting Facebook® updates, and watching videos while the teacher and other students are talking is rude and disrespectful. If cell phones have to be turned off in movie theaters, libraries, during exams, at border controls, and on planes, why are classrooms any different? In addition, texting back and forth in class might generate unnecessary gossip and make everybody uncomfortable. People don't want to think they're being talked about behind their backs. Finally, it's important for students to get used to not going online whenever they want to. Self-discipline and the ability to focus are critically important in today's hyper-connected world. For all of these reasons, I strongly believe that schools should implement stricter phone rules.

B Read *Write it right!* Then underline the topic sentence in A.

Write it right!

A topic sentence is the most important sentence in any paragraph because it summarizes the rest of the paragraph for the reader. The topic sentence is sometimes, but not always, the first sentence.

When building your argument, use connectors to add each new idea:

First,
To begin with,
↓
In addition,
Besides that,
Moreover, (more formal)
↓
Finally,
Lastly,

C Read the Common mistakes. Then punctuate the beginning of the paragraph below.

Common mistakes

Hyper-connected kids get bored ~~easily,~~ *easily.* ~~in addition they~~ *In addition, they* find it hard to focus.

There are several advantages to texting over voice calls~~,~~ *.* ~~to~~ *To* begin with it allows shy people to say things they wouldn't otherwise besides that when you text someone you can think carefully about the message before hitting send.

D Your turn! Write a 100-word paragraph arguing in favor of the statement you chose in 11B.

Before
Order your arguments clearly and logically. Write a topic sentence expressing the main idea of your paragraph.

While
Use a variety of connectors to link your ideas.

After
Proofread your paragraph carefully and check punctuation. Email it to a classmate before sending it to your teacher.

2 What's most on your mind right now?

1 Vocabulary: Noun modifiers

A 2.1 Listen and match people 1–6 to topics a–g. Pause and answer when you hear *Beep!* There is one extra topic.

Different people, different concerns

We asked people what was most on their minds.

a romantic relationships
b family dynamics
c material possessions
d financial problems
e physical appearance
f leisure activities
g peer pressure

B 2.1 Listen again. In pairs, who do you relate to most?

I felt sorry for the guy who had an argument with his father. I'm going through that, too.

C Read *Types of noun modifiers*. Then label the modifiers a–g from A as either A (adjective) or N (noun). Can you add three other combinations of these words?

Types of noun modifiers

We can use both nouns and adjectives to create new expressions:
a **family dinner** (noun + noun) = a dinner for the family
social issues (adjective + noun) = issues in society

romantic relationships – A

How about "family pressure"?

That's a good one. There's a lot of pressure in my family!

D Make it personal What's most on your mind these days? Share your thoughts in groups. Ask for and give more details. Any surprises?

I can't stop thinking about my dog. She's been sick for a week now.

Sorry to hear that. Have you taken her to a vet?

Common mistakes

I'm considering / thinking about ~~to go~~ *going* back to school.

Romantic ~~relations~~ *relationships* take up a lot of energy!

I'm thinking about ~~family's~~ / ~~families~~ *family* problems a lot.

I'm considering ...

I keep worrying about ...

I think about ... night and day.

I can't seem to focus on anything but ...

Lesson Aims: Sts learn vocabulary to talk about their worries, and listen to other people talking about what things they worry about.

Skills	Language	Vocabulary
Listening to someone conducting a survey about people's worries Discussing the optimum age for doing things, e.g. traveling abroad, getting married	Talking about worries and anxieties, e.g. *I can't stop worrying about ... , I keep worrying about ...* Expressing surprise, e.g. *I had no idea at all.*	Noun modifiers (nouns and adjectives), e.g. *family dinner, material possessions, peer pressures, social issues*

Warm-up

Board the following adjectives: *anxious, calm, trouble-free, concerned, preoccupied, laid-back*. Check understanding and elicit the stress. Ask sts: *Which of the adjectives best describes you? What sort of things make you anxious?*

Board the lesson title question: *What's most on your mind right now?* Elicit other ways of asking the question, e.g. *What's bothering / worrying you?* You could also teach the expression *to have a lot on your mind*. In pairs, sts discuss the title question, then feedback anything interesting to the class.

1 Vocabulary

A 2.1 Ask sts, in pairs, to describe the people in the photos, e.g. A describes one until B picks out who it is, then they swap roles. You could board some adjectives to help them, e.g. *thoughtful, relaxed, worried, confident*.

Go through topics a–g and check understanding. Explain that sts are going to listen to each of the people in the photos 1–6 answering the question *What's most on your mind right now?* Sts have to listen and say which of the topics a–g they mention. Point out that there is one extra topic they do not mention. Play the audio. Pause and paircheck each time when you get to the beep, then classcheck.

Answers

1 b 2 e 3 d 4 a 5 c 6 g

See Teacher's Book p.313 for Audio script 2.1.

Optional activity

Ask sts which of the concerns a–g they worry about most. Ask them to rank them in order 1–7 (1 = worry about most), then compare their lists in pairs. Which is the class' number one worry?

B 2.1 Have sts read the example in the speech bubble and check they understand the meaning of *to go through* (= to experience). Tell sts we often use the expression *to go through a bad / difficult time*.

Sts listen again to get a deeper understanding of each person's issue. Get them to note, for example, three key words for each speaker, then compare the ones they choose. In pairs, ask them to discuss the people from A and decide who they relate to most, explaining why. Monitor for accuracy of language they picked up from the audio.

Tip

Ask sts to record their conversation on a cell phone, and listen to it later to check pronunciation and fluency.

C Go through **Types of noun modifiers** with the class. Then ask sts, in pairs, to classify the modifiers in A as either adjectives or nouns. Do the first one with them as an example.

Elicit other examples (e.g. *family party / outing / car; social work / life / club*). Ask sts how they would say these phrases in their own language. Explain that we sometimes call these phrases compound nouns. Do the first one with them as an example.

Answers

Adjective: romantic relationships, financial problems, physical appearance

Noun: family dynamics, material possessions, leisure activities, peer pressure

Other combinations of the words: family problems, family relationships, physical activities

D **Make it personal** Before sts do the activity, refer them to **Common mistakes**. Ask: *Are these mistakes you have made? Who do you imagine might be saying these things?*

Put sts into small groups to discuss what's most on their mind these days. Encourage them to use the expressions in the speech bubbles. At the end, invite volunteers to tell the class something surprising they have learned about one of their classmates.

Tip

Weaker classes: Before a groupwork activity like the one in D, have sts note down some ideas on paper first before they share their ideas in groups.

Song lyric: See Teacher's Book p.335 for notes about the song and an accompanying activity to do with the class.

2 Listening

A Ask sts what they can say about pictures 1–4. Ask: *Where are the people? Who do you think they are? What's happening?* Encourage sts to speculate, e.g. *Maybe the man is ... . The boys might ... It looks as if the teacher is ... .*

Optional activity

To lead into B, play Hangman quickly on the board with the word *adolescent*. When sts have guessed the word, elicit behaviors they associate with adolescents, e.g. *they go to bed late, get up late, are easily influenced by their peers, don't respect authority.*

B 2.2 Ask sts to read through the opinions and check meaning. Ask: *Which do you agree / disagree with?*

Explain that sts are going to listen to April and her dad discussing an article he has read about the adolescent brain. Sts should number the opinions in the order they hear them mentioned. Play the audio. Paircheck, then classcheck.

Answers

1 Young people don't think about the consequences of their actions.
2 It's hard for young people to plan and organize so they can reach their goals.
3 Natural body rhythms in young people are different from adults.
4 Young people listen to their friends more than adults.

See Teacher's Book p.313 for Audio script 2.2.

C 2.2 Read through the opinions with the class. Then re-play the audio for sts to mark who believes each one. Make sure they understand that for some of the opinions, both April and her dad agree with them. Classcheck. To end, ask: *What do you think of them both and their relationship?*

Weaker classes: Pause the conversation after the relevant answers.

Answers

1 D 2 B 3 B 4 D 5 D 6 A

See Teacher's Book p.313 for Audio script 2.2.

D Go through the example and refer sts back to the types of noun modifiers on p.16.

Sts rephrase the underlined parts of the sentences, then peercheck. You could re-play audio 2.2 so they can listen and check.

Answers

1 schoolwork 2 the adolescent brain 3 scientific facts
4 instant decisions 5 sleep patterns, our body clocks
6 car crashes

E Ask sts to try and complete the speech bubble, e.g. *She clearly didn't think about what her hair would look like*. In pairs, sts describe the pictures in A using noun modifiers. Invite pairs to share their sentences with the class.

Answers

1 bad / instant decisions (Young people don't think about the consequences of their actions.)
2 car crashes (Young people don't think about the consequences of their actions.)
3 adolescent brain (Young people listen to their friends more than adults.)
4 sleep patterns, body clocks (Natural body rhythms in young people are different from adults.)

Optional activity

Give sts two minutes to think of as many other compound nouns as they can, e.g. *film star, musical instrument, modern language, winter sport*.

F Make it personal

1 2.3 **How to say it** Ask sts to complete the sentences from memory. Play the audio to classcheck. Then ask them who said the expressions (1 April, 2 Dad, 3 April, 4 April).

Re-play the audio for sts to listen and repeat. Then ask them to practice the expressions in pairs. Monitor, checking they use the correct intonation.

Answers

1 all 2 occurred 3 kidding 4 amazes

2 Go through the list of things with the class and ask: *Which of these things have you done? How old were you when you first did it? How old do you legally have to be before you can do these things?* Take a range of responses.

In small groups, sts discuss what age they think you should be to be able to do these things. Elect a spokesperson for each group to report back their ideas to the rest of the class. If there are disagreements, take a vote to find the majority class opinion.

Optional activity

Discuss how old you have to be in the U.S. to do these things. Ask sts for homework to research how old you have to be in other countries.

Workbook p.8.

2 Listening

A What's each person's problem in pictures 1–4? What do you think happened?

> This guy was driving with his feet out the window!

B 2.2 Listen to a conversation between April and her dad. Number the opinions 1–4 in the order you hear them.

- [ ] Young people listen to their friends more than adults.
- [ ] It's hard for young people to plan and organize so they can reach their goals.
- [1] Young people don't think about the consequences of their actions.
- [ ] Natural body rhythms in young people are different from adults.

C 2.2 Listen again. Who believes 1–6, Dad (D), April (A), or both (B)?

1 Young people's brains are immature until the age of 25.
2 April's last haircut was bad.
3 Teenagers are often tired during the day.
4 April is easily influenced by her friends.
5 Children under 25 should live with their parents.
6 Young people are adults at 18.

D Rephrase 1–6 using noun modifiers to replace the underlined text.

1 I'm worried about the work you're doing for school.
I'm worried about your schoolwork.
2 I was just reading an article about the brain of the adolescent.
3 You can't argue with facts that are scientific.
4 They make decisions in an instant they often regret.
5 Our patterns of sleep, clocks regulating our bodies, are different.
6 Lots of crashes involving cars are caused by young drivers.

E In pairs, how many noun modifiers can you use to describe the pictures in A? Which reasons in B explain the situations? Similar opinions?

> She sure has an awful haircut! She clearly didn't think about ...

F **Make it personal** Discuss young people's responsibilities.

1 2.3 **How to say it** Complete these expressions from the conversation in B. Then listen to check.

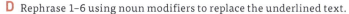

Expressing surprise

What they said	What they meant
1 I had no idea at *all* (that) ...	I had absolutely no idea (that) ...
2 It never ________ to me (that) ...	I never thought (that) ...
3 You've got to be ________ !	This is a joke, right?
4 It ________ me (that) ...	It really surprises me (that) ...

2 In groups, decide at what age young people should be able to do these things and why. Use *How to say it* expressions.

babysit   drive a car   get a tattoo   get married   join the army   travel abroad alone   vote

> It amazes me that some people say you should be 25 or over to drive a car. I'm 19 and I'm a really careful driver.

> Well, maybe you're the exception and not the rule.

3 Language in use

A 2.4 Listen and fill in the missing words. As you listen, notice the silent /t/ at the end of some words.

the best thing   the biggest problem   the hardest thing

Sign in | Join

Online Quick Survey

Do you have a sweet tooth?

We asked our readers what sweet **treats** they can't resist. Here's what they told us!

I usually have an [1] ___________ every afternoon. The best thing about it is that it wakes me up for my afternoon classes.

Carmen, 17

[2] ___________!! The biggest problem is **weight gain** if I have one every day.

Greg, 24

I love a big [3] ___________ for dessert in restaurants. The hardest thing is sharing it with other people!

Marcella, 16

I have two or three [4] ___________ a day. The good thing is the [5] ___________, which gives me energy. It **keeps me going**, and I really need it because I play a lot of sports.

Dieter, 19

[6] ___________ is my favorite! Going to our local [7] ___________ is a **big deal** for my family. The best part is all the different [8] ___________, so it never gets boring!

Nancy, 18

There's definitely an advantage to [9] ___________! I eat a lot of them to pick me up. However, the **disadvantage** is that they make you feel even more tired later, when the effect **has worn off**.

Ben, 20

In my family, we don't have [10] ___________ like ice cream and cookies, only fruit. My mom says fruit has [11] ___________.

Jackie, 21

B Complete the definitions with the **highlighted** words from A. Change the form if neccesary.

1 To ___*keep*___ someone ___*going*___ (v) means to give someone strength to continue.

2 A ___________ (n) is the opposite of an advantage.

3 It's a ___________ (n) means it's important.

4 A ___________ (n) is something that gives pleasure or enjoyment.

5 To ___________ (v) means to diminish in effect.

6 ___________ (n) is the process of becoming heavier.

C Make it personal Who in the survey do you identify with most / least? What foods can't you resist? Survey the class to find your top five.

Do you have a sweet tooth?

Not really, but I really can't resist pizza! It's such a great comfort food.

Lesson Aims: Sts learn vocabulary to talk about their diet and discuss their preferences.

Skills	Language	Vocabulary	Grammar
Listening to people talking about their diet Discussing preferences	Talking about food habits, e.g. *I have two or three soft drinks a day. I usually have an energy drink every afternoon.*	Food vocabulary, e.g. *candy bar, chocolate, cookies, energy drink, ice cream, sugar, sweets* Expressions for food habits, e.g. *keep me going, wear off, weight gain.*	Noun, verb, and sentence complements

Warm-up

Board these food items: *cake, chocolate, sweets, ice cream, French fries, chicken, candy bar, soft drink*. Ask: *Which of them are sweet / non-sweet?* You could teach the word *savory*. Explain that it means 'salty' or 'spicy', not 'sweet'. Ask sts, in pairs, to add five more words to the list. Classcheck.

In pairs, ask sts to discuss which of the foods they like / dislike. Board these questions to keep their conversation going: *Do you have a healthy diet? Do you think you eat too many sugary foods? Do you worry about your diet? Why? If you could make one change, what would / should it be?* Classcheck any interesting answers.

3 Language in use

A 2.4 Board *have a sweet tooth* and ask sts to guess what it means (= to like sugary foods). Ask if there is a similar expression in their language. Discuss the meaning of *resist* (= to refuse to accept, to do without). Ask: *What can't you resist?*

Draw sts' attention to the three superlative phrases above the survey and model pronunciation. Have them repeat after you. Explain that this silent 't' is common in English in fast connected speech when a word ends with a fricative sound (when air is pushed through a small space between your teeth and your tongue or lips) and the next word starts with a consonant.

Explain that sts are going to listen to the seven people in the photos talking about what sweet foods they like. Play the audio for sts to complete the gaps. Paircheck, then classcheck.

Answer key

1 energy drink 2 Candy bars 3 piece of cake
4 soft drinks 5 sugar 6 Ice cream 7 ice cream parlor
8 flavors 9 chocolate bars 10 sweet stuff
11 natural sugar

See Teacher's Book p.314 for Audio script 2.4.

Song lyric: See Teacher's Book p.335 for notes about the song and an accompanying activity to do with the class.

B First, have sts cover up the survey text in A, then try and complete the gaps in sentences 1–6. When they have completed as many as they can, allow them to check back in the survey.

Answer key

1 keep going 2 disadvantage 3 big deal 4 treat
5 wear off 6 Weight gain

Optional activities

Have sts write each of the highlighted words in the survey in a personalized sentence of their own. Elicit the class favorite.

Stronger classes: Ask sts to cover up B, and write their own definitions for the highlighted words in the survey. Have them compare their definitions with those in the Student's Book.

C Make it personal In groups of four or five, sts discuss the questions. Then tell them to take turns to interview the other sts in their group and find the five most popular sweet foods. Ask a spokesperson from each group to report back their results, and find out what the five most popular sweet foods are in the class. Do they know the ideal recipe for them?

Weaker classes: Elicit some useful questions and board them, e.g. *Which sweet / sugary foods do you find most difficult to resist? Which sweet foods do you eat too much of / eat every day?*

Optional activity

For homework, ask sts either to write the recipe for their perfect dessert, or research and write a paragraph about the health problems associated with eating too much sugary food or too much salt. Encourage them to use the *-ing* form from Unit 1, e.g. *Eating too much sugary food can cause diabetes*.

4 Grammar: Using noun, verb, and sentence complements

A Go through the grammar box. Make sure sts understand the example sentences. Focus on sentence 2 and explain that we sometimes add *about* + noun / pronoun or verb in the *-ing* form to clarify what we are talking about.

Refer sts to **Common mistakes**. If necessary, remind them of the rules for count and non-count nouns, and elicit others which have caused them problems in the past, e.g. *news, information*.

Ask sts to find five similar sentences in the survey on Student's Book p.18 (note that there are six in total), then complete the rules in the grammar box. Paircheck, then classcheck.

Weaker classes: Revise the basic spelling rules for the *-ing* form with sts. See Unit 1 Teacher's Book p.26.

Answers

1 The best thing about it is that it wakes me up for my afternoon classes. (S)
2 The biggest problem is weight gain if I have one every day. (N)
3 The hardest thing is sharing it with other people. (V)
4 The good thing is the sugar which gives me energy. (N)
5 The best part is all the different flavors. (N)
6 The disadvantage is that they make you feel even more tired. (S)

Rules:

After *is*, the form of the verb is an *-ing* form.

When a sentence follows *is*, the word *that* is optional.

Refer sts to the **Grammar expansion** on p.140.

Tip

Vary classes by checking **Common mistakes** before or after the production exercise. If you prefer to head off mistakes by anticipating them, do it before the activity. If you prefer sts to make mistakes and then correct them, do it after the activity.

B Books closed. Do the first matching with the class as an example. Board sentence 1 beginning: *The best thing about energy drinks is …* and elicit ideas for completing the sentence. Books open. Have sts choose the correct sentence ending from a–e.

Sts continue matching. When checking the answers, ask sts to identify the types of complement used in a–e (noun, verb or sentence).

Answers

1 c 2 a 3 e 4 b 5 d

Optional activity

Stronger classes: Ask sts to cover up the second half of the sentences a–e, and then complete the sentences themselves. When they have finished, they can compare their sentences with those in the Student's book.

C Do the first sentence together as a class. Focus on the example answer in the speech bubble. Elicit as many other answers as you can.

In groups, sts complete the sentences. Encourage them to use a mixture of noun, verb and sentence complements.

Invite volunteers to share their sentences with the class. Who thought of the most original sentences?

Optional activity

If they need more practice, board these gapped sentences for sts to complete:

The best thing about living in the city / country is … , but the worst thing is …

The problem with cooking for yourself / eating out is …

The worst thing about working at home / traveling by plane is … , but the best thing is …

D Make it personal

1 First, brainstorm ideas with the class for choice a. Then ask sts individually to note down the advantages and disadvantages for the other situations b–d.

Weaker classes: Brainstorm ideas together as a class and board them.

2 Have sts find a partner who thinks the opposite to them. For choice a, ask sts to show their hands if they'd prefer to go out. Have the remaining sts find a partner from those with their hands up. Do the same for choices b–d. Monitor round the class and make a note of common errors. Class feedback.

3 Take a class vote for each of the choices a–d.

Tip

Allow enough time for this activity. Weaker sts will need more preparation and thinking time. However, this is a great opportunity for them to practice the target language in a less controlled way. Resist correcting sts while they are talking. If necessary, write down any key mistakes and correct them later.

Workbook p.9.

4 Grammar: Using noun, verb, and sentence complements

A Study the sentences 1–3 in the grammar box. Find five similar ones in the survey, and write N (noun), V (verb) or S (sentence) next to each. Then check (✔) the correct rules.

Noun, verb, and sentence complements to describe advantages and disadvantages

1 The problem with cafés **is noise**. (N)
2 The good thing about going to one **is being able to sit down**. (V)
3 The best thing **is (that) they serve nice food**. (S)

After *is*, the form of the verb is an ☐ **infinitive** ☐ ***ing* form**.
When a sentence follows *is*, the word *that* ☐ **is** ☐ **isn't** optional.

Be careful with subject-verb agreement, and make sure sentences have a subject!

One of the best things about restaurants **is** good food.
One disadvantage of **restaurants** is that **they are** often crowded.

Common mistakes

The best thing about ~~fruits~~ *fruit* (NC) is that ~~they have~~ *it has* ~~less~~ *fewer* calories (C) than chocolate.

Remember that count (C) and non-count (NC) nouns are different!

Grammar expansion p.140

B Match the sentence halves. Do you agree with the statements?

1 The best thing about energy drinks is ...
2 The problem with fruit is ...
3 The biggest advantage of vegetables is ...
4 The most difficult thing about eating well is ...
5 The worst thing about junk food is ...

a ☐ that it's expensive, especially if it's organic.
b ☐ knowing what's good for you and what isn't.
c ☐ that they help you stay alert.
d ☐ that it's irresistible!
e ☐ vitamins and minerals, but less sugar.

I definitely agree with the first one. And another good thing about them is ...

C Complete 1–4 with your ideas. In groups, whose were the most original?

1 The best thing about paying taxes is ... , but the worst thing is ...
2 The most difficult thing about studying English is ... , but the most rewarding thing is ...
3 The easiest part of meeting someone new is ... , but the hardest part is ...
4 The biggest advantage of my neighborhood is ... , but the biggest disadvantage is ...

The best thing about paying taxes is that it feels good to be honest, but ...

D **Make it personal** Choices and more choices!

1 Note down the pluses and minuses of each choice (a–d). Then make a decision.

a On your birthday, would you rather go out to eat or throw a party at home?
b If you want to see a movie with your family, would you rather go to a theater or watch it on TV?
c If you want a new phone, would you rather buy it unlocked or sign up for a plan?
d On vacation, would you rather lie on the beach, hike in the mountains, or go sightseeing in your city?

2 Find a partner who thinks the opposite. Share your arguments. Use expressions from A and B. Can you change people's minds?

Well, the good thing about having a party is that you can invite more people.

Yes, but it's a lot of work.

3 Finally, take a class vote. Which choices win?

5 Vocabulary: Describing ability

A 2.5 Listen to a lecture on six types of intelligence. Number the pictures 1–6.

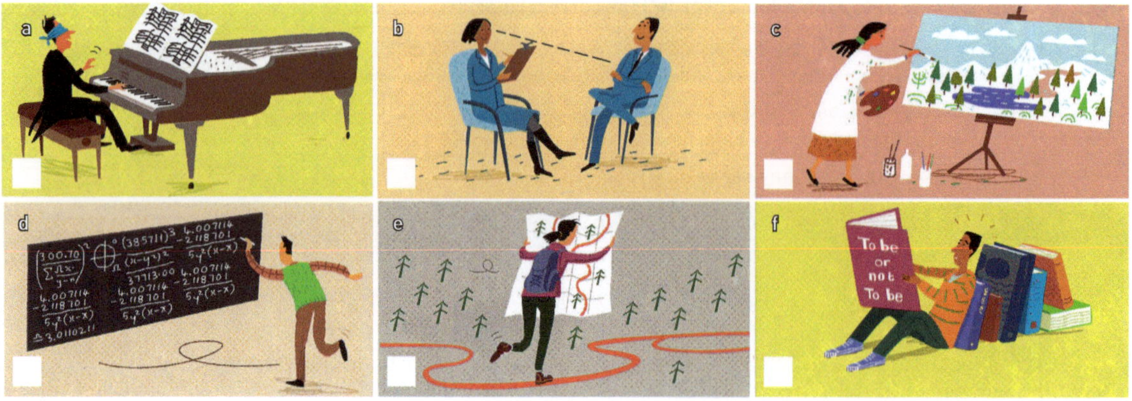

B 2.5 Guess the missing words in the notes (1–6) on the right. Be careful with verb forms. Listen again to check.

C Write the highlighted expressions from the notes in **B** in the chart. Then test your memory in pairs:

A Use the pictures and chart to describe the six types of intelligence.

B Prompt **A** and offer help when needed. Then switch roles.

	☺	☹
at	1 *be good at* 2 ________ 3 ________	be bad / hopeless at (music / singing)
for	4 ________	have no talent for (sports / playing ...)
of	5 ________	be incapable of (learning ...)
to	6 ________	be unable to (learn ...)

Someone who has logical-mathematical intelligence is really good at ...

Common mistake

I find it easy to speak / I'm good at speaking
~~I have facility to speak / speaking~~ in public.

NOTES

Intelligence types / people's abilities:

1 Logical-mathematical: They're good at analyzing and *solving* problems.

2 Verbal-linguistic: They find it easy to tell stories and ________ new concepts.

3 Musical: They're capable of remembering whole songs and ________ notes and tones.

4 Bodily-kinesthetic: They often have a gift for drawing and ________ .

5 Spatial: They're adept at interpreting graphs and ________ maps.

6 Interpersonal: They're skilled at interacting with other people and ________ their emotions and intentions.

D **Make it personal** In pairs, answer 1–3.

1 Which are your two strongest types of intelligence? How do you know?
2 Which one(s) do you think you should work on? Have you tried?
3 Do you think it makes sense to divide intelligence into different types? Why (not)?

I think my spatial intelligence is good. I find it easy to give directions, and I never get lost.

I'm just the opposite. I can barely understand my GPS!

Lesson Aims: Sts learn vocabulary to talk about types of intelligence, what they are good/bad at, people's abilities and the skills needed for different jobs.

Skills	Language	Vocabulary	Grammar review
Listening to an expert talking about different types of intelligence Reading about a theory of multiple intelligences	Talking about abilities, e.g. *be bad / hopeless / good at ... , have no talent for ... , be capable / incapable of ... , be unable to learn ... , find it easy to ... , have a gift for ... , be adept / skilled at ...*	*bodily-kinesthetic, interpersonal, logical, mathematical, musical, spatial, verbal-linguistic*	Reference words

Warm-up

Ask sts: *What are you good / bad at?* Elicit some examples to ensure they use the gerund, then have them discuss in pairs. Classcheck any surprising answers they heard.

Tell the class about the smartest person you know. Say: *The smartest person I know is .... He / She can .... He / She is amazing at ..., He / She always knows ....*

Ask: *Who's the smartest person you know? Why do you think they are smart?* Have sts discuss in pairs.

5 Vocabulary: Describing ability

A 2.5 Focus on the pictures. Ask sts, in pairs, to describe what the person is doing in each one.

Ask: *What do you think these people are good at?* Encourage as many suggestions as they can for each, e.g. *playing a musical instrument/reading music/hearing and playing new tunes, composing music.*

Play the audio for sts to number the pictures in the order the presenter talks about them.

Answers

1 d 2 f 3 a 4 c 5 e 6 b

See Teacher's Book p.314 for Audio script 2.5

B 2.5 Have sts read through the pink page notes first and identify the types of words which are missing from each gap, e.g. 2 verb (infinitive) 3 verb (*-ing* form) before they guess what the missing words are. Re-play the audio to classcheck. As a follow-up, go through the highlighted words and drill pronunciation. Point out that the prepositions in the highlighted expressions are unstressed.

Answers

1 solving 2 explain 3 recognizing 4 dancing
5 following 6 identifying

See Teacher's Book p.314 for Audio script 2.5.

C Focus on the chart. Go through the expressions in the column with the sad face, checking sts understand and can pronounce them.

Elicit a variety of true sentences from individual sts using the expressions, e.g. *My team are hopeless at scoring goals.*

Explain that the expressions they need to write in the column with the smiley face have the opposite meanings.

Read the example in the speech bubble and go through the **Common mistake** with them. Then in pairs, sts describe the six types of intelligence.

Answers

1 be good at 2 be adept at 3 be skilled at
4 have a gift for 5 be capable of 6 find it easy to

Optional activity

Have sts write true sentences about themselves on pieces of paper, using a range of the expressions, e.g. *I'm good at math, but I'm hopeless at spelling.* Then shuffle them for sts to read and guess who each one is.

D Make it personal Use the speech bubble to set this up by example. Elicit further examples to give additional thinking time for weaker sts. Then, in pairs, sts answer questions 1–3. Encourage them to use the expressions from both columns of the chart in C, and to ask each other follow-up questions.

When sts have finished, invite one or two sts to report back to the class what they have learned about their partner. If there's time, have a class vote on the answer to question 3.

Optional activity

Stronger classes: After they've discussed the questions in pairs, ask: *What ways can you think of to improve the different intelligence types?* (e.g. to improve verbal-linguistic intelligence you could do a crossword every day). Discuss with the whole class.

As a follow-up, you could ask sts to write a paragraph entitled *Five ways to become a smarter person*, including some of the ideas you have discussed.

Song lyric: See Teacher's Book p.335 for notes about the song and an accompanying activity to do with the class.

6 Reading

A 2.6 Ask sts to read the title of the text and the opening paragraph. Elicit what they remember about Howard Gardner's theory of intelligence from the listening in A on p.20. (He disagrees with the traditional view that you are either intelligent or not, and suggests that there are, in fact, nine types of intelligence.)

Ask what they think the author of the text might mean by *Fish and Trees*. Board the question from the opening paragraph: *Is it a valid way of looking at learning?* Encourage guesses about the author's view of the theory using the title as a clue. Don't confirm or deny their guesses until they have read the whole article. You can play the audio while they read.

Answer

No

Tip

While it's generally a good idea to separate reading from listening, by asking sts to read and listen at the same time, you make them read at the same pace. This saves time for the next activities and encourages sts to pay attention to pronunciation.

B Read through the statements with the class. Then ask sts to re-read the article and decide which ones the author would agree with. Ensure sts underline the evidence for each answer. Paircheck, then classcheck and encourage a range of sts to contribute.

Weaker classes: Ask sts to first identify where in the text the author talks about his opinion and where he talks about the views of others. This will help them do the activity.

As a follow-up, discuss the meaning of *meme* (= an idea, image, etc. that spreads quickly on the Internet).

Answers

1 N (*This, to me, denies the whole point of education, which is to enable people to master new skills and deal with challenges.*)
2 N (*In a way, we all like to think of ourselves as unappreciated geniuses, whose brilliance remains undiscovered.*)
3 Y (*The fact that my three-year-old can draw a four-legged horse on a rooftop doesn't make her a genius.*)
4 N (*... which may or may not help her make a decent living in the future.*)
5 N (*... the whole point of education ... is to enable people to master new skills and deal with challenges.*)
6 Y (*... the importance of motivation, passion, and hard work ...*)

Optional activities

Ask sts to find expressions for describing ability in the text (*be gifted at, have a high degree of, excel at, be hopeless at, be skilled at, have no talent for*).

Stronger classes: In small groups, sts discuss the statements in B and say whether they agree / disagree with each one. Encourage them to justify their opinions.

C Have sts study **Reference words** on their own. Highlight the lack of apostrophe in *its*. Remind sts that *its* is the possessive form of *it*, whilst *it's* is the contracted form of *it is* or *it has*. Write the following examples on the board:

It's a very interesting theory. (It's = it is)

The theory hasn't lost its relevance. (its = possessive form of it)

It's been a very popular theory. (It's = it has)

Sts then look at the highlighted words in the text and work out what they refer to. Paircheck, then classcheck.

Answers

It = Howard Gardner's theory of multiple intelligences
one = meme on Facebook
themselves = people with a high degree of musical intelligence
their = people with a high degree of musical intelligence
whose = unappreciated geniuses
her = the author's three-year-old daughter
which = her skill at drawing animals
it = the idea that some people have no talent for certain things

Optional activity

Have sts write their own sentences with each of the highlighted words in A. Ask them to swap their sentences with a partner and peercheck.

D **Make it personal** Divide the class into groups of three or four to discuss the questions. Encourage them to use the expressions for describing ability in C on p.20. Ensure they use *a/an* when they talk about jobs in the singular form.

Class feedback. Ask a spokesperson from each group to report back anything unusual or unexpected to the rest of the class. If there's time, each st could choose their favorite of the jobs and describe which would be their own ideal job, too.

Tip

Ask sts to work in different groups and report what their colleagues said.

Workbook p.10.

6 Reading

A 2.6 Read the introduction. Guess the author's answer to the question there. Then listen to or read the article to check.

FISH AND TREES: GARDNER'S MULTIPLE INTELLIGENCES REVISITED

Howard Gardner's theory of multiple intelligences was published in 1983. It is still relevant today and accepted by many as true. But is it a valid way of looking at learning?

Of all the memes I see on my Facebook® wall day after day, there's one that looks particularly clever. It claims that "Everybody's a genius, but if you judge a fish by its ability to climb a tree, you will think it's stupid." In other words, we're all gifted at different things, so we should concentrate on our strengths, not on our weaknesses. People with a high degree of musical intelligence, for example, will excel at playing instruments, but may be hopeless at expressing themselves in writing, or doing math problems in their heads. Fair enough. Who can argue against the notion that each and every one of us is different?

Maybe this explains why Gardner's theory is still popular. In a way, we all like to think of ourselves as unappreciated geniuses whose brilliance remains undiscovered. We're fish, and our teachers and bosses are making us climb trees. But are we really that special? Stephen Hawking is a genius. Mozart was a genius. The fact that my three-year-old can draw a four-legged horse on a rooftop doesn't make her a genius. It simply means she's skilled at drawing pictures of animals, which may or may not help her make a decent living in the future.

Worse still, the theory seems to reinforce the idea that some people have no talent for certain things and that little can be done about it. This, to me, denies the whole point of education, which is to enable people to master new skills and deal with challenges. In my view, you don't need highly developed linguistic intelligence to be able to write a clear essay, or a good degree of bodily intelligence to become a dancer or an athlete.

Any theory that overlooks the importance of motivation, passion, and hard work should not be taken seriously, I believe.

B Re-read. Infer which statements the author would agree with and write Y (yes) or N (no). Underline the evidence in the article.

1 We should only focus on what we're naturally good at.
2 People tend to underestimate their own intelligence.
3 Parents tend to overestimate children's talents.
4 Children with special talents generally become rich later in life.
5 Schools should focus on what students can already do well.
6 You can learn most things if you put your mind to it.

C Read *Reference words*. Then explain what the eight highlighted words in the text refer to.

Reference words

Reference words often refer back to a specific, stated word, but they can refer to a concept, too.

You can't judge a **fish** by **its** ability to climb a tree. **This** idea makes perfect sense to me.
(*Its* = the fish's ability; *This* = the fact that we can't judge a fish.)

D Make it personal Answer 1–3 in groups. Any surprises?

1 Choose a statement in B you agree / disagree with. Explain why.
2 How does / did your school deal with students' different abilities and learning styles?
3 Which skills do these jobs require? Which is the most important intelligence type for each?

actor athlete chef manager nurse parent politician taxi driver teacher

I think it's really important for a teacher to be good at explaining things.

I don't know. A teacher needs to be intuitive – you know, have a gift for reading people's expressions.

7 Listening

A 2.7 Listen to three friends discussing a news report. Who's most convinced that intelligent alien life exists, Theo or Ruby?

B 2.7 Listen again and check (✔) the name(s). In pairs, share your opinion on these statements.

Who believes ...	Theo	Judd	Ruby
1 most UFO stories have a lot in common?		✔	✔
2 it's likely that there's some extraterrestrial life?			
3 maybe aliens talk to each other mentally?			
4 the pyramids were built by aliens?			
5 there's a lot of reliable evidence that aliens do exist?			
6 it's likely that if aliens exist, they are physically similar to us?			

C 2.8 Read the excerpts in the speech bubbles and guess Theo's story. Then listen and number the speech balloons (1–6). How close were you to guessing Theo's story?

1 So I thought, "There must be someone following me."

__ You're saying it might have been a joke?

__ Oh, come on! It can't have been a vacuum cleaner.

__ The whole thing must have been planned.

__ Walking the dog after midnight? You can't be serious!

__ A toy? Yeah, that could explain the whole thing.

Let's see. It was late at night, and he thought somebody was following him. So he was walking outside, right?

Yeah, but what about the vacuum cleaner? What does it have to do with the rest of the story?

Lesson Aims: Sts learn vocabulary and expressions to talk about strange happenings, and tell their own stories.

Skills	Language	Vocabulary	Grammar	Pronunciation
Listening to people discussing the possibility of the existence of aliens	Modal verbs in informal speech: *must have, might have, could have*	*alien, extraterrestrial, flying object, galaxy, planet, sighting, spaceship, UFO, universe*	Degrees of certainty with modal verbs (present and past tense): *may, might, must, can* and *could*	Modal verbs in informal speech

Warm-up

Write *UFO* on the board and elicit what it stands for (Unidentified Flying Object). Ask: *Do you believe there is life on other planets? Why? / Why not? Has anything strange or inexplicable happened to you? Do you remember any news stories about UFOs?* Have sts discuss in pairs. Invite volunteers to share their partners' stories with the class.

Board the lesson title question: *Do you enjoy science fiction?* Ask: *More generally, do you enjoy reading/ watching science fiction? Are there any TV shows, films or books you'd particularly recommend? Why?*

7 Listening

A 2.7 Focus on the picture and the title of the news report. Ask: *What can you see?* (A spaceship / flying saucer). *Where?* Explain that sts are going to hear three friends (Theo, Ruby and Judd) talking about the news report. Play the audio for them to answer the question.

Weaker classes: Before playing the audio, board the following words: *spaceship, genius, flying object, cellphone, galaxy, extraterrestrial life, airplane, ticket, wood, alien, universe, planet, passenger*. Ask sts to predict which five words / phrases they expect to hear in the recording. Then they listen and see if they were right. (They will hear the underlined words.) Re-play the audio for them to do the listening task.

Answer

Theo

See Teacher's Book p.314 for Audio script 2.7.

B 2.7 Have sts read questions 1–6, and check understanding. Re-play the audio for them to check the correct names. Ask: *Who do you agree with most, Theo, Judd or Ruby? Why?*

Answers

1 Judd, Ruby 2 Theo and Ruby 3 Theo and Ruby
4 Theo 5 Theo 6 Theo and Ruby

See Teacher's Book p.314 for Audio script 2.7.

Tip

Intensive listening is often very challenging, especially for weaker classes. In order to help sts, you can ask them to read the questions carefully and anticipate the answers. Break the listening into shorter chunks, pausing to paircheck comprehension to avoid them glazing over once they fail to understand something, and help each other through. Re-play one or two short parts which they failed to understand, focusing on how the words connect and distort, to make them feel the activity is worthwhile and they are learning something about listening and how to listen better.

C 2.8 This exercise practices guessing the contents of a listening. Sts read six speech bubbles extracted from the conversation, then try to guess Theo's story. Encourage all manner of speculation as there are lots of possibilities!

Then ask sts to read the model exchange in the speech bubbles at the bottom of the page. Highlight the expression *What does it have to do with ... ?* (= How is it connected / related to ... ?)

Ask: *What can you guess about Theo's story from the speech bubbles?* Accept any answers but don't confirm or deny until sts have listened to the audio. Play the audio for them to number the speech bubbles and check their ideas to see how near they got. After so much speculation, sts will probably want to read the audio script to confirm they have fully understood it all.

Answers

1 So I thought, "There must be someone following me."
2 Walking the dog after midnight? You can't be serious!
3 Oh, come on! It can't have been a vacuum cleaner.
4 A toy? Yeah, that could explain the whole thing.
5 The whole thing must have been planned.
6 You're saying it might have been a joke?

See Teacher's Book p.315 for Audio script 2.8.

Tip

Use the recording for shadow reading. Play it with sts simultaneously reading the speech bubble statements aloud. You'll need to prompt them when each line is coming up, or pause the audio immediately after each one, so they can echo what they have heard.

Song lyric: See Teacher's Book p.336 for notes about the song and an accompanying activity to do with the class.

8 Grammar: Degrees of certainty with modal verbs

A In pairs, sts study the example sentences in the grammar box. If appropriate, elicit how sts would say them in their own language.

Then sts read the rules and choose the correct words. Classcheck. Go through **More about *can* and *could*** and check understanding.

Answers

1 passive 2 affirmative
Passive sentence: The whole thing must have been planned.

Refer sts to the **Grammar expansion** on p.140.

Tip

Board ~~*It can be an alien*~~. Explain that this is a very common learner mistake, as we never use *can* to talk about possibility. Point out, however, that we do use the negative *can't* to express impossibility, e.g. *It can't be an alien*.

B Ask sts to read sentences 1–6. Do they remember whose opinions they are from audio 2.7 ? (1 Theo, 2 Ruby, 3 Theo, 4 Judd, 5 Ruby, 6 Theo).

Set this activity up using the example. Sts individually complete this task. Paircheck, then classcheck.

Answers

1 We can't (couldn't) be alone in the universe.
2 There could (may, might) be life on other planets.
3 They could (may, might) use a different form of communication.
4 The pyramids can't (couldn't) have been built by aliens.
5 They must look a lot like us.
6 We must have been visited by extraterrestrials.

C **Make it personal** Read the example in the speech bubble with the class. Elicit other possible answers, encouraging them to use all the modal forms they know, e.g. *There has to be /must be other life in the universe*.

Go through **Common mistakes** with the class.

Have sts rephrase the other sentences they disagree with and write them down. Ask volunteers to read them out, and their classmates to correct them.

Optional activity

Stronger classes: Books closed. Write the incorrect sentences from **Common mistakes** on the board and ask sts to correct them.

9 Pronunciation: Modal verbs in informal speech

A 2.9 Read through sentences 1–3 with the class and check understanding. Play the audio for sts to listen to the rules, then listen and repeat the sentences. Elicit which letter(s) 'disappear'.

Tip

It could be useful to focus on the highlighted words in the box first and drill them in isolation before the class repeats the three sentences with all the contractions. Say each phrase at natural speed and ask the whole class to repeat in chorus.

B **Make it personal** Think of an example situation yourself and share it with the class, e.g. *I went shopping yesterday and met a friend of mine. While I was talking to her in the street, a passer-by bumped into me, and nearly knocked me over. When I got home, I couldn't find my cellphone or my house keys*. Elicit appropriate responses from individuals, e.g. *You must have dropped them when the person bumped into you. / The passer-by might have stolen your cellphone and keys*. Encourage use of the contracted forms *musta / mighta / coulda*.

Then, in groups, sts discuss their own stories. Monitor and help with vocabulary as necessary. Invite groups to tell the class any interesting stories they discussed and invite the rest of the class to offer logical explanations.

Tip

If sts are struggling to think of stories, they could search for 'unexplained stories / mysteries' on the Internet and share those with the group.

Workbook p.11.

8 Grammar: Degrees of certainty with modal verbs

A Study the grammar box and check (✔) the correct rules. Then identify the passive sentence in 7C.

Degrees of certainty: *may, might, must, can,* and *could*

	Present	Past
Maybe it's true.	They **might / may** (**not**) **look** like us.	It **might / may** (**not**) **have disappeared**.
I'm pretty sure it's true.	It **must** (**not**) **be** a UFO.	You **must** (**not**) **have felt** scared.
I **really doubt** it's true.	You **can't / couldn't be** serious!	It **can't / couldn't have been** a UFO.

1 Use a modal verb + *be / have been* + past participle to form ☐ **active** ☐ **passive** sentences:
Other planets **might be inhabited** by humans. The scene **could have been captured** on video.

2 Could means *may* or *might* in the ☐ **affirmative** ☐ **negative only**:
It **could have been** a UFO. The scene **could have been captured** on video.

More about *can* and *could*

Can is not used in the affirmative to express possibility:
It **could** / **may** / **might be** an alien.

Grammar expansion p.140

B Rephrase 1–6 beginning with the underlined words.

1 I doubt we are alone in the universe.
We can't (couldn't) be alone in the universe.
2 Maybe there is life on other planets.
3 Maybe they use a different form of communication.
4 I doubt the pyramids were built by aliens.
5 (If there are aliens out there), I'm pretty sure they look a lot like us.
6 I'm pretty sure we have been visited by extraterrestrials.

C **Make it personal** In pairs, rephrase the sentences you disagree with, using a different modal. Are you more like Theo, Ruby, or Judd?

First one ... I think we might be alone in the universe. I mean, who knows.

Common mistakes

That legend must have ~~invented~~ *been invented* by our ancestors.
I think The Loch Ness Monster might ~~had~~ *have* actually existed.

9 Pronunciation: Modal verbs in informal speech

A 2.9 Read and listen to the rules. Then listen to and repeat examples 1–3.

In rapid, informal conversation, it's important to understand these common reductions:
must have = *musta* might have = *mighta* could have = *coulda*
In less informal speech, say *must've*, *might've*, and *could've*.

1 He must have been confused. 2 It might have been a joke. 3 It could have been a UFO.

B **Make it personal** Think of something hard to explain that happened to you or someone else. Share your stories in groups. Whose explanation is the most logical?

And then when I opened the door, there was nobody there.

Wow! That must have been scary. Were you alone at home?

10 Listening

IQ QUIZ

1 Which number should come next in this series: 25, 24, 22, 19, 15 ...?

2 *Library* is to *book* as *book* is to ...
A copy B page C cover D bookshop

3 Mary, who is 16 years old, is four times as old as her brother. How old will Mary be when she is twice as old as her brother?

4 Which of the following diagrams doesn't belong?

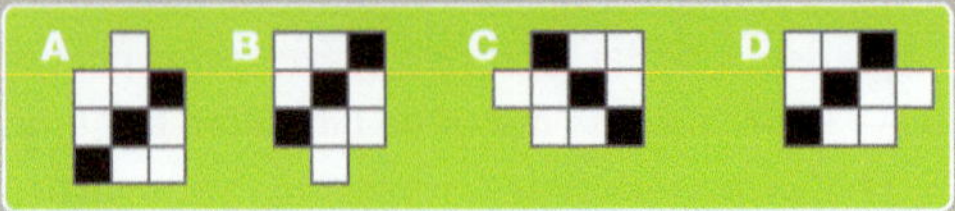

A 2.10 Answer 1–4 in the IQ quiz as fast as you can. Listen to two friends to check. For you, which was the hardest question?

B 2.11 Listen to the rest of their conversation. Circle a or b.

1 Carol thinks IQ tests ...
- a are boring.
- b have more disadvantages than advantages.

2 Flavio ...
- a doesn't have strong feelings for or against IQ tests.
- b sees many advantages to IQ tests.

C 2.11 Listen again and complete 1–6 with one to three words.

Advantages	Disadvantages
1 Internet IQ tests are *fun* .	4 They focus on specifics like ________ .
2 They ________ your brain.	5 They pay no attention to your ________ .
3 They can help teens ________ .	6 They might negatively affect your ________ .

D Go online and take an IQ quiz in English and check your score. Is there an argument in **C** you strongly (dis)agree with?

Common mistakes

I ~~made~~ *took* one of those online tests and ~~took~~ *got* a perfect score. IQ ~~signifies~~ *stands for* Intelligence Quotient.

11 Keep talking

A Choose a question 1–6. Note down two advantages, two disadvantages, and your conclusion.

What are the advantages and disadvantages of ...

1 being considered the family genius?
2 getting into college when you're very young?
3 being rich and famous?
4 being extremely good-looking?
5 being very tall?
6 being an only child?

B **How to say it** Share your views in groups using the expressions in the chart. Who has the best arguments?

Advantages	Disadvantages	Agreeing / Disagreeing
One of the best things about ... is (that) ... Another plus is (that) ...	The trouble with ... is (that) ... Another problem with ... is (that) ...	Absolutely! That's one way to look at it. I wouldn't be so sure.

I think being an only child has more advantages than disadvantages. For one thing you get a lot of attention.

Well, I wouldn't be so sure. The trouble with being an only child is you're lonely.

Lesson Aims: Sts learn to discuss advantages and disadvantages referring to testing, then write a for-and-against essay.

Skills	Language	Vocabulary
Listening to two friends talking about IQ tests Writing a for-and-against essay, listing pros and cons, contrasting, and reaching a conclusion	Expressing advantages and disadvantages, agreeing and disagreeing	*continuous evaluation, essay, evaluate, grade, performance, score, test*

Warm-up

Ask sts: *What was the last test you took? What type of test was it?* Elicit what IQ stands for (Intelligence Quotient). Elicit that IQ tests aim to measure the level of people's intelligence. Ask: *Have you ever taken an IQ test? Are you good / bad at them? Do you think they are a good way to measure intelligence?* If possible, have an example from a real online IQ test ready to show them.

10 Listening

A 2.10 Focus on the IQ quiz. Give sts 90 seconds to answer the questions individually, and then compare, discuss and justify their answers with a partner. Don't check or confirm answers yet.

Tell sts to listen to two friends, Carol and Flavio, doing the quiz together. Play the audio for sts to check their answers. Ask: *Which questions did you find easy / difficult?*

Answers

1 10 2 page 3 24 4 diagram C N.B. A, B, and D are the same figures at a different angle. C is a mirror image. Ask sts to rotate their pages to be able to see this clearly.

See Teacher's Book p.315 for Audio script 2.10.

B 2.11 Have sts read the options a and b for each item before they listen. They might well be able to guess the answers before they listen. Play the audio for them to check their answers. Ask: *Who do you agree with: Carol or Flavio?*

Answers

1 b 2 b

See Teacher's Book p.315 for Audio script 2.11.

C 2.11 Encourage sts to complete the missing words from memory before they listen. Then re-play the audio for them to check their answers.

Answers

1 fun 2 exercise 3 choose a career
4 logic and numbers 5 social skills 6 self-image

D If pressed for time or without in-class online access, set the IQ test search as homework. In pairs, sts discuss which statements in C they agree / disagree with. Classcheck by asking sts to report their opinions using, e.g. *We both agree with … . Neither of us agree … . My partner agrees with … but I agree with …*

Go through **Common mistakes** with the class, and ask which, if any, they (used to) make.

Optional activities

Stronger classes: Books closed. Board the incorrect sentences in **Common mistakes**. Tell sts there are three mistakes, and to find and correct them.

Ask sts, in groups of four, to write four IQ questions, one each, similar to those in the IQ quiz in 10A. Groups swap questions and try to answer them.

11 Keep talking

A Go through questions 1–6 with the class to check understanding. Ask: *Do you know anyone who falls into these categories?* Ask sts to think of one person for each of 1–6.

Brainstorm a few advantages / disadvantages with the class before they begin, as examples.

Ask sts individually to choose one of the questions and note down two advantages and two disavantages. Encourage them to choose different questions so that all are discussed in B. Monitor as they do so to help eradicate likely errors.

B **How to say it** Check the meanings of the expressions in the chart. Elicit other expressions for agreeing / disagreeing, e.g. *I'm not so sure. That's true, but on the other hand … .* Ask two sts to model the example dialogue in the speech bubbles.

In groups, sts share their views. Classcheck by asking volunteers to report back their classmates' views.

Tip

It is important for sts to have the opportunity to express their own views, as in 11B. This allows them to use recently learned language to make their own meaningful sentences. Don't worry too much about grammatical errors, but give sts positive feedback for successfully expressing their opinions.

Song lyric: See Teacher's Book p.336 for notes about the song and an accompanying activity to do with the class.

12 Writing

A Ask sts to read through the essay quickly (e.g. in two minutes) to get the general meaning. Elicit the arguments which are given first 'for' and then 'against' tests. Elicit and drill the pronunciation of any words students mispronounce or you think they need help with. Ask: *Do you agree with these advantages / disadvantages?*

Answers

Arguments for: tests are objective and easy to grade; sts with low scores can be given extra help before it is too late.
Arguments against: sts who do well might think they are better than everybody else, and sts with lower grades might lose confidence and have a poor self-image; they emphasize memorization instead of creativity and social skills.

Optional activity

Ask: *How often do you take formal tests at school? Do you like / respect them? Why / Why not? Why do you think teachers use them? What other ways are there to evaluate sts' progress? Which of them are the fairest?*

B Go through the expressions in **Write it right!** and check understanding. Point out that we also use *However*, (in paragraph 1) for contrasting ideas. Ask sts to re-read the essay and put the expressions in the correct places. Warn them that they will need to change the punctuation in places.

Paircheck, then classcheck.

Answers

Paragraph 1: while (whereas)
Paragraph 2: One advantage of, A further advantage
Paragraph 3: On the other hand, there are a number of drawbacks to, whereas, Another disadvantage of
Paragraph 4: To sum up

C Focus on the paragraph numbers, 1–4. Tell sts to use them to complete the guide. Classcheck.

Then refer them to the **Common mistake** and highlight the common punctuation problems. Ask in which paragraphs they might use *On the other hand ...* (paragraphs 1 and 2). Get sts to notice the use of *other* and *others*, and elicit the difference.

Answers

Present both sides of the question in paragraphs 1 and 2.
Give your own opinion in paragraph 3 and summarize it in paragraph 4.

D Read the three speech bubbles with the class and ask sts to complete them with their own opinions. Give examples of your own to help them first, as necessary.

Stronger classes: Encourage sts to write more than one idea for each sentence.

Weaker classes: Complete 1 together with the class, as an example. Elicit a few different ideas from volunteers and write the sentences on the board.

Put sts into groups to compare their ideas.

Tip

Bring in a different topic, tailored to the specific group you teach, for your examples. That way, you ignite imagination and don't kill off one of the three examples on the page, e.g. *While it's true televised sport is mainly controlled by money, there's still nothing more exciting than a winner-takes-all, live sport moment.*

E Your turn! Read the instructions with the class to check everyone understands what to do. Highlight the three key stages: *Before, During* and *After*.

Weaker classes: Elicit and, in note form, board the advantages and disadvantages that were discussed in 11B, so sts have prompts to help them.

If possible, it's generally better to set this up in class, but sts could both prepare and write the essay successfully for homework, provided you ensure all the stages here are clear. Encourage sts to take sufficient time when they have finished to edit their essay and correct any obvious mistakes.

Class feedback after sts have written and read each other's essays. Either in this lesson or the next, ask: *Which essay do you most agree with?*

Tip

You could get sts to swap their essay with another to peer correct. They could use the correction guide on p.38 of the Teacher's Book. Remind them that peer feedback should always include a combination of positive comments and some suggestions on what to work on.

Optional activity

When reading their classmates' essays, ask sts to consider and answer the following questions:

1 Does the essay present both sides of the argument?
2 Does the writer use the expressions from 12B correctly?
3 Does the last paragraph include a logical conclusion?

Have them give their feedback to their classmates who wrote the essay.

Workbook p.12.

12 Writing: A for-and-against essay

A Read this upper-intermediate student's essay. Ignoring the blanks, find two arguments for tests and two against them.

1 Most schools in my country still evaluate students using formal tests. However, more and more schools are beginning to evaluate students based on their performance, instead. This includes essays, projects, presentations, and real-world activities. Some people think tests are a necessary evil, *while (whereas)* others say students need to be evaluated after every class. Personally, I agree with the second group.

2 ____________ tests is that they're objective and easy to grade, which is useful for teachers who teach large classes. ____________ is that students with low scores can be given enough extra help before it's too late.

3 ____________ , I believe ____________ using test scores to evaluate students. First, students who do well might think they're better than everybody else, ____________ students with lower grades might lose confidence and have a poor self-image. ____________ tests is that they emphasize memorization, instead of creativity and social skills. When performance is evaluated continuously, every class is important. Students try harder, and teachers take more interest in every individual.

4 ____________ , I believe formal tests should be replaced by continuous evaluation. This way, students can also evaluate themselves, and this is really the whole point of education.

B Read *Write it right!* Then complete the essay with items 1–8, changing the punctuation as necessary.

Write it right!

In a for-and-against essay, use expressions like these to help readers follow your train of thought.

Listing pros and cons	1 One advantage of ... 2 A further advantage ... 3 There are a number of drawbacks to ... 4 Another disadvantage of ...
Contrasting	5 On the other hand ... 6 While ... / 7 Whereas ...
Reaching a conclusion	8 To sum up ...

C Complete the guide with the numbers of the paragraphs 1–4.

- Present both sides of the question in paragraphs ___ and ___ .
- Give your own opinion in paragraph ___ and summarize it in paragraph ___ .

Common mistake

Some people are in favor of school ~~uniforms, on~~ *uniforms. On* ~~the other hand~~ *the other hand,* others want to ban them.

D Complete 1–3 with an opinion of your own. Then compare sentences in groups. Any similarities?

1 While it's true that schools ... , personally, I believe that ...

2 Retiring early gives you a chance to reinvent yourself, whereas ...

3 Living in a big city has both pros and cons. On the one hand, ... On the other hand, ...

E Your turn! Write a four-paragraph essay (250 words) discussing one of the questions in 11A.

Before
List the pros and cons. Order them logically. Anything you can add?

While
Write four paragraphs following the model in A. Use at least five expressions from B.

After
Post your essay online and read your classmates' work. What was the most popular topic? Similar arguments and conclusions?

Review 1

Units 1–2

1 Listening

R1.1 Listen to Joe and Amy and choose the best inferences A–D. What did they say that supports your answers? Check in AS R1.1 on p.162.

1 When he was a teenager, Joe probably did something ...
   A embarrassing but not serious.
   B dangerous and illegal.
   C motivating and exciting.
   D cool and fun.

2 Joe uses the expression "Need I say more?" because ...
   A he doesn't want to go into details.
   B he's already told the whole story.
   C he might have forgotten what happened.
   D he'd like to continue with his story.

3 Amy keeps the conversation going by ...
   A talking about herself.
   B showing interest.
   C being overly curious.
   D changing the subject.

4 Joe and Amy are probably ...
   A close friends.
   B brother and sister.
   C just getting to know each other.
   D teacher and student.

2 Grammar

A In pairs, rewrite 1–6 about Joe. Begin with the underlined words and use modal verbs.

1 Maybe <u>Joe</u> was arrested when he was 16.
2 I doubt <u>he</u> has a criminal record. He seems like such a nice guy.
3 I'm pretty sure <u>they</u> moved because of something more minor.
4 Maybe <u>his grandparents</u> liked change in general.
5 I'm pretty sure <u>his grandparents</u> had an interesting life.
6 I doubt <u>they</u> made much money, though.

B Role play the conversation between Joe and Amy, changing the details to those of a story you've heard or read about. Act out your conversation for the class. Whose is the most creative?

C **Make it personal** Write sentences with your opinion. Share in groups. Any disagreements?

1 The best thing about moving to a new city is ...
2 A problem with our school is ...
3 One advantage of this city (town) is ...
4 The most difficult thing about getting up in the morning is ...
5 A disadvantage of having a part-time job is ...
6 A good thing about having older parents is ...

Tip

Revision is at least as important as other language learning activities. Motivate those focused on taking an exam / getting a certificate by telling them the Review exercises are similar to what they can expect there, so this is good practice.

To add value to the review lessons, after each exercise ask sts to feedback on/assess their own performance, 0–4:

4 *Excellent*, 3 *Very Good*, 2 *Good*, 1 *Not good enough*, 0 *Awful!*

They can note their mark after each exercise, then add it up at the end and share it with you/compare with others. Self-evaluation is, in many ways, the most important test there is.

Warm-up

In pairs, sts look at the Phrasal verbs list on pp.165–167 of the Student's Book. Together they tick off the ones they covered in Units 1 and 2, and create a useful example of their own for each.

In pairs or groups of three, sts ask and answer the lesson title questions from Units 1 and 2 in random order. Ensure sts respond appropriately (Do you? Really?, Wow, That's interesting, No way, etc.) and ask follow-up questions too to try to produce more natural conversation, not just a barrage of questions and quick answers.

In pairs, sts review the **Common mistakes** in Units 1 and 2 and make a new, personally-relevant example for any that they aren't yet comfortable with.

1 Listening

R1.1 Have sts look at the photo and, in pairs, discuss what they think the relationship might be between the two people.

Tip

Sts read through questions 1–4 carefully then play the audio for them to choose the best ending for each sentence. Paircheck, then classcheck. Ask: *How many of your initial guesses about Joe and Amy were right?*

Answers

1 B – dangerous and illegal.
2 A – he doesn't want to go into details.
3 B – showing interest.
4 C – just getting to know each other.

See Teacher's Book p.315 for Audio script R1.1.

Optional activity

In pairs, sts turn to the audio script on p.162 and act out the conversation, taking turns to play both Joe and Amy.

2 Grammar

A If necessary, refer sts back to the grammar section on p.23 before this exercise.

Do the first one as an example. Sts rewrite the remaining sentences, beginning with the underlined words and using modal verbs.

Paircheck, then classcheck. Ask: *Any questions about modal verbs? Do you feel you're using them more/better now?*

Answers

1 Joe might have been arrested when he was 16.
2 He can't have a criminal record. He seems like such a nice guy.
3 They must have moved because of something more minor.
4 His grandparents might have liked change in general.
5 His grandparents must have had an interesting life.
6 They can't have made much money, though.

B Go through the instructions with the class. Brainstorm some alternative details if necessary.

In pairs, sts plan and rehearse. Feed in vocabulary and accuracy. Ask volunteer pairs to perform their conversations for the whole class. Vote for the most creative.

Weaker classes: Sts can write out their role plays first, but have them try to act them out from memory.

Tip

Allow enough time for this activity, as weaker sts need more preparation . However, this is a great opportunity to practice the target language from Units 1 and 2 in a less controlled way. Resist correcting while roleplaying unless they get stuck. Note and correct key mistakes afterwards. When you do, asks sts to classify the mistakes *S* (serious) or *NS* (not serious) to understand your correction criteria better and help them relax more.

C Make it personal Read the sentence beginnings and elicit possible endings for each. Then sts complete the sentences with their own opinions. Refer them back to the Grammar section on p.19, if necessary, before the exercise.

Groupcheck, then classcheck. Find out which sentences, if any, students didn't agree about.

3 Reading

Ask: *Do you like science fiction? What are your favorite science fiction movies/novels?*

Read the text title and elicit what it means, and what the article might be about. Elicit what the image brings to mind too.

Give sts two minutes to read the text for gist and find out if they were right. Paircheck. Ask: *Which parts of it did you find interesting/difficult?*

Weaker classes: Instead of checking vocabulary afterwards, add dynamism by selecting a few words you believe sts will find difficult beforehand. Provide them with definitions and ask them to find the words in the text.

Optional activity

Sts re-read and say whether 1–5 are true or false, correcting the false ones.

1 The writer believes a lot of ideas in science begin as science-fiction stories. (True)

2 The aim of the Center for Science and the Imagination is to encourage writers, artists, and scientists to work together. (True)

3 The 1964 picture phone was initially a failure because it was too big. (False. Service was only available in three cities and calls were too expensive.)

4 The author thinks all scientific innovation starts as science fiction. (False. Much scientific innovation happens without science fiction stories.)

5 The CSI consider scientists are wasting their time dreaming. (False. Scientists should be encouraged to keep dreaming.)

4 Writing

Refer sts back to the Writing section on p.15, if necessary.

Weaker classes: Brainstorm the main ideas from the text in 3 and board them in note form.

Discuss the statement and brainstorm ideas and locally relevant examples (e.g. of successful innovation) before they begin.

Set a two-minute time limit to frame the activity and keep sts on task, writing at a brisk pace. If they take an age just to produce a single sentence, in-class writing can get very dull, so insist the main aim is to get a draft written as quickly as possible, then you can polish it together.

Individually, sts write their own paragraph, but they should ask each other for help where they have doubts. Have (online) dictionaries available so they all keep busy.

Sts swap paragraphs with a new partner to give peer feedback.

Tip

Try to get behind sts as they write so you can monitor without having to interrupt. Point out errors for sts to self-correct if possible, and refer to each other for help too.

5 Point of view

Note: This is a very flexible exercise. It can be an in-class writing activity (with sts making their recording at home), a structured in-class speaking activity, or a combination of both. Best is usually when sts talk from their own notes. It's more natural, more fun in class and will avoid some of the dangers of sts just reading aloud their scripts, with the resultant poor pronunciation this usually brings. Much will depend on time and whether you can record in class or not. The topics they don't choose now can all be used later for pair, group or class discussion/revision at any time.

Go through topics a–d with the class, and brainstorm a few ideas for each one. Individually, sts choose one of them and make some preparatory notes. Tell sts to take the notes they feel they need to be able to speak for about 80 seconds on the topic. You don't want full sentences or a script, just prompts from which they can talk naturally. Refer sts back to 11 on p.14, and review the expressions for developing an argument.

Weaker classes: Sts can write out their argument in full, ensuring they structure it logically and use expressions from p.14. However, get them to rehearse so they don't just read it aloud.

Group together sts who chose the same topic so that they can compare, share, expand on, and improve their ideas. Monitor and correct as much as you can.

If possible, sts record their opinion in class using a cell phone. Allow sts to re-record if they aren't happy. It's all good practice and everybody wants the best possible end product. Encourage sts to swap recordings with a partner and give each other feedback.

Optional activity

Hold a debate on one of the topics from 5. Divide the class into four groups. Tell two of the groups they are going to argue 'For' and two of the groups they are going to argue 'Against'. In their groups, have sts brainstorm ideas.

Have sts note down their ideas, then present them to the class. Make sure each member of the group speaks. Encourage them to explain and justify their points of view. The groups arguing the opposing viewpoint are allowed to ask questions and challenge the ideas presented. Give each group a time limit to present their arguments.

When all groups have spoken, have sts vote for the most convincing group (not their own!).

3 Reading

Read the title. What do you think the article is about? Skim the article quickly. Were you right?

Science fiction may soon be fact!

Do great new developments in science start as science fiction? And does the creative process of science fiction encourage breakthroughs in science? According to the Center for Science and the Imagination (CSI) at Arizona State University, founded in 2012 to foster cooperation between writers, artists, and scientists, the answer to both questions may be yes.

Science fiction authors have a long history of imagining life-changing technology. Rockets for space travel were popular in science fiction long before they became reality, culminating in the Apollo mission that put a man on the moon in 1969. During the most exciting periods of innovation, science has had many "dreamers."

While space travel is still too expensive, other elements of science fiction stories have become part of everyday life. The "picture phone" of the 1964 World's Fair was a failure initially. For one thing, service was only available in three cities, and customers had to schedule screen time in advance. Calls were prohibitively expensive, with a three-minute call between New York and Washington, D.C. costing $16, or the equivalent of $120 today. By 1968, the project had been judged a failure. Yet today, free video calls over WiFi are a fact of life around the world.

Of course, much scientific innovation happens without science fiction stories. Future computers may be a big theme in science fiction today, but the foundations of modern computing were established in the 1940s and 50s. The most imaginative ideas may lack funding, and surprising innovation may happen spontaneously. Nevertheless, according to CSI, even though failed ideas can be expensive, scientists should be encouraged to keep dreaming.

4 Writing

Using the ideas in the article and three of the words or expressions below, write a paragraph to support the following statement.

Ideas that sound like science fiction today may be real tomorrow, and companies should fund scientists' innovative ideas.

First, To begin with,	→	In addition, Besides, Moreover,	→	Finally, Lastly,

5 Point of view

Choose a topic. Then support your opinion in 100–150 words and record your answer. Ask a partner for feedback. How can you be more convincing?

a You see many advantages to owning a pet. OR
You think pets are a lot of unnecessary work.

b You feel there are far too many rude people using technology inappropriately. OR
You feel technology is a wonderful modern invention.

c You think there's no such thing as types of intelligence, and you can learn anything if you put your mind to it. OR
You think people have unique talents and should spend their time developing those.

d You don't believe what appears in science fiction will ever be real. OR
You think the world is a mysterious place, and it's impossible to know what's true.

3 »

Do you get embarrassed easily?

1 Vocabulary: Physical actions

A 3.1 Read and match the highlighted verbs in the radio station's countdown to pictures a–g. Listen to check.

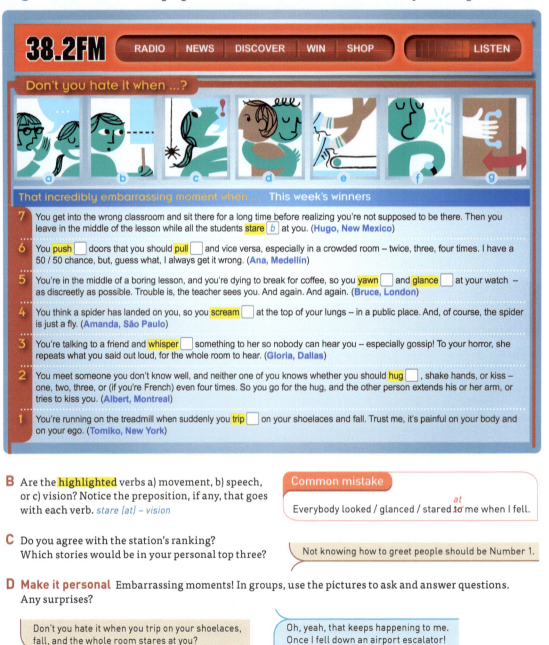

38.2FM RADIO | NEWS | DISCOVER | WIN | SHOP | LISTEN

Don't you hate it when ...?

That incredibly embarrassing moment when ... This week's winners

7 You get into the wrong classroom and sit there for a long time before realizing you're not supposed to be there. Then you leave in the middle of the lesson while all the students **stare** [*b*] at you. (Hugo, New Mexico)

6 You **push** [ ] doors that you should **pull** [ ] and vice versa, especially in a crowded room – twice, three, four times. I have a 50 / 50 chance, but, guess what, I always get it wrong. (Ana, Medellín)

5 You're in the middle of a boring lesson, and you're dying to break for coffee, so you **yawn** [ ] and **glance** [ ] at your watch – as discreetly as possible. Trouble is, the teacher sees you. And again. And again. (Bruce, London)

4 You think a spider has landed on you, so you **scream** [ ] at the top of your lungs – in a public place. And, of course, the spider is just a fly. (Amanda, São Paulo)

3 You're talking to a friend and **whisper** [ ] something to her so nobody can hear you – especially gossip! To your horror, she repeats what you said out loud, for the whole room to hear. (Gloria, Dallas)

2 You meet someone you don't know well, and neither one of you knows whether you should **hug** [ ], shake hands, or kiss – one, two, three, or (if you're French) even four times. So you go for the hug, and the other person extends his or her arm, or tries to kiss you. (Albert, Montreal)

1 You're running on the treadmill when suddenly you **trip** [ ] on your shoelaces and fall. Trust me, it's painful on your body and on your ego. (Tomiko, New York)

B Are the **highlighted** verbs a) movement, b) speech, or c) vision? Notice the preposition, if any, that goes with each verb. *stare (at) – vision*

Common mistake

Everybody looked / glanced / stared ~~to~~ *at* me when I fell.

C Do you agree with the station's ranking? Which stories would be in your personal top three?

Not knowing how to greet people should be Number 1.

D **Make it personal** Embarrassing moments! In groups, use the pictures to ask and answer questions. Any surprises?

Don't you hate it when you trip on your shoelaces, fall, and the whole room stares at you?

Oh, yeah, that keeps happening to me. Once I fell down an airport escalator!

Lesson Aims: Sts learn language to talk about embarrassing situations and how they feel in them, and then write their own embarrassing stories.

Skills	Language	Vocabulary	Grammar
Listening to a radio show Writing an embarrassing story Using the present tense for dramatic effect	Creating suspense: *The next thing I know …, You won't believe what happens next.* Listening to a story: *OK, go on. So, what happens next?*	Physical actions: *glance, pull, push, scream, stare, trip, whisper, yawn*	Narrative style: using present tenses for dramatic effect

Warm-up

Ask: *When were you last embarrassed? How did you react? What physical changes occur when we feel embarrassed?* Elicit / introduce and board the phrases they want to say, e.g. *feel uncomfortable, get hot, change color, go / turn red, blush, laugh loudly, quickly change the subject.*

Pairs discuss the last time they felt embarrassed, why and what happened. Invite volunteers to tell the class anything interesting about their partner (with their partner's permission, of course!).

Ask the title question: *Do you (usually) get embarrassed easily? What sort of situations do you find embarrassing?*

1 Vocabulary: Physical actions

A 3.1 Focus on the text. Ask: *What is it?* (a radio webpage). Ask: *Do you listen much to the radio online?*

Ask: *What are the people doing in each of the seven pictures? What do you think's happening?* Focus on picture e to set this up by example. Elicit the word for *treadmill*. Ask: *How do you think he/she is feeling?* Elicit *embarrassed*.

Ask: *What's the purpose of the text?* Sts skim quickly to find the answer. (Listeners have sent in their examples of embarrassing moments, and the radio station has ranked them in order of how embarrassing they are.)

Highlight the title *Don't you just hate it when …?* and elicit when they might say this increasingly common phrase.

Sts re-read the text more carefully, to work out the meanings of the highlighted verbs. Get them to demonstrate meaning by miming the actions they know. Check the meanings of *to be dying for / to do something* (= very eager to do something).

Sts do the matching activity. Tell them that some pictures go with two verbs. Play the audio to classcheck. For fun, get the class to mime them as they hear them.

Answers

a whisper b stare c scream d hug e trip
f yawn, glance g push, pull

See Teacher's Book p.315 for Audio script 3.1.

B Board the words *movement*, *speech* and *vision*, and do this activity verbally with the whole class. Write the verbs in the correct groups. Elicit that verbs of speech and vision are often followed by the preposition *at*.

Focus on the **Common mistake** and ask sts what preposition they use after these verbs in their language, if any.

Answers

a movement: push, pull, yawn, hug, trip (over)
b speech: scream (at), whisper
c vision: stare (at), glance (at)

Optional activity

Stronger classes: Ask sts to write their own useful contextualized sentences using the highlighted verbs in A.

C Begin by asking: *Have any of these situations happened to you?* Elicit one or two examples, but save the rest till D.

When they have chosen their top three stories, in pairs, sts compare their answers. Do they agree?

Song lyric: See Teacher's Book p.336 for notes about the song and an accompanying activity to do with the class.

D Make it personal Focus on the example speech bubbles. Highlight the negative question *Don't you hate it when …?* Elicit other examples using the negative question, e.g. *Don't you hate it when you are late for a lesson?*

Elicit other questions they can ask each other about the pictures, e.g. *How do you feel when …? Have you ever …? Has somebody ever (done this to you)? Has that ever happened to you?*

In groups of four or five, sts discuss any embarrassing moments. Classcheck the stories they enjoyed the best.

Optional activity

Sts write their own examples of embarrassing moments, in the same style, to send in to Radio 38.2FM. Encourage creativity. Monitor and help as necessary. When they are finished, (or next lesson if you set this for homework) sts display their stories on the class walls to mingle, read and vote on the most embarrassing.

2 Listening

A 3.2 Explain that sts are going to listen to three friends, Ana, Lucas, and Marco, doing the activity in 1C. They have to guess which two embarrassing moments the friends are talking about.

Play the audio. Classcheck, and ask sts to give you as much detail about Ana and Lucas's embarrassing moments as they can remember. Build up the story as a class, then re-play it if necessary.

Answers

Stories 1 and 2

See Teacher's Book p.316 for Audio script 3.2.

B 3.3 Explain that the third friend, Marco, did ... something even more embarrassing. Play audio 3.3 for sts to find out what happened and answer the questions. Paircheck, then classcheck.

Answers

1 To the movies; it had been a stressful day, and he wanted to relax before going home.
2 A woman that he thought he knew; he thought it was his sister-in-law.
3 He whispered in her ear and pulled her hair.

See Teacher's Book p.316 for Audio script 3.3.

C 3.3 Read the statements with the class. Point out that one is not correct. Perhaps get sts to try to do this from memory, or guess first, to get them more motivated to listen again.

Answer

Wrong statement – He'd been looking forward to that movie.

D 3.4 Before listening to the conclusion of the story, ask: *What would you have done in that situation?* Sts discuss the possible endings in pairs. Invite a few sts to share their guesses with the class, boarding them accurately to help eliminate any errors.. Play the audio for sts to check how close their ideas were to what actually happened. and elicit their reactions to his choices.

See Teacher's Book p.316 for Audio script 3.4.

E Go through **Narrative style** with the class. Sts turn to p.162 of their Student's Books and underline the examples in audio script 3.3 and 3.4. Tell them there are sixteen examples in total, but they just need to find seven.

Stronger classes: Ask them to listen without looking at the audio script and note down the present tenses they hear.

Answers

Audio 3.3:
So, anyway, I glance across the room, and I see someone who looks familiar.
Well, the lights go out, the movie starts, and the next thing I know the woman moves three rows back and sits right in front of me.
You won't believe what happens next.
Audio 3.4:
The woman's hair comes off.
So she turns around and screams
Before I know it, everybody's staring at us, telling us to be quiet, and ...
So what happens next?

F Make it personal

1 3.5 **How to say it** In pairs, sts complete 1 to 6 from memory. Play the audio for them to listen and check. Ask: *Which expressions does the narrator of the story use?* (1, 2 and 3) *Which are the listener's?* (4, 5 and 6). Point out that 4, 5 and 6 are expressions the listener can use to encourage the speaker to continue with the story.

Elicit gestures and facial expressions you could use when telling or listening to a story such as Marco's, e.g. for 1–3, they can open their hands to convey surprise, for 4–6, they could make a circular motion to show that the other speaker should continue. They could also exaggerate their facial expressions to show / share in the embarrassment of the situation.

Re-play the to drill the expressions. Focus on intonation and using appropriate gestures.

Answers

1 next 2 won't 3 know 4 on 5 then 6 happens

2 Explain that sts are going to tell their own embarrassing moment story. If they prefer, it can be something that happened to someone they know. Guide through the instructions and seven suggestions. Check the meaning of *appointment* (an arranged time for something, e.g. doctor's appointment, a meeting).

In groups, sts tell their stories and write each student's name on the embarrassment continuum according to how embarrassing they consider each story to be. Ask volunteers to share their stories with the rest of the class. Have a class vote on the most embarrassing story.

Workbook p.13.

2 Listening

A 3.2 Listen to three friends doing activity 1C. Which two stories from 1A are they talking about?

B 3.3 Listen to the rest of the story. Answer 1–3.

1 Where did Marco go and why? 2 Who did he see here? 3 What did he do?

C 3.3 Listen again. What can you infer about Marco? Check (✔) the wrong statement.

- ☐ He sometimes goes to the movies alone.
- ☐ He and his sister-in-law get along.
- ☐ He'd been looking forward to that movie.
- ☐ Marco is a friendly person.

D 3.4 In pairs, how do you think the story will end? Listen to check. How close were you?

E Read *Narrative style*. Then underline seven examples in AS 3.3 and 3.4 on p.162.

Narrative style

When telling stories or jokes, we sometimes use present tenses to create a dramatic narrative effect. Don't mix present and past tenses in the same sentence.

Then I click "send" and ~~realized~~ realize I ~~had~~ 've sent a message to the wrong person, so I start to sweat.

F Make it personal Tell your own "embarrassing moment" story.

1 3.5 **How to say it** Complete these expressions from Marco's story. Then listen, check, and repeat, first at normal speed and then faster. Be sure to use appropriate gestures.

Creating suspense	
After that	What next?
1 The ________ thing I know (the woman moves three rows back.)	4 OK, go ________ .
2 You ________ believe what happens next.	5 And ________ what?
3 Before I ________ it, (everybody's staring at us).	6 So what ________ next?

2 Choose an idea below for inspiration, or think of your own.

You're never going to believe what happened to me! Last week ...

a Note down what happened, using the past tense.
b In groups, tell your story. Use the present tense for dramatic moments.
c Use physical action verbs and *How to say it* expressions.
d Write each student's name on the "embarrassment continuum" and compare your rankings!

being caught doing something wrong breaking something texting / emailing the wrong person forgetting your wallet mistaking people spilling drinks / food forgetting appointments

3 Language in use

A 3.6 Guess how these photos are connected. Listen to a radio show to check. How close were you?

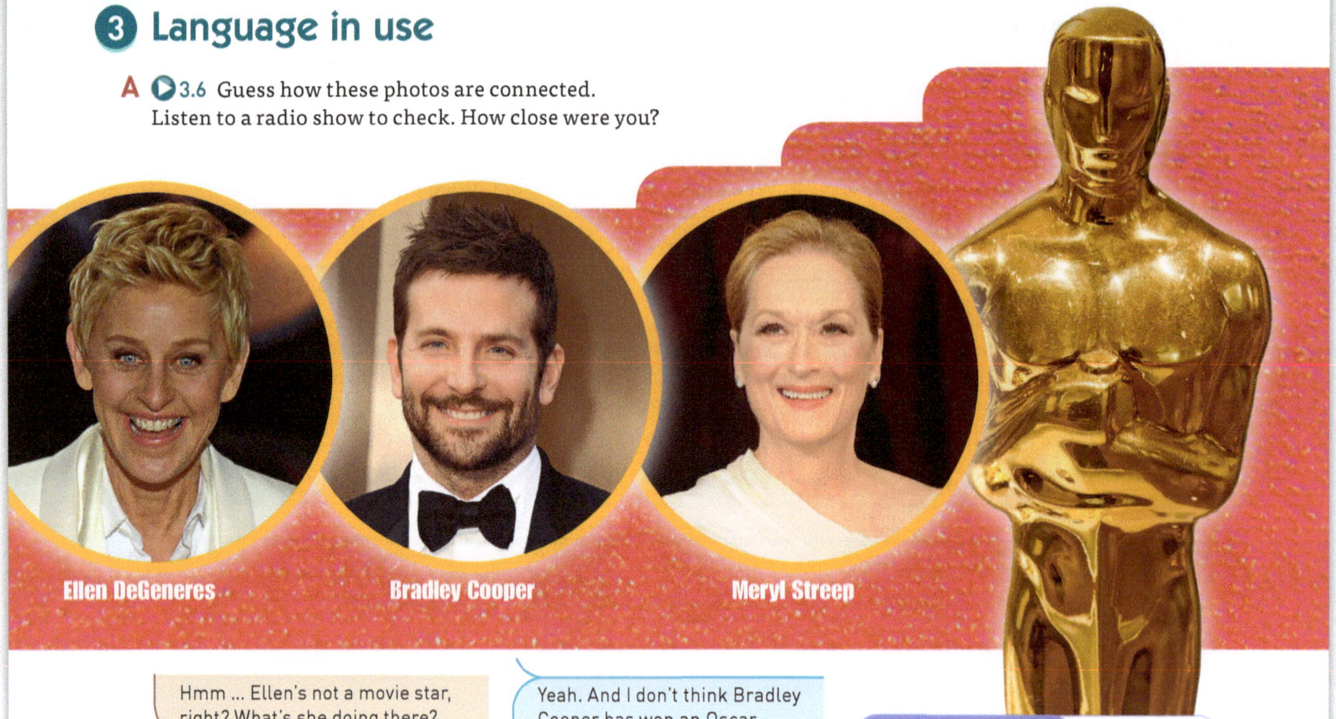

Hmm ... Ellen's not a movie star, right? What's she doing there?

Yeah. And I don't think Bradley Cooper has won an Oscar.

Longer numbers

In informal writing, longer numbers are sometimes simplified:
23**k** followers = 23 **thousand**
1.1**m** retweets = 1.1 **million**
2m **plus** views = **over** 2 million

B 3.7 Read *Longer numbers* and listen to the rest of the story. Which two longer numbers do you hear?

C In each paragraph, check (✔) the action that happened first. Did you hear the correct numbers?

DeGeneres then **posted** ☐ the photo online, and it reached nearly 800k retweets in about half an hour, temporarily crashing Twitter®. Before the three-and-a-half hour show **was** ☐ over, it **had become** ☐ the world's most retweeted photo ever, with 2m plus tweets. The selfie had just made history. "We're all winners tonight," said DeGeneres.

Was it 100% spontaneous? No one knows for sure. The photo was taken with a popular phone, so some people say it **was** ☐ a multi-million dollar deal with the phone company, which **had been sponsoring** ☐ the Oscars for years. Others believe it was totally unplanned.

HOW ABOUT YOU? WHAT DO YOU THINK? LEAVE A MESSAGE ON OUR WEBSITE.

D Make it personal In pairs, answer 1–6. Any major differences?

1 Is the word *selfie* used in your language?
2 Should selfie sticks be banned?
3 Are you both into taking selfies? Looking at others' selfies?
4 Where and when was the last one you took?
5 Would you have the courage to ask a celebrity to take a selfie with you?
6 Find the Ellen DeGeneres selfie. Why do you think it was retweeted so many times?

I'd never have the courage. I'm way too shy to ask a celebrity for a selfie!

Lesson Aims: Sts learn language to talk about celebrities and selfies.

Skills	Language	Vocabulary	Grammar
Listening to a radio show Writing an embarrassing story Using the present tense for dramatic effect	Creating suspense: *The next thing I know ... You won't believe what happens next.* Listening to a story: *OK, go on. So happens next?*	Physical actions: *stare, pull, push, yawn, glance, scream, whisper, trip*	Narrative style: using present tenses for dramatic effect

Warm-up

If appropriate, ask sts to take out their phones, take a quick selfie of themself and partner, and then decide if they are happy with it. Ask: What do we say in English when we pose for a photo? (*Say Cheese, Smile, Ready, Don't move, Hold still, Freeze.*)

Ask: *How often do you take selfies? Do you post them on social-media sites? Have you ever taken a selfie of yourself with a famous person?* Discuss the questions as a class.

3 Language in use

A 3.6 Ask sts what they know about the three people, where they've seen them, their opinions, etc. Elicit the following words: *comedian, TV host, actor / actress*. Elicit *Oscar-winning* too and ask if they can remember last year's Oscar winners. Encourage guesses about the connection between the photos, but try to keep it mysterious, neither confirming nor rejecting answers at this stage. Play the audio for them to check. Sts could do an online search for the photo. How many of them watched it live?

Answer

All three people were in Ellen DeGeneres' selfie photo, taken at the Academy Awards (Oscars) in 2013.

See Teacher's Book p.316 for Audio script 3.6.

Background information

Elicit *Oscar* is the nickname for the gold statuette (officially named the Academy Award of Merit), awarded each year at the Academy Awards (or The Oscars) ceremony for the film industry. Main categories include: Best Picture / Actor / Actress / Director / foreign film. In 2016, there were 24 different categories.

B 3.7 Ask: *How many of you use Twitter? Do you follow famous people on Twitter? Why / Why not?* Ask: *When was the last time Twitter/YouTube/your computer crashed?* to pre-teach the word *crash* when used to talk about computer-related systems (= to stop working or functioning properly).

Read **Longer numbers** with the class and ask if they use similar abbreviations in their language.

Play the audio for sts to write down the two numbers. Either classcheck now, or go straight into the next exercise, then check with the listening.

As a follow-up, ask the class if they think Ellen DeGeneres took the photo spontaneously or whether it was planned by the phone company.

Answers

800k (800,000) 2m (2,000,000)

C Ask sts to read the text and decide which action happened first in each paragraph.

Weaker classes: You could re-play audio 3.7 for sts to follow the text in their books.

After deciding which action happened first, ask sts to identify the tenses of the verbs in bold (*posted* – past simple; was – past simple; *had become* – past perfect; *was* – past simple; *had been sponsoring* – past perfect continuous).

Answers

Paragraph 1 – DeGeneres then posted the photo online
Paragraph 2 – the phone company had been sponsoring the Oscars

Song lyric: See Teacher's Book p.336 for notes about the song and an accompanying activity to do with the class.

D Make it personal In pairs, sts discuss the questions. For fun, set this up yourself by giving an extreme answer to each question first, e.g. *I think selfies are the worst thing ever, they should be banned, people taking them in public places ought to be fined, celebrities should never be allowed to take them with fans.* This will greatly add to the discussion!

Class feedback to find out which of the questions sts agreed / disagreed on. If you have already googled the image, get them to google celebrity selfie and find a few they are interested in to comment on as a class.

4 Grammar: Narrative tenses

A Read through the grammar box with the class. Check they understand the example sentences.

Individually, sts match the examples with the rules. Paircheck, then classcheck.

Answers

1 d 2 b 3 a 4 c

Refer sts to the **Grammar expansion** on p.142.

Tip

Ask sts to compare the form and use of each of the tenses in English with their own language. You could represent the example sentences in the grammar box as time lines to help sts understand the meaning and different uses for each tense.

Optional activity

Elicit sts' own past perfect / past perfect continuous examples by asking them to complete the following sentences:

1 I had been waiting two hours when ...

2 When I arrived at the party ...

3 I hadn't enjoyed many of my English classes until ...

4 I had been ... for two years when ...

B Sts to read the sentences and choose the correct form of the verbs in parenthesis. Do the first one with the class as an example. Paircheck, then classcheck. Elicit what is implied by the other form.

Answers

1 turned 2 had changed 3 had seen 4 wasn't paying
5 had been sleeping

C Go through the rules in **Spoken grammar** with the class. Elicit examples for each of the rules, e.g.

1 I need a new computer (not ~~I'm needing a new computer~~).

2 It was the first time I'd watched the Oscars.

3 She'd been learning English for six years.

Explain that we sometimes break these rules when we are speaking, as in tweets 1–4.

Have sts rewrite them in grammatically correct English. Paircheck, then classcheck. Perhaps board a few more sentences with typical mistakes you know they would make if translating directly from their own language for further practice.

Answers

1 I bet Ellen had wanted to host the show for a long time. Good for her.
2 Hated she show. It was the first time I had seen it. First and last.
3 Ellen said that people had been tweeting for half an hour when the site crashed.
4 I really liked the show at first until I saw that dumb selfie!

D Before reading, ask sts what they know about the man in the photo. Ask: *What is he doing?* (sticking his tongue out at the photographer).

Weaker classes: If necessary, revise *had (just) done something* before the exercise. Elicit / Explain *just* here is used to talk about an action which happened immediately before a new event, i.e. seconds or minutes earlier.

Sts individually complete the text. Paircheck, then classcheck. Ask: *How rude is sticking out your tongue in your culture?*

Answers

1 was returning 2 had taken place 3 was just getting / had just gotten 4 asked 5 had been 6 agreed

Background information

Albert Einstein was a German physicist, born in 1879, who lived in Germany, Switzerland and the USA. He developed the theory of relativity. He died in 1955.

E Make it personal Read through the instructions with the class and make sure that everyone understands what they have to do. If sts don't have selfie photos, they can google famous selfies, and tell the class about these instead.

In groups of three or four, sts share their selfies. Ask each group to share the most interesting story with the rest of the class. Have a class vote on which selfie story is the most memorable/funniest/weirdest/most special, etc. Use a range of adjectives to achieve a range of winners, not just one!

Tip

Keep instructions objective and concise otherwise sts may get lost mid-task. Boarding the key stages in note form will help you explain and conduct the activity as sts will be able to refer to them. An example is usually the clearest form of instruction, so set this up by taking them through a selfie of your own first, answering each of the questions.

Workbook p.14.

4 Grammar: Narrative tenses

A Read the grammar box and match examples a–d with rules 1–4.

Past narration: simple, continuous, and perfect tenses

When telling a story, use a variety of tenses to sequence events logically:

a Ellen took her phone out of her pocket and **went** into the audience. (past simple)
b The photo was taken while she **was hosting** the show. (past continuous)
c Later she announced that the photo **had crashed** Twitter®. (past perfect)
d Ellen was tired because she **had been working** really hard. (past perfect continuous)

1 *d* : longer action in progress before the time of a new event
2 __ : longer action in progress at the same time as a new event
3 __ : two single or short events that happened at the same time
4 __ : a single or short event before the time of a new event

Grammar expansion p. 142

B Circle the most logical way to complete **five people's reactions to the show.**

1 I thought the Oscars were a bit boring, so I [**turned** / **had turned**] off the TV and went to bed.
2 I could hardly recognize some of the actors! They [**had changed** / **had been changing**] a lot.
3 Ellen was the best host I [**had seen** / **had been seeing**] in years! She did a wonderful job.
4 When they took the selfie, I [**hadn't paid** / **wasn't paying**] attention. Too bad I missed it!
5 When the show finally ended, I [**was sleeping** / **had been sleeping**] for hours!

C Read *Spoken grammar*. Then rewrite the underlined sentences in tweets 1–4 to make the grammar traditional.

Spoken grammar

Here are three traditional grammar rules that people sometimes break in informal spoken English:

1 Avoid continuous forms with stative verbs, such as *like*, *need*, and *want*.
2 Use the past perfect after "It was the first second / third / time ... "
3 Use the past perfect continuous for earlier actions when you say how long they were in progress.

1 I bet Ellen had ~~been wanting~~ *wanted* to host the show for a long time. Good for her.
2 Hated the show. It was the first time I saw it. First and last.
3 Ellen said that people were tweeting for half an hour when the site crashed.
4 I was really liking the show at first until I saw that dumb selfie!

D Complete the text with the verbs in the correct tense.

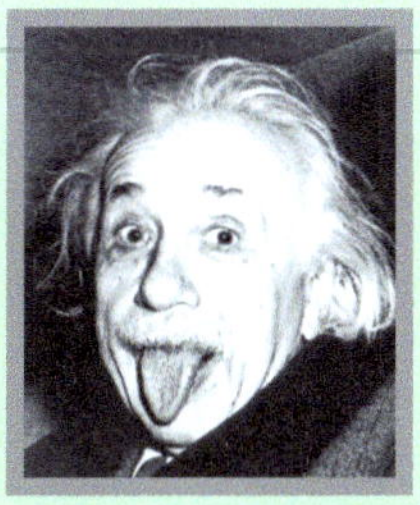

This photo was taken on Einstein's 72nd birthday in 1951, while he [1] __________ (return) from an event that [2] __________ (take place) in his honor.

Einstein [3] __________ (just / get) into his car to go home when photographer Arthur Sasse [4] __________ (ask) him to smile for the camera.

It [5] __________ (be) a long day and Einstein was exhausted. But Sasse wouldn't give up. Einstein finally [6] __________ (agree), but stuck out his tongue. The photo became a cultural icon!

E **Make it personal** Share a selfie (or recent photo) and tell the story behind it. Which is the class favorite? Think through these three questions:

- The event: When did it happen? Where were you? What were you doing?
- Background: What had just happened? What had you been doing?
- The aftermath: What happened after the event? Why do you think you still remember it?

This is me right here ... This photo was taken in 2014, and I was 17 at the time. I had just graduated from high school.

5 Reading

A 3.8 Read the blog quickly and check (✔) the meaning of *serendipity*.

- [ ] The ability to make logical connections.
- [ ] Something good that happens by accident.
- [ ] Scientists' ability to create new inventions.

BLOGADMIN **THE POWER OF SERENDIPITY**

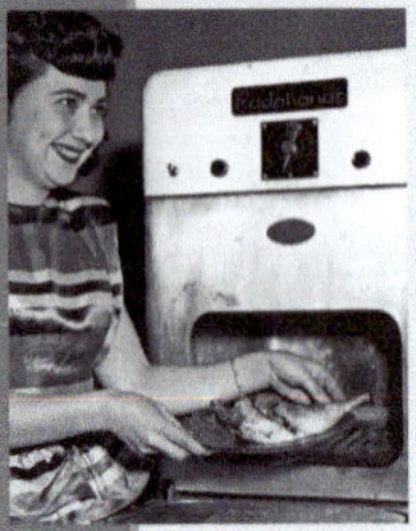

A lot of the things we buy, eat, and drink today were not designed and created **step by step**. Here are two examples of chance discoveries you might be unaware of.

If potato chips are ruining your diet, blame it on chef George Crum. According to one legend that became popular after Crum's death, in the 1850s, he had an impossible customer who kept sending his French fries back to the kitchen because they were "not crunchy enough." Eventually, Crum got **sick and tired** of the customer's never-ending complaints and decided to ignore all the **dos and don'ts** of potato frying: He sliced the potatoes extra thin, fried them in hot oil, and drowned them in salt. To his surprise, the customer, completely unaware of the changes, loved the new recipe and kept going back, **again and again**. Before long, Crum's fries became the house specialty, changing the history of junk food forever!

Speaking of food ... sometimes all you need to make a groundbreaking discovery is a snack. In the early 1940s, American engineer Percy Spencer was conducting an experiment to generate microwaves – a form of electromagnetic radiation – when he felt an odd sensation in his pants. Spencer reached for his pocket and found out that the chocolate bar he'd been saving for later had melted. He then tried to replicate the same experiment with popcorn – sure enough, it worked. A few years later, Spencer gave us the first microwave oven, which weighed 750 pounds and cost between $2,000 and $3,000. Little did he know that one day, his invention would become one of the most widely used household appliances in the whole world.

Some scientists and inventors are understandably reluctant to report accidental discoveries out of fear that they might appear foolish. Fair enough, but I can't help wondering, though, how many other discoveries and inventions we would have if all of us were more willing to admit that necessity isn't always the mother of invention and that serendipity does seem to play a major role in innovation. What do you think?

B Check (✔) the correct statement in each group. Which story did you enjoy more?

Crum ...

- [ ] was surprised by his customer's feedback on the new chips.
- [ ] invented a very popular story about a customer.

Spencer ...

- [ ] knew the microwave oven would become very popular.
- [ ] suspected that the microwaves might pop the corn.

C What's the writer's main point in the last paragraph? Do you agree?

- [ ] If we were more open-minded about serendipity, we might have many more good inventions.
- [ ] If we focused more on necessity, we would have more good inventions.

D 3.9 Look at the highlighted words in the blog and choose the correct alternatives. Listen to check.

1 *Crunchy* sounds like a [**positive** / **negative**] adjective to describe [**food** / **places**].
2 *Slice* probably describes a way of [**cutting** / **cooking**] food.
3 *Groundbreaking* sounds like a [**positive** / **negative**] adjective that describes [**minor** / **major**] events.
4 *Odd* sounds like a [**positive** / **negative**] adjective.
5 *Widely* is an adverb that probably describes [**frequency** / **size**].

E Make it personal Choose one item from each pair that you couldn't live without. Compare in groups. Can you change everyone's mind?

bed / sofa
buses / trains
fridge / air conditioning
fruit / vegetables
microwave / stove
wide-screen TV / tablet

I'd die without a microwave. I don't know how to cook!

32

Lesson Aims: Sts learn language to discuss inventions and the nature of serendipity.

Skills
Reading a blog about serendipity
Telling personal stories about serendipity

Language
Using binomials in everyday speech, e.g. *It's going to happen sooner or later. We've had our ups and downs.*

Vocabulary
Words to describe inventions: *accidental, crunchy, discovery, experiment, groundbreaking, household appliance, serendipity, sliced*
Binomials, e.g. *face to face, pros and cons, heart and soul*

Warm-up

Ask: *Can you name any great inventors?* In pairs, sts write down the names of as many as they can remember.

Board the lesson title question: *What invention can't you live without?* Give an example yourself first, and perhaps allow them three as narrowing it down to one isn't easy!

5 Reading

A 3.8 Focus on the photos. Ask: *When do you think each was taken? Where? By whom? What for?, etc.* Get as much out of them as you can at this stage as it will heighten their motivation to read.

Have sts read the blog text quickly and elicit the meaning of *serendipity*. You could play the audio for sts to listen and read at the same time. Classcheck.

For fun, get them to cover the text and share in pairs all they remember. Again this will increase their desire to re-read it later, as well as helping weaker sts get more help from the stronger ones.

Answer

Something good that happens by accident.

Tip

Asking sts to retell all they can remember from a reading text is helpful in many ways. It adds dynamism and communicative practice. It also allows you to monitor how they are getting on pronouncing the new, pink-stressed words.

B Read the statements with the class first. Sts re-read and check the correct statement for each person. Ask sts: *Who was Crum?* (a chef) *Who was Spencer?* (an engineer)

Paircheck, then classcheck. Ask: *Which story did you enjoy more?*

Answers

Crum was surprised by his customer's feedback on the new chips.
Spencer suspected that the microwaves might pop the corn.

C Focus on the final paragraph and the expression *necessity is the mother of invention*. Explain or elicit that this is a proverb in English, meaning if you really need to do something, you will find a way of doing it. Do they have a similar proverb in their language?

Sts re-read the last paragraph and decide what the writer's main point was.

Classcheck the answer. Do they agree with the writer? Encourage them to justify their reasons.

Answer

If we were more open-minded about serendipity, we might have many more good inventions.

Optional activity

Ask individuals to read out the last paragraph sentence by sentence to check their stress on the new words with pink syllables. Asking them to do this as a class, reading aloud simultaneously in pairs and having to say it together, rather than round the class one at a time, is more dynamic and productive.

D 3.9 Focus on the highlighted words in the blog. Sts work out their meaning from the context and choose the correct alternatives to complete the sentences. Play the audio to classcheck. Which, if any did they know already? Any other onomatopoeic words they know?

Answers

1 positive, food 2 cutting 3 positive, major 4 negative 5 size

See Teacher's Book p.316 for Audio script 3.9.

Tip

Encourage sts to add details and examples to the definitions e.g.*crunchy items include fresh biscuits and potato chips*.

E Make it personal Go through the instructions and focus on the example. Explain *I'd die without ...* (= I can't live without). Teach or elicit also the expression *I'm dying to ...* (= I can't wait to ....).

In groups, sts discuss which of the items they can't live without. Encourage them to justify their choices.

6 Vocabulary: Binomials

Tip

Before this exercise, google Binomials yourself, to choose and board a few you think the sts will know or enjoy learning. This will add context and fun to the lesson.

A Read **Binomials** with the class and check that everyone understands. Highlight the fact that these are set expressions and we don't change the order, e.g. it is incorrect to say ~~cons and pros~~.

Ask sts to scan paragraphs 1 and 2 of the blog text in 5A and complete the chart with binomials for the definitions.

Highlight the error in the **Common mistake**. Read the sentences aloud to the class. As ever, try to personalize, e.g. by asking who might have said this.

Answers

1 sick and tired 2 again and again 3 step by step
4 dos and don'ts

Tip

When recording new words and expressions in their notebooks, encourage sts to write them in a personal contextualized sentence as this will help them to remember the word and its meaning more rather than simply writing its translation.

Optional activity

Board these binomials for sts to try and guess the meanings in pairs:

more or less (approximately)

short and sweet (very quick and directly to the point)

odds and ends (small unimportant items)

by and large (generally)

safe and sound (not in danger)

ups and downs (times when things are going badly and times when things are going well)

Ask sts to write their own sentences with each of the expressions. Paircheck.

B 3.10 Ask sts if they have heard of the singers and groups in brackets, and whether they are familiar with any of the song lyrics.

Sts complete the activity in pairs. Play the audio to classcheck.

Answers

1 time 2 downs 3 over 4 later 5 worse 6 then
7 miles

C 3.11 Explain that sts are going to listen to two friends, Sue and Ann, discussing how Ann met her boyfriend. Get sts to read the questions carefully before you play the audio.

Play the audio for sts to answer the questions. Paircheck, asking them to tell each other anything else they understood, then classcheck.

Answers

1 She bumped into him by chance when walking her dog late one night.
2 He was her boyfriend at high school.

See Teacher's Book p.316 for Audio script 3.11.

Song lyric: See Teacher's Book p.337 for notes about the song and an accompanying activity to do with the class.

D 3.11 Re-play the audio for sts to note down the binomials they hear. Ask sts to turn to p.162 in their Student's Book to check in the audio script.

Discuss the meaning of 'it's in the stars'. Ask what Ann is referring to when she says this (marriage). Elicit that she thinks that fate or destiny will determine that they marry.

Ask: *What's Ann's favorite word?* (serendipity). Ask sts if they have their own favorite English words, and have them explain what they like about these words, e.g. the sound, meaning, connotation. Give examples of your own first and why you like them so much: common choices include *mother* or *home*, or more 'exotic' words like *flabbergasted* or *disgruntled*.

Answers

sick and tired, now and then, face to face, ups and downs, for better or worse, sooner or later

See Teacher's Book p.316 for Audio script 3.11.

E **Make it personal** Ask sts if they have seen the movie *Serendipity*, and what it is about. In groups, sts discuss their own serendipity stories. They can use the prompts or their own ideas. Ask: *Which story is the best proof that serendipity is real?* Invite that student to relate the story to the rest of the class. They can vote for the best story and on the existence of serendipity, or not.

Background information

Serendipity is a 2001 American romantic comedy, starring John Cusack and Kate Beckinsale. It's about a couple who meet in their twenties and fall in love. Both are involved in other relationships, but Sara believes that destiny (or serendipity) will bring them back together some time. Ten years later, through a series of coincidences, they end up together proving that fate / destiny / serendipity does exist!

Workbook p.15.

6 Vocabulary: Binomials

A Read *Binomials*. Then scan paragraphs 1 and 2 of the blog in 5A and complete the chart with the bold expressions.

Binomials

Remember that binomials are expressions where two words are joined by a conjunction, most frequently "and." The word order is usually fixed. Binomials may have:

1 Repeated words: *I've never met a famous scientist* ***face to face*** (in person).

2 Combined opposites: *What are the* ***pros and cons*** (advantages and disadvantages) *of microwave cooking?*

3 Combined related words: *Creativity is the* ***heart and soul*** (essence) *of successful businesses.*

1 fed up *sick and tired*	3 done in stages ________
2 repeatedly ________	4 rules ________

Common mistake

I'm sick and tired ~~to eat~~ *of eating* junk food.
I need some vegetables for a change!

B 3.10 Use your intuition to complete these song lines. Listen to check.

1 "If you fall, I will catch you. I'll be waiting, **time after** *time*." (Cindy Lauper)
2 "We've had some fun, and yes, we've had our **ups and** ________." (Huey Lewis and The News)
3 "It's not the game; it's how you play. And if I fall, I get up again, **over and** ________." (Madonna)
4 "**Sooner or** ________, we learn to throw the past away." (Sting)
5 "For **better or** ________, till death do us part, I'll love you with every beat of my heart, I swear." (All4one)
6 "Every **now and** ________ I get a little bit tired of listening to the sound of my tears." (Bonnie Tyler)
7 "You've got a friend in me when the road looks rough ahead, and you're **miles and** ________ from your nice warm bed. You've got a friend in me." (Randy Newman)

C 3.11 Listen to two friends and answer the questions.

1 How did Ann start dating her boyfriend?
2 Where did she know him originally?

D 3.11 Listen again. Write down the six binomials Ann uses. Check AS 3.11 on p.162. Do you have a favorite word in English, like Ann?

E **Make it personal** In groups, share good things that have happened to you by accident. Use at least one binomial. Does the whole class believe serendipity is both real and powerful?

winning money unexpectedly
meeting old friends / your soulmate
near misses
a lucky find
an amazing coincidence
an accidental / fortunate discovery
following your intuition successfully

I had an amazing experience last month! I'd just left home for work when all of a sudden … and …

7 Listening

A 3.12 Read the webpage and check (✔) the meaning of *fad*. Then listen to a conversation. Which fad from the website are they talking about?

A fad is something that ...

☐ is really fun and enjoyable. ☐ wastes people's time. ☐ is very popular for just a short time.

I MISS THAT FAD *Our favorite fads from years past!* *What are yours?*

2000s			2010s		
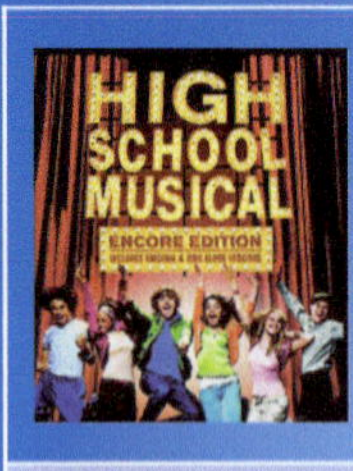					
High school Musical	**Oversized sunglasses**	**MP3 players**	**Psy's Gangnam Style dance moves**	**Angry Birds**	**Photo bombing**
Every teenager's dream; every parent's nightmare.	For those who want to be noticed.	Yes, people didn't always use their phones!	Biggest YouTube hit ever.	A cell-phone game with over 500m downloads!	The art of sabotaging people's photos.

B 3.12 Listen again. T (true) or F (false)?

1 The fad was very popular in Joe's class.
2 He didn't want the teacher to see what he was doing.
3 He never played at home.
4 He usually played with friends.
5 He lost his enthusiasm after a while.

C 3.13 Write the missing letters. Listen carefully. How are the sounds pronounced?

JOE: I was crazy about [beep], you know. Actually, everyone in my class, boys and girls, _sed to love it.
PEDRO: Oh, yeah?
JOE: Uh huh. It was such an _bsessi_n. I used t_ sit in the back row so the teacher w_ _ldn't see me. Then I'd get home from school, l_ck myself in my r_ _m, and start again, playing the same game over and over.
PEDRO: S_ _nds b_ring.
JOE: No, it was fun, actu_lly, though a bit s_l_tary. I'd spend hours and hours alone, trying to get r_d of the pigs. I j_st kept playing the same game again and again.
PEDRO: How good were you?
JOE: I was OK, I guess. Well, eventu_lly I beg_n to use it less and less ... , and then I just del_ted th_ app from my phone.

D Re-read the conversation in **C** and underline the evidence supporting 1–5 in **B**.

E **Make it personal** In pairs, answer 1–4. Anything in common?

1 Are you familiar with the fads in **A**? Which ones are still popular?
2 Can you think of any other fads, past or present?
3 If you could bring a fad back from an earlier time, which would it be?
4 Which would you love to kill off forever?

Oh, I'd get rid of those stupid online contests – like the ice-bucket challenge that was so popular a few years back.

Lesson Aims: Sts learn language to talk about fads from the past.

Skills	Language	Vocabulary	Grammar review
Listening to a conversation about a fad Reading about popular fads from the past Discussing childhood obsessions	Talking about past habits, e.g. *I used to have really long hair. I'd spend hours combing it.*	*bellbottoms, childhood, come back, fad, hair straightener, MP3 player*	Describing past habits and states: simple past, *used to*, and *would*

Warm-up

In groups, sts discuss some current trends among their age group. Board: *Which is the most popular TV show / book / computer game / hair style / social media site / weekend activity?* Ask one volunteer from each group to feed back to the rest of the class. Agree, as a class, on one item for each category.

Ask the lesson question title: *What was your favorite activity as a child?* Brainstorm a list and help them to find the names of activities older sts may have enjoyed in English.

7 Listening

A 3.12 Focus on the webpage and title. Ask: *Who knows the meaning of fad?* (something very popular for a short time). Hands up. Insist they read the text to find out, even if some think they know it. Classcheck. Ask: *Is there a similar word in your language?* Focus on the photos in the webpage and ask: *Which of the fads in the photos were you into?* Keep it short for now as they will come back to this in 7E.

Explain that sts are going to hear two friends discussing fads they were into. Play the audio for sts to say which fads in the photo it is. Classcheck. Drill the new pink-stressed words.

Answers

They are talking about the game *Angry Birds*.

See Teacher's Book p.316 for Audio script 3.12.

Background information

High School Musical an American teen movie made in 2006. It starred Zac Efron.

MP3 player is a small electronic device very popular in the 2000s, used to listen to digital audio files.

Psy is a Korean rapper who rose to stardom in 2012 on the basis of a music video for his song *Gangnam Style*. It became one of the most-watched YouTube videos ever.

Angry Birds is a video game, released in 2009. It involves catapulting birds into pigs.

Photo bombing is a practical joke. It involves spoiling someone's photo by unexpectedly appearing in the camera's field of view as the picture is taken.

B 3.12 Have sts read statements 1–5 and check they understand. Re-play the audio for sts to mark the sentences T (true) or F (false). Paircheck, then classcheck. Ask: *Does anybody empathize with Joe?*

Answers

1 T 2 T 3 F 4 F 5 T

See Teacher's Book p.316 for Audio script 3.12.

C 3.13 In pairs, sts complete the missing letters in the dialogue. Classcheck. Re-play the audio for sts to shadow how the sounds are pronounced. Monitor to check they say them all accurately as, surprisingly, sts at this level can still get some wrong.

Answers

Actually, used, obsession, to, wouldn't, lock, room, Sounds, boring, actually, solitary, rid, just, eventually, began, deleted, the

See Teacher's Book p.316 for Audio script 3.12.

D Sts re-read conversation and underline the sections of the text which gave them the answers to the True / False questions in B. Classcheck.

Answers

1 everyone in my class, boys and girls, used to love it
2 I used to sit in the back row so the teacher wouldn't see me
3 Then I'd get home from school, lock myself in my room and start again
4 it was fun, actually, though a bit solitary
5 eventually, I began to use it less and less

E **Make it personal** Focus on the example in the speech bubble. Explain or elicit what the 'ice-bucket challenge' was and if any of them did it. If you can, have a YouTube clip ready to show them.

In pairs, sts discuss the questions.

Background information

The ice-bucket challenge was initiated to raise money for charity. It involved nominating a friend or relative to be filmed having a bucket of ice water poured over their heads.

8 Grammar: Describing past habits and states

A Get sts to try to do the grammar box without you for a change to see better how individuals are getting on. In pairs, sts study the examples and rules, then complete the rules for *used to*. Ensure they understand *used to* is for an action that happened regularly in the past, but no longer happens.

Elicit the negative and question forms: *There didn't use to be ... / Did there use to be ...?* Highlight the **Common mistakes** and ask why we can't use *would* in the second sentence (because it's describing a state).

Answers

	a single action	a habit	a state
used to	✗	✓	✓

Refer sts to the **Grammar expansion** on p.142.

Tip

Another common learner mistake is to confuse *used to* with *be used to doing*. Board the following sentences: 1) *I used to go to bed very late*. 2) *I'm used to going to bed very late*. Get them to explain the difference in meaning:

1) In the past I went to bed very late, but now I don't.
2) I often go to bed very late. / I'm accustomed to going to bed very late.

The contrast with *get used to* comes in Lesson 10.4.

B Focus attention on the photos and ask what they can see. If you have a whiteboard, show them the photos without the text and get them to speculate what's coming up next.

Have them read the texts quickly and find out what fads they are describing.

Board the **bold** expressions and identify together as a class which can be replaced with *used to*. Ask why the other expressions cannot be replaced with *used to*. Drill the harder words, e.g. *alarmed, fashionable, ironing, straightener*. Focus on the final question in the text and see if anyone is prepared to confess what's in their closet!

Answers

was – used to be
would spend – used to spend
became – not possible because it's one single action
would wear – used to wear
saw – not possible because it's a state, not a repeated action
came back – not possible because it is one single action

Optional activity

Sts use the models of the example sentences in the grammar box to write personalized sentences with *used to, would* and the simple past. Sts then swap their sentences with a partner to check they have used *used to* and *would* correctly.

Song lyric: See Teacher's Book p.337 for notes about the song and an accompanying activity to do with the class.

9 Pronunciation: Weak form of *and*; *used* vs. *used to*

A 3.13 Look at the linked phrases in the box with the class. Ask sts to underline where they occur in the conversation in 7C.

Play the audio, pausing after each phrase for sts to repeat. Make sure they pronounce *and* as /n/, where appropriate and elicit where you can/can't hear the 'd' elide into the next word.

Weaker classes: Model and drill the phrases in isolation first. Elicit other pairs they know, e.g. *fish n chips, salt n pepper, rock n roll, hot n cold*.

B 3.14 Elicit that *used to* is pronounced with /s/ not /z/. Elicit that when we say the verb *to use*, we pronounce it with /z/.

Play the audio for sts to write which sounds they hear.

Stronger classes: Sts can mark the sounds first and then listen to check.

Classcheck, then ask sts to practice the sentences in pairs.

Answers

1 /s/ 2 /z/ 3 /s/ 4 /z/

C Make it personal Focus on the example in the speech bubble with the class. Elicit the meaning of *rerun* (a TV program which is repeated). Ask *Is this true of anyone you know?* Exemplify yourself by getting sts to ask you the four questions and giving your answers. Exaggerate a bit if you think it will help!

In groups, sts discuss the questions. Monitor and help with vocabulary as necessary. Ask a few sts to share their stories with the rest of the class.

Optional activity

For homework, sts research and write a short paragraph about a fad, like the ones in 8B, explaining what they were, and who was into them, e.g. Crazy Bones, Rubik's cube, Pac-Man, Heelys, neopets, Mario. Younger sts could interview their (grand)parents and write up their memories.

Workbook p.16.

8 **Grammar:** Describing past habits and states

A Read the grammar box and complete the chart for *used to*.

Past habits and states: simple past, *used to*, and *would*

a Once I **got** a Tamagotchi for my birthday. I **played** with it every single day. I really **liked** it. (simple past)
b **I didn't use to** / **never used to** collect DVDs. (*used to*)
c I **used to** have really long hair. **I'd** spend hours combing it. (*used to* and *would*)

We often start with *used to* and then continue with *would*. Past tenses can express:	a single action	a habit	a state
simple past	✔	✘	✔
used to			
would	✘	✔	✘

Grammar expansion p.142

Common mistakes

In the 90s, ~~it~~ *there* used to be a show on TV called *Dinosaurs*. It ~~would be~~ *was / used to be* very popular.

B Read about two more fads. Which verbs in **bold** can be replaced by *used to*? Have you ever tried these or similar fashion fads?
In the 60s, straight hair used to be very fashionable.

Don't be alarmed by the photo – there's a logical explanation! In the 60s, straight hair **was** very fashionable. Teenagers all over **would spend** hours and hours ironing their hair, trying to look their best! Thank goodness for modern technology. Today's hair straighteners are much safer!

Bellbottoms **became** extremely popular in the 60s, partly because artists like Elvis Presley and James Brown **would wear** them in their shows, night after night. Also, in the 70s, hippies **saw** bell-shaped pants as a way to rebel against their parents. Bellbottoms **came back** a few years ago and haven't completely disappeared. Are there any in your closet?

9 **Pronunciation:** Weak form of *and*; *used* vs. *used to*

A 3.13 Listen to 7C again. Notice the links and the pronunciation of *and* (/n/).

boys and girls   over and over   hours and hours   again and again   less and less

B 3.14 Pronounce *used to* with /s/, not /z/. Which do you hear? Write "s" or "z."

1 _s_ I used to have an MP3 player.
2 __ We used that book in class last year.
3 __ My mom used to play that game over and over.
4 __ Have you ever used a PlayStation?

C **Make it personal** Did you have a childhood ob**ses**sion? In groups, share your stories.

- How old were you at the time?
- How did your obsession start?
- How often did you use to do it?
- How long did it last? When did you lose your en**thus**iasm?

I used to be crazy about *Friends*. I'd spend hours and hours watching *Friends* reruns.

10 Listening

A 3.15 What do you think makes these people happy? Listen and fill in the missing words.

1 Getting good ________ on my ________

3 Learning how to ________ ________ ________

2 Spending ________ ________ with my child

4 Enjoying life's ________ ________

B 3.15 Listen again. Note down one reason for each person's answer.

11 Keep talking

A 3.16 Competition! In teams, complete each quote with one word. Listen to check. Which team guessed the most words correctly?

1 "For every minute you are *angry*, you lose sixty seconds of happiness." (Ralph Waldo Emerson)
2 "Happiness is not something ready-made. It comes from your own ________." (Dalai Lama)
3 "Joy is not in ________; it is in us." (Richard Wagner)
4 "One of the keys to happiness is a bad ________." (Rita Mae Brown)
5 "If you spend your whole life waiting for the storm, you'll never enjoy the ________." (Morris West)
6 "The true way to make ourselves happy is to love our ________ and find in it our pleasure." (Madame de Motteville)

B Which is your favorite quote and why?

I love number 4. If you think about … too often, you can't enjoy it.

C **Make it personal** In groups, answer 1–5 and compare your choices. You can't say "both" or "It depends." Can you change anyone's mind?

What do you really need to be happy?

1 a very high IQ or very good looks
2 a loving family or a circle of very close friends
3 a well-paid job or a job you love
4 luck or persistence
5 perfect health and not enough money or less-than-perfect health and lots of money

I think a high IQ is much more important. Looks are temporary; IQ is permanent!

D In pairs, complete this sentence in as many ways as you can.

My idea of perfect happiness is …

My idea of perfect happiness is having a long weekend lunch with my family.

36

Lesson Aims: Sts learn language to talk about people's values and the nature of happiness.

Skills	Language	Vocabulary
Listening to people talking about what makes them happy Writing a story and sequencing events using linking words	Sequencing events, e.g. *Initially, I enjoyed my classes. Suddenly, it all made sense.*	*follow your heart, key to happiness, pleasure, quality time, simple pleasures* *Sequencing words: after a while, as, eventually, in the meantime, initially, suddenly*

Warm-up

Say: *Imagine you are going to spend 12 months on your own on a desert island. You can take ten of your belongings with you. Decide what you will take.* Encourage sts to think of the things which are most important to them, not necessarily realistic essentials for survival. In groups, sts compare their ideas. Class feedback. Ask: *What have you learned about your classmates' values?*

Ask the lesson title question: *What makes you really happy?* and elicit as many answers as you can. Give a couple of examples yourself first to be sure sts use the gerund: *Not having to spend my weekend checking homework. / Somebody cooking and serving me an exquisite meal.*

Song lyric: See Teacher's Book p.337 for notes about the song and an accompanying activity to do with the class.

10 Listening

A 3.15 Focus on the photos. Ask: *What can you say about the people? What are they doing?* Encourage sts to speculate, e.g. *She might be a student who's just passed her final exams. The man in picture two looks like he's reading to his daughter.*

Explain that sts are going to listen to someone interviewing the four people for a survey about what makes people happy. Ask sts to try and complete the sentences before they listen. Play the audio for them to check their ideas.

Answers

1 feedback, writing 2 quality time 3 use social media 4 simple pleasures

See Teacher's Book p.317 for Audio script 3.15.

Tip

Predicting content before listening helps sts in several ways. It generates interest, but it can also set the context and pre-teach anticipated vocabulary, making it easier for sts to understand what they hear.

B 3.15 Re-play the audio for sts to write down one reason for each speaker's answer. Paircheck, then classcheck.

Answers

Person 1: but I want to be reassured I'm on the right track
Person 2: And that way I can be a real parent, not a weekend dad.
Person 3: feeling of being connected
Person 4: it's the little things that count

See Teacher's Book p.317 for Audio script 3.15.

11 Keep talking

A 3.16 Sts look at the quotes and say if they have heard of any of the people who said them. In groups of three or four, sts complete the quotes. Play the audio (see Student's Book p.36 for Audio script). Classcheck.

Answers

1 angry 2 actions 3 things 4 memory 5 sunshine 6 work

Background information

Ralph Waldo Emerson (1803–1882) was an American essayist, lecturer and poet.

Dalai Lama is a Tibetan Buddhist monk. The quote was made by the 14th Dalai Lama, Tenzin Gyatso born in 1935.

Richard Wagner (1813–1883) was a German composer, famous for his operas.

Rita Mae Brown, born in 1944, is a writer and feminist.

Morris West (1916–1999) was an American playwright.

Madame de Motteville (1621–1689) was a French memoir writer.

B In pairs, sts discuss their favorite quote. Encourage them to explain their choices. Class feedback. Which was the most popular quote?

C **Make it personal** Read the instructions, the five questions and the example speech bubble with the class. In groups, sts discuss the questions. Ask a spokesperson from each group to report back to the class. Ask: *Which choices did you all agree on?*

D In pairs, sts complete the sentence. Monitor and help with vocabulary as necessary.

12 Writing: Telling a story (1)

A Get sts to cover the website and either board or focus on the competition title only. Sts brainstorm things the author might say in answer to this question.

Give sts two minutes to read through the story quickly to see if any of their ideas were mentioned and to get the general idea. Elicit the missing text in the first paragraph. Ask: *Do you think Bob did the right thing giving up Law School?*

Answer

... a job you love

Optional activity

Ask: *Do/Did you feel pressure from your parents to follow a certain career path? Do you think parents should try and influence their kids' decisions about what job they might do in the future?*

B Read and complete the guidelines with *Do* or *Don't* as a class. Check understanding.

Look back at the story in A and ask: *How many paragraphs are there? How does the writer try and build suspense? In which paragraph does he reveal the main event? What background information does he include?*

Answers

1 do 2 do 3 don't 4 do

C Read **Write it right!** with the class and look at the linking words in the box.

In pairs, sts match the highlighted words to the linking words in the chart. Classcheck.

Answers

a initially b after a while c eventually d as
e in the meantime f suddenly

Optional activity

Elicit other synonyms, or write the words in italics below in random order on the board, and ask sts to add them to the chart.

(at first): *to begin with, in the beginning*

(some time later): *by and by, subsequently*

(finally): *in the end*

(meanwhile): *during that time*

(all of a sudden): *all at once, out of the blue*

D 3.17 Go through the instructions with the class First, sts improve the extracts adding two linking words from 1–6 to each extract. Then they use the original extracts and improve them again, this time adding two linking words from a–f to each extract.

Ask sts to work individually. Paircheck, then classcheck. Play the audio for sts to hear some sample answers. How did theirs compare with the audio?

Answers

1–6

1 We moved to London in 2010. At first I hated the neighborhood, our house, and my new school. Some time later (Finally), I began to change my mind, though, little by little.

2 While I was on my way back home from work, my phone rang, and I got the best news ever: My wife had just had twins! All of a sudden, I realized that our lives had changed forever.

3 I lost my job last year and spent months looking for a new one. Meanwhile (Some time later), I started learning another language to increase my chances. Finally (Some time later / All of a sudden), I found the job of my dreams, but it took a long time.

a–f

1 We moved to London in 2010. Initially I hated the neighborhood, our house, and my new school. After a while (Eventually), I began to change my mind, though, little by little.

2 As I was on my way back home from work, my phone rang, and I got the best news ever: My wife had just had twins! Suddenly, I realized that our lives had changed forever.

3 I lost my job last year and spent months looking for a new one. In the meantime (After a while), I started learning another language to increase my chances. Eventually (After a while / Suddenly), I found the job of my dreams, but it took a long time.

See Answer key for Audio script 3.17

E **Your turn!** Read through the instructions and ask sts to think back to their answers to 11C. Tell them they can tell a story about someone else if they don't have any personal stories to illustrate the items in 11C.

Weaker classes: In groups, sts choose one of the items in 11C. Then they can brainstorm ideas together and plan their paragraphs before writing them up individually.

Sts could starts this in class and finish it for homework. When they have finished their stories, ask them to swap them with a partner, and give feedback to each other following the guidelines in 12B, and suggest improvements where possible.

Suggest sts put their texts into a 'talking' website (search online for 'text to speech'), which will read them back in English. Hearing your own text helps you notice errors you might not otherwise have spotted.

Workbook p.17.

12 Writing: Telling a story (1)

A Read Bob's story and complete the first sentence with a choice from 11C. Do you identify with his story?

WHAT DO YOU REALLY NEED TO BE HAPPY?

This week's winner: Bob Goldman, from Chicago

Last year I made a decision that completely changed my life and taught me that in order to be really happy all you need is ______________________ .

I come from a family of well-respected lawyers who had always expected me to follow in their footsteps. Day after day, Mom and Dad would spend hours talking about cases they'd won, trials they'd attended, and people they'd helped – just to get me interested in law. Eventually, they were able to persuade me to go to law school.

Initially, I enjoyed my classes, but after a while, I realized that law was probably not for me. I started missing classes, and my grades kept getting worse and worse. In the meantime, a friend who had a small band invited me to be the bass player, and I jumped at the chance. We played mostly at weddings and birthday parties, usually on the weekends, but it was wonderful.

One day, as we were packing up after a gig, a man who had come to see us several times introduced himself as an agent. He said he loved our music, and he offered us a record deal – just like that! Suddenly, it all made sense: Music, not law, was my destiny. So I quit law school, got into music school, and continued playing with the band on a part-time basis. I know I might only make half as much money as I would as a lawyer, but I don't care. I followed my heart, and I'm happier than I've ever been.

B Write *Do* or *Don't* at the beginning of guidelines 1–4.

When you write a narrative ...

1 ___do___ include at least three paragraphs.
2 ________ try to build suspense.
3 ________ reveal the main event right in the first paragraph.
4 ________ include enough background information.

C Read *Write it right!* Then find and match the highlighted linking words in the story to the synonyms in the chart.

Write it right!

When you are writing a story, use linking words, such as *at first*, *while*, and *immediately*, to make the sequence of events clear and build interest and suspense.

Sequencing		
1 at first	2 some time later	3 finally
a ___initially___	b ________	c ________
Simultaneous events		**Interruptions**
4 while	5 meanwhile	6 all of a sudden
d ________	e ________	f ________

D 3.17 Improve these extracts from other competition entries by adding two linking words from 1–6 in C to each. Then do the same for a–f. Listen to some sample answers. Did you choose the same words?

1 We moved to London in 2010. *At first* I hated the neighborhood, our house, and my new school. *Some time later*, I began to change my mind, though, little by little.
2 I was on my way back home from work, my phone rang, and I got the best news ever: My wife had just had twins! I realized that our lives had changed forever.
3 I lost my job last year and spent months looking for a new one. I started learning another language to increase my chances. I found the job of my dreams, but it took a long time.

E **Your turn!** Write your own competition entry in about 200 words.

Before
Pick an item from 11C and think of a story that illustrates your choice.

While
Check the guidelines in B and use at least four linking words from C.

After
Proofread, especially the tenses. Share your story with the class. Which one should win the competition?

4 Are you ever deceived by ads?

1 Vocabulary: False advertising

A Read the guide. In pairs, share five tips to protect yourself from false ads.

> I haven't stayed in a hotel in years. Can you recognize a fake review?

> Yes ... if it doesn't give many details, it's probably fake.

Common mistake

Our hotel was filthy!
What a ~~deception~~ disappointment!

home | articles | guide | SEARCH

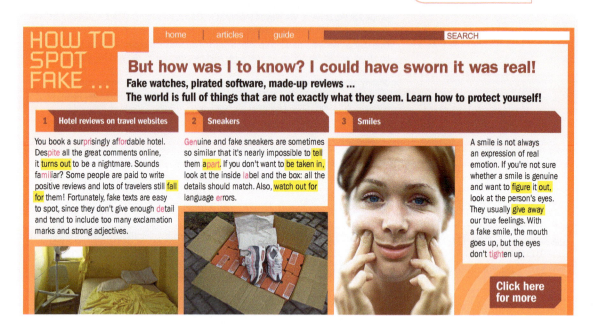

HOW TO SPOT FAKE ...

But how was I to know? I could have sworn it was real!

Fake watches, pirated software, made-up reviews ...
The world is full of things that are not exactly what they seem. Learn how to protect yourself!

1 Hotel reviews on travel websites

You book a surprisingly affordable hotel. Despite all the great comments online, it turns out to be a nightmare. Sounds familiar? Some people are paid to write positive reviews and lots of travelers still fall for them! Fortunately, fake texts are easy to spot, since they don't give enough detail and tend to include too many exclamation marks and strong adjectives.

2 Sneakers

Genuine and fake sneakers are sometimes so similar that it's nearly impossible to tell them apart. If you don't want to be taken in, look at the inside label and the box: all the details should match. Also, watch out for language errors.

3 Smiles

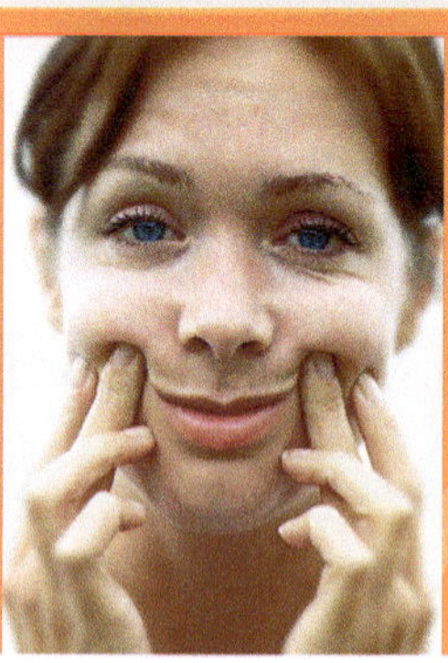

A smile is not always an expression of real emotion. If you're not sure whether a smile is genuine and want to figure it out, look at the person's eyes. They usually give away our true feelings. With a fake smile, the mouth goes up, but the eyes don't tighten up.

Click here for more

B 4.1 Complete dictionary entries 1–7 with the highlighted phrasal verbs in the correct form. Listen to check.

Separable:

1 reveal something secret: "I can't lie. My voice always _gives_ me _away_."
2 passive when meaning to fool or deceive someone: "I've never ________ by a TV ad."
3 recognize the difference between two people or things: "The twins look so much alike that no one can ________ them ________."
4 discover an answer or solve a problem: "It took me weeks to ________ how to use our new washing machine."

Inseparable:

5 look out or be on the alert for: "What problems should I ________ when buying a used car?"
6 be deceived by something: "I can't believe you ________ that trick!"
7 prove to be the case in the end: "This jacket was cheap, but it ________ to be really warm."

C 4.2 Re-read and listen to the guide in A. Then use only the photos to remember at least three tips. Use phrasal verbs.

> If you look at the shoe label, you won't be taken in.

Lesson Aims: Sts talk about being deceived by fake adverts, products and reviews.

Skills
Reading a *How to ...* guide
Listening to a conversation between friends about fake goods
Discussing ethical issues

Language
Developing an argument, e.g. *You're missing the point. Let me put it another way.*

Vocabulary
brand new, deceive, fake, fool (v), *genuine, lie, refund, second-hand, suspicious*
Phrasal verbs: *be taken in, fall for, figure (something) out, give away, tell apart, turn out (to be), watch out for*

Warm-up

Board these adjectives: *authentic, counterfeit, dishonest, fake, false, forged, fraudulent, genuine, honest, original, pirated, real, true, untrue.*

Sts divide them into two groups: positive and negative.

Board these nouns and ask which of the adjectives can be used with each one:

a painting (*fake, forged, original*)
a name (*false, real*)
money (*counterfeit, real, genuine*)
video (*pirated, genuine*)
leather (*fake, genuine, real*)
story (*true, untrue*)
Italian food (*authentic*)
person (*honest, dishonest*)
business (*fraudulent*)

In pairs, sts write down as many other noun and adjective combinations as they can, using the adjectives on the board. Make the activity competitive by giving sts a point for each adjective used correctly that no one else has.

Stronger classes: Ask sts to use the adjectives in full sentences.

Board the lesson title question: *Are you ever deceived by fake ads?* In pairs, sts share any experiences they've had. Get them going with a good personal (or invented) example if you can. Elicit any good stories back to the class.

Write the title of the forthcoming text on the board *How to spot fake ...* and elicit what they think it might say. Don't confirm answers yet.

1 Vocabulary: False advertising

A Focus quickly on the three photos, ask sts to cover the text with their hands so they can't read it, and get them to speculate what each section might say. Tell sts to read the guide quickly and find five pieces of advice. Paircheck. Classcheck, boarding and drilling any words they struggle to pronounce.

Focus on the **Common mistake**, and elicit the difference in meaning between *deception* and *disappointment*. Highlight the use of the article after *What a*. What other phrase do they know with *What a*/an/zero article, e.g. *What a disaster/nuisance, an escape/idiot, terrible news/bad luck.*

Then focus on the speech bubbles to model how they can talk about their own experiences of the five tips. Expand by asking a couple of (stronger) sts the same question to get some different responses. In new pairs, sts discuss the tips in the same way. Prompt, praise and encourage fluency, noting any key errors of form, use or pronunciation, then correct them collectively afterwards.

Answers

To help spot fake hotel reviews: watch out for those that don't give enough detail, and contain a lot of exclamation marks and strong adjectives.
To spot fake sneakers: check the label inside the shoe and the box to see if the details match. Also check for language errors.
To spot a fake smile: check the person's eyes to see if their smile is revealing their true feelings.

B 4.1 Sts read the dictionary entries, ignoring the gaps. Check any unknown vocabulary. Ask them to fill the gaps with the highlighted phrasal verbs in the guide. Play the audio for them to check their answers.

Answers

1 gives, away 2 been taken in 3 tell ... apart
4 figure out 5 watch out for 6 fell for 7 turned out

See Teacher's Book p.317 for Audio script 4.1.

C 4.2 Play the audio while sts re-read the guide. Get them to underline any words/phrase/connected speech where the pronunciation is difficult / not what they expected. Take feedback.

Tip

It's important that sts listen, not just glaze over and read. It's also difficult to synchronise the activities too as our eyes tend to run ahead of our ears. So pause the audio just before any parts you expect them to struggle with, and have them guess how it will be said, then play it to check. Do this several times during any 'listen and read' to ensure they are listening as well as reading.

In pairs, sts look at the photos in the guide and remember the tips. Monitor to check they are using the phrasal verbs correctly.

D Board some questions for students to answer in groups of three: *Do you have a Facebook account? How often do you look at it/post things? Which features do you use most? Do you have Facebook friends that you have never met? Do you always accept friend requests?* Class feedback any unusual answers.

Focus on the next section of the guide. Sts read it quickly first (ignoring the gaps) to understand the general meaning. Cover the text and, in pairs, sts paraphrase the advice to check what they understood.

Sts then complete the text with the correct phrasal verbs. Paircheck, then classcheck. Ask: *Do you think this is good advice? Can you add any other tips for spotting fake profiles? Why do you think people create fake profiles?*

Answers

taken in, give away, figure out, turn out, tell ... apart

Song lyric: See Teacher's Book p.337 for notes about the song and an accompanying activity to do with the class.

E Make it personal Board these questions: *Have you ever been taken in by a fake discount or special offer? Have you ever received suspicious emails? Have you ever accepted a Facebook request from someone who pretended to know you? What did you do?* Invite sts to share their experiences with the class. With larger classes, do this in small groups.

In groups, sts brainstorm ideas on one of the topics, and make notes. Encourage different groups to choose a different topic so that each one is discussed.

Class feedback. Invite groups to tell you their advice. As a class, draw up a list of advice on the board for each one.

Optional activity

As a follow-up, or for homework, ask sts to write a paragraph using their notes from E for the *How to Spot Fake ...* guide on p.38.

2 Listening

A 4.3 Explain that sts are going to listen to three friends, Kim, Mark and Linda talking about a new phone that Mark has bought. Sts read through the activity, and guess from their own experience, which three of the problems they think are most likely to come up.

Pre-teach / check the meaning of *brand new* and *second hand*.

Play the audio for sts to check the correct answers. Paircheck, then classcheck. If sts have wrongly opted for 3, explain that although this statement may well be true, it cannot be inferred from the audio text.

Answers

1, 2 and 4

See Teacher's Book p.317 for Audio script 4.3.

B 4.4 Before they listen to the end of the conversation, ask: *What would you do in Mark's position? Would you keep the phone or return it? Why?*

Play the audio for sts to listen and answer the questions. Classcheck.

Answers

He wants to return it.
Yes, Kim agrees in the end.

See Teacher's Book p.317 for Audio script 4.4.

C 4.4 Read the four arguments with the class and check understanding. Re-play the audio for sts to number the arguments in the order they are mentioned. Classcheck.

As a follow-up, ask: *Have you ever bought fake goods by accident? What did you buy? What did you do about it?*

Answers

1 might discourage new products
2 are made under bad working conditions
3 could hurt the country's economy
4 may harm the environment

See Teacher's Book p.317 for Audio script 4.4.

D Make it personal

1 4.5 **How to say it** Look at the sentences in the box with the class. Discuss the meaning of *ethical* (= conforming to a moral code of conduct). Ask sts to try to complete the sentences from memory. Play the audio to classcheck.

Answers

1 mean 2 Surely 3 missing 4 put 5 way

2 Go through the dilemmas with the class and brainstorm a few ideas. Discuss the different ways you might cheat at sports (= taking drugs, diving in football, match fixing, feigning injury, bribing officials).

Individually, sts then choose one of the dilemmas and note down the arguments for and against. Monitor, helping with vocabulary as necessary.

Background information

A *radar detector* is an electronic device used by motorists to detect if their speed is being monitored by the police using a radar gun. The idea is that a driver can reduce their speed so that they don't get fined for speeding.

3 In groups, sts take it in turns to present their arguments. Encourage the other members of the group to agree or disagree, using the expressions from the *How to say it* box.

Workbook p.18.

D Complete the next item in the guide with phrasal verbs from B.

E Make it personal In groups, choose a topic from those below. What information would you include in a "how to spot" guide?

HOW TO SPOT ...
- fake discounts and special offers
- suspicious emails
- fake friends

4 Facebook® profiles

Be careful before accepting friend requests from strangers. You might be ________ . Studies suggest that there may be more than 100 million fake Facebook® accounts worldwide. Here are two signs that can ________ a fake profile and help you ________ if you're talking to a real person:

- Pages with few status updates, but lots of "likes," often ________ to be fake.
- You can also ________ real and fake profiles ________ because the average Facebook® user has over 300 friends. An impostor will often have far fewer.

Let's see ... how about this: Emails from banks sometimes turn out to be viruses.

Yeah. And watch out for other signs too, like spelling mistakes.

2 Listening

A 4.3 Listen to Kim, Mark, and Linda talking about fake goods. Which ways to identify a fake product can you infer? Check (✔) the correct answers.

Fake goods ...

1 ☐ often come without the original packaging.
2 ☐ are often more affordable.
3 ☐ don't always work well.
4 ☐ can't always be returned.

B 4.4 Listen to the rest of the conversation. What does Mark want to do with his phone? Does Kim agree in the end?

C 4.4 Listen again and order their arguments against fake goods 1–4. Can you think of any others?

Fake goods ...

☐ may harm the environment.
☐ might discourage new products.
☐ could hurt the country's economy.
☐ are made under bad working conditions.

Fake goods can be expensive. You think you're saving, but they don't last.

D Make it personal Try to persuade the class!

1 4.5 **How to say it** Complete the sentences. Then listen to check.

Developing an argument (2)

What they said	What they meant
1 Just because (it's legal) doesn't ________ (it's ethical).	Being (legal) doesn't make it (ethical).
2 ________ you'd agree that ...	I know you'd also agree that ...
3 You're ________ the point.	You don't understand my argument.
4 Let me ________ it another way.	Let me make the same point differently.
5 Look at it this ________ .	Listen to my (convincing) argument.

2 Choose a dilemma from the list on the right, or think of your own, and note down arguments for or against.

3 In groups, present your arguments. Who was the most convincing?

Is it ever acceptable to ...
- use a radar detector?
- cheat at sports?
- take someone's photo without permission?
- genetically modify food?
- break the law to save someone's life?
- lie on your résumé?

I think it's wrong to use a radar detector while you're driving. I'm not sure it's illegal, though.

Yeah, just because you can use one doesn't mean you should.

3 Language in use

A 4.6 Read the homepage. Then listen to / watch a teacher and circle the correct alternatives.

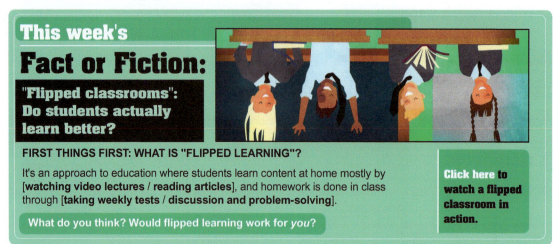

This week's

Fact or Fiction:

"Flipped classrooms": Do students actually learn better?

FIRST THINGS FIRST: WHAT IS "FLIPPED LEARNING"?

It's an approach to education where students learn content at home mostly by [**watching video lectures / reading articles**], and homework is done in class through [**taking weekly tests / discussion and problem-solving**].

What do you think? Would flipped learning work for *you*?

Click here to watch a flipped classroom in action.

B In pairs, are / were your science lessons like that?

> My physics teacher was horrendous. I used to fall asleep.

C Read the comments on a discussion forum and predict the missing words 1–5 from the box. There are two extra words.

coffee	communication	~~focus~~	grades	language	sleep	smile

1 **Location: Australia** Learning through video at home might be enjoyable. But in spite of all the fun, it would take a lot of self-discipline and _focus_ not to check my Twitter® feed or upload a photo to Instagram® every five minutes.

2 **Location: U.S.** I'd definitely miss having live lectures. I think my ______ and test scores might improve, though, since I'd be able to watch all the explanations again and again, go at my own speed, stop, drink coffee, take notes …

3 **Location: Brazil** Despite its advantages, "flipped learning" wouldn't work for me. I need a real live teacher to ______ at me, nod, look me in the eye … you know, just generally encourage me.

4 **Location: Mexico** Although "flipped learning" is becoming very popular and even though it might work well for math and science, I think "hands-on" skills should be taught traditionally. I mean, just imagine what it would be like to learn how to drive like that. Or to learn a ______ !

5 **Location: Canada** Absolutely. Unlike other subjects, languages should be learned through ______ – and preferably in the country where they're spoken.

D Answer 1–4 in groups. Any disagreements?

1 Who do you agree with?
2 Can you think of another (dis)advantage?
3 Do you think there should be a minimum age for "flipped learning"?
4 Would you like to learn English in a flipped classroom?

> I think it would be fun. Plus, we'd have more time to speak in class.

> I don't know … I hate spending too long in front of a screen.

Lesson Aims: Sts learn language to talk about flipped learning, and discuss popular misconceptions about a selection of topics.

Skills	Language	Vocabulary	Grammar review
Reading a webpage about flipped learning Watching / listening to a video lesson Discussing popular misconceptions	Comparing ideas: *Unlike my classmates, I can't stand the "flipped" classroom.* Conceding: *Despite having a bad internet connection, I still manage to do my homework.*	*encourage, flipped learning / classroom, independently, lecture* (v), *multiply*	Conjunctions to compare and contrast ideas: *although, (even) though, despite, in spite of, unlike, while,* and *whereas*

Warm-up

Board these questions for sts to answer as they enter the class: *Who is / was your favorite or most interesting teacher? Why? What makes a good / bad teacher? How can teachers help to make lessons interesting?*

Discuss the lesson title question as a class: *Are teachers important in the digital age? Are they still essential? Why? / Why not?*

Song lyric: See Teacher's Book p.338 for notes about the song and an accompanying activity to do with the class.

3 Language in use

A 4.6 Board: : *Flipped learning*. Books closed, sts try to guess what it means. Don't confirm or deny at this stage.

Sts read the text and think about which of the alternatives is the correct answer. Play the video for them to find out if their guesses were right. If you don't have access to video in the classroom, sts listen to the audio version.

Classcheck. Ask: *Do you think flipped learning works/ would work for you? Why (not)? Has anyone tried much of it?* And if relevant: *How much flipped content has there been in this course?*

Answers

watching video lectures
discussion and problem-solving

See Teacher's Book p.318 for Audio script 4.6.

Background information

Flipped learning is the reverse of traditional teaching models, whereby the content is delivered outside the classroom, usually online, and activities normally considered as homework are carried out in the classroom, guided by a teacher. The aim is to create a more learner-centred teaching environment, in which the classroom is used to explore topics in more depth, and the teacher is a less central focus.

B Ask: *What did you see the sts doing in the video?* (Working together in pairs, sitting on the desks, using digital devices, working independently, problem-solving).

In pairs, sts compare their lessons with the lesson they saw on the video. Invite individual sts to tell the class about their science lessons.

C Check the meanings of the words in the box with the class. Then sts read through the comments on a discussion forum and complete the blanks with the boxed words two of which they will not need to use. Paircheck.

Tip

For a change, get sts to close books and listen to you read the text aloud to check their answers, just to change skills and add variety. Read slower and faster for different texts, adding different accents if you can and, add fun to a couple of them by turning your back to the class so it's a pure listening, where they can't see your lips. This gives you the opportunity to elicit why listening is harder than speaking and talk about aspects of body language, the advantage of video over radio, etc.

Classcheck. Ask sts which of the comments they agree with the most and why. Have a quick class vote for a general consensus.

Answers

focus, grades, smile, language, communication

D Focus on questions 1-4. Clarify that questions 1 and 2 refer to the text in C and the speech bubble exchange refers to question 4.

In groups, sts discuss the questions. Monitor, helping with vocabulary and noting any really good utterances as well as general mistakes for a feedback session.

Ask a spokesperson from each group to feed back to the class, summarizing their answers to questions 1-4 and saying whether they agree or not within their groups, e.g. *We (don't) all agree there should be a minimum age for flipped learning. It very much depends on the individual.* Discuss what they think the minimum age should or could be. Expand the range of (school) subjects they might learn through flipping, e.g. exercise classes, how to drive.

4 Grammar: Conjunctions to compare and contrast ideas

A Highlight the two headings in the box, Comparing and Conceding. Read aloud the first example under each using your own intonation to show the contrast.

In pairs, sts read the other four example sentences and check off rules a–c. Don't rush them on this as they will need to think it through.

Tip

Tell them to resist trying to translate if they can, even if they can't mentally find the exact equivalents, they ought to be able to work out the rules.

Classcheck. Highlight the position of the commas in each sentence. Ask sts which conjunctions are followed by noun phrases (*unlike, despite / in spite of*).

Then refer sts to the **Common mistake**. Ask them why we need to use *the fact that* after *despite* in this example (because it is followed by a clause). Depending on their mother tongue, it might now be worth asking which of the words do/don't have an exact translation in their L1, as they might not have so many, and if their L1 punctuation would be more similar to English or to the **Common Mistake**, to help consolidate/avoid similarities and differences in future.

Answers

a ✓ b ✓ c ✓

Tip

In rule b in the grammar box, point out that we can also use a clause after *despite* or *in spite of*, but you need to add *the fact that* after *despite*, as in the **Common mistake** example.

Refer sts to the **Grammar expansion** on p.144.

B Use the speech bubble to set this up, referring sts back to the first example sentence in the grammar box. In pairs, sts rephrase the other sentences in the grammar box using *but*. Remind them that they need to use a comma before *but*. Classcheck.

Weaker classes: Do a few more examples together on the board.

Answers

I can't stand the "flipped classroom," but my classmates like it.
My grades improved, but my sister's stayed the same.
Teenagers can learn independently, but small children need more guidance.
The sts work at home, but the teacher is still essential.
Learning on your own is practical, but it can be a bit lonely.
Results are good, but some people are still skeptical.
I have a bad Internet connection, but I still manage to do my homework.

Optional activity

Sts write their own sentences using each conjunction, e.g. *Unlike my sister, I don't like pizza*. If time, a partner could rephrase or 'flip' them, as in 4A.

C Re-read comment 5 in 3C. Then, in pairs, sts read the opinions on the comment and choose the correct alternatives.

Classcheck. Still in their pairs, discuss whether they agree / disagree with the statements. Have a class feedback session to compare opinions.

As a follow-up, ask sts to add their own comment.

Answers

1 though 2 although 3 in spite of
4 Unlike, even though 5 while

D **Make it personal** Read the topics with the class and check meaning and pronunciation. Focus on the speech bubble examples, then brainstorm a few ideas of misconceptions for each topic by getting them to use the phrases, e.g. *Even though some believe (famous person X) isn't very smart, she actually (has a PhD in Y).*

Tip

With a less imaginative class, it might be a good idea to prepare a slide of ideas to get them going, e.g. photos of some locally known controversial faces, covers of children's books, foods/types of exercise which are(n't) considered good for you.

In groups of four or five, sts brainstorm more misconceptions. Encourage sts to use their cell phones to search online if they struggle to think of many. Invite sts to share their ideas with the rest of the class. Praise their use of conjunctions.

Workbook p.19.

4 Grammar: Conjunctions to compare and contrast ideas

A Read the examples. Then check (✔) the correct grammar rules a–c.

Conjunctions: *although, (even) though, despite, in spite of, unlike, while,* and *whereas*

Comparing	Conceding (but ...)
1 **Unlike** my classmates, I can't stand the "flipped" classroom. 2 My grades improved **while** my sister's stayed the same. 3 Teenagers can learn independently **whereas** small children need more guidance.	4 **Although** / (**Even**) **though** the students work at home, the teacher is still essential. 5 Learning on your own is practical. It can be a bit lonely, **though**. 6 Some people are still skeptical **despite** / **in spite of** the good results. 7 **Despite** / **In spite of** having a bad Internet connection, I still manage to do my homework.

a **Though** can come at the end of a sentence. ☐
b Use the *-ing* form or a noun phrase after **despite / in spite of**. ☐
c Use a complete sentence after **while** and **whereas**. ☐

Common mistake

Despite ~~it is convenient~~ *the fact that it is convenient*, online learning is not for me.

Grammar expansion p.144

B In pairs, rephrase the examples (1–7) in the grammar box using *but*.

OK, number 1: I can't stand the "flipped classroom," but my classmates like it.

C Read the opinions on comment 5 in 3C. Circle the correct words. Which ones do you agree with?

1 **Location: Peru** I agree you need to spend some time abroad to master a language. Or marry a native! Lots of people, of course, disagree with me, [**though** / **although**].

2 **Location: Colombia** Well, I disagree. Have you heard of that guy who's fluent in 11 languages [**although** / **despite**] he's never left his country? How do you explain that?

3 **Location: India** I'd say he's exaggerating. But I speak fluent French [**even though** / **in spite of**] the fact that I've never been to France or Canada.

4 **Location: U.S.** How about the opposite? Take my grandma. [**Unlike** / **Whereas**] my grandpa, she speaks very poor English [**even though** / **despite**] she's lived in the U.S. for nearly forty years.

5 **Location: Japan** Well, [**while** / **in spite of**] there are exceptions, I still think you need to be surrounded by the language 24/7 to become truly fluent.

Well, I'm not sure. Although some people say you can only learn a language abroad, I actually think ...

D Make it personal In groups, can you think of misconceptions usually associated with the topics below? Search online for "popular misconceptions" for more ideas. Use conjunctions!

controversial celebrities   health and fitness   kids' beliefs   current events   intelligence   sleeping

Although some say we need eight hours of sleep every night, I've read it's not necessarily true.

It really varies. ... whereas ...

Even though some believe ...

Despite what many kids are told ...

People think ... That's not necessarily true, though.

Unlike most of us, I actually think ...

5 Reading

A In pairs, read the first part of the article, a paragraph at a time. Answer the questions in bold. Then read the next paragraph to check.

MY COUSIN'S NEIGHBOR SWEARS HE SAW IT TOO!

1 If you're planning a visit to New York City any time soon, be careful if you use the subway. It's filled with danger. "**What kind of danger?**" you must be wondering.

2 The kind that purses are made of. Apparently, the sewers under the city are filled with mutant alligators, waiting for their next victim. Back in the day, southern migrants moved to New York City and took their pet alligators (!) with them. At first, it seemed like a good idea, but in the end, Manhattan and alligators turned out to be a bad match. So some owners got tired of their pets and simply dumped them into the city's sewers. They started multiplying, of course, and, in no time, formed an underground city of reptiles. **Now, why would anybody fall for a story like that?**

3 Oh, human nature, I guess. Although it seems logical that underground Manhattan wouldn't be hospitable to cold-blooded reptiles, this particular urban legend, like many others, refuses to go away. In the process of writing my latest book, *What if it turns out to be true?* I tried to figure out why these myths persist. But first things first: **What exactly is an urban legend?**

4 It's like a modern-day fairy tale, except it's retold as a true story and usually includes an element of fear. An urban legend tends to spread very quickly. All it takes is one person to share it with someone else and, soon enough, it's all over the Internet. These are some common questions people ask about urban legends.

B Read the second part. Match the questions and answers. There's one extra question.

a Why do people create urban legends?
b How do urban legends originate?
c Are all urban legends false?
d Do all cultures have urban legends?

5 *Are all urban legends false* ?
Nine times out of ten, that turns out to be the case. However, some urban legends are based on actual events that are changed and exaggerated so much that, at some point, they become fictional stories with bits of truth in them – pretty much like some of today's journalism. New versions of classic legends also appear from time to time, which means they're never out of date.

6 ____ ?
Experts think they do, although since urban legends are often passed on as stories that "happened to a friend," it's virtually impossible to trace them back to their original source. Most people, though, tend to enjoy these stories for what they are – stories – and don't ask their origin because they know they're being taken in.

7 ____ ?
To me, this is perhaps the most intriguing question. While we don't know the reasons exactly, we do know that urban legends are an integral part of popular culture. They represent who we are as a society and reflect our own concerns and fears. Plus, as my grandmother used to say, "Life is much more interesting if there are monsters in it." I couldn't agree more.

C 4.7 Re-read and listen to both parts. In which paragraphs (1–7) are these points made? Did you enjoy the article?

[4] Urban legends spread rapidly and are often meant to make people afraid.
[ ] Some urban legends make no sense, but they remain popular.
[ ] Some of today's news stories are not very reliable.
[ ] Urban legends make our lives more exciting.
[ ] People like urban legends even though they suspect they might be fake.

D Make it personal Do you know the two urban legends below? Search online for more "urban legends".

There's that one about the hitchhiker that disappears. Or is that a movie?

I heard that if you leave a tooth in a glass of soda overnight, it will completely dissolve!

Common mistake

Last week I ~~listened~~ heard Katy Perry had retired. It turned out to be a rumor.

Lesson Aims: Sts learn language to discuss inventions and the nature of serendipity.

Skills	Language	Vocabulary
Reading an article about urban legends Discussing false news stories and gossip on social media	Using similes: *I ran like the wind. This dress fits like a glove.*	*alligator, cold-blooded, exaggerate, fictional, intriguing, sewer* Time expressions: *at first, at some point, back in the day, from time to time, in no time, in the end, out of date*

Warm-up

Play *Telephone*, a fun activity to show how rumours become distorted! Sts stand in a line. Write a rumor of at least eight words on a piece of paper (e.g *I've heard that X has been dating Y for ages*), and give it to the first in line. He/She whispers the message to the next in line. Then this person whispers whatever they heard to the next person, and so on down the line. When it gets to the end of the line, the last person should say aloud what they heard, and compare it with the original message.

Ask the lesson title question: *What was the last rumor you heard? How did it get to you? Did it turn out to be true or false?* Invite sts to tell the class.

Song lyric: See Teacher's Book p.338 for notes about the song and an accompanying activity to do with the class.

5 Reading

A Focus on the title of the article and the picture. Ask sts what they think the text is about. Don't confirm or deny guesses at this stage.

In pairs, sts cover the text with a piece of paper or their hands. Sts read only the first paragraph, then together quickly answer the question in bold before they read on. Repeat this process with paragraphs 2 and 3. Tell sts to ignore any words/expressions they don't know or can't pronounce for now. This will come at stage 5C.

Ask: *Are urban legends common in your culture?*

Answers

What kind of danger? Mutant alligators
Why would anyone fall for a story like that? Human nature
What exactly is an urban legend? It's like a modern-day fairy tale, which is retold as a true story.

B Sts read questions a–d and try to guess the answers before they read. Then ask them to read the second part of the text and match the questions to the paragraphs. Paircheck, then classcheck.

Answers

5 c 6 d 7 a

C 4.7 Read through the five points with the class and check understanding. Highlight paragraph numbers 1-7, and that there are only five points to match.

Play the audio while sts re-read the text and match the points to the paraghraphs. To ensure they are listening, get them to underline any words/phrases they find hard to pronounce. If you choose to play it twice, be sure they have a different task each time, e.g. pause after some of the more interesting sentences, so they can shadow read them aloud in pairs, or re-cap in pairs the gist of each paragraph after you've listened to it.

Classcheck, then discuss the meanings of the words and phrases highlighted in yellow. If appropriate, ask what the equivalent expressions are in their language. Board any new words from both parts of the article and discuss the meanings.

Answers

4 Urban legends spread rapidly and are often meant to make people afraid.
3 Some urgan legends make no sense, but they remain popular.
5 Some of today's news stories are not very reliable.
7 Urban legends make our lives more exciting.
6 People like urgan legends even though they suspect they might be fake.

D **Make it personal** Sts read the example speech bubbles. Have they heard of these urban legends? Elicit what they know about them. Encourage sts to search online for more information about each if necessary (See Background information below).

Focus on the **Common mistake**. Elicit the differences, e.g. that we can use the verb *hear* to ask someone if they 'know about something or someone'.

Background information

The 'Vanishing or disappearing hitchhiker' is an urban legend in which people travelling by vehicle meet up with a hitchhiker who then disappears without explanation. The story has been reported globally for centuries.

Many people have heard the myth that a glass of soda will dissolve a tooth or a nail if left overnight in it. This is not true, of course, but probably originates from the fact that sodas contain acids that will eventually dissolve some items over a very long period of time.

6 Vocabulary: Time expressions

A 4.8 Focus attention on the pictures and ask sts what they can see. Discuss the meaning of *breaking news* (= a news story happening right now). Get them to predict which urban legends might be represented in the pictures. Don't confirm or deny their ideas until after they have listened.

Play the audio for sts to listen and match audios 1-3 to pictures a-c. Ask sts if they have heard of any of these urban legends before. Board the expression *spread like wildfire* from conversation three, and elicit the meaning (= to circulate quickly). Elicit/Explain this expression to talk about news or rumors, and also disease, e.g. *The disease spread like wildfire*.

Answers

1 b 2 c 3 a

See Teacher's Book p.318 for Audio script 4.8.

Tip

It's vital to follow up listening exercises by exploring the task and skill itself, e.g. *Which speaker/ conversation was easiest to understand? Why?* so sts learn to self-assess. Useful questions include: *Was the person speaking fast or slowly? Throughout? Which bits were(n't) hard? Why? When did you switch off? Why? Was it a problem of (accent/a dull topic/difficult vocabulary)? Was this exercise useful? How will you try to listen differently next time? Any questions (about listening)?* to encourage reflection on Listening, the most difficult skill to teach.

B 4.9 Pre-check understanding of *refresh the page* in conversation 3.

Sts complete the task individually, then peercheck. Play the audio to classcheck. Any surprises?

Answers

1 At first, in the end
2 back in the day, from time to time
3 out of date, at some point, in no time

C **Make it personal** Use the example to set this up and give further examples yourself, e.g. *Back in the day, I was a goth! I started this great diet last year and lost ten kilos in no time!*

In groups, sts make true statements using four of the expressions in B. Monitor, helping with vocabulary. Get groups to feedback their favorites and take a vote on which is the most interesting.

D 4.10 Read the **Similes** box with the class , then define the word *similes* if they don't know it (= a figure of speech where two unlike things are compared). Drill pronunciation /'simili:z/. If need be, elicit examples of similes in students' L1.

Focus on the words in the circles. You might want to explain that *record* in circle 3 refers to a vinyl disc of music.

When sts have done the matching task, play the audio to classcheck. Ask sts if they know any other similes in English, e.g. *swim like a fish, sleep like a log*.

Answers

fight like cats and dogs
eat like a bird
sound like a broken record
spread like wildfire

See Teacher's Book p.318 for Audio script 4.10.

E Explain the aim: to role play and expand the dialogs from B in their own words, using the pictures and the time expressions to help them. Play audio 4.10 again before they begin, if necessary.

In pairs, sts practice the dialogs. Monitor and help as necessary. Check they're using time expressions and the similes correctly. Invite any willing pairs to act out their dialogs to the class.

Weaker classes: As an alternative to E, give out a copy of audio script 4.10, and get them to act them it out. Then have them block out some of the words, and act out the scripts again completing the gaps as they go. Depending on the level of the sts, block out more gaps, and repeat the activity, until they are memorizing much of it. Finally, they can try and act out the dialogs without the scripts.

F **Make it personal** Ask: *Do you read gossip or news stories on social media? Do you believe what you read? How much of what you read do you think is true? Can you give any examples?* Discuss as a class.

Focus on the questions and the example speech bubble. Elicit that "A little bird told me" means that the speaker knows who said it but has decided to keep the person's identity a secret – this is usually used when repeating gossip or a rumor.

In pairs, sts discuss questions 1 and 2. Open up into class discussion.

Workbook p.20.

6 Vocabulary: Time expressions

A 4.8 Listen and match three conversations to pictures a–c. Which was the easiest to understand? Why?

B 4.9 Complete parts of conversations 1–3 with the highlighted expressions in the article in 5A and B. Listen to check.

1 A: *At first* (= initially), I wasn't sure whether the story was real.
B: ... So I guess ________ (= it turned out that), Don was lying.

2 A: Well, ________ (= in the past), people used to say that taking a shower after a meal could kill you.
B: I eat and then shower ________ (= occasionally) – maybe once a month – and I'm still here.

3 A: Try refreshing the page. Maybe it's ________ (= not updated).
B: Oh, don't worry! ________ (= sooner or later) we're going to find out that the rumors are false.
A: You post something and, ________ (= very quickly), it's all over the web.

C Make it personal In groups, make true statements with four of the expressions in B. Whose were the most interesting?

> Last week, I was walking home when ... At first ...

D 4.10 Read *Similes*. Then match the words in the circles. There are three extra words or phrases in circle 3. Listen to check.

Similes

Using a verb + *like* + a noun can make your descriptions more vivid:
I was so scared (that) **I ran like the wind.** (= very fast)
This dress **fits like a glove**. (= fits perfectly)
Remember: These are fixed combinations. You can't change the words!

1: fight, eat, sound, spread

2: like

3: a bird, a goldfish, a broken record, cats and dogs, bacteria, wildfire, lions

E Using only the pictures and new expressions, improvise and expand the three mini dialogs in B.

> Have you lost your mind? You can't throw a coin from here.

> Why not? They say it brings good luck ...

F Make it personal In groups, answer 1–2. Anything in common?

1 Do you ever check if a news story is true before you share it on social media?
2 Are you into gossip? Have you ever accidentally spread a false rumor?

> I'm really into celebrity gossip. I love expressions like "A little bird told me (that) ..."

7 Listening

A 4.11 Listen to Bill and Rachel on a radio show describing an experiment. Order the pictures 1–3.

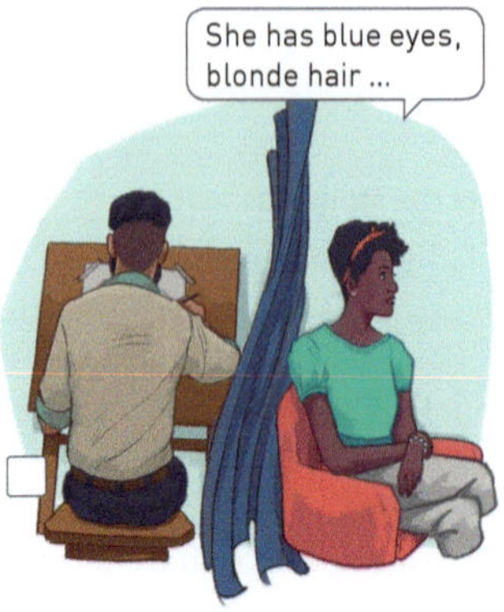
She has blue eyes, blonde hair ...

I have blue eyes, blonde hair ...

B 4.11 Listen again. T (true) or F (false)?

1 The experiment was designed to sell a product.
2 After each woman described herself, the artist drew her.
3 He then drew a second sketch looking at the woman.
4 The participants had all met before the show.

C 4.12 Guess the experiment results. Circle *more* or *less*. Listen to check. Any surprises?

BILL: As it turns out, the sketches based on self-descriptions were [**more** / **less**] attractive than the other drawings – all of them! In other words, when participants were asked to describe each other, they were [**more** / **less**] positive than when they talked about themselves.

RACHEL: Well, I'm not surprised, really.

BILL: I was a bit puzzled myself, to be honest. Anyway, the moral of the story is that maybe you're [**more** / **less**] attractive than you give yourself credit for.

RACHEL: Yeah. In other words, how we see ourselves is one thing; how others view us, quite another.

D Read *Avoiding repetition*. Then connect the highlighted words in **C** to their (near) synonyms.

Avoiding repetition

Writers often use (near) synonyms to avoid repetition. When you come across an unknown word, look for related words nearby. They can help you guess the meaning!

This experiment was **conducted** by a New York psychologist. It was **carried out** to change the way people see themselves.

E **Make it personal** In pairs, choose three questions to discuss. Are your answers similar?

1 Do you remember what product was being advertised? Was this a good experiment for it?
2 What do you think might have happened if they'd picked men instead of women?
3 What's your favorite recent photo of yourself? Why? Who has seen it?
4 Do others usually see you the same way you see yourself?
5 Has your personality / self-image changed much as you've grown older?

My friends say I'm really outgoing, but I think I'm a bit shy, actually.

I don't think you're shy at all.

Lesson Aims: Sts learn about an experiment (Who's the real you?) and discuss how we see ourselves, compared with how other people see us.

Skills	Language	Vocabulary	Grammar
Listening to radio presenters describing an experiment Discussing how we see ourselves	Using synonyms to avoid repetition: *This experiment was conducted by a New York psychologist. It was carried out to change the way people see themselves.*	*advertising campaign, mirror, puzzled, sketch*	Reflexive pronouns with *-self / -selves*: reciprocal actions with *each other / one another*

Warm-up

Brainstorm vocabulary for facial features on the board, then elicit adjectives you can use to describe them, e.g. (*thin / thick*) eyebrows, lips, (*wide / narrow*) forehead, (*long / thick*) eyelashes, (*brown / auburn / dark / long / short / curly*) hair, etc. Sts note down as many other facial features and adjectives as they can. Ask: *How would you describe yourself?*

Extra game: In pairs. A chooses a classmate and, without telling B who it is, describes their face. B draws the face. When finished, B should try and guess who it is. Sts swap roles, with B describing a classmate, and A drawing them. Class feedback. Ask: *Were you able to recognize the person in the drawings? What was similar / different? Did you find it difficult to describe your classmates?*

Board the lesson title question: *How would you describe yourself?* In pairs, sts describe themselves first physically to each other. Do so yourself first as an example, or, if feeling brave, get them to do it to you!

7 Listening

A 4.11 Focus on the pictures. Ask: *What do you think is happening in each picture?* Explain that sts are going to listen to two radio presenters describe the experiment taking place in the pictures. Ask sts if they can guess what the experiment is. Don't confirm or deny their ideas until after the listen.

Play the audio for sts to listen and number the pictures. Classcheck. Ask which sts guessed correctly what the experiment entailed.

Answers

3, 2, 1

See Teacher's Book p.318 for Audio script 4.11.

Tip

Before a listening activity, encourage sts to establish the following: a) who they are listening to; b) the topic; c) the situation. They can do this by reading the rubric carefully, and looking at any pictures.

B 4.11 Before listening again, ask sts to read the statements carefully, so they are clear about what information they are listening for.

Play the audio again. Paircheck, then classcheck.

Answers

1 T 2 T 3 F 4 F

See Teacher's Book p.318 for Audio script 4.11.

C 4.12 In pairs, sts read the dialog and guess the results of the survey by circling *more* or *less*. Don't confirm or deny the answers yet. Play the audio to classcheck (see Student's Book p.44 for Audio script). Ask: *Were you surprised by any results? Why do you think the sketches were different in each case?*

Answers

1 less 2 more 3 more

D Read **Avoiding repetition** with the class. Elicit what a *synonym* is (= a word with a similar meaning). Point out that it's helpful to identify what type of word the unknown word is, e.g. *conducted* is a verb in the past, therefore the synonym they are searching for will also be a verb in the past, *carried out*.

Answers

sketches – drawings
puzzled – surprised
see – view

E Make it personal In pairs, sts read and choose three of the questions to discuss. Monitor helping with vocabulary and making a note of any common errors to go over in a feedback stage at the end.

After discussing the questions, ask individual sts to share their ideas with the class. Encourage others to say whether they agree / disagree.

Tip

To help sts assess their spoken English, have them record speaking activities from time to time. After they have finished the activity, ask them to listen to the recording and discuss in their groups what they did well / badly, and how they could have improved their performance.

8 Grammar: Reflexive pronouns and *each other / one another*

A If necessary, quickly revise reflexive pronouns on the board (*myself, yourself, himself, herself, ourselves, yourselves, themselves*).

Go through the grammar box to check they understand the different uses. Explain that *each other* and *one another* in box 4 mean the same.

Ask sts to find an example of the use of a reflexive pronoun for emphasis in 8C.

Answer

I was a bit puzzled myself, to be honest.

Tip

It can be useful to write the following sentences on the board to clarify the difference in meaning between -*selves* and *each other*:

Sally and Jo described themselves. (= Sally described herself, and Jo described herself.)

Sally and Jo described each other. (= Sally described Jo, and Jo described Sally).

Optional activity

Stronger sts: Sts write their own versions of the four types of sentences from the grammar box. Paircheck their sentences and help each other with any mistakes.

Song lyric: See Teacher's Book p.338 for notes about the song and an accompanying activity to do with the class.

B Focus on sentence 1 and the speech bubbles. Check that everyone understands the difference in meaning between a and b, e.g. by volunteers roleplaying the two options:

a) Student A: *Hello, I'm Kitty Smith, I'm a politician*.

Student B: *Hello, I'm Paul Jones, I'm also a politician*.

b) Student A: *Hello, this is Paul Jones. He's a politician*.

Student B: *Hello, this is Kitty Smith. She's a politician*.

In pairs, sts work through the remaining sentences and explain the differences to each other. Monitor and help as necessary.

Classcheck and invite volunteers to explain, or better, roleplay the differences.

Answers

1 Different – **themselves** = A introduced A, and B introduced B; **each other** = A introduced B, and vice versa.
2 Different – **themselves** = A motivated A, and B motivated B; **each other** = A motivated B, and vice versa.
3 Different – **a lot with each other** emphasizes that their arguments were reciprocal, not with other people.
4 Different – **ourselves** = no one else taught us; **one another** = A taught B, and B taught A.
5 Different – **herself** = emphasizes that she did it; **by herself** = she had no help.
6 Different – **by themselves** = with no help; **of themselves** = A drew A, B drew B, etc.

C 4.13 Sts read **Common mistakes** and, in pairs, explain who might be saying them and why each is wrong. Point out that English doesn't use reflexive verbs for daily routines, unlike many languages, e.g. *He has a shower every morning*, NOT ~~He showers himself every morning~~. *They get up at 8 am*. NOT ~~They get themselves up at 8 a.m~~.

Ask sts to look at the underlined words in each sentence and correct them where they are incorrect. Paircheck. Play the audio to classcheck.

Answers

1 yourselves 2 yourself 3 correct, ourselves
4 themselves 5 correct

9 Pronunciation: Final /l/

A Sts read through the box. To clarify the difference, ask sts to say these words and notice where the tongue is when pronouncing the "l": *follow, silly, class, flat* (at the top of the mouth behind the front teeth). Then ask them to say the words in the box and compare: *Paul, all, level, will*, and notice where the tongue is when pronouncing the "l" (still on the roof of the mouth but further back, not right behind the front teeth).

Play the audio for sts to listen and repeat the sentences. Ask them to practice in pairs.

Tip

Sts practice repeating the sentences under their breath first before trying to say it aloud. It's a useful way to practice the language alone.

B Make it personal Ask individuals to read each question aloud to check they pronounce the final "l" correctly.

In groups, sts discuss the questions. Listen out for the correct pronunciation of the "l" sound, and use of reflexive pronouns.

Workbook p.21.

8 Grammar: Reflexive pronouns and *each other / one another*

A Read the grammar box. Then find an example of emphasis in 7C.

Reflexive pronouns with *-self / -selves*; reciprocal actions with *each other / one another*

When the subject and object are the same person: 1 **We** can be too critical of **ourselves**.	3 To express "all alone" or "without help": **The artist** sketched the pictures **(by) himself**.
2 For emphasis: **I myself** was surprised by the results. **I** was surprised by the results **myself**.	4 To express reciprocal actions: **We** were asked to describe **each other / one another**.

Grammar expansion p.144

B Do a) and b) have the same or a different meaning? In pairs, explain the differences.

1 The two politicians introduced **a) themselves b) each other**.
2 Before the debate, they had really motivated **a) themselves b) each other**.
3 They argued **a) a lot b) a lot with each other**.
4 We taught **a) ourselves b) one another** how to play the guitar.
5 My daughter wrote her name **a) herself b) by herself**.
6 The children drew pictures **a) by themselves b) of themselves**.

In sentence a), the politicians say their own names, but in sentence b), they say the name of the other politician.

C 4.13 Read *Common mistakes*. Then check (✔) the correct pronouns in sentences 1–5 and change the wrong ones. Listen to check.

1 You see ~~yourself~~ in mirrors often, so your minds internalize that image. *yourselves*
2 If you see an ugly angle, you can instantly correct itself.
3 We stand closer to mirrors than to each other, so we see us from the same height.
4 When people see theirselves in a photo, their imperfections are magnified.
5 On some level, we will always be a mystery to ourselves. But maybe not to others!

Common mistakes

You can both put on your shoes ~~yourself~~ *yourselves*.
Sarah and ~~myself~~ *I* are going to the meeting.
I got ~~myself~~ up at six yesterday.
The survivors consider ~~theirselves~~ *themselves* fortunate.

9 Pronunciation: Final /l/

A 4.14 Read about final /l/. Then listen and repeat 1 and 2.

The /l/ at the end of a syllable or word is pronounced with the tongue further back in the mouth.
1 Paul, I don't see myself as a celebrity at all.
2 On some level, we will always be a mystery to ourselves.

B **Make it personal** In groups, answer 1–5. Then share the most surprising answers with the class. Remember to pronounce final /l/ carefully.

1 Do you like looking at yourself in the mirror, or do you look better in photos?
2 How often do you and your closest friends call / email / text each other?
3 Have you ever tried to teach yourself something? How successful were you?
4 What exactly is your usual morning routine? What are the first six things you do?
5 Have you ever formed a false perception of someone? What made you change it?

Well, when I look at myself in the mirror, I look thin, but in photos I often look heavier.

4.5 How many pairs of glasses do you own?

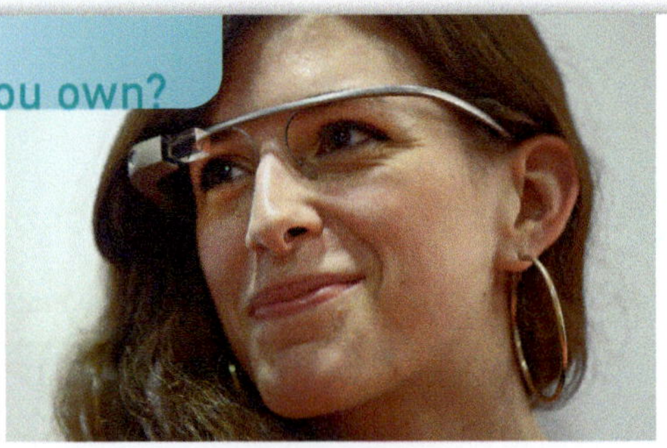

10 Listening

A 4.15 Listen to Liz talking to her friend Ryan. Answer 1–3.

1 What's special about Liz's glasses?
2 Did she buy them herself?
3 Where were they made?

B 4.16 In pairs, guess six things the X29 can do. Listen and take notes. Any surprises?

I never knew smart glasses could ...

Me neither. And I had no idea it was possible to ...

C 4.16 Listen again. Check (✔) the correct answer.

It can be inferred that Liz ...

1 ☐ speaks good Portuguese.
2 ☐ wishes the X29 was a better translator.
3 ☐ doesn't mind speaking in public.
4 ☐ exercises.

D 4.17 Listen to the end of the conversation. Order Liz's feedback 1–4. Which aspect(s) was she surprised by?

The glasses ...

☐ can be socially isolating.
☐ make multitasking difficult.
☐ are a little uncomfortable to wear.
☐ are kind of unnatural in a way that's hard to explain.

E 4.18 Read *Figurative expressions with 'die'*. Then complete 1–3. Listen to check.

Figurative expressions with *die*

You can use the verb *die* figuratively to emphasize your ideas:

I'm dying for / **to get** a pair of smart glasses. (= I really want ...)
My mother's **scared to death** of technology. (= She's very afraid of ...)
I **wouldn't be caught dead** wearing that thing! (= I would never do it.)

1 I'm __________ ____ go to Rio de Janeiro.
2 I nearly __________ ____ embarrassment when my mind went blank.
3 The kids love them ____ __________ .

F **Make it personal** In pairs, answer 1–3. Any surprises?

1 Would you like to test the X29? Why?
2 What else do you think smart glasses should be able to do?
3 What other products would you volunteer to test?

I'd love to test a 3D printer. I mean, that would be so cool!

I'd never be a guinea pig for anything. I'd be too scared.

11 Keep talking

A Talk about a product that let you down. Think through 1–6 first.

1 Was it (a) a gift or (b) did you buy it yourself?
2 If (b), how did you choose it? Did you fall for a misleading ad / fake reviews?
3 Do you still have it? How much longer do you intend to keep it?
4 What are three things that turned out to be disappointing about this product?
5 Is / Was there anything positive about it? If so, what?
6 Would you recommend this product?

B In groups, share your stories. Who's had the worst experience?

Well, I once bought a new bicycle, and I regretted it immediately!

Lesson Aims: Sts learn language to talk about smart products, and learn how to write a product review.

Skills	Language	Vocabulary
Listening to two friends discuss smart glasses Discussing products that have let you down Writing a product review	Using figurative expressions: *My mother's scared to death of technology.* Language for generalizing: *as a rule, by and large, on average, generally*	Expressions with *die*: *to die for, be scared to death, to be caught dead ...*

Warm-up

Board and discuss these questions as a class: *What is a smart phone?* (a phone which performs many of the functions of a computer) *Has anyone seen or used any other smart products, e.g. a smart watch, a smart fridge?* Ask: *Do you think these smart products are always a good idea? If not, why? Do you feel optimistic or pessimistic about their future uses?*

Ask the lesson title question: *How many pairs of glasses do you own?* If appropriate, give your own fun answer to get them going, e.g. *About 10 pairs, mainly sunglasses, but a couple of pairs of reading glasses.* Who has the most pairs at home?

10 Listening

A 4.15 Focus on the photo of Liz. Ask: *Do they look like a normal pair of glasses? What's strange about them?* (the cable that goes down behind her neck) Play the audio for sts to listen to a conversation between Liz and a friend and to answer the questions. Classcheck.

Answers

1 They're smart glasses.
2 No, her husband bought them.
3 In Japan.

See Teacher's Book p.318 for Audio script 4.15.

B 4.16 In pairs, sts make a list of six things. Then elicit their ideas onto the board. Play the audio for sts to note the uses Liz mentions. Paircheck, then classcheck. Ask: *Were your guesses correct?*

Answers

Help the wearer to make phone calls, text, search the Internet, use social media
Translate street signs; translate simple conversations
Act as a teleprompter while the wearer is making a speech
Monitor heart rate and blood pressure

See Teacher's Book p.319 for Audio script 4.16.

C 4.16 Explain that the information is not directly stated in the listening text, and they must listen for clues. Re-play the audio. Classcheck. After confirming the correct answer, ask: *How do you know Liz exercises?* (Because she mentions that she has a personal trainer.)

Answers

4 – It can be inferred that Liz exercises.

See Teacher's Book p.319 for Audio script 4.16.

D 4.17 Play the audio for sts to number Liz's feedback 1–4. Classcheck, then ask sts which aspects surprised Liz.

Answers

The glasses ...
1 are a little uncomfortable to wear. 2 make multitasking difficult. 3 can be socially isolating. 4 are kind of unnatural in a way that's hard to explain.

See Teacher's Book p.319 for Audio script 4.17.

Song lyric: See Teacher's Book p.338 for notes about the song and an accompanying activity to do with the class.

E 4.18 Read **Figurative expressions with *die*** with the class. Ask for an example of a figurative expression in their own language. Discuss the meanings of the expressions in the box. Sts complete the gapped sentences. Paircheck. Play the audio to classcheck.

Answers

1 dying to 2 died of 3 to death

F **Make it personal** Focus on the speech bubbles. Explain that *guinea pig* is a pet animal, but that the phrase *be a guinea pig* is figurative and means 'be the subject of experimentation or research' or, in other words, 'to try out something new'. In pairs, sts then open up to a class discussion.

11 Keep talking

A Highlight the stages of the task. Discuss the meaning of *let down* (to disappoint). Ask sts, individually, to make notes.

B In groups, sts take turns to tell the others about their experience, using their notes. Encourage the other group members to ask questions. When they have finished, invite groups to share their stories with the class.

12 Writing: A product review

A Board and discuss these questions: *Do you normally read product reviews before buying things? What type of information do they normally include? Have you ever written a product review and posted it online?*

Focus on Liz's review and just read the headings. Ask sts what they think Liz will mention in the review.

Sts read the review quickly to check their ideas and to answer the question. If time, paircheck what they can remember. Then classcheck. Get them to analyze it as far as you can, e.g. *Do you think it's an effective review? Why (not)? How could it be improved, shorter, less formal, etc.? What might readers do as a result?*

Answers

She has changed her mind about the comfort of the X29.
In the product review she says: *On the whole, the glasses are comfortable.*
In the audio she says: *the X29 is still a bit awkward to wear, so I find myself taking the glasses off from time to time.*

B Go through the guidelines about writing reviews and check understanding. Using Liz's review as a model, which advice do they think is wrong? In pairs, sts underline examples of the guidelines in Liz's review. Classcheck. Ask: *Is any of it irrelevant?*

Answer

Wrong guideline – Use a very formal style.

C Sts read **Write it right!**, then, in pairs, share what they have understood. Deal with any doubts or errors you picked up during monitoring and elicit any further questions. Ask sts what expressions they use to generalize in their language. Are any of them similar?

Sts re-read the review and find the five expressions. Paircheck, then classcheck.

Answers

generally speaking, on the whole, for the most part, overall, in general

Tip

If time, sts can google the word *quotation* + any of the phrases to find a real example to consolidate them.

Optional activity

Sts find as many adjectives or adjective phrases as they can in Liz's review. Board them: *well built, reliable, easy to use, comfortable, tough, stylish, tasteful, uncomfortable*. Sts add other adjectives they know for describing products to the list.

D Explain that sentences 1–5 are quotes from product reviews. Ask sts to read them and cross out the wrong alternatives, if any. Paircheck then classcheck.

The 'if any' is just to seed doubts, and make them think more. In general, this is a good technique to get them more involved, rather than telling them all are right or wrong, as they actually think less!

Answers

1 ~~a mistake on page 22~~
2 ~~started on Monday~~
3 ~~has a sunroof~~
4 ~~didn't write a review of my last phone~~
5 ~~I'm disappointed~~

Tip

If possible, ask sts to research other product reviews on the internet, and bring them in to class to use as examples to look at before they do E.

E Your turn Focus on the **Common mistake** and elicit why the present perfect is needed in the sentence (because it refers to a period of time which started a week ago and is continuing).

Read through the instructions with the class and check that everyone understands what they have to do. If you did the optional activity after C, encourage sts to use some of the adjectives.

When sts have finished and proofread their reviews, ask them to swap them with a partner and double check their partner's review, before they share it with the rest of the class. Ask: *Which reviews did you think were most useful?*

Tip

To ensure they also focus on the positive, sts can collect an example from each other's work of a phrase or point they wish they'd used in their own review.

Workbook p.22.

12 Writing: A product review

A Read Liz's review. Which feedback in 10D has she changed her mind about?

B Re-read the review. Cross out the wrong guideline.

- Use headings to make your review easy to read.
- Start with an introduction.
- Use a very formal style.
- Try to find something positive to say, even if you don't like the product.
- Be careful to include only relevant details and information.
- Finish by saying whether or not you recommend the product.

C Read *Write it right!* Then underline five more similar expressions in the review.

Write it right!

Notice how the bold words and expressions can help you generalize:
As a rule, the product worked well.
Customer support was **generally** helpful.
The experience was, **by and large**, satisfactory.
The battery lasted five hours **on average**.

D Cross out the wrong alternatives, if any.

1 I read the manual and, on the whole, I found [**it complicated** / ~~**a mistake on page 22**~~].
2 Overall, my experience with your new 4D TV [**was disappointing** / **started on Monday**].
3 Generally speaking, the car [**has a sunroof** / **handles great**].
4 As a rule, I [**don't write product reviews** / **didn't write a review of my last phone**].
5 I've had the R34 for a week and, for the most part, [**I'm disappointed** / **it works well**].

E Your turn! Write a review of the product you talked about in 11A in 175–200 words.

Before
Re-read questions 4–6 and think of any details you can add.

While
Check the guidelines in B and use at least four phrases from C to express generalizations.

After
Proofread your review. Share it with the class.

Add photos

Your Review

17 Reviews | Follow | + Add Review

Rate the X29!

I've had the X29 for thirty days and, generally speaking, I find the device well built, reliable, and easy to use. The glasses work well as a translator and mini-teleprompter, and the battery life is better than I expected. I'm not sure, though, if they have made my life easier.

Comfort

<u>On the whole</u>, the glasses are surprisingly comfortable. Even though the first few days were tough, I soon got used to wearing them. My husband, on the other hand, never did – possibly because he wears prescription glasses.

Multitasking

For the most part, it's nearly impossible to carry on everyday activities such as driving – or even crossing the street – while actively using the device, which has often made me wonder what the whole point of the X29 is.

Look

Overall, the X29 is stylish and tasteful. However, the screen is way too big, and the device attracts a lot of stares, which makes me feel really uncomfortable. It's possible, of course, that people are still not used to smart glasses and that this will change in the future.

Conclusion

In general, I believe the X29 is a solid product that people who are interested in technology will enjoy. However, if you're a more casual user like me, stick to your phone – at least until an improved version is available.

Common mistake

I have ^had this product for about a week and I love it.

Review 2

Units 3–4

1 Speaking

A Look at the photos on p.38.

1 Note down two questions for each, using the phrasal verbs below.

be taken in   fall for   figure out   give away   tell apart   turn out   watch out for

2 Take turns giving advice.

A Choose a photo. Ask your questions.

B Give **A** suggestions on how to avoid being taken in.

How can you tell apart fake sneakers and real ones?

Well, if you don't want to be taken in, you should ...

B **Make it personal** Choose three question titles from Units 3 and 4 to ask a partner. Ask at least three follow-up questions for each. What did you learn about each other?

Do you get embarrassed easily?

Yes! The other day, I had just arrived at school when ...

C Search on "common embarrassing moments" and in groups, share a story about someone you know who's experienced one of them, using *used to*, *would*, or the simple past.

My little brother always used to have food in his teeth!

2 Listening

A R2.1 Listen to a radio show on embarrassing incidents. Put the events in order. Write an X for any events that aren't mentioned.

The caller ...

- [ ] complains about her boss.
- [ ] explains how she feels.
- [ ] is thanked by her boss.
- [ ] breaks up with her boyfriend.
- [ ] apologizes.
- [ ] goes to her boss's office.
- [ ] is working on a deadline.

B **Make it personal** In pairs, have you or has anyone you know ever had a similar experience? Share your stories using the expressions below.

all of a sudden   at first   finally   meanwhile some time later   while

You'll never believe what once happened to me! ...

Warm-up

See page 61 of the Teacher's Book for warm-up ideas.

1 Speaking

A Sts look back at the photos on p.38. Can they remember what the article is about? (how to avoid being taken in by fake reviews / goods / smiles). Sts will probably need to re-read it, so give them a minute or so to skim it, then tell each other in pairs what they remember.

1 Explain that sts are going to write questions about the photos to ask their classmates. Focus on the boxed phrasal verbs and speech bubbles below as an example, and get them to complete the answer. Note that this is the model for exchange one. When they do it, they respond to the question they're asked, just like the model.

In pairs, sts write their questions. Monitor and try to eliminate as many errors as you can before they begin talking.

Weaker classes: Brainstorm a few questions as a class first.

2 Put sts into new pairs to ask and answer the questions. Insist they ask follow-up questions too.

Possible questions

Photo 1: How can you avoid falling for fake hotel reviews?
How can you figure out if a review is fake?
Photo 2: How can you tell fake sneakers apart from real sneakers?
What should you watch out for when buying sneakers?
Photo 3: How can you figure out if a smile is genuine or not?
What do people's eyes give away?

B Make it personal Sts look back at the lesson title questions in Units 3 and 4 and choose three to ask a partner, plus follow-up questions. Allow time to think of other questions they might ask, and give some examples yourself first, e.g. *Do you get embarrassed easily? Why (not)? If not, do you know anyone who does? Can you remember a recent embarrassing situation? How did you react physically?*

Sts can swap partners again, mingle and use different lesson title questions.

Tip

As with any speaking activity, make sure there's a clear task/endpoint, e.g. they will have to tell the class at least two things they learned about their partner.

C Brainstorm and board some embarrassing moments with the class, e.g. walking into a glass door, sending a text message to the wrong person, forgetting someone's name.

Ask: *Which of these have happened to people you know?* In groups, sts share their stories and push each other for details. Monitor for positives and negatives and pick up on any key ones during or after the activity.

Class feedback. Ask: *What's the funniest thing you heard?*

Tip

This is worded to talk about other people to avoid any discomfort at having to share their own embarrassing stories. With a well-knit, more extrovert class, sts will, of course, want to talk about themselves, so let them.

2 Listening

A Focus on the cartoon and ask sts to suggest a thought bubble for the woman.

R2.1 Ask: *Have you ever called in to a radio show?* Invite any sts who have done so to share their experience.

Explain they will hear a listener call in about something embarrassing which happened to her. Sts first read the events and try to guess what happened. Elicit suggestions but don't confirm or deny their ideas at this stage. Highlight the X option for what's not mentioned.

Play the audio for sts to listen and order the events. Paircheck, then classcheck. Re-play it to clarify any doubts as necessary.

Answers

3, 5, 6, 1, X, 4, 2

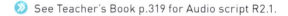

See Teacher's Book p.319 for Audio script R2.1.

B Make it personal Check sts remember the meaning and pronunciation of the boxed connectors. Refer them back to the Writing page on p.37 in Unit 3 if necessary to see them used in context.

Give sts two or three minutes to prepare their stories and build in the linkers. They can make notes if necessary, but shouldn't write out their stories, as this should be an opportunity to practice fluency.

Weaker classes: Start by building up the story from A as a class using the linkers.

In pairs, sts share their stories. They should start with *You'll never believe what happened to me!*

Encourage sts to listen attentively and use phrases from p.29 to prompt the speaker to continue, e.g. *OK, go on. And then what? So what happened next?* Monitor.

Invite volunteers to share their stories with the class.

3 Grammar

A Focus on the photo and ask these questions for sts to discuss in pairs, e.g. *Where could it be? Why? What time of day is it? How long has it been snowing? When was the last time you experienced weather anything like this?* Don't feedback their answers, just keep asking more questions, and give them a few seconds to answer each one. Classcheck their best ideas.

Sts read the text individually and circle the correct forms of the verbs. Paircheck, then classcheck.

As a follow-up, ask: *Do you think most off-duty taxi drivers would do this in your country?*

Answers

1 used to leave 2 had stayed 3 had just left 4 was already falling 5 weren't running 6 had injured 7 wasn't able to 8 decided 9 kept falling 10 were freezing 11 stopped 12 had stopped working 13 took

B Refer sts back to the grammar section on p.41 before this exercise, if necessary.

Go through the example, and ask sts which verb has been changed (*leave* > *finish*).

In pairs, sts rewrite the rest of the paragraph. Focus on the example and brainstorm the first line with them to get them started. (Note: They don't have to agree a single version.)

Weaker classes: Brainstorm some synonyms they can use, e.g. *hurt* (injured), *thought I would* (decided) *was already descending / coming down* (was already falling).

Swap pairs or allow sts to mingle to compare versions. How similar are they?

Possible answers

Although I usually finished work every day at 6:00 p.m., that day I had stayed late to finish a project. Even though the snow was already falling, at 8:00 p.m. I had just left work. The buses weren't running, though, so my only choice was to take the subway. But unfortunately, I had hurt my ankle two weeks before. Since I wasn't able to walk down stairs, I thought I'd take a taxi. The snow kept coming down, and my feet were freezing. In spite of the fact (Despite the fact) that the snow kept falling, a nice taxi driver stopped. Even though (In spite of the fact / Despite the fact / Although) he had stopped working for the day, he took me home anyway.

4 Self-test

This exercise revises **Common mistakes**. Explain to sts that it not only helps them review and consolidate vocabulary and grammar, but helps practice their proof-reading skills.

Sts do it individually, then paircheck. Encourage sts to look back through Units 3 and 4 if they're unsure of how to correct the mistakes.

If sts score less than 15 out of 20, suggest they re-do the exercise in a few days' time, to see if they get a better score. If they do really well, they could also repeat the exercise later, but without referring to Units 3 and 4 this time.

Answers

1 Everyone was staring at me because I glanced at my watch in class.
2 Jean sounded like a broken record with that false rumor, but it spread like wildfire.
3 So then he heard a really loud noise, so he looked around and opened the door. / So then he hears a really loud noise, so he looks around and opens the door.
4 Sometimes I'm really tired of studying English and hate hearing my accent over and over.
5 I didn't use to like bellbottoms and used to always wear straight pants.
6 That program used to be very popular, but personally, I didn't use (never used) to like it.
7 They should consider themselves lucky and do more to help ~~each~~ others.
8 John and I are planning a trip, and maybe you'd both like to join us yourselves.
9 I have had this phone for a week, and by and large, I like it.
10 Unlike my little brother, I can't ~~learn to~~ swim, in spite of really trying.

5 Point of view

See page 62 of the Teacher's Book for notes about this section.

Go through topics a–d with the class, and brainstorm a few ideas for each one. Individually, sts choose one of them, and make some preparatory notes. Tell sts to make the notes they feel they need to be able to speak for about 80 seconds on the topic. You don't want full sentences or a script, just prompts from which they can talk naturally. Refer sts to the language for developing an argument in 2D on p.39, and encourage use of the expressions in their answers.

Weaker classes: Sts can write out their argument in full, ensuring they structure it logically and use expressions from p.39. However, get them to rehearse so they don't just read it aloud.

Group together sts who chose the same topic so that they can compare, share, expand on and improve their ideas.

If possible, sts record their opinion in class using a cell phone. Allow sts to re-record if they aren't happy. Encourage sts to swap recordings with a partner and give each other feedback.

Optional activity

Hold a class debate on one of the topics in 5. See technique on Teacher's Book p.62.

3 Grammar

A Circle the correct forms of the verbs.

I [1][used to leave / was leaving] work every day at 6:00 p.m., but that day I [2][had stayed / would stay] late to finish a project. So at 8:00 p.m. I [3][just left / had just left] work, but the snow [4][already fell / was already falling]. The buses [5][didn't run / weren't running], so my only choice was to take the subway. But unfortunately, I [6][had injured / was injuring] my ankle two weeks before. Since I [7][wasn't able to / am not able to] walk down stairs, I [8][decided / used to decide] to take a taxi. The snow [9][kept falling / would keep falling], and my feet [10][were freezing / froze]. Finally, a nice taxi driver [11][would stop / stopped]. He [12][had stopped / was stopping] working for the day, but he [13][took / used to take] me home anyway.

B In pairs, rewrite the paragraph, without changing the meaning, using at least four of these conjunctions. How many verbs can you change also?

although	despite	even though	in spite of	though	unlike	whereas	while

Although I usually finished work every day at 6:00 p.m., that day ...

4 Self-test

Correct the two mistakes in each sentence. Check your answers in Units 3 and 4. What's your score, 1–20?

1 Everyone was staring me because I glanced my watch in class.
2 Jean sounded like a broken cassette with that false rumor, but it spread like fire.
3 So then he hear a really loud noise, so he look around and opened the door.
4 Sometimes I'm really tired to study English and hate hearing my accent over and again.
5 I didn't used to like bellbottoms and use to always wear straight pants.
6 That program would be very popular, but personally, I don't like it.
7 They should consider theirselves lucky and do more to help each others.
8 John and myself are planning a trip, and maybe you'd both like to join us yourself.
9 I have this phone for a week, and for and large, I like it.
10 Whereas my little brother, I can't learn to swim, in spite of really trying.

5 Point of view

Choose a topic. Then support your opinion in 100–150 words, and record your answer. Ask a partner for feedback. How can you be more convincing?

a You think false advertising is a serious problem. OR
You think, by and large, companies do a good job of advertising their products.
b You think everyone buys fake goods, and it's nice to save money. OR
You think the purchase of fake items is truly unethical.
c You think urban legends can be fun and persist because everyone enjoys them. OR
You think urban legends can do serious damage when people start to believe them.
d You think "flipped learning" is a wonderful idea. OR
You think "flipped learning" is only the latest fad and just a way for teachers to do less work.

5 What's your biggest life decision so far?

1 Vocabulary: Adversity

A 5.1 What do you know about these people? Guess the missing words. Then listen to check. Were you close?

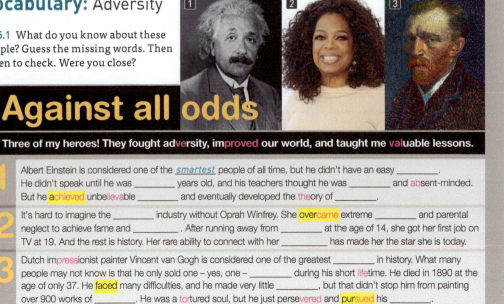

Against all odds

Three of my heroes! They fought adversity, improved our world, and taught me valuable lessons.

1 Albert Einstein is considered one of the *smartest* people of all time, but he didn't have an easy ________. He didn't speak until he was ________ years old, and his teachers thought he was ________ and absent-minded. But he achieved unbelievable ________ and eventually developed the theory of ________.

2 It's hard to imagine the ________ industry without Oprah Winfrey. She overcame extreme ________ and parental neglect to achieve fame and ________. After running away from ________ at the age of 14, she got her first job on TV at 19. And the rest is history. Her rare ability to connect with her ________ has made her the star she is today.

3 Dutch impressionist painter Vincent van Gogh is considered one of the greatest ________ in history. What many people may not know is that he only sold one – yes, one – ________ during his short lifetime. He died in 1890 at the age of only 37. He faced many difficulties, and he made very little ________, but that didn't stop him from painting over 900 works of ________. He was a tortured soul, but he just persevered and pursued his ________.

> I don't know very much about ... yet. Was he/she the one who ...

B Read *Collocation*. Then complete the mindmaps with the highlighted words in **A**.

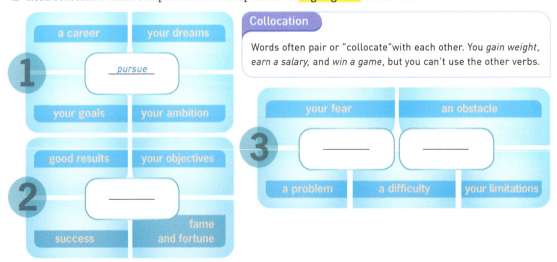

1: *pursue* — a career, your dreams, your goals, your ambition

2: ________ — good results, your objectives, success, fame and fortune

3: ________ / ________ — your fear, an obstacle, a problem, a difficulty, your limitations

Collocation

Words often pair or "collocate"with each other. You *gain weight*, *earn a salary*, and *win a game*, but you can't use the other verbs.

C Which phrases from **B** can you use to describe 1) the people in **A** and 2) famous people from your own country?

> Let's see. Despite her family background, Oprah has achieved a lot of success.

Lesson Aims: Sts learn language to talk about adversity and people they look up to.

Skills	Language	Vocabulary
Reading about famous people who overcame adversity Listening to people talking about their heroes Telling a narrative with suspense	Building a narrative: *My cousin is a total inspiration. My friend is amazing! She's been in a wheelchair her whole life, but she ...*	Collocations with *achieve* (e.g. *success / fame*), *face* (e.g. *a problem / an obstacle*), *overcome* (e.g. *fear / a difficulty*), *pursue* (e.g. *a career / your goals*)

Warm-up

Board: *Facing / Overcoming adversity*. Illustrate it with a suitable image / story if you can. In pairs, sts brainstorm as many words / phrases as they can associated with these phrases, e.g. *(be in) serious trouble, continued difficulty, constant hardship, traumatized, poverty, sorrow, depressed/relieved*. See if they can say where they've seen / heard them before and which are cognates in their L1. Set a time limit of two minutes. Board the items sts feedback. If you like, the pair with the most 'correct' wins.

Board the lesson title question: *What's your biggest life decision so far? How did the decision affect you?* Sts discuss in pairs.

1 Vocabulary: Adversity

A 5.1 Sts cover the text and look at the photos. Ask who the people are, and elicit as much information as possible before sts read the text (see Background information below).

Sts read the text and guess the missing words. Encourage them to guess several words if they want to.

Weaker students: Get them to look at the word before and after the gap, and, if they can't guess the word itself, at least say what type of word is missing, e.g. gap 1 – noun, gap 2 – number.

Paircheck before you play the audio for them to listen and check. Ask if they had different words in the gaps to those on the audio. Their answers may well be correct and praise them if this is the case. Ask: *What do the three people have in common?* (They all achieved amazing things despite their adversity.)

Answers

1 smartest, childhood, four, lazy, success, relativity
2 entertainment, poverty, fortune, home, guests
3 artists, painting, money, art, dream

Background information

Albert Einstein (1879–1955) was a German physicist. Besides the theory of relativity, he was involved in many other influential theories and projects. He won the 1921 Nobel Prize in Physics.

Oprah Winfrey, born in 1954, is one of the most successful and influential women in American TV history. In her talk show, *The Oprah Winfrey show*, she interviewed celebrities and discussed social issues. She has also acted and was nominated for an Oscar in her first film *The Color Purple*.

Vincent Van Gogh (1853–1890) was a remarkable Dutch post-impressionist painter. He is famous for his vivid, thickly-painted portraits, self-portraits, and landscapes.

Optional activity

Ask: *Which of these three people do you admire most? Why?* Sts discuss in pairs, then write a short paragraph about why they admire the person they have chosen. Display the paragraphs around the classroom for the others to read.

B Board the highlighted words from A, and elicit synonyms / meanings. Read **Collocation** and elicit other examples of pairs of words which go together, e.g. *take / pass an exam, take a photo, lose / gain weight*.

Go through the mind maps and four options for *pursue*. Then have sts study maps 2 and 3. Elicit which of the nouns are positive (1 and 2) and which are negative (3). Explain that the highlighted words in A collocate with the words in the mind maps, and have them match them with the correct mind map. Classcheck, and check sts understand all the collocations.

Answers

1 pursue 2 achieve 3 face, overcome

Tip

Encourage sts to create a few mind maps in their vocabulary notebooks for collocations sharing the same verb. They can keep going back and adding to their mind maps as they learn more collocations.

C In pairs, sts use the mind maps to create sentences. Encourage them to write six sentences: three about the people in 1) and three about the people in 2).

2 Listening

A 5.2 Give sts ten seconds to glance at the text and two photos, then cover it and remember what they can in pairs.

Board the following questions: *What's its purpose?* (to encourage people to send in stories about their heroes). *What do people have to do?* (send in a video). *What could they win?* ($1,000 gift card). Sts read the webpage quickly to find out. Classcheck. Highlight pronunciation of the three stressed words.

Explain that sts are going to listen to the videos that two readers, Carol and Fernando, have sent in. Play the audio for sts to complete the chart. Paircheck, then classcheck.

Weaker classes: Pre-teach: *quit a job* (give up or leave a job), *drop out of college* (give up college or leave college), *to be bedridden* (to have to stay in bed through illness).

Answers

	Tara	Fernando
Speaker's relationship to ...	friend	grandson
Problem(s)	single mom, lost her home, hard to earn a living	serious medical condition
Most impressive thing	pursued her dreams and wrote a book	kept on going

See Teacher's Book p.319 for Audio script 5.2.

Optional activity

In pairs, sts write their own definition of the word *hero*, e.g. *A hero is someone you look up to or someone who inspires you*. Then put pairs into groups to compare their definitions and come up with the best one they all agree on. Groups tell the class, then try to agree on a single, class definition for hero.

B 5.2 Sts may be able to do this from memory. Let them try to do it, then have them listen again to check. If you play it a third time, add on an additional task, e.g. to spot aspects of pronunciation like elision, words which 'disappear', silent *ts* at the end of words.

Answers

Incorrect statements:
made a fortune on her first book
used to lead a stress-free life

C Read the questions and the speech bubble with the class. Highlight the phrases *(greatly / really) impressed (me) (very much indeed)* and *made a big / strong impression on (me)* and elicit variations.

In pairs, sts discuss the questions. Encourage them to give their reasons, as in the speech bubble. In class feedback, ask: *Do you know anyone who has had a similar experience to Tara or Fernando?*

D **Make it personal** Give sts thirty seconds to read through the rubric and instructions silently, then try to tell each other in pairs what they have to do. Check they understand what to do by asking simple questions, e.g. *Are you going to speak or write? In pairs or groups? About whom?* Tell sts they can choose a friend, family member or a famous person.

Weaker classes: Before sts do D1, give them a copy of the audio script 5.2, and ask them to underline ways in which the speakers create suspense.

1 Give sts two minutes to make notes about their chosen hero, using questions 1–3. Refer them to **Beginning a narrative**, and ask them to write a short paragraph about their hero using their notes. Encourage them to use some of the collocations in 1B.

2 Focus on **Common mistakes** and elicit what the st did wrong. Get them to change the sentence into the present continuous (*is facing, is overcoming*, etc.) to doublecheck.

Tip

With a monolingual class, when going through **Common mistakes**, add a couple of additional typical mistakes you can anticipate sts making, based on direct translation from their mother tongue, to help them achieve greater accuracy in group work.

In groups of four or five, sts share their ideas. Closely monitor to 'capture and kill off' as many errors as you can, e.g. note down and pass any erroneous phrases to the speaker for them to study and try to self-correct. Giving sts a sense of audience and making them feel you are really listening to them makes all the difference to pair and groupwork.

When they have voted for the best story, have one group member tell the rest of the class about their group's chosen hero. Then ask which should win the class prize, and have a class vote, if appropriate.

Song lyric: See Teacher's Book p.339 for notes about the song and an accompanying activity to do with the class.

Workbook p.23.

2 Listening

A 5.2 Read the webpage, listen to two people's stories, and complete the chart.

Our magazine is looking for heroes.
Who are yours?
They're your friends, neighbors, relatives – maybe even your parents. And their personal stories have inspired you and have had an impact on your lives.

Share your story with us. Three questions to help you get started: Tara

1 Who's your chosen hero?
2 What kind of problem has he / she been able to overcome?
☐ health ☐ relationships ☐ money ☐ other (what?)
3 What did he / she do that so impressed you?

Send us a short video telling us about your hero.
The ten most convincing entries will win a $1,000 gift card.

	Tara	Fernando
Speaker's relationship to ...	*friend*	
Problem(s)		
Most impressive thing		

B 5.2 Listen again. For each person, cross out the incorrect statement.

Tara ...	Fernando ...
couldn't afford her home.	is very close to his grandson.
didn't get along with her mom.	used to lead a stress-free life.
made a fortune on her first book.	had always been in good health.

C In pairs, whose story impressed you more? Why do you feel that way?

Fernando's story really made a big impression on me because he never gave up.

D **Make it personal** For the webpage competition, who would you nominate as your own hero and why?

1 Think about questions 1–3 in A for two minutes. Read *Beginning a narrative*.
2 In groups, share ideas, and then take a vote. Which are the most convincing narratives? Whose story should win the prize?

Beginning a narrative

A good narrative creates suspense and gives only relevant details. Always start by capturing your listener's attention:
My cousin Bruno is amazing / unbelievable / a total inspiration!

My friend Sara is amazing! I'd like to nominate her. She's been in a wheelchair her whole life, but she ...

Common mistakes

My grandmother faced lots of setbacks, but she ~~overcome~~ *overcame* most of her problems and ~~turn~~ *turned* her life around.
Don't forget! When you tell a story, be careful with both tense consistency and, in the present, third person *-s*.

3 Listening

If only I could multitask!

A Which skills (1–9) from the website have(n't) you learned?

9 NINE LIFESAVING SKILLS YOU'LL REGRET NOT LEARNING BEFORE YOU'RE 18!

1 cooking	4 playing a sport well	7 learning self-defense
2 driving	5 saving money	8 swimming
3 multitasking	6 speaking a second language	9 touch typing

I haven't learned how to swim yet, and I'm already 16!

B 5.3 Listen to two colleagues. Which skill is Anthony talking about?

C 5.3 Listen again. T (true) or F (false)? Guess what they will say next.

1 Anthony was surprised he didn't pass.
2 He's taken the test four times this year.
3 Claire thinks instructors are usually friendly.
4 When Anthony had to turn, he got even more nervous.
5 There was an accident at the end of the test.

D 5.4 Complete the rest of the conversation with the sentences. Listen to check.

I wish she wouldn't do that.	If only I'd started in my late teens.	I wish I knew, though.

CLAIRE: Don't let it get you down. You can do it! You're taking lessons, right?
ANTHONY: Oh, yeah. It's been two years now.
CLAIRE: Two years? Wow! Same instructor?
ANTHONY: Yeah. She's all right. But she keeps yelling, "Watch out!" whenever I do something wrong. [1] ______________ . It's really annoying.
CLAIRE: Why do you think you always get so nervous?
ANTHONY: No idea. [2] ______________ . If I did, I'd be able to do something about it. But here's the thing ... I started taking lessons in my late 20s.
CLAIRE: So?
ANTHONY: Too late, I guess. [3] ______________ . For example, I still don't know how to park! Can you believe it?
CLAIRE: Look, just take the test again, and do the best you can. You'll do better next time.
ANTHONY: I don't think there will be a next time. After more than a hundred lessons and eight exams, I'm calling it quits. Enough is enough.
CLAIRE: Oh, no! Keep at it! It's never too late to learn.
ANTHONY: Maybe it's not meant to be.
CLAIRE: Don't be silly! Just stick with it.

E Make it personal Answer 1–4 in groups. Any big disagreements?

1 Guess how their conversation ends. Will Anthony retake the test?
2 If you were in Anthony's shoes, what would you do now?
3 Is it essential for adults to know how to drive?
4 Do you know anyone who took a long time to learn something? How about you?

Well, if I was Anthony, I'd take a break and spend my money on something else.

Lesson Aims: Sts learn to talk about skills they have learned, and regrets they have about the past and present.

Skills	Language	Vocabulary	Grammar
Listening to friends discussing a driving test Role playing a conversation about a situation that went wrong	Expressing encouragement: *You'll do better next time. Do the best you can. Don't let it get you down.*	*accident, driving test, instructor, let something get you down, pass / fail*	Imaginary situations (1): *wish* and *if only*

Warm-up

Board the word *Dreams* and get sts, in pairs, to brainstorm what it makes them think of. Classcheck their best ideas. They may come up with all sorts of dreams, past, present and future, which lead nicely into the lesson.

Refer sts to the list of skills in A. Explain what *touch typing* is, if necessary (using all your fingers to type without looking at the keys).

In pairs, ask sts to rank them in order of importance or difficulty (1 = most important / difficult to learn and 9 = least important / difficult). Do they all agree? Compare their ranking lists with the rest of the class. Do they agree? Ask the lesson title question: *What would you love to be able to do?*

3 Listening

A Sts go through the list of skills and tick the ones they have learned. Focus on the speech bubble, and highlight the use of *yet* with the present perfect. Elicit that this means that it is a skill the speaker intends to learn at some stage. In pairs, sts make similar sentences about the skills they haven't learned.

Focus on the photo and speech bubble *If only I could multitask!* Ask: *Is this a verb in your language? Do you know anyone like this?* Elicit some true *If only* sentences about the skills.

Optional activity

Revise other language for talking about skills. Remind sts that we use *can / could* to talk about the skills we have, e.g. *I can / can't cook. I could / couldn't drive when I was seventeen*. Point out that we can also say *I know / I don't know how to drive*. Elicit the question forms (*Can you ...? Could you ... when you were ...? Do you know how to ...?*) In pairs, sts ask and answer questions about the skills in A, e.g. *Do you know how to touch type? Do you know how to drive?*

B 5.3 Focus on the photo. Explain that sts are going to listen to a conversation between these two friends, Anthony and Claire. Anthony has been trying to learn how to do something. Play the audio for sts to find out which skill from A he is talking about. Classcheck.

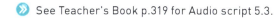

Answer

Driving

See Teacher's Book p.319 for Audio script 5.3.

Tip

When listening for general understanding, encourage sts to listen out for the stressed words, as normally these are the key words conveying the main meaning.

C 5.3 Sts read the statements before they listen again, and can guess the answers they don't remember. Replay the audio for them to mark the statements as true or false.

Classcheck. Discuss together how they think the conversation will continue.

Answers

1 F 2 T 3 F 4 T 5 T

See Teacher's Book p.319 for Audio script 5.3.

D 5.4 Sts read the rest of the conversation quickly. Ask: *Why do you think Anthony keeps failing his test?* Elicit that he gets nervous.

Sts complete the gaps. Play the audio for them to check their answers. Discuss the meaning of the expression *let something get you down* (= allow something to make you feel disappointed or downhearted).

Answers

1 I wish she wouldn't do that.
2 I wish I knew, though.
3 If only I'd started in my late teens.

E Make it personal In small groups of three or four, sts go straight into the questions. Encourage all members of the group to give their opinions. In a class feedback, invite volunteers to share their ideas with the rest of the class. Ask: *Did you learn anything surprising?*

Tip

Remind sts that you can use *were* instead of *was* in *if* sentences, e.g. *If I was / were Anthony ....* or they can say *In Anthony's shoes, I would ... .*

Song lyric: See Teacher's Book p.339 for notes about the song and an accompanying activity to do with the class.

4 Grammar: Imaginary situations (1)

A In pairs, sts read examples 1-3 and match them to their meanings.

Tip

First get sts to **mentally** translate the example sentences and count if the same number of words is used in English and their L1. They don't need to say a word in their L1, but just noticing which words are/aren't used or are in a different position in the two languages both helps consolidate meaning and notice/pre-empt potential problems. All second language sts, especially in part-time language classes, translate anyway, so build this into your pedagogy, rather than trying forever in vain to get them to *Think in English* in spite of their L1.

Go through **More about *wish***. Then refer sts to the **Common mistake**. Explain that we can use *would* or *could* with the third person, e.g. *I wish he would speak French slowly. I wish he could speak French fluently.*

Answers

1 b 2 a 3 c
For wishes about the present and the future, we use a verb in the simple past.
For regrets about the past, we use a verb in the past perfect.

Refer sts to the **Grammar expansion** on p.146.

Tip

Sts may be confused about which tense to use in English, as often a subjunctive tense is used in other languages, so it is useful for them to compare with their L1.

B Board sentences 1–3 from the grammar box in A, then elicit the correct endings. Explain that when using *I wish* ... or *If only* ... , adding these endings will help sts clarify whether the situation they are wishing for is in the past or the present, and will help them to decide which tense to use.

Answers

1 didn't 2 don't 3 doesn't

C 5.5 Focus on the example and warn sts that they need to think carefully about which subject to use for each gap. Classcheck using the audio.

Weaker classes: You could board the subjects, and ask sts to match them with sentences 2–6: *there, she, that, you, he*.

Answers

1 I knew 2 he had taught 3 there was (were) 4 you didn't / wouldn't miss 5 she would change 6 that was (were)

Optional activity

Board the following sentence beginnings:

If only my English teacher ...

I wish my best friend ...

Sts write six sentences using *I wish / If only* about people they know. Encourage affirmative and negative sentences, e.g. *I wish my English teacher didn't give us so much homework. If only my English teacher would speak more slowly!* Classcheck.

D Make it personal

1 5.6 **How to say it** Sts look at the expressions in the box. Ask: *When would you use these expressions?* (when encouraging someone to do something that they aren't very good at).

Sts complete the expressions, then listen to the audio to check their answers. Re-play the audio, pausing after each one for sts to repeat, focusing on the correct stress and intonation.

Answers

1 get 2 do 3 best 4 at 5 with

2 Go through the instructions and check that the A and B sts understand what they have to do.

Ask the As: *Which of these situations have you been in? Did they go well or badly?* Tell them they can either talk about a real situation that went wrong, or use a made-up situation.

In pairs, sts act out their own conversations. Monitor and help as necessary. Praise those sts who use the grammar correctly and the *How to say it* expressions.

Weaker classes: Have sts write out their conversations first, but encourage them to act them out from memory. If necessary, they can write down five or six prompt words.

Invite one or two pairs to act out their conversation to the class.

Workbook p.24.

4 Grammar: Imaginary situations (1)

A Match statements 1–3 to their meaning (a–c). Then check (✔) the correct rules.

Imaginary situations (1): *wish* and *If only*

1 I **wish I had started** when I was younger.	a ☐ a strong wish for the present to be different
2 **If only I knew how** to park the car!	b ☐ a wish for the past to be different
3 **I wish** my instructor **would give** clearer instructions.	c ☐ a wish for a situation or another person to change

For wishes about the present and future, we use a verb in the ☐ **simple present** ☐ **simple past**.
For regrets about the past, we use a verb in the ☐ **simple past** ☐ **past perfect**.

Grammar expansion p.146

More about *wish*

Other verbs and tenses can also be used with *wish* to express the present or future:
I can't draw. → I wish I **could draw**.
He's coming with us. I don't like him.→ I wish he **wasn't** / **weren't coming** with us.
The simple past and *would* are often interchangeable for repeated actions:
I wish my mom **listened** to me. = I wish my mom **would listen** to me.

Common mistake

I wish I ~~would~~ *could* speak French fluently.
Don't use *wish* or *if only* + *would* to talk about yourself.

B Choose the correct ending for sentences 1–3 in A.

1 ... but I [**don't / didn't**]. 2 ... but I [**don't / didn't**]. 3 ... but she [**doesn't / didn't**].

C 5.5 Complete six reactions to the website in 3A with a subject and the correct verb form. Listen to check.

1 I wish _I knew_ (know) how to cook so I wouldn't spend so much on fast food.
2 I had the best dad in the world, but I wish __________ (teach) me how to save money.
3 Why are languages so hard? If only __________ (be) a magic pill to speak English.
4 Carlos, I wish __________ (miss) so many classes. Please try to come more often!
5 Mom says I'm not ready to get my driver's license yet. I wish __________ (change) her mind.
6 They say you can learn how to multitask at any age. If only __________ (be) true!

D Make it personal Role play "What went wrong?"

1 5.6 **How to say it** Complete the chart. Listen to check.

Expressing encouragement

	What they said	What they meant
1	Don't let it ______ you down.	Don't let it make you sad.
2	You'll ______ better next time.	Your performance will be better next time.
3	Do the ______ you can.	Try hard.
4	Keep ______ it!	Don't give up.
5	Stick ______ it!	Don't give up.

2 Role play in pairs. Explain what went wrong, and tell **B** two things you regret.

A Choose a situation.
an exam a job interview a sports event
a meal you cooked an audition

B Support and encourage **A**, and ask for more details. Use *How to say it* expressions.

So, how did it go?

Terrible. I wish I'd studied more. I mean I couldn't even answer some questions.

53

5 Reading

A In pairs, what can you learn about Victoria from the photo and title of the article? Then read the first paragraph to check. Were you close?

Up and coming

From dull dinosaurs to glorious Greek food

Meet Victoria Sánchez, the 25-year-old college dropout behind *Fossil.*

We all know the stories – talented individuals who didn't graduate from college, never regretted it, and still managed to make absurd amounts of money despite lots of setbacks. According to a recent survey, 63 of the 400 wealthiest people in the U.S. don't have a college degree. That's about one in six. *Up and coming* spoke to Victoria Sánchez, the archeology dropout behind *Fossil*, elected best Greek restaurant of the year.

Q: *Why archeology* ___?

A: Mostly because I had a wonderful archeology teacher as a freshman. So I wanted to follow in her footsteps and pursue a career in science, as well.

Q: ___?

A: It took a while. I guess it wasn't until my sophomore year when it just hit me that there was life beyond dinosaurs and fossils and rocks. So at the end of the year, I dropped out, which hardly anyone in my family had done before. Since I knew that eventually I wanted an international career, I decided to spend some time traveling around Europe. That's when I fell madly in love with Greece.

Q: ___?

A: My friends couldn't believe their ears when I told them I'd decided to start my own business. But they were generally supportive – most of them, that is. They kept reminding me of all the famous dropouts who'd made a fortune, while secretly wondering, I think, if I had the skills to be my own boss. Mom was cool about it, too. She used to say, "Better to be stressed out and overworked than underpaid and unhappy." Dad wasn't exactly thrilled, though. He still wishes I'd stuck with archeology, even now! He's always had such an interest in it.

Q: ___?

A: Europe was great, but after that, being back home was pretty much the same since I had to study again! Before opening *Fossil*, I spent about a year reading about Greek cuisine, learning from experts, seeking mentors, and learning the basics of running a restaurant, which I knew virtually nothing about. Now I'm happier than I've ever been. *Fossil* is winning award after award, and we're opening our first restaurant abroad next month.

Q: ___?

A: Well, above all, I've learned that formal education, with its overemphasis on theory, doesn't necessarily lead to actual learning. Learning can take place at work with a boss mentoring you, by going abroad and immersing yourself in a new culture, while starting your own business – or in a million other ways. It's wrong to underestimate the power of practical, real-life experience.

Q: ___?

A: Well, I wouldn't go as far as that. For every mega-success, there are a thousand students who drop out of college and, after a few years, wish they hadn't. College can help you develop social skills, self-discipline, and good study habits. So, despite what some people might say, college is anything but a waste of time. In my case, though – and I don't want to generalize beyond my own experience – there were more effective ways to reach my goal.

B 5.7 Skim the interview to put the questions back in the article. Listen to check. Any difficult parts?

1 So are you saying that a college education is a complete waste of time?
2 What was life after college like?
3 How did people react when you broke the news?
4 When did you realize you'd had enough of college?
5 Why archeology?
6 Looking back, what have you learned from the whole experience?

C Read *Expressing negative ideas*. What does Victoria say to express 1–4? Underline the relevant sentences in **A**.

1 There were very few college dropouts in my family. *I dropped out, which hardly anyone in my family had done before.*
2 My father wasn't happy with my decision.
3 I knew very little about how to manage a restaurant.
4 I disagree with those who say college is useless.

Expressing negative ideas

There are many subtle ways to express negativity:
Being a student is **far from** / **anything but** easy. (= very difficult)
I have **hardly any** / **virtually no** free time. (= very little free time)
Some subjects **aren't exactly** interesting. (= They're boring)

Lesson Aims: Sts read and talk about going to college, and discuss the advantages and disadvantages of a college education.

Skills	Language	Vocabulary
Reading a magazine article about a girl who dropped out of college Discussing the advantages and disadvantages of going to college	Expressing negative ideas: *Being a student is far from easy. Some subjects aren't exactly interesting.*	*archeology, dropout, footsteps, freshman, sophomore, talented* Prefixes: *over-*, *under-*, and *inter-*, e.g. *overemphasis, underestimate*

Warm-up

Ask: *Did your parents go to college?* Sts put up their hands if the answer is yes. Work out what percentage of sts' parents went to college.

Discuss these questions as a class: *What percentage of teenagers go to college today? Do you think more people go to college these days? Why do you think that is? What are the advantages / disadvantages of going to college?* This will lead naturally into the lesson title question: *How important is a college degree?*

5 Reading

A Get sts to cover the text and focus only on the title of the article with the class. Discuss the meaning of *up and coming* (= something or someone who is new to the scene, but is progressing well and gaining success).

Now refer sts to the photo and the rest of the title, and elicit what they think the article is about (a chef who cooks Greek food and is becoming very successful). Ask what they think *Fossil* is (the name of a restaurant). Ask sts to read the first paragraph of the article to check their ideas. Ask: *Any surprises? How do you pronounce the five pink–stressed words?*

Tip

It's better for sts to guess the pronunciation of new words than you keep telling and drilling them. Unlike Romance languages, English has no stress system, which is why iDentities gives this additional help. The more sts guess, the greater their sensitivity to English spelling / pronunciation relationships will develop, and so too, their confidence to try on their own. And, since there are so many cognates between English and Romance languages, learning to Anglicize words from their L1 is a skill which is really worth cultivating.

B 5.7 Sts read the questions first before re-reading the article. In pairs, get them to guess what her answers might be, especially as they may only need to read the first sentence in each paragraph to be able to match the questions.

Paircheck, then classcheck with the audio.

Discuss the meaning of *freshman* (= first year student) and *sophomore year* (= 2nd year at college).

Answers

5 Why archeology?
4 When did you realize you'd had enough of college?
3 How did people react when you broke the news?
2 What was life after college like?
6 Looking back, what have you learned from the whole experience?
1 So are you saying that a college education is a complete waste of time?

Optional activities

Write the following events on the board. Ask sts to read the article again and put them in chronological order.

She spent a year studying Greek cuisine. (4)
She opened a restaurant called Fossil. (5)
She went to college. (1)
She traveled round Europe. (3)
She dropped out of college. (2)

After 5B, ask sts to find and note down five words each that they don't know in the article. In pairs, they try to work out the meanings. If they can't, then do so using the context, get them to mingle and help each other, or allow them to check in a dictionary. Class feedback.

C Refer sts to **Expressing negative ideas**. Sts read and notice the different options and meanings.

To test comprehension, board: *Being a student is far from / anything but easy*. Ask how they'd express this using *very difficult*. (*Being a student is very difficult.*) Ask: *Which sentence do you prefer?* Discuss why you might want to say it using *far from / anything from*. (It's less direct and more subtle.)

Ask sts to look back to how Victoria expresses these sentences in the article. Classcheck.

Answers

1 I dropped out, which hardly anyone in my family had done before.
2 Dad wasn't exactly thrilled, though.
3 ...running a restaurant, which I knew virtually nothing about.
4 College is anything but a waste of time.

D Have sts read the questions. You might want to brainstorm some ideas with the whole class first. In groups of four or five, sts discuss the questions. Monitor, helping with vocabulary as much as you can, without getting too stuck either with one st or group, or the others won't feel the activity is worthwhile. Encourage sts to use the expressions they have just looked at for expressing negative ideas.

Invite individual sts to feed back to the class. Ask: *Did your group mainly agree or disagree? What did you disagree on?*

Song lyric: See Teacher's Book p.339 for notes about the song and an accompanying activity to do with the class.

6 Vocabulary: Prefixes *over-*, *under-* and *inter-*

A Elicit examples of prefixes, then ask for a definition (a letter or group of letters added to the beginning of a word or root, to form a new word,) *Why is it useful to recognize patterns of prefixes?* (It helps you to guess the meaning of unknown words.)

Once sts have circled the correct answers, re-elicit pronunciation of the highlighted words in the reading text in A. Ask: *Where is the stress on words which have the prefix 'under' / 'over'?* (on the third syllable, i.e. the next syllable after the prefix). Are there any strong prefix pronunciation rules in their language? Highlight that it helps to record / try to remember prefixed roots in pairs, *over / underestimate*, for example.

Answers

1 "between" or "among" 2 over 3 Under 4 a verb, an adjective or a noun

B 5.8 Sts cover and look only at the title and initial question of the radio show page. Elicit what sort of answer they might have got so they get the idea that they're going to read quotes from listeners calling in to a radio show.

Sts first read the statements and work out what type of word is missing (noun, verb or adjective) from each gap.

Sts complete the gaps. Highlight that there is one extra root. Paircheck, then play the audio to classcheck.

Answers

1 overrated 2 overqualified 3 underperform, interact 4 oversimplify 5 overachiever 6 underprivileged

Optional activity

In groups, sts write as many words as they can beginning with *under-*, *over-* or *inter-*. Groups get a point for each word they think of, and two points for each word they think of which none of the other groups has thought of. The group with the most points wins.

C Make it personal Refer to the **Common mistake**.

In groups, sts discuss the questions. Encourage sts to discuss them one at a time, setting a time limit for each question, so the lesson doesn't drift. Monitor and note common errors or good uses of English to share at the end. Invite sts to feed back to the rest of the class. Ask: *Did your group all agree? Which questions did you disagree on?* Finally, provide the language feedback you noted, e.g. by boarding half a dozen common mistakes for them to correct.

Tip

Weaker classes: In group activities like these, where weaker sts may be overshadowed by more able ones, suggest that sts discuss the questions in pairs first, then join with another pair to exchange their ideas.

Workbook p.25.

D In groups, discuss 1–3. Do you generally agree?

1 How would your parents / friends (have) react(ed) if you('d) dropped out of college for whatever reason?
2 Do you think you have the skills to run your own business?
3 Is it better to be self-employed or to work for somebody else?

I think it's much better to be self-employed, without a boss telling you what to do.

6 Vocabulary: Prefixes *over-*, *under-* and *inter-*

A Look at the highlighted words in the article in 5A and circle the correct answer.

1 The prefix *inter-* means [**"between" or "among"** / **"in the middle"**].
2 The prefix [**over-** / **under-**] means "too much" or "more than necessary."
3 [**Over-** / **Under-**] means "too little" or "not enough."
4 *Under-* and *over-* can be followed by [**only a verb or an adjective** / **a verb, an adjective, or a noun**].

B 5.8 Complete the call-in statements to a radio show about Victoria Sánchez. Use *under-*, *over-*, and *inter-* and the words in the box. There is one extra word. Listen to check.

achiever (n)	act (v)	paid (adj)	perform (v)	privileged (adj)	qualified (adj)	rated (adj)	simplify (v)

THIS WEEK'S HOT ISSUE:

Do you need a college degree to get ahead in life? What some of our callers had to say:

No, of course not!

1 "College education is *overrated*. Intelligence and flexibility are more important. Victoria's living proof of that."
2 "I have an MBA and a PhD, but I'm having trouble finding a job. They say I'm ________. So, not very helpful!"
3 "Not having a degree doesn't necessarily mean you're going to ________ at work. Talent and the ability to ________ with people are far more important."

Yes, absolutely!

4 "We shouldn't ________ things. For some careers, like engineering and medicine, you do need a college degree."
5 "Not everyone's an ________ like Oprah Winfrey or Bill Gates. Most people need a college degree to make a decent living."
6 "A college degree is a passport to a better life. The government ought to help ________ students fund their college education, I think."

C Make it personal In groups, answer 1–4. Do you mainly agree?

1 Which statement in B best describes your own views?
2 If you were to start college (again) tomorrow, what would you study?
3 Do you think online courses will replace traditional teaching?
4 Do you think it's a good idea to take a year off before college?

I've always thought taking a break after 12 years of school was a good idea, so I agree with ...

Common mistake

My dad never *went to / attended* ~~did/made/studied~~ college.

7 Language in use

A 5.9 In pairs, imagine the story behind each photo. Listen to a radio show to check. Were you close?

Well, maybe the first one is an album photo.

B 5.9 Listen again. In groups, share the additional details you understood. Then check AS 5.9 on p.162. Did you miss anything?

Let's see ... the Beatles got that letter in 1962.

C Do the speech balloons 1–3 mean the same as a–c below? Write S (same) or D (different).

1 I bet they wouldn't have sent that letter if they'd had a crystal ball.

2 What a fighter she is. If she didn't have such willpower, she might have given up.

3 Maybe if he hadn't had so much faith in himself, we wouldn't have Mickey Mouse today!

a The executives sent the letter because they didn't have a crystal ball.
b Rowling has a lot of willpower, but she gave up.
c Mickey Mouse might exist because Disney had faith in himself.

D Which of the people mentioned would you most like to meet / have met?

I wish I'd met Walt Disney. I bet he was a lot of fun!

E **Make it personal** Search online for "famous people who weren't successful at first." Find an interesting fact to tell the class.

I bet you didn't know this! Guess what I learned about ...

Lesson Aims: Sts listen to a radio show about famous people who had bad starts to their careers, and then discuss good or bad decisions in their own lives.

Skills	Vocabulary	Grammar	Pronunciation
Listening to a radio show about the Beatles, J. K. Rowling and Walt Disney Discussing situations in the past where sts made bad decisions	*crystal ball, willpower, faith, reject, fire s.o. (v), have faith in ...*	Imaginary situations (2): mixed conditionals	Sentence stress

Warm-up

Board some famous quotes about mistakes, e.g.:

He who never made a mistake never made a discovery. (Samuel Smiles)

If you're not making mistakes, you aren't really trying. (Coleman Hawkins)

I've learned so much from my mistakes, I'm thinking of making some more. (Anon)

Ask: *Have you heard the quotes before? Any similar ones?* Ask sts if they agree / disagree with the quotes, and how they feel when they make mistakes in their English classes. If time, they can google more quotes very easily.

Ask: *What do you think makes a successful person?* Sts discuss in groups and try to think of five pieces of advice on "How to be successful in life.", e.g. *Don't be afraid of failure. Don't let discouragement deter you. Be determined to succeed.*

Ask the lesson title question: *Did you make any mistakes yesterday? What did you do about it? How did you react?* Invite sts to share their experiences with the class.

7 Language in use

A 5.9 In pairs, sts answer: *Who are the people in the photos? What are / were they famous for?* Elicit any and everything you can of interest, e.g. how many Harry Potter films / books they have seen / read, if they've been to a Disney theme park, whose parents learned English by listening to the Beatles, what song lines of theirs do they know.

Narrow it down, asking: *Can you guess which experience they all had?* Don't confirm or deny their ideas yet.

Play the audio for them to check their ideas. (They were rejected at the beginning of their careers.)

Answers

The Beatles were rejected by Decca records.
J. K. Rowling was rejected by 12 publishers.
Walt Disney was fired from his job as a newspaper editor in 1919.

See Teacher's Book p.320 for Audio script 5.9.

Background information

The Beatles (John Lennon, Paul McCartney, George Harrison and Ringo Starr) were an English rock band formed in Liverpool in 1960. They were the most successful rock band of the era.

J. K. Rowling, born in 1965, is a British novelist, screenwriter and film producer, best known for her Harry Potter books, published 1997–2007.

Walt Disney (1901–1966) was an American cartoonist, animator and film producer; a pioneer of cartoon films. He founded the Walt Disney Film Company. His famous character, Mickey Mouse, has become a cultural icon.

B 5.9 Sts listen again, and note down any additional facts they hear. In groups, sts compare their notes. Then have them check against the audio script on p.162. Get them to underline any parts they missed/ didn't understand. Play these parts again and try to help them.

Discuss the reasons why all were rejected. (The Beatles were told that guitar groups were on their way out; J. K. Rowling was told her book was too long; Disney was told that he lacked imagination and had no good ideas.) Ask: *Which of them was the biggest mistake, do you think?*

C Sts read the speech bubbles, and discuss the meaning. Concept check by asking: 1 *Did they have a crystal ball?* (no) 2 *Did she have willpower?* (yes) 3 *Did he have faith in himself?* (yes) Then have sts read sentences a–c, and decide in pairs if they mean the same as sentences 1–3. Classcheck.

Answers

1 S 2 D 3 S

D In pairs, sts tell each other who they would choose, explaining their reasons why. Be careful to distinguish between Rowling and the two living Beatles, McCartney and Starr, who sts might like to meet as they are still alive, and the others.

E **Make it personal** Set this task for homework if short of time. Back in the classroom, sts share their information with the class. Class feedback. Ask: *What is the most interesting / surprising fact you learned?*

Song lyric: See Teacher's Book p.339 for notes about the song and an accompanying activity to do with the class.

8 Grammar: Imaginary situations (2)

A If necessary, quickly revise second and third conditionals by boarding the following examples:

Second conditional: *If I didn't have a lot of homework, I would come out with you.*

Third conditional: *If I hadn't been late, I wouldn't have missed the film.*

Ask sts what tenses are used in each sentence. Elicit and board this chart:

	Conditional clause	Main clause
Second	*If* + simple past	*would* + infinitive
Third	*If* + past perfect	*would have* + past participle

Sts study the examples in the grammar box. Ask: *Which tenses are used in the If-clauses? Which tenses are used in the main clauses?* Compare with the examples on the board.

Finally, ask sts to check the correct rules.

Answers

A = a past situation, and its present consequence
B = a present situation, and its past consequence

Refer sts to the **Grammar expansion** on p.146.

B 5.10 Ask sts to look at the pictures in the Student's Book and read the text below each one.

In pairs, sts complete the gaps. Before they listen and check, ask: *Who do you think is speaking? Who are they talking to? What can you say about the situations the people are in?* Play the audio for them to check their answers.

Answers

1 We wouldn't be lost now if you had checked the directions.
2 I would've maybe joined you last week if I hadn't been so short on money these days.
3 If I'd stayed in my old job, I'm sure I would be miserable right now.

C Focus on **Common mistakes** to highlight what to avoid. Elicit some other possibilities that people in the pictures could have said to help them prepare.

In pairs, sts role play each situation using only the pictures. Monitor, help and congratulate on their successful performances.

Weaker classes: Do the first one together with the class. Write on the board: *We wouldn't be lost now if you had checked the directions*. Ask sts: *Do you remember who said that?* (the man) *What did the woman say before that?* (I have no idea where we are!) Elicit other ideas for what she could have said, e.g. *I think we're lost. / I haven't a clue where we are. / I think we're going the wrong way*. Write it on the board, building up a mini-dialog. Ask: *What did the woman say afterwards?* Elicit ideas, e.g. *It's not my fault. / I thought you had checked. / I'm sorry I forgot*. Ask two sts to role play the dialog. Have sts do role plays for the other two pictures. They can write them out first if they want to.

Tip

Tell sts to be careful with contractions when using conditional sentences. We use *'d* for both *would* and *had*. Remind them also that we never use *would* in the *if*-clause.

9 Pronunciation: Sentence stress

A 5.11 Read through the pronunciation box with the class. Explain that they will hear each sentence twice, once slowly and then a second time more quickly.

Play the audio for them to listen and repeat, paying particular attention to the pronunciation of the contracted forms. Then have them practice in pairs.

B Make it personal

1 Ask sts to think of a situation where they made a good or a bad decision. Have them look through the topics in 1 for ideas. Then ask them to read through questions a–d, and make a note of their answers.

2 In groups, sts share their stories. Monitor round the class and make a note of common errors, and good uses of the conditional.

Class feedback. Ask volunteers to recount their stories to the rest of the class. Encourage other sts to comment on them, using the conditional, e.g. *If you hadn't quit your job ..., If you had taken your mother's advice ..., If you hadn't changed schools ...* .

Optional activity

For homework, sts write about the decision they discussed in B. Remember to check their homework assignment during the next class. Alternatively, sts swap paragraphs with a partner for peer checking. If necessary, board the following correction code for them to use:

G = grammar mistake *Sp* = spelling *P* = punctuation
T = tense *WO* = word order *M* = missing word
? = not clear *!* = silly mistake

Workbook p.26.

8 Grammar: Imaginary situations (2)

A Read the example sentences and check (✔) the correct rules.

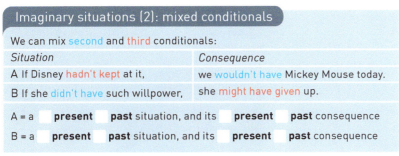

Imaginary situations (2): mixed conditionals

We can mix second and third conditionals:

Situation	*Consequence*
A If Disney hadn't kept at it,	we wouldn't have Mickey Mouse today.
B If she didn't have such willpower,	she might have given up.

A = a ☐ **present** ☐ **past** situation, and its ☐ **present** ☐ **past** consequence

B = a ☐ **present** ☐ **past** situation, and its ☐ **present** ☐ **past** consequence

» Grammar expansion p.146

B ▶ 5.10 What are they saying? Complete 1–3 with the correct forms. Listen to check.

1 We __________ (be) lost now if you __________ (check) the directions.

2 I __________ (maybe join) you last week if I __________ (be) so short on money these days.

3 If I __________ (stay) in my old job, I'm sure I __________ (be) miserable right now.

C In pairs, use only the pictures to expand and role play each situation.

Common mistakes

If ~~you would have~~ *you'd* taken your phone, we ~~would have been~~ *'d be* able to call now.

9 Pronunciation: Sentence stress

A ▶ 5.11 Read about sentence stress. Listen to and repeat the sentences, slowly and then faster.

Auxiliary forms are often contracted, as in these songs, and sentence stress is on a content word.

If I'd /aɪd/ never **met** you.

I would have /ˈwʊdəv/ **loved** you anyway.

You've /yuv/ lost that loving **feel**ing.

I've /aɪv/ been **wait**ing for a girl like you.

B Make it personal Tell a story about a good or bad decision you've made.

1 Choose a topic and think about a–d.

accepting or rejecting advice
buying an expensive item
changing schools
adopting or buying a pet
getting or quitting a job
taking a trip

a When / Where / How did your decision happen?

b What happened afterwards?

c What if something different had happened?

d What have you learned from the experience?

2 In groups, share your stories. Use different conditionals and pay attention to sentence stress. Any similar experiences?

Last month I adopted a puppy. I'd always wanted to have a pet and ...

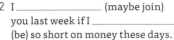

10 Listening

A 5.12 Ron is telling his friend Holly about his very unlucky birthday last week. Guess what happened. Listen to the first part of the conversation and answer 1–3.

1 Where did Ron go?
2 What did Ron's boss, Barry, find out?
3 What did Barry do?

B 5.13 Listen to the complete conversation and circle the correct answers.

1 Holly [**remembered** / **forgot**] Ron's birthday.
2 Ron and Aimee are [**just friends** / **a couple**].
3 Ron and Aimee [**had** / **hadn't**] been looking forward to the show.
4 Holly [**approves** / **disapproves**] of the story Ron told Barry.
5 Ron suspects Barry was watching the show [**live** / **on a recording**].
6 Ron is [**worried** / **confident**] about Monday.

C In pairs, answer 1–3. Any differences? Has anything like this happened to you?

1 What do you think Ron's boss wants to talk about on Monday?
2 Do you think Ron's boss really saw him on TV? Is there another hypothesis?
3 If you'd been Ron, what would you have done (a) before the show and (b) when you got the text message?

Well, maybe he just wants to catch up on Ron's work.

Are you kidding!

11 Keep talking

A Read the quotes. How strongly do you agree? Write ++ (= strongly agree) to -- (= strongly disagree). Compare your ideas in groups. Which is the most controversial quote?

1 "Luck is what happens when preparation meets opportunity." (Seneca)
2 "Remember that sometimes not getting what you want is a wonderful stroke of luck." (Dalai Lama)
3 "Luck is believing you're lucky." (Tennessee Williams, *A Streetcar Named Desire*)
4 "I believe in a lot of things ... magic, vampires, and even ghosts, but I don't believe in luck. Good or bad." (Hillary DePiano)

I totally agree with the first one. I mean, without hard work, luck means nothing.

Hmm, I'm not sure. I believe some people are just born lucky.

B **Make it personal** In groups, tell each other about a stroke of good / bad luck you've had. Prepare using 1–5.

1 When / Where did it happen?
2 What were you doing at the time?
3 What is the main event? Why were you so (un)lucky?
4 What if something different had happened?
5 What did you learn from the experience?

Mine is about how I came to live in Lima. I was 12 at the time and had just started high school...

Lesson Aims: Sts learn language to talk about the nature of luck, and write a story about the worst / best luck they have ever had.

Skills	Language	Vocabulary
Telling a story; using synonyms Discussing quotes about luck Telling stories about lucky / unlucky situations	Agreeing / disagreeing: *I totally agree with the first one.*	Adjectives: *amazed, delighted, devastated, filthy, terrified* Synonyms

Warm-up

Board the phrase *Common superstitions*. Get them going by asking: *Do you walk under ladders? Do you avoid opening umbrellas indoors?* If necessary, explain / elicit that some people believe these actions are unlucky, and will always try to avoid doing them.

In groups, sts think of as many superstitions as they can. If necessary, brainstorm a few ideas to get them started, e.g. *breaking a mirror, dropping salt, seeing a black cat, the number 13*. Class feedback. Ask: *Which ones do you believe in? Do they really bring bad luck?*

Ask: *Do you believe in bad / good luck? How lucky are you? On a scale of 0–10, what rating would you give yourself today?* Use a show of hands to check answers and elicit *'why?'* for any of the more extreme high or low scores!

10 Listening

A 5.12 Read through the instructions and look at the pictures with the class. Ask: *Can you guess what is happening? Where are the people?* (at a concert) *What is the man looking at in the bottom picture?* (his cell phone) Don't confirm or deny their guesses at this stage.

Sts guess the answers to the questions. Play the audio for sts to listen and check their ideas. Classcheck.

Board: *I made up a lame excuse*. Ask: *Who said this in the audio?* (Ron) *What do you think it means?* (He invented a poor reason for leaving work.)

Answers

1 To see a Lana Del Rey concert.
2 He found out that Ron had been to the show.
3 He sent Ron a text asking him about the show, and then saying he wanted to see him on Monday.

See Teacher's Book p.320 for Audio script 5.12 / 5.13.

B 5.13 Before they listen to the complete conversation, ask: *How do you think Barry knew Ron was at the concert?* Encourage them to make a few guesses. Read through the sentences with the class. Ask sts to guess which are the correct answers. Play the audio to classcheck.

Answers

1 remembered 2 a couple 3 had 4 disapproves
5 live 6 worried

See Teacher's Book p.320 for Audio script 5.13.

C When sts have discussed the three questions in pairs, open up to a class discussion. Ask sts: *Do you consider the situation Ron found himself in to be the result of "bad luck"? Has anything like this ever happened to any of you?*

11 Keep talking

A Ask individuals to read out the quotes. Ask: *What, if anything, do you know of the people who said these quotes?* Discuss the meaning of the quotes with the class.

In groups, sts discuss which of the quotes they agree / disagree with, and score them accordingly to the four options. Ask sts to share their views with the rest of the class, and decide together which is the most controversial quote.

Background information

Seneca (4BC–65 AD) was a Roman philosopher.

Dalai Lama is a Tibetan Buddhist monk. The 14th and current Dalai Lama, whose quote this is, is Tenzin Gyatsu.

Tennessee Williams (1911–1983) was a great American playwright. Two of his most famous plays are *A Streetcar Named Desire* and *The Glass Menagerie*.

Hillary DePiano is an American playwright, fiction and non-fiction author, best known for her play *The Love of Three Oranges*.

B Make it personal Tell sts to think about the questions and make notes if they want to. Ask one or two volunteers to tell the class about their experience. Prompt them by asking them the questions, e.g. *When did it happen? What were you doing at the time?* etc. In groups, sts tell each other their stories.

Song lyric: See Teacher's Book p.340 for notes about the song and an accompanying activity to do with the class.

12 Writing: Telling a story (2)

A Focus on the title and genre so sts know what sort of text they're going to read. Give them two minutes to read the text at a good speed, then, in pairs, share what they can remember, trying to recall as many details as possible.

Check the meaning of any new vocabulary they really want to know at this stage, and drill pronunciation of the pink-stressed words. But don't become a 'walking dictionary' for every word, as sts will match the highlighted words to synonyms in C.

Elicit some details of the story from the class by prompting. Ask: *Why did Paul go away? Where did they go? What happened on the seventh day?*

B Highlight the use of the past perfect in the story to sequence events, e.g. *there had been a fire, ... I'd left the toaster on*. Elicit that this tense is used in stories to say that something happened before another event in the story.

Sts read through the events and order them 1 to 7. Paircheck, then classcheck.

Answers

2 There was a fire in Paul's house.
4 Paul found out about the fire.
3 Paul's neighbor put out the fire.
5 Paul wasn't sure if he'd left the toaster on.
7 Paul discovered the freezer had melted.
1 Paul spent six days relaxing.
6 Paul went back home.

Note: If sts express scepticism or incredulity about the story, please note that it's true, and actually happened to the course author at his home in Santa Teresa, Rio de Janeiro!

Weaker classes: Sts could now try to reconstruct the story, adding details to the skeleton provided by 12B.

C Read **Write it right!** with the class. Then sts match the synonyms to the highlighted words in the text.

Check answers, then elicit other (near) synonyms they might know, e.g. *thrilled, delighted, disgusting, stunned, petrified, traumatized*.

Answers

1 delighted 2 filthy 3 devastated 4 amazed
5 terrified

Optional activity

Revise adjectival word order with the class. Board these headings in this order and explain that this is the general order of adjectives before a noun:

Opinion, Size, Shape, Condition, Age, Color, Pattern, Origin, Material, Purpose, Noun.

Elicit adjectives to go under each heading, e.g. *beautiful, small, thin, brand-new, red, striped, Japanese, cotton, sleeping (bag)*. Point out that it doesn't sound natural to use three or more adjectives in the same sentence.

In pairs, sts write three lists of three adjectives on a piece of paper, choosing adjectives from the different categories on the board, e.g. 1 *flowery, funny, broken*. 2 *gardening, paper, round*. 3 *tall, young, Italian*. Pairs swap lists and try to write three sentences with the adjectives they are given. Encourage creativity. Class feedback and take a vote on the most imaginative sentences.

D Ask: *What was the main event?* (the fire) *What was unusual about the event?* (the fire was started by the fridge) *What background information did Paul give?* (He'd suffered three very stressful years, and so had decided to go on a trip.)

Sts re-read the story to find out in which paragraph each fact is mentioned.

Answers

The main event: 2
What was unusual about the event: 3
Background information to create suspense: 1

E Your turn! Read through the instructions for each stage quickly to ensure everyone understands the overall aim. Then go back and add detail to each step.

Sts can write about the stories they discussed in 11B. Encourage them to use questions 1–5 in 11B to help them structure their stories into paragraphs, and add the ingredients requested at the *While* stage.

Once sts have written their stories, insist they proofread them. Tell them to pay special attention to tenses and verb endings.

Suggest some websites or cellphone techniques for sts to record (or video) themselves (google 'online voice recorder' for suitable websites). Less tech-savvy sts can read them to a classmate, or simply pin them up on the classroom walls for others to read.Ask: *Who do you think has had the worst luck / best luck ?*

Workbook p.27.

12 Writing: Telling a story (2)

A Read Paul's story. In pairs, how many details can you remember?

Forum BLOG INBOX MEMBERS YOU

What's the best / worst luck you've ever had? Tell us your stories.

1 Last year, after the most stressful three years of my life, I decided that my wife and I deserved at least two weeks away from it all. Amanda was delighted with my suggestion that we go on a trip, so we took our savings and booked a five-star hotel in sunny Rio de Janeiro. If only I'd known what those two weeks had in store for me!

2 The first six days were everything we'd dreamed of. We were amazed by the beauty of the city, especially the gorgeous views. Our nightmare began on the seventh day when I got an email from our neighbor Ed saying that there had been a fire in the house! I was terrified! I wondered if I'd left the toaster on, but I thought that couldn't have caused a fire six days later! We were both devastated and, needless to say, our well-deserved vacation was ruined. Miraculously, Ed, who fortunately had our keys, managed to put the fire out. If he'd arrived five minutes later, our 80-year-old house might have burned to the ground.

3 When we got back home, we discovered that actually the fridge had started the fire – the fridge! The freezer had slowly melted, giving off awful toxic fumes. Everything was black and filthy. The insurance company was as surprised by our bad luck as we were. They had never seen anything like it before. One thing is for certain, though: We will never leave the fridge – or any household appliance – plugged in when we go away for a long break.

SHARE

B Order the events in the story 1–7.

___ There was a fire in Paul's house.
___ Paul found out about the fire.
___ Paul's neighbor put out the fire.
___ Paul wasn't sure if he'd left the toaster on.
___ Paul discovered the freezer had melted.
_1_ Paul spent six days relaxing.
___ Paul went back home.

C Read *Write it right!* Match the synonyms (1–5) to the highlighted adjectives in the story.

Write it right!

When you write a story, use a good range of adjectives, both simple (like *angry*) and more intense (like *furious*), to make your story more vivid and interesting.

1 very happy ________
2 very dirty ________
3 very upset ________
4 very surprised ________
5 very frightened ________

D Write the number of the paragraph:

The main event: ___
What was unusual about the event: ___
Background information to create suspense: ___

E **Your turn!** Write a story of 200–250 words about the best / worst luck you've ever had.

Before

Note down the main events and organize them into paragraphs.

While

Use highlighted adjectives from A to make your story vivid. Make sure the first paragraph creates suspense. Be careful with tenses, and use linking words to connect your ideas (Unit 3).

After

Record your story, and ask a classmate to listen and react. Is it what you intended?

6 Have you ever Googled yourself?

1 Vocabulary: Online privacy

A Which of the experiences shown in pictures a–e on page 61 have you had?

Once I bought something online, and my credit card number was stolen!

B Read the article. Guess what text is missing.

PROTECTING YOUR ONLINE PRIVACY—

- Rule number one: Choose your passwords carefully, and stay away from obvious choices, such as your date of birth. Also, avoid using the same password across lots of different sites. Cyber criminals are everywhere these days, and ______________________ .
- How would you feel if you were at the mall and someone followed you around with a camera, writing down every single item you looked at? That's what happens when you shop online. Even if you don't buy anything, the store is keeping an eye on you, which means ______________________ .
- Do you have a health concern you need to talk to someone about? Or maybe a family problem you want to get off your chest? Be careful with sites containing discussion forums. ______________________ , and this information could be accessed by future employers.
- Well, at least there's Google. Surely running a simple search is pretty safe? Well, no. ______________________ , and your search will be kept in Google's files for months or even years.

C Extracts 1–4 are from the article. Match the highlighted words to their meanings a–d.

1 whatever you look up may appear in your search history
2 they might break into a vulnerable site and steal your password
3 they might sell all your shopping habits to third parties
4 they might keep records of every status update you post and every *like* you click on

a ☐ people not directly involved in something
b ☐ try to find a particular piece of information
c ☐ save information in order to refer to it in the future
d ☐ access illegally

D 6.1 Put the extracts back into the article. Listen to check. Think of one new way to fill in each blank.

E **Make it personal** In groups, discuss the concerns in the article. Do you think they pose serious dangers? Which of you is the most security-conscious online / in the real world?

I don't understand what's wrong with the last one.

Hmm, I don't know. What if Google remembers confidential information?

I live in a dangerous neighborhood, so I'm always thinking about safety!

Lesson Aims: Sts learn language to talk about online security, and discuss their attitudes to risk-taking.

Skills	Language	Vocabulary
Reading a magazine article about online security Listening to conversations related to aspects of online security Asking and answering questions about taking risks	Talking about risk: *You know you're at risk, right? Isn't online shopping a bit risky?*	*break into, cyber criminal, keep records of, look up, third party* Risk words: *at risk, at your own risk, risk* (v), *risk-free, risky*

Warm-up

Board: *The Internet*. In small groups, sts think of as much associated language as they can. Class feedback, and see which group has the most items. Elicit or pre-teach: *website, cloud, online shopping, password, cookies, search engine, cyber crime, browser, discussion forum, virus*.

In pairs, sts discuss these questions: *Do you shop online? Do you use search engines like Google? Do you go on to discussion forums? Do you have a secure password?*

Ask the lesson title question: *Have you ever Googled yourself? Were you surprised / worried by anything in the search results?*

1 Vocabulary: Online privacy

A Focus on the pictures on p.61. Discuss as a class what's happening in each one. (a: *The girl is shopping online for a smart phone*. b: *The computer network has worked out the location of the computer user*. c: *The woman's user name and password doesn't work because it is considered unsafe*. d: *The man is Googling himself*. e: *The girl has found a friend's search results for Miley Cyrus, much to his embarrassment*.)

Ask sts to tell the class about any experiences they have had of these situations.

B Focus on the title. Discuss the meaning of *my two cents* (= here's what I think ...). Ask sts to read the article and try to guess the missing text. Elicit suggestions as a class, but don't confirm or deny their guesses at this stage as sts will check in D.

C Explain that extracts 1 to 4 are the missing texts from the article. Focus on the highlighted words, and ask: *Which do you recognize? What do they mean?*

Sts read through the meanings and match them with the correct words. Paircheck, then classcheck.

Answers

1 b 2 d 3 a 4 c

Optional activity

In pairs, sts write their own sentences with each of the highlighted words. Monitor and help with vocabulary, checking that sts have understood the words correctly. Invite volunteers to read their sentences to the class.

D 6.1 Sts put the extracts back in the correct places in the article. Play the audio for them to listen and check their answers, or if you are short of time, check answers as a class.

Answers

Paragraph 1: they might break into a vulnerable site and steal your password Paragraph 2: they might sell all your shopping habits to third parties Paragraph 3: Whatever you look up may appear in your search history Paragraph 4: They might keep records of every status update you post and every like you click on

In pairs, sts can try to think of other ways to complete the paragraphs, e.g. 1: ... *they can easily work out what your password is*. 2: *they can build up a profile of your shopping habits and target you with specific advertising*. 3: *Any comment or opinion you post cannot later be deleted* ... 4: *The websites you visit are visible to your internet service provider*.

Class feedback, and board their best suggestions.

E Make it personal Read out the questions in the instructions. Get a volunteer to read aloud each speech bubble dramatically.

In groups, sts discuss the concerns in the article. Set a clear aim: to agree on which concern poses the most serious danger, and which of the group is the most security-conscious.

Weaker classes: Board the aims and main points in the article to prompt them.

Class feedback each group's answers. Finally, ask: *Who here will be more security-conscious after reading the article?*

Tip

With large classes, to ensure greater participation / involvement, get one st from each group to move and report back to another group instead of each group doing so slowly to the whole class.

Optional activity

Stronger classes: Ask what advice they'd add to the article "Protecting your online privacy." For homework, they could write a fifth paragraph to add to the article.

2 Listening

A Focus on the example speech bubble, and then ask the class to guess what problems could arise from each situation. Point out that there are no right or wrong answers so encourage sts to brainstorm.

Possible answers

- b The computer is storing personal information about the man. This could be used by companies to try and sell you things.
- c The woman might be at risk from cyber crime if she doesn't have a secure password.
- d If anyone Googles Don Doe, they can see he's been searching romantic advice online. This might lead to problems if he were applying for a job, for example.
- e The girl has found the man's search history. If she'd been his girlfriend, she might get jealous.

B 6.2 Play the audio for sts to match the conversations to the pictures. Classcheck and re-play the audio, if necessary.

As a follow-up, ask: *What's the relationship between the speakers in each conversation?* (1 husband and wife; 2 mother and daughter; 3 two work colleagues; 4 two friends; 5 two friends) *Was this similar to your original guess in 1A?*

Answers

1 b 2 d 3 e 4 c 5 a

See Teacher's Book p.320 for Audio script 6.2.

C 6.2 Read the statements to the class. Elicit that *is* in questions 2 and 5 could also be contracted.

Explain that sts will need to listen more carefully this time, as the information is not directly given in the audio. They need to listen for clues and make inferences.

Re-play the audio for sts to mark the sentences *probably true* or *probably false*. Paircheck, then classcheck.

When checking answers, get sts to tell you what the clues were.

Weaker classes: Give / Show the audio script for them to underline the information which provides the answer.

Answers

1 F (His mother-in-law had told his wife she'd married a 15-year-old. In other words he was like a child.)
2 T (B mentions that Jerry makes sure they get their work done, which implies he's the boss.)
3 T (Daniel lets Cathy use his laptop, and he doesn't mind too much that she has seen his search history.)
4 F (She uses the same password on 20 different websites.)
5 F (She thinks online shopping's a bit risky.)

See Teacher's Book p.320 for Audio script 6.2.

D 6.3 Focus on the words in the box.

Elicit what *risk* means (= being exposed to danger or loss).

Elicit or tell sts that we use an *-ing* form after the verb (*to risk* + *-ing* form), e.g. *I didn't want to risk telling them my password*.

Elicit that *-free* means "free from".

Elicit other phrases with *-free*, e.g. *trouble-free, lead-free, stress-free, sugar-free*.

Sts read the gapped sentences, then ask: *Do you remember who said these things?* Set sts a minute to complete the sentences with the words in the box. Play the audio to classcheck.

Sts cover the sentences, try to remember them using the pictures as prompts.

Stronger classes: Sts could role play some or all of the conversations.

Answers

1 at your own risk 2 risk-free 3 risk 4 at risk 5 risky

Optional activity

Sts create their own sentences using the boxed words. Monitor and check. Tell them to copy them out again, leaving a gap where the *risk* phrase should go. Sts exchange sentences with a partner, and try and complete their partners' sentences.

E Make it personal Read through the scenarios 1–4 with the class and check understanding. Refer to **Common mistakes** and highlight the use of the preposition with each verb.

In groups of four, sts work through the scenarios one at a time, giving each group member an opportunity to say something before moving on to the next one.

Class feedback and invite groups to share anything interesting from their discussions. Ask: *Who's the biggest risk-taker in your group?*

Tip

The size of your groups obviously depends on class numbers. Generally speaking, six or seven should be a maximum, as sts get much less interaction time. Fours or fives are usually best, an odd number being a good idea where a decision has to be arrived at, to avoid a fifty–fifty decision.

Song lyric: See Teacher's Book p.340 for notes about the song and an accompanying activity to do with the class.

Workbook p.28.

2 Listening

A Which problems are shown in pictures a–e?

> In the first one, she's shopping, and someone could steal her personal information.

B 6.2 Listen and match five conversations about online privacy to pictures a–e.

C 6.2 Listen again. T (probably true) or F (probably false)?

1 Rob's mother-in-law likes him.
2 Jerry is Don's boss.
3 Cathy and Daniel are close friends.
4 Lynette worries about her online privacy.
5 Sophie's mother is a frequent online shopper.

D 6.3 Complete 1–5 with *risk* words. Listen to check. Then remember the sentences using only the pictures.

risk (v)	risky (adj)	risk-free (adj)
at risk	at your own risk	

1 Well, OK, whatever. Play it ________.
2 I thought the whole thing was ________. How was I to know they'd use my real name?
3 I don't want to ________ losing her over a stupid Google search.
4 You know you're ________, right? I mean, using the same password.
5 Isn't online shopping a bit ________?

E **Make it personal** In groups, discuss 1–4. Any surprises?

1 Something you did at your own risk, despite your parents' advice.
2 Something risky you do more often than you should.
3 Three things worth risking your life for.
4 The greatest risk to the survival of humanity.

Common mistakes

Parents shouldn't listen ^*to* / eavesdrop ^*on* / spy ~~in~~ *on* their kids' private conversations.

> My parents wouldn't let me ride a motorcycle, but as soon as I got a job, I bought one.

> Mine wouldn't let me skateboard.

> Crazy! Not even walking is risk-free!

3 Language in use

A Read the blog. In pairs, answer 1–4 with A (Andrew) or Z (Zoë), and underline the evidence.

1 Who's afraid of past secrets hurting him / her?
2 Who called someone and demanded action?
3 Whose career is suffering because of online information?
4 Who has been confused with a relative?

The online privacy blog

HOME | BLOG POSTS

There are lots of reasons why you might want to delete yourself from the web: embarrassing photos, opinions you no longer have, fake social media accounts – you name it. Our readers share their stories of how they **attempted** to disappear from the web. Forever.

Sept 14, 10:03 a.m. Reply to post #1

Andrew, Chicago: A distant relative with the same first and last name was **arrested** for tax evasion a while back. He had his sentence **reduced** for good behavior and is now out of jail. So it all **ended** well, right? Wrong. Whenever people Google me, his arrest is the first thing **linked** with my name. I'm unemployed at the moment and, because of this mix-up, I have been **turned** down by three different employers this month, which isn't fair. I shouldn't be **penalized** for something I didn't do!

Sept 14, 10:42 a.m. Reply to post #2

Zoë, Calgary: About ten years ago I wrote a comment on an article in a well-known newspaper in Canada, including personal details about myself. Last year, I Googled myself and, to my horror, saw my response in the archive section of the newspaper. Now, who knows how this information might be **used**? I **picked** up the phone and told them I **wanted** to have my profile **deleted** immediately. So far they haven't been very cooperative.

Reply to Thread

B Make it personal In groups, answer 1–3.

1 Who do you feel most sorry for? Why?
2 Who do you think will have the most trouble in the future?
3 What advice would you give someone whose privacy has been invaded? Online? Offline?

> If your identity is stolen, you should contact the bank immediately.

C 6.4 Read *"-ed" endings*. Then, in the blog, circle the /t/ or /d/ verbs and box the /ɪd/ verbs. Listen to check, echoing the verbs as you hear them.

"-ed" endings

Remember, "-ed" endings are pronounced either /t/ (*liked, kissed, stopped*) or /d/ (*played, rained, called*). The "-e" is silent. Only pronounce the final "-e" /ɪd/ when the verb ends in "t" (*started*) or "d" (*needed*).

Lesson Aims: Sts learn language to talk about online privacy, and discuss their attitudes to social networking.

Skills	Language	Vocabulary	Grammar
Reading a blog about people who have tried to remove themselves from the web Discussing attitudes to social networking	Responding to an argument: *I couldn't agree more. I don't see it that way. OK, point taken.*	*arrest, attempt, delete, identity, penalize, profile*	Using passive structures: *be*, modal verbs and *have*

Warm-up

Discuss these questions as a class, e.g. board them for sts to answer as they come in: *Do you use social media sites? What kind of things do you post? What are the advantages / disadvantages of social media sites? Do you write blogs?*

Ask the lesson title question: *Do you worry about your privacy 1) online? 2) more generally? Why (not)?* In groups, give sts three minutes to discuss as a lead-in to the lesson / reading.

3 Language in use

A Focus on the photo. Ask: *Does this remind you of anyone? Why do so many people use their computers lying on the floor like this?*

Move on to the title of the blog. Discuss the meaning of *confuse someone / something with ...* (= to be mistakenly identified as ...).

Set sts three minutes to read the blog and answer the questions. Paircheck, then classcheck.

In pairs, have sts re-read the blog together and try to pronounce the highlighted words. Classcheck and drill any they struggle with.

Answers

1 Z (*About ten years ago I wrote a comment on an article in a well-known newspaper in Canada, including personal details about myself.*)
2 Z (*I picked up the phone and told them I wanted to have my profile deleted immediately.*)
3 A (*I have been turned down by three different employers this month.*)
4 A (*A distant relative with the same first and last name ... Whenever people Google me, his arrest is the first thing linked with my name.*)

Tip

Instead of checking any new vocabulary from a reading text with the whole class, you can make the activity more dynamic by selecting a few words you believe sts will find difficult beforehand. Provide them with definitions and ask them to find the word in the text, e.g. *the practice of avoiding doing something that you should do* (evasion).

B **Make it personal** Go through the three questions. When you get to 3, focus on the speech bubble. Elicit other ways to give advice and board them, e.g. *If I was in that situation, I'd ... The sooner you ... the better, If it was / were me, I'd ..., It's a good idea to ... Make sure you (don't) ... Whatever you do, ...* .

In groups, sts discuss the questions. Encourage them to use your boarded expressions when answering question 3. Class feedback. Which group thought of the best advice?

Weaker classes: Brainstorm advice for question 3 and write it on the board.

C 6.4 Take sts through the pronunciation box, drilling a few verbs they often struggle with. If necessary, remind sts of the rules for the pronunciation of *-ed* endings. Verbs ending in:

- *t* or *d* (e.g. *want* or *end*), *-ed* ending is pronounced /ɪd/.
- an unvoiced sound, *-ed* ending is pronounced /t/, e.g. *hope* /p/, *laugh* /f/, *fax* /s/, *wash* /ʃ/, *watch* /tʃ/, like /k/.
- any other sounds (e.g. *play*), *-ed* ending is pronounced /d/.

Sts circle and box all the *-ed* verbs in the blog. Then either play the audio (the entire blog text) or model the pronunciation of each verb for them to listen and repeat. For further practice, ask sts to add other *-ed* endings to the lists, and practice them in pairs.

Answers

/t/ or /d/ verbs – reduced, linked, unemployed, turned, penalized, Googled, used, picked
/ɪd/ verbs – attempted, arrested, ended, wanted, deleted

Tip

Remind sts that the *t* ending is voiced at the front of the mouth with the tongue at the top of the mouth behind the front teeth, while the *d* ending is voiced further back with the tongue up against the roof of the mouth.

Optional activity

Ask: *Have you ever tried to delete your name from a website or social media site?* For homework, sts write a short paragraph to add to the online privacy blog page.

Song lyric: See Teacher's Book p.340 for notes about the song and an accompanying activity to do with the class.

4 Grammar: Using passive structures

A Go through the grammar box with the class and check understanding of example sentences 1–3. Ask sts to complete the rules, then classcheck. Ask sts to find two examples of each passive in the blog text.

Stronger classes: Explain that we can also use *have* + object + *done*, meaning to arrange for someone to do something for us, e.g. *I had my hair cut last week. He had his car repaired at the local garage*. If you think sts can handle it, explain the potential ambiguity in example 3, i.e. Tom arranged for his phone to 'disappear' so he could then claim for it on his insurance!

Answers

a the action b Someone else c use the passive voice
1 *be* + past participle: *A distant relative ... was arrested, I have been turned down ...*
2 Modal verb + *be* + past participle: *I shouldn't be penalized ... , ... this information might be used*
3 *have* + object + past participle: *He had his sentence reduced, I wanted to have my profile deleted*

Refer sts to the **Grammar expansion** on p.148.

B Focus on the title and elicit any predictions for content. Read the text with the class, inviting individuals to read out each of the seven sentences. Check the meaning is clear each time and ask: *Do you think this is good / bad advice?*

Go through the **Common mistake** with the class. Point out that sts make this mistake because *being* and *been* sound very similar. Model pronunciation of the two words, and help sts recognize the difference.

Sts work individually to rewrite the underlined parts. Remind them that the modal verbs don't change, e.g. *You* ***can't*** *undo the steps below. > The steps below* ***can't*** *be undone*. Paircheck, then classcheck. Personalize and extend the text content by asking: *Which of these steps have you (or people you know) tried? What happened?*

Answers

1 are you being bullied?
2 the steps below can't be undone
3 your profile can be deleted
4 they must be completely removed
5 have your name removed
6 you haven't been listed online
7 you can have your identity erased by him / her

C Make it personal

1 Sts read statements a–d. Check they understand them. Have them work individually and mark each one *A*, *D* or *NS*. Paircheck quickly for all of you to see where any disagreements will come, but don't go further yet.

2 6.5 Discuss what's behind statement a in 1. Ask: *What sort of things do your friends post on Facebook? Do you get annoyed with some of the posts? Do you think people should be able to post what they want?*

Play the audio for sts to find out what the three friends think. Ask: *Do they all agree? Which phrases can you remember them using?* Re-play it quickly if they want to try to pick up more.

Answer

No, they disagree.

See Teacher's Book p.320 for Audio script 6.5.

3 6.6 **How to say it** Sts complete the chart from memory, then play the audio for them to check their answers.

Re-play the audio and have sts mark the stress on the phrases as they listen. Classcheck, then practice them in pairs. Monitor round the class and check their stress and pronunciation.

Answers

1 couldn't 2 see 3 point 4 thing 5 take

4 Give time for individuals to formulate their views on topics a–d in step 1. Remind sts to think about the advantages of social networking as well as the disadvantages.

In groups of four or five, sts share their views. Encourage them to give reasons for their opinions, and to respond to their partners' opinions using the expressions for agreeing / disagreeing in **Responding to an argument**. Monitor round the class and give help where necessary.

Have a class feedback session. Does the class generally agree or disagree with the statements?

Workbook p.29.

4 Grammar: Using passive structures

A Study 1–3 and complete the grammar box. Then find two examples of each type of passive in the blog.

Using passive structures: *be*, modal verbs, and *have*

1 ***Be*** + past participle: I **have been offered** a job by three different employers.
2 Modal verb + ***be*** + past participle: I **shouldn't be arrested** for something I didn't do.
3 ***Have*** + object + past participle: Tom **had his cell phone stolen**.

a In 1–3, which is more important? ☐ the action ☐ who did the action
b In 3, who stole the cell phone? ☐ Tom ☐ someone else
c When you don't want to emphasize who did the action, you can use the ☐ active voice ☐ passive voice.

» Grammar expansion p.148

B Rewrite the underlined items in the passive.

Common mistake

My brother is ~~been~~ *being* bullied on Facebook®.

Seven ways to say good-bye to the Internet – *forever!*

1 First, ask yourself why you're leaving the web. Just fed up, or is anyone bullying you?
2 Stop and think things through carefully. Remember: You can't undo the steps below.
3 Focus on well-known sites first, where you can delete your profile more easily.
4 If you've created sites on the Internet, you must completely remove them.
5 Check all the mailing lists you've subscribed to, and have somebody remove your name.
6 Check with your phone company to make sure they haven't listed you online.
7 Sometimes you'll need help from a real person so you can have him / her erase your identity.

C Make it personal Take part in a discussion about digital technology.

1 Answer A (agree), D (disagree), or NS (not sure).
   a Facebook® should be treated like a social network, not a diary.
   b You can have your "real" life ruined by too much social networking.
   c Teenagers' Internet activity must be closely monitored by their parents.
   d Digital technology is beginning to control us.

2 ▶ 6.5 Listen to three friends discussing topic a. Do they all agree?

3 ▶ 6.6 **How to say it** Complete the chart. Listen to check.

Responding to an argument

	What they said	What they meant
1	I ________ agree more.	I agree.
2	I don't ________ it that way.	I disagree.
3	OK, ________ taken.	That makes sense, I admit.
4	Look, here's the ________ .	Listen to what I'm about to say.
5	What's your ________ on it?	What do you think?

4 For two minutes, plan what you can say about topics a–d in step 1. Then in groups, compare ideas. Use *How to say it* expressions. Any disagreements?

Facebook® shouldn't be a diary!

I couldn't agree more.

5 Reading

A Using only the title and photo, guess what the magazine article is about.

Home | World | Business | Sports | Health | Tech | Entertainment | Search

I, the Spy

by Jo O'Donnell

This isn't easy to admit, but I felt slightly embarrassed a while back when I was watching a news report about the National Security Agency's (NSA) surveillance program – the one that allowed the government to spy on its citizens, eavesdrop on phone calls, and monitor Internet traffic. Why? Because over the past decade, I have kept my children under strict surveillance in pretty much the same way: capturing instant messaging logs, eavesdropping on Skype® conversations, and even using spy software to keep tabs on what they typed. I have been the biggest threat to my children's privacy.

A few years ago, when I casually mentioned this to a friend, she was horrified. How could I do this, she asked, when it was such an invasion of my children's privacy? At the time, I made the same argument that generations of parents before me have probably made, which is that my children have no expectation of privacy while they are still living under my roof. If invading their privacy was what it took to protect them, then obviously I had every right to do so. Or did I?

The NSA once stated that what the agency did could be justified on security grounds, since it allowed the agency to identify potential terrorist threats to the U.S. So I made a similar argument to myself about monitoring my sons' online activity – after all, all I wanted was to protect them from the kinds of trouble teens get into, especially drug abuse and bad relationships. Was I right to do so? To be honest, I'm not sure. Yes and no, I suppose. Anyway, it's been quite a while since I last spied on my two sons (the youngest of whom is now turning 17), but looking back, I think I've learned some important lessons.

B Quickly read the article in two minutes to check. Does Jo ...

☐ feel spying on the kids was the right thing to do? ☐ regret it? ☐ have mixed feelings about it?

C 6.7 Re-read and listen. T (true) or F (false)?

1 Jo thinks government / parental surveillance are two completely different things.
2 She told a friend it was OK to spy on the kids until they left home.
3 She used to spy on the kids mostly to keep them safe from cyberbullying.
4 She hasn't spied on the kids for some time.

D What nouns do the underlined words in the article refer to? Draw lines to them.

E 6.8 Listen to part of an interview with Jo. Number the lessons she learned 1–3. Then circle A or B.

Lessons		
☐ I learned my son had impressive talents.	☐ It's important for couples not to have secrets.	☐ None of the dangers I'd anticipated came true.
A He wrote fiction online. B He was leading an online book group.	A My husband already knew I was spying. B My husband was really upset.	A They talked about homework and school stress. B There was very little cyberbullying.

Lesson Aims: Sts learn language to talk about the right to privacy, and discuss whether it is ever OK to spy on other people.

Skills	Language	Vocabulary
Reading an article about a mother who spied on her children Listening to an interview with the mother who spied on her children Discussing whether it is OK to spy on people in certain situations	Discussing people's rights to privacy: *I think employers have a right to eavesdrop on conversations.*	Privacy words and expressions: *cyber bullying, eavesdrop, invasion, keep tabs on, spy, surveillance*

Warm-up

Board: *Privacy is a fundamental human right.* Ask: *Do you agree / disagree? Are there any circumstances in which it is OK to violate an individual's right to privacy? Do you think children have a right to privacy?* Sts discuss the questions in pairs, then open up to a class discussion.

Ask the lesson title question: *What makes you suspicious?* Focus on people, not e.g. institutions or dodgy emails. Elicit actions, demeanor, body language people display that make them wary, e.g. not making eye contact. Provide contexts to help, e.g. when traveling, meeting new people, dealing with authority.

5 Reading

A Focus attention on the magazine article and ask: *What is the woman in the photo doing? What is she holding?* (a magnifying glass). Elicit the meaning of *spy* (noun) and *to spy* (verb). Get the class to predict what the article will be about and some ideas they might find in it.

B Have sts read the questions first before they read the text. Remind them that they are reading to get a general understanding of the text, and that they should ignore unknown words.

Answers

Jo has mixed feelings about it.

C 6.7 Have sts read sentences 1–4. Check understanding of *cyberbullying* in 3 (= using electronic communication to send threatening messages).

Sts re-read the article and mark the sentences true or false. You can play the audio while they listen and 'echo drill' the pink-stressed words after they hear them.

Classcheck. As a follow-up, ask: *How would you feel if you were Jo's children? Do you think she was right to spy on her children? Could you ever be 'a spy'?*

Answers

1 F 2 T 3 F 4 T

Tip

When doing True / False exercises, encourage sts to underline key words in the statements. This will help them focus better on the information they're looking for in the text.

D Focus on the first underlined word, *one*. Ask: *What's it referring to? Why do we use words like this?* (to avoid repetition).

Sts do the exercise individually, then paircheck. As they do it, board a list of the underlined words.

Classcheck. Board the answers next to the underlined words.

Answers

one – surveillance program
its – government
this – the fact that she kept her children under surveillance
which – the same argument
so – invade their privacy
it – what the agency did
so – monitoring her son's online activity
whom – her sons

Tip

It's very useful for sts to work through a text from time to time underlining all the pronouns / reference words and identifying what each refers to.

E 6.8 Explain that sts are going to hear Jo (from 5A) reflecting on her experience of 'spying' on her children. Ask: *What do you think she learned from this?* Elicit suggestions, but don't confirm or deny their ideas yet.

Read through the Lessons and the A / B options with the class. Check understanding.

Play the audio for sts to number the lessons she learned and to choose the correct options. Paircheck, then classcheck.

Answers

1 None of the dangers I'd anticipated came true; A
2 I learned my son had impressive talents; A
3 It's important for couples not to have secrets; B

See Teacher's Book p.320 for Audio script 6.8.

Song lyric: See Teacher's Book p.340 for notes about the song and an accompanying activity to do with the class.

F Make it personal Read through the questions, and, for number 2, the example dialog below in the speech bubbles.

In small groups, sts discuss the questions. Monitor round the class and offer help where necessary.

Ask individual sts: *Did you learn anything surprising about your classmates?*

Tip

When monitoring group work, help the weaker ones to get involved so all get the opportunity to speak. Encourage good listening skills as well as good speaking skills.

Optional activity

Have a class debate. Board: *Teenagers are entitled to 100% privacy.*

Divide the class into four groups. Two groups will argue 'For' and the other two 'Against'. In their groups, sts brainstorm ideas.

Group presentations: ensure each group member speaks. Encourage sts to explain / justify their points of view. Allow groups arguing against to pose questions and challenge the ideas presented. Set a time limit for each group to present their arguments.

When all groups have spoken, sts vote for the most convincing argument (not their own!).

6 Vocabulary: Privacy words and expressions

A 6.9 Ask: *What do you think is happening in the pictures?* You could prompt them by asking:

Picture 1: *Whose bedroom is it?* (a teenager's), *Who's at the computer?* (the teenager's mother), *What do you think she's doing?* (spying on her son / daughter's Internet activity)

Picture 2: *Who is standing outside the room?* (a father), *What is he doing?* (eavesdropping), *Whose bedroom is it?* (his son or daughter's)

Sts listen to the five conversations and say which two match the pictures. Check that sts understood *surveillance camera* in conversation 1.

Classcheck. Ask: *Do any of these parents remind you of your own?*

Answers

Picture 1 – conversation 4
Picture 2 – conversation 3

See Teacher's Book p.321 for Audio script 6.9.

B 6.10 Model and drill pronunciation of the highlighted words. Have sts repeat the words after you.

Sts match the words to their meanings. Encourage guessing the meanings from context by looking back at the text in 5A. Play the audio for sts to check their answers. Ask: *Do you like the teacher from the audio?*

Stronger classes: Cover exercise B. Sts find the words in paragraph 1, and to try and write their own definitions for each word. Then they compare their definitions with those in the Student's Book. How similar were they?

Answers

1 b 2 e 3 c 4 a 5 d

C Focus on the example speech bubbles for both stages of the activity and get sts to tell you in their own words what they have to do.

In pairs, assign roles. Ensure sts take turns to play both the role of the parent and the teenager.

Invite several pairs to act out their conversations to the class.

Weaker classes: Give gapped copies of the audio script 6.9 to help them with their role plays.

D Make it personal Sts complete the questions individually. Paircheck, then classcheck.

In groups, sts discuss their answers. Use the example to set this up. Where sts answer "Sometimes", encourage them to discuss the circumstances in which they think it is OK, e.g. *If you suspect your girlfriend / boyfriend is cheating on you, then I think it is OK to check their text messages.*

Appoint one student in each group to time the five minutes per question, and to organize the vote. Have a class feedback session to compare groups' opinions on each situation.

Answers

1 eavesdrop on 2 surveillance, spy on 3 threat
4 keep tabs on

Tip

Do not worry about sts making mistakes in a **Make it personal** exercise such as this. The aim is to get their message across, so encourage them. If necessary, write down common mistakes and correct them later.

Workbook p.30.

F Make it personal In groups, answer 1–4. Any surprises?

1 Do you think Jo acted appropriately? Are the lessons she learned important?
2 How much freedom do / did you have as a teenager?
3 Do you think teenagers have too much, too little, or just enough freedom these days?
4 What do you think of people who read others' texts or WhatsApp® messages? Is it ethical?

My parents were too strict, so I'll be easier on my kids. How about you?

I'm not sure I'll ever have kids, but I wouldn't spy on them.

6 Vocabulary: Privacy words and expressions

A 6.9 Listen to five short conversations between parents and their teenagers. Which two match the pictures? Do any of the people remind you of your parents?

B 6.10 Re-read paragraph 1 in 5A. Match the highlighted words to their meanings. Listen to check.

1 surveillance	a	☐	keep yourself informed about something
2 spy on	b	☐	the act of watching someone who might be doing something illegal
3 eavesdrop on	c	☐	listen secretly to a private conversation
4 keep tabs on	d	☐	someone or something that is potentially dangerous
5 threat	e	☐	watch someone secretly

C In pairs, cover and remember both pictures in A. Then role play the conversations.

In the first one, the woman was about 50 and she was wearing ...

Mom, I just can't believe you were using my computer! Are you ...?

Yes, I am. As your mother ...

D Make it personal Complete 1–4 with a word or expression from B. Answer Y (yes), N (no), or S (sometimes). In groups, compare ideas. After five minutes, take a vote on each question. How many unanimous opinions?

Is it OK for ...

1 employers to ________ their employees' phone conversations when they're talking?
2 parents to install ________ equipment in their children's cars and ________ their driving?
3 the government to monitor people's Internet activity to identify a potential ________?
What do you think of people who expose government surveillance? Is it ethical?
4 couples to ________ each other's text messages and recent calls?

Hmm ... I'm not sure. Isn't everyone entitled to a little privacy?

I think employers have a right to eavesdrop on conversations.

6.4 Are you into social media?

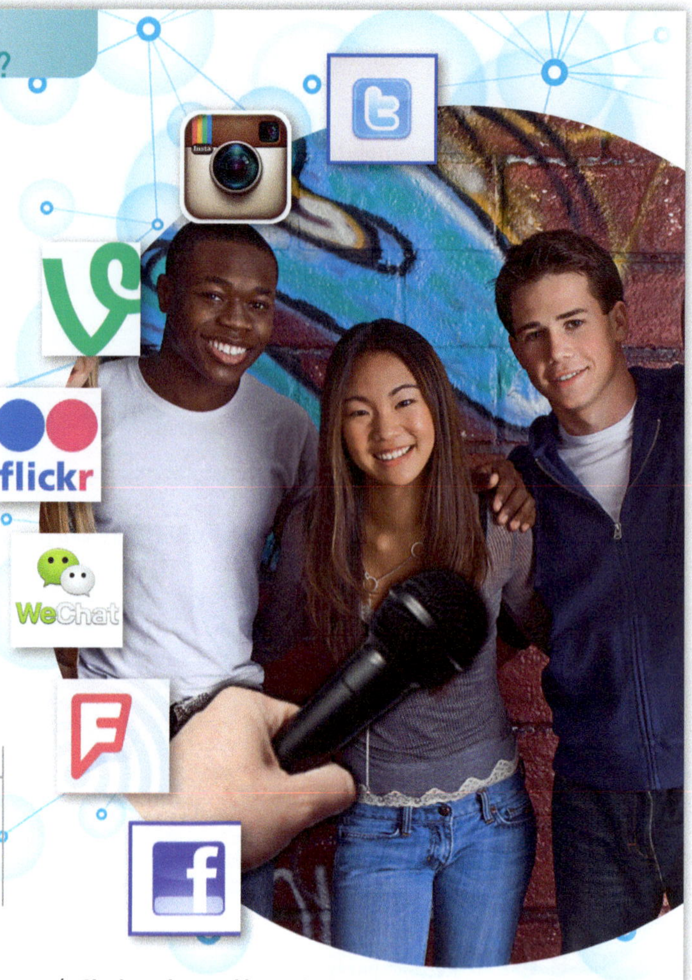

7 Listening

A In pairs, answer 1–3. Any surprises?

1 Guess what the people in the photo are doing.
2 Why do some people feel the need to keep tabs on their friends?
3 Do you know any apps that make it easy for friends to spy on each other?

> All of my friends spy on me on Foursquare®, and I hate that!

Common mistake

Facebook® lets your friends ~~to~~ see all the stuff you like.

B 6.11 Listen to James, Audra, and Tom, and match the three columns. There's one extra threat. Do you identify with any of the speakers?

Speaker	App	Privacy threats
1 James	Instagram®	teachers
2 Audra	Foursquare®	friends
3 Tom	Facebook®	boss
		family

C 6.11 Listen again. T (true) or F (false)?

1 James's parents respect his privacy on Facebook®.
2 His friends like Facebook® better than he does.
3 Audra posts photos of where she's been.
4 She has changed her privacy settings.
5 Tom uses Foursquare®.
6 He knows how to use apps correctly.

8 Pronunciation: Blended consonants

A 6.12 Listen to the rule and examples. Then complete 1–4 with the words you hear.

> Two similar consonant sounds are usually pronounced as one.
> Do you have a minute to spare?
> My parents seem totally obsessed with Facebook®.

1 It's __________ __________ ask before you take a photo.
2 __________ __________ app take a picture of you?
3 What if I __________ __________ stay home?
4 __________ __________ addictive.

B **Make it personal** Draw lines connecting the similar consonant sounds in these questions 1–4. Then ask and answer them.

1 Do your (grand)parents seem to value the Internet?
2 Do you see any future reasons to maintain libraries?
3 How do you think communication will change over the next 100 years?
4 How could the World Wide Web bring more peace to the world?

> My grandparents are amazing. They're really into technology.

Lesson Aims: Sts learn language to talk about social media apps, and discuss whether they are a threat to our privacy.

Skills	Language	Vocabulary	Grammar
Listening to an interview for a survey Discussing favorite social apps	Asking and answering interview questions: *What's your favorite social app? I love Vine. Whenever I see something funny, I just video it.*	*stay in touch with ... , have a love / hate relationship with ...* **Pronunciation** Blended consonants	Question words with *-ever: whoever, whatever, whichever, whenever*, and *wherever*

Warm-up

Ask: *What song lines have you listened to / sung along with in English this week?* In pairs, sts brainstorm.

Discuss the lesson title question as a class: *Are you into social media? How important a role does it play in your life? How would your life be different if it didn't exist?* Brainstorm a few ideas together to flow naturally into the lesson.

7 Listening

A Focus on the photo. Ask: *Do you recognize the social media icons around it? What are they? Which of the apps do you have? How frequently do you use them? Which do you use the most / the least?*

Give sts time to discuss the three questions in pairs, then open up into a class discussion. Focus on the **Common mistake**. Remind sts that we can also use *allow* or *enable* with the same meaning, and that both are followed by *to*.

Background information

Twitter is an online social networking service where users read and send short messages called "tweets".

Instagram is an online mobile service for sharing videos and photos.

Vine is a video sharing app.

Flickr is a photo management and sharing app.

WeChat is a free messaging and calling app.

Foursquare is a free app which allows you to share your location with friends, and see where your friends are.

Facebook is a social networking website.

B 6.11 Talk sts through the choices in each column so they know what to expect and to look out for. Play the audio for sts to match the speakers, apps, and threats. Classcheck.

Answers

1 James – Facebook – family
2 Audra – Instagram – friends
3 Tom – Foursquare – teachers

See Teacher's Book p.321 for Audio script 6.11.

C 6.11 Sts read statements 1-6 carefully before listening again. They can pre-mark any they think they already know. Re-play the audio to answer true or false.

Classcheck. Ask: *Which of the speakers do you agree / disagree / identify with?* Discuss with the class.

Answers

1 F 2 F 3 F 4 F 5 T 6 F

8 Pronunciation: Blended consonants

A 6.12 Go through the rule with the class, then play the audio for sts to listen to the examples. After sts complete 1–4, re-play the audio to drill both sentences. In pairs, sts practice saying the sentences to each other.

Weaker classes: Back-chain drill the sentences, if necessary. Start by focusing on the two blended words, then build up to sts repeating the whole sentence, e.g. *best to, It's best to, It's best to ask, It's best to ask before you take a photo*.

Answers

1 best to 2 Does the 3 want to 4 It's so

B Make it personal Sts work through the questions, drawing connecting lines to the similar consonant sounds, as in the rule above. Classcheck, asking individual sts (or groups if your class is shy) to repeat the questions. Get the rest of the class to applaud good examples of pronunciation.

Having practiced the similar consonant sounds, in pairs, sts ask each other the questions. Ensure both take turns to ask the questions. Monitor and note down any common errors. Class feedback, with pairs sharing anything interesting from their discussion with the class.

Answers

1 grandparent**s s**eem 2 futu**re r**easons
3 thin**k c**ommunications 4 We**b b**ring

Song lyric: See Teacher's Book p.341 for notes about the song and an accompanying activity to do with the class.

9 Grammar: Question words with *-ever*

A 6.13 Sts match the phrases. Then play the audio for them to check.

Sts underline the *-ever* words in the first column: *whatever, whoever, whenever, however, wherever* and *whichever*. Ask: *How would you translate these words?*

Tip

Don't be concerned if sts sometimes whisper quickly to each other in L1 in pairs to confirm any doubts. Managing L1 efficiently is more effective than banning it bluntly, as we miss so many subtle opportunities to help different sts in all sorts of ways. Prohibiting L1 is a very narrow approach, blocking many potential alternative learning strategies for each individual in your class.

Sts study the rules and examples to check the correct options, 1-3. Classcheck.

Stronger classes: Sts match who from James, Audra, and Tom said each sentence and what they were talking about. Re-play audio 6.11 for them to check. (1 James, talking about his dad commenting on all his Facebook posts. 2 James, talking about how all his friends feel they are too exposed on Facebook. 3 Audra, talking about people constantly taking photos to post on Instagram. 4 Audra, talking about how pointless Instagram is. 5 Tom, talking about how to use the Foursquare app. 6 Tom, talking about how he isn't very good at using apps.)

Answers

1 d 2 c 3 e 4 f 5 b 6 a
1 all 2 sometimes 3 Use

Refer sts to the **Grammar expansion** on p.148.

B 6.14 Ask: *What do you remember from the interview with James, Audra and Tom in 7B? What were they talking about?*

Before listening, have sts quickly read the rest of the interview for gist, ignoring the gaps. In pairs, they compare what they got from this and see if their guesses were close.

Sts go back through the interview and complete the gaps with words with *-ever*.

Paircheck before you play the audio for them to check their answers.

In pairs, sts ask and answer the reporter's three questions. Monitor, encouraging the use of words with *-ever*.

Class feedback where sts share anything interesting from their discussion.

Answers

1 Whenever 2 wherever 3 whoever 4 whichever
5 Whatever

Optional activity

Sts write out their answers to the interview questions from B.

C Make it personal

Uncover and go through statements 1–4 with the class. Were any of their guesses remotely close? Have fun while they react to how near they were(n't), and what they think of each person after reading what they were really saying.

Board: *Whenever I hear the song ..., I ... .* Ask a few sts to complete the statement so that it is true for them. Have them do the same with the other statements.

In pairs, sts compare their sentences. Any similar responses?

Workbook p.31.

9 Grammar: Question words with *-ever*

A 6.13 Match the phrases. Then listen to check. Check (✔) the correct rules in the grammar box.

1 He comments on whatever ...
2 The answer is always the same whoever ...
3 They stop and take a photo whenever ...
4 However you look at this Instagram® craze, ...
5 Wherever you are, ...
6 Whichever app I use, ...

a ☐ I always end up doing something wrong.
b ☐ you just access the app and check in.
c ☐ you talk to.
d ☐ he sees on my newsfeed.
e ☐ they see something "interesting."
f ☐ it's just pointless.

Question words with *-ever*: *how, who, what, which, when* and *where*

1 ***Ever*** means "no matter who, what, or which" in ☐ **all** ☐ **some** of the examples.
2 Question words with *-ever* ☐ **always** ☐ **sometimes** go at the beginning of the sentence.
3 ☐ **Use** ☐ **Don't use** a comma at the end of the clause when an *-ever* word begins the sentence.

Grammar expansion p.148

B 6.14 James, Audra, and Tom continue the interview from 7B. Complete 1–5 with a question word with *-ever*. Listen to check. How would you answer the reporter's questions?

REPORTER: And what's your favorite social app?
JAMES: I love Vine®. [1] *Whenever* I see something funny, I just video it. I mean, how cool is that? Wechat® is another favorite. I can stay in touch with my friends [2] ________ I am.
REPORTER: And are there any apps you like?
AUDRA: Flickr® is OK for [3] ________ likes photographs. Tumblr® isn't bad, either. I just use [4] ________ I click on first.
REPORTER: OK. What about your favorite app?
TOM: [5] ________ people may say about Facebook®, it's still my number one app. I love it.

C Make it personal Make 1–4 true for you. In pairs, compare. Any similar answers?

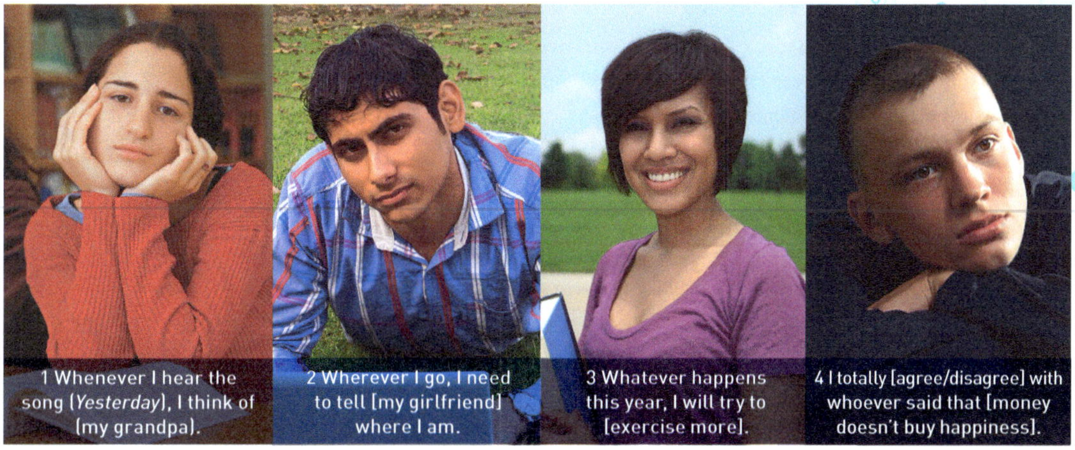
1 Whenever I hear the song [*Yesterday*], I think of [my grandpa].
2 Wherever I go, I need to tell [my girlfriend] where I am.
3 Whatever happens this year, I will try to [exercise more].
4 I totally [agree/disagree] with whoever said that [money doesn't buy happiness].

Whenever I hear the song *Summer*, I think of my ex. He used to love Calvin Harris.

Yeah, that's a great song. It reminds me of my trip to New York in 2015.

10 Listening

"We no longer look at résumés. We go straight to your Facebook® page."

A In groups, answer 1–2. Any surprises?

1 Why does the interviewer in the cartoon prefer to look at candidates' Facebook® profiles?

2 How can your Facebook® page help you to get a job / stop you from being hired? Think about:

AREAS OF CAUTION

a Pages you like

b Your choice of words

c Photos you post

d Religion and politics

e Photos you're tagged in

The photos you post might make them think you're not serious enough for the job.

B 6.15 Listen to Larry, from the cartoon, talking to his wife about the interview. Which area of caution in A did he ignore?

C 6.15 Listen again and circle the right alternative.

1 The interview was [**short** / **long**].
2 They said they wanted someone [**younger** / **more experienced**].
3 Larry [**worked** / **didn't work**] at Apple®.
4 Larry [**was** / **wasn't**] late for the interview.
5 Larry's photo was taken [**indoors** / **outdoors**].
6 His wife is [**supportive** / **critical**] of him.

11 Keep talking

A In groups, what advice would you give for each area of caution in 10A? Any differences of opinion?

B **Make it personal** What advice would you give for these areas?

be happy · look your best 24/7 · spend your money more wisely · impress your English teacher · make a perfect burger · stay out of trouble at college · live to be a hundred · shop online safely

1 Brainstorm as many ideas as you can.
2 Share the best ones with the class.

I think to be happy, it's important not to worry.

Yes, but you should be careful not to spend too much money, though!

Lesson Aims: Sts learn language to talk about the dangers of Facebook, and discuss how it might affect their careers.

Skills
Listening to a conversation about a job interview
Writing a "how to ..." guide

Language
Giving advice: *Do your best to reply within 24 hours. To be happy, it's important not to worry.*

Vocabulary
interview, hire, inappropriate, candidate
Phrases for giving advice: *Do your best to ... , Be sure to ... , As far as possible, Try to ... , Avoid ... , Whatever you do, don't ... , Never, ever ...*

Warm-up

Ask: *Do you use Facebook? Is there anything on your Facebook page that you'd be unhappy for a potential employer to see? Have you been tagged in any embarrassing photos?* Sts discuss in pairs, then share anything interesting with the class.

Ask: *Do you have many secrets? Mainly big ones or smaller ones? Who do you share your secrets with?*

10 Listening

A Focus sts on the cartoon. Ask: *Who do you think the men are and what are they doing?* (The man behind the desk is interviewing the other man for a job.)

Read the questions and look at the areas of caution with the class. Highlight the phrases: *help you to* + infinitive, and *stop you from* + *-ing* form in the questions.

In groups of four or five, sts discuss the questions, using the photos for ideas. Feedback as a class.

Background information

In recent surveys, around 44% of employers said they'd hired a candidate through social media. An even larger number of employers (around 93%) have checked candidates' social media profiles during the interview process.

B 6.15 Focus on the cartoon again. Ask: *Do you think Larry got the job? Why?* Have a class vote.

Then explain he was turned down for it, and congratulate those who voted correctly. Explain that sts are going to hear him tell his wife about the interview. Again, they might like to guess why, from the areas of caution a-e., and what his wife's reaction is going to be.

Play the audio for sts to find out which area of caution Larry ignored.

Answer

c Photos you post

See Teacher's Book p.321 for Audio script 6.15.

C 6.15 Sts read the six options. They might be able to recall some of the answers without listening again. If so, let them have a go, then play the audio for them to check their answers.

Answers

1 short 2 more experienced 3 didn't work 4 wasn't 5 outdoors 6 supportive

See Teacher's Book p.321 for Audio script 6.15.

Tip

Don't forget to ask a final 'overall' task after a series of listenings or readings. Try both to draw them back to the skill, as well as giving some kind of emotional reaction to the text. Even if they say they hated it, this will help you re-shape the lesson next time you teach it.

11 Keep talking

A Elicit and board phrases for giving advice, e.g. *You (really) should / shouldn't ... , It's important not to ... , Never ... , Avoid ... , Whatever you do, ...*

In small rather than large groups, sts decide what advice they would give for each area of caution a–e in 10A. Elicit an original example from them to set this up.

Answers

Make sure you use correct spelling and grammar.
Don't share inappropriate posts / photos.
Avoid making religious comments.
It's important not to be rude.
You should always check the photos you've been tagged in.
Be careful what you post and what pages you like, as they will reflect on the kind of person you are, and may give the wrong impression.

B Make it personal Ensure sts can clearly envisage the eight advice-giving situations. Give pairs a topic each.

For three minutes, pairs brainstorm advice and write notes on their topic.

Sts exchange their ideas, either in plenary with a small group or on their feet and mingling with a larger one, so they all say more. As sts listen to each other, get them to try to react, comment and help each other if they spot any errors.

To finish, invite volunteers to share their best moments / ideas / exchanges with the class.

Song lyric: See Teacher's Book p.341 for notes about the song and an accompanying activity to do with the class.

12 Writing: A *how to …* guide

A Focus on the title and photo. Ask: *What comes to mind / is going to come up?* and give them the chance to respond freely.

Tell sts to read the *Watch out!* text quickly and ask: *What is the purpose of this text?* (to give advice about using Facebook.)

Give sts 45 seconds to fill in the headings using areas of caution a–e, from 10A. Use the example to set this up and narrow it down for them.

Classcheck, then discuss the meaning of polarizing opinions in the last paragraph. To *polarize* means to cause two directly opposite opinions.

Ask: *Did they enjoy it? Do you like the mantra? Do you have any of your own?* e.g. ours as teachers is to *Think in English!* Encourage sts to pick up on any other verbal ticks you have, too.

Answers

1 Pages you like
2 Photos you post
3 Photos you're tagged in
4 Your choice of words
5 Religion and politics

B Ask sts what a *"how to …"* guide is (= advice / guide about how to do something).

Read through the guidelines with the class, then ask sts to find and underline examples in the *Watch out!* text.

Answers

1 Facebook could be sabotaging your career
2 Pages you like, Photos you post, etc.
3 Do the math; A mantra for you
4 don't post pictures of alcoholic beverages

C Ask: *Do you send many emails? How quickly do you reply to emails you receive?*

Read **Write it right!** together. Then refer sts to the example in 1. Have them use the prompts in 2–4 and the verbs in the box to write more advice about writing emails. Paircheck, then classcheck any doubts.

Answers

1 Do our best to reply within 24 hours.
2 Avoid including huge attachments.
3 Be sure to scan your messages for viruses.
4 Whatever you do, don't write in CAPS.

Optional activity

For further practice of the phrases in **Write it right!**, ask sts to complete the phrases with their own words, e.g. *Never, ever accept friend requests from people you don't know on Facebook. Whatever you do, don't open emails from suspicious email addresses.*

D Your turn! Read the instructions with the class, pausing at each stage to elicit any questions.

Focus on the **Common mistake** and ask if this is a mistake they used to make, or have heard others make.

In pairs, sts choose a topic from 11B. Encourage them to choose one that they have knowledge or experience of. Advise them to write simple instructions which are easy to read.

Weaker classes: Brainstorm and board a few ideas with the class first for each of the topics.

Stronger classes: When they have finished and checked their guides, have them write a *"how to …"* guide for a topic of their own, maybe a skill they have learned to do, a recipe they know, or a sport they are good at.

Optional activity

Rhythmically read out the mantra below the *Watch Out!* text. Elicit the meaning of *leave a trace* (= evidence that you have been somewhere) and the meaning of the mantra as a whole. Ask sts: *Do you think fewer young people are using Facebook these days? Do you think Facebook will exist in five years' time? Why / Why not? Do you think it will be replaced by something else? What, for example?* Class discussion to end lesson.

Workbook p.32.

12 Writing: A *how to* ... guide

A Read *Watch out!* Write the correct area of caution in 10A for each paragraph.

B Read the guidelines for an effective "how to ... " article. Underline examples in *Watch out!*

1. Create a catchy title.
2. Use section headings.
3. Write a short introduction / conclusion.
4. Add details.

C Read *Write it right!* Write guidelines for email etiquette (1–4).

Write it right!

When writing a "how to ..." guide, it's important to be very specific and tell the reader the dos and don'ts.

Dos	Don'ts
1 Do your best to ...	1 Avoid + noun / *-ing* verb
2 Be sure to ...	2 Whatever you do, don't ...
3 As far as possible, try to ...	3 Never, ever ...

include reply scan write

1 within 24 hours – ✓ [your best]
Do your best to reply within 24 hours.

2 huge attachments – ✗ [avoid]
____

3 your messages for viruses – ✓ [sure]
____

4 in CAPS - ✗ [whatever]
____

D Your turn! Write a "how to ... " article in about 150–180 words.

Common mistake

Try ~~to don't~~ *not to* spend money on things you don't need.

Before
Choose a topic from 11B and in pairs, brainstorm your "Top five guidelines."

While
Pay attention to the guidelines in B, and use at least four expressions from C.

After
Share your work with your classmates. What was the most popular guideline?

WATCH OUT!

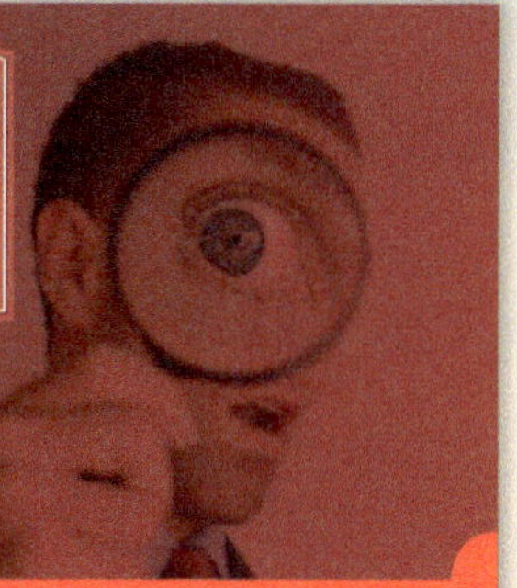

Facebook® could be sabotaging your career.

Do the math: If you joined Facebook® in, say, 2010 and have posted an average of two comments every day since then, there are currently more than 4,000 comments floating around the site with the potential to ruin you reputation. Here are five things to keep in mind.

1 *Pages you like*
The pages you're a fan of say an awful lot about you. When you respond to like requests, be selective. Do your best to keep your likes as neutral as possible.

2 _______________
Watch out! If you don't want to be seen doing something embarrassing, don't post it on Facebook®. Also, avoid posting inappropriate photos. And whatever you do, don't post pictures of alcoholic beverages.

3 _______________
Even if you're careful when posting status updates and photos, other Facebook® users could still get you in trouble. Be sure to keep tabs on the photos you are tagged in, and have them removed if necessary.

4 _______________
Never ever – ever – use foul language in a Facebook® post. Period.

5 _______________
As far as possible, try to stay away from controversial topics and avoid giving polarizing opinions.

A mantra for you: "Whatever you say leaves a trace in cyberspace!" If you're afraid of being seen, you can bet your life: you probably will be!

Review 3

Units 5–6

1 Speaking

A Look at the photos on p.50.

1 Note down everything you can remember about these people, using these verbs.

achieve face overcome pursue

2 Take turns describing the person who you admire the most.

My hero is ... He / She managed to overcome ...

B Make it personal Choose three question titles from Units 3 and 4 to ask a partner. Ask at least three follow-up questions for each. What did you learn about each other?

What's your biggest life decision so far?

Breaking up with my girlfriend. I had to face ...

2 Grammar

A Rewrite the underlined sentences using the passive.

Even before the Internet, there were many security risks. Once I was in a train station, and I thought (1) someone was watching me. I wasn't sure, though, and I needed to make a phone call, so I took out my phone card. The phones were all in a row, and (2) anyone could see them, but it never occurred to me that might be a problem. Two weeks later, the phone bill arrived. (3) They had charged me $1,200! (4) Hundreds of people had placed calls from all over the world! A police officer explained that (5) they had read my phone card with a pair of binoculars, and (6) they had captured my password as I typed it, too. Even before the technology we have today, (7) criminals victimized many people.

B Make it personal In pairs, use the words below to tell a story about yourself or someone you know. Use at least six passive sentences.

capture eavesdrop on post remove see spy on tag watch

I knew someone who was spied on as he was ...

3 Self-test

Correct the two mistakes in each sentence. Check your answers in Units 5 and 6. What's your score, 1–20?

1 I'm sick of my mom listening my conversations and my dad spying my friends.
2 Jenny has been turn down for the first job, but she been interviewed for another.
3 I had stolen my computer by some thieves, and however I looked, I couldn't find it.
4 It's important to achieve a career and solve any obstacles.
5 My dad face a lot of setbacks, but after he moved to the U.S., he find work immediately.
6 I wish I would speak English better – if only I learn those verb tenses!
7 My job isn't precisely easy, and I have hardly no free time.
8 My mom wasn't able to do college, and it bothers her not to have studies.
9 If I hadn't keep at it, I wouldn't have been so successful now.
10 She's an underachiever, but if she didn't have determination, she wouldn't have win the race.

Warm-up

See page 61 of the Teacher's Book for warm-up ideas.

1 Speaking

A 1 Sts work individually and note down as much information as they can about Einstein, Oprah Winfrey, and Vincent van Gogh. Paircheck.

Weaker classes: Let them quickly check with the text and add a few more notes.

2 Sts choose the one from the three people that they admire the most and, in pairs, describe him/her to their partner.

B **Make it personal** Sts look back at the lesson title questions in Units 5 and 6 and choose three to ask a partner, plus follow-up questions.

Sts can swap partners again, mingle and use different lesson title questions.

2 Grammar

A Explain/Elicit that before the advent of cellphones, most public places had fixed public pay phones that people could use either by inserting coins or by using a phone card which worked a bit like a credit card today. There was a personal number on the phone card, and to activate it you needed a password.

Give sts a minute to read the text quickly to find out what problem the writer had. Paircheck. Then sts rewrite the underlined sentences using the passive.

Paircheck, then classcheck. Ask: *Do you know of anyone who has been spied on / hacked like that?*

Weaker classes: Do the first item as an example.

Answers

1 I was being watched.
2 they could be seen by anyone,
3 I had been charged $1,200!
4 Calls had been placed by hundreds of people from all over the world!
5 my phone card had been read with a pair of binoculars
6 my password had been captured
7 many people were victimized by criminals.

B **Make it personal** Review meanings and pronunciation of the boxed words by asking sts to give a useful example with each. Highlight *capture* /ˈkæptʃə/ and brainstorm more words ending in *–ture* to show the pattern (e.g. culture, adventure, picture).

Give sts time to think about their stories and make notes.

In pairs, sts tell each other their stories. Monitor and give help where necessary.

As feedback, board the passive structures (a mixture or incorrect and incorrect), for sts to correct any errors.

Weaker classes: Brainstorm a story as a class.

Tip

Weaker sts will need more preparation and thinking time but it's time well invested as this is a great opportunity to practice the target language from Units 5 and 6 in a less controlled way.

3 Self-test

This exercise reviews **Common mistakes**. Explain to sts that it not only helps them review and consolidate vocabulary and grammar, but helps practice their proof-reading skills.

Sts do it individually, then paircheck. Encourage sts to look back through Units 5 and 6 if they're unsure of how to correct the mistakes.

If sts score less than 15 out of 20, suggest they re-do the exercise in a few days' time, to see if they get a better score. If they do really well, they could also repeat the exercise later, but without referring to Units 5 and 6 this time.

Answers

1 I'm sick of my mom listening <u>to</u> my conversations and my dad spying <u>on</u> my friends.
2 Jenny has been <u>turned</u> down for the first job, but <u>she's</u> been interviewed for another.
3 I had <u>my computer stolen</u> by some thieves, and <u>wherever</u> I looked, I couldn't find it.
4 It's important to <u>pursue</u> a career and <u>overcome</u> any obstacles.
5 My dad <u>faced</u> a lot of setbacks, but after he moved to the U.S., he <u>found</u> work immediately.
6 I wish I <u>could</u> speak English better – if only I <u>had learned</u> those verb tenses!
7 My job isn't <u>exactly</u> easy, and I have hardly <u>any</u> free time.
8 My mom wasn't able to <u>go to</u> college, and it bothers her not to have <u>studied</u>.
9 If I hadn't <u>kept</u> at it, I wouldn't <u>be</u> so successful now.
10 She's an underachiever, but if she <u>hadn't had</u> determination, she wouldn't have <u>won</u> the race.

Tip

Board any other Common mistakes, either those from their L1 background, and/or those you've heard recently to expand this exercise.

4 Reading

A Cover the text and focus on the title. Elicit suggestions about the content of the article. Board their best ideas.

Give sts two minutes to read the article to check their ideas. Classcheck. Who guessed correctly?

As a follow-up, board these three topics and ask: *Which is the main topic of the article?* (a)

Why you should:

a) not allow other people to use your Facebook password.

b) make sure you have a secure Facebook password.

c) change your Facebook password every month.

B Tell sts the article mentions four reasons. Brainstorm as a class onto the board any reasons they remember. Then sts re-read the article, and find all four. Ask them to underline the relevant sections of the text.

Classcheck. Elicit the meaning of *to grant permission (give)*, *to sue someone* (= to bring legal action against them). Elicit their emotional reaction to the text (e.g. bored, angry, couldn't care less as I'd never do it), and their answer to the last question in it.

Answers

Your friends have not given permission for their correspondence to be read.
Your friends haven't given permission for their photos to be shared.
One of your friends might apply for a job at the same company.
Employers may be accessing information that they could not legally ask for in an interview.

C Tell sts they're going to read five actions that may or may not be legal/illegal.

In pairs, sts read and complete the sentences, then write A or E depending on whether the action may be illegal for either an applicant for a job or the potential employer.

Weaker classes: Give sts the first letter of each missing word to help them.

Classcheck. Ask: *Do you think your Facebook account has ever been accessed by a current or potential employer? Do you think this is fair/ethical? If your son/daughter/partner left their account open or messages readable, would you take advantage?*

Answers

1 private – A
2 photos – A
3 discrimination – A
4 interview – E
5 third – E

5 Point of view

See page 62 of the Teacher's Book for notes about this section.

Go through topics a–c with the class, and brainstorm a few ideas for each one. If necessary, board a few sentence stems for sts to refer to, e.g. *In my opinion / view … , I really / strongly believe that … , It seems to me that … , As far as I'm concerned …* . Point out they might also find the Expressions for expressing negative ideas on p.54 useful.

Individually, sts choose one of them, and make some preparatory notes. Tell sts to make the notes they feel they need to be able to speak for about 80 seconds on the topic. You don't want full sentences or a script, just prompts from which they can talk naturally.

Weaker classes: Sts can write out their argument in full, ensuring they structure it logically. However, get them to rehearse so they don't just read it aloud.

Group together sts who chose the same topic so that they can compare, share, expand on and improve their ideas. Monitor and correct as much as you can.

If possible, sts record their opinion in class using a cell phone. Allow sts to re-record if they aren't happy. It's all good practice and everybody wants the best possible end product. Encourage sts to swap recordings with a partner and give each other feedback.

Optional activity

Hold a class debate on one of the topics in 5. See technique on Teacher's Book p.62. When all groups have spoken, have sts vote for the most convincing group.

4 Reading

A Read the title. In pairs, what do you think the article might be about? How many ideas can you think of?

Your Facebook® password and you

You might find this incredibly hard to believe, but more and more employers are asking job candidates for their Facebook® passwords. Get ready. It could happen to you on your next interview. But do you have to agree? Absolutely not! Protect yourself. Never, ever give your Facebook® password, under any circumstances, to a potential or current employer.

Why not? You might think if you're a discreet person and haven't posted anything risky. Be aware. You could still find yourself in legal trouble. First of all, your friends, who have posted on your timeline or written you what they thought were private messages, have not granted permission. They may sue you and your company for invasion of privacy if they find out a company is reading their correspondence. They also haven't given permission for your company to see their photos. And just imagine what might happen if one of your friends applies for a job at the same company and is turned down. You could be in big trouble if your friend suspects discrimination.

And what if you're the employer? You may think your right to information is protected, but you may be wrong. You could be accessing sensitive personal information that would be illegal to ask for in an interview. And again, your candidate's friends have not given you permission for third-party access. Even if you escape legal action, is what you're doing ethical? You wouldn't ask to read through your candidate's personal mail before making a job offer – or would you?

B In pairs, note down reasons not to give your employer your Facebook® password. How many can you remember?

C Fill in the missing words in these actions that may be illegal and write A (Applicant) or E (Employer). Did any of them surprise you?

1 Letting an employer read ________ messages from friends.
2 Allowing an employer to see ________ taken of friends.
3 Allowing access to information if your friend applies for a job and suspects ________ .
4 Gaining access to sensitive information that you could not ask for during an ________ .
5 Not having been given ________ -party access by a candidate's friends.

5 Point of view

Choose a topic. Then support your opinion in 100–150 words, and record your answer. Ask a partner for feedback. How can you be more convincing?

a You think people who overcome illness are more inspiring than those who overcome poverty. OR
You think people who overcome poverty are more inspiring than those who overcome illness.
b You think protecting your online privacy is very important. OR
You're not too worried about online privacy because you have nothing to hide.
c You think college is essential for success. OR
You think college is one option, but there are many other ways to suceed.

7

How important is music to you?

1 Vocabulary: Success expressions

A In groups, share what you know about musicians 1–5. Remember any lines from their songs?

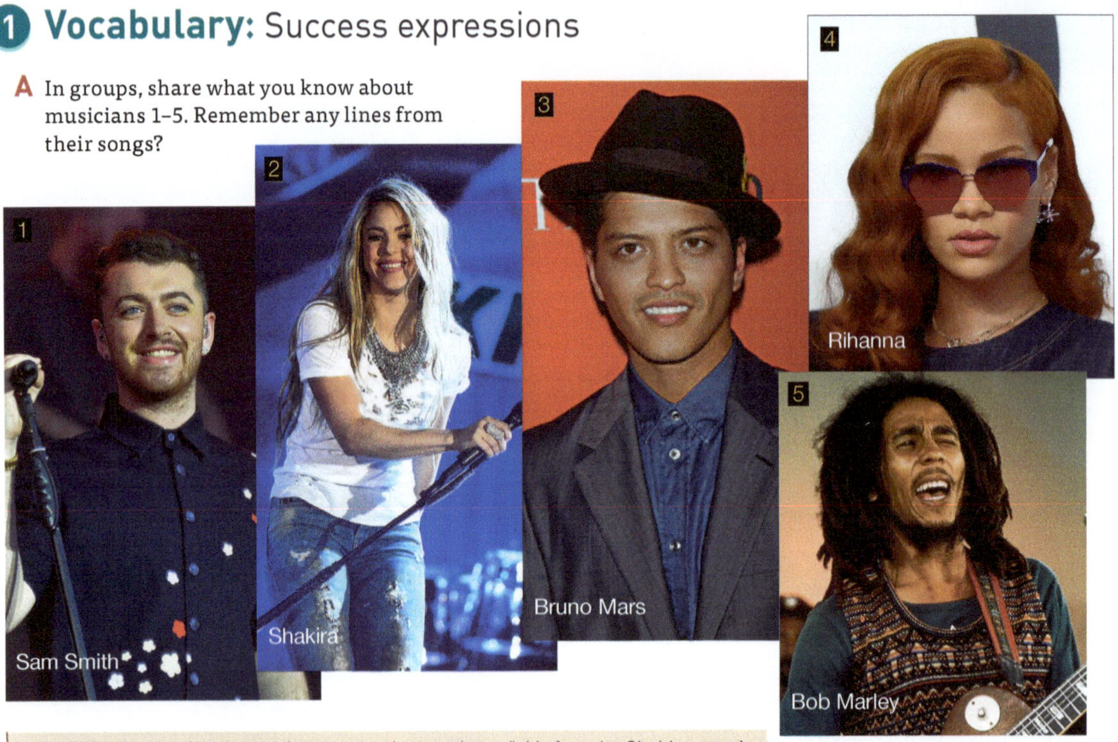

Yes! "Whenever, wherever, we're meant to be together ...". My favorite Shakira song!

B 7.1 Take the quiz. Listen to a radio show to check. Did you get any right?

RU an expert on pop-music trivia?
Try these four tricky questions to find out

1 Sam Smith **rose to fame** in 2012. What was his job before he became a **high-profile** celebrity?

a a taxi driver
b a bartender
c a pet groomer

2 Jamaican Bob Marley (1945–1981) **is generally regarded as** the king of reggae. Which is true?

a As a child, he could predict people's futures by reading their palms.
b He only released three albums in his lifetime.
c His biggest hit is *Don't worry, be happy.*

3 Adele's *21*, the best-selling album that **came out** in 2011, topped the charts for nearly six months. What does 21 refer to?

a her lucky number
b the number of songs on the CD
c her age at the time

4 The first U.S. edition of the Rock in Rio music festival **took place** in 2015 and featured the singer behind the smash hits *Uptown funk* and *Grenade*. Was it ...?

a Bruno Mars
b Rihanna
c Shakira

Lesson Aims: Sts learn vocabulary to talk about musicians and musical tastes.

Skills	Language	Vocabulary
Listening to a music quiz on a radio show Discussing musical tastes in the past and present, and how sts' tastes (or something similar) have changed	Talking about changing musical tastes: *I grew tired of playing the same old songs.*	*album, be regarded as, come out / be released, get / be hooked on, high-profile, radio station, rise to fame, take place, taste*

Warm-up

Discuss the lesson title question as a class: *How important is music to you? Who are your favorite singers? What sort of music do they sing?* Brainstorm types of music (*reggae, jazz, pop, folk, blues, classical, hip hop, indie pop, R&B, soul, rock*).

Briefly elicit music genres and get to know sts' favorites. Ask sts to write down their top five favorite songs of all time. In groups, sts compare and look for similarities. Classcheck.

1 Vocabulary: Success expressions

A Focus attention on the photos and ask sts if they recognize each musician (see Background notes below). Ask: *What nationality are the musicians in the photos? What type of music do they sing?* Ask how many songs they know by each of the artists.

In pairs, sts note down as many facts as they can about the musicians and any lines they know from their songs. Then pairs join up with two other pairs to form groups of six, and have them share their information. Have a class feedback session to compare information. Which of them do/don't they like (best)?

Background information

Sam Smith is an English singer-songwriter. He was born in 1992 and is a soul-inspired vocalist singing modern soul and pop. He won an Oscar in 2016 for his James Bond theme song, *Writing's on the Wall*.

Shakira, born in 1977, is a Colombian singer, songwriter, and dancer. She sings a mixture of pop, rock, and Latin. She has set up charitable organizations, and uses her celebrity status to campaign for important social issues such as children's' education.

Bruno Mars is an American singer, songwriter, and record producer, born in Honolulu, Hawaii in 1985. He sings pop, R&B, and reggae.

Rihanna, born in 1988 in Barbados, is an R & B / pop singer. She is known for her no. 1 hits such as *Umbrella*, *SOS*, and *We found love*.

Bob Marley (1945–1981), a Jamaican reggae singer and songwriter, has been described as a world ambassador for reggae music.

Song lyric: See Teacher's Book p.341 for notes about the song and an accompanying activity to do with the class.

B 7.1 Focus on the title and use of RU. Ask: *Do you know/use other texting abbreviations like this in English?*

Ask: *Are you into pop trivia? Do you buy/read music magazines? Listen to/watch pop quizzes on the radio/TV? How good are you? Good enough to go on TV/the radio? Why / Why not?*

Pre-teach *bartender, pet groomer, palm (of the hand)*, e.g. by miming the jobs and showing an image/your hand.

In pairs, sts answer quiz.

Play the audio for sts to check their answers. Ask: *How did you do?* With a more extrovert class, encourage sts to sing lines from any of the songs they recognize.

Answers

1 b 2 a 3 c 4 a

See Teacher's Book p.321 for Audio script 7.1.

Tip

Monitor and help with any expressions sts struggle with, e.g. by miming or exemplifying rather than always explaining with definitions. Generally, the more willing you are to mime and exemplify, the more they will too, which helps reduce the amount of L1 in circulation.

C 7.2 Elicit pronunciation of the highlighted words in 1B in their context/phrases, not just the words themselves, including links to the words around them and schwas, and drill as necessary.

Sts look back at the quiz and work out their meaning from the context. Then match them with their definitions. Paircheck, then classcheck by playing the audio.

NB Some might know/ask about another meaning for *come out*, i.e. declare their homosexuality, so be careful.

Answers

1 b 2 e 3 c 4 a 5 d

See Teacher's Book p.322 for Audio script 7.2.

Optional activity

Sts write their own sentences with each of the new phrases in C. Monitor and help at this stage, weeding out any errors. Then sts rewrite the sentences leaving a gap for the new phrase.

Sts swap their sentences with a partner, and try to fill in the gaps in their partner's sentences correctly.

Weaker classes: Sts write these sentences in pairs, then swap with another pair.

D Make it personal In groups of four or six, sts write their music trivia questions. Encourage them to search on the Internet for interesting questions. They need to find three multiple-choice answers for each question.

A spokesperson from each group reads out the questions. The other groups write down their answer choice for each question. At the end, check answers. Which group is the winner?

2 Listening

A 7.3 Focus on the photo and elicit they're the two DJs from 1B. Ask: *Who's your favorite DJ? Have you ever DJ-ed?* Sts read and guess the reasons why Tim might be tired of his job at the radio station.

Clarify *taste in music* (= preference or liking for something). Elicit other expressions with taste, e.g. *to have good / bad taste, to lack taste, to have a taste of something*, e.g. *I had a taste of the high life!* (to have a brief experience of something).

Play the audio for sts to listen and choose the correct reason. Classcheck. How many guessed correctly?

Answer

His taste in music has changed.

See Teacher's Book p.000 for Audio script 7.3.

Tip

Keep pre-teaching new words before a listening task to a minimum, especially if the task is listening for gist. Sts need to get used to understanding the general meaning, even when there are words they don't know, as in real-life. Encourage them to ignore these words, and listen for the key words they do know.

B Read through the sentences for sts to remember/guess if they're (likely to be) true or false.

Play the audio. Sts complete the exercise.

Classcheck, and ask sts to correct the false statements. Sts discuss what they think of her advice and what they think Tim should do.

Weaker classes: You could pre-teach the following phrases before sts listen a second time: *to have a background in ... , undergraduate degree*.

Answers

1 T 2 T 3 F (He thinks the lyrics are very repetitive.) 4 T 5 T 6 F (He's considering applying for a job on a jazz radio station.)

C Make it personal Board the rubric: *How have your tastes changed over the last decade?* to frame the activity for them.

1 7.4 In pairs, sts complete the sentences. Play the audio for them to listen and check. Re-play the audio, pausing after each sentence for sts to repeat. Sts practice 1-6. Monitor to check correct pronunciation, reductions and stress.

Weaker classes: Give them the initial letter for each gapped word to help them.

Answers

1 fond 2 into 3 grew 4 getting 5 get 6 enough

2 Tell sts to choose topics where their tastes have changed over the years. Set them three or four minutes to make notes about each topic under the headings "past" and "present."

3 Focus on the **Common mistake**. Elicit other examples with *be hooked on ... , be tired of ... , be into ...* , and write them on the board.

In groups, sts share their ideas. Monitor round the class, and make a note of common errors and good uses of English.

Optional activity

Ask sts to write their notes up as a short paragraph, and explain how/why their tastes have changed.

Workbook p.33.

C 7.2 Match the highlighted words in **B** to their definitions. Listen to check.

1 rose to fame		a ☐	was officially released, became available
2 high-profile		b ☐	suddenly became very famous
3 is regarded as		c ☐	is considered
4 came out		d ☐	happened, occurred
5 took place		e ☐	prominent and well known

D **Make it personal** In groups, search online for *music trivia*. Write three questions to ask the class. Try to use some words from **C**. Who are the most popular artists?

> OK, Calvin Harris is a high-profile Scottish DJ and singer. Which song did he produce? Was it a) ...

2 Listening

A 7.3 Listen to DJs Tim and Nina after their show. Why is Tim tired of his job?

☐ The pay's not good enough.
☐ His taste in music has changed.
☐ Music has changed.

B 7.3 Listen again. T (true) or F (false)? What do *you* think Tim should do?

1 Tim studied music in college.
2 Nina likes Coldplay.
3 Tim thinks pop songs have predictable melodies, but fine lyrics.
4 Nina seems to dislike the commercial side of pop music.
5 Their station probably has very young listeners.
6 Tim's considering applying for a non-radio job.

> I think Tim should follow his heart and just quit.

> Definitely, that's what I would do.

C **Make it personal** How have your tastes changed over the last decade?

1 7.4 **How to say it** Complete the sentences from the conversation. Listen to check.

Talking about changing tastes

	What they said	What they meant
Past	1 I used to be really ______ of (pop music).	I used to like pop music.
	2 I was really ______ (their music).	I really liked their music.
	3 I ______ tired of (playing the same songs).	I lost interest in playing the same songs
Present	4 I'm ______ hooked on (jazz).	I'm becoming fascinated by jazz.
	5 I can't ______ enough of (it).	I really, really like it.
	6 I've had ______ of (this job).	I'm sick of this job.

2 Choose three topics. Note down your tastes under "past" and "present."

clothes exercise food / drink movies music
radio / TV shows reading shopping sports

3 Share your ideas in groups. Use *How to say it* expressions. Many similarities?

> I used to be really fond of *The Simpsons* when I was a kid. I wouldn't miss a single episode.

Common mistake

I'm really into / hooked on / tired of ~~read~~ reading gossip magazines.

3 Language in use

A 7.5 Listen to Liz sharing her experience with Josh. Choose the correct headline.

- [ ] MILEY CYRUS CANCELS CONCERT DUE TO SUDDEN ILLNESS
- [ ] DISAPPOINTING TICKET SALES FORCE CYRUS TO CANCEL KANSAS CONCERT
- [ ] CYRUS CONCERT CANCELED BECAUSE OF POWER OUTAGE

B 7.6 Read and predict the missing words. Listen to more of their conversation to check. Do you think Josh is a good listener?

KANSAS CITY, MO

Pop star Miley Cyrus has canceled Tuesday night's concert at the Sprint Center as she had a viral infection.

In a press release, the concert organizers said Cyrus was in a local __________ due to a severe allergic reaction to the __________ she was taking and would not be able to perform.

Ticket holders were told to proceed to the box office so that they could get a __________, but no further information was provided on whether the show would be rescheduled.

Cyrus tweeted a message in order to apologize to her __________: "Kansas, I promise I'm as heartbroken as you are. I wanted so badly 2 be there 2 night." ■

C 7.7 Read four extracts from what Liz said next and guess how 1) her story ends and 2) she feels about Miley now. Listen to check. Were you close?

Since I was on vacation, I thought I'd give her a second chance.

I left home early so I'd have plenty of time to get to the airport.

We nearly froze to death.

In the end, I downloaded the show just to have a taste of what I missed.

I think in the end Liz might not have ...

D **Make it personal** In pairs, which of these would(n't) you do in order to see and briefly meet your favorite artist(s)?

go into debt · miss school or work · sell something valuable · take an overnight bus · travel abroad · wait in line all day

I wouldn't mind waiting in line all day to meet Leonardo DiCaprio.

I might wait all day for an Alicia Keys concert, but it would depend on ...

E Read *Uses of so*. Then write 1–5 next to the examples in AS 7.7 on p.162.

Uses of *so*

So is in the top 50 most common words in spoken English. It is used to ...

1. keep the conversation going: *So, as I was saying, it was really cold and ...*
2. express a result: *It was a long journey,* ***so*** *I'm really exhausted.*
3. avoid repetition: *"Is Metallica playing in Peru this year?" "Yeah, I think* ***so****."*
4. intensify meaning: *Why do you have to be* ***so*** *difficult?*
5. express purpose: *Here's my number* ***so*** *you can text me.*

Lesson Aims: Sts learn vocabulary to talk about canceled events, and discuss their own disappointing experiences.

Skills	Language	Vocabulary	Grammar
Listening to a conversation between friends about a concert being cancelled Sharing stories about their own disappointing experiences	Expressing purpose and reason: *Liz took a day off to see her idol. She was hospitalized due to an allergic reaction.*	*backstage, box office, cancel, perform, postpone, re-schedule, stage* Uses of so: intensify meaning, express purpose, avoid repetition, express a result, keep the conversation going	Conjunctions to express purpose and reason: *(in order) to, so (that), as, since, because (of), and due to*

Warm-up

Board *Expressing disappointment* and draw an unhappy emoticon. Elicit adjectives/phrases they know and add any new ones, e.g, *I was disappointed, upset, devastated, destroyed, in tears*. Elicit adverbs they can use to augment them: *pretty, really, so, hugely, immensely, absolutely, totally, completely, utterly*, and revise the rules for use of extreme adjectives.

Board the lesson title question: *What was your most recent disappointment?* Sts ask and answer in pairs.

3 Language in use

A 7.5 Focus on the photo in B and ask: *Do you like Miley Cyrus? Have you ever seen her in concert? Would you like to? Why / Why not?* Ask sts to read the headlines. Ask: *Which is most likely?*

Play the audio for sts to listen to Liz telling Josh why the show was canceled.

Classcheck. Ask: *How do you think the fans felt?*

Answer

Miley Cyrus cancels concert due to sudden illness

See Teacher's Book p.322 for Audio script 7.5.

Background information

Miley Cyrus, born in 1992, is an American singer, songwriter, and actress. In 2006, she played the role of Miley Stewart in the TV series *Hannah Montana*, which turned her into a teen idol.

B 7.6 In pairs, sts read through the newspaper story and predict the missing words. Play the audio for sts to check their answers. Explain any new vocabulary from the newspaper story.

Discuss whether the class think Josh is a good listener (No, he interrupts a lot).

Answers

hospital, antibiotics, refund, fans

See Teacher's Book p.322 for Audio script 7.6.

Optional activity

Ask: *What do good listeners do?* (make eye contact, mirror body language, ask questions, etc.) *What phrases do they use to encourage a story?* (*Go on ... , What happened next ... ?, Really ... and then what?*) Give sts a copy of the audio script for 7.6, and ask them to rewrite Josh's responses to make him a better listener.

C 7.7 Invite individuals to read each extract aloud as meaningfully as they can, as if they were Liz. Have sts guess in pairs how her story ends.

Quick class discussion, then play the audio for sts to check answers.

Answers

1 She didn't see the concert.
2 She would still like to see Miley one day.

Teacher's Book p.322 for Audio script 7.7.

D Make it personal Ask: *Have you ever done anything extreme to see a favorite artist? Did you travel a long way? Pay a lot of money?* Go through the list and elicit an individual example of someone doing each of them if you can.

Focus on the example speech bubbles with the class, then, in pairs, sts discuss which they would or wouldn't do. Open up into a class discussion.

E Read **Uses of *so***, then cover the box and see how many uses they can remember.

Direct sts to the audio script on p.162 of the Student's Book to find examples for each use of so. Classcheck.

Answers

2 I have friends there, so finding a place to stay wouldn't be a problem. ...
1 So, anyway, I borrowed money for the tickets and ...
5 I left home early so I'd have plenty of time to get to the airport.
1 So I got on the plane and, guess what ...
2 we nearly froze to death, so the plane was diverted back to ...
4 I was so fed up with the whole thing
3 I hope so!

Song lyric: See Teacher's Book p.341 for notes about the song and an accompanying activity to do with the class.

4 Grammar: Conjunctions to express purpose and reason

A Highlight the two columns and go through the examples under each with the class. Sts notice words which follow conjunctions in **bold**, and check the correct rules.

Paircheck, classcheck. Elicit a few examples of sts' own, using the conjunctions, and board the best ones.

Answers

a verb b sentence c noun

Refer sts to the Grammar expansion on p.150.

B Focus on the title of the text, and discuss *to make it* (= to be successful in doing something or to happen). Tell sts we also use *make it* with *in time*, e.g. *I didn't make it in time for the meeting* (= I didn't arrive in time.)

Sts to circle the correct words, then paircheck. Classcheck and get them to choose the one which surprised them most. Ask: *Do these remind you of any similar stories?*

Use the example to set this up. They have to to rewrite the three texts in the same way, using the incorrect choice each time. Do the second line with them to be sure they get the idea.

Sts write the text out individually using the alternative choices. Paircheck, then classcheck.

Weaker classes: Rewrite at least the first text together with the class.

Answers

1 so that 2 as 3 in order to 4 because of 5 because of 6 so

2 However, it was canceled after only one episode because of terrible reviews.
3 Soccer fan Ric Wee made news in 2014 when he traveled 7,000 miles from Malaysia to the UK so that he could see his favorite team play live.
4 But the game was postponed because the weather was bad.
5 Eighties British superstar Morrissey, who's a vegetarian, walked off stage a number of years ago in California since there was the smell of barbecue coming from backstage.
6 To his fans' relief, Morrissey went back to finish the show.

C Go through headlines 1–5, and check the meaning of any new words. Focus on the **Common mistakes** and elicit different endings to *The show was postponed due to ... .*

Go through the example together. Point out that we usually omit indefinite and definite articles in headlines (e.g. *due to water shortage*).

In pairs, sts complete the other headlines, then invent one more of their own. Fast finishers can invent more.

Classcheck with them reading out their headlines as dramatically as they can. Putting them all into a poster might make a nice activity too.

Optional activity

Ask sts to choose a headline, and expand it into a short newspaper article, referring to the articles in 3B and 4B to help them. Use conjunctions where appropriate.

D **Make it personal** Give sts a minute to read the rubric, stages and example and digest what they have to do. To test comprehension, they can try to summarize it for each other. Boarding a title for the activity can help, e.g. something fun like *Oh no! That sucks, What a let-down!* or even *What a bummer!* as this is so common.

In groups, sts share their stories. Encourage them to

- encourage (*Really/and then what?*, etc.)
- react sympathetically (using the language and phrases from the warm-up)
- use the conjunctions in 4A

Weaker classes: Elicit more examples first by asking individual sts the questions, e.g.

You: *Have you ever missed an event?*

Student: *Yes, I missed my friend's birthday party.*

You: *Oh dear! What happened exactly?*

Student: *I was ill, and couldn't get out of bed.*

You: *What a shame. Did you call and let her know or sleep through it?*

Workbook p.34.

4 Grammar: Conjunctions to express purpose and reason

A Study the grammar box and check (✔) the correct rules.

Conjunctions: *(in order) to, so (that), as, since, because (of),* and *due to*

	Purpose	Reason
Neutral	Liz took a day off **to** see her idol. She bought front-row tickets **so** she could be near the stage.	**Because** / **Since** expectations were high, people were very frustrated. She canceled **because of** health reasons.
More formal	Cyrus tweeted **in order to** apologize. We went back **so that** we could get our money back.	**As** Cyrus had a viral infection, she had to take antibiotics. She was hospitalized **due to** an allergic reaction.

Use: a *In order to* + ☐ noun ☐ sentence ☐ verb
b *So (that), as, since,* and *because* + ☐ noun ☐ sentence ☐ verb
c *Because of* and *due to* + ☐ noun ☐ sentence ☐ verb

Grammar expansion p.150

B Circle the correct answers. Then rewrite the text correctly using the incorrect choices.

CANCELED! THREE THAT (ALMOST) DIDN'T MAKE IT!

In 2009, MTV aired *The Osbournes Reloaded* [1][**so that / in order to**] they could repeat the success of the original reality show. However, it was canceled after only one episode [2][**because of / as**] it got terrible reviews.

Soccer fan Ric Wee made news in 2014 when he traveled 7,000 miles from Malaysia to the UK [3][**in order to / so that**] see his favorite team play live. But the game was postponed [4][**because / because of**] the bad weather.

Eighties British superstar Morrissey, who's a vegetarian, walked off stage a number of years ago in California [5][**since / because of**] the smell of barbecue coming from backstage. To his fans' relief, Morrissey went back [6][**to / so**] he could finish the show.

1 In 2009, MTV aired the Osbournes Reloaded in order to repeat the success of the original reality show.

C In pairs, complete headlines 1–5. Use *due to* and your own ideas. Then write one more headline.

1 SMALL MEXICAN TOWN IN TOTAL PANIC ...
Small Mexican town in total panic due to water shortage.
2 ALL NEW YORK-BOUND FLIGHTS SUSPENDED ...
3 FINAL GAME MOVED TO (CHOOSE COUNTRY) ...
4 FAMOUS RESTAURANT CHAIN (CHOOSE ONE) CLOSES DOWN ...
5 MEGA-LOTTERY WINNER FAILS TO COLLECT PRIZE ...

Common mistakes

The show was postponed because of / due to ~~it was raining heavily.~~ *heavy rain*

D Make it personal In groups, share your stories about events that were canceled, postponed, or that you missed. Use 1–5 to help you. Any happy endings?

1 Remember a(n) show / game / party / date / interview / trip ...
2 What happened exactly and why?
3 Whose fault was it?
4 How did you feel?
5 What happened in the end?

I missed my sister's wedding last year because of a power outage in my neighborhood.

Oh, no! What happened?

I got stuck in the elevator. And they couldn't get me out in time!

5 Reading

A Read paragraph 1 of the article. What do you think *flop* means?

B 7.8 Read and choose the best headings for paragraphs 2–4. There is an extra one. Listen to check.

Risk-taking Reviews The cost Timing

Top of the Flops

– when the best made plans go wrong

① In 2014, to promote the release of the iPhone 6, U2 made their new album available as a free download to iTunes users worldwide. In theory, a match made in heaven. But thousands of music fans resented the album being added to their libraries! In the end, what looked like a brilliant marketing strategy backfired and became one of the decade's biggest flops. But why? After all, how can anyone say no to a present? This episode shows just how hard it is to predict when something will make millions or flop embarrassingly and go nowhere. Here are three factors that we wrongly assume determine what's hot and what's not.

② ________________: 2014's *Legends of Oz: Dorothy's Return* had a lot going for it. Loosely based on the *Wizard of Oz* story, it had tons of promotion and featured famous voices such as Lea Michele's, from *Glee*. Yet the movie made only $19 million worldwide – 27% of the production cost. Most people blame it on the critics. But if that's the case, how could a movie like *Teenage Mutant Ninja Turtles*, which critics disliked just as much, make nearly 200 million dollars in the same year?

③ ________________: Unless you were hiding in a cave in the late 2000s, there was no escaping the first *Twilight* movie, a smash hit despite the mixed reviews. Why did it become so massive? Possibly because it hit the screens just four months after the final *Twilight* novel, a cultural phenomenon. But then surely the same formula should have worked for *Joey*, released a few months after the wildly popular *Friends* finale in 2004. Yet *Joey* never caught on and was canceled due to poor ratings. So what did *Friends* have that *Joey* lacked? Maybe the chemistry between the characters, but it's hard to tell.

④ ________________: In the competitive New York theater scene, investors often base their musicals on proven hits. Take *Rocky the Musical*. Based on Sylvester Stallone's Oscar-winning movie, the show couldn't go wrong. It was far from a work of art, but it had an impressive production, masculine appeal, and pleasant songs. But, for whatever reason, *Rocky* failed to impress the public and didn't live up to expectations, running for six months only. Why did it never match the success of *Lion King*?

⑤ The truth is that no one really knows. Sometimes things just don't work as planned. Even with the most important ingredients in place, there is always an element of luck. C'est la vie!

C Re-read. T (true) or F (false)? Underline all the evidence.

1 iTunes users' reaction didn't come as a surprise.
2 *Legends of Oz* had a lot of potential.
3 The *Twilight* movies were extremely popular in the 2000s.
4 Musicals based on movies tend to be financially risky.
5 Broadway shows are never aimed at men.

D 7.9 Read *Noun, verb, or both?* In which two pairs of underlined words in the article does the meaning change? Listen to check.

Noun, verb, or both?

Nouns and verbs usually have the same meaning: *I sometimes* ***shop*** *(v) for rare CDs in a small record* ***shop*** *(n).*
But sometimes the meaning changes: *I'll be very upset if somebody's phone* ***rings*** *(v) during* ***Lord of the Rings*** *(n).*

Same	answer, cause, delay, damage, email, fight, guess, help, need, offer, practice, promise, rain, request, search, support, tweet, vote
Different	book, rock, show, trip

Lesson Aims: Sts learn vocabulary to talk about flops, and the reasons for their failure.

Skills
Reading an article about big projects with high hopes that fail

Language
Talking about flops: *It didn't live up to my expectations. The movie lacked depth and soul.*

Pronunciation
Stress patterns in nouns and verbs

Vocabulary
backfire, catch on, fail to, lack, live up to
Words that can be nouns, verbs, or both, e.g. *flop, hit, match, release*

Warm-up

Prepare slips of paper or board the questions: *How often do you go to the movies? Do you read movie reviews to help you choose which movie you go and see? Do the reviews affect whether you go and see the movie or not? How often do you agree / disagree with the movie reviews? What's the best movie you've ever seen? What's the worst movie you've ever seen?* Sts mingle and discuss.

Seated in pairs, sts ask and answer the question title, '*What's the best movie you've ever seen?*' Classcheck. Help them find (or search online) the name in English if they don't know it.

5 Reading

A Cover the article and focus only on the title. Quickly in pairs and then as a class, sts guess what 'flop' means. Don't confirm, as sts now read paragraph 1 to check. Paircheck. Classcheck.

Elicit synonyms for *flop*, e.g. *failure, disaster*. Ask: *Why do you think the writer chose to use "flop" in the title?* (because it rhymes with top). *Have they ever heard the expression Top of the pops?*

B 7.8 Read the boxed headings to the class. Then set 90 seconds to read the rest of the text (to force reading quickly for gist), and match the headings to the paragraphs.

Paircheck. Ask: *How was that?* to get sts to talk about the experience of trying to read quickly, struggling with new words, and still not being sure about the answers. This may be painful, but the aim is to get sts asking genuine questions about the skill of Reading, how they struggle to read in English, and how to improve things.

Classcheck. Have sts echo the pinked words after hearing each paragraph. Drill any harder ones. There's still a detailed reading task in C, so refrain from a lot of explanation. Tell sts you're experimenting, trying to help them live without knowing every word and practice specific, real-life reading skills.

Answers

2 Reviews 3 Timing 4 Risk-taking

Optional activity

Stronger classes Use the recording for shadow reading, i.e. play it with sts simultaneously reading aloud at the same time. This can help sts improve their fluency and intonation.

C Sts read the statements carefully, then re-read the text to decide if the statements are true or false. Give sts a little longer this time to read the text for detail. Tell them to underline the evidence in the text. Paircheck, then classcheck.

Answers

1 F – *how can anyone say no to a present?*
2 T – *had a lot going for it, it had tons of promotion and featured famous voices*
3 T – *Unless you were hiding in a cave in the late 2000s, there was no escaping the first Twilight movie, a smash hit*
4 F – *investors often base their musicals on proven hits … , Based on … the show couldn't go wrong*
5 F – *it had … masculine appeal*

D 7.9 Read **Noun, verb, or both?** and go through the meanings of the words in the table. Ask sts to look up the unknown words in a dictionary. Remind them to check the abbreviations after the words (*n.* = noun, *vb.* = verb, *adj.* = adjective).

Ask sts to look at the underlined words in the article and find the two pairs where the meaning changes between the noun and verb.

Play the audio to classcheck. Write the underlined words from the text on the board, and ask whether they are nouns or verbs. Write n. or v. next to each word. Elicit the meanings for each of the words, and have sts say which pairs of words have different meanings. Ask: *Is this common in your language?*

Answers

hit (n.) = big success / hit (v.) = appear on
match (n.) = pairing or combination / match (v). = compare favorably with

See Teacher's Book p.322 for Audio script 7.9.

6 Vocabulary: Failure expressions

A Sts read the rubric and example to see what to do. They ought to be able to do it without needing any vocabulary first, but a still of *House of Cards* (a Netflix series) or Adam Sandler would help.

Paircheck after two minutes. Classcheck one sentence at a time, and personalize each of them, asking: *Do you like House of Cards/Maroon 5/Sandler? How many of you watched the Brazil-Germany game?*

Weaker classes: Work through the remaining sentences together as a class, and write them on the board.

Stronger classes: Sts can try immediately to create a brand new example of their own while the rest finish.

Answers

1 I had high hopes for the third season of *Game of Cards*, but it didn't live up to expectations.
2 The latest Stephen King novel failed to generate any interest. Nobody talked about it.
3 I'll never understand why the latest Maroon 5 single never caught on. It was such a good song.
4 Most critics say the latest Adam Sandler movie lacked "depth and soul", but I thought it was awesome.
5 Brazil was confident of winning the 2014 World Cup, but maybe this confidence backfired. Their team lost to Germany 7–1.

B Make it personal Read the instructions with the class and and use the speech bubble to exemplify. Go through the **Common mistake box** as many sts at this level still have difficulty using names as adjectives.

Each st chooses a topic and writes two more sentences. In pairs, they share opinions and ask follow-up questions. Encourage them to expand on their views and really explore the potential content. Time permitting, turn this into a class mingle.

Stronger classes: Ask sts to rewrite all the sentences in 6A, replacing the underlined words with their own ideas.

7 Pronunciation: Stress patterns in nouns and verbs

A 7.10 Focus on the sentences. Ask sts if "present" is a noun or a verb in each sentence.

Elicit/Use the audio to listen and check where the stress falls. The pink stress gives it away, but no matter! Ask: *What do you notice?* (the stress changes).

Sts complete the rules. Replay the audio for sts to listen and repeat both sentences as well as they can.

Answers

Some words are stressed on the first syllable when they're used as nouns and on the second syllable when they're used as verbs.

Optional activity

Elicit other pairs of words (nouns and verbs) sts know where the stress changes, e.g. *insult* (noun) / *insult* (verb), *object* (noun) / *object* (verb), *export* (noun) / *export* (verb), *conflict* (noun) / *conflict* (verb).

Song lyric: See Teacher's Book p.342 for notes about the song and an accompanying activity to do with the class.

B 7.11 In pairs, sts predict the stress, then say the sentences to each other as they think it will be said, including the rising or falling intonation.

Play the audio for them to check. Did they get all the pronunciation right, stress and intonation? Quickly practice any they didn't.

Answers

1 project 2 increased 3 rebel 4 record 5 progress 6 refund

C Make it personal In groups, sts discuss the questions. Monitor for stress and intonation and add some prompts/extra questions to help them open out their discussion.

Classcheck by getting sts to report their partner's most interesting answer(s).

Weaker classes: Have sts do 7C in pairs first to give them more practice before going on to discuss in groups.

Workbook p.35.

6 Vocabulary: Failure expressions

A Rewrite 1–5, substituting the bold words with the highlighted words in the article in 5B.

1 I had high hopes for the third season of *House of Cards*, but it **didn't** really **meet** my expectations.
I had high hopes for the third season of House of Cards, but it didn't live up to expectations.

2 The latest Stephen King novel **didn't manage to** generate any interest. Nobody talked about it.

3 I'll never understand why the latest Maroon 5 single **didn't become popular**. It was such a good song.

4 Most critics say the latest Adam Sandler movie **didn't have** "depth and soul," but I thought it was awesome.

5 Brazil was confident of winning the 2014 World Cup, but maybe this confidence **had the opposite effect**. Their team lost to Germany 7–1.

B Make it personal In pairs, share opinions on recent flops you remember. Any surprises?

A Choose two examples in A and replace the underlined words with your own opinions.

B Ask follow-up questions and continue the conversation.

books movies music plays restaurants soccer teams TV shows

I had high hopes for that new Turkish restaurant, but it didn't really live up to expectations. The service was great, but the food really wasn't anything special.

Common mistake

I've just streamed ~~the new John Legend's album~~ *the new John Legend album / John Legend's new album*.

7 Pronunciation: Stress patterns in nouns and verbs

A 7.10 Listen to the examples from the article. Then complete with "verbs" or "nouns."

How can anyone say *no* to a **present**?
Sometimes unexpected problems **present** themselves.

Some words are stressed on the first syllable when they're used as ______ and on the second syllable when they're used as ______ .

B 7.11 Predict the stressed syllable in the bold words. Then listen, check, and repeat.

1 Are you in the middle of an important **project** right now?

2 Have noise, pollution, and traffic **increased** in your city recently?

3 Who's the **rebel** in your family?

4 Do you ever **record** yourself in English?

5 How much **progress** have you made with English this year?

6 When was the last time you got a **refund**?

C Make it personal In groups, ask and answer 1–6 in B. Anything in common?

It's not exactly a project, but I'm midway through my final exams. What a nightmare!

I know the feeling. How's it going?

7.4 When was the last time you went to a museum?

8 Language in use

A In groups, which of the three paintings do you like most / least? Why?

I'm not sure. The da Vinci is beautiful, but there's nothing to see in the background.

I love Kahlo's hair. But the portrait itself doesn't do anything for me.

I'm not really into modern art at all. The one I like least is ...

1

Pre-impressionism

Lady with an Ermine
Leonardo da Vinci

2

Impressionism

Dancers in Blue
Edgar Degas

3

Modern

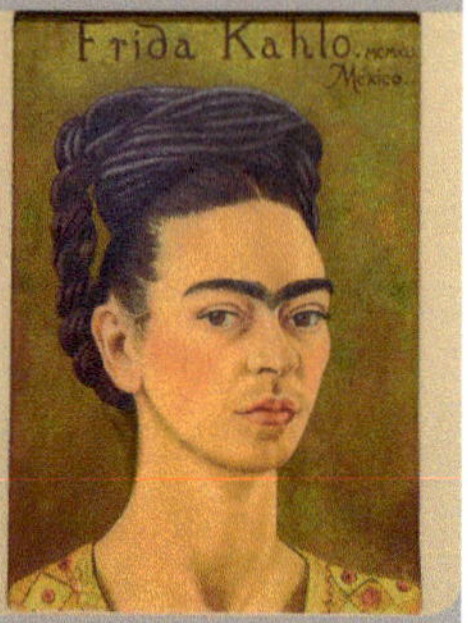

Self Portrait
Frida Kahlo

B 7.12 Listen to Rick and his friend Peter. Why is Rick worried? What does Peter suggest?

C 7.13 Read the guide and match the highlighted verbs to pictures 1–5. Listen to check. When do you do each action?

How to pretend you're ... an art expert

1 Stare thoughtfully, but don't squint as if you need glasses. Act classy.

2 Rub your chin to look intellectual, but don't scratch your head. You'll appear dumb!

3 Examine the piece closely, walk back two steps, and deliver an enigmatic "hmmm." And another one.

4 Listen carefully to the others in your group. If asked a question, frown a little, as if searching your vast mental repertoire.

5 Let the other person do most of the talking by replying with another question.

6 Learn to invent words with the prefix *meta*, meaning "of a higher order." Say, "What an interesting metaperspective!" People may look puzzled, but will probably nod in agreement.

1

2

3

4

5

I scratch my head when it itches, or when I'm thinking.

D Make it personal In groups, answer 1–4. Anything in common?

1 What can go wrong when you try to impress people like that?
2 Would you ever date someone with completely different interests from you?
3 Do you have a favorite painting, photo, statue, or museum?
4 Have you ever pretended to be knowledgeable about something?

One day my girlfriend's dad started quizzing me on classical music. Not my specialty!

Lesson Aims: Sts learn vocabulary to talk about art, and read advice on how to pretend you're an art expert.

Skills	Language	Vocabulary	Grammar
Listening to two friends talking about a date that one of them is going on Reading a "How to ..." guide about bluffing in art	Talking about art: *The portrait doesn't do anything for me.*	*background, date* (n. and v.), *frown, impressionism, nod, portrait, rub, scratch, squint*	Modifying nouns: *another, some other, the other, the others*

Warm-up

Board the name of some world famous pieces of art, e.g. *Mona Lisa* (Da Vinci), *The Last Supper* (Da Vinci), *The Thinker* (Rodin), *Starry Night* (Van Gogh), *Aphrodite of Milo* (Antioch), etc. In pairs, sts share/ guess information about them, e.g. *Is it a sculpture or paiting? What is it about? Which museum can you see it in?* If technology available, Google images and show the pieces of art to classcheck.

In pairs, sts ask and answer the lesson title question: *When was the last time you went to a museum?* They can ask you first to exemplify. Encourage follow-up questions.

8 Language in use

A Focus on the three paintings. Ask: *What do they have in common?* (all women). Elicit what sts know about each one, the artist and the three genres in white. Board adjectives for each in two groups (and leave them up for later):

\+ *striking, dramatic, impressive, stunning, extraordinary,*

– *dull, unexceptional, boring, weird.*

Go through the comments in the speech bubbles. Add *It doesn't do anything for me* to the list on the board.

In groups, sts discuss which painting they like most / least and why.

Background information

Lady with an Ermine, painted by Leonardo da Vinci in around 1489–1490. Commissioned by the Duke of Milan, the subject of the painting is a 16-year-old girl called Cecilia Gallerani, who was reputedly the Duke's mistress. The white winter fur of the ermine is a traditional symbol of purity.

Dancers in Blue, painted in about 1895, features a small group of ballerinas back stage. Opera and ballet were a fashionable part of Parisian cultural life, and more than half of Degas' work featured dancing bodies.

Self Portrait (in Red and Gold dress), painted in 1941, is one of the many self-portraits which made up her work. They are striking and shocking self-portraits which reflect the physical and psychological suffering she endured during her life.

B 7.12 Explain that Rick is telling Peter about a date he is going on. Sts listen and answer the questions. Paircheck.

Answers

Rick has a date with a woman who knows a lot about art. Rick knows nothing about art, and is afraid she will think he's stupid. Peter suggests Googling ways to pretend to be an art expert.

See Teacher's Book p.322 for Audio script 7.12.

Optional activity

Ask sts to listen again and answer these questions:

When did Rick last go on a date? (six months ago)

Where did Rick meet the woman? (at a party)

How does he describe her? (amazing, good-looking, funny, sweet, smart)

C 7.13 Focus on the pictures and elicit that he's an art expert. Ask: *What's he doing in each picture?* Encourage guesses if they don't know. Have them read the guide quickly and match the highlighted words to the pictures.

Play the audio for sts to check their answers. Ask: *What did you think of the advice in the text? Would doing these things make you look/sound like an expert?* Elicit situations where sts would do each action, e.g. *frown*: when you are annoyed, worried, or thinking hard.

Answers

1 frown 2 rub 3 scratch 4 squint 5 nod

See Teacher's Book p.323 for Audio script 7.13.

Optional activity

In pairs, ask sts to mime the highlighted words in C. Student A mimes one of the words, and Student B has to guess what it is.

D Make it personal Get sts to ask you the questions one by one to set this up, adding follow-up questions too. Clarify any problems. e.g. *to bluff* (= pretend you know a lot about a topic you know nothing about).

In groups, sts discuss questions 1–4.

Class feedback, inviting a few sts to share their ideas (especially question 4) with the class.

9 Grammar: Modifying nouns

A Sts study sentences 1–5 and underline the nouns in each sentence. Ask: *Which of the nouns are singular / plural / uncountable? Mark them S, P or U.* Sts check the correct rules in the table. Classcheck and deal with any queries.

Focus on sentence 5, and ask: *What does "the others" refer back to?* (choices)

Sts individually race to find three more examples in 8C, and raise a hand as soon as they've found them. Board the examples, underlining both noun and modifier.

Go through the **Common mistakes**. Ask: *Have you made these mistakes?*

Answers

What follows …	another?	some other?	the other?	the others?
a singular noun	✓	✓	✓	
a plural noun		✓	✓	
an uncountable noun		✓	✓	
no noun at all				✓

Some in some other is not optional when nouns are singular.

Examples from 8C:

And another one.

Listen carefully to the others in your group.

Let the other person do most of the talking … replying with another question

Refer sts to the **Grammar expansion** on p.150.

B 7.14 Ask sts: *Do you have any friends who know a lot about art? How do you think the date between Rick and Sue went?*

Give sts 30 seconds to skim their conversation and get the general meaning. Ask: *Do you think Rick has impressed Sue with his knowledge of art?*

Sts complete the extract individually, then paircheck. Play the audio to classcheck. As a class, speculate about how their date ended.

Answers

1 the others 2 another 3 other 4 Other 5 another

See Teacher's Book p.323 for Audio script 7.14.

Optional activity

Have sts roleplay the dialogue in 9B. Make sure they swap roles.

Song lyric: See Teacher's Book p.342 for notes about the song and an accompanying activity to do with the class.

C Set this up as a class, and make some suggestions. Student A will be a knowledgeable art critic, B someone who's trying to bluff! In pairs, sts brainstorm ideas for their roles and google a painting. Monitor and help as necessary. Sts can note down phrases / a skeleton for their ideas to help them.

Note: If nothing else is available, sts could use a photo from their phone, pretending it's a painting.

Get them to rehearse in pairs and swap roles to see who is more comfortable in each. Invite pairs to act out their roleplay for the class. With a larger class, group pairs to role play to each other. Classcheck. Ask: *Who sounds like the most convincing art critic. And the best bluffer?*

D Make it personal Give individuals a minute to read the quotes and choose the correct form. Tell them to use their instinct, even if they don't entirely understand it. Paircheck, then classcheck. Elicit the meaning of *close-knit* and *impulse*.

Brainstorm what the class knows about the five authors. In pairs, sts interpret and discuss the quotes, as in the example. Open up to a class discussion. Ask: *Which of the quotes do sts agree with most?*

Answers

1 another 2 others 3 the other 4 another 5 other

Background information

George Burns (1896–1996) was an American comedian, actor, singer and writer, whose career spanned vaudeville theatre, radio, film and TV.

Rosa Parks (1913–2005) was an African-American civil right activist. She was called "the first lady of civil rights," and the "mother of the freedom movement."

Walter Annenberg (1908–2002) was an American media tycoon. He made a huge success of his family's magazine business extending it into radio and TV.

Angelina Jolie, born in 1975 is an American actress, film-maker and humanitarian.

John Lennon (1940–1980) was a British singer and song-writer. He was co-founder and member of the Beatles, one of the most commercially successful pop groups of all time.

Workbook p.36.

9 Grammar: Modifying nouns

A Study sentences 1–5 and check (✔) the correct rules. Find three more examples in 8C.

1 Let's look at **another** website.
2 I'd like to find **(some) other** information / opinions.
3 There must be **some other** way to do it.
4 I think **the other** advice / idea / people might be more helpful.
5 I like the first three choices, but **the others** don't appeal to me.

Modifying nouns: *Another, some other, the other,* and *the others*

What follows ...	*another?*	*some other?*	*the other?*	*the others?*
a singular noun	✔			
a plural noun				
an uncountable noun				
no noun at all				

Use ***the*** to refer back to a noun already mentioned. ***One*** is often added when the noun is singular: *Do you prefer this* ***photo*** *or* ***the other*** *(****one****)?*

Some in ***some other*** is not optional when nouns are ☐ singular ☐ uncountable ☐ plural.

Common mistakes

I'm sorry, I can't tonight. I have ~~another / others / the other~~ *(some) other* plans. Maybe ~~other~~ *another* time?

Grammar expansion p.150

B 7.14 Complete the extract with *another, other,* or *the others*. Listen to check. Imagine how their date ended.

SUE: This one's nice. I like it better than [1] ________ .
RICK: Hmm ... Let me look at it [2] ________ time. Yes, I agree. It really captures the essence of passion, conflict, and ... and some [3] ________ things.
SUE: I guess.
RICK: And don't you just love his use of color? Experimental, but structured.
SUE: Err ...
RICK: [4] ________ artists may try, but nobody comes close to Picasso.
SUE: But that's a Kandinsky.
RICK: Oh, yes, you're right. It's [5] ________ metaperspective, isn't it?
SUE: What's that supposed to mean?

C In pairs, find another painting and adapt / role play the conversation in 9B. Role play for the class. Who sounds most like an art critic?

D Make it personal Choose the correct form. In pairs, explain each quote. Who do you agree with most?

1 "Happiness is having a large, loving, caring, close-knit family in [**another** / **other**] city." (George Burns)
2 "Each person must live life as a model for [**others people** / **others**]." (Rosa Parks)
3 "Live rich, die poor; never make the mistake of doing it [**other** / **the other**] way round." (Walter Annenberg)
4 "I believe in living on impulse as long as you never intentionally hurt [**other** / **another**] person." (Angelina Jolie)
5 "Life is what happens while you are busy making [**other** / **others**] plans." (John Lennon)

I think Annenberg is saying we worry too much about the future and don't enjoy the present.

10 Listening

A Do you recognize the musician on the right? His initials are M.D. Guess what the quote refers to, too.

It is one of the single greatest achievements in recorded music.

B 7.15 Listen to two friends talking about *Kind of Blue*. Match the musicians to the comments (1–3). Then search *Kind of Blue* and listen to a few minutes of the album. Do you agree with these quotes?

1 How do you go to the studio with minimum stuff and come out with eternity?

2 If there's one record and we've all said it, but it's true, that captures the essence of jazz for a variety of reasons, it would have to be *Kind of Blue*.

3 It's a cornerstone record, not only for jazz. It's a cornerstone record for music.

Definitely. I closed my eyes and started dreaming. Beautiful!

It's a bit slow, with no lyrics. It made me feel kind of lonely.

C 7.16 Listen to the rest of the conversation. T (True) or F (False)? Correct the false statements.

1 In the 1950s, jazz in New York City was played mainly in Harlem.
2 Jazz was so popular that players were in the media regularly.
3 Duke Ellington and Count Basie were popular before Miles Davis.
4 In the 1950s, if you liked R & B (Rhythm and Blues), you couldn't possibly like jazz.
5 Miles was the "essence of hipness" (ultra cool) because he went to Juilliard Music School.

11 Keep talking

A Choose a favorite album. Note down answers to 1–6. Search online as necessary.

1 What's the album called and who recorded it? When?
2 What type of music would you say it is?
3 What makes the music really special?
4 Which is your favorite track? Who wrote it?
5 Are there any tracks that were a letdown? Ones you usually skip?
6 Was the album commercially successful? Locally? Globally?

My all-time favorite is Ivete Sangalo's live album. It came out in 2014. Her music is so easy to dance to.

She's fun, but I'm not really into her music or the lyrics. I prefer songs with a message.

B In groups, discuss your chosen albums. Is everybody familiar with them?

Lesson Aims: Sts listen to a discussion about jazz music, and write their own album reviews.

Skills	Language	Vocabulary	Grammar
Listening to two friends talking about jazz music Discussing a favorite album Writing an album review: using adverbs	Talking about music: *My all-time favorite album is ... , She has an amazingly good voice*	*all-time, capture the essence, awesome, catchy, track, lyrics, melody, cornerstone, letdown, skip*	Adverbs: to modify nouns, verbs, adjectives and whole ideas

Warm-up

Have some jazz playing as they come in, ideally Miles Davis, *Kind of Blue*. Board *Famous jazz musicians*. Sts brainstorm a few. Younger classes may not know any, so brainstorm the music their (grand)parents listened to. Ask: *What instruments do you associate with jazz music?* Elicit *saxophone, piano, guitar, trumpet, trombone, drums, clarinet, double bass*. Ask: *Do you play a musical instrument? Have you played jazz music? Do you ever listen to jazz music?* Sts discuss the questions in pairs.

Ask the lesson title question: *Which musician do you listen to most?* and natural follow-up questions. Sts brainstorm answers and call them out or do this as quick mingle.

10 Listening

A Ask: *Do you recognize the musician on the right? Use his initials as a clue. What instrument is he playing?* Read the quote together and encourage sts to guess what it refers to. Elicit the photo is Miles Davis and the quote is about his album *Kind of Blue*. Show an image of the cover if you can. Do any of them know it?

Background information

Ed Bradley (1941–2006) American journalist best-known for working on a television program called *60 Minutes*, and interviewed musicians like Mick Jagger, Michael Jackson, and Bob Dylan.

Miles Davies (1926–1991) American jazz musician and trumpeter. His most famous album was *Kind of Blue*, released in 1959, and generally regarded as the definitive jazz album.

B 7.15 Ask: *What do you know about the musicians in the photos?* In trios, sts could quickly Google one each.

Sts read comments 1–3. Play the audio for sts to listen and match the people with the quotes. Paircheck. Classcheck.

Sts search online and listen to a few minutes of *Kind of Blue* to see if they like it. Focus on the example. Ask if they agree with the quotes and for their own opinions.

Answers

1 Carlos Santana 2 David Liebman 3 Herbie Hancock

See Teacher's Book p.323 for Audio script 7.15.

Background information

Herbie Hancock, born in 1940, is an American pianist, and played with Miles Davis in the Miles Davis quintet.

Carlos Santana, born in 1947 is a Mexican and American musician, famous in the late 60s and 70s with his band Santana.

Dave Liebman, born in 1946, is considered one of the most important saxophonists in contemporary music.

C 7.16 Sts read the statements carefully and underline the key words. Then play the audio for sts to listen and mark the statements true or false. Play the audio a second time, if necessary, for sts to correct the false statements. Classcheck.

Answers

1 F (Jazz was played everywhere across the city from Greenwich village to Harlem.)
2 T 3 T
4 F (Teenagers who liked R & B came to appreciate the jazz their parents listened to.)
5 F Miles was hip because of the way he looked, dressed, and played.

See Teacher's Book p.323 for Audio script 7.16.

11 Keep talking

A Read through the instructions. Point out that they can choose any type of music. It doesn't have to be jazz.

Elicit the meaning of *letdown* (= disappointment), and *to skip a track* (= to miss it out). Read through the speech bubbles, and highlight the expression *all-time*. Tell sts we can also say *My favorite album of all time is ...* . Give sts time to make notes for each question.

B In groups, sts discuss their favorite albums, or, alternatively, interview each other in pairs (see Optional activity below).

Optional activity

In pairs, sts interview each other about their favorite albums. A plays the role of music journalist and asks questions 1–6 in 11A, and B answers the questions about their favorite album. Then swap roles.

12 Writing: Writing a review

A Cover up the text, and ask: *Who is the singer in the photo? Do you like her music?* In pairs, sts note down as much as they know about Beyoncé. Class share their ideas. Ask: *Is there a better/more famous/powerful female singer around today?*

Sts read the review and find the answers to the questions in 11A. Point out that part of one of them is not answered.

Paircheck, then classcheck. Highlight the expression *catchiest* from the adjective *catchy*, and elicit the meaning (= pleasant and easily remembered). Elicit pronunciation of the pinked words. *Which if them are (near) cognates?*

Answers

1 *Beyoncé*, recorded by Beyoncé in 2013.
2 Electronica, hip-hop, disco, and R&B.
3 She experiments with different genres / powerful / catchiest melodies.
4 *Heaven* and *Rocket* (the review doesn't say who wrote the songs)
5 No, there's not a single letdown.
6 It managed to sell close to a million copies in two weeks.

Song lyric: See Teacher's Book p.342 for notes about the song and an accompanying activity to do with the class.

B Read **Write it right!** with the class. Ask what they notice about the position of the adverb in each case (The adverb comes before the noun, adjective or adverb. When modifying a whole idea, the adverb comes at the beginning of a the sentence, and is followed by a comma.)

Ask sts to find more examples of *-ly* adverbs in the review, and classify them a–c. Classcheck.

Answers

a truly great album, a deeply powerful song
b she cleverly experiments, I firmly believe
c Thankfully, her fifth album, *Beyoncé*, released at the end of 2013, proved me wrong, honestly, there's not a single letdown, Incredibly, it managed to sell close to a million copies ...

Tip

Comparing adverb use for Romance language speakers, for example, is very motivating as their form is mainly easy, and their use similar and there are a lot of near cognates. Spelling can be an issue, so give them the rules.

To make adverbs from adjectives that end in:

- *-l* or *-e*, add *-ly*: *specia**lly**, nice**ly***
- *-y*, remove the *-y* and add *-ily*: *happ**ily***
- consonant + *le*, remove the *-e* and add *-y*: *terrib**ly***
- *ic*, add *-ally*: *enthusiastic**ally***

C Go through the **Common mistakes** and ask sts what is wrong in each case (the position of the adverb). As ever, personalize, asking: *Are these mistakes you have made/ might make?*

Sts complete the sentences with the correct adverbs. Classcheck.

Weaker classes: Before the exercise, elicit, and board the adverbs for each one. Sts can also practice saying them together enthusiastically at the end to feel more confident.

Answers

1 easily 2 consistently 3 Unfortunately 4 Sadly
5 absolutely 6 wonderfully 7 disappointingly
8 consistently, occasionally

D **Your turn!** Explain that sts are going to write their own album review. It can be a singer or a group, and any genre of music.

Ask sts to look at the review in 12A again. Ask them which of the paragraphs:

a) describes the album itself? (2)
b) gives the writer's opinion of the album? (4)
c) describes how well it did? (3)
d) says how long, and why you are fan of this singer / group? (1)

Encourage sts to use this paragraph structure as a guide.

Read through the instructions with the class and check that everyone understands what they have to do. Sts could start this in class and then finish for homework. Set a deadline for sts to post their review online. Assign each student a partner to read each other's review and peer correct.

Optional activity

Have sts read each other's reviews. Ask them to say which review they found most useful, and which album they would most like to listen to. They can always swap albums together, and even write follow-up reviews!

Tip

If this is the first time you use the book, ensure you keep the best ones, and use them as models next time you teach this lesson. Seeing models from previous sts about locally well-known albums is highly motivating, and it will save you a lot of marking the second time if you leave your corrections in place, for the next class of sts to learn from them in advance, a sort of personalized **Common mistakes**!

Workbook p.37.

12 Writing: Writing a review

A Read the review on the right and underline the answers to the questions in 11A.

B Read *Write it right!* Underline seven more examples of *-ly* adverbs in the review and mark them a–c.

Write it right!

In a review, use adverbs to make your attitude clear and your ideas more "colorful." Adverbs can modify:

a An adjective or another adverb: She has an ***amazingly*** *good* voice. *She sings* ***extremely*** *well.*

b A verb: *I* ***highly*** *recommend this album.*

c A whole idea: ***Surprisingly****, sales didn't live up to expectations.*

Common mistakes

Chris Botti plays ~~incredibly well the trumpet~~ *the trumpet incredibly well*.

I ~~recommend highly his music~~ *highly recommend his music / recommend his music highly*.

C Complete music review excerpts 1–8 in the most logical way. Check your spelling!

consistent	~~easy~~	unfortunate

1 This is easily their best album in a decade – no doubt about it.
2 This collection is ______ awesome, from beginning to end.
3 ______, some of the tracks leave you a bit cold.

absolute	wonderful	sad

4 I really wanted to love their live performance. ______, I didn't.
5 I ______ adored the new CD. It exceeded all my expectations.
6 Throughout, it is fun, romantic, and has ______ written lyrics.

occasional	disappointing	consistent

7 I enjoyed this CD, but, ______, there are only 10 tracks in the standard edition.
8 It's ______ good, from start to finish, rather than only ______ great.

She rules the world!

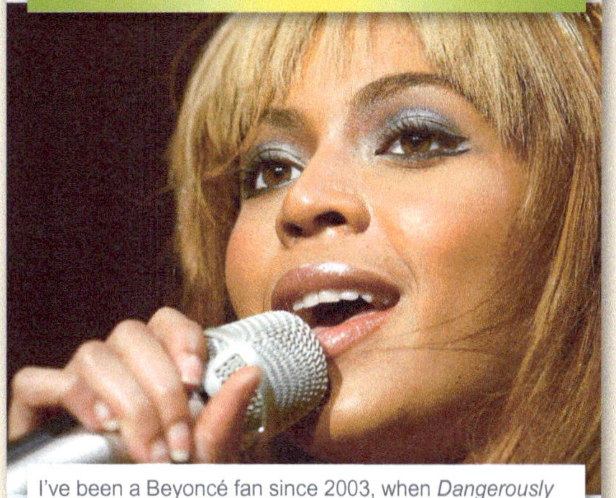

I've been a Beyoncé fan since 2003, when *Dangerously in Love* came out. Her last truly great album was the 2008 smash hit *I Am ... Sasha Fierce*, so I was starting to lose hope and doubt that she would ever release another masterpiece like that. Thankfully, her fifth album, *Beyoncé*, released at the end of 2013, proved me wrong.

What I love about this album is the way she cleverly experiments with different genres. There are elements of electronica, hip-hop, disco, and R&B, of course. The album starts off with *Pretty Hurts* (co-written by superstar Sia), a deeply powerful song about the pressure to look perfect. The other 14 tracks will take you on the musical journey of a lifetime, with some of the catchiest melodies you'll ever hear. My personal favorites are *Heaven* and *Rocket*, but, honestly, there's not a single letdown. And *Blue* as a finale is just a great way to end the album.

As everyone knows, *Beyoncé* was a surprise release, with zero promotion other than an Instagram® post. Incredibly, it managed to sell close to a million copies in two weeks, which I bet even *Queen Bey* herself wasn't expecting. But even more impressive is the fact that the album featured 17 music videos – something no one had ever done before.

I'm not a professional critic, but I firmly believe that *Beyoncé* is one of the best albums of the 2010s. It's mature without being boring, courageous without being forced, and entertaining without being silly. It's just the sort of album that both fans and non-fans will fall in love with.

D Your turn! Write your own review in about 200 words.

Before
Order your notes from 11A into three paragraphs, including an introduction. Then think of a conclusion.

While
Use at least four adverbs from 12C.

After
Proofread and then post your review online. Share the link with your class.

8 Has fear ever held you back?

1 Listening

A 8.1 Listen to the ad. Brainstorm other common fears and add them to the three groups in the ad.

Another real fear is that your boyfriend or girlfriend might meet someone new.

F.E.A.R. = False Evidence Appearing Real
Fear is everywhere!
• **Real fears** (losing your job, getting ill, offending people)
• **Fears we love** (scary movies, theme park rides)
• **Exaggerated or even irrational fears** (flying, public speaking, confined spaces, the dark), which can be really upsetting
Email a video to IQYP TV talking about your worst fear, and you could be invited to our groundbreaking show, *Making F.E.A.R. disappear*.

B 8.2 Listen to the beginning of three stories. What is each person afraid of? Are any of your ideas in A mentioned?

C 8.3 Listen to the full stories. Who answer(s) each question, Lucy, Rob, or Donna?

1 How long have you had this fear?
2 How did your fear begin?
3 Do you experience any physical symptoms?
4 How supportive are your family and friends?
5 What have you done to overcome your fear?

D 8.3 Listen again. In pairs, answer one question for each person.

E **Make it personal** Don't panic! In groups, share your fears.

1 8.4 **How to say it** Complete the sentences from the conversation. Listen to check.

Expressing fears

	What they said	What they meant
1	I'm ____ of (spiders).	I'm really afraid of ...
2	(Clowns) freak me ____ .	
3	I ____ (flying) if I can.	I'm not comfortable with ...
4	(Cockroaches) make me a bit ____ .	
5	(Dolls) don't ____ me.	I'm not afraid of ...
6	I don't ____ (bats) at all.	

Lesson Aims: Sts learn vocabulary to discuss fears and the physical symptoms of fears, and talk about scary experiences.

Skills	Language	Vocabulary
Listening to interviews with people talking about their fears Discussing scary experiences	Expressing fears: *I'm petrified of flying. Clowns freak me out.*	*burst into tears, fear, get butterflies, get dizzy, pass out, race, sweat, symptom* Expressing fears: *be terrified of, freak s.o. out, avoid + -ing* form, *make s.o. uneasy, bother*

Warm-up

Ask: *Do you get frightened easily? What sort of things are you afraid of? How do you feel when you get frightened?*

Board the lesson title question: *Has fear ever held you back (from doing something)?* Personalize with an example yourself, e.g. *I've never been able to bungee jump.* In pairs, sts discuss. Classcheck their best ideas.

1 Listening

A 8.1 Cover the text and focus on the large yellow title title. *F.E.A.R* Ask: *What is it?* (an acronym) *What do you understand by 'False Evidence Appearing Real'?* Elicit that it means feeling afraid for irrational reasons. Ask: *Do you think most fears are real or irrational?*

Ask: *What's the text about?* Elicit that it's an ad (inviting people to appear on a TV show about fear).

Play the audio for sts to listen, read and note the sound effects.

See Teacher's Book p.323 for Audio 8.1.

Tip

You'll have to pause the audio a lot for this to work, but breaking audios into small chunks like this is 1) great fun and 2) excellent pronunciation practice as they're trying to echo short chunks accurately, without being asked to remember too much.

Ask: *Do you agree with this division of fears into three categories?* Brainstorm other common fears and add them to the right category. Monitor and help with new vocabulary as necessary.

B 8.2 Focus on the photos and explain that sts are going to listen to the three people talking about their fears. Ask them to listen to the beginning of each story, and find out what they are afraid of. Peercheck, then classcheck asking: *Which of their fears from A were mentioned?*

Answers

Lucy – being a passenger in a vehicle
Rob – spiders
Donna – clowns

See Teacher's Book p.323 for Audio script 8.2.

C 8.3 Sts read the questions before they listen. Play the audio for them to write *Lucy, Rob*, or *Donna* next to each question. Paircheck, then classcheck.

Answers

1 Lucy 2 Rob, Donna 3 Lucy, Rob 4 Rob, Donna 5 Lucy

See Teacher's Book p.323 for Audio script 8.3.

D 8.3 Look back at questions 1-6. Re-play the audio for sts to note each person's answers. Emphasize first that each person does not answer all of the questions.

In pairs, sts answer one question for each person (Lucy, Rob and Donna), e.g. A: *Lucy, how long have you had this fear?* B: *About ten years.*

Class feedback working through the questions answering them for each person. If necessary re-play parts of the audio. Ask: *What do you think of each person and their fear?*

Answers

1 Lucy: About ten years.
2 Rob: When I found a huge spider under my pillow.
Donna: I think it comes from TV.
3 Lucy: I get really dizzy ... my heart starts to race ... I get butterflies in my stomach.
Rob: I can't breathe whenever I see a picture of a spider ... and I start to sweat.
4 Rob: My wife tries to keep bugs out of the house ... my parents aren't exactly sympathetic.
Donna: Someone has to hold my hand until I stop crying.
5 Lucy: I've read a couple of self-help books.

E Make it personal

1 8.4 **How to say it** In pairs, sts pre-read gapped sentences 1-6 trying to remember who said them.

Sts complete them, then listen and check. Re-play the audio, pausing after each sentence for sts to repeat, copying the stress and intonation.

Elicit other synonyms for *terrified* (*petrified, really scared, scared stiff*). Many will know the Gloria Gaynor song beginning: *First I was afraid I was petrified*, which is a nice prompt.

Answers

1 terrified 2 out 3 avoid 4 uneasy 5 bother 6 mind

2 Get them to interview you to set this up. Stop before question d so you don't pre-empt their answers.

In groups, sts do the same. Monitor round the class, and make a note of any common errors or good uses of English for delayed correction.

Tip

If you choose to board some errors at the end, get sts both to correct them and then classify the mistakes: *I* (important) or *NI* (not so important), so they have to think. This helps them see that not all mistakes are equal and begin to share a bit more of your correction policy and criterion.

Classcheck. Ask if they learned anything surprising or interesting about each other. If appropriate, take a class vote on question d.

2 Vocabulary: Physical symptoms of fear

A 8.5 Sts cover the speech bubbles, looking only at the cartoons. Ask: *What's happening in the first picture?* Elicit: *He's hot/sweaty/perspiring/nervous/over-heating. What do you think he's saying?* to elicit *I start to sweat.*

In pairs, get sts quickly to do two things: 1) describe what's happening and 2) imagine/note down what each person is saying. Get them to try to say something about each of the pictures, no matter how off they might be! Elicit answers, but don't correct just yet.

In pairs sts uncover and match the speech bubbles to the pictures.

Play the audio for sts to check their answers. Deal with any questions now about the other things they thought of, and help with any errors they made. Ask: *When do you feel these symptoms?* Then personalize more *Have you ever felt like this? When?*

Answers

1 f 2 b 3 a 4 e 5 d 6 c 7 g
People feel these symptoms when they are frightened.

See Teacher's Book p.341 for Audio script 8.5.

Optional activity

In pairs, sts cover speech bubbles and remember/drill the symptoms from the pictures. They can do this in a number of ways, e.g. A pointing to a picture, B saying the sentence or, much more fun, A miming and B having to say that person's words.

Song lyric: See Teacher's Book p.342 for notes about the song and an accompanying activity to do with the class.

B Make it personal

1 Have sts think of a scary experience and make notes. Read through the example in the speech bubble, and highlight the use of the past continuous. Remind sts that we use the past continuous in this way to say that someone was in the middle of doing something when a second action occurred.

Give another example yourself, add in some false details and include three expressions from A to show them they will have to do the same. Get them to guess what was/wasn't true. Then in pairs, sts do the same and share their experiences. Ask: *Do you believe your partner's story? Which bit of it don't you believe?*

Stronger classes: Sts may not feel the need to write notes beforehand.

2 a Tell sts they are going to talk about their fears on the TV show, *Making FEAR disappear*. Have them prepare what they are going to say.

Weaker classes: Give sts time to prepare what they are going to say. Monitor as they do to help with vocabulary, and weed out any errors as early as you can.

b Sts take turns role playing the TV show. Roleplay it twice yourself first to help set this up; once as the interviewer, then with them interviewing you. Remind them to use the questions in 1C and the expressions in 1E. Make sure they take turns to play the role of presenter. Some volunteers might want to do it for the whole class at the end. With the right class, you could get them to video this stage, then watch each other afterwards.

Optional activity

In groups, or as a class, sts offer and discuss suggestions to alleviate the symptoms of fear, e.g. breathe deeply from your stomach, relax your muscles, talk to someone about how you are feeling. Sts feed back to the rest of the class. Ask: *Did you come up with any good ideas? Do you think this would help if you are feeling frightened?*

Workbook p.38.

2 In groups, answer a–d. Use *How to say it* expressions on p.82. Any surprises?

a What are you / others you know most afraid of?

b What have you / they tried to do about it?

c Would you ever send your own testimonial to a show like this? Why (not)?

d Do you agree with the acronym F.E.A.R.? Are most of our fears false?

2 Vocabulary: Physical symptoms of fear

A 8.5 Match 1–7 to pictures a–g. Listen to check. When do you feel these symptoms?

1 I get really dizzy. ☐

2 I can't breathe. ☐

3 I start to sweat. ☐

4 I burst into tears. ☐

5 I almost pass out. ☐

6 My heart starts to race. ☐

7 I get butterflies in my stomach. ☐

My hands start to sweat on a plane when there's turbulence.

B Make it personal Share your scary experiences!

1 In pairs, share a frightening experience (true or made up!), using three expressions. Guess what is (not) true.

I was walking home alone late one night when I heard footsteps right behind me. My heart started to race ...

2 Take turns role playing the TV show. Who's the best actor?

a Plan what to say using the questions in 1C and expressions in 1E.

b Share your fear and answer the "interviewer's" questions.

So, welcome to *Making F.E.A.R. Disappear*. Please introduce yourself and share your fear with us.

Hi, my name's Dan and, please don't laugh, but I'm terrified of going anywhere without my cell phone. I've felt like this for as long as I can remember, and ...

3 Language in use

A 8.6 In pairs, guess the story behind the photo. Listen to check.

I have no idea. Maybe her house was on fire.

But then she wouldn't be smiling, would she?

B 8.7 Listen to the rest of the story. Answer 1–3. Has anything like this ever happened to you?

1 Did Louise try to contact her parents?
2 Was she afraid of heights as a child?
3 Why didn't she enjoy the party?

C 8.6 and 8.7 Who said these lines, L (Louise) or D (Diego)? Order them logically as you think you heard them. Listen again to check.

☐☐ I couldn't find the spare one.

☐☐ So you're telling me you were able to climb the fence?

☐☐ I could climb just about anything.

L 1 I wasn't able to get there until after 10.

☐☐ I think he could see it in my eyes.

☐☐ But you were able to make it to the party ...

D Scan AS 8.6 and 8.7 on p.163. Replace the underlined expressions with 1–6.

1 This might be hard to believe, but ...
2 That's really typical of you.
3 To summarize ...
4 I don't understand.
5 How often does that happen?
6 Why?

E Make it personal In groups, answer 1–5. Any coincidences?

1 Would you have the courage to do what Louise did?
2 Have you ever run into someone you didn't want to see at a party?
3 Name three things that are a) essential for b) can ruin a good party?
4 Are there any items you keep losing?
5 What spare items do you keep, just in case? Where do you keep them?

We keep a spare key hidden outside our apartment, in case we're locked out.

I thought of doing that, but I'm scared someone might get in.

Lesson Aims: Sts talk about improvising in difficult situations.

Skills	Language	Vocabulary	Grammar
Listening to a conversation between two friends about a difficult situation	Talking about ability in the past: *I was able to climb just about anything. My friends weren't able to.*	*climb, escape, fence, spare (key)*	Describing past ability: *could* and *was / were able to*

Warm-up

Ask the lesson title question:

Are you good at improvising? as a follow-up to the game. If time, add other questions: *How do you react in a crisis? Have you been in any difficult situations where you've had to make a quick decision?* Have sts discuss in pairs, then share anything interesting with the class. Teach sts the expression *think on your feet* (= to react quickly to a situation and find a solution).

3 Language in use

A 8.6 Focus on the photo and the example speech bubbles. Ask: *What is the girl wearing? Why do you think she's climbing the fence at night? Does she look unhappy?* Encourage sts to speculate about what is happening. Board the following expressions to help them: *She might be ..., Perhaps ..., She could be ..., It's possible that ...* .

Play the audio for sts to listen and check their ideas. Ask: *Who was closest/furthest from the 'answer'? What do you think's going to happen next?*

Answers

She was going to a party, but she'd lost the key to the gate around her apartment complex so had to climb over the fence. Her brother took a photo and posted it on Instagram.

See Teacher's Book p.324 for Audio script 8.6.

B 8.7 Sts read the questions. Ask them what they already know about the situation (she was going to a party). Play the rest of the story to answer the questions.

Stronger classes: Invite sts to tell the rest of the class about any similar situations which have happened to them.

Weaker classes: Students might need a minute or two to plan their thoughts and get some new vocabulary from you.

Ask: *Did you have nickname at school?* Share yours, if you had one.

Answers

1 Yes, but there was no cell coverage where they were.
2 No. She was called "spider girl."
3 She ran into her old boyfriend and his new girlfriend.

C 8.6 and 8.7 Go through the speech bubbles. Ask: *What does spare one refer to in the first speech bubble? (key)*

In pairs, sts label each bubble *L* or *D* depending on who said them and then try to order them from memory. Re-play the audio for sts to check their answers. Classcheck.

Answers

L 2: I couldn't find the spare one.
L 4: I could climb just about anything.
L 6: I think he could see it in my eyes.
D 5: So you're telling me you were able to climb the fence?
L 1: I wasn't able to get there until after 10.
D 3: But you were able to make it to the party?

See Teacher's Book p.324 for Audio script 8.6 and 8.7.

Tip

After listening exercises, encourage self-evaluation, and get feedback by asking: *How much of the listening did you understand? 70%? 80%?* With larger classes they can show you with their hands, each finger representing 10%.

D Have sts do this individually, then paircheck. Encourage sts to note new/similar expressions such as these in their vocabulary notebooks.

Answers

1 Believe it or not ... 2 That's so like you. 3 Long story short ... 4 I don't get it. 5 What are the odds of that happening? 6 How come?

Optional activity

In groups of four, sts re-tell Louise's story. Sts take turns to continue the story, the next one taking over as soon as you shout *Change!*

E Make it personal In pairs, sts name the items in the photo. Make sure they use determiners/interesting phrases, not just individual words (e.g. *some/an open pack of tissues, a (folded) pair of glasses*).

In groups, sts discuss questions 1–5. Refer them to the model dialogue in the speech bubbles. Highlight the expression *keep + -ing* in question 4 (= to repeatedly do something).

Classcheck, and ask: *Were there any coincidences?*

4 Grammar: Describing past ability

A Go through the example sentences in the grammar box and check everyone understands them. Elicit other examples of stative verbs, e.g. *see, hear, smell, taste, feel, remember, believe*, and *understand*.

Focus on the **Common mistakes**. Ask why the sentences are incorrect. (*In the first sentence, "believe" is a stative verb. In the second, you use "was able to" for a specific occasion in affirmative sentences.*) Personalize by asking: *How often do you/your parents/kids say something like this?*

In pairs, sts complete the rules, then classcheck.

Answers

often, 1 affirmative 2 could

Refer sts to the **Grammar expansion** on p.152.

Tip

Explain that when we want to say that someone managed to do something, we always use *was / were able to* (not *could*), e.g. *Luckily she was able to climb the fence*. (= She managed to climb the fence.)

Optional activity

Board: *When I was younger, I couldn't / wasn't able to … , but now I can*. Sts complete the sentence in as many ways as they can to make it true for them.

Song lyric: See Teacher's Book p.343 for notes about the song and an accompanying activity to do with the class.

B Sts look back at the sentences in 3C, and decide where be able to could be replaced by *could*.

Elicit the answer *I couldn't get there until after 10*. Explain or elicit that *couldn't* or *wasn't able to* are both possible because it refers to a specific occasion in the negative. Ask sts why *could* is not possible in the other sentences. (Because they refer to specific occasions in the affirmative).

Answer

I couldn't get there until after 10.

C Get sts to cover the texts and elicit what you can from the photos before reading. With a little lateral thinking you can get a lot from them, e.g. *Who's been to Berlin? What do you know about that city now and in the past? Who's been to San Francisco? What else is it famous for?*

Sts read the texts quickly. Ask: *Who escaped?* (Text 1 – Hans Strelczyk and his family; text 2 – three prisoners) *Where did they escape from?* (Text 1 – East Berlin; text 2 – Alcatraz).

Sts correct the mistakes individually, then paircheck. Classcheck.

Answers

1 was able to 5 were able to

Background information

The **Berlin Wall** divided Berlin from 1961–1989. It was built by the German Democratic Republic (East Germany) to protect the East Germans from Fascism. It also stopped people from defecting from the East.

Alcatraz Federal Penitentiary was in operation on the island of Alcatraz in San Francisco Bay from 1934–1963. America's most difficult and dangerous criminals were kept there. The prison, now a museum, is open to the public.

D Make it personal Go through the questionnaire. Pause to highlight each verb and the potential collocates. Get sts who do understand to mime any unfamiliar vocabulary to those who ask, e.g. running out of gas, getting caught or *pretend*, which is a false friend for learners who speak Romance languages.

Ask: *Which of these situations have you been in? When? What did you do? How did the situation end?*

In pairs, sts relate their experiences to each other. When listening to their partner, encourage them to push for detail with follow-up questions and to use good listening expressions, e.g. *Really? What then? What happened next? No way!*

Class feedback. Ask: *Were there any coincidences? Did you experience any similar situations?* Invite sts to relate their stories to the class. Obviously these might well lend themselves to being written up afterwards, if your class need a lot of writing practice.

Workbook p.39.

4 Grammar: Describing past ability

A Read the grammar box and *Common mistakes*. Then check (✔) the correct answers.

Describing past ability: *could* and *was / were able to*

General	Louise **could** / **was able to** climb just about anything, but her friends **couldn't** / **weren't able to**. They weren't as athletic.
Specific occasion	She **couldn't** / **wasn't able to** reach her parents. Luckily, she **was able to** climb the fence and get a taxi.
Stative verbs	Her neighbors **could** see her climbing the fence. They **couldn't** understand why.

Can and *be able to* are ☐ **often** ☐ **never** interchangeable. However, to talk about ...

1 a specific past occasion in the ☐ **affirmative** ☐ **negative**, use *be able to*.

2 a past state, with verbs like *see*, *believe*, and *feel*, use ☐ **could** ☐ **was able to**.

Common mistakes

The traffic was awful. I ~~wasn't able to~~ *couldn't* believe it. But I ~~could~~ *was able to* get to work on time. Just barely!

Grammar expansion p.152

B Which *be able to* sentences in **3C** can be replaced by *could(n't)*?

C Correct any mistakes in the use of *could* and *be able to*.

TWO FAMOUS ESCAPES!

Before the Berlin Wall came down in 1989, people from East Germany sometimes tried to escape to the West. In 1979, for example, a man called Hans Strelczyk (1) **could** build a hot air balloon using old bed sheets, and his family (2) **was able to** drift over to the other side! Those who saw it (3) **couldn't** believe their eyes!

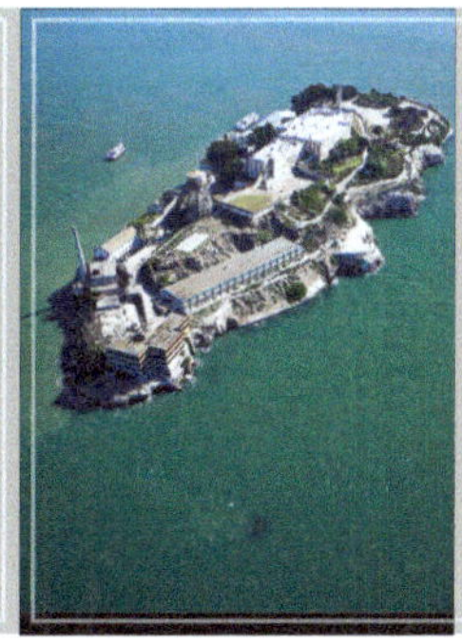

Alcatraz, the most legendary prison in the world, was supposedly escape-proof. However, one day, three inmates disappeared, and Alcatraz officials simply (4) **couldn't** find them. No one knows if the three men (5) **could** escape or if they jumped in the sea and drowned. My grandfather was a guard there, and he told me everything! I (6) **could** spend hours listening to his stories!

D Make it personal In pairs, answer the questionnaire, adding plenty of detail. Use expressions from **3D**. Any coincidences?

R U calm and creative in a storm? | **How well do you improvise?**

Think of times when you ...

1 ran out of gas / money / clean clothes at the worst possible moment.
2 got stuck in traffic and missed something important.
3 got caught doing something you shouldn't.
4 pretended to be enjoying yourself.
5 escaped from a very difficult situation.

We both ran out of gas, and neither of us had a clue what to do.

8.3 How much attention do you pay to the news?

5 Reading

A Look at the title and choose a meaning for *fear-mongering* (1–3). Read paragraph 1 of the article to check.

1 relevant safety warnings   2 scare tactics   3 strategies to deal with fear

B Guess how Lee will answer his own question at the end of paragraph 1. Then read the rest and choose his most likely answer (1–3). Underline sentences supporting your choice.

1 "No doubt it is."   2 "Not exactly."   3 "To a certain extent."

Be Afraid. Be Very Afraid:
Fear-mongering in the 21st century

By Lee Corelli

1 As part of my job as a freelance reporter, I've been practically glued to the screen lately. Here's a snapshot of my daily routine. Wake up in the morning: "New bomb scare. FBI on the alert." Go to bed: "Unemployment at an all-time high." Wake up: "Broccoli can kill you." The list is endless, and if we took all these scary stories to heart, we might never leave home again. It's no secret that in order to grab the audience's attention and boost ratings, the media rarely fails to make things look worse than they actually are. But is this kind of fear-mongering such a big deal after all?

2 ____. The fear spread by the media shapes the way we think and act, often without us being fully aware of what's really going on. The evening news reports a "worrying increase" in plane crashes, and we rethink our travel plans. It warns of a nasty new virus, and we start to wonder if leaving home without a mask on is worth the risk. We're living as if our lives were in a constant state of imminent danger. But why are we so easily influenced?

3 ____. A number of major studies have examined how our brains cope with all the negativity that surrounds us. A recent one, carried out at Ohio State University, found a significant increase in brain activity when subjects were shown negative images as opposed to positive ones. This is especially frightening in this day and age, when we're bombarded with bad news after bad news, not only on TV, but via social media, too.

4 ____. Back in the day, our grandparents only had about half a dozen TV stations to get their news from, so it was easier for them to see through cheap fear-mongering on the rare occasions they encountered it. But the media has undergone a lot of major changes in recent years, and now, with so many channels and websites, it's much harder to tell fact from fiction. In the end, we're left with a hundred different versions of the same story, wondering which ones to trust.

5 ____. The shocking images we see of war zones and natural disasters can and do inspire fear, of course, but they can also inspire action. For example, would people have mobilized so many resources to help the victims of hurricane Katrina in 2005 if the images hadn't been all over the media 24/7? Probably not. It's up to us, though, to make sure the media does not manipulate our fears in a way that's not proportional to the problem itself.

C 8.8 Match topic sentences a–d to paragraphs 2–5. Listen to check. Did the audio help you understand the text?

a The number of news channels has also greatly increased.
b All this negativity is affecting our thoughts and actions.
c But maybe there's hope, after all.
d One reason might be neurological.

Lesson Aims: Sts learn vocabulary to talk about the way news is reported, and discuss the effect bad news has on us.

Skills

Reading an article about fear-mongering by the media

Language

be glued to the screen, bombard, grab, see through

Common verb + noun collocations with *boost, carry out, cope with, spread* and *undergo*

Warm-up

Board: *The news wasn't / weren't good* and elicit the correct form. Board: *Uncountable nouns*. Give sts, in pairs, one minute to brainstorm a list, then try to group them logically, (concepts, substances, liquids, etc.), e.g.:

- advice, information, news, knowledge, evidence
- electricity, gas, power, air, technology
- rice, sugar, salt, butter, flour
- unemployment, work, homework, progress

Ask: *Which aspects of countability do you still find hard?* to see what sts come up with.

Board the lesson title question: *How much attention do you pay to the news?* In pairs, sts discuss the question. As they do, board follow-up questions, e.g. *How do you get/keep up with it? Which aspects of local/national/ international news do/don't usually interest you? What was the last good/bad news item that really caught your attention? Do you believe every story you hear/read? If not, give examples.*

5 Reading

A Cover the article to focus only on the title. Individually sts read the options and choose/guess the best meaning for *fear-mongering*. Insist those who know, don't call out the answer! Paircheck very quickly, then give them a minute to skim the first paragraph to check. Paircheck again quickly, then classcheck.

Tip

Lots of quick pairchecking keeps sts interacting more, and gives you much more feedback, from their faces as well as what they say. It also helps you avoid getting stuck explaining too much vocabulary at this stage. The aim is to practice different reading skills.

Focus on the photos. Sts describe what they can see. (*The guy's reading an article on his tablet about ways to prevent living in fear. His response is to turn off the tablet.*)

Answer

2 scare tactics

B Ask: *What's Lee's question?* Board it: *But is this kind of fear-mongering such a big deal after all?* Ask sts what their view is. Have them read the three likely responses, and guess what Lee's answer will be.

Sts read the rest of the article, and check their idea. Ask them to underline the sentences in the article that support their answer.

Answers

3 "To a certain extent."
Supporting sentences:
The fear spread by the media shapes the way we think and act, often without us being fully aware of what's really going on.
We're living as if our lives were in a constant state of imminent danger.
... a significant increase in brain activity when subjects were shown negative images, as opposed to positive ones.
... we're left with a hundred different versions of the same story, wondering which ones to trust.
... do inspire fear, of course, but they can also inspire action. It's up to us, though, to make sure the media does not manipulate our fears in a way that's not proportional to the problem itself.

C 8.8 Go through the topic sentences and check sts understand them. Sts re-read and match them with the correct paragraphs. Play the audio for sts to check their answers. Classcheck.

Answers

2 b 3 d 4 a 5 c

Optional activity

Highlight the idiomatic expressions in the text: *be glued to the screen, grab the audience's attention, be bombarded with bad news, see through cheap fear-mongering*. Elicit (or help sts write) definitions for the expressions, and another example when they might use each.

D Ask sts to read points a–f and underline the key words. If they don't remember which paragraphs the points were made in, have them skim the text again to find them. Classcheck.

Answers

a 3 b 1 c 2 d 5 e 4 f 4

Optional activity

Sts do a class survey on the most popular means of finding out the news. Board these: *TV, newspaper, radio, Internet, apps, social media, gossip.*

In groups, or as a class mingle, give each a source to find out how many sts in their group use it to access their news, and how often. In their group, then as a class, sts agree on which is the most popular news source. Class feedback. Use the board to collate results to see which is the class favorite news source.

Song lyric: See Teacher's Book p.343 for notes about the song and an accompanying activity to do with the class.

E Make it personal Give sts 40 seconds to read through the questions and match the example to the right one (Q4). Check they understand *boost* (= to help something increase, improve or become more successful). Ask: *What else can you boost?* (e.g. confidence, strength).

In pairs, sts discuss the questions, then open up to a class discussion. Ask: *Did you mostly agree /disagree with your partner?* In relation to question 3, you might want to discuss whether they trust some newspapers more than others. Beware of getting into political deep water, and move on at the first sign of trouble! They can always write up their opinions afterwards.

Weaker classes: Discuss the questions as a class.

6 Vocabulary: Common verb + noun collocations

A Go through **Noticing collocations** with the class. Ask sts to find the highlighted verbs in the text in 5B, and work out which nouns each verb relates to (*boost ratings, spread fear, cope with negativity, carried out studies, undergone changes*).

Sts write the verbs in the correct places on the mind maps. Paircheck, then elicit the stress and quickly drill the other words in each box. Get sts to explain to each other any some might not be sure of.

Strong classes: Get them to add one more collocate to each box.

Answers

1 undergo 2 carry out 3 boost 4 spread 5 cope with

B Focus on the gapped sentences and do the first one with together with the class as an example. Tell sts to be careful with the form of the verbs.

Sts complete the other sentences individually, then paircheck. Classcheck.

Answers

1 cope with, loss 2 undergone, changes 3 carry out, promises 4 spreading, rumors 5 boost, confidence

Optional activity

Sts write an additional question to add to 6B with a verb from the mind maps, and a new noun collocate. Monitor to weed any errors. Then ask sts to rewrite their questions, gapping the verb and noun. In pairs, sts swap questions, fill in each other's gaps, then discuss the answers to both questions.

C Make it personal Give sts two minutes to prepare, re-reading the questions in B and note down any answers that spring to mind to see which they find most interesting. Encourage them to try to think of anecdotes of their own they'd like to tell. A good story from you first usually always helps with this, e.g. *I remember when our puppy suddenly died when I was a kid. I was devastated …*

In small groups, sts vote on two questions to discuss first.

Tip

If they can't agree, tell sts to start with two, then move on to a third option once done. The aim of giving choices is to keep speaking activities more personal, feasible if you are short of time and couldn't discuss all five, and motivating as they feel they are covering 'all the material'.

Monitor to help weaker sts to participate more, and correct where necessary. If there's time, get sts to swap groups and compare their answers before wrapping up. Were their ideas and answers similar? Were there any exceptionally ingenious answers?

Workbook p.40.

D In which paragraph (1–5) does Lee make points a–f?

a ☐ There is an increase in brain activity when we see bad news.
b ☐ The media knows what kinds of stories will keep people interested.
c ☐ People don't always realize how the media influences their daily lives.
d ☐ People are more likely to help others when they can see the problem.
e ☐ Having access to many different sources of information is not always a good thing.
f ☐ TV stations were more consistent in the past.

E **Make it personal** In pairs, answer 1–4. Any similarities?

1 Besides fear-mongering, how else does the media boost ratings?
2 Did any recent news stories a) scare you b) shock you c) make you laugh out loud?
3 What do you trust more, TV, the radio, the Internet, or the newspapers?
4 What other institutions use scare tactics with you? Do they work?

> Oh, my school, for sure. My teachers keep telling me I'll fail this year unless my grades improve.

6 Vocabulary: Common verb + noun collocations

A Read *Noticing collocations*. Then complete the mind maps with the highlighted verbs in the article.

Noticing collocations

It's easy to notice collocations when the words occur together: *We tend to **pay attention** to bad news.*
But sometimes the words appear far from each other: *This is a key **issue** that people really need to **address**.*

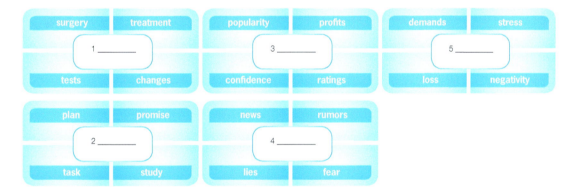

surgery, treatment, tests, changes — 1 ________

popularity, profits, confidence, ratings — 3 ________

demands, stress, loss, negativity — 5 ________

plan, promise, task, study — 2 ________

news, rumors, lies, fear — 4 ________

B Complete 1–5 with words from A in the correct form.

1 How can children ________ the ________ of a pet when it dies?
2 How different is your neighborhood from ten years ago? Has it ________ many ________ ?
3 Do you always ________ the ________ you make to friends, or do you sometimes find excuses?
4 Have you ever found out that a friend or colleague was ________ false ________ about you? What's the best way to deal with gossip?
5 What successes have you had in life? In what ways did these positive experiences ________ your ________ ?

C **Make it personal** Choose two questions from B to answer in groups. Ask for / give more details. Similar ideas?

> I guess their parents should simply explain that pets die, just like people.

7 Language in use

A 8.9 Guess the missing words from an interview about the author's recent trip to Europe. Listen to check.

LAURA GÓMEZ *author of Fearless traveler*

Milan, in northern Italy, is a very happy city. So much so that you're not allowed to frown unless you're at a [1]__________ or at the hospital. Yes – smiling is required by law … a pointless law, I know! So, if you ever visit, you'd better [2]__________ about your troubles, or else you might have to pay a fine.

In general, tourists are not supposed to eat and drink in [3]__________, but Rome has recently enforced a law banning eating and drinking at all historical sites. The fine? Up to [4]$__________! So maybe you ought to eat an extra slice of bread before leaving the hotel.

In countries like Denmark and [5]__________, driving with your headlights off is considered a violation of the law. You have to keep them on even during the day! This may sound [6]__________, I know, but you've got to obey the local laws.

B 8.10 Listen to the full interview. Note the reasons behind each law. Do they make sense to you?

C Scan A to find law expressions with meanings 1–4. Did you know them all?

1 obligatory
2 illegal
3 a law serving no purpose
4 make people obey a law

D Make it personal Crime and punishment! Answer 1–4 in pairs. Any disagreements?

1 "The heavier the punishment, the more likely we all are to obey a law." Do you agree?
2 Where you live, are some laws not enforced?
3 If you could create a new law to legalize, reward, or ban something, what would it be?
4 Search online for "stupid laws." Any funny ones?

Here's one that says it's a violation of the law for French people to name a pig Napoleon!

8 Grammar: Expressing obligation, permission, and advice

A Match meanings 1–5 to the examples in the grammar box on p.89.

1 You (don't) have permission to do it.
2 This is(n't) an obligation. You have a / no choice.
3 My advice or suggestion: (Don't) do it.
4 My strong advice or warning: You *really* should(n't) do it, or else …
5 People expect you (not) to do it, but it's a rule we often break.

Lesson Aims: Sts learn vocabulary and modal verbs to talk about strange laws in other countries.

Skills	Language	Vocabulary	Grammar
Listening to an interview with an author about her recent travels Discussing things you're not supposed to do	Expressing obligation, permission and advice: *You'd better not forget your coat. You're not supposed to turn it on. You shouldn't miss it.*	*ban, crime, enforce, legalize, obey the law, pay a fine, punishment*	Modals: *must / have to, had better, be allowed to, be supposed to,* and *should / ought to*

Warm-up

Board the word: *Traveling* and ask: *Have you traveled recently?* In pairs, sts brainstorm what *traveling* makes them think of, and list all the phases traveling involves, in order to revise useful collocates/phrases, e.g. *work out a route, book tickets, pack bags*.

Board the lesson title question: *What prevents you from traveling more?* Sts brainstorm their answers, e.g. *expense, stress, lack of time/vacation options*.

7 Language in use

A 8.9 Focus on the photo and heading. Ask: *What can you surmise about Laura Gomez?* Brainstorm answers (she's a traveler/of Latino origin/author of a blog, etc.)

Focus sts on the pictures. Ask: *What is the man doing in each picture?* (1 smiling, 2 eating an ice cream, 3 driving without his lights on).

Have sts read the text quickly for gist, ignoring the gaps, and ask: *What is the purpose of the text?* (to advise travelers about laws in different countries). Sts re-read and guess the missing words. Paircheck.

Play the start of an interview with the woman in the photo for sts to check their answers.

Answers

1 funeral 2 forget 3 museums 4 650 5 Sweden 6 unnecessary

B 8.10 Get sts to brainstorm in pairs the reasoning behind each law. Play the full interview for sts to listen to and note down the reasons she gives. Classcheck.

Ask: *Which laws do you think are sensible / silly?* Highlight these words and expressions from the audio: *obey the law, pay a fine, enforce, ban*. Elicit what they mean.

Answers

Smiling – they want to build the city's reputation as a happy, friendly place
Eating – they want to protect the city's monuments
Driving – moving lights are easy to notice, and this can reduce the number of accidents

See Teacher's Book p.324 for Audio script 8.10.

C Sts skim the text in A quickly for the relevant expressions for the four meanings. Classcheck.

Answers

1 required by law 2 a violation of the law 3 a pointless law 4 enforce a law

D Make it personal Ask: *Are there strange / silly laws in your country?* Elicit and board a few using appropriate legal language if you can. Use this opportunity to brainstorm some vocabulary sts may need in their discussion.

Read the questions and brainstorm a few answers as a class. In pairs, sts discuss the questions.

If you don't have Internet access in class, have sts research "stupid" laws for homework. Start the next lesson by asking sts to share what they found out.

8 Grammar: Expressing obligation, permission, and advice

A Give sts one minute to read through the ten example sentences in the grammar on p.89. Then, in pairs, get them to imagine the context and speaker for each.

Weaker classes: Have sts, at least mentally, translate each phrase into their language to see if there are any obvious similarities/differences that will help them remember and use these modal forms more.

Sts match them with meanings 1–5 at the bottom of page 88. Paircheck, then classcheck.

Tip

Remind sts that *You mustn't ...* means that "it is necessary that you don't do something," and has a different meaning from *You don't have to ...* , which means "it is not necessary to do something" (but you can if you like).

Answers

1 You can / are allowed to ... , You can't / 're not allowed to ...
2 You must / have (got) to ... , You don't have to ...
3 You should / ought to ... , You shouldn't ...
4 You'd better ... , You'd better not ...
5 You're supposed to ... , You're not supposed to

Refer sts to the **Grammar expansion** on p.152.

B In pairs, sts read the laws and choose the correct options. Quickly elicit/pre-teach *light bulbs* using a mime or one in the room. Monitor and help with pronunciation, e.g. Saudi Arabia.

Classcheck. Ask: *Do you think these are all sensible laws? Are there any in our country you disagree with?*

Answers

1 're not allowed to, 'd better 2 must, ought to
3 have to, ought to 4 're not supposed to

Optional activity

Board three locations: In a library, In a museum, In the classroom.

In groups, sts brainstorm all the rules they can for each, using the modals in 8A, e.g. *You're not supposed to talk in a library. You're not allowed to touch the paintings. You mustn't talk over the teacher*. Maybe award a point for each correct rule, the group with the most wins.

9 Pronunciation: *have to, got to, ought to, supposed to* in informal speech

A 8.11 Play the audio for sts to listen to the sentences. Then re-play for sts to repeat first the phrase and then the complete sentences.

Ask sts to practice the sentences in pairs. Monitor, checking that sts are not pronouncing the silent letters and are using the schwa for the unstressed "to."

» Song lyric: See Teacher's Book p.343 for notes about the song and an accompanying activity to do with the class.

B 8.12 Model the pronunciation of the underlined phrases using informal pronunciation (i.e. *have to* = /'hæftə/, *got to* = /'gɑːtːə/, *ought to* = /'ɔːtə/). Then play the audio, and have sts repeat the song lines.

In pairs, sts practice the song lines. Invite volunteers to sing them if they know them!

C **Make it personal** Read through sentences 1–4 with the class. Make sure sts understand that they have to substitute the phrases in brackets with their own phrases. Go through the example in the speech bubble to demonstrate. Sts can write out the sentences first if they prefer.

In groups, sts tell each other their sentences. Monitor to check that their communication sounds as natural as possible, and they're using informal pronunciation as best they can. At the end congratulate them on sounding so 'nativelike'!

Tip

Encourage sts to react to each sentence. Elicit/Board some key phrases to help them do so: *Me too, That's pretty much the same for me, I don't/Neither did I, My case completely*. Add others as they come up with them.

Class feedback. *Ask: Who has the best / worst excuses?*

» Workbook p.41.

Obligation, permission, advice: *must / have (got) to, had better, be allowed to, be supposed to,* and *should / ought to*

You **must** / **have (got) to** get a visa to enter Russia.	You **don't have to** get one to go to Bermuda. Your passport will do.
You**'d better** pack some warm clothes or you'll freeze!	You**'d better not** forget your coat!
You**'re supposed to** keep your phone off at the theater.	You**'re not supposed to** turn it on.
You **can** / **are allowed to** use computers on a plane.	You **can't** / **'re not allowed to** use them during takeoff.
You **should** / **ought to** visit Times Square.	You **shouldn't** miss it.

Grammar expansion p.152

B Circle the most logical options. Are there any laws in your country you disagree with?

1 In Saudi Arabia, you [**'re not allowed to** / **don't have to**] photograph government buildings. So you [**have to** / **'d better**] leave your camera at home – just in case you forget.
2 In France, between 8:00 a.m. and 8:00 p.m., 70% of radio music [**must** / **ought to**] be by French artists. I don't think the government [**must** / **ought to**] decide what gets played!
3 In 2013, China passed a new law saying adult children [**have to** / **are allowed to**] visit their parents. Hmm ... Maybe I [**ought to** / **must**] call my mom right now!
4 In Victoria, Australia, you [**'re not supposed to** / **'d better not**] change your own light bulbs! There's no need to be afraid, though. I doubt the police will go after you for this one.

9 Pronunciation: *have to, got to, ought to, supposed to* in informal speech

A 8.11 Listen to and repeat the examples. Notice the silent letters and schwas.

1 Tourists are not ~~supposed~~ to eat and drink. /ə/
2 Maybe you ~~ought~~ to eat an extra slice of bread. /ə/
3 You ~~have~~ to keep headlights on. /f/ /ə/
4 You'~~ve got~~ to obey the laws. /ə/

B 8.12 Read aloud the song lines, using informal pronunciation. Listen to check.

1 "How many times do I have to tell you, even when you're crying, you're beautiful, too." (John Legend)
2 "It's the way I'm feeling, I just can't deny, but I've got to let it go. We found love in a hopeless place." (Rihanna)
3 "Ah, but working too hard can give you a heart attack. You ought to know by now." (Billy Joel)
4 "Make me your selection, show you the way love's supposed to be." (Mario)

C **Make it personal** In groups, take turns personalizing 1–4. Use informal pronunciation. Who feels the guiltiest? Who has the best excuses?

Yeah, I'm guilty, I know. It's not much of an excuse, but ...

1 I know I ought to (do the laundry) more often. What's stopping me is (my dad likes doing it).
2 We have to (keep our phones off) in (class), but sometimes (I check mine quickly under my desk).
3 This week I've got to (change all my passwords). I've been putting it off for (months) because (I'm too lazy to create new ones).
4 I know I'm not supposed to (eat junk food), but I can't help it. I mean, (it tastes so good).

I know I ought to visit my grandparents more often. What's stopping me is ...

10 Listening

A 8.13 Take a test-anxiety quiz. Listen once to note down the key words from the questions. Listen again to answer each question. Then add up your score.

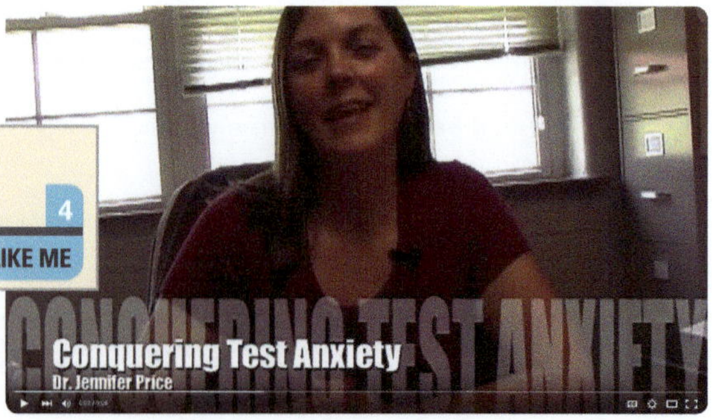

ANSWER ON THE FOLLOWING SCALE:

1 — 2 — 3 — 4

NOT AT ALL LIKE ME … VERY MUCH LIKE ME

B 8.14 Listen to / Watch a psychologist's views on test anxiety. Pause at 1.37. In pairs, how accurate is your test anxiety index?

> Very accurate! I scored 17, and I freak out whenever I take a test.

C 8.15 Listen to / Watch the rest and number her recommendations 1–6 in the order she makes them. Which is the most important one for you?

- [ ] Study a little and often.
- [ ] Focus on your breathing.
- [ ] Remind yourself how to succeed.
- [ ] Learn how to relax.
- [ ] Find somewhere quiet to study.
- [ ] Remember: preparation is key.

> My choice would be finding somewhere quiet. It's hard to learn with noise.

D 8.14 & 8.15 In pairs, complete 1–5 with the words in the correct form. Listen to both parts to check. Which ones were easy?

cram   blank (v)   lower (v)   no matter what   way in advance   on a daily basis

1 You studied really hard for a test, but when you got it, you just ______ (= forgot everything).
2 Even if your anxiety was low, these things can be helpful for you ______ (= in any case).
3 The first strategy is just to spend your time preparing ______ (= ahead of time).
4 It really does not work to ______ (= learn too much too quickly) the night before a test.
5 If you practice relaxation ______ (= every day), it ______ (= reduces) your overall anxiety.

11 Keep talking

Read and note down three recommendations. In groups, compare your advice. What would be best for each person?

1 I'm terrified of flying, but in a moment of madness, I bought a ticket to Peru. What should I do?
Mayumi

2 I've always been petrified of public speaking, but I've been asked to give a 20-minute presentation next week!
Roger

3 In three days, I'm supposed to be getting married, but now I'm really not sure I'm ready. What should I do?
Ellen

> The smartest thing for Mayumi to do would be to cancel her flight.

> ______ might want to think about ______ *-ing*.

> If I were in ______'s shoes, I'd probably ______.

Lesson Aims: Sts do an anxiety test, listen to advice about how to deal with exam anxiety and write a message of advice

Skills	Language	Vocabulary
Watch / Listen to a psychologist giving advice about exam anxiety Writing a message of advice	Giving advice, e.g. *If were in ...'s shoes, You might want to think about ...*	*blank, cram, distraction, no matter what, relaxation, way in advance*

Warm-up

In a corner of the board, write up some typical mistakes you anticipate coming up in this lesson, e.g. with *advice. I asked her an advice. (for some) She advised me to not eat there. (not to)*

In pairs, sts correct them. Classcheck. Leave the corrected version up for latecomers to immediately get the message when they come in, and as a prompt for more st–st correction throughout the lesson.

Ask: *What's the best piece of advice anyone ever gave you?* Give an example or two yourself and see what they come up with. Then ask: *When you have a problem do you usually prefer to keep it to yourself, or talk about it? Who do you usually turn to for advice?* In pairs, sts discuss the lesson title question, then feedback to the class.

10 Listening

A 8.13 Ask: *How do you feel when you take an exam? Do you always get nervous?*

Explain that sts will hear five statements from people who feel nervous about taking an exam. Explain the answer scale: for each statement they have to rate it on a scale of 1–4: 4 if it sounds very much like them, and 1 if it doesn't, 2 or 3 if they fall somewhere in between.

First, play the audio for sts to note down the key words from the five questions. Paircheck. Re-play it for sts to rate each question. Paircheck to allow you time to clarify individual doubts / sort out whole class problems.

Sts add up their scores. Class feedback. Ask: *Who scored more than 10? Who scored less than 10?*

See Teacher's Book p.324 for Audio script 8.13.

B 8.14 Play the video or audio for sts to listen to a psychologist, analyzing the test scores. Pause the video at 1.37. Ask: *Do you think your test anxiety score is accurate? Why / Why not?*

See Teacher's Book p.324 for Audio script 8.14.

C 8.15 Sts quickly read the six recommendations. Play the video from 1.37, or play the audio, for sts to number the recommendations in her order.

Classcheck, then ask: *Which of these things do you do / not do before an exam? Do any of them not work for you?*

Answers

1 Remember: preparation is key.
2 Find somewhere quiet to study.
3 Study a little and often.
4 Remind yourself how to succeed.
5 Learn how to relax.
6 Focus on your breathing.

See Teacher's Book p.324 for Audio script 8.15.

D 8.14 and 8.15 Go through the words in the box, and ask which ones sts know. Assuming they know some, have them first match these to the correct sentences, then try to guess where the remaining items go. Remind them they might need to change the verb forms. Sts check with their partner to help / teach each other.

Re-play the video or audio for sts to check their answers or check answers as a class.

Answers

1 blanked 2 no matter what 3 way in advance 4 cram
5 on a daily basis, lowers

See Teacher's Book p.324 for Audio script 8.14 & 8.15.

Optional activity

Ask: *What are the best things to do when you feel stressed/nervous before any important event?* Sts write four pieces of advice. Ask: *What's your best tip?*

11 Keep talking

Ask sts to read the text in the purple boxes. Ask: *What problems do Mayumi, Roger, and Ellen have?*

Focus on the speech bubbles, and highlight the phrases for giving advice.

Have sts think of advice they would give each person, and make notes. Encourage them to use the phrases in the speech bubbles.

In groups, sts exchange their ideas, and decide what the best advice would be. Have a member of each group report back their best advice for each person to the class.

Tip

Space-permitting, this makes a good mingle, so all speak more intensively and exchange more ideas.

Song lyric: See Teacher's Book p.343 for notes about the song and an accompanying activity to do with the class.

12 Writing: A message of advice

A Focus on the cell phone. Ask: *Have you ever written a single message as long as this? Or a (handwritten) letter or postcard? What's the longest thing you've ever written?* to personalize straight away and get them thinking about the genre. This can expand as much as you want, e.g. *Do you enjoy writing (in English)? Has your writing improved since the start of the course?*

Ask sts to read Sonia's email quickly, and find out what Cynthia's problem is (*She's worried about a test she has next month*).

Weaker classes: Before doing 12A, get sts to go through the email and underline all the bits of advice. Then look back and match it with 10C.

Sts read questions 1–3, then re-read the message, this time in much more detail, and answer the questions.

Tip

Give sts a time limit so they don't read slowly, e.g. three minutes, then put them into pairs to change the dynamic, talk more, and complete the exercise together.

Classcheck. Encourage a range of responses to question 2, e.g. *Background music can sometimes help people to concentrate better than silence*. For Q3, elicit how they chose the most important paragraph.

Finally, elicit pronunciation/meaning of the pinked words and drill any they find tricky.

Answers

1 Study a little and often, learn how to relax, find somewhere quiet to study.
2 Sts' own answers
3 Paragraph 3 (because she starts with 'Above all')

B Go through **Write it right!** with the class and check understanding.

Explain that the highlighted expressions in Sonia's message are informal expressions we often use in emails or letters to friends. Ask sts which of the expressions they know already. Have them match them to the meanings 1–6. Paircheck, then classcheck.

Answers

1 Above all 2 so to speak 3 Other than that
4 For starters 5 Needless to say 6 That said

C Focus on the second message. Ask: *Why is Sonia texting Cynthia?* Give sts 20 seconds to read it quickly, then paircheck the answer, plus share all else they can remember from it. (to give her advice for the day of the exam)

Sts re-read and choose the correct options. Paircheck, then classcheck. Get their overall reaction to all they've read, e.g. *What do you think of the relationship between Cynthia and Sonia? Do you have any close friends/relatives like her?*

Answers

1 For starters 2 so to speak 3 That said 4 above all
5 needless to say 6 Other than that

D Your turn! Tell sts they are going to write their own message of advice. Read through the instructions with the class, and check that everyone understands what they have to do.

Refer sts back to 11, and ask them to choose one of the people, Mayumi, Roger and Ellen, to be their 'close friend' to write to.

Tip

With the right class, get them to speculate what each of the three people might be like, their age, visualize them, etc. for fun, to help them assign a character they can relate to. This will help them write with greater conviction.

Ask if they remember the advice they discussed earlier. Get them to brainstorm again, jot down their ideas in note form, and add any additional advice they may have thought of since.

Monitor while sts write or set the task for homework if you are short of time. Get them to swap messages before the next class if you can for some peer correction.

When sts have finished, you could have them display their advice on the walls, and ask sts to read their classmates' advice. Class feedback. Ask: *What was the best / worst / most original advice?*

Optional activity

Ask sts to write a few sentences about something they are worried about. Put sts in pairs, and ask them to swap their problems. Have them write a message of advice for their partner. Encourage them to use the highlighted phrases in Cynthia's email, and also the phrases in the speech bubbles in 11. Ask: *Was your partner's advice useful?*

Workbook p.42.

12 Writing: A message of advice

A Read Sonia's message to Cynthia and answer 1–3.

1 Which recommendation(s) in 10C does she mention?

2 Is there anything in Sonia's message you disagree with?

3 Which paragraph includes her most important recommendation?

B Read *Write it right!* Then match the highlighted expressions in Sonia's message to their uses 1–6.

Write it right!

When writing to someone close to you, use a variety of friendly comments to sound natural:

You shouldn't take an exam on an empty stomach. **Trust me**, it's not good for you. I did it once and almost fainted. **I mean**, I didn't literally pass out, but I came close. **Thank goodness** there was a doctor on campus.

1 Most of all, you should remember this.

2 I'm using a metaphor. Don't take my words literally.

3 Besides what I've just said ...

4 This is the first item on a list.

5 This is obvious.

6 In a way, I'm contradicting what I've just said.

C Circle the correct options in Sonia's next message.

Oh, I almost forgot. On the day of the exam, here's what you should keep in mind. [1] **[For starters / Other than that]**, make sure your head is in a good place, [2] **[other than that / so to speak]**. Think positive thoughts, relax your muscles, and watch your breathing – your brain needs enough oxygen to work well. [3] **[That said / For starters]**, don't breathe too deeply or you may feel dizzy. Remember to read the instructions very carefully and [4] **[so to speak / above all]** trust your instincts – you know your stuff! Oh, and [5] **[needless to say / that said]**, keep your phone off! But I'm sure you know this. [6] **[Above all / Other than that]**, I can't think of anything else to tell you; you'll be fine!

Hi Cynthia,

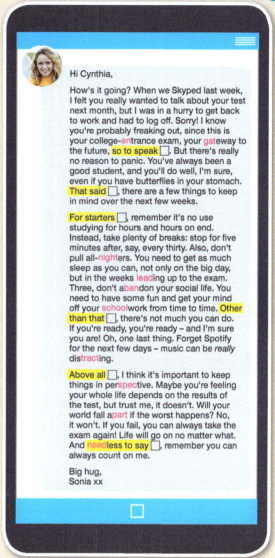

How's it going? When we Skyped last week, I felt you really wanted to talk about your test next month, but I was in a hurry to get back to work and had to log off. Sorry! I know you're probably freaking out, since this is your college-entrance exam, your gateway to the future, so to speak ☐. But there's really no reason to panic. You've always been a good student, and you'll do well, I'm sure, even if you have butterflies in your stomach. That said ☐, there are a few things to keep in mind over the next few weeks.

For starters ☐, remember it's no use studying for hours and hours on end. Instead, take plenty of breaks: stop for five minutes after, say, every thirty. Also, don't pull all-nighters. You need to get as much sleep as you can, not only on the big day, but in the weeks leading up to the exam. Three, don't abandon your social life. You need to have some fun and get your mind off your schoolwork from time to time. Other than that ☐, there's not much you can do. If you're ready, you're ready – and I'm sure you are! Oh, one last thing. Forget Spotify for the next few days – music can be *really* distracting.

Above all ☐, I think it's important to keep things in perspective. Maybe you're feeling your whole life depends on the results of the test, but trust me, it doesn't. Will your world fall apart if the worst happens? No, it won't. If you fail, you can always take the exam again! Life will go on no matter what. And needless to say ☐, remember you can always count on me.

Big hug,
Sonia xx

D Your turn! Choose a person from 11. Imagine you are close friends. Write him / her a three-paragraph message in about 250 words.

Before

Rank your recommendations from most to least important.

While

Follow the model in A. In paragraph 1, introduce the problem. In paragraph 3, give your most important advice. Use at least four friendly comments.

After

Share your message with classmates. Who has the most original suggestions?

Review 4
Units 7–8

1 Speaking

A Look at the photos on p.72.

1 Note down everything you can remember about the people, using these words and expressions.

be regarded as	come out	high-profile	rise to fame	take place

2 In groups, share information. Did you remember everything?

3 Take turns describing your favorite singer and explaining why.

> I used to be really hooked on ..., but now I'm into ...

B Make it personal Choose three question titles from Units 7 and 8 to ask a partner. Ask at least three follow-up questions for each. What did you learn about each other?

> How important is music to you?

> Very! I look for new songs on Spotify every day so I can keep up.

2 Grammar

A Circle the most logical words or expressions to complete the paragraph.

As recently as 20 years ago, air travel was a pleasure. But things have changed [1][**because / because of**] the number of passengers and increased security, and you [2][**have to / 're supposed to**] expect delays. Now you [3][**'d better / can**] get to the airport three hours in advance [4][**be supposed to / in order to**] catch your flight. When you go through security, you [5][**must / ought to**] place your carry-on liquids in a plastic bag, and in some countries, you [6][**'d better / have to**] take off your shoes, too. You [7][**ought to / 're not allowed to**] take any sharp objects on the plane, so check your carry-on luggage before leaving home. [8][**Since / Because of**] even a dead cell phone might be a weapon, you might have to turn your cell phone on [9][**so that / as**] it can be inspected. I know I [10][**'d better / should**] be calm at the airport, but I never am!

B Make it personal In pairs, are there regulations at school or at home that you disagree with? Use at least three of these expressions.

above all	for starters	needless to say	other than that	thank goodness	trust me

> My roommate has too many rules. For starters, when I come in the house, I'm supposed to ...

3 Point of view

Choose a topic. Then support your opinion in 100–150 words, and record your answer. Ask a partner for feedback. How can you be more convincing?

a You think popular music used to be better: better lyrics, better melodies, better performers. OR
You think music is always changing, and today's popular music is very good.

b You think culture is important, and everyone should keep up with music, art, and literature. OR
You think people have different interests, and culture is just one of them.

c You think everyday fears can really hold people back. OR
You think everyone is afraid of something, and it's usually no big deal.

d You think the news, for the most part, is accurate and well researched. OR
You think the news is often influenced either by politics or business considerations and may not be accurate.

Warm-up

See page 61 of the Teacher's Book for warm-up ideas.

1 Speaking

A 1 Before sts look back at p.72, elicit definitions and useful personal examples for the words and phrases in the box. Sts turn to p.73 and compare their definitions to those in 1C.

Sts work individually, and note down as much information as they can about the musicians in the photos.

2 In groups, sts share their information, adding anything else of their own, e.g.

A: *What do you know about Sam Smith?*

B: *Well, he's English. He sang the theme song for a James Bond movie.*

C: *And I remember he was born in 1992.*

Tell sts to make a note of any information their classmates have that they don't have.

3 Ask sts to choose their favorite singer, and tell the others in the group about them and why they like them so much. Monitor and praise their use of the boxed expressions. Invite volunteers to give a short class presentation about them, saying what they particularly like, and why they chose them.

B Make it personal Sts look back at the lesson title questions in Units 7 and 8 and choose three to ask a partner, plus follow-up questions. Focus on the example to see how many use Spotify (or a similar music-streaming site). Allow time to think of other questions they might ask.

Sts can swap partners again, mingle, and use different lesson title questions, so this can become a full class revision.

Class feedback. Ask: *What was the most surprising thing you learned about your partner?*

2 Grammar

A Explain that the text is about what causes delays at the airport. Brainstorm what they think it might say.

Sts read the text quickly to answer the following question: *Why, according to the writer, is air travel no longer a pleasure?* (Because an increased number of passengers and security mean long delays.) *What other problems did it mention?* Paircheck, then classcheck.

Sts re-read the text and circle the most logical words or expressions. If necessary, suggest sts refer back to the grammar section on p.88 to help them. Classcheck.

Answers

1 because of 2 have to 3 'd better 4 in order to
5 must 6 have to 7 're not supposed to 8 Since
9 so that 10 should

B Make it personal Review the meaning and pronunciation of the boxed expressions.

Brainstorm some regulations at school that sts disagree with, e.g. not being able to take drinks into class, or chew gum when they have an exam. Then, in pairs, sts discuss regulations at home or at school that they disagree with, following on from the example.

3 Point of view

See page 62 of the Teacher's Book for notes about this section.

Go through topics a–d with the class, and brainstorm a few ideas for each one. Review and board phrases for giving opinions, e.g.

In my opinion / view ...

I really / strongly believe that ...

It seems to me that ...

As far as I'm concerned ...

Individually, sts choose one of them, and make some preparatory notes. Tell sts to make the notes they feel they need to be able to speak for about 80 seconds on the topic. You don't want full sentences or a script, just prompts from which they can talk naturally.

Weaker classes: Sts can write out their argument in full, but should rehearse it so they don't just read it aloud.

Group together sts who chose the same topic so that they can compare, share, expand on and improve their ideas. Monitor and correct as much as you can.

If possible, sts record their opinion in class using a cell phone. Allow sts to re-record if they aren't happy. It's all good practice and everybody wants the best possible end product. Encourage sts to swap recordings with a partner and give each other feedback.

Class feedback. You could play some of the answers to the whole class, and ask: *Which argument did you think was most convincing?*

Optional activity

Hold a class debate on one of the topics in 3. See technique on Teacher's Book p.62. When all groups have spoken, have sts vote for the most convincing group.

4 Reading

A Cover the text and ask sts to note down three things they remember or learned about jazz from Unit 7. If necessary, they can look back at p.80 to remind them. Invite individuals to tell the class what they have written down.

Uncover the title of the text and ask: *What comes to mind?* Let sts call out ideas but don't confirm just yet.

Sts uncover and look at the photo. Ask: *What's the man doing?* (turning on the radio)

Sts read the title and first sentence of the article, and choose the best answer, 1–3. Then give them two minutes to read the rest of the article to check their answer.

Ask: *What else do you remember from the text?* In pairs, sts share what they remember. Don't let them re-read it yet.

Answer

2 a time before the 1950s

B In pairs, give sts three minutes to complete the word web, looking back in the text to check. Classcheck.

Answer

1 big band dance music 2 dance halls 3 ballrooms
4 black 5 white 6 white

Optional activity

Stronger classes: Cover up B and ask sts to read through the text and make a note of all the words connected to jazz music and radio. You could also give them a copy of audio scripts 7.15 and 7.16, and ask them to note down words from these. Have them design a word web to include all the words.

C Sts re-read the article and put the events in order, 1–5. Classcheck. Elicit pronunciation and any problems of meaning with *migrating, characterized, rebellion, improvised, rhythms, broadcasts, amateurs, racial, emerged* and *maturity*. Ask: *Did you find the text informative? Anything you didn't know or can add to it? Have you heard of any of the other musicians mentioned (Parker, Gillespie, or Monk)?*

Answers

1 Jazz was played down south before the migration to the north.
2 Jazz gained popularity along with the innovative style of the decade.
3 Radio helped to spread jazz in urban areas.
4 Bebop, a more serious kind of jazz, developed.
5 Miles Davis released *Birth of the cool.*

5 Writing

Go through the instructions with the class. Brainstorm and board a checklist of things they could mention, e.g. how long they have liked this type of music, how they got into it, whether it's "popular," and who with, where they'd recommend you begin if you want to get into it.

They may want to say whether they've always liked this music or how their tastes have changed (refer them back to 2C on p.73). Elicit/Board useful expressions, e.g.

I've liked reggae music since I was ...

I didn't use to like ... but now I love it ...

I'm really hooked on ...

I grew tired of listening to ...

If you want to hear (him) at (his best), a good starting point would be ...

If they do this in class, some inevitably finish first. As they do so, sts swap and read each other's paragraphs to give the rest more time.

Sts swap paragraphs with a (new) partner, read and proofread each other's writing. Display the texts on the wall or post them on the class website.

Ask: *How would you define our class taste in music, e.g. eclectic, typical of a mixed bunch of people from our country?*

4 Reading

A Read the title and first sentence of the article. Choose the best answer. Then read the rest to check.

"The jazz age" probably refers to ...

1 the 1950s. 2 a time before the 1950s. 3 a time after the 1950s.

The jazz age and beyond

By the 1950s, when Miles Davis was performing in Harlem, jazz had already come into its own. The birth of jazz is generally credited to African Americans, who began migrating to the American north in the 1920s and brought their music with them to the large cities of New York and Chicago. The "roaring 20s" or "jazz age," which ended with the Great Depression, was a period characterized by rebellion. Traditions were questioned, women got the right to vote and began to work in large numbers, and a new and innovative style of dress emerged. The improvised rhythms and sounds of jazz went hand in hand with the new age.

The spread of jazz was encouraged by the introduction of large-scale radio broadcasts in 1932. From the comfort of their living rooms, Americans could now experience new and different kinds of music. Originally, there were two types of live music on the radio: concert music and big band dance music. Concert music was played by amateurs, often volunteers, whereas big band dance music was played by professionals. As commercial radio increased, big band dance music took over and was played from nightclubs, dance halls, and ballrooms. Musicologist Charles Hamm, who studied American popular music in the context of its complex racial and ethnic dynamics, described three types of jazz on the radio: black music for black audiences, black music for white audiences, and white music for white audiences. In urban areas, African American jazz was played frequently and its popularity spread.

In the early 1940s, bebop emerged, led by Charlie Parker, Dizzy Gillespie, and Thelonius Monk. This was a more serious art form that moved jazz away from popular dance music. Other types of jazz followed, including cool jazz, a melodic style that merged the traditions of African American bebop and white jazz traditions. The original cool jazz musican was Miles Davis, who released *Birth of the cool* in 1957. Jazz had reached maturity, soon to have an international following.

B In pairs, complete the word web on the kinds of jazz played on the radio.

concert music

[1] ______ ______ dance music

nightclubs, [2] ______ ______, and [3] ______

black music for [4] ______ audiences; for [5] ______ audiences

white music for [6] ______ audiences

C Put the events in order.

☐ Radio helped to spread jazz in urban areas.
☐ Jazz gained popularity along with the innovative style of the decade.
☐ Miles Davis released *Birth of the cool*.
☐ Jazz was played down south before the migration to the north.
☐ Bebop, a more serious kind of jazz, developed.

5 Writing

Write a paragraph about a type of music that's important to you or a musician that you admire. Include *-ly* adverbs, such as *amazingly*, *surprisingly*, and *extremely*.

9 How much time do you spend on your own?

1 Listening

A 9.1 Listen to Angela and Marco. Match them to a photo 1–3. Who's more like you?

B 9.1 Match the sentence halves and write A (Angela) or M (Marco). Listen again to check. Which opinions do you agree with most?

1 People who talk the loudest ...
2 Group work is better than ...
3 All my good ideas ...
4 Most great leaders ...
5 Introverts ...
6 The people I work best with ...

a [ ] happen when I think things over.
b [ ] haven't been outgoing at all.
c [1] always get their ideas accepted! A
d [ ] love talking.
e [ ] should be valued more.
f [ ] working alone.

I definitely think it's introverts who ...

2 Vocabulary: Interacting with people

A Take the quiz. Don't check your score yet! Which situations 1–6 have you been in recently?

ARE YOU MORE OF AN INTROVERT OR AN EXTROVERT?

1 At a party, you ...
A mingle as much as possible.
B talk to and stick with just one person.

2 On a long plane or bus trip, you ...
A reveal personal information to strangers.
B stick to small talk.

3 When you're upset, you ...
A open up to a friend.
B keep things to yourself.

4 When making a hard decision, you ...
A think out loud and ask for advice.
B sit by yourself to think things over.

5 In a group meeting, you ...
A suggest lots of ideas.
B say little and think up ideas on your own.

6 When people discuss politics, you tend to ...
A give your opinion.
B keep quiet.

Lesson Aims: Sts learn vocabulary to talk about interacting in group situations, and discuss whether they are extroverts or introverts.

Skills	Language	Vocabulary
Listening to a conversation about the advantages and disadvantages of groupwork	Word order for objects and phrasal verbs	Verbs and expressions for interacting with people: *keep quiet, mingle, open up, reveal, small talk, think something over, think up*

Warm-up

Ask sts to go to Phrasal Verbs on pp.165–167 and, in pairs, test each other, e.g. A says a phrasal verb, B says what it means.

Begin by saying: *It's amazing how rarely most of us are truly alone these days.* Ask the lesson title question: *How much time do you spend on your own?* Follow up with: *Do you need more time alone than you get? How much of your time alone are you really entirely alone, i.e. offline, unable to contact or be contacted by the world?* In pairs, sts discuss the questions.

1 Listening

A 9.1 Ask: *Do you like doing group work in class? Why / Why not?* Focus on the photos. Ask: *What are the people doing? Which of the people do you think enjoy / don't enjoy working in a group?*

Set the task to listen and spot which photo shows Angela and Marco. Play the audio. Paircheck. This will let you know how many got it the first time.

Classcheck and re-play if necessary. Then ask sts if they are more like Angela or Marco. Encourage them to explain why. Ask for a show of hands for who is most like Angela, then Marco.

Answer

Photo 2

See Teacher's Book p.325 for Audio script 9.1.

B 9.1 Ask sts to match the sentence halves and then decide who said each one, Angela or Marco.

Paircheck, then classcheck. Again ask: *Whose opinions do you agree with most? Anyone changed their mind?*

Stronger classes: Discuss the meaning of outgoing in ending b. Elicit synonyms, e.g. *sociable, gregarious, extroverted*. Have sts think of opposite adjectives, e.g. *unsociable, reserved, introverted*. Also highlight the expression from the audio *The squeaky wheel gets the grease*. Ask: *Who says this?* (Angela). Discuss what she is referring to and what the expression means. (She is referring to Max, meaning that the person who talks the loudest gets the attention.)

Answers

1 c – A 2 f – M 3 a – A 4 b – A 5 e – A 6 d – M

See Teacher's Book p.325 for Audio script 9.1.

2 Vocabulary: Interacting with people

A Focus on the title of the quiz. Ask: *Would you say you are an introvert or an extrovert?*

Go through each situation. Clarify meaning, so they can mark their choice to each question as you go along.

Tip

Use your arms, hands, fingers and head to gesture as much as you can to explain new vocabulary. Helping sts to visualize words can stop them having to try to find an exact translation for everything at this stage.

Exemplify the meaning of *small talk* (general conversation about trivial impersonal topics).

Have sts do the quiz, then put them into pairs to tell each other about any similar situations they have been in, e.g. *I had a very hard decision to make last week ... . I had to decide whether to ...* . A personal example or two from you first will make this more productive.

Optional activity

Stronger classes: Sts write another quiz question (with A and B answers). Then they mingle, asking classmates their question, collate the answers and feed the results back at the end.

B 9.2 Sts look back at the highlighted words in the quiz and put them in the correct column in the chart. Play the audio for them to check their answers.

Ask if they can think of any other words they could add to the three groups, e.g. *Socializing – circulate, mix with other people, chat; Sharing – communicate, gossip, spread, mention, transmit; Thinking – ponder, contemplate, reflect, consider*.

Answers

Socializing: mingle, small talk
Sharing: reveal, open up
Thinking: think over, think up, keep quiet

See Teacher's Book p.325 for Audio script 9.2.

Tip

Elicit/Contrast which words in the chart are more formal (usually those of Latin origin). Discuss the pros and cons of using both. Shorter, phrasal-type ones tend to be more common in native/fluent speaker speech but are less frequent between lower level 'International English'/EFL learners. Over 80% of the world's conversations in English no longer involve a native speaker at all, so sts need to learn both. Always going for 'native speaker' models is not necessarily in sts' best interests, as none will ever be native speakers.

C 9.3 Read **Word order** with the class, using the errors to highlight the grammar and problems. Elicit other examples for 1, 2 and 3 to check sts have understood, e.g. *She communicated the information to her bosses*. Go through the **Common mistake**, and check sts understand when to use *on* and *by*.

In pairs, sts check if samples 1–5 are correct or not, fixing the wrong ones. To add context, tell sts these are all from sts' homework.

Weaker classes: Give the clue that four are wrong/ only one is correct.

Play the audio for sts to check, or classcheck by inviting individual sts to board the corrected sentence.

Answers

1 I don't mind revealing my phone number to people, but not my address.
2 Correct
3 Whenever I have things bothering me, I always open up to my friends.
4 I guess I'm more likely to keep things to myself.
5 I tend to keep my opinions quiet. I hate disagreements.

See Teacher's Book p.325 for Audio script 9.3.

Optional activity

Weaker classes: To clarify the difference between a direct object and indirect object, board the following sentences:

1 *He gave me some help.*
2 *They communicated the news to everyone.*

Ask: *Which of the underlined words is a) a direct object b) an indirect object?*

Optional activity

Ask sts to complete the following sentences using the correct pronouns and the phrasal verbs in brackets. Tell them to refer to point 2 in the Word order box for help.

1 *Here are your glasses, why don't you* __________ ? (put on)
2 *You know smoking it bad for your health , why don't you* __________ ? (give up)
3 *You must be hot in that coat on, why don't you* __________ ? (take off)
4 *If there are any words you don't know,* __________ *in the dictionary*. (look up)
5 *Put those newspapers in the recycling bin. Don't just* __________ . (throw away)
6 *I can't see in here. We need more lights on. Can you* __________ *, please?* (switch on)

(Answers: 1 put them on, 2 give it up, 3 take it off, 4 look them up, 5 throw them away, 6 switch them on)

Song lyric: See Teacher's Book p.343 for notes about the song and an accompanying activity to do with the class.

D Make it personal

1 In groups, sts compare their quiz answers and talk more generally about their usual preferences in the situations. Encourage them to expand on their answers, as in the speech bubble. Monitor, prompt and correct. To end, ask: *Who in your group gave the most similar answers to you?*

2 Groups should be able to move straight onto stage 2 as the situations are 'universal'. Quickly highlight the example, then tell them to imagine and keep talking about each situation. Board a prompt to help: *Have you been in any of these situations? What did/ would you do?*

3 Finally, sts score their results to the quiz in 2A to find out what it means. Ask: *Did you get mostly As or Bs? Read the quiz results. Do you agree with them? If not, explain why*. To end, focus on the cartoon characters, and ask: *Who are you most alike? What are you doing tonight?*

Workbook p.43.

B 9.2 In pairs, put the highlighted words in A into three categories. Listen to check. Which are phrasal verbs?

Socializing	Sharing	Thinking

C 9.3 Read *Word order*. In pairs, decide which of 1–5 are correct. Rephrase the wrong ones. Listen to check.

1 I don't mind revealing people my phone number, but not my address.
2 I'm not really very good at thinking new ideas up. I guess I'm not very creative.
3 Whenever I have things bothering me, I always open my friends up.
4 I guess I'm more likely to keep to myself things.
5 I tend to keep quiet my opinions. I hate disagreements.

Word order

1 Some verbs only allow indirect objects with *to*: I **revealed** the answer **to him**. (Not: ~~I revealed him the answer~~.)
2 Pronouns must go between the verb and the particle in many separable phrasal verbs: I thought **it** over for a long time. (Not: ~~I thought over it~~.)
3 Objects go between the verb and the adverb: She raised **her voice** angrily. (Not: ~~She raised angrily her voice~~.)

Common mistake

I like to solve problems ~~by my own~~. *on my own / by myself*

D Make it personal Find out how introverted you really are!

1 In groups, using your quiz answers, share your own preferences.

> When I'm at parties, I really like to mingle. You never know who you'll meet!

2 How would you react in these situations?

a You're at a wedding where you know no one.
b A new neighbor moves next door.
c You go to a cooking class alone.
d You're sitting next to a stranger on a long bus trip.
e You go to a cafeteria for lunch, but there are no free tables.

> I'd smile and speak to the first person who smiled back. But it's still hard to open up to strangers.

3 Do you agree? Who are most alike? Check your quiz score below.

QUIZ SCORE – WHAT IT MEANS

Mostly As: You're the type who has to tell people what you're thinking. You don't like spending too much time alone, either. A true extrovert.

A balance of As and Bs: You're happy being alone, but also like to socialize. You prefer to think things over before expressing your opinions. Public speaking makes you nervous, but it excites you, too.

Mostly Bs: You're a classic introvert, a "strong silent type." At social events, you look for chances to be alone. You like intimate conversations and love to read.

I'm staying in tonight
I'm staying in tonight

3 Listening

A 9.4 What do you know about China? Look at 1–6. T (true) or F (false)? Listen to / Watch the travel advice to check.

1 You can eat before a senior person if you're told to start.
2 Don't leave a business card on the table in front of you in a meeting.
3 It's OK to hold hands, but don't kiss your wife in public.
4 China and Japan have a positive history together.
5 If you invite a translator to dinner, you don't have to pay.
6 At someone's home, your host will give you slippers that are your size.

B 9.4 Listen / Watch again. In pairs, remember the 11 behaviors to avoid. Did any surprise you?

C **Make it personal** In groups, answer 1–3. Any surprising stories?

1 How (im)polite are people from your country? What customs might be rude somewhere else?
2 When was the last time you were mistreated in a store / restaurant? What happened?
3 What is the rudest thing anyone has ever said to you? Use "bleep" for any words you don't want to repeat.

I used to work part-time in a supermarket. And one day, a woman pointed at me and told her son, "This is why you have to stay in school!"

4 Language in use

Read the discussion forum. Underline six expressions to show annoyance or anger. Do you agree with the opinions?

It really gets to me when I'm shopping and the employee at the checkout counter doesn't smile. I don't mean saying "thank you" or even "please," **which most of them manage to do**. I'm talking about trying to be genuinely friendly, **which is the most important thing of all**. Ji-min, Seoul

I hate it when I'm watching a movie and the people around me start talking – even if they're just whispering. It drives me insane! Or, eating! The noise! And don't get me started on the smell of popcorn, **which literally makes me sick**, especially if there's butter on it. Diego, Bogotá

It gets on my nerves when I'm riding on the bus or subway next to people whose headphones are so loud I can hear the music from several meters away. I tell you, it drives me up the wall. So I just stare at the person and start singing along, **which, strangely enough, usually does the trick**. Birgit, Munich

Loud headphones don't bother me at all.

Really? They drive me crazy, especially when people are singing, too. You have no idea!

Lesson Aims: Sts talk about customs in other countries, and discuss what makes them angry or annoyed.

Skills	Language	Vocabulary	Grammar
Listening to someone giving advice about customs in China Discussing what makes you angry	Expressing annoyance, e.g. *I hate it when … , It really gets to me when …*	*get on s.o.'s nerves, rude, polite* Phrases to express annoyance: *It really gets to me when … , I hate it when … , It drives me insane, Don't get me started on… , It gets on my nerves when … , It drives me up the wall*	Uses of *which* in non-restrictive clauses

Warm-up

Discuss the following questions as a class: *Do you have any customs in your country that people find strange? Which customs do you like / dislike? Which do you think are silly?*

Ask the lesson title question: *What behavior is considered rude in your culture?* e.g. In Brazil, blowing your nose in a restaurant. In the UK, talking too loudly, or over others. Brainstorm more as a class.

3 Listening

A 9.4 Ask: *Have you ever been to China? What do you know about the country and Chinese customs?*

Read advice 1–6 with the class, check understanding, and ask sts to guess whether they are true or false. Explain that they are going to listen to / watch a businessman giving advice about eleven different customs, of which he will mention 1–6.

Play the video / audio for sts to listen and check their guesses. Classcheck, and sts correct the false ones.

Answers

1 T
2 F. It is polite to leave the business card on the table in front of you.
3 T
4 F. China and Japan have a negative history.
5 F. If you invite a translator to dinner, or anyone, you are expected to pay.
6 F. They will give you slippers, but maybe not your size.

See Teacher's Book p.325 for Audio script 9.4.

B 9.4 After they have listened / watched again, have sts cover up 3A and try to remember all the behaviors to avoid. In pairs, sts compare their lists and see if they can remember all eleven.

Answers

1 When you are doing business, you need to give a gift, and if you are offered a gift, don't open it until later.
2 At business lunches, don't eat first. The most senior person goes first, or the oldest.
3 People give business cards with two hands. If someone gives you a card in a meeting lay it on the desk in front of you.
4 Don't put chopsticks straight down into rice.
5 Don't give kisses and hugs in public.
6 Don't make comparisons with Japan.
7 Don't point at people.
8 If you invite someone out to have dinner, you are expected to pay.
9 Don't give anyone a green hat. This means that your spouse is cheating on you.
10 Don't give people clocks as gifts, as this means you want them to die.
11 If you go to a Chinese person's house, take off your shoes.

See Teacher's Book p.325 for Audio script 9.4.

C Make it personal In groups, sts discuss questions 1–3.

Weaker classes: For question 1, board the following prompts to help them: *greeting people, eating in restaurants, standing in line, taking photos, clothes, crossing the road, driving*.

Have a class feedback session. For question 2, ask: *How are you generally treated in restaurants / stores in your country? Is the 'customer always right'?* When discussing question 3, ask: *Have you ever offended a stranger by saying something rude?*

Song lyric: See Teacher's Book p.344 for notes about the song and an accompanying activity to do with the class.

4 Language in use

Ask sts to read the comments on the discussion forum quickly. Ask: *What are the people complaining about?* (sales clerks not smiling, people talking or eating at the movies, people playing loud music through headphones on the bus or subway). *Do these things make you angry?*

Sts re-read the comments and underline the six expressions to show annoyance / anger. Classcheck, then ask sts to discuss the comments, and say if they agree with the people.

Stronger classes: Elicit more expressions with *drive*, e.g. drive someone *mad / crazy / insane / nuts*.

Answers

It really gets to me when … , I hate it when … , It drives me insane!
Don't get me started on … It gets on my nerves when …
It drives me up the wall

5 Grammar: Uses of *which*

A Read the example sentences with the class, and check sts understand them.

Have sts complete the rules. Paircheck, then classcheck.

Answers

a 1, 4 b 2, 3

Refer sts to the **Grammar expansion** on p.154.

Tip

Board these sentences to illustrate the difference between *restrictive* (defining) and *non-restrictive* (non-defining) clauses:

My new ringtone, which I love, is driving my colleagues crazy! (non-restrictive)

The new ringtone (that) you bought for me is driving my colleagues crazy! (restrictive)

Elicit that in 1 *which* introduces additional information, whereas in 2 *(that)* introduces information which tells us which ringtone is being referred to (in other words, it defines the noun). Ask: *When do we need a comma?* (with non-restrictive clauses)

B 9.5 Read the **Common mistakes**, and check that everyone understands. Emphasize that we never use *that* in non-restrictive clauses. Remind sts, however, that we use *that* in restrictive clauses, e.g. *Kissing people on both cheeks is a custom that people find strange in some countries*.

Sts read and correct sentences 1–7.

Classcheck. Then have sts practice saying the sentences in pairs, pausing between the two clauses as in the example.

Answers

1 My car is always breaking down, which drives me up the wall.
2 My WiFi signal keeps dropping every five minutes, which is getting on my nerves.
3 Whenever I'm sad, my mom says "life is too short," which usually makes things worse.
4 I've been thinking of moving abroad, which my friends say is a bad idea.
5 I can't stop biting my nails, which is a terrible habit, I know.
6 Yesterday, my supervisor told me to shut up, which was very rude of her.
7 Today is Thursday, which means I have to help with the housework.

Tip

Suggest sts record themselves saying the sentences on their cell phone. Then they can listen to the recording to check their pronunciation and fluency.

C Go through the examples in the speech bubbles to illustrate what to do. Then have sts rewrite the sentences in 5B with their own ideas and exchange sentences with a partner. Monitor hard to help weed out errors. In pairs, A says their answers to B who responds appropriately, giving advice or asking for more information. Congratulate sts on their successes, and pick up on any serious errors.

Weaker classes: Sts can swap and read each other's sentences first to help prepare more complex/accurate responses.

Classcheck to give individuals a chance to show off their best exchanges.

D Make it personal Give sts three minutes to complete the chart with their own annoying habits column and their reactions. Feed in vocabulary and all the correction/guidance you can.

Refer sts to the speech bubbles as an example, then invite a st to talk about shopping, beginning with *Whenever I'm shopping, people ... .*

In pairs, sts compare what makes them mad. Monitor, checking they are using *which* correctly.

Class feedback and invite sts to tell you anything interesting / funny that their partner said. Do any sts get annoyed by the same things?

Weaker classes: Brainstorm examples for each category as a class first.

Optional activity

Sts write a short comment about what makes them mad for the discussion forum in 4. Display the paragraphs on the classroom wall, then ask sts to mingle and read each other's opinions. Class feedback. Ask: *Who did you agree with? Did you find any of the comments surprising/amusing/outrageous?*

Workbook p.44.

5 Grammar: Uses of *which*

A Complete rules a and b with the sentence numbers (1–4). Then write a or b next to the bold examples in the discussion forum on p.96.

Uses of *which* in non-restrictive clauses

Non-restrictive clauses often reveal the speaker's opinions and feelings, as well as give information.

1 My new ringtone, **which** I love, is driving all my colleagues crazy!
2 Judy has unfriended me on Facebook®, **which** means she's probably mad at me.
3 My boss is always taking credit for people's work, **which** I think is really unfair.
4 Most of my friends like hip hop, **which** personally I can't stand.

a In sentences ______ and ______ , *which* refers to the noun before it.
b In sentences ______ and ______ , *which* refers to the whole idea before it.

» Grammar expansion p.154

B ▶ 9.5 Read *Common mistakes* and correct 1–7. Listen to check. Notice the pause and the slight drop in intonation between the two clauses.

1 My car is always breaking down, this drives me up the wall.

My car is always breaking down, which drives me up the wall.

2 My WiFi signal keeps dropping every five minutes that is getting on my nerves.
3 Whenever I'm sad, my mom says "life is too short" which usually makes things worse.
4 I've been thinking of moving abroad, my friends say it's a bad idea.
5 I can't stop biting my nails what is a terrible habit, I know.
6 Yesterday, my supervisor told me to shut up that was very rude of her.
7 Today is Thursday what means I have to help with the housework.

Common mistakes

My boss is always whistling ~~what / that~~ *, which* really ~~get~~ *gets* on my nerves.

I hear message tones constantly, ~~it~~ *, which* really gets to me.

Use a comma before *which* in non-restrictive clauses, but not to separate sentences.

C In pairs, change the underlined words in **B** to make 1–7 true for you. Any unusual stories?

> My cell-phone case is always coming off, which drives me up the wall.

> Maybe it's time to buy a new one. Mine never comes off.

D **Make it personal** Complete the "Makes me mad!" chart. In pairs, compare ideas using *which*. Do you get annoyed by the same things?

Place / situation	Annoying habit	Your reaction
eating out	*People speak too loud.*	*It drives me insane.*
shopping		
school / work		
public transportation / driving		
home with my family		
telemarketers and call centers		

> Whenever I'm eating out, people always speak too loud, which drives me insane.

> Yeah, I hate that, too.

6 Reading

A Read the introduction and paragraph 1 in 6B. Then complete the dates for Generation Z. Search online to complete the chart. Which generations are the members of your immediate family from?

Generation Z: ________ to present
Millenials (Generation Y): ________ to ________
Generation X: ________ to ________
Baby boomers: 1946 to ________

My parents were born in ... , so they must be Generation ...!

B Read the article. Complete the introduction with *better* or *worse*. Did you enjoy the interview?

THE Z FACTOR by Gloria Blanco

Already the largest generational group in the U.S., Generation Z-ers are forming a demographic tsunami that will change the country forever – and probably for the ____. Adam Smith, author of *Generating generations*, tells us why.

1 **Q:** *Why Z? I don't remember hearing that term before.*

A: It's just an arbitrary label to describe children who were born after 1997. I know that these terms don't always mean much – especially outside the U.S. – so let's call them *Screenagers*, a word coined by writer Douglas Rushkoff, which I myself [**also like better / tend to avoid**].

2 **Q:** *Interesting term.*

A: It makes perfect sense, since Generation Z kids spend over 40% of their time staring at different screens. But unlike us, *screenagers* have been using computers, tablets, and phones practically since they were born, which means that, to them, multitasking across devices [**is as natural as breathing / takes a lot of effort**]. These kids have a totally different outlook on technology than you and I do.

3 **Q:** *What else makes them unique?*

A: *Screenagers* are growing up in an unpredictable world filled with danger: extreme weather, massive poverty, endless wars and financial crises. Because of all these threats, they've developed a different attitude to risk-taking, which means they will probably seek [**more / less**] stability as adults. Also, they're fully aware of how interconnected the world is, take an interest in all kinds of social issues and are far more tolerant of diversity than I ever was. These are all very encouraging signs.

4 **Q:** *It seems they have very different priorities.*

A: Yes. In a recent study, thousands of kids were asked whether they'd rather be smarter or better looking. Nearly 70% chose "smarter," which means they seem to value [**intelligence over beauty / beauty over intelligence**] – a very welcome change, in my opinion. Just ask my thirteen-year-old! She couldn't care less about fashion, brands and accessories – unlike her older brother, who spends the whole day at the mall. No wonder they don't see eye to eye on anything!

5 **Q:** *One last question, what kind of employees will they be?*

A: Resourceful and creative, I'm sure, but with alarmingly short attention spans because of the number of distractions from their many devices, which means they'll find it [**easy / hard**] to keep focused. I'm under the impression they'll prioritize self-fulfillment over financial gains and will have a strong preference for green, socially responsible companies. Whether they'll find it easy to deal with hierarchy is hard to tell, but my philosophy has always been "rebelliousness is better than blind adherence to authority."

C Re-read. T (true), F (false) or NS (not sure)? Underline the evidence in the interview.

1 "Generation Z" is a carefully chosen term.
2 *Screenagers* will only feel comfortable with people like themselves.
3 Adam's son probably likes to wear what's in fashion.
4 Adam thinks *Screenagers* will want to have meaningful jobs that make them happy.
5 *Screenagers* will have trouble dealing with people in positions of power.
6 Adam believes authority is very important.

Lesson Aims: Sts read about Generation Z, and learn vocabulary to talk about different generations' values and attitudes

Skills	Language	Vocabulary
Reading an interview with an author about Generation Z Discussing people from different generations	Describing attitudes: *Most of my friends couldn't care less about politics or green issues*	Describing attitude: *outlook on ... , be aware of ... , be tolerant of ... , value, not care less about ... , see eye to eye on ... , be under the impression ...*

Warm-up

Board: *Common worries*. Brainstorm ideas/phrases, e.g. *crime levels, the area I live in, health, appearance, work/study-related issues, being a good parent, family matters, finding the right partner, financial issues, ageing, diet, the latest technology.*

Ask the lesson title question: *What does your age group worry about most?* In groups, sts decide how old their 'age group' is and their top three worries. If they can't generalize/order them, sts can at least agree a few key ones. Class feedback.

Tip

With sophisticated classes, add questions like: *How does the world around you affect your attitudes and values? What influence does technology have on generations? If you could've chosen a different generation, which would it have been?*

Song lyric: See Teacher's Book p.344 for notes about the song and an accompanying activity to do with the class.

6 Reading

A Focus on the title and introduction. Ask: *What is the article about?* (a specific generation of people referred to as *Generation Z*). Ask if they have heard of this term. Focus on the chart, and the names of other generations. Ask if sts can guess what the dates are.

Sts research the dates on the Internet, or tell them what they are (see Background information below). Ask: *Which is your generation? Which generations are your (grand)parents from? Do they have any characteristics in common? Do you use these or similar terms in your language/culture?*

Answers

Generation Z: 1997 to present
Millennial (Generation Y): early 1980s to 2000
Generation X: early 1960s to early 1980s
Baby boomers: 1946 to 1964

Background information

These terms are used to identify specific cohorts of people; to understand their taste, their fashion, and what defines them as a generation.

Generation Z: 1997 to present

Millennial (Generation Y): early 1980s–2000, the babies of the baby boomers, and one of the largest cohorts

Generation X: early 1960s–early 1980s, also known as the latchkey kids (who return from school to an empty home) because of the increase in divorce and working mums

Baby boomers: 1946–1964, born in the post Second World War years, when there was a temporary marked increase in birth rate

B Sts read the text quickly and ignore any new words. Set a time limit of two minutes to encourage them to read quickly.

Ask how they would complete the introduction, with *better* or *worse*.

Answers

better

C Go through the statements for sts to underline the key words in them. Sts re-read the interview and answer *T*, *F*, or *NS*. Tell them to underline the evidence in the interview.

Paircheck, then classcheck. Did they underline the same evidence for each item?

Answers

1 F – *an arbitrary label ... I know that these terms don't mean much ...*
2 F – *are far more tolerant of diversity ...*
3 T – *who spends the whole day at the mall*
4 T – *they'll prioritize self-fulfillment over financial gains*
5 NS – *Whether they'll find it easy to deal with hierarchy is hard to tell*
6 F – *my philosophy has always been "rebelliousness is better than blind adherence to authority."*

Optional activity

Sts find and look up six new words in the reading text. Tell them to write a definition for each word. In pairs, ask them to exchange their definitions. Ask them to try and match their partner's definitions with the words they correspond to in the text.

D 9.6 Sts re-read the interview and find the **bold** text in parenthesis. Ask them to choose the best option in each case. Paircheck then play the audio for them to check their answers, or if you are short of time, classcheck.

Model the pronunciation of the words in **Pronunciation**, and have sts repeat after you. Elicit other words with similar spellings, e.g. *Biology, stability, geography*.

Answers

Para 1 also like better
Para 2 is as natural as breathing
Para 3 more
Para 4 intelligence over beauty
Para 5 hard

E Make it personal Ask: *Who are screenagers?* (= people born after 1997, who have never known a world without screens) *Are you a screenager? Do you know any screenagers? Are they friends or relatives?*

Read through the questions together, giving a quick answer yourself to each one to help them digest it. Use the example for Q5. In groups, sts discuss the questions more fully. Have one person from each group report back their groups' views to the class.

Stronger classes: During the class feedback, ask: *What do you think the next generation will be like? What worries will they have? Will their lives be easier / more difficult than the current generation's.*

Song lyric: See Teacher's Book p.342 for notes about the song and an accompanying activity to do with the class.

7 Vocabulary: Describing attitude

A 9.7 Explain that sts are going to listen to Gloria and Adam (from the interview text in 6B) chatting about Gloria's family.

Ask sts to listen first to find out which family members she mentions (13-year-old sister, 70-year-old grandma, and her mom) and match the family members with the photos (1 – grandma, 2 – mom, 3 – sister).

Re-play the audio for sts to match the family members with the descriptions a–d. Classcheck, and elicit which Gloria thinks is more important – generation or personality. Do sts agree with Gloria?

Answers

1 d 2 c 3 a 4 b
Personality is more important in Gloria's opinion.

See Teacher's Book p.326 for Audio script 9.7.

B 9.8 Sts read extracts 1–6 from the audio in 7A, and complete them with the highlighted expressions in 6B. Point out that the text in parenthesis after each gap is a definition for the highlighted phrases, and that in some cases, they will have to change the form of the verb.

Paircheck, then play the audio to classcheck.

Answers

1 couldn't care less about
2 is aware of
3 'm under the impression
4 see eye to eye, outlook on
5 value
6 was more tolerant of

See Teacher's Book p.326 for Audio script 9.8.

C Make it personal Focus on the speech bubbles. Elicit one or two other sentences about people they know using the expressions in 7B. Tell sts they can change the expressions from negative to positive, and vice versa, e.g. *cares a lot about ..., I really value ..., He / she isn't aware of ...* .

In pairs, sts make up more sentences.

Have a class feedback session, and invite sts to tell the class their sentences. Are there many similarities?

Optional activity

Sts research and write a paragraph about one of the other generations in the chart in 6A. Tell them to include information about:

- background information about the world when they were growing up
- what they spent their time doing
- their knowledge and attitude towards technology
- what their values and attitudes were
- what they worry about
- what makes them unique

Encourage them to use the highlighted expressions in 6B.

Display the paragraphs either on the wall or class website for sts to read each other's work.

Workbook p.45.

D 9.6 Circle the most logical option in the *which* clauses in the interview. Listen to check. Notice we stress the third syllable from the end in words ending in *-gy*, *-ty*, and *-phy*.

Pronunciation of *-gy*, *-ty*, and *-phy*

Notice we stress the third syllable from the end in words ending in *-gy*, *-ty*, and *-phy*.

psychology curiosity biography

E Make it personal In groups, answer 1–5. Similar opinions?

1 How accurately does Adam describe the *screenagers* you know?
2 Are older people necessarily wiser? Why (not)?
3 Which problems from paragraph 3 do you worry about most?
4 Do you agree with Adam's philosophy in paragraph 5?
5 Will *screenagers* have an easier life than their parents? Why (not)?

Well, I think life will be more difficult. Everything is more unpredictable and ...

7 Vocabulary: Describing attitude

A 9.7 Listen to Adam and Gloria from 6B. Label the women in her family photo a–d. In Gloria's opinion, which is more important – generation or personality?

a environmentally-aware
b happiness-seeking
c conservative
d technology-minded

B 9.8 Use the correct form of the highlighted expressions in 6B to complete 1–6. Listen to check.

1 My younger sister ________________ (= is not interested in) what's going on in the world.
2 Grandma ________________ (= knows) all the latest technology and enjoys using it.
3 Sometimes I ________________ (= believe) that I have more in common with my grandma than with my parents.
4 My parents and I don't really ________________ (= agree on) lots of things. My ________________ (= attitude to) life is totally different from theirs.
5 I don't ________________ (= give importance to) money and status as much as my parents do.
6 I wish my mother ________________ (= open to) other people's lifestyles.

C Make it personal In pairs, modify 1–6 in B to describe people you know from different generations. Many similarities?

Most of my friends couldn't care less about politics or green issues.

Unlike me! Call me a nerd, but I watch the evening news every day!

Common mistake

~~Not like~~ Unlike you, I'm really interested in politics.

8 Listening

A 9.9 Listen to the start of an interview with a police officer. Check (✔) the correct option.

The officer thinks the robbery suspect …

- [ ] was watching TV.
- [ ] may have hurt someone.
- [ ] was at the crime scene.
- [ ] worked at a store.

B 9.10 Listen to the rest. Number the actions (1–3) in the order you hear them. There are two extra pictures.

C 9.10 Listen again. Match the officer's explanations to the correct pictures. Which explanations might explain the extra pictures, too?

The suspect …

1 [ ] wanted to run away.
2 [ ] didn't want to fall asleep.
3 [ ] was lying.
4 [ ] was making up a story.
5 [ ] was embarrassed.

D 9.11 Complete 1–6 with words from the interview, without changing the meaning. Then listen to check.

1 I questioned someone believed to have taken part in a robbery.	=	I questioned someone s*uspected of* taking part in a robbery.
2 A guy saying he was at home was the key suspect.	=	A guy c________ he was at home was the key suspect.
3 He said he wasn't involved.	=	He d________ being involved.
4 He said it was true, but it wasn't.	=	He wasn't t________ the t________ .
5 What showed the most that he was lying was …	=	What g________ him a________ the most was …
6 It's a story you're inventing.	=	It's a story you're m________ u____ .

E **Make it personal** Crime time! Work in pairs.

1 Use only the pictures and the words in D to remember the lies.
2 Are you good at spotting a liar? What unusual crime stories have you heard?

> I once heard a story where a guy was suspected of … He claimed …

100

Lesson Aims: Sts learn about how to detect whether someone is lying, and role play a trial.

Skills	Language	Vocabulary	Grammar
Listening to a detective giving tips on how to detect whether someone is lying Role playing a trial	Defending yourself: *But Officer, I was only making a left turn.*	*catch someone, claim, crime, deny, detective, give s.o. away, make up a story, suspect, suspicious, tell the truth, violate the law*	Reduced relative clauses: active and passive

Warm-up

Board *crime* and give sts, in pairs, two minutes to think of as many words as they can connected with the word. Class feedback, and board them. Elicit or teach the following: *confess, suspect, robbery, prison, interview, detective, police officer, closed circuit TV camera, robbery, witness, guilty, innocent*.

Ask the lesson title question: *What makes a good detective? Would you be a good detective?* Have sts discuss the questions in pairs, then class feedback.

8 Listening

A 9.9 Explain that sts are going to listen to a reporter interviewing a police officer about how to tell if a suspect is lying. Sts listen and choose the correct option. Paircheck and share all else they understood, then classcheck. Ask: *What does he do to tell if a suspect is lying?* (He watches the body for signs of stress).

Answer

was at the crime scene

See Teacher's Book p.326 for Audio script 9.9.

B 9.10 Focus on the pictures. Ask: *What is happening?* (The police officer is interviewing the suspect.) Ask sts to describe the suspect's actions in each picture (a He has his head bowed. b He is leaning back in his chair, and moving his feet up and down. c His eyes are looking up to the right. d He is rubbing his eye. e He is scratching his nose). Play the audio for sts to say which three of these actions the inspector mentions, and in which order.

Classcheck, then re-play the audio if necessary.

Answers

1 b 2 e 3 c

See Teacher's Book p.326 for Audio script 9.10.

C 9.10 Read through explanations 1–5. Ask sts which of the explanations they heard the inspector give (1, 3 and 4).

Sts listen and match them with the pictures. Ask which of the explanations they think match the other pictures.

Weaker classes: Let sts refer to the audio script if they find this difficult.

Answers

1 b 2 d 3 c 4 e 5 a

See Teacher's Book p.326 for Audio script 9.10.

D 9.11 In pairs, sts read through the gapped sentences from the interview and try to complete them.

Play the audio for them to check their answers.

Highlight the use of *the* definite article in the expression *tell the truth*. Elicit the opposite expression tell a lie using the indefinite article. Tell them we often use *To tell you the truth ...* meaning *I have to admit* or *To be frank ...* , e.g. *To tell you the truth, I don't really like watching crime movies.*

Answers

1 suspected of 2 claiming 3 denied 4 telling, truth
5 gave, away 6 making up

E Make it personal

1 In pairs, sts brainstorm all they can remember from each picture, the detective and criminal's words, lies and actions that gave him away. Do the first picture with them to set this up and show just how much they can say.

Stronger classes: Sts can roleplay the officer-criminal dialog from the pictures. Video them once they've rehearsed.

2 Sts discuss the questions in pairs, then feedback to the class anything interesting from their discussions. Praise sts for using any of the new vocabulary from 8D. Ask: *Are you a good liar?*

Optional activity

Sts list five things they did yesterday evening, including one thing which is not true. In pairs, have them tell each other what they did, and try to guess which thing is true / untrue. Ask: *Were you right? How did you tell your partner was lying?*

Song lyric: See Teacher's Book p.344 for notes about the song and an accompanying activity to do with the class.

9 Grammar: Reduced relative clauses

A Go through the examples and clarify the color coding: blue = relative clause, pink = reduced relative clause. Explain that we can leave out the blue words in brackets to make 'reduced' relative clauses. Discuss the meaning of *to catch someone doing something* (= to discover or find someone doing something).

In pairs, sts to complete the rules. Classcheck, then ask them to find an active and passive example of reduced relative clauses in 8D.

Tip

Elicit/Explain that a relative clause tells us exactly who or what (or the kind of person or thing) the speaker means.

Answers

1 If a relative clause refers to a subject, you can delete the pronoun and *be*.
2 An active verb in a reduced clause is always an -ing form and a passive one is always a past participle.

Examples from 8D:
Active – *A guy claiming he was at home was the key suspect.*
Passive – *I questioned someone suspected of taking part in a robbery.*

Refer sts to the **Grammar expansion** on p.154.

B Focus on the signs, and ask: *Where might you find these?* Elicit suggestions for each. Monitor for correct use of *at/in/on* + the places, e.g. *at an airport*, and revise if necessary. Elicit the meaning of *holding up* (= blocking).

In pairs, sts rewrite the text with reduced relative clauses.

Pairs compare their versions with another pair. Classcheck by asking sts to read out their signs to the class.

Answers

1 Luggage left unattended will be removed and destroyed. You might see it in an airport, bus station, or a railway station.
2 $20,000 reward for information leading to an arrest. You might see it in a police station.
3 Anyone suspected of entering will face serious consequences. You might see it outside private property.
4 Those caught littering will be fined. You might see it in a park.
5 Cars moving at excessive speeds will be identified by radar. You might see it on a highway.
6 Protesters holding up traffic will be arrested. You might see it on a road.
7 Anyone swimming here will be in for an unpleasant surprise. You might see it by a river or lake, or the sea.

Optional activity

Sts write two signs for their classroom, using reduced relative clauses, e.g. *Any teachers giving out homework will face serious consequences.*

C Ask sts to mentally translate the sentences into their own language. Ask if a relative pronoun is always needed in their language.

Do the first with them as an example. In pairs, sts cross out all optional words. Classcheck answers.

Answers

1 The man ~~who was~~ sitting next to me on the bus was very suspicious-looking.
2 None
3 That's the place ~~that~~ I told you about that said "No pets or children allowed."
4 The girl ~~who was~~ accused of taking my notebook totally denied it.
5 None

D Make it personal Read through the instructions as a class, and make sure everyone understands what they have to do.

1 In groups of three, sts think of five behaviors they'd like to change or ban.

Weaker classes: Elicit examples as a class, e.g. *Playing music loudly on public transport. Using smart phones in restaurants.*

2 Groups create a sign for each behavior. Tell sts they can make their signs serious or funny. Create a sign on the board, as an example, e.g. *Anyone heard playing their music loudly on the bus will be forced to sing out loud.*

3 In their groups, sts carry out the role plays. Make sure they take turns to play each role.

Weaker sts: Before they start, elicit phrases sts can use for the trial, and write them on the board to refer to during the role play, e.g. *You have been seen on CCTV camera eating with your mouth open. You are accused of playing your music very loudly on the bus. A witness saw you using a smart phone in the restaurant. It wasn't me, it was my twin brother. That's not true, I wasn't eating anything. I was only laughing at my friend.*

Monitor while sts carry out the trial and help with vocabulary.

At the end, invite groups to role play their trial to the class.

Have a class feedback session. Ask: *Who was good at lying / making up excuses?*

Workbook p.46.

9 Grammar: Reduced relative clauses

A Study the sentences and complete the rules. Then find an active and a passive example of reduced relative clauses in 8D.

Reduced relative clauses: active and passive

Relative clauses can be reduced:

Active	Students	who cheat / cheating	on their final exams will not graduate.
	A passenger	(who was) riding	on the train robbed the conductor.
Passive	Anyone	(who is) caught	cheating will be suspended.
	The conductor	(who was) robbed	last night is very upset.

1 If a relative clause refers to a subject, you can delete ☐ only the pronoun ☐ the pronoun and *be*.

2 A(n) ☐ active ☐ passive verb in a reduced clause is always an *-ing* form and a(n) ☐ active ☐ passive one is always a past participle.

Grammar expansion p.154

B Rewrite these signs with reduced relative clauses to make them more natural. Where might they appear?

1 LUGGAGE THAT'S LEFT UNATTENDED WILL BE REMOVED AND DESTROYED.

2 $20,000 REWARD FOR INFORMATION THAT LEADS TO AN ARREST.

3 ANYONE WHO IS SUSPECTED OF ENTERING WILL FACE SERIOUS CONSEQUENCES.

4 THOSE WHO ARE CAUGHT LITTERING WILL BE FINED.

5 CARS THAT ARE MOVING AT EXCESSIVE SPEEDS WILL BE IDENTIFIED BY RADAR.

6 PROTESTERS WHO ARE HOLDING UP TRAFFIC WILL BE ARRESTED.

7 ANYONE WHO SWIMS HERE WILL BE IN FOR AN UNPLEASANT SURPRISE!

1 Luggage left unattended will be removed and destroyed. You might see it in an airport or a bus station.

C Cross out all optional words in these relative clauses. If no words can be crossed out, write "none."

1 The man who was sitting next to me on the bus was very suspicious-looking.
2 People are always pushing against my seat in airplanes, which is incredibly annoying.
3 That's the place that I told you about that said "No pets or children allowed."
4 The girl who was accused of taking my notebook totally denied it.
5 I'm always stepping on gum, which drives me up the wall.

D **Make it personal** You're under arrest! In groups, role play a trial.

1 List five behaviors you'd like to change or ban. Use ideas from 5D on p.97 or think up others.
2 Create signs for each one. Include the penalty.
3 **A** You're a police officer. Accuse **B** of violating the law.
B Defend yourself. Explain why you did nothing wrong.
C You are the judge. Guilty or innocent? Make a fair decision.

But Officer, I was only making a left turn ...

SCHOOL
THOSE CAUGHT SPEEDING IN FRONT OF THE SCHOOL WILL DO 500 HOURS OF COMMUNITY SERVICE!

10 Listening

A 9.12 In pairs, explain the cartoon. Then listen to two students and choose the correct option.

Laura [**agrees** / **disagrees**] with Alfredo that consumerism is a serious problem.

B 9.13 Listen to and order Alfredo's ideas 1–5. Which one(s) do you agree with?

Consumerism is a problem because ...

- ☐ it has an impact on the planet's resources.
- ☐ it affects people's relationships.
- ☐ people end up overspending.
- ☐ people buy things just to feel better.
- ☐ buying things doesn't bring long-term happiness.

I definitely agree that ...

C 9.14 Listen and note down two solutions to B. Any other possible ones?

D 9.15 Listen again to excerpts from the conversation. Number them 1–4.

Alfredo's purpose is to ...

- ☐ begin to build an argument.
- ☐ explain an idea in a different way.
- ☐ try again to persuade Laura to accept his point of view.
- ☐ tell Laura she doesn't understand his argument.

11 Keep talking

A 9.16 **How to say it** Complete the chart. Then listen, check, and repeat, copying the intonation.

Developing an argument (3)

	What they said	What they meant
1	That's a ______ question.	It's hard to answer that question.
2	Why (people think it's a problem) is ______ me.	I don't understand why ...
3	There's ______ to it than that.	It's not so simple.
4	Wouldn't you ______ that (it's just a quick fix)?	Don't you think that ...
5	I know what you're ______ at.	I know what you're trying to say.

B **Make it personal** Choose a problem from the survey. Note down (a) why it's serious and (b) what could be done to solve it.

What's the biggest problem facing society today?

Our readers' top picks:

1. social injustice
2. selfishness
3. overpopulation
4. lack of respect for nature
5. corruption
6. urban violence
7. prejudice
8. unemployment
9. hyperconnectedness

C In groups, compare ideas. Use *How to say it* expressions. Where do you (dis)agree?

Hmm ... that's a tough question, but to me, the biggest problem we face today is corruption.

What makes you say that?

Well, for one thing ...

Lesson Aims: Sts consider some of the biggest problems facing our society, and discuss possible solutions

Skills	Language	Vocabulary
Listening to someone giving his views about the problem of consumerism Writing a problem-solution essay about a social problem	Developing an argument: *There's more to it than that, Wouldn't you agree that ... ?* Using conjunctions: *although, as, despite, due to, in order to, so that, unlike, while*	*afford, defining, discard, mindless, pay off*

Warm-up

Board *shopping*, and ask: *Do you enjoy shopping? How often do you go? Do you ever buy things you don't really need? How does shopping make you feel?* In pairs, sts discuss the questions.

Board the lesson title question: What *do you spend most money on?* Brainstorm phrases onto the class: accommodation, domestic bills, food and drink, clothes, transportation, going out. Gets sts to choose and perhaps vote for their top three.

Song lyric: See Teacher's Book p.344 for notes about the song and an accompanying activity to do with the class.

10 Listening

A 9.12 Ask sts to explain the cartoon. Elicit *consumerism* (= the theory that an increasing consumption of goods is economically desirable). Ask: *Do you think consumerism is a problem? Why / Why not?*

Explain that sts are going to listen to two sts, Laura and Alfredo. They listen and choose the correct option about consumerism. Play the audio, then classcheck.

Answer

disagrees

See Teacher's Book p.326 for Audio script 9.12.

B 9.13 Ask: *What was the last thing you bought? Why did you buy it?* Sts read Alfredo's thoughts on consumerism and quickly decide which they (dis)agree with. They could mark them A or D before listening.

Sts listen to more from Alfredo and Laura and order his statements, 1-5. Paircheck, then classcheck. Highlight the expression *a quick fix* (= an easy, but only temporary, solution).

Answers

1 people buy things just to feel better
2 buying things doesn't bring long-term happiness
3 people end up overspending
4 it affects people's relationships
5 it has an impact on the planet's resources

See Teacher's Book p.326 for Audio script 9.13.

C 9.14 Sts listen and note two suggested solutions from Alfredo. Paircheck, then classcheck. Ask: *Do you like his solutions? Would you try these yourself?* In pairs, sts think of other solutions (e.g. learn to barter and trade, become self-reliant and make / build the things you need, grow your own vegetables, walk or cycle everywhere).

Answers

Shop less; buy only what you need
Get rid of things you don't need

See Teacher's Book p.327 for Audio script 9.14.

D 9.15 Sts read the choices, then listen again to say what the purpose of each excerpt is. Classcheck.

Answers

1 tell Laura she doesn't understand his argument
2 begin to build an argument
3 try again to persuade Laura to accept his point of view
4 explain an idea in a different way

See Teacher's Book p.327 for Audio script 9.15.

11 Keep talking

A 9.16 **How to say it** Go through the expressions in the chart, elicit the missing words. Play the audio for sts to listen, check, and repeat.

Sts practice the expressions in pairs. Monitor and correct their stress and pronunciation where necessary.

Answers

1 tough 2 beyond 3 more 4 agree 5 getting

B **Make it personal** Go through the survey problems with the class, elicit definitions, and give examples where appropriate. Have sts choose one of the problems, and make notes.

C In groups, sts compare their ideas. Monitor round the class and give help where necessary. Encourage them to use the expressions from 10D and 11A. When they have all finished, ask one or two sts to present their ideas to the whole class. Class feedback. Ask: *Did you agree on what the biggest problems are? Did you think of any good solutions?*

12 Writing: A problem-solution essay

A In pairs, sts summarize all they've learnt about Alfredo. Class feedback.

Have sts read Alfredo's essay, and find the ideas from 10B and 10C that he mentions.

Classcheck, then ask: *Do you think the essay is persuasive / convincing? Why / Why not?* Ask sts to underline three key sentences in the essay which they personally find most persuasive and compare them with a partner. Did they choose the same sentences?

Answers

Buying things doesn't bring long-term happiness.
It has an impact on the planet's resources.

Optional activity

Sts underline three phrases they like in the essay. They choose the criteria, e.g. sounds similar to a phrase in their language, incredible spelling – sound combination. Mingle, compare and say why they chose them.

B Read through **Write it right!** take sts back to the suggested pages, if necessary. In pairs, sts talk each other through the different categories too, to allow you to monitor individual perceptions.

Tip

Sts will mentally translate, however briefly, so consider letting them whisper translations to their neighbor too, so the class, weak and strong, stay together and help each other.

Sts put the conjunctions back into the essay. Paircheck, then classcheck.

Answers

Paragraph 2: (h) due to globalization, (f) despite the recent bad economy
Paragraph 3: (g) as it encourages us, (a) In order to solve them
Paragraph 4: (d) unlike shopping
Paragraph 5: (b) material possessions so that

C Look at conjunctions 1–8 with the class, and ask sts which they already use. Elicit and board example sentences including each of the conjunctions. Then sts reword the sentences from the essay using the conjunctions a–h. Classcheck.

Answers

1 unlike 2 as 3 due to 4 so that 5 although
6 in order to 7 despite 8 while

D Sts re-read the essay and match each paragraph to the functions. Classcheck.

Stronger classes: Sts could think of a heading for each paragraph.

Answers

1 define the problem?
3 offer more supporting arguments?
5 conclude his argument?
2 put the problem in a historical perspective?
4 propose possible solutions?

E **Your turn!** Explain the aim: to write a five-paragraph, problem-solution essay. Give them a choice: to write either about the topic they discussed in 11C or choose a new one from the survey in 11B.

Best is usually to set it up in class, then finish it for homework. Set a date for them to post their essays online.

Tip

Having sts do extended writing in class, either alone or in pairs (with both writing the same agreed text), is often very useful as they have you for support and means they talk more about any difficulties or issues they have with the skill of writing.

Encourage sts to read each other's work. Then class feedback to discuss the most popular problem and if sts proposed similar solutions.

Tip

Help sts avoid the traps of direct translation when writing. Have them write a quick first draft, without using a dictionary or reference materials. Then, when writing their final versions, encourage them to check spellings, grammar and look for synonyms / antonyms, etc.

Discourage them from using an online translator – as an experiment, you could ask them to put the text in twice, from L1 to English and then back again to their L1, so they can see where the difficulties lie.

Workbook p.47.

12 Writing: A problem-solution essay

A Read Alfredo's essay. Which ideas in 10B and C are mentioned?

B Read *Write it right!* Then put a–h back into the essay. There are two extra words or phrases.

Write it right!

In essays, use a variety of conjunctions to connect your ideas well. Refer back to lessons 4.2 and 7.2, too.

Purpose: (a) *in order to*, (b) *so that*

Comparing: (c) *while*, (d) *unlike*

Conceding (*but* ...): (e) *although*, (f) *despite*

Reason: (g) *as*, (h) *due to*

C Which conjunctions (a–h) could be replaced by these?

1 as opposed to *unlike*
2 since ________
3 because of ________
4 so ________
5 even though ________
6 to ________
7 in spite of ________
8 whereas ________

D In which paragraph (1–5) does Alfredo ...

☐ define the problem?
☐ offer more supporting arguments?
☐ conclude his argument?
☐ put the problem in a historical perspective?
☐ propose possible solutions?

E Your turn! Choose a problem from the survey in 11B and write a five-paragraph essay in about 280 words.

Before
Note down problems and solutions. Follow the structure in D to order them logically.

While
Write five paragraphs following the model in A. Search online for facts, as necessary. Use at least four conjunctions from B and C.

After
Post your essay online and read your classmates' work. What was the most popular problem? Similar solutions?

1 Think about the last time you wanted something *badly* – say, new designer sunglasses. When you got them, you felt great. As time went on, the sunglasses probably lost most of their initial appeal. And then you lost them and regretted spending so much in the first place! Sound familiar? Blame it on consumerism, a cultural phenomenon that encourages us to find happiness by buying what we don't need. In other words: "Buy, use, discard, buy more."

2 Consumerism is not a new phenomenon. It had its origins in the Industrial Revolution. What's new is that in today's world, partly ________ globalization, whole societies are organized around the need to consume. Some studies, for example, have found that, ________ the recent bad economy, people in the U.S. spend 100 billion dollars every year on shoes, jewelry, and watches – more than what they invest in higher education.

3 It's a mistake to believe that material possessions can make us feel better. Many studies show that focusing on owning things can lead to anxiety and even depression. Also, consumerism can affect our self-esteem, ________ it encourages us to compare ourselves with others. Finally, the worst environmental problems we face have been caused by consumerism. ________ solve them, we must confront consumerism whenever we can.

4 It's hard to escape materialism, but it's not impossible. Here's a small first step: The next time you buy something, ask yourself "Do I need it?" rather than "Do I want it?" Also, be clear about what *really* matters to you. In other words, concentrate on the things that, ________ shopping, can bring long-term happiness – your family? your career? an important cause? a new challenge? Then, instead of going to the mall, focus your energy on those things.

5 Having a less materialistic lifestyle – and ultimately saving the planet – doesn't mean giving up on life's pleasures. It simply means giving less importance to material possessions ________, over time, they become less and less important to you.

10 How do you like to get around town?

1 Listening

A In pairs, read the ad and take turns guessing the problems. Then add four more.

A Mime a problem.

B Guess what it is.

From your expression and gestures, that must be annoying kids!

the Travel blog
THIS WEEK: TRAVEL NIGHTMARES
We've all been there: road rage, flat tires, running out of gas, (near) crashes, reservation problems, cancelations, missed connections, annoying kids, unpleasant fellow travelers …
The list goes on and on. Do you have a tale to tell? Click here to tell us about your worst travel experience ever!

B 10.1 Listen to three friends, Joel, Ana, and Ian. Which travel nightmare in **A** is each talking about?

C 10.2 Guess how each story ends, picture A or B. Listen to check. Did you get them all right?

Story 1 | Story 2 | Story 3

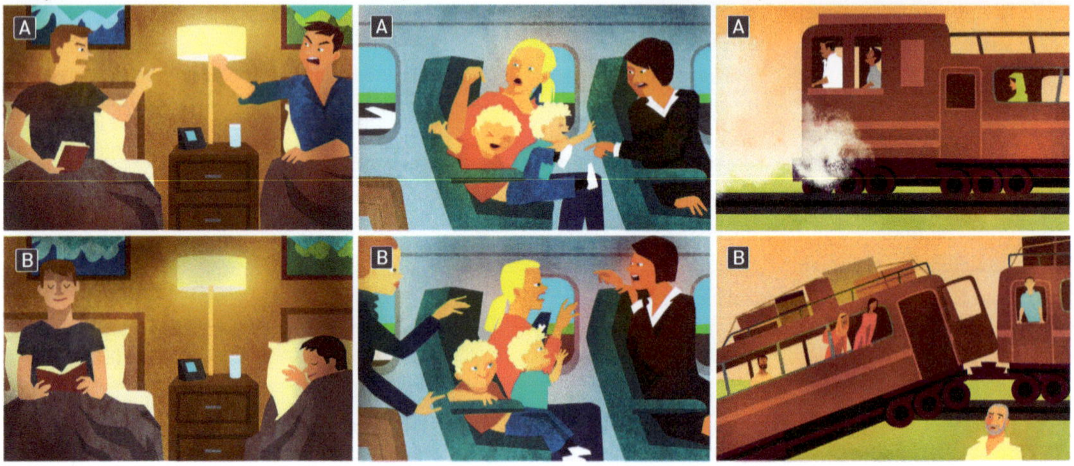

D 10.2 Listen again. T (true), F (false) or NI (no information)? Whose story was the most surprising?

1 John was afraid at first that Barry couldn't be trusted.
2 John and Barry didn't talk about work.
3 When Ana saw the twins on the plane, she was sure they'd misbehave.
4 She asked them not to kick her seat, several times.
5 The conductor left the train to get something to eat.
6 Ian says he was never in real danger.

E Make it personal Which quotes 1–5 are good advice for Joel, Ana, or Ian? Which ones do you like best?

1 "Once a year, go someplace you've never been before." (Dalai Lama)
2 "Everything is funny as long as it's happening to someone else." (Will Rogers)
3 "You get educated by traveling." (Solange Knowles)
4 "When traveling with someone, take large doses of patience and tolerance with your morning coffee." (Helen Hayes)
5 "Wherever you go becomes a part of you somehow." (Anita Desai)

Ana seems to work hard. Maybe the first one is good for her.

And me! I wish I had the money to travel, though!

Lesson Aims: Sts learn vocabulary related to traveling, listen to three travel nightmare stories, and relate their own travel stories.

Skills	Language	Vocabulary
Listening to three people talking about bad travel experiences Discussing your own travel nightmare	Talking about unexpected events: *For whatever reason, the conductor stepped off the train. It turned out the hotel had made a mistake.*	*cancelation, check in, flat tire, reservation, scheduled* Phrasal verbs: *dawn on, end up, get away, get through, look forward to, mix up*

Warm-up

Revise means of transportation with the class. Brainstorm modes of transport, travel verbs, and elicit the difference between *get in/out* and *get on/off*.

Ask the lesson title question: *How do you like to get around town?* In pairs, sts ask and answer, e.g. *How often do you use public transport? Have you ever had a crash / flat tire / been in an argument with another driver?* Classcheck any interesting stories.

1 Listening

A Focus sts on the ad and ask: *What are the problems associated with traveling mentioned in the ad?* Elicit and board them: *road rage, flat tires, running out of gas, (near) crashes, reservation problems, cancelations, missed connections, annoying kids, unpleasant fellow travelers*. Ask: *Which of these things have you experienced?*

In pairs, A mimes one of the problems and B guesses what it is. Sts then swap roles.

B 10.1 Talk sts through the task. Explain that they are going to listen to Joel, Ana, and Ian talk about their own travel nightmare and match it to one of the nine in the ad. Play the audio. Paircheck, then classcheck, and re-play the audio if necessary. Ask: *Which one sounds the worst?*

Answers

Joel – reservation problems; Ana – annoying kids; Ian – (near) crashes

See Teacher's Book p.327 for Audio script 10.1.

C 10.2 Focus on the cartoons. Ask: *Which pictures are Joel, Ana and Ian?* (Story 1 – Joel, Story 2 – Ana, Story 3 – Ian.)

Explain that they illustrate two possible endings for each story. Sts describe what's happening in each picture (Story 1: A The two men are arguing. B There's no conflict; one of the men is sleeping, the other's reading a book. Story 2: A Ana and the mother are telling the children off. B Ana is arguing with the mother's children. Story 3: A The train stopped in time. B The train crashed.)

Sts guess which are the correct endings. Paircheck. Play the audio. Paircheck, then classcheck.

Answers

Story 1 B Story 2 B Story 3 A

See Teacher's Book p.327 for Audio script 10.2.

D 10.2 Sts read the statements and mark the ones they remember T, F or NI. Have them at least guess the others. Re-play the audio for them to listen and check. Ask: *Which situation was the most frightening / annoying / surprising?*

Answers

1 T 2 T 3 F 4 T 5 NI 6 F

Optional activity

In groups of three, sts recount one story each from the audio. The other two help with the details and vocabulary as necessary. Have the audio script ready to help sts read before re-telling.

E **Make it personal** Go through the quotes and check understanding. Ask: *Have you heard of any of the authors?* (see Background information). In groups, sts interpret the quotes. Then, following the example, choose the best quotes for Joel, Ana, and Ian, and explain why. Ask: *Which is your favorite quote?*

Background information

Dalai Lama – the name given to Tibetan people's spiritual leader. Dalai Lamas are Buddhist monks of the Gelug school.

Will Rogers (1879–1935) – a cowboy from Oklahoma. Became an actor and author, known for his wit and wisdom on Broadway and in movies.

Solange Knowles – born in 1986 in Houston, Texas. Singer, songwriter, model, and actress. She's Beyoncé's younger sister.

Helen Hayes (1900–1993) – famous American actress whose career spanned over 80 years.

Anita Desai – born in 1937. Indian novelist, lives in the US.

2 Vocabulary: Phrasal verbs

A 10.3 Books closed. Board the phrasal verbs. Ask: *Do you know any of them?* and try to elicit examples, or a simple paraphrase, if they claim to, e.g. *dawn on* (= become clear to), *end up* (= finally happen), *get away* (= escape), *get through* (= survive), *mix up* (= confuse). Highlight that phrasal verbs often have a more formal sounding synonym, but are often subtly different, and generally more common in fluent-speaker speech. Refer them to the list on pp.165–167.

Tip

Remind sts to record the phrasal verbs in a separate section in their vocabulary notebooks, headed "Phrasal verbs," and highlight the particle in some way to help them remember it.

Books open, sts read the definitions, and examples. Clarify any doubts.

Sts complete sentences 1–6 with the correct form of the phrasal verbs. Paircheck. You could use the audio for sts to check their answers and shadow read for pronunciation.

Focus on the speech bubble. Then in pairs sts retell the stories in 1C, including all six phrasal verbs.

Weaker classes: Let sts read the audio script, match each phrasal verb to a story and make a few notes for each story first.

Monitor hard both to encourage fluency, and praise accuracy. Classcheck.

Answers

1 looking forward to 2 get through 3 mixed up
4 dawned on 5 get away 6 ended up

Optional activity

In different pairs, sts take turns to ask and answer questions about the stories, using the phrasal verbs, e.g. *How did Joel get through the week? Did the train driver mix up the controls? Why did Ana want to get away?*

B Focus on the speech bubble example, and go through the **Common mistakes**. Ask: *Is either error familiar?*

Sts rewrite the example definitions to make them true for them. Emphasize writing personalized examples with new language is a great way to remember it.

In pairs, sts compare sentences, and see what they might have in common. Classcheck by inviting volunteers to report their partner's answers to the class.

Song lyric: See Teacher's Book p.345 for notes about the song and an accompanying activity to do with the class.

C Make it personal

1 10.4 **How to say it** Do sentence 1 with the class as an example, then in pairs, sts complete sentences 2–5.

Play the audio for sts to listen, check, and repeat. In pairs, they practice the expressions. Monitor and correct stress and pronunciation as necessary.

Answers

1 turned 2 happened 3 reason 4 luck 5 enough

2 Set this up by telling your own travel nightmare story. Get sts to ask you each of the questions in a in full (i.e. *What exactly happened?, When did it happen?*, etc.) Highlight when you include the phrasal verbs and the *How to say it* expressions.

Give sts a few minutes to make notes and plan their stories. Monitor and help with vocabulary.

In groups, sts tell their stories. Monitor and note the feedback you're going to give.

Tip

Take notes for feedback discreetly. Initially this may put sts off, but they soon get used to it. Your monitoring is more credible when you do this. Be sure to refer to them when you feedback!

Finally, invite some sts to share their stories with the rest of the class.

Optional activity

Sts write up their stories as if for the Travel blog in 1A. Display them on the walls or post on the class website. Encourage readers to write a comment below each one.

Workbook p.48.

2 Vocabulary: Phrasal verbs

A 10.3 Read the definitions and complete 1–6 with the correct phrasal verb. Listen to check. Then, in pairs, use only the pictures in 1C to remember each story.

dawn on: To begin to be perceived or understood. *It only dawned on me that I could actually speak English when I finally went abroad.*

end up: Eventually arrive at a place or situation. *When shopping, I always end up spending more than I ought to. My parents say I'll end up with a huge credit card debt.*

get away: To escape. *College is driving me crazy. I wish I could get away for a week or so.*

get through: To manage to deal with or survive a difficult experience. *If I lived in Canada, I'd find it very difficult to get through winter there. I hate the cold!*

look forward to: To await eagerly or anticipate with pleasure. *I'm really looking forward to (watching) this year's Super Bowl.*

mix up: To confuse two people or things, or spoil the arrangement of something. *My closet is a mess! My winter clothes are all mixed up with my summer clothes.*

1 I was really ________ relaxing after a long flight.
2 How did you manage to ________ a whole week with that guy?
3 The poor man probably got ________ and pulled the wrong switch.
4 When it finally ________ the passengers that they were in trouble, everyone started screaming.
5 It'd been a rough year and all I wanted was to ________ from it all for a few days.
6 The woman got really mad, and we ________ arguing.

Joel had just flown from Washington to London, and he was really looking forward to relaxing after a long flight ...

B In pairs, modify the examples in A so they are true for you. Anything in common?

It only dawned on me how hungry I was when I ...

Common mistakes

I'm not really looking forward to ~~meet~~ *meeting* my in-laws. What if they end up ~~dislike~~ *disliking* me?

C **Make it personal** Describe your worst travel nightmare ever.

1 10.4 **How to say it** Complete the sentences from 1B and C. Then listen to check.

Talking about unexpected events

	What they said	What they meant
1	It ________ out (the hotel had made a mistake).	In the end, it proved to be true that ...
2	I ________ to (know who the man was).	By chance, I ...
3	For whatever ________, (the conductor stepped off the train).	No one knows why ...
4	As ________ would have it, (they were able to stop the train).	Luckily, ...
5	In the end, strangely ________, (it wasn't nearly as bad as I thought).	It may seem strange, but ...

2 Plan or make up your story. Use the travel nightmares in 1A to help you.

a Note down the main events. Ask yourself *what, when, where, why,* and *how?*
b Include three or more a) phrasal verbs and b) *How to say it* expressions.
c In groups, tell your stories. Whose experience was the most unpleasant?

I've got to tell you what happened on my vacation last year ...

3 Listening

A 10.5 Marty Falcon is on vacation. Listen and match the start of three conversations to three of the pictures (a–d). How does his tone suggest he is feeling?

To me, it sounds like he wants to go home!

a 
b 
c 
d 

B 10.6 Listen to the full conversations. Check (✔) all the statements that can be inferred. Have you ever had / heard of a tourist experience like this?

1 Marty ...
- ☐ wants to leave the hotel and go straight to the airport.
- ☐ won't take no for an answer.

2 The salesperson ...
- ☐ has no idea if the pants will shrink.
- ☐ agrees they're expensive.

3 Marty ...
- ☐ hasn't used the app before.
- ☐ stopped the car as soon as he noticed the light.

Well, it didn't happen to me personally, but a friend of mine went to ... and ...

Common mistake

a friend of ~~me / him / her~~ *mine / his / hers*

4 Pronunciation: Word stress in nouns and phrasal verbs

A 10.7 Read *Nouns from phrasal verbs* and listen to the examples. Check (✔) the correct rule.

Nouns from phrasal verbs

Some nouns formed from phrasal verbs are hyphenated; others are written as one word.
- I was wondering if I could get a late **checkout** (n) tomorrow. I need a **wake-up call**, too.
- Sorry, you need to **check out** (v) by noon. Just dial 00. The system will **wake** you **up**.

The stress in most phrasal verbs is on the ☐ **verb** ☐ **particle**.
The equivalent nouns are usually stressed on the ☐ **first** ☐ **second** part of the word.

B 10.8 Underline the stressed syllables in the bold words. Listen to check. Then find three comments in AS 10.6 on p.163 that show Marty is an inexperienced traveler.

1 Almost 100 dollars? That's a **rip-off**! Aren't these things supposed to cost about 20 bucks?
2 My car **broke down** and I don't know what to do! I'm lost in the middle of nowhere.
3 The fastest way to report a car **breakdown** is via our app. Do you know whether you have it installed on your phone?
4 Yeah, but I don't have a **login** or a password. Can't you help me over the phone?
5 It seems there's been a **mix-up**. Let me see if I can correct it and **fix** things **up**.

C Make it personal Complete 1–3 with words from B. Then ask and answer in pairs. Any good stories?

1 When was the last time you said, "I got confused. Sorry for the ________"? What happened?
2 Is 500 dollars for a watch a fair price or a ________? How much would you be willing to pay? Do you ever feel you're being overcharged when you shop?
3 What would you do if your car ________ late at night and your phone was dead?

I'd be terrified if there was no one around!
I guess I'd lock the doors and wait until it got light.

Lesson Aims: Sts talk about things that go wrong on holiday, and role play everyday conversations.

Skills	Language	Vocabulary	Grammar
Listening to short everyday conversations in a store, restaurant, and hotel Role-playing everyday conversations	Asking negative and indirect questions: *Isn't there free Wi-Fi? Could you tell me what time the gym closes?*	Forming nouns from phrasal verbs: *checkout, wake-up call, rip-off, mix-up*	Negative and indirect questions: *Wh- and yes-no*

Warm-up

Board these questions: *When did you last go on vacation? Did anything go wrong? Did you complain to anyone? Did you get annoyed? How did the situation turn out?* In pairs, sts discuss the questions.

Board the lesson title question: *What's your idea of a perfect vacation?* Sts discuss as a class.

3 Listening

A 10.5 Focus on cartoons a–d, and explain they show Marty Falcon on vacation. Ask: *Where is Marty in each picture? What do you think is happening?* (a – he is buying some trousers, b – he's complaining about his soup, c – his car has broken down, d – he's getting annoyed with the receptionist).

Sts listen and match the start of three conversations to three of the four pictures. Classcheck. Ask: *Do you think Marty sounds polite or rude? How do you think he's feeling? How would you feel?*

Answers

1 d 2 a 3 c

His tone suggests he is feeling annoyed.

See Teacher's Book p.328 for Audio script 10.5.

B 10.6 Sts read the statements before listening, and guess which is more likely. Highlight *infer*, elicit a synonym (suggest) and the phrase *make an inference*. Play the full audio for sts to listen, and check the statements they can infer.

Paircheck, then classcheck. Ask: *Do you think Marty is an experienced traveler? What information did you hear which allowed you to infer the statements?* (1 He insists on speaking to the manager when the receptionist refuses to let him check out late. 2 The sales assistant looks at the label and says she will check with her manager. 3 Marty doesn't know his login or his password.)

Sts tell the class about any similar experiences they have had.

Answers

1 Marty won't take no for an answer.
2 The salesperson has no idea if the pants will shrink.
3 Marty hasn't used the app before.

See Teacher's Book p.328 for Audio script 10.6.

4 Pronunciation: Word stress in nouns and phrasal verbs

A 10.7 Go through **Nouns from phrasal verbs**. Explain that sadly, there are no spelling rules for this, sts just have to learn them.

In pairs, sts should be able to work out the rules from the pink stressing before they listen and check.

Classcheck. Elicit other examples of nouns from phrasal verbs, e.g. *warm-up, break-up, workout, break-in, rip-off, handout, mix-up*.

Answers

The stress in most phrasal verbs is on the particle.
The equivalent nouns are usually stressed on the first part of the word.

B 10.8 Sts read the statements. Ask: *Who said these things?*

In pairs, sts look at the sentences, and work out where the stress is. Use the audio to check. Sts then take turns to practice saying the sentences.

Refer sts to audio script 10.6 to find three comments that show Marty is an inexperienced traveler.

Answers

1 <u>rip</u>-off! 2 broke <u>down</u> 3 <u>break</u>down 4 <u>log</u>in
5 <u>mix</u>-up, fix things <u>up</u>
Comments:
You mean I have to use the phone in the room?
Do you accept international credit cards? I'm living in London now.
My car broke down and I don't know what to do

C Make it personal Sts complete the questions with words from B. Classcheck, and highlight *be willing to* (= be prepared to).

Focus on the example answer in the speech bubble and ask which question it goes with (3).

In pairs, sts ask and answer the questions. Classcheck by inviting volunteers to share their best answers.

Answers

1 mix-up 2 rip-off 3 broke down

Song lyric: See Teacher's Book p.345 for notes about the song and an accompanying activity to do with the class.

5 Grammar: Negative and indirect questions

A Read through the grammar rules and examples with the class, and check understanding.

Have sts underline the verbs in the indirect questions. Classcheck. Ask: *What do you notice about the word order?* Elicit that in indirect questions the word order is different from a simple question. Focus on **Common mistakes**, which highlights this point.

Ask: *When do we need to use if / whether in indirect questions?* (with yes / no questions). Sts then look back at 4A and 4B to find two indirect questions and two negative questions. Classcheck.

Answers

1 contracted 2 have 3 can
Indirect questions:
I was wondering if I could get a late checkout tomorrow.
Do you know whether you have it installed on your phone?
Negative questions:
Aren't these things supposed to cost about 20 bucks?
Can't you help me over the phone?

Refer students to the **Grammar expansion** on p.156.

Tip

Tell students that we can also say ***Can*** *you tell me what time the gym closes?*

Optional activities

1 **Weaker classes:** Board these for sts to change first into negative questions.

Do I have to use a password? (Don't I have to ...?)

Is there a TV in the room? (Isn't there ...?)

Then to change them into an indirect question (*Could you tell me if I have to use a password? Do you know whether there is a TV in the room?*).

2 Sts write five indirect questions they might ask a hotel receptionist, e.g. *Could you tell me what time breakfast is, please? Do you happen to have a band aid?*

In pairs, sts roleplay the questions, A as the hotel receptionist, B the guest. Swap roles.

B 10.9 Sts correct the questions, then listen to the audio to check answers. Ask: *Who might have said this and when?* to contextualize, and: *Which are your mistakes?* to personalize and help them remember.

In pairs, sts role play the conversations. Monitor and praise/prompt good use of question forms.

Answers

1 Can you tell me what time she'll be back?
2 Would you happen to know whether these are machine-washable?
3 Can't you help me over the phone?
4 Do you remember if any warning lights came on?
5 Do you know what your exact location is?

C Set this up by doing the first transformation with them: *Do you happen to know if anyone ever died in this room?* Sts work through the questions individually. Paircheck. Then in pairs, sts complete the negative questions. Classcheck.

Weaker classes: Together with the class, board the beginnings of the indirect questions and elicit the rest. Then sts complete the negative questions.

Answers

1 Do you happen to know if anyone ever died in this room?
2 Can you check if / whether this is gluten-free?
3 Do you have any idea how much you have spent on shoes this year?
4 I'd like to know how long it will take me to speak fluent Chinese.
5 I wonder if you could help me, please.
Follow-up questions
1 Can't you check with your manager?
2 Isn't there a gluten-free option?
3 Don't you have enough shoes already?
4 Isn't there a miracle method or something?
5 Can't the other customer wait?

D **Make it personal** Read the instructions with the class, then focus on the examples in the speech bubble. Ask: *Who might say these things? Where?*

In pairs, give sts 4–5 minutes to choose their situations, map out their role plays and rehearse. They can take a few notes, but don't let them write it all out, or this will take an age. Help as much as you can at this stage.

If appropriate, get sts to video each other as they roleplay to the class. After each one, ask the class a few questions, e.g. *Where did that take place? Who were they? What do you think happens next? Who was the most annoying?* Have them vote on the funniest one.

Workbook p.49.

5 Grammar: Negative and indirect questions

A Read the grammar box and check (✔) the correct rules 1–3. Then in 4A and B, underline two indirect questions and circle two negative questions.

Negative questions; indirect questions: *Wh-* and *yes-no*

Use negative questions when you expect a positive answer:
Isn't there free WiFi? Yes, the network name is "guest123."
Don't I have until noon to check out? Well, no, actually, checkout is at 11:00.

Use indirect questions to soften the tone of your questions or requests:
Where**'s** the nearest ATM? → **Do you (happen to) know** where the nearest ATM **is**?
What time **does** the gym **close**? → **Could you tell me** what time the gym **closes**?
Did anyone **leave** me a message? → **I'd like to know if / whether** anyone **left** me a message.

1 Use ☐ **full** ☐ **contracted** forms to start negative questions. Answer yes to confirm them.
2 Indirect questions ☐ **have** ☐ **don't have** the same word order as statements.
3 The word *If* ☐ **can** ☐ **can't** be replaced by *whether*.

Grammar expansion p.156

Common mistakes

Do you know how long ~~does it take~~ *it takes* to get there?
Could you tell me where ~~are the restrooms~~ *the restrooms are*?

B 10.9 Correct the mistakes in 1–5. Listen to check. Then, in pairs, use only the pictures in 3A and questions to role play each dialogue in 3B.

1 Can you tell me what time will she be back?
2 Would you happen to know are these machine-washable?
3 Cannot you help me over the phone?
4 Do you remember did any warning lights come on?
5 Do you know what is your exact location?

C Annoying questions! Turn 1–5 into indirect questions. Then complete the follow-up negative questions.

	Annoying question	Annoying follow-up question
At a hotel	1 Did anyone ever die in this room? (Do you happen to know ...?)	No idea? _____ you check with your manager? Please?
On a flight	2 Is this gluten-free? (Can you check ...?)	Really? _____ there a gluten-free option?
At home	3 How much have you spent on shoes this year? (Do you have any idea ...?)	Wow! _____ you have enough shoes already?
At a language school	4 How long will it take me to speak fluent Chinese? (I'd like to know ...)	That long? _____ there a miracle method or something?
At a store	5 Could you help me, please? (I wonder ...)	_____ the other customer wait?

D **Make it personal** Be annoying! In pairs, role play and expand two situations in C. Include indirect and negative questions. Then present one to the class and vote on the funniest.

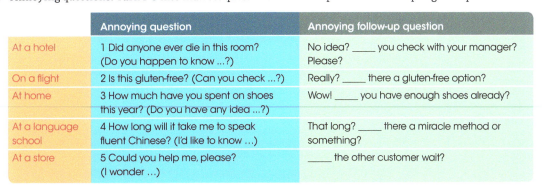

Can't the customer wait? I'm important, too!

Please be patient, sir ... what can I do for you?

This phone is driving me nuts. Could you tell me how I turn it on?

10.3 Which foreign country would you most like to live in?

6 Reading

A Read paragraph 1 of Arturo's blog. Use the photo to guess his nationality and answer 1 and 2.

1 Was the party in the U.S. or his country of birth?

2 Which five habits did he change when he went abroad?

B Read paragraph 2. Check (✔) the true statement(s). Is the story interesting so far?

Arturo ...

- ☐ got a degree abroad.
- ☐ was starting to lose touch with friends.
- ☐ found it easy to adjust when he returned home.
- ☐ sometimes questions his decision to live abroad.

C Read the rest. How would he answer the last question in paragraph 2?

☐ absolutely ☐ not really ☐ not at all

WINDS OF CHANGE

HOME | ABOUT | ARTICLES | CONTACT

1 Two years ago I was at a birthday party when an old friend called my name. It went in one ear and out the other. "Arturo? Are you deaf?" he repeated. For a split second, I didn't recognize Arturo as my name! I'd grown so used to being called Art by my American friends that now, back home, my birth name sounded as if it belonged to somebody else. That was the first time I'd experienced reverse culture shock; that is, culture shock not from going abroad, but from coming back. Other symptoms followed, of course: being more punctual than anyone else, driving more slowly, eating earlier, giving better tips, telling fewer jokes – you name it. What was going on with me?

2 I'd just returned from doing an MA in San José, CA, in information technology. I was thrilled to see my family and reconnect with all the friends I'd left behind and was beginning to drift apart from. I was also looking forward to going back to work so I could put all the theory I'd learned into practice. I wanted to get on with my old life in Madrid, but something was missing and I couldn't put my finger on what. Strangely enough, after all this time, I still can't. My time in the U.S. is still a powerful magnet that constantly pulls me back to all the sights, the smells, and the little joys and annoyances of the life I left behind. I think I'm finally coming to terms with the fact maybe I'll never have a clear sense of home again, which sometimes makes me wonder: was my time abroad worth it?

3 Studying or working abroad, trying to express your personality in another language, and fitting into a different culture can be frustrating, especially at first. You have to get used to both being and sounding foreign, and you have to grow to like your new self – your new identity. But here's the good news: Your self-awareness develops, and your outlook on life changes. Many of your old pre-conceived ideas crumble like buildings in an earthquake. You learn that "normal" means socially acceptable in different cultures – nothing more than that. And, most of all, you finally begin to remove all the labels that had come to define you. At home, people always thought of me as the family genius, but back in California I was just "the nice guy from Madrid," which means I can be whoever I choose to be.

4 When you move abroad, you're forced to abandon your roots and take a leap into the unknown. Things can and do go wrong, but you learn that you can get through the rough times without your family. You also realize that the ugly haircut or the wrong meal you got because of your limited vocabulary, at the end of the day, mean absolutely nothing. And, most of all, you realize that – pardon the cliché – you become a better person. Not better than those around you, but definitely better than your former self, no matter where you are – "home" or otherwise.

D Does Arturo make these points in paragraph 3 or 4?

When you live abroad, you ...

- ☐ become more accepting of diversity.
- ☐ learn to rely more on yourself.
- ☐ can reinvent yourself.
- ☐ don't get bothered by small problems.

Lesson Aims: Sts read about someone's experience of living abroad, and discuss the effect living abroad has on your life.

Skills	Language	Vocabulary
Reading a blog about what it feels like to return home after living abroad	Giving your own view about living abroad: *I think I'd miss my hometown most of all.*	Words with literal and figurative meanings: *crumble, fit, label, leap, magnet, root*

Warm-up

Board the following questions: *Have you (or any of your family/close friends) ever been/lived abroad? Was it a positive experience? Would you like to live abroad? Why / Why not?* In groups of three, sts take turns asking and answering.

In their groups, sts discuss the question title: *Which foreign country would you most like to live in?* Encourage follow-up questions and extended responses. Classcheck to share anything interesting.

6 Reading

A Cover the text and refer sts only to the photo. Ask questions for them to speculate, e.g. *How old do you think Arturo is? Guess his nationality, job, marital status, where he lives.*

Explain Arturo spent a year abroad, and is writing about how he feels he changed while he was away. Sts read questions 1 and 2, then give them one minute to scan the first paragraph to find the answers. It helps to get them to underline the evidence in the text. Classcheck.

Answers

1 In his country of birth
2 Being more punctual than anyone else, driving more slowly, eating earlier, giving better tips, telling fewer jokes.

Tip

Make it clear you are trying to stick to the reading tasks and postpone dealing with non-essential vocabulary until later. Living with doubts/the unknown is very much part of any authentic reading experience, and sts do need to get used to this.

B Tell sts to read the statements carefully before reading paragraph 2. Help with *adjust* (= get used to it). Give sts two minutes to read and check the true statements.

Paircheck, then classcheck. Elicit corrections of the false ones. Ask: *Is the text interesting so far? Are you enjoying this? How do you feel about not understanding every word?*

Answers

Arturo ...
got a degree abroad.
was starting to lose touch with friends.
sometimes questions his decision to live abroad.
(He didn't find it easy to adjust when he got home. He wanted to get on with his old life, but something was missing.)

C Sts read the rest of the blog and choose the correct answer for the question in paragraph 2.

Classcheck. Get the class to list five good things about living abroad that Arturo mentions: 1 your self awareness develops, 2 your outlook on life changes, 3 you can be whoever you choose to be, 4 you learn you can get through the rough times without your family, 5 you become a better person.

Answer

Absolutely

Optional activity

As an alternative in C, in pairs, first get A to read paragraph 3 in a minute, while B reads paragraph 4. Then, from memory sts tell each other what they read.

D Sts skim the blog again to find where Arturo make these points. Ask them to underline the relevant points in the blog. (1 *You learn that "normal" means socially acceptable ... – nothing more than that.* 2 *You can get through the rough times without your family.* 3 *I can be whatever I choose to be.* 4 *You realize that the ugly haircut or the wrong meal ... mean absolutely nothing.*)

Paircheck, then classcheck. Do they agree with him?

Answers

become more accepting of diversity. – 3
learn to rely more on yourself. – 4
can reinvent yourself. – 3
don't get bothered by small problems. – 4

Optional activity

Tell sts to write a short comment or question they could post on Arturo's blog. Then ask them to read it aloud to their classmates.

Song lyric: See Teacher's Book p.345 for notes about the song and an accompanying activity to do with the class.

E 10.10 In pairs, sts go back through the blog and try to pronounce the pink-stressed words. Use the audio for them to check. Pause after each paragraph to deal with any questions, and check meanings. Between them, sts ought to be able to guess/paraphrase most new items, so try to let them but save the highlighted phrases until 7C if you can.

F **Make it personal** Go through the questions, e.g. by getting sts to ask you first. Highlight the example for sts to match to the right question (5).

In groups, sts discuss the questions. Monitor to pick up on their most interesting answers, so you can ask them to tell the class later.

Class feedback. Ask a few to say something they remember from their partners. Ask: *Which countries did you choose to spend a year abroad in? Which was the most popular choice for questions 2, 3 and 5? How do you feel about your accent?* There's ample room for discussion here.

7 Vocabulary: Words with literal and figurative meanings

A Sts cover the boxed words, and look at the pictures. In pairs, sts write down as many words/phrases as they can associated with each. Classcheck.

Uncover the words. Ask: *How many of them did you think of, if any?* Sts can guess which are verbs and nouns, and the meaning too before matching them with the pictures. Teach *crumb(s)* as well as *crumble*. Classcheck. Have sts make a sentence with each word.

Answers

1 leap 2 label 3 crumble 4 root 5 magnet 6 fit

Tip

It's nearly always better to get sts to make phrases at least, not just say words in isolation, e.g. *She's about to leap.*

B Go through **Literal or figurative?** with the class and check understanding. Ask: *Why might you want to use a figurative expression?* (for variety, or to add impact to speech/writing.) Tell sts figurative expressions are especially common in poetry or literary writing.

Sts find the highlighted words in the blog and match them with the definitions. Paircheck, then classcheck.

Elicit other words with figurative meanings, e.g. *path* meaning "course" or "direction" (e.g. *path to success, to be on the wrong / right path*), *shoes* meaning "position" (*I wouldn't like to be in your shoes*).

Answers

1 fitting 2 roots 3 label 4 leap 5 crumble 6 magnet

C Sts complete the discussion points 1–6. First elicit the opposite of *good* (evil) and synonyms for *unfit* (in poor shape/condition) to help with tricky vocabulary. Paircheck, then classcheck. Highlight the phrasal verb *fit in*.

Answers

1 label 2 crumbling 3 root 4 magnet 5 leap 6 fit

Optional activity

Sts can write their own "useful sentences" with items in 7A (i.e. ones they can imagine saying often) to test they've fully grasped them and remember better too.

D **Make it personal** Sts match the speech bubble to the correct question in C (1).

Weaker classes: Brainstorm a few more ideas before they choose their questions.

In pairs, give sts five minutes to discuss the three questions they have chosen. Classcheck. Ask: *Which question lead to the best discussion?*

Stronger classes: Sts swap partners, and discuss the other three questions.

Workbook p.50.

E 10.10 Try to pronounce the pink-stressed words. Listen to check. Did you get all the vowels right?

F Make it personal In groups, answer 1–5. Any surprises?

1 Which benefit(s) of living abroad in 6D would be most important to you? Can you think of any others?
2 If you could spend a year abroad, where exactly would you go and why?
3 Would you prefer to move abroad or to another place in your own country? Why?
4 If you moved abroad, would it bother you having a foreign accent?
5 Which aspects of your identity might be hardest to abandon?

> I think I'd miss my hometown most of all. After all, I've lived here since I was born. It's part of my identity.

7 Vocabulary: Words with literal and figurative meanings

A Match the words to the pictures 1–6.

crumble	fit	label	leap	magnet	root

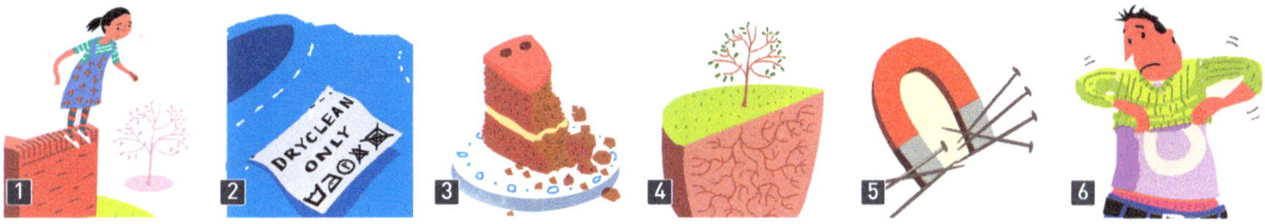

B Read *Literal or figurative?* Then match the highlighted words in Arturo's blog to the definitions 1–6. Do you know any other words with figurative meanings?

Literal or figurative?

Words can have literal (concrete) or figurative (abstract) meanings. Knowing a word's literal meaning can help you guess what it means when it's used figuratively:
My older sister was scared to **dive** into the pool (literal) / into a new relationship (figurative).

1 *fitting* : being in harmony with or belonging to
2 ______ : origins or source
3 ______ : arbitrary description or identifying words
4 ______ : make a sudden change or transition
5 ______ : fall apart or break down completely
6 ______ : a force that attracts

C Complete 1–6 with the correct form of the words in A.

1 Think of a ______ often attached to your country or city. Do you think it's a fair description?
2 How's the economy doing in your country? Is it in good shape, so-so, or ______ ?
3 "Money is the ______ of all evil." Do you agree?
4 Some people seem to be a ______ for bad luck or trouble. Do you know anyone like that?
5 Can you think of an artist that successfully made the ______ from music to movies?
6 At school, how hard do / did you try to ______ in with the "cool kids" in your class?

D Make it personal In pairs, choose three questions in C to answer. Any surprises?

> Well, Montevideo is known as "a culinary paradise" because our meat and fish are so good. Of course!

» 10.4 Has your daily routine changed over time?

8 Language in use

A 10.11 Listen to the start of a podcast. Who is being interviewed and why?

B 10.12 Listen and order the photos 1–5. Who do you think is having the hardest time?

a ☐

b ☐

c ☐

d ☐

e ☐

C 10.12 Listen again. T (true) or F (false)?

1 Mariana had a sedentary lifestyle in Venezuela.
2 Ignacio mostly blames his roommate for their cold relationship.
3 Ines says she lacks self-discipline.
4 Diego found it hard to adapt to life in the U.S.
5 Elena's parents are going to take her back home.

D Match the highlighted words in podcast excerpts 1–5 to definitions a–f. Which feelings and opinions can you relate to?

1 I was born and raised in Caracas, so I kind of miss the **hustle and bustle** of life there. ... I'm sure I'll get used to the peace and quiet eventually.
2 I'm not used to sharing a room with anyone – **let alone** someone I **barely** know.
3 Here we have regular assignments, quizzes, projects, and exams, which can be a little **overwhelming**. I wonder if I'll ever get used to working this hard.
4 When I came here, I was used to life in the States. I mean, there was less of a culture **clash** than I'd anticipated.
5 I started to feel terribly **homesick**. I wasn't used to being away from my parents for more than a couple of days.

a a conflict ____________
b much less, not to mention ____________
c noisy, energetic activity *hustle and bustle*
d scarcely, hardly ____________
e sad because you're away from home and family ____________
f so confusing and difficult, it's hard to deal with ____________

> I can definitely relate to the last one. I felt so homesick when I ...

E **Make it personal** How would you feel about leaving home to study or work?

1 Do you make new friends easily?
2 Are you a good roommate? How many people have you shared an apartment or dorm with? Have you had good experiences?
3 Would you mind sharing a kitchen and a bathroom? Is there anything you couldn't share?
4 How badly would you miss your family? How often would you contact them?
5 How often do you need peace and quiet? What do you do to find it?

> Well, I actually went away to school. The first year was a nightmare because ...

Lesson Aims: Sts listen to people talking about difficult life changes, and discuss tough changes in their own lives.

Skills	Language	Vocabulary	Grammar
Listening to sts talking about their experiences of moving abroad to study Discussing difficult life changes	Talking about life changes: *Ignacio isn't used to sharing a room, I've gotten used to going to work by bike, I wasn't used to being away from my parents*	*adapt, homesick, let alone, overwhelming, sedentary*	Talking about acquired habits: *be* and *get used to*

Warm-up

In small groups, sts discuss: *Have you had any big changes in your life recently?* Encourage follow-up questions, e.g. *How did you react to that? How different is your life now? Was it a positive experience?* Classcheck by asking sts to report their partners' answers.

Board the lesson title question: *Has your daily routine changed over time?* Ask students to write down five things that are different e.g. *I used to share an apartment with my best friend, but now I live with my husband. I used to live downtown, but now I live in the suburbs. I used to get up at 6.30, but now I get up at 8 a.m.*

Have sts discuss their answers in pairs, and if they like it better now or before. Classcheck to share anything interesting.

8 Language in use

A 10.11 Focus on the first photo. Ask lots of 'teacher-like' questions, e.g. *Guess who she is, Where?, Why?, What's she thinking?*

Answers

Five overseas students at college in Vermont. They're talking about the first few months away from home, and adapting to college life.

See Teacher's Book p.328 for Audio script 10.11.

B 10.12 Play the next part of the podcast for sts to listen and order the photos.

Paircheck. Classcheck, then ask who they think is having the hardest time.

As a follow-up, ask: *Who finds Vermont too quiet?* (1 – Mariana) *Who doesn't like the weather?* (4 – Diego) *Who misses her family?* (5 – Elena) *Who finds the work hard?* (3 – Ines) *Who doesn't get along with his roommate?* (2 – Ignacio).

Answers

3 (Ines), 4 (Diego), 1 (Mariana), 5 (Elena), 2 (Ignacio)

See Teacher's Book p.328 for Audio script 10.12.

C 10.12 Go through statements 1–5, and elicit the meaning of *sedentary* (= tending to sit about without doing much exercise).

Re-Play it for sts to say whether the statements are true or false. Classcheck.

Answers

1 T 2 F 3 T 4 F 5 F

See Teacher's Book p.328 for Audio script 10.12.

Optional activity

Ask: *What advice would you give them?* Elicit phrases for giving advice, e.g. *If I were Mariana , I'd ... , I think Diego should ... .* In pairs, discuss, then report back to the class.

D Sts read the excerpts and say who said each one (1 Mariana, 2 Ignacio, 3 Ines, 4 Diego, 5 Elena).

Focus on the highlighted words and have sts say what type of word they are (adverb, noun, conjunction or adjective). Then ask them to match them with the definitions. Paircheck, then classcheck.

Ask: Which of the statements can you relate to? Refer sts to the speech bubble. Elicit other answers, e.g. *I can't relate to Ines. You expect to work hard when you go to university, you have to be prepared for that! Would you like to go to Vermont? Which of them would(n't) you choose to be friends with?*

Answers

a clash b let alone c hustle and bustle d barely
e homesick f overwhelming

E **Make it personal** Board the rubric question and ask too: *Have you ever been away from home to study or work?*

Go through questions 1–5 eliciting *dorm* is short for *dormitory*. In small groups, sts discuss them. Help with tricky vocabulary and note any useful language you can feed in.

Classcheck. Ask: *Which question was the most productive?* Invite volunteers to say what they learned about their partners.

9 Grammar: Talking about acquired habits

A Clarify meaning by boarding these sentences:

At first Ignacio wasn't ***used to*** *sharing a room.* (= He found it unusual/difficult).

But he soon ***got used to*** *it.* (= It became less strange/ more normal.)

*Now he'****s used to*** *it.* (= Now, it feels totally normal.)

Sts read the grammar box, then check the rules *T* (true) or *F* (false). Paircheck, then classcheck. Associating *used to* with *accustomed to* is helpful as that's how it translates in Romance languages.

Answers

1 T   2 T

Refer students to the **Grammar expansion** on p.156.

Tip

Use the **Common mistakes** to highlight the possible confusion between *be used to doing* and *used to do*.

I used to have my own room. (= In the past I had my own room, but not anymore.)

I'm used to having my own room. (= I'm accustomed to having my own room.)

Song lyric: See Teacher's Book p.345 for notes about the song and an accompanying activity to do with the class.

B 10.13 Sts correct the sentences, paircheck, then listen to check.

In pairs, sts practice the sentences. Check the pronunciation of *used* /juːst/ and also the schwa sound in *to* /tə/.

Weaker classes: Correct the sentences on the board together as a class.

Answers

1 Mom says we'll get used to living together.
2 I'm not used to being treated as an adult.
3 It took me a while to get used to the weather.

C Sts cover 8C and 8D, looking only at the photos. In pairs, sts note down as much information as they can remember about each student. Focus in particular on using *used to* forms correctly.

Class feedback. Invite students to tell the class what they have remembered, then allow them to check against the audio script to see if they missed anything.

D Sts look at the webpage *Tough changes!* Elicit the opposite to establish meaning (easy) Ask: *What changes did Marco and Kathleen experience in their lives?* Give sts two minutes to read the text and fill in the gaps 1–7 appropriately. Paircheck, then classcheck. Ask: *Who do you empathize with most?*

Answers

1 wasn't   2 to get   3 was   4 getting   5 ride   6 working   7 going

E Make it personal Ask: *Have you had any big changes in your life recently?* Elicit an immediate answer or two.

Refer sts to the webpage (*Search our archive section*) in D. They can choose a topic from the list or their own idea. Give them a minute or two alone to prepare the stages in the instructions.

In pairs, sts interview each other. As well as questions a, b and c from the webpage, elicit and board others they can ask, e.g. *What was the hardest thing? What else did you find tricky? How did you get used to it? Are you used to it now?*

Monitor, and make a note of common errors for delayed correction.

Class feedback. Ask sts to tell the class something they learned about their partner. Ask: *Who had the worst experience?*

Workbook p.51.

9 Grammar: Talking about acquired habits

A Read the grammar box. Check (✔) T (true) or F (false) in rules 1 and 2.

Talking about acquired habits: *be* and *get used to*

***be used to* (the state)**	***get used to* (the process)**
Ignacio **isn't used** to sharing his room.	He'll have **to get used to** it.
Diego **was** already **used to** living abroad.	He still **hasn't gotten used to** the weather.
Ines **is** still **not used to** college life.	She'**s** slowly **getting used to** doing more homework.

1 ***Be used to*** means *be accustomed to* and ***get used to*** means *become accustomed to*. T F
2 After ***be / get used to***, you can use a verb in the *-ing* form or a noun. T F

Grammar expansion p.156

Common mistakes

I ~~use to wake~~ *'m used to waking* up early. But I'll never ~~used to go~~ *get used to going* to bed late.

How often did you ~~used~~ *use* to go skiing when you lived in Argentina?

B 10.13 Correct the mistakes in 1–3. Listen to check. Notice the /s/ sound in *used*.

1 Mom says we'll get used to live together.
2 I'm not used to been treated as an adult.
3 It took me a while to used to the weather.

C In pairs, use only the photos in 8B to remember all you can about each person. Check in AS 10.12 on p.163. Anything you missed?

D Complete 1–4 with *be* or *get* in the correct tense. Then complete 5–7 with a form of the verbs in parentheses.

TOUGH CHANGES!

	Marco, from Colombia: moving out of your parents' house	Kathleen, from Denver: selling your car and buying a bicycle
a Was it tough at first?	I come from a large family, so at first I (1) _____ used to the silence. I found it really weird.	Not as hard as I thought. I used to (5) _____ (ride) my bike everywhere when I lived in Amsterdam, which certainly helped.
b Any other problems?	It took me a long time (2) _____ used to doing all the housework by myself because I (3) _____ used to having a housekeeper.	Not really. I don't mind the effort. I go to the gym every day, so I'm used to (6) _____ (work) out.
c How are things now?	I guess I'm slowly (4) _____ used to being on my own, and I kind of like it.	I've gotten so used to (7) _____ (go) to work by bike, I don't think I'll ever need a car again.

SEARCH OUR ARCHIVE:
changing schools / getting into college / getting married / moving to a new city / becoming a vegetarian / starting an exercise program / switching from iOS to Android (or vice versa!)

E Make it personal Choose a topic from the website in D, answer questions a–c mentally, and make notes. Then, in pairs, interview each other. Who had the hardest time adapting?

I started college last year, and it was a bit of a shock at first.

What was hard about it?

Well, I was used to smaller classes and ...

10 Listening

A 10.14 Take the quiz. T (true) or F (false)? Listen to check. How many correct guesses?

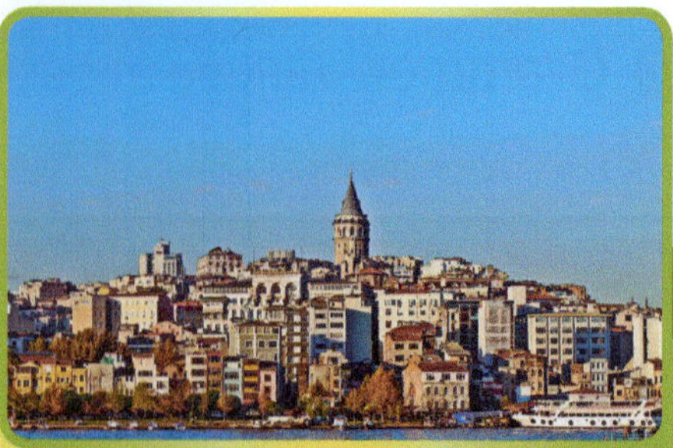

How much do you know about Istanbul?

1 Istanbul is one of the five largest cities in the world.
2 Two-thirds of the city is located in Europe and one-third in Asia.
3 Istanbul's subway is the oldest in the world.
4 As the city is surrounded by water, it doesn't snow there.
5 Over time, it has been the capital of three different empires.
6 The Grand Bazaar is the world's most visited tourist attraction.

B 10.15 Listen to Bill and Gail's first impressions of Istanbul and answer 1 and 2.

1 List three reasons why Bill loves Istanbul.
2 List three things you can do there. Would you like to visit the city?

C 10.16 Listen to the second part. T (true), F (false), or NI (no information)? Have you been anywhere at all like this?

1 The Grand Bazaar is smaller than a city block.
2 Bill thinks The Grand Bazaar is still getting bigger.
3 You can buy rugs, slippers, and jewelry.
4 According to the conversation, you can also buy live animals.
5 It's less crowded early in the morning.

D 10.17 Complete 1–5 with the correct prepositions. Use your intuition! Listen to check. Any surprises?

1 I can't wait to explore the city ___ the next few days.
2 We should definitely stock up ___ these for an afternoon snack or two.
3 And then we can go ___ some Turkish ice cream.
4 Istanbul is love ___ first sight, isn't it?
5 It [the Grand Bazaar] is one of the largest markets ___ the entire world.

11 Keep talking

A What's the most amazing place you've ever been / imagined going to? Think through 1–7. Search online, if necessary.

1 What's it called and what country is it in?
2 Is it historically significant in any way?
3 When did you first go (first imagine going) there?
4 What was your first reaction to the place?
5 What are the highlights? What else is there to do?
6 Did you need to take any precautions?
7 Have you been back there since (or in your dreams)? How many times?

B In groups, describe the places. Be sure to answer 1–7. Which sounds the most irresistible?

I think Rio is the most unbelievable place I've ever been.

Oh, I'd love to go. What's so special about it?

Well, as you know, it's famous for Sugarloaf Mountain ...

112

Lesson Aims: Sts listen to tourists giving their impressions of Istanbul, and tell each other about their favorite cities.

Skills	Language	Vocabulary
Listening to tourists talking about their impressions of Istanbul Writing a travel report: using synonyms and figurative expressions in descriptions	Talking about places you have visited, e.g. *Rio is the most unbelievable place I've ever been to. Rio is famous for Sugarloaf Mountain.*	Synonyms for *nice / beautiful: breathtaking, gorgeous, stunning, awe-inspiring*

Warm-up

Before sts come in, board vocabulary from the last class, e.g. *hustle and bustle, let alone, barely, overwhelming, clash, homesick*. Ask sts to choose three items and create three different questions with them. In pairs, sts take turns asking and answering.

Ask the lesson title question: *Which are your two favorite cities and why?* In pairs, sts answer the question. Tell sts these can be cities they have visited or just heard/read/dreamed about. Individuals tell the class which ones they have chosen. *Which are the most popular cities?*

10 Listening

A 10.14 Focus on the photos (of the Galata Tower and Grand Bazaar). Ask: *Have you ever been to Istanbul? What do you know about it? Would you like to go/live there?* Class brainstorm. Ideally, bring in / show some more images too, or a short tourist video.

In pairs, sts read the quiz questions and say which they think are true or false.

Sts listen and check. Ask them to correct the false sentences.

Answers

1 F (Istanbul is one of the ten largest cities in the world.)
2 T
3 F (London's underground system is the oldest in the world.)
4 F (It occasionally snows in winter.)
5 T
6 T

See Teacher's Book p.328 for Audio script 10.14.

Background information

Istanbul straddles two continents, Europe and Asia. It's the most populated city in Turkey, with two-thirds of the population occupying the European part of the city, where the commercial and historic center lie. That makes it the largest population in Europe too! People often mistake Istanbul for the capital, which is Ankara.

B 10.15 Explain that sts will hear two friends, Bill and Gail, who have just arrived in Istanbul. Sts listen and answer the questions. Paircheck, classcheck, then ask if this has made them want to visit the city more.

Answers

1 He likes the food, Istanbul is affordable, and it's pedestrian-friendly.
2 A boat tour down the Bosphorus River; have Turkish ice-cream, *Domdurma*; get a good cheap shave.

See Teacher's Book p.329 for Audio script 10.15.

C 10.16 Sts read the statements, and underline the key words. Play the audio for them to make them *T* (true), *F* (false) or *NI* (no information). Classcheck. Elicit meaning of *jet lag* (= tiredness / physical effects caused by long distance flying over different time zones). Ask: *Have you ever had jet lag?*

Answers

1 F 2 T 3 T 4 NI 5 T

See Teacher's Book p.329 for Audio script 10.16.

D 10.17 Ask *Do you remember who said these things?* (1 Gail, 2, 3, 4 & 5 Bill). Sts try to complete with the correct prepositions, using their intuition.

Play the audio for them to check. Highlight *love at first sight* and ask: *Is there a similar expression in your language?*

Answers

1 over 2 on 3 for 4 at 5 in

11 Keep talking

A Go through the instructions and give sts a few minutes to think about questions 1–7, make basic notes, look things up online, etc.

B Go through the example in speech bubbles. Ask: *Has anyone been to Rio?*

In small groups, sts exchange their ideas. Monitor and help where necessary. Class feedback. Sts report back to the class on places they have learned about. Ask: *Which seems the most fascinating place? Why?*

Song lyric: See Teacher's Book p.346 for notes about the song and an accompanying activity to do with the class.

12 Writing: A travel report

A Focus on the photo. Ask: *Where is it? Has anybody been there? What do you think Lucy might say in her report?*

Give sts two minutes to read the travel report with three tasks:

1 to read quickly without stopping for unknown words.

2 to underline anything they find particularly interesting or makes them want to visit the place.

3 to find out how many times she has been there.

Paircheck, then classcheck. Ask: *How much of what you guessed was in the text?*

Answers

She's been there once.

B Sts look back at the questions in 11A, then re-read the travel report to find where Lucy has answered them. They write the question numbers 1–7 next to the correct paragraphs. Set a two-minute time limit to keep up momentum and avoid dwelling on vocabulary until they finish.

Weaker classes: Do Paragraph 1 with them to set this up and ensure they realize it's more than one question per paragraph.

Paircheck, then classcheck. Elicit pronunciation of the pinked words which aren't highlighted in yellow.

Answers

Paragraph A – Questions 1, 2 Paragraph B – Questions 3, 4, 5 Paragraph C – Question 5 Paragraph D – Question 6 Paragraph E – Question 7

C Go through **Write it right!** Ask: *Can you remember any figurative expressions from earlier in the course?*

Sts study the highlighted example in the report and mark them 1 or 2.

Classcheck. Now elicit stress and pronunciation of all the yellow items. Elicit and board more alternatives for *nice / beautiful*, e.g. *charming, attractive, appealing, delightful, magnificent, impressive, pretty, striking, dramatic, jaw-dropping*.

Answers

set my imagination on fire – 2
blown away – 2
stunning – 1
gorgeous – 1
awe-inspiring – 1
take your breath away – 2
beyond your wildest dreams – 2

D Go through each **Common mistake** and elicit why it is wrong. Ask: *Which adverbs can you use with extreme adjectives?* (*really, absolutely, quite, totally*).

Sts then correct the mistakes in the sts' draft paragraph. Paircheck, then classcheck. Ask: *What mark would you give this st?*

Tip

In exercises like this, tell sts how many mistakes they are aiming to correct (6 here), to give a clear goal and avoid them inventing all sorts of other problems!

Answers

If you ~~never went~~ **have never** been to Cartagena, located on Colombia's northern coast, you don't know what you're missing. It's a ~~very~~ gorgeous city and one of the most popular tourist ~~attraction~~ **attractions** ~~of~~ **in** the country. My favorite place is the Café del Mar, a great spot to watch the sunset over the old city walls. It's ~~very~~ amazing! ~~I've been~~ **I went** there last December and it was very crowded, so I suggest you go in October or November.

Optional activity

Sts find four superlatives in the report: *Peru's most popular tourist attraction ... the world's most famous archeological sites, the best chocolate in the country, the best time to visit Machu Picchu.*

Revise superlatives by asking: *When do we use "-est."?* (with short adjectives) *"most"?* (with longer adjectives). Elicit examples: *It's the cheapest hotel/ most convenient hotel in Cartagena. Highlight use of in + place, e.g. Machu Picchu is the best Incan ruin* ***in*** *Peru.*

Sts write sentences for a guidebook for their own city/capital using superlatives, e.g. *interesting, old, good, famous, popular, large*. In pairs, sts compare their sentences.

E **Your turn!** Read through the instructions with the class and check sts understand what they have to do.

Weaker classes: Board expressions from Lucy's report for sts to use, e.g. *I was ... when I first learned about ..., When I saw ... for the first time ..., ... is located ..., Don't miss ...*

Sts can start their writing in class, and finish for homework. Be sure they follow the *While* and *After* steps and use superlative expressions where appropriate. Monitor and help as necessary.

Allocate a 'study buddy' for each student to email their description to before sending their final draft to you. Post the descriptions on the class website or class walls, and encourage sts to read each other's work.

Class feedback. Ask: *Which was the most interesting travel report you read? Where would you like to visit?*

Workbook p.52.

12 Writing: A travel report

A Read Lucy's travel report. Does it make you want to visit both places? How many times has she been there?

B Write the question numbers 1–7 in 11A next to each paragraph A–E.

Our readers' favorite vacation spots
THIS WEEK: Machu Picchu and Cusco, by Lucy Aurey

A I was twelve when I first learned that Machu Picchu, which means "old mountain," is Peru's most popular tourist attraction and one of the world's most famous archeological sites. The textbook images of that isolated stone city, built by the Incas more than 550 years ago, set my imagination on fire ☐. I had so many questions: Why was it built? Why was it abandoned? I convinced myself that I had to go there one day.

B That day finally came. Last year my fiancé and I spent a week in Peru, and all I can say is that Machu Picchu exceeded my expectations in every possible way. When I saw the Inca ruins for the first time, I was blown away ☐ by the perfection. Was it the giant stones, so well preserved? The extraordinary temples? Maybe the stunning ☐ views? It's hard to tell.

C Machu Picchu lies just fifty miles from Cusco, the starting point for any visit. It's an amazing city with colorful markets, fine restaurants, and gorgeous ☐ monuments. If you have a sweet tooth, check out the ChocoMuseo, where you'll eat the best chocolate in the country. Plus, it'll give you the energy you'll need to climb up the Inca trail. Once in Machu Picchu, don't miss the Temple of the Sun – it's truly awe-inspiring ☐.

D Machu Picchu is located nearly 2.5 kilometers above sea level, so it'll take your breath away ☐! Take it easy and drink plenty of water so your body can get used to the altitude. As a rule, the best time to visit Machu Picchu is between May and August, outside the rainy season. But, beware! Daily visitor numbers are strictly controlled, so be sure to book your trip way in advance.

E Machu Picchu is magnificent beyond your wildest dreams ☐. No wonder it's been named one of the New Seven Wonders of the World. I'm already looking forward to going back next year!

C Read *Write it right!* Then scan the report and write 1 or 2 next to the highlighted examples.

Write it right!

Two ways to make your description come alive are:

1 Avoid the word *nice*, and try not to overuse *beautiful*. Use more "colorful" synonyms:
The place was absolutely **breathtaking**.

2 Use figurative expressions:
It was a gorgeous beach spoiled by **a sea of tourists**.

D Read *Common mistakes*. Then correct six mistakes in the paragraph.

Common mistakes

The place was ~~very~~ *absolutely* stunning.

New York is one of the most multicultural ~~city of~~ *cities in* the world.

I~~'ve been in~~ *went to* Bangkok in 2010.

Don't use *very* with extreme adjectives, and be careful with plurals and tenses!

If you never went to Cartagena, located on Colombia's northern coast, you don't know what you're missing. It's a very gorgeous city and one of the most popular tourist attraction of the country. My favorite place is the Café del Mar, a great spot to watch the sunset over the old city walls. It's very amazing! I've been there last December and it was very crowded, so I suggest you go in October or November.

E Your turn! Describe the place you talked about in 11B. Write about 200 words.

Before
Organize your notes into five paragraphs to answer the questions from 11A.

While
Use colorful and figurative expressions from Lucy's report and *Write it right!* Check your grammar, too, for common mistakes.

After
Proofread carefully. Email your text to a classmate before sending it to your teacher.

Review 5
Units 9–10

1 Speaking

A Look at the photos on p.94.

1 Note down your impressions of the people using these expressions:

keep quiet	mingle	open up	reveal	small talk	think out loud	think over	think up

2 In groups, share information. Who seems introverted? Who seems extroverted?

3 Take turns describing how you usually react in these situations.

At parties, I like to mingle and get to know new people.

Really? I hate small talk.

B Search "extrovert or introvert" and take a new personality quiz. Then share something new you learned about yourself.

I learned a new word. I'm an "ambivert." I really like to socialize, but I also like time by myself.

2 Listening

A R5.1 Listen to a conversation between Daisy and an employee of a car rental company. Number the problems in the order mentioned.

- [ ] The employee doesn't know much about the device.
- [ ] The only office is at the airport.
- [ ] Daisy can't hear a voice on the GPS.
- [ ] Refunds are only given through the website.
- [ ] The boss is away.
- [ ] The directions are wrong.

B **Make it personal** In pairs, discuss these questions.

1 Describe a specific travel problem that you've had. What happened in the end?

2 Was anyone able to help you?

Once I was locked in the bathroom of a hotel, and I couldn't get out ...

3 Grammar

A Eileen would like to take a study-abroad vacation. Change her questions to a program director to indirect questions, using the words in parentheses.

1 Are there any two-week Portuguese programs in Salvador Bahia? (Do you happen to know ...?)
2 Where do students stay? (Do you have any idea ...?)
3 How many hours a day are classes? (I wonder ...)
4 Is there a placement exam? (Could you tell me ...?)
5 What methodology does the teacher use? (I'd like to know ...)
6 Are there organized social activities? (Can you ask someone ...?)

Warm-up

See page 61 of the Teacher's Book for warm-up ideas.

1 Speaking

A 1 Sts work individually, and note down their impressions of the people in the photos using some of the expressions in the box.

Possible answers

Photo 1: They are making small talk. The girl on the left is keeping quiet.
Photo 2: The girl on the left is thinking things over / keeping quiet. The other three are thinking up ideas.
Photo 3: The lady on the left is thinking out loud.

2 In groups, sts share the ideas they noted down in 1. Class feedback. Sts discuss which of the people in the photos they think is introverted/extroverted, and why. Class feedback.

3 Sts reflect on the situations in the photos on p.94. Ask: *How do you feel in these situations? How do you normally react? Do you keep quiet and withdraw or do you like to be the center of attention?* Refer to the examples in the speech bubbles. Sts discuss the questions in their groups.

B Either in class if possible, or at home, sts find an extrovert / introvert personality quiz on the Internet, and take it.

In pairs, sts tell each other what they discovered about themselves. Alternatively, they can find a quiz and ask a partner the questions.

Tip

Monitor and help sts to move on / avoid getting stuck on anything which is obviously too hard / inappropriate / long. There are a lot of short ones. As soon as one student finds a good one, they could all do that.

Optional activity

Stronger classes: Sts write their own *Extrovert or Introvert?* quizzes with two or three multiple-choice answers for each question. Encourage them to refer to 2A on p.94 as a model. In pairs, sts exchange quizzes and take each other's.

2 Listening

A R5.1 Focus on the photo and elicit all you can. Ask a few questions, e.g. *Who are they? What's going on? How are they both feeling?* Then, in pairs, sts quickly speculate before feeding back their ideas to the class.

Explain that the woman, Daisy, is talking to an employee of a car rental company. Have sts guess how their conversation might go, e.g. *She doesn't look happy so there's probably a problem with the car.*

Read through the problems. Then play the audio for sts to number the problems in order. Classcheck.

Answers

3 The employee doesn't know much about the device.
5 The only office is at the airport.
1 Daisy can't hear a voice on the GPS.
6 Refunds are only given through the website.
4 The boss is away.
2 The directions are wrong.

See Teacher's Book p.329 for Audio script R5.1.

B **Make it personal** Go through the instructions and example speech bubble. Ask: *Has anyone had this problem, being locked in (or out) of somewhere?*

In pairs, sts discuss a travel problem they have had. Encourage the listener to be supportive and ask for lots of details. Monitor, helping with vocabulary.

Classcheck. Invite individuals to share their travel problem. Ask: *Were most people helped out of their situations by others, or did they have to "fix" the problem themselves?*

3 Grammar

A Set the context by asking: *Have you ever had a study-abroad trip? Are you thinking of taking one? If so, which language and where?*

Remind sts we often use indirect questions in formal situations, like this interview.

Board question 1 as an example and elicit the answer. Sts then change the other questions into indirect questions using the prompts in parentheses. Refer sts to the grammar on p.107 if necessary.

Paircheck, then classcheck.

Answers

1 Do you happen to know if there are any two-week Portuguese programs in Salvador Bahia?
2 Do you have any idea where students stay?
3 I wonder how many hours a day classes are.
4 Could you tell me if / whether there is a placement exam?
5 I'd like to know what methodology the teacher uses.
6 Can you ask someone if there are organized social activities?

Optional activity

Sts roleplay the interview, inventing the answers, or changing the context to a local course they do know about.

B **Make it personal** Elicit and board a couple of example questions, then sts write four more indirect questions a tourist might ask. Encourage sts to use a variety of indirect question expressions.

In pairs, A pretends to be a visitor to your town, and asks B, a local person, their questions. Sts role play, then swap roles.

Possible questions

Could you tell me where the train station is, please?
I'd like to know where the nearest hotel is.
Do you happen to know what time the museum opens?
Do you have any idea how I can get to the airport?

C Tell sts Eileen is now on her study tour in Brazil. Sts read through sentences 1–5 quickly, ignoring the gaps. Ask: *What can you infer about Eileen's vacation?* Elicit that she's staying with a family, is learning Portuguese, struggled at first with a number of things but is now happy and doing well.

Go through the example. Sts complete the rest of the exercise individually. Paircheck, then classcheck. Ask: *Do you think her experience sounds typical of anybody studying abroad? Why (not)?*

Answers

1 In the beginning, I had some trouble getting used to the food, which was very spicy.
2 I wasn't used to speaking Portuguese either, which was overwhelming at first.
3 But it was easy to get used to early morning classes, which was great because I had the rest of the day to sightsee.
4 I also got used to singing in Portuguese every day because my teacher loved music, which was amazing.
5 And now I'm used to / 'm getting used to living with a family and speaking Portuguese at breakfast which is such a great way to improve my language skills!

4 Writing

A Elicit and board some problems sts may encounter if they moved abroad. Then brainstorm some possible solutions, e.g.

Problems: You might miss your friends and family. It's hard to understand people at first.

Solutions: Although it's tempting to keep messaging people back home, try to spend the time making new friends. Don't be discouraged if you don't understand people at first, as after a few weeks you'll find it easier. Ask people to speak more slowly or repeat things so you can understand them.

Sts choose one of the problems discussed, or think of their own, and write a paragraph. Ensure they include the boxed items.

Sts can start the writing in class and finish it for homework. Make time in the next lesson for sts to read each other's work and for you to check them over.

Weaker classes: Sts could refer back to **Write it right!** and the notes in 12E on p.103.

5 Self-test

To revise and consolidate the **Common mistakes**, sts do this individually then paircheck. Encourage sts to look back through Units 9 and 10 if they're unsure of how to correct the mistakes.

Classcheck by boarding the corrected sentences.

Answers

1 I'd like to live <u>by myself</u> (on my own), but I might have trouble <u>getting</u> used to the quiet.
2 I was <u>telling</u> the truth, but the police thought I was making <u>up</u> the story.
3 Students <u>cheating</u> (who cheat) on their exams will end <u>up</u> being expelled.
4 People are always <u>chewing</u> gum in class, <u>which</u> drives me up the wall.
5 If you raise a lot your voice <u>a lot</u>, it doesn't make people see eye <u>to</u> eye with you.
6 I'm really looking forward <u>to</u> my trip with an old friend of <u>mine</u>.
7 You have to <u>check out</u> by 11, so you'd better ask for a <u>wake-up</u> call.
8 I'd like to know <u>if (whether) anyone called</u> and where the nearest bank <u>is</u>.
9 I miss the <u>hustle and bustle</u> of city life, and I can't <u>get</u> used to the country.
10 The view was <u>awe-inspiring</u> and it took my breath <u>away</u>.

6 Point of view

See page 62 of the Teacher's Book for notes about this section.

Go through topics a–d with the class, and brainstorm a few ideas for each one.

Individually, sts choose one of them, and make some preparatory notes.

Group together sts who chose the same topic so that they can compare, share, expand on and improve their ideas. Monitor and correct as much as you can.

If possible, sts record their opinion in class using a cell phone. Allow sts to re-record if they aren't happy. It's all good practice and everybody wants the best possible end product. Encourage sts to swap recordings with a partner and give each other feedback. You could play some of the answers to the whole class, and get class feedback. Ask: *Which argument did you think was most convincing?*

Optional activity

Hold a class debate on one of the topics in 6. See technique on Teacher's Book p.62.

B **Make it personal** Note down four indirect questions a visitor to your town or city might ask. In pairs, role play helping the "tourist."

C Complete Eileen's reactions to her vacation (1–5) with a form of *be used to* or *get used to*. Then combine the sentences using *which*.

1 In the beginning, I had some trouble _getting used to_ the food. It was very spicy.
I had some trouble getting used to the food, which was very spicy.
2 I ______________ speaking Portuguese, either. It was overwhelming at first.
3 But it was easy to ______________ early morning classes. It was great because I had the rest of the day to sightsee.
4 I also ______________ singing in Portuguese every day because my teacher loved music. It was amazing.
5 And now I ______________ living with a family and speaking Portuguese at breakfast. It's such a great way to improve my language skills!

4 Writing

Write a paragraph about a problem you may encounter when you move abroad and offer a solution. Include at least four of these words or expressions.

in order to	while	although	as
so that	unlike	despite	due to

5 Self-test

Correct the two mistakes in each sentence. Check your answers in Units 9 and 10. What's your score, 1–20?

1 I'd like to live by my own, but I might have trouble get used to the quiet.
2 I was claiming the truth, but the police thought I was making the story.
3 Students cheat on their exams will end being expelled.
4 People are always chew gum in class, that drives me up the wall.
5 If you raise a lot your voice, it doesn't make people see eye and eye with you.
6 I'm really looking forward my trip with an old friend of me.
7 You have to checkout by 11, so you'd better ask for a wakeup call.
8 I'd like to know did anyone call and where is the nearest bank.
9 I miss the bustle and hustle of city life, and I can't used to the country.
10 The view was awe-inspire and it took my breath.

6 Point of view

Choose a topic. Then support your opinion in 100–150 words, and record your answer. Ask a partner for feedback. How can you be more convincing?

a You think small talk is a total waste of time. OR
You think small talk is a good way to meet new people and feel comfortable with them.
b You think social injustice is the worst problem facing society. OR
You think a lack of respect for the environment is far worse.
c You think living abroad is something everyone should do. OR
You think living abroad is very difficult and not for everyone.
d You think a foreign accent is something people should try to get rid of. OR
You think a foreign accent is like a foreign culture and should be respected.

11 What recent news has caught your eye?

1 Listening

A 11.1 Listen and match news items 1–6 to photos a–f. Then decide the section each is from.

arts business local science sports style

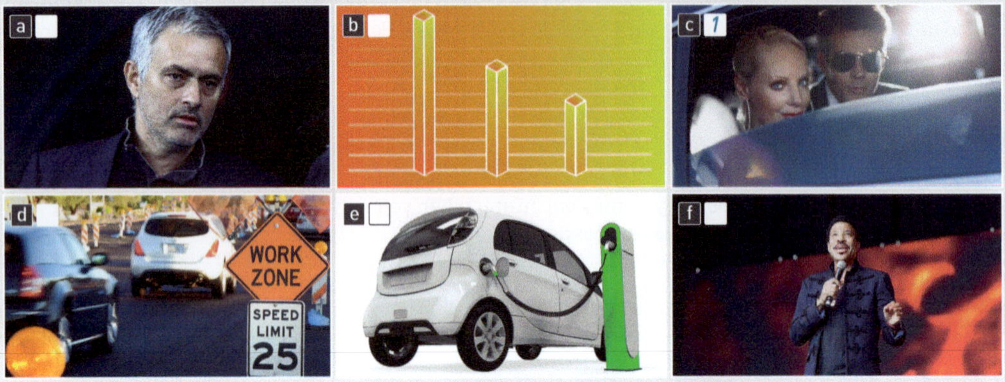

News story 1 must be the style section. That's where they talk about celebrity gossip.

Talking about the news

News is singular and uncountable.

I read **some** news that **was** shocking.
I'm interested in business **news** / **the** arts.
I enjoy reading **the** science **section**.

B 11.2 A reporter from A is doing a survey. Listen and note down Jack's answers in 1–3 words.

1 Favorite news topic?	
2 How often?	
3 In print or on digital media?	
4 Favorite news source?	
5 News alerts?	

C 11.2 Memory test! Try to complete 1–5. Listen again to check. Anything in common with Jack?

1 Jack follows the news so he won't seem ________ in front of his friends.
2 He is also interested in ________ , but he doesn't follow this area.
3 He only watches ________ when he's away from home.
4 He likes the ________ in his online magazine, but he would like to see more ________ and ________ .
5 He looks at his news feed on ________ and ________ .

Call me old-fashioned, but I still read a printed newspaper almost every day.

D Make it personal Choose a news story you've followed. In groups, share and ask follow-up questions. Any surprises?

Well, I'm studying politics, so I've been following the news story about ...

Oh, I didn't hear about that at all. When did it happen? ...

Lesson Aims: Sts learn language to talk about different types of news, and discuss different news sources.

Skills	Language	Vocabulary	Pronunciation
Listening to different news stories Listening to a reporter interviewing someone about the type of news stories they like reading Carrying out a survey about news reading habits	Asking and answering questions about news habits: *How often do you follow the latest news? What is your favorite news source? I look at the news feed on Facebook.*	Words and expressions for talking about the news: *accurate, behind-the-scenes, biased, breaking news, catch one's eye, in favor of, keep up with, skip*	Question intonation

Warm-up

Explore the verb *catch*. Ask: *What can you catch?* to see how many collocations sts can come up with: a ball, a cold, your breath (after exercise), fire, sb doing something (red-handed), a friend as in *Catch you later*. We also use it to ask for repetition: *Sorry, I didn't catch what you said*, and *What's the catch?* (when we are suspicious, e.g. meaning are there any hidden problems?). Finally, move on to *catching somebody's attention*, i.e. your eye.

Board the lesson title question: *What recent news has caught your eye?* In pairs, sts discuss, then class share ideas.

1 Listening

A 11.1 Ask: *What can you see in the photos? Do you recognize a and f?* (José Mourinho and Lionel Richie) *What do you know about them?* In pairs, sts brainstorm ideas. Monitor then classcheck.

Play the audio for sts to match the news items 1–6 with the photos. The first is given as an example to help you set this up. Paircheck, then classcheck.

Focus on the list and discuss which category of news each one comes from (arts, business, local, science, sports, or style).

Go through **Talking about the news**. Ask: *Is news singular or plural in your language?* Highlight use of the definite article, e.g. *Have you seen the news today?*

Answers

c 1 (style) e 2 (science) a 3 (sports) f 4 (arts)
b 5 (business) d 6 (local)

See Teacher's Book p.329 for Audio script 11.1.

Background information

José Mourinho – Portuguese football manager. He hcurrently manages Manchester United.

Glastonbury Festival – one of the world's most famous music festivals. Held annually over five days in June on a farm in Somerset, England. There are many different stages. Attended by around 175,000 people each year.

Lionel Richie – born 1949, was a member of the musical group The Commodores in the 1970s. Had a hugely successful solo career in the 1980s with songs including *All Night Long* and *Hello*.

B 11.2 Sts study the table. Ask if they can guess what the interviewer's questions were, e.g. 1 *What's your favorite news topic?*

Play the audio for sts to listen and note down Jack's answers.

Paircheck, then classcheck.

Answers

1 the arts 2 at least once a day 3 digital media
4 Rolling Stone 5 none

See Teacher's Book p.329 for Audio script 11.2.

C 11.2 Ask: *How good is your memory?* to see what they come up with. Then test them! Sts try to complete the sentences individually, then paircheck. Re-play the audio for them to check their answers. Classcheck.

Ask: *Which of the sentences are also true for you?* Tell your partner, e.g. *I'm also interested in sport, but, unlike Jack, I follow it every day.*

Answers

1 stupid 2 sports 3 TV 4 movie reviews, photos, gossip
5 Twitter, Facebook

Song lyric: See Teacher's Book p.346 for notes about the song and an accompanying activity to do with the class.

D **Make it personal** Give sts time to think of a news story they have been following and make notes about it.

In groups, sts discuss their stories. Monitor to give them all a better sense of audience, and correct what you can.

Afterwards, ask: *Which is the most interesting story you have learned about? Which is the most popular news section, e.g. the arts, sports?*

2 Vocabulary: The news

A 11.3 Sts read sentences 1–6, Jack's answers from the audio in 11B, and guess the meaning of the expressions highlighted in yellow. Use number 6 as the example, as they will have covered this from the question title.

Play the audio for sts to check, or if short of time, check answers as a class.

Answers

1 A 2 A 3 B 4 A 5 B 6 A

See Teacher's Book p.330 for Audio script 11.3.

Optional activity

Stronger classes: Books closed. If you think sts already know some of these expressions, board the sentences, gapping the yellow-highlighted expressions. Board the highlighted expressions separately in random order, or just give the first half of each word: e.g. *ke__ u_ wi___*. Sts match and complete the expressions with the correct sentences.

B Sts complete sentences 1–5 with the highlighted phrases from A. Paircheck, then classcheck.

Sts change the underlined words to make the sentences true for them. Give two examples yourself first then ask a volunteer to do another as an example, e.g. *The news feed on ... is usually accurate, but not always. Sometimes they don't seem to use reliable sources.*

3 Pronunciation: Question intonation

A 11.4 Cover the text and ask: *What intonation rules do you know?* to see what they come up with.

Tip

Emphasize how few watertight rules there really are. Generalizations are helpful, especially when sts notice the exceptions. Suggest the best ways to learn are through extensive listening, as they did with their mother tongue, and noticing patterns, e.g. echoing lines they hear in movies.

Play the audio for students to listen to the questions, paying attention to the intonation, and repeat.

In pairs, sts check the correct rules. Classcheck. Then, sts practice the questions in pairs.

Answers

1 rising 2 falling 3 rising, falling

B 11.5 Elicit what the arrows mean (rising, falling, rise-fall).

Play the audio for sts to listen and mark the correct intonation. Check answers by replaying it, pausing after each question for sts to tell you the intonation pattern.

Board the questions from the audio script (see p.330) for sts to practice in pairs.

Weaker classes: Mark the intonation over the relevant words for sts to refer to.

Answers

1 ↘ 2 ↘ 3 ↗↘ 4 ↘ 5 ↗↘

C Make it personal

1 Ask sts if they can remember the interviewer's questions from 1B. Elicit and board them, or give sts a copy of the audio script (see p.329), to find and underline the questions:

Can I ask you a few questions please?

What would you say your favorite news topic is?

How often do you follow the latest news on the arts?

Do you prefer to get the news in print, or on a computer or mobile device?

What's your favorite news source?

Do you ever get news alerts sent to you?

In pairs, sts ask and answer, noting down their partner's answers. Class feedback. Have a few report their partner's answers to the class.

2 If you have online access and a digital board, get sts to suggest a story, possible sources for it in English, and search for it together. Looking at authentic English, live in class, is totally real and usually motivating, even though they will almost certainly come across tricky language.

But unless they can all do the same work easily for their individual stories in class, sts research them for homework. However they do it, be sure they discuss questions 1–3 afterwards. Dealing with authentic English is ever more essential nowadays. If time, volunteers can tell their story to the class.

Optional activity

Sts write their own short reports about the stories they discussed in 1D. Tell them to think of a good headline. Remind sts we don't use articles in news headlines.

In pairs, sts swap reports to peer check, and suggest ways of improving it.

Workbook p.53.

2 Vocabulary: The news

A 11.3 Circle the choice that is closest in meaning to the highlighted words. Listen to check.

1 I try to **keep up with** what's going on.
A stay informed
B tell people

2 It's such an **accurate** source of information.
A free from error and true
B with errors or not true

3 I wish they'd post more **behind-the-scenes** stuff.
A official
B usually hidden

4 They're **not biased** in favor or against any particular artist.
A neutral
B unfair

5 I tend to **skip** most stories.
A read in detail
B maybe glance at headlines, but not read

6 If a headline **catches my eye**, I click on the link.
A attracts my attention
B worries me

B Complete 1–5 with items from A. Then, in pairs, change the underlined words to make them true for you.

1 The evening news is usually ________ , but not always. Sometimes they don't seem to check their facts .
2 I always try to ________ the latest news about sports.
3 Our main TV network is ________ against the government.
4 When presidents get together, it would be fascinating to know what actually happens ________ .
5 When I check the news, I ________ most of it and move straight to the horoscope section.

3 Pronunciation: Question intonation

A 11.4 Listen to and repeat the examples. Then check (✔) the correct rules.

1 Do you have a favorite news source?
2 What does that include?
3 Can I pick several topics or only one?

1 *Yes / No* questions usually have a ☐ rising ↗ ☐ falling ↘ intonation.
2 *Wh*-questions usually have a ☐ rising ☐ falling intonation.
3 Questions with *or* have a ☐ rising ☐ falling intonation on the first choice(s), but a ☐ rising ☐ falling intonation on the last one.

B 11.5 Listen to 1–5 and write a ↗, b ↘ or c ↗ ↘. Then listen again, copying the speaker's intonation.

1 ________ 2 ________ 3 ________ 4 ________ 5 ________

C **Make it personal** Give your opinions on the news!

1 Interview a new partner to complete the survey in 1B. Ask for lots of detail. Use words and expressions from 2A.

Common mistakes

Turn up the radio, I can't ~~listen to~~ *hear* the news.

OK. What's your favorite news topic?

Well, I really like to keep up with sports, but I usually skip the style section.

Do you mainly follow local teams or international ones?

2 Search for and read a news story about your city or country in a well-known English-language newspaper. Discuss 1–3.

1 Was it easy to understand, or were some parts difficult?
2 Was everything included, or were some important parts left out?
3 Overall, did the English version seem fair or biased?

11.2 Have you ever laughed at the wrong moment?

4 Language in use

A 11.6 In the news, a "blooper" refers to a mistake made in public. Guess bloopers 1–3. Then listen and fill in the blanks. How close were you?

Some of our favorite news bloopers of all time
1
A reporter was doing a story on pets that act like humans when, suddenly, the dog he was holding ________ on live TV.
2
A news anchor ________ in the middle of a news story, before millions of viewers.
3
A TV network interviewed a woman, who they believed was an economist. However, she ________ .

B 11.6 Listen again. T (true) or F (false)?

1 The dog had been behaving strangely.
2 Viewers had no idea whether the reporter was OK.
3 The news anchor woke up by himself.
4 He made a joke about his mistake.
5 The candidate lost her temper during the interview.

C Write R (relaxed) or VN (very nervous) for the highlighted expressions. Which ones were you familiar with?

1 No one really knows why the dog lost it like that. The reporter himself **claimed** that everything had been going well behind the cameras.
2 He kept his cool, though, and **reassured** viewers that he was fine.
3 The news anchor was woken up by his colleague, who stayed calm and **reminded** him he was on live TV!
4 He was able to keep it together and simply denied that he had fallen asleep. Then he **admitted** he was just kidding, of course.
5 Instead of freaking out, the candidate **warned** them they'd made a mistake, then she calmly got up and left the studio!

D **Make it personal** In pairs, answer 1–4.

1 Which story did you like best?

> The last story was great. I would have totally lost it, but she really kept her cool.

2 Can you recall any "bloopers," either by famous people or in comedy?
3 Have you ever made a "blooper" of your own, or been caught on camera at the wrong moment? How did you react?
4 What kinds of things make you laugh? Have you ever laughed at the wrong time?

cartoons   Internet memes   animals doing silly things
comedy shows / funny movies   people falling   stand-up comedians

Lesson Aims: Sts hear about bloopers made by news presenters live on TV, and use reporting verbs to tell classmates about situations they have been in.

Skills	Language	Vocabulary	Grammar
Listening to a TV presenter talking about bloopers made by news anchors	Reporting what people say, e.g. *I told my boyfriend that he needed to save money.*	Expressions to describe being relaxed or very nervous: *lose it, keep your cool, stay calm, keep it together, freak out* Reporting verbs: *claim, reassure, remind, admit, warn, deny*	Reporting what people say (1)

Warm-up

Ask: *What live radio/TV shows do you listen to or watch? Do things ever go wrong? What's the funniest thing you've ever seen on TV?* Teach/Elicit the word blooper (i.e. the name for this sort of mistake). Brainstorm possible radio/TV bloopers with them, e.g. presenters who forget their lines, start laughing at an inappropriate moment, get hiccups, or mispronounce a word.

Board the lesson title question: *Have you ever laughed at the wrong moment?* In pairs, sts discuss the question. Get them to follow-up with further questions. Class feedback to share the best stories.

4 Language in use

A 11.6 Explain that sts are going to hear a presenter on a show called *Behind the Scenes*, talking about mistakes presenters made live on TV. The presenter is going to talk about the three "bloopers" in the pictures. Before they listen, ask sts to read the text under the pictures, and guess what words are missing.

Play the audio for sts to listen and check their ideas. Paircheck, then classcheck. Play the audio again if necessary.

Answers

1 attacked him
2 fell asleep
3 had come for a job interview

See Teacher's Book p.330 for Audio script 11.6.

B 11.6 Sts read the statements carefully before listening again. Have them guess the answers.

Re-play the audio for sts to say whether the statements are true or false, correcting the false ones. Did they guess many correctly?

Answers

1 T
2 F The reporter reassured viewers that he was fine.
3 F He was woken by a colleague.
4 T
5 F She just calmly got up and left the studio.

See Teacher's Book p.330 for Audio script 11.6.

C In pairs, sts quickly read and decide (guessing from the context) if the highlighted expressions (are likely to) mean relaxed or very nervous, marking them accordingly, R or VN.

Classcheck and clarify their meaning. Ask: *How would you say the expressions in your language? Which ones did you already know and use?*

Answers

1 VN 2 R 3 R 4 R 5 VN

Optional activity

Sts think of two different situations, one where they "kept their cool," and one where they "freaked out." In pairs, sts share their situations.

Class feedback. Individuals tell the class what happened to their partner. Ask: *How would you have reacted in that situation?*

D Make it personal Go through question 1 and the model in the speech bubble, then speed them through the other questions. For 3, add an anecdote of your own, and for 4 give your opinion of each category to give them more time and inspiration.

In pairs, sts do the same, discussing the questions one by one. Monitor and discreetly correct all you can.

Once finished, sts can swap partners and do it again, as they ought to have a lot to say, and they should be more confident/fluent the second time.

Finally, ask volunteers: *Tell us something funny you've been told.*

Song lyric: See Teacher's Book p.346 for notes about the song and an accompanying activity to do with the class.

5 Grammar: Reporting what people say (1)

A Cover the grammar box. Ask: *What rules do you know for reported speech?* In pairs, sts compare what they know. Classcheck to see if there are any 'experts'!

Read through the grammar box with the class. Point out that the text in the left column shows what the person actually said, and the text in the right-hand column is how it was reported at a later date by someone else.

Look at the text in pink in each column and ask: *What tense are they?* Write the following table on the board with the second column blank, and complete it as a class.

Direct speech	Reported speech
Present >	[Past]
Past >	[Past perfect]
Present continuous >	[Past continuous]

Then look at the blue text and show students how these words change when reporting speech.

Ask students to read the rules, and, referring back to the example sentences in the grammar box, check the correct alternatives. Paircheck, then classcheck and take any questions. Ask: *Is reporting speech similar in your language?*

Answers

1 back 2 can 3 change

Refer sts to the **Grammar expansion** on p.158.

Tip

Remember sts don't need to use their language to describe similarities and differences to English. Helping them to express these things in English is positive, and trains them to avoid it better.

Optional activity

Weaker classes: Board reported time adverbials for sts to provide direct speech equivalents: *the day before* (yesterday), *that day* (today), *the next day* (tomorrow), *the week before* (last week), *a month before* (last month), *the following week* (next week).

B Go through **Reporting verbs and indirect objects** with the class.

Board: *Say sth / Tell sb sth*. Explain that a common mistake made by sts is to use an indirect object after *say*, e.g. *He said me that …* . However, we can use *to* + indirect object with *say*, e.g. *She said hello to me*.

Sts complete the chart with the words in bold from 4C and 5A. Paircheck, then classcheck.

Answers

Indirect object required: tell, reassure, remind, warn
No indirect object or optional: say, claim, admit, explain, ask (optional)

Optional activity

Board these sentences for sts to complete with an appropriate reporting verb from 5B (answers in parenthesis). Ask: *In which ones can you add "that" after the verb?* (all of them).

1 He ________ me the car was unsafe to drive. (told)
2 She ________ the accident was her fault. (explained)
3 Paul ______________ me everything would be OK. (reassured)
4 I __________ her she'd said she'd do the shopping this time. (reminded)
5 The kids __________ their mom if she could help with their homework. (asked)
6 She _________ she knew how to get home without the GPS. (claimed)

C Ask two sts to read aloud the dialog. Ask: *What does Andy mean by "positive buzz"?* (= people are saying positive things about what happened). *Do you think he's right? If not, what do you think people will be saying?*

Highlight the problems in **Common mistakes** and elicit his original words. Sts report the dialog by completing sentences 1–7. Paircheck, then classcheck. Elicit all possible contractions.

Answers

1 Sam asked Andy if (or whether) he had really fallen asleep.
2 First he denied (that) he had fallen asleep, then he admitted (that) he had.
3 Sam warned Andy (that) everyone was probably talking about him.
4 Andy reassured Sam (that) that didn't worry him.
5 Sam reminded Andy (that) the video had already been posted online.
6 Andy explained (that) it would create a lot of positive buzz.
7 Sam asked Andy how he could be so sure.

D Make it personal Go through the instructions and situation options. Expand as you do so by giving natural examples for each situation to provide more ideas, e.g. had a small disagreement, such as who would pay the check in a café or whose turn it was to do the dishes, or a big one, such as when you had a real argument with somebody about something, as in the example here.

Sts choose one situation, prepare for two minutes, with your help as need be and then share their story in groups. Did they find anything in common?

Workbook p.54.

5 Grammar: Reporting what people say (1)

A Read the grammar box and check (✔) the correct rules 1–3.

Reported statements and questions

The news anchor said, "You're right, I'm exhausted. I went to bed late last night."	The news anchor **admitted** (to us) (that) he was exhausted. He **said** (that) he'd gone to bed late the night before.
She asked, "Can I have a day off?"	She **asked** her boss if she could have a day off.
The announcer asked, "What are you doing here?"	The candidate **explained** (to the announcer) what she was doing there.

In reported speech:
1 You often move one tense ☐ **back** ☐ **forward**.
2 You ☐ **can** ☐ **cannot** omit *that* after a reporting verb.
3 Pronouns, time, and place expressions often ☐ **change** ☐ **stay the same**.

Grammar expansion p.158

B Read *Reporting verbs and indirect objects*. Put the bold verbs in 4C and 5A in the chart.

Reporting verbs and indirect objects

Memorize which reporting verbs are followed by indirect objects!

*He **told me** he was tired.* *She **said** she was fine.* *He **explained (to us)** he was tired.*

Indirect object required	No indirect object or, for some verbs, optional
tell	*say*

C Report the dialogue between a news anchor (Andy) and co-host (Sam). Do you think Andy's right?

Sam: Did you really fall asleep?
Andy: Of course I didn't fall asleep! Erm ... Well, actually, I did.
Sam: Everyone is probably talking about you.
Andy: Really? Well, that doesn't worry me.
Sam: Erm... The video has already been posted online.
Andy: Yeah, but it will create a lot of positive buzz.
Sam: Hmm ... How can you be so sure?

1 Sam asked Andy ...
2 First he denied ... Then he admitted ...
3 Sam warned ...
4 Andy reassured ...
5 Sam reminded ...
6 Andy explained ...
7 Sam asked ...

Common mistakes

I asked him whether ~~he's~~ *he was* OK. He ~~explained / admitted / said me~~ *explained / admitted / said* that he was sick.

D Make it personal Choose a situation and think through 1–3 to prepare. Share your stories in groups. Anything in common?

1 What was the situation?
2 What questions did you ask? What was the response? Use a variety of reporting verbs.
3 What happened in the end?

I told my boyfriend that he needed to save money, but he didn't listen and ...

When was the last time you ...?

had a small / big disagreement
denied you'd done something
reminded someone of a promise
tried to get out of doing something boring
explained something again and again
were warned about something

6 Reading

A Read the title and questions 1–4, and imagine the answers. Then read the text and put the questions back into the interview. There is one extra question.

1 What kind of content do people tend to connect with?
2 Are there dangers involved in posting a video that goes viral?
3 Are there specific things I can do to make my video go viral?
4 Can viral videos be created? Or do they happen by chance?

How to make your video go viral

Of the many millions of videos posted online every day, why do some clips stand out from the crowd and go on to attract millions of viewers – sometimes in a matter of hours? Media experts Stacey Wright and Kevin Murray explain to our readers why some videos go viral.

"We've postponed the wedding until we come up with something we can do at the ceremony that will become a viral video."

Q: ______________________________?

Stacey: Basically, the latter. Having a video go viral is like winning the lottery. It's incredibly hard – though certainly not impossible – to achieve. For every success story out there, there are thousands of flops.

Kevin: Stacey's answer got me thinking about what our goal should be when we create a video. It's important to catch people by surprise. As a rule, I think we should try to leave them speechless. Whether our content will go viral is another story – it may or may not happen. But we shouldn't focus on that goal right from the beginning.

Q: ______________________________?

Stacey: People's brains are wired to pay close attention to anything that goes against their expectations. This means that a video that contains an unusual image, a bold statement, or some sort of unexpected turn of events tends to strike a chord with viewers, otherwise it may do nothing for them.

Kevin: The most shareable videos convey strong emotions. In a world obsessed with money and deadlines, people want to get in touch with their humanity. They want romance, entertainment, anger, and joy. They want to burst out laughing. They want to be moved to tears. So, the more intense a video is, the more likely it is to be passed along.

Q: ______________________________?

Stacey: The first thing most people do before they decide whether or not to watch a video is check how long it is, so the main thing is to keep it short and sweet. When your video is ready, cut it in half, and then cut it in half again. Keep in mind that you're creating content for the 140-character Twitter® generation – people with increasingly short attention spans.

Kevin: Recent evidence actually suggests nearly one fifth of your viewers will leave your video after ten seconds. By a minute in, nearly half will have clicked away, so you can't save the best for last, really. One more thing, people can be incredibly cruel online! You can't let their comments get to you.

B ▶ 11.7 Listen to check. Notice the /eɪn/ sound in the underlined words.

Lesson Aims: Sts learn vocabulary to talk about how to make a video go viral, and discuss their emotional reactions to videos they watch.

Skills	Language	Vocabulary
Reading an article about how to make your video go viral Discussing how we react to video clips	Describing your emotional reaction to something: *The documentary on forest fires left me speechless. I burst out laughing when I saw it.*	Expressions to describe emotional reactions: *get you thinking, leave you speechless, catch you by surprise, do nothing for me, burst out laughing, move to tears*

Warm-up

Ask: *Have you seen "Gangnam Style" on YouTube?* (or any more recent video you think most will have seen) *Do you like it? How many views has it had?* (more than 2,550 million views, and rising). *Why was it so successful? Did you watch it more than once? What other really popular videos are trending now?*

Board the lesson title question: *What was the last video you shared?* plus follow-up questions, e.g. *How many views did it get? Did anybody post any comments?* In pairs, sts discuss the questions. Class feedback anything interesting from their discussions.

6 Reading

A Sts read the title of the text and discuss the meaning of *go viral* (see Background information). Get sts to predict how best to make a video go viral.

Focus on the cartoon. Ask: *Do you find it funny? Does it remind you of anyone? Any other suggestions now as to ways to go viral?*

Ask them to read the text quickly to get the gist, and put questions 1–4 in the correct place. Explain that there is one question that they do not need. Paircheck quickly so you can monitor how all are feeling about the text and activity, but don't classcheck answers yet.

Answers

(in order) 4, 1, 3

Background information

"Going viral" is an Internet phenomenon, where a story or video or comment from an independent source catches the attention of a large number of people around the world who then post links to it on social media networks. Content can go viral in a matter of hours. Marketing departments spend a lot of time trying to work out how to get something to "go viral" which will bring their brands to the attention of the world.

B 11.7 Sts listen and read to check they put the questions in the correct place. Pause after each paragraph for sts to practice the pink-stressed words together.

Discuss the extra question: *Are there dangers involved in posting a video that goes viral? What do you think?*

In pairs, sts practice the /eɪn/ sound in the underlined words. Encourage them to correct each other's pronunciation. Finally ask: *Did you enjoy the interview? Did the listening help?*

Optional activity

Stronger classes: Sts imagine how Stacey and Kevin would respond to the extra question above. They can write a response for Stacey or Kevin to include in the article.

C In pairs, sts work through the statements. Explain that even though some of the statements are not made directly, they may be inferred.

Paircheck, then classcheck.

Answers

1 B 2 K 3 S 4 N 5 B 6 K

D Make it personal In groups, sts discuss the questions. Monitor, help and make a note of language to pick up on later, e.g. common errors, awkward phrases they could express much better, good uses of English.

Discuss questions 1 and 2 as a class. Ask: *Did you mostly agree/disagree?*

Invite sts to report back to the class anything interesting from their discussions from questions 3 and 4.

Tip

If online access is available, sts could show the class some of their comments.

7 Vocabulary: Emotional reactions

A 11.8 Focus on the photos, text below covered. Ask: *Have you seen any of these? What (do you think) happens?*

Sts read the comments below quickly and check if they were right.

Refer sts back to the highlighted expressions in the text in 6A. They re-read and complete the comments in 7A with the correct form of the verbs. Point out that there's an extra one.

Play the audio for sts to listen and check.

Answers

1 get 2 moved 3 gets 4 caught 5 burst 6 did 7 left

See Teacher's Book p.330 for Audio script 11.8.

B Focus on the example and mime scratching your head. Doing some yourself will get them miming better. Ask a volunteer to mime another expression, 1–7, from 7B for the class to guess.

In pairs, sts continue. After they have finished, they could swap partners and repeat it, with improved mimes.

Classcheck. Get sts to repeat any that were particularly amusing.

Optional activity

Sts write their own examples with each of the highlighted expressions. They then swap sentences and check each other's. Ask: *Did your partner use the expressions correctly?*

C Make it personal

1 If you haven't got online access, sts can search for the videos as homework. Get them to vote for their favorite, and perhaps quickly show any other recent ones they know. If in L1, sts could subtitle them in English, or even dub them.

2 Have sts discuss their reactions to things they've watched recently, as in the example. Use the categories in the Student's Book. Classcheck. *Any similar reactions?*

Weaker classes: Elicit and board questions they could ask, e.g.

What movie has moved you to tears?

Has anything you've seen in the news lately left you speechless?

Has anybody made comments on your Facebook page which have really got to you?

What was the last sitcom episode you saw which made you burst out laughing?

Optional activity

In groups, sts think up, plan and script their own short video. It must be short with something of interest in the first ten seconds.

Refer sts to the advice in the article in 6A. If feasible to actually make it, record their video on a cellphone. If not, each group presents and explains their planned video, and who they're trying to attract. The class decides if it would go viral and votes for the best video. They can even write a comment too using highlighted expressions in 6A.

Song lyric: See Teacher's Book p.346 for notes about the song and an accompanying activity to do with the class.

Workbook p.55.

C Who made points 1–6? S (Stacey), K (Kevin), B (both), or N (neither)?

1 It's no use trying to make a video go viral.
2 People are interested in content that moves them.
3 People are interested in content that surprises them.
4 Twitter® is not a good platform for sharing videos.
5 You have to grab the viewer's attention from the beginning.
6 If your video goes viral, you can't be too sensitive.

D Make it personal In groups, answer 1–4. Similar opinions?

1 Who do you think made the best points, Stacey or Kevin?
2 Why else might a video go viral? Would you like one of yours to go viral? Why (not)?
3 How often do you leave a comment on a video? Do you tend to say mostly positive or negative things?
4 Have you ever posted a video yourself? Were you happy with the reaction?

7 Vocabulary: Emotional reactions

A 11.8 Review the highlighted expressions in 6A, then complete expressions 1–7 with the correct form of these verbs. There is one extra. Listen to check. Which expressions do you already use?

burst catch do get (two expressions) give leave move

My favorite viral videos of the past few years!

Emotional baby This one will **(1)** get you thinking, I'm sure. A ten-month-old baby gets teary-eyed as she watches her mother sing an old Rod Stewart song. This video **(2)** _____ me to tears when I first saw it, and it still **(3)** _____ to me whenever I play it again.

Sneezing baby panda A baby panda sneezes and the mother panda is **(4)** _____ by surprise. No big deal, right? Wrong. This clip is hilarious. When I first watched it, I **(5)** _____ out laughing so loud my family came running.

***Friday* by Rebecca Black** *Friday* is about a girl who's bored Monday through Thursday, but cheers up, well, guess when. When the video took off, people either loved or hated the clip. Nobody said, "It **(6)** _____ nothing for me." Did I like *Friday*? Well, let's just say it **(7)** _____ me speechless.

B In pairs, take turns miming and guessing the expressions in A (1–7).

You're scratching your head. That must be "It gets you thinking."

C Make it personal Talk about viewing tastes!

1 In groups, search online for the videos in A. Vote for your favorite.
2 Share impressions of other clips you've seen. Use expressions in A. Any similar reactions?

music video movie sitcom episode soap opera amateur video documentary

What was the last documentary you watched?

I saw a terrifying one on forest fires a few weeks ago. It really left me speechless.

8 Language in use

HERE SHE COMES WITH THE ONE O'CLOCK NEWS

A Read the website. In pairs, answer 1–3.

1 What's the difference between gossip and news?
2 Which of the three types of gossip might the worker be? Which do you think is most common?
3 Rank the three gossip types most to least harmful.

Three types of gossip we've all met!

1 **The forwarder** Forwarders don't start rumors. They simply pass on gossip that comes to them.
2 **The seeker** Seekers are always on the lookout for gossip. They're always seeking someone to fill them in on the latest "news."
3 **The creator** Creators are the ones that start gossip and pass it on, even if they're not 100% sure.

Well, to me, the forwarder is the worst. If you just pass the news on, you're gossiping behind someone's back.

B 11.9 Listen to three conversations taking place in an office. Identify the gossip types.

1 ________ 2 ________ 3 ________

C 11.9 Listen again. M (the man), W (the woman), or N (neither)? Who do you think Truman is?

Who seems ...

Conversation 1	Conversation 2	Conversation 3
1 jealous of Lorrie?	3 to have trouble keeping a secret?	5 sure two people are dating?
2 to dislike gossip?	4 concerned about inconvenience?	6 most worried the rumor might spread?

D 11.10 Complete 1–4. Listen to check. Which expressions describe a) gossip? b) secrecy?

between you and me | my big mouth | keep it to myself | spread it around

1 I asked Truman for a raise last week, but he **refused** to even listen. By the way, this is ________, OK?
2 Truman **made** me swear I'd ________ .
3 If this leaks, Truman will kill me. Once he **threatened** to fire me because of ________ , remember?
4 I **begged** him not to ________ , and I'm sure he won't. Well, at least, I **expect** him not to.

E **Make it personal** Read the quotes. How strongly do you agree? Write ++ (strongly agree) to - - (strongly disagree). Then compare in groups. Which is the most controversial quote?

1 "I get accused all the time of having a big mouth. But if you ask me, guys gossip way more than girls do." (Meg Cabot)
2 "Whoever gossips to you will gossip about you." (Unknown / graffiti)
3 "Show me someone who never gossips, and I'll show you someone who isn't interested in people." (Barbara Walters)
4 "There is only one thing in the world worse than being talked about, and that is not being talked about." (Oscar Wilde)

Gender terms

Use *woman* and not *girl* to refer to someone who's not a child. Using "girl" can easily offend.

I disagree with the first one. My experience is that women find it harder than men to keep things to themselves.

Hmm ... I don't think gossip has anything to do with gender, actually. It has to do with personality.

Lesson Aims: Sts learn vocabulary to talk about people who gossip, and use reporting verbs to pass on gossip themselves.

Skills	Language	Grammar	Vocabulary
Listening to conversations about gossiping Talking about gossiping	Gossiping, e.g. *You'll never guess who I saw, Promise you'll keep it between you and me*	Reporting what people say (2): Using reporting verbs + infinitive / base form	Reporting verbs: *refuse to, make sb. do sth, threaten to, beg sb to, expect sb to, promise to, persuade sb to, urge sb to, let sb do sth* Expressions: *between you and me, my big mouth, keep it to myself, spread it around*

Warm-up

Board *gossiping* and questions for sts to answer in pairs: *Why do people like gossiping? Do you know a "real gossip"? Are you careful what you say to gossips? Do you ever gossip? Why / Why not?* Classcheck.

Board the lesson title question: *What's your definition of gossip?* Together decide on a class definition (e.g. a conversation about unimportant things, particularly people's private lives).

8 Language in use

A Focus on the cartoon. Ask: *What's happening? Where are they? What are the women doing?* (one's serving hot drinks, the other chatting to the guy) *Who's talking about who? What does the lady mean by her comment "Here she comes with the latest gossip"? Do you think it's funny? Does it remind you of anything?*

Set sts a minute to read the webtext and answer questions 1–3. Explain that question 2 refers to the trolley lady in the cartoon. Use the speech bubble to help them answer Q3. Classcheck to discuss which is the worst.

Suggested answers

1 Gossip may or may not be true 2 A forwarder
3 Students' own answers

B 11.9 Explain that students are going to listen to three office gossips.

Play the audio for sts to identify what type of gossip each person is.

Tip

From their faces/reaction, gauge what to do next. If most got the answers, try to resist playing the audio again at this stage. If most haven't, listen again with a new task, e.g. to remember two phrases used by each gossip.

Classcheck. Ask: *Is there a gossip in the place you work/ study/live? What type of gossip are they?*

Answers

1 seeker 2 forwarder 3 creator

See Teacher's Book p.330 for Audio script 11.9.

C 11.9 Sts read questions 1–6, then re-play the audio for them to answer.

Paircheck, then classcheck. Ask: *Did you find it difficult to understand? Did you understand more than 50 percent?*

Answers

1 M 2 W 3 W 4 M 5 W 6 M
Truman is most likely the boss.

See Teacher's Book p.330 for Audio script 11.9.

D 11.10 Discuss the expressions in the box. Ask: *Which of these do you know? Are there similar expressions in your language?* Tell students another common expression is to *keep something a secret*.

Sts complete the sentences. Use the audio to check answers and repeat, copying the stress and intonation.

Classcheck. Sts divide the expressions into the two categories: gossip and secrecy.

Answers

1 between you and me (secrecy)
2 keep it to myself (secrecy)
3 my big mouth (gossip)
4 spread it around (gossip)

E Make it personal Ask individuals to read the quotes aloud to the class. Ask if they know the people who made the quotes. Discuss what each one means. Refer to **Gender terms** when discussing quote 1.

In groups, sts compare their ideas. Class feedback. Ask: *Did you mostly agree? Are there any you all disagreed with?*

Background information

Meg Cabot (born 1967) – best selling US author of romantic / paranormal fiction for teens and adults. Famous for *Princess Diaries* series, turned into a movie in 2001.

Barbara Walters (born 1929) – US broadcast journalist, author, and TV personality. Hosted popular morning TV shows like *Today* and *The View*.

Oscar Wilde (1854–1900) – Irish playwright, novelist and poet. Hugely popular in the 1890s, and still an icon today.

Song lyric: See Teacher's Book p.347 for notes about the song and an accompanying activity to do with the class.

9 Grammar: Reporting what people say (2)

A **Stronger classes:** Get sts to try to do this without looking back at 8D, then use it to check.

Refer sts to the bold verbs in 8D, and elicit a synonym/ paraphrase for each (e.g. said No way, forced me to, tried to scare me by saying strongly, on my knees, believe something will/won't happen).

In pairs, sts read through and complete the grammar box with the verbs from 8D. Classcheck. Personalize by asking: *Which of the verbs in the box do you already use? Are there any you have problems with?*

Answers

1 refuse, threaten 2 beg, expect 3 make

Refer sts to the **Grammar expansion** on p.158.

B Ask: *What was the last thing we heard from Julia? What's going to happen next?*

In pairs, sts read the dialog. Perhaps ask a lively pair to act it out to the class.

Go through item 1 using the example in blue, to clarify what to do. Refer sts to the **Common mistake**. Elicit we can also say *He forced me to promise to keep it to myself* (NOT *obliged me* as some may think)

In pairs, sts complete 2–6.

Weaker classes: Do 2 and 3 as well together first to help them.

Classcheck. In pairs, sts practice reporting the conversation, as in the longer blue example sentence. Monitor, for correct use of reporting verbs.

Answers

1 Ann promised to keep it to herself.
2 Julia refused to tell her.
3 Ann begged Julia not to keep her in suspense.
4 Julia made Ann promise she wouldn't say a word.
5 Then she threatened to unfriend Ann on Facebook if she did.
6 She finally agreed to tell Ann the gossip.

C Make it personal

1 11.11 **How to say it** Have sts read through the "What they said" column, and decide who might say each of the sentences: the "gossiper" or the "receiver" of the gossip.

Sts guess the missing words, then play the audio for them to check their answers and repeat. In pairs, sts practice the sentences, paying particular attention to the stress and intonation.

Answers

1 guess 2 lips, soul 3 keep 4 word

2 Have sts read through the situations. Allow sts thinking time to choose a situation and develop details. Board prompts:

1: *how much, how felt when found out, plans for winnings*

2: *what makes you suspect this, who else knows, what 'agent' was doing*

3: *who dating, how they met, what celebrity is like*

4: *what secret, about who/what/where/when, how found out*

In pairs, sts share their gossip. Monitor, praising correct use of the reporting structures and expressions to ask for discretion.

3 Refer sts to the example speech bubble, then elicit other ways to spread gossip, e.g.

Guess what Paula told me. She said she'd seen Ricardo spying on ...

You'll never guess who's won the lottery. She told me to keep it to myself, but ...

Bet you can't guess who's going out with ...

In new pairs, sts spread the gossip they just learned from their partner.

Class feedback. Ask: *Who's the ultimate class gossip?* Decide together a suitable prize!

Tip

This works well as a class mingle, all gossiping at once to as many classmates as they can.

Optional activity

For homework, sts search for authentic items of celebrity gossip in English. In class, groups share their news. A spokesperson feeds the group's gossip back to the class.

Workbook p.56.

9 Grammar: Reporting what people say (2)

A Read the grammar box. Then fill in the blanks with the bold verbs from 8D.

Reporting patterns with the infinitive and base form	
1 Verb + (not) + infinitive	She **agreed to tell** me a secret. I **promised to keep** it. Other verbs include ________ and ________ .
2 Verb + object + (not) + infinitive	I **persuaded him to reveal** what he knew. He **urged me not to spread** it around. Other verbs include ________ and ________ .
3 Verb + object + base form	I tried to talk about something else, but she didn't **let me change** the subject. ________ follows the same pattern.

Grammar expansion p.158

B Julia couldn't keep Truman's secret! Complete 1–6 using the verb given and a pattern from the grammar box. Then take turns reporting the whole conversation.

ANN: What were you two gossiping about?
JULIA: Erm ... Nothing.
ANN: (1) I'll keep it to myself. I promise!
JULIA: We weren't gossiping.
ANN: Well, I heard Truman's name. And Lorrie's.
JULIA: Hmm ... (2) I can't tell you. Sorry.
ANN: It must be something big. (3) Don't leave me in suspense!
JULIA: (4) Promise you won't say a word.
ANN: I swear.
JULIA: (5) I'll unfriend you on Facebook® if you do!
ANN: You have my word.
JULIA: (6) All right. I'll tell you.

1 Ann promised *to keep it to herself*.
2 Julia refused ...
3 Ann begged ...
4 Julia made ...
5 Then she threatened ...
6 She finally agreed ...

Ann asked Julia what she and her friend had been gossiping about.

Common mistake

He made me ~~to~~ promise to keep it to myself.

C Make it personal Gossip!

1 11.11 **How to say it** Complete the chart. Then listen, check, and repeat.

	Gossiping	
	What they said	What they meant
1	You'll never ____ (who I ran into at the mall).	You have no idea (who ...)
2	My ____ are sealed. I won't tell a ____ .	I won't tell anyone.
3	Promise you'll ____ it between the two of us.	Promise you won't tell anyone.
4	You have my ____ .	I promise.

2 Choose a situation, imagine the details, and tell a partner. Ask him / her to be discreet! Use *How to say it* expressions.

You've won a small fortune on the lottery.
Someone in class is actually a secret agent.
You're dating a celebrity.
You've discovered a secret about a classmate.

3 Form new pairs and spread the news. Use reporting verbs. Who's the best gossip?

You'll never guess in a million years who I ran into at the mall over the weekend!

10 Listening

A 11.12 Listen to Rita Sycamore, a young actress, complaining to her friend, Jeb, about a news story. Note down three facts that were wrong.

B 11.13 Listen to the rest of the conversation. Check (✔) the correct answers.

1 Rita is bothered most by the ...
- [ ] invasion of her privacy.
- [ ] inaccuracies in the story.

2 Jeb's main point is that ...
- [ ] fame has more advantages than disadvantages.
- [ ] fame comes at a price.

C 11.13 Listen again and try to complete the sentences. Then check your answers against the definitions. Did you catch all the words and expressions?

1 You'll be ________________ for a day or two. And you know what they say, "Bad publicity is always better than no publicity."
2 Well, if you ask me, celebrity gossip is as ________________ as other more "serious" topics.
3 When you're a celebrity, there's no such thing as privacy. You're ________________ 24/7, and that's exactly the way it should be.
4 I think newspapers are ________________ to publish whatever they like.

entitle (v) (often passive): give someone a legal right or just a claim to receive or do something

in the spotlight (idiom): receiving public notice or attention

newsworthy (adj): important or interesting enough to report as news

the talk of the town (idiom): someone or something everyone is talking about

D Make it personal Choose a statement 1–4 in C you (dis)agree with, and share your opinions in pairs. Any major differences?

> I don't agree with the last one. Newspapers should try to be selective about what they publish.

11 Keep talking

A Check (✔) the problems you've experienced for 1–4. Then add one more problem to each group.

1 A TV channel you watch ...
- [ ] presents news that's biased or inaccurate.
- [ ] shows endless reruns of sitcoms.
- [ ] shows content inappropriate for children.

2 Your phone, cable, or Internet company ...
- [ ] keeps sending wrong bills.
- [ ] has terrible customer service.
- [ ] has lots of coverage and stability problems.

3 A recent documentary or news story about your country ...
- [ ] had wrong factual details.
- [ ] made too many generalizations.
- [ ] exaggerated small problems.

4 Your favorite online store ...
- [ ] makes it difficult to find what you want.
- [ ] has security problems.
- [ ] doesn't give enough product information.

B In groups, compare your ideas. Add more details and examples. Which are the most common complaints?

> WEID seems really biased. They only present one side of a story!

> Yeah, I know what you mean. The news just isn't accurate these days.

Common mistakes

There's too ~~many~~ *much* violence on TV.

There's not *enough* educational content ~~enough~~.

Lesson Aims: Sts listen to a conversation where someone is complaining, discuss common reasons for complaining, and then write a letter of complaint.

Skills	Language	Vocabulary
Listening to an actress complaining about an inaccurate newspaper article written about herself Writing a letter of complaint	Phrases for complaining, e.g. *I am writing to complain about … , To make matters worse, my age was incorrect. I would like to call your attention to a number of inaccuracies in your article*	*biased, entitled, in the spotlight, inaccurate, newsworthy, the talk of the town*

Warm-up

Ask: *What are the advantages / disadvantages of being famous?* Brainstorm and board ideas in two columns.

Board the lesson title question: *Would you enjoy being world-famous? Why (not)?* and let them run with it. Obviously it would depend what for. If you were e.g. a famous sportsperson, actor or president, it would be very different from being a criminal! Pairs discuss for two minutes, then class feedback. Monitor for some good responses, to share when you classcheck. What's the majority feeling?

10 Listening

A 11.2 Look at the photo of Rita with the class, and ask: *How old do you think she is?* Explain that Rita has just seen an inaccurate article in the local newspaper about herself, and is telling her friend Jeb about it.

Play the audio for sts to note down the three incorrect facts. Paircheck, then classcheck.

Answers

The man in the photo is her vocal coach, not a new boyfriend.
She doesn't have plans for a movie.
She's not 32.

See Teacher's Book p.331 for Audio script 11.12.

B 11.13 Go through statements 1–4 and elicit meaning of *be bothered by* (= to be worried / upset about something that is important to you).

Sts guess the correct answers, then listen and check. Paircheck, then classcheck.

Answers

1 invasion of her privacy 2 fame comes at a price

See Teacher's Book p.331 for Audio script 11.13.

C 11.13 Play the audio for sts to complete the sentences.

Sts then check their answers against the definitions.

Classcheck, and check understanding of the definitions. Then ask: *Do you think the statements are more likely to have been written by a celebrity or a journalist? Which of the statements do you agree/disagree with?*

Answers

1 the talk of the town 2 newsworthy 3 in the spotlight
4 entitled

D Make it personal Ask: *Which statements in C do you (dis)agree with? In pairs, set sts a minute to answer all four so they get a taste of them, without going into too much depth.*

Together, sts choose one of them to talk about, then individually make notes about why they (dis)agree with it.

Back in pairs, sts share their opinions. Use the speech bubble to show they should justify and develop their ideas. Encourage use of *So do I. / Neither do I. / Me neither*.

Stronger classes: In new pairs, sts share views on another statement in C.

11 Keep talking

A Have sts read through the problems, then ask others around them to clarify anything they don't understand. Monitor, helping individuals as necessary, then classchecking any more general issues.

Sts check each problem they've experienced, then add one more problem to each group. Monitor to help to express their ideas.

B Go through the speech bubbles and elicit meaning of *present one side of the story, and its opposite*, asking: *How should newspapers present the news?* (by presenting both sides of the story).

Ask sts to tell you why the **Common mistakes** are wrong. *Why much not many? What's the rule about the position of enough?*

Weaker classes: Board *There are too many violent programs on TV* to elicit *too much* + uncountable nouns, *too many* + plural nouns. Ask for an example with *not enough* + plural noun, e.g. *There aren't enough kids' programs on TV*.

In groups, sts compare their ideas from A. Note common errors / good examples for delayed correction.

Class feedback. Ask: *What's the most common complaint in your group?*

Song lyric: See Teacher's Book p.347 for notes about the song and an accompanying activity to do with the class.

12 Writing: A letter of complaint

A Ask: *What was Rita's problem? What were the three wrong facts in 10A? What did she decide to do?*

Focus on the letter. Ask: *Where does she live? Who's it to? Why's she writing the letter?* (to complain about the article). Give sts a minute to read and say which of the three facts she fails to mention. Paircheck, then classcheck.

Answer

The fact that she is not making a movie.

Tip

Use a range of questions to explore the text and get sts talking as much as possible, e.g. *Why she doesn't talk about the movie? Is it a secret or is she saving it for Round 2 in case they fail to answer? What do you think of her letter, the tone, what she asks for? What impact will her letter have? Does she go far enough? Does she threaten them? Will she have to?*

Optional activity

Sts add two sentences to paragraph 2 about the fact she isn't making a movie, e.g. *Furthermore, you say that I am making a movie. This is not the case at all. / This is completely untrue, and shows that you did not do enough research.*

B Sts work through the paragraph, looking back at her letter and circling the correct options.

Weaker classes: You could do the first one together as a class.

Classcheck. *Any questions?*

Answers

situation, problem, an opinion, makes a request

C Books closed. Board: *Formal letters: Beginning and ending, punctuation, contractions, language*.

Weaker classes: Let sts refer back to the letter, but not look at **Write it right!**

In small groups, sts brainstorm rules they already know. Classcheck, inviting individuals from each group to summarize their 'rules' for one of the headings on the board.

Now sts uncover and read through **Write it right!** to check / see if they missed anything. Class feedback. Get sts to compare the rules and letter in A to a formal letter in their language. Ask: *How is it the same / different?*

Sts complete the chart with the highlighted expressions in the letter. Paircheck, then classcheck.

Answers

1 in reality 2 in regard to 3 It is my belief 4 I would like to call your attention to 5 To make matters worse

D Sts read 1–5 quickly, ignoring the gaps. Ask: *What are the people complaining about in each one?*

Sts complete the gaps using formal expressions from C. Paircheck, then classcheck.

Answers

1 in regard to 2 in reality 3 I would like to draw your attention to 4 It is my belief 5 To make matters worse

E **Your turn!** Read through the instructions and set out the aim of the task, which is to write a formal complaint, letter or e-mail in about 180 words (that means not more than 195!).

Focus on the problems in 11A, for them to choose one.

Go through the *Before* and *While* stages and get sts to highlight the things they have to remember.

Sts can start their letter / email in class, and finish it for homework. Assign each student a partner to exchange letters with to proofread.

Tip

Elicit what a proof reader might do, e.g. give positive feedback, underline what they think are errors of form, spelling, tone, use a marking code – like the one in Unit 1.5, etc., or just make the correction if they're sure. Get sts to talk about their preferences, and decide what they want their partner to do when checking their work.

Finally, collect the letters in or sts email them to you, or the class website.

Optional activity

Stronger classes: Sts swap letters with a partner, but have to write a reply. Elicit and board phrases they can use, e.g.

Thank you for your letter of May 23 regarding ...

I am sorry to learn that ...

We must apologize for ...

We agree that ...

I am surprised that ... , as usually ...

We assure you that ...

Workbook p.57.

12 Writing: A letter of complaint

A Read Rita's letter to the editor of an online newspaper. Which wrong fact from 10A is not mentioned?

Rita Sycamore
101 Maryland Avenue
Pittsburgh, PA 15212

Mr. Jerome Sacks
ID News and Views

May 23, 2016

Dear Mr. Sacks:

I am writing in regard to the photo and the article published in the entertainment section of your home page this morning ("TV star Rita Sycamore spotted with new boyfriend"). I happen to be the woman in the photo and I would like to call your attention to a number of inaccuracies in your article.

You claimed that the man in the photo was my new boyfriend, when, in reality, he is my vocal coach, and our relationship is strictly professional. To make matters worse, my age was incorrect, which shows a lack of attention to detail.

Above all, I am very surprised that a reputable newspaper like yours would even consider publishing stories like this one. It is my belief that celebrities are entitled to the same level of privacy as the general public.

I would like to ask you to remove the photo and article from your website in the next few hours. Tomorrow I will check to confirm that these steps have been taken. Thank you very much for your attention to this matter.

Sincerely,

Rita Sycamore

Rita Sycamore

B Circle the correct options.

A well-organized complaint letter presents the [**situation / solution**] in paragraph 1. It then moves on to a [**problem / suggestion**] in paragraph 2. In paragraph 3, it sometimes presents [**an opinion / only facts**]. Finally, in the last paragraph, the letter often [**makes a request / only gives a summary**].

C Read *Write it right!* Then write the more formal highlighted expressions 1–5 in the chart.

Write it right!

In a formal email or letter:

1 Begin your email with *Dear* + full name or *Dear Sir / Madam*. Sign off with *Sincerely (yours)*.

2 Put a colon (:) after the full name when you begin, but a comma (,) when you sign off.

3 Avoid contractions: ~~*I'm*~~ ***I am*** *writing to complain about ...*

4 Avoid informal language: *There were* ~~*lots of*~~ ***a number of*** (more formal) *inaccuracies in the article.*

"Well, actually ..."	1 ________
"about ..."	2 ________
"I think ..."	3 ________
"I want to point out ..."	4 ________
"Another problem is ..."	5 ________

D Complete 1–5, from different letters and emails, using formal expressions from C.

1 I am writing ________ the programming on your channel.

2 While you claim to have excellent customer service, ________, I had to call five times before someone could help me.

3 ________ the fact that there were a number of factual errors in your recent documentary.

4 ________ that there should be fewer stories on urban violence, especially in that time slot.

5 Your online store is not only hard to navigate. ________, it often lacks sufficient product information.

E **Your turn!** Write a 180-word letter or email complaining about a problem from 11A.

Before
Check the guidelines in B, and decide the main points you will make in each paragraph.

While
Re-read *Write it right!* Use at least four expressions from C, and check the level of formality.

After
Proofread your work carefully. Show it to another student before sending it to your teacher.

12 » How optimistic are you?

1 Listening

A ▶ 12.1 Complete the quotes from a radio show with *an optimist* or *a pessimist*. Listen to check. Which is your favorite?

1 "I used to be ________, but now I know nothing is going to turn out as I expect." Sandra Bullock
2 "________ sees the difficulty in every opportunity; ________ sees the opportunity in every difficulty." Winston Churchill
3 "The man who is ________ before 48 knows too much; if he is ________ after it, he knows too little." Mark Twain

Common mistakes

Overall, I'd say I'm ~~optimist~~ *an optimist*, but I'm a bit ~~pessimist~~ *pessimistic* about the interview.
Optimist and *pessimist* are nouns. *Optimistic* and *pessimistic* are adjectives.

B ▶ 12.2 Listen to the radio show survey and circle the correct answers. Do you feel the same way?

Are we becoming a city of pessimists?

Take the survey to help us find out!
How optimistic are you about ...?

☺ optimistic
😐 not sure
☹ pessimistic

1 your final exams ☺/😐/☹

2 your (future) career ☺/😐/☹

3 your team's chances ☺/😐/☹

4 this country's economy ☺/😐/☹

C ▶ 12.3 Complete the highlighted expressions in 1–4, using your intuition. Listen to check. Do you have similar ones in your language?

feet	fingers	proportion	store	tunnel	world

1 I keep telling myself that it's **not the end of the ________** (= not a tragedy) if I fail an exam or two, but deep down, I know I'll be really upset. Anyway, I'm **keeping my ________ crossed** (= hoping for the best).
2 They're going through a rough time right now, so who knows **what the future has in ________** (= what will happen) for me.
3 I know we've lost all the games so far this season, but now with this new coach, there might be **a light at the end of the ________** (= some hope).
4 The media tends to **blow things out of ________** (= exaggerate), but, on the whole, I think we're doing OK. Anyway, I try to **keep my ________ on the ground** (= be practical and sensible).

Lesson Aims: Sts listen to a radio show presenter interviewing people about how optimistic or pessimistic they are, and role play situations where they are optimists / pessimists.

Skills	Language	Vocabulary
Listening to a radio presenter carrying out a survey about how optimistic people are	Cheering people up / being optimistic: *Look on the bright side, Cheer up. It's not the end of the world.*	Phrases for expressing optimism / pessimism: *Look on the bright side. No news is good news. Let's hope for the best.*

Warm-up

In pairs, asks sts to look through all the song lines from Units 1–11 to find all the phrasal verbs in them. Then turn to Phrasal verbs on pp.165–167. Get sts to test themselves/each other and ask any questions. *Any there they don't yet feel comfortable using?*

Board the lesson title question: *How optimistic are you?* Bring a glass to the lesson, half-filled with water. Ask: *Is the glass half full or half empty?* If sts answer "half full," say it means they're optimists; if "half-empty," they're pessimists! Ask if they agree and if they have a "measure" like this in their language. In pairs, sts come up with a definition of *optimistic* and *pessimistic*. Have a few sts read out their definitions. Does the class agree?

1 Listening

A 12.1 Focus on the optimist / pessimist caricature. Elicit more words and phrases for each side, e.g. *Think positive. / There's a light at the end of the tunnel. / Every cloud has a silver lining / Let's face it. / Be realistic. / Anything that can go wrong will go wrong.*

Sts complete the quotes, then play the audio for them to listen and check.

Classcheck, by asking individuals to read each quote aloud. Check the meaning after each one. Ask: *Do you know anything about the authors? Which do you agree/ disagree with?*

Go through the **Common mistakes**. Highlight use of the indefinite article with the nouns: *I'm **an** optimist / **a** pessimist*. Is it the same in their language.

Tip

As this is the last unit, look for new ways to help sts remember words/expand their vocabulary. Get half the class to brainstorm/list words they know ending in *-ic*, the other half words ending in *-ist*. Elicit the stress for the longer ones. Ask: *Which are cognates in your language? What other suffix stress rules do you know to help with cognates?*

Answers

1 an optimist 2 a pessimist; an optimist
3 a pessimist; an optimist

See Teacher's Book p.331 for Audio script 12.1.

Background information

Sandra Bullock (born 1964). American actress/ producer. One of Hollywood's highest-paid actresses.

Winston Churchill (1874–1965) British Prime Minister 1940–45, and 1951–1955. Led Britain to victory in the Second World War.

Mark Twain (1835–1910) American author, best known for *The Adventures of Tom Sawyer*, and its sequel *Adventures of Huckleberry Finn*.

Song lyric: See Teacher's Book p.347 for notes about the song and an accompanying activity to do.

B 12.2 Focus on the radio survey title. Ask: *What's your immediate answer to their question about our (city/ town)?* Focus on the photos and topic beneath that each will talk about. In pairs, sts guess what they're going to say (how optimistic we are) and which of the three emoji categories each will fall into. Encourage free brainstorming from the photos, e.g. age, nationality, profession, personality.

Play the audio for sts to listen and circle the correct answers. Paircheck, then classcheck. Ask: *Do you feel the same way as them? Who's most like you? Which topic(s) do you feel (more) optimistic / less sure / (more) pessimistic about?* Do this as plenary with a small class, if not in small groups, then feedback to the class.

Answers

1 not sure 2 pessimistic 3 not sure 4 optimistic

See Teacher's Book p.331 for Audio script 12.2.

C 12.3 Cover the boxed words. Sts read and try to remember who said them.

Individually, sts complete sentences 1–4 with the first words that come into their heads, even if they don't think it was what was said. Paircheck.

Uncover the boxes. Sts look to see if they got the right words, check their spelling, and make any alterations.

Play the audio for sts to check their answers. Ask: *Is your intuition for English getting better?*

Classcheck. Ask: *Do you/we have similar expressions in your/our language?*

Answers

1 world, fingers 2 store 3 tunnel 4 proportion, feet

D In groups, sts play Charades (see Background information) using the expressions in C, giving their classmates clues about how many words are in the expression, how many syllables in each word, what the word sounds like, etc. Alternatively, they can act out the whole expression, e.g. cross their fingers for *keeping my fingers crossed*.

Background information

Charades is a guessing game. Players act out a word or phrase, often by miming the word (or a word with a similar sound), for their teammates to guess. Their teammates can ask questions, but the person miming can only nod / shake their head, not say a word. Search online for more detailed instructions, if necessary.

E Make it personal Read through the instructions with the class, and check everyone understands what to do.

In pairs, sts work through the questions. Set a time limit for them to spend on each question (e.g. two minutes), so the class progresses at more or less the same pace.

Swap or change pairs halfway through to slow down faster sts to give the others more time.

2 Listening

A 12.4 First cover exercise B below, so sts can't look ahead.

Explain that sts will hear three conversations to decide if each speaker is an optimist or a pessimist.

Play the audio. Sts listen and mark each speaker O or P. As they do, board more questions: *What was the context? What else did they pick up from each conversation?* Paircheck and discuss.

Classcheck. Highlight the expression from conversation 1 *to have a long face* (= look fed up).

Weaker classes: Sts listen for gist first, and find out in which conversation someone: *is going to Paris* (3 – Linda), *has just been fired* (1 – Ed), *has had their car stolen* (2 – Kate). Then they listen again to do the O/P task.

Answers

1 Ed – P 2 Sonia – O 3 Peter – O 4 Kate – P
5 Tom – O 6 Linda – P

See Teacher's Book p.332 for Audio script 12.4.

B 12.4 Read through the statements. Some they may be able to remember, but don't let them call out answers. Sts listen again to check what they can infer about the people.

Paircheck, then classcheck. Personalize and get feedback on the task, e.g. *Who do you feel most sorry for, Ed or Linda? Which of these situations have you/close friends been in?*

Answers

1 ✓ (*Looks like it finally happened. Wonder why it took this long.*)
2 ✓ (*Ed, times have changed. Age is no longer an issue.*)
3 ✗ (*I don't want a better model. I want my Fiesta back.*)
4 ✗ (*... it's the only one I can park easily! It's so nice and compact.*)
5 ✗ (*Just the thought of it* (packing) *makes me exhausted.*)
6 ✓ (*I hope there's something for me to do there ... I mean something I haven't done before.*)

See Teacher's Book p.332 for Audio script 12.4.

C Make it personal

1 12.5 **How to say it** Go through the expressions in the chart, and elicit the missing words.

Play the audio for sts to listen and check, then repeat. Ask: *Which are similar sayings in your language?*

Answers

1 best 2 news 3 bright 4 sorry 5 dream 6 thinking

Optional activity

In pairs, copy out the expressions from the chart marking the stress, e.g. by underlining the correct stressed syllable or as below, with stressed words/syllables in capitals. Do the first with them as an example. Classcheck, then in pairs, sts practice the expressions.

Let's HOPE for the BEST.

NO news is GOOD news.

LOOK on the BRIGHT SIDE.

BETter SAFE than SORry.

Yeah, DREAM ON!

THAT's WISHful THINking.

2 Read through the situations and highlight the smileys showing who is the optimist/pessimist.

In pairs, sts choose and imagine they're in one of the situations and role play it. Allow a minute or so to brainstorm ideas and vocabulary, helping as necessary.

Tell sts to take turns being the optimist/pessimist. Encourage them to use the expressions in 1C, and *How to say it* expressions.

Weaker classes: Brainstorm and board a situation , e.g.

A: *Why the long face?*

B: *Oh, I just failed my driving test. I've been learning for more than a year, and I still can't drive!*

A: *Well, it's not the end of the world. You can take it again.*

B: *I've already taken it twice. I'm never going to pass!*

A: *Never say never! You just need to practice a bit more.*

Invite volunteer pairs to act out their role plays.

Workbook p.58.

D In groups, take turns miming and guessing the expressions in **C**. Then remember all you can of each conversation. Check in **AS** 12.2 on p.164. Anything you missed?

E **Make it personal** In pairs, answer 1–4. Any surprises?

1 Take the survey in **B**. Use expressions from **C** in your answers.
2 Create two other questions to ask each other. Who's more optimistic?
3 Who's the most / least optimistic person in your family? How well do you get along?
4 Does the weather affect your general feelings of optimism / pessimism?

I love cold, rainy days, you know. The grayer the better! I feel really good.

Really? Rainy days always get me down.

2 Listening

A ▶ 12.4 Listen to three conversations. Are the people O (optimistic) or P (pessimistic)? Have you ever had a similar experience?

Conversation 1	Conversation 2	Conversation 3
1 Ed ______	3 Peter ______	5 Tom ______
2 Sonia ______	4 Kate ______	6 Linda ______

B ▶ 12.4 Listen again and check (✔) what you can infer about each person.

1 Ed wasn't surprised he got fired.
2 Sonia thinks Ed's age might have been a problem in the past.
3 Kate likes expensive cars.
4 Kate probably had a big car before.
5 Linda doesn't mind packing.
6 Linda has probably been to Paris before.

C **Make it personal** Take turns role playing an optimist / pessimist.

1 ▶ 12.5 **How to say it** Complete the chart. Listen, check, and repeat, copying the intonation.

Optimism and pessimism

	What they said	What they meant
1	Let's hope for the ______ .	Let's hope things will turn out well.
2	No ______ is good news.	
3	Look on the ______ side.	Try to find something good about this situation.
4	Better safe than ______ .	It's better to be cautious so you don't regret it later.
5	Yeah, ______ on! (informal)	What you want probably won't happen.
6	That's wishful ______ .	What you want is not realistic.

2 Choose two situations and role play them with a partner. Use *How to say it* expressions.

A ☹ You've just failed an important test. You think you might have to take the course again.
B ☺ Convince **A** that taking the course again will be a good idea.

A ☺ You've just inherited $1 million. You want to quit your job, invest the money, and live off the interest.
B ☹ You think quitting a steady job is too risky.

A ☺ You love to live dangerously. You want to go mountain climbing next weekend.
B ☹ You're scared of extreme sports. Remind **A** of all the risks involved.

12.2 Will the world be better in 100 years?

3 Language in use

A 12.6 Listen to part 1 of an online program and match conversations 1–4 to pictures a–d. Label the items.

DYING TECHNOLOGIES: WHAT WE SAY ABOUT WHAT THE EXPERTS SAY

a ☐ ______

"Wireless chargers for smartphones are already on the market, and the possibility of Power WiFi is not that far off."
Yes, definitely. Soon you won't have to shout "Watch out! You're going to trip over that thing!" anymore. But we're talking [1] ______ years from now, at least.

b ☐ ______

"Very soon, people are going to be driving into a gas station for a recharge. Or maybe to fill up the tank with a clean [2] ______ , like ethanol."
Gas is bound to be replaced **by** ☐ greener fuels, but the combustion engine won't be going anywhere until electric cars become less [3] ______ .

c ☐ ______

"In the past few years, subscriptions have dropped **by** ☐ more than 50%. By the end of the decade, we'll be using [4] ______ only."
Yes, this trend is likely to continue, except in more remote areas, where there are relatively few cell phone [5] ______ .

ALL NEWSPAPERS
NOW ON MEMORY STICK
USB

d ☐ ______

"**By** ☐ 2020, printed newspapers and magazines will have disappeared without a trace. Online subscriptions are much cheaper."
Newsstands are still going to be around for a while. They'll attract new customers **by** ☐ selling [6] ______ and lottery tickets, for example.

B 12.7 Read the infographic in A and predict the missing information. Listen to part 2 to check. Did you guess correctly? Any you disagreed with?

> I'm not so sure about the first one. I think it will take ... years.

C Read *Uses of by*. Then write 1–4 next to the bold words in A.

Uses of *by*

By is the 30th most common word in English. Here are four important uses:

1 Expresses "not later than":
I'll get back to you ***by*** *Monday.*

2 Answers the question *how*:
We're going ***by*** *car.*

3 Indicates the amount:
Prices have increased ***by*** *20%.*

4 Identifies the "doer" in passive sentences:
The telephone was invented ***by*** *Bell.*

D Make it personal In pairs, answer 1–4. Similar opinions?

1 Order the technologies in A in the order you think they will disappear.
2 Will you miss them? Why (not)?
3 Which other everyday items / jobs / activities would you like to disappear?
4 What do you think they should be replaced by?

doing dishes   ironing   plastic bags   postal workers   watches

> I think watches are totally useless. I know what time it is by looking at my phone.

Lesson Aims: Sts talk about dying technologies, and make predictions about the future.

Skills	Language	Vocabulary	Grammar
Listening to an online program about dying technologies Reading short texts about dying technologies Speaking about the future, and making predictions	Making predictions, e.g. *Next year is likely to be better than this year. TV sets will become increasingly rare.*	Uses of *by* Phrases for making predictions: *be likely to …, be bound to …*	Talking about the future (1): predictions with *going to*, *will*, future perfect, and future continuous

Warm-up

Say: *Imagine it's 1920, and you're interviewed by a journalist, who asks, "What will the world be like in 100 years?"* In pairs, sts role play, taking turns to be the journalist, e.g.

A: *What will the world be like 100 years from now?*

B: *I think it will be a lot easier. We will all drive around in cars. Everyone will have a radio. Housework will be easier. Women will go to work … .*

A: *Do you think the world will be better or worse? Why?*

Ask: *What about now? Are you optimistic / pessimistic about the future? Will the world be better in 100 years?* Discuss with the class.

3 Language in use

A 12.6 Cover the text and board the program title: *Dying technologies* to see which ones sts suggest.

Uncover only cartoons a–d. In pairs, sts describe what they can see, which technologies it refers to and what might be said. Classcheck. Try to elicit: *cables* (picture a), *gas pump* (picture b), *landline phone* (picture c), *newsstand* (picture d).

Play the audio for sts to listen to the four conversations, and match them to pictures a–d. Paircheck, then classcheck.

Answers

Conversation 1 c   Conversation 2 b   Conversation 3 d
Conversation 4 a

See Teacher's Book p.332 for Audio script 12.6.

B 12.7 Give sts 90 seconds to read the texts, ignoring the gaps and boxes, to find out if their guesses from A were right. Paircheck.

Pairs re-read and work out what type of words are missing from each gap (i.e. noun, adjective or number). Encourage them to guess the exact words. Classcheck their guesses onto the board.

Sts listen to check their ideas. Classcheck. Ask: *Do you agree with the predictions? If not, explain why.*

Answers

1 10 2 fuel 3 expensive 4 smartphones
5 towers 6 food

C Go through the **Uses of *by*** and elicit other examples for each use, e.g. *I'll do the homework by tomorrow. We're traveling to Europe by plane. He won by two sets to one. They reduced the price by $20. The book was written by Stephen King.*

Sts look back at the text in A, and match uses 1–4 to each instance of *by*, writing 1–4 in the boxes. Paircheck, then classcheck.

Answers

by greener fuels – 4
by more than 50% – 3
by 2020 – 1
by selling – 2

Optional activity

In pairs, write their own sentences for each use of *by*, indicating (or having another pair indicate) which use 1–4 it matches.

Song lyric: See Teacher's Book p.347 for notes about the song and an accompanying activity to do.

D Make it personal Go through the questions and example speech bubble. Ask: *Which question (1–4) is this a response to?* (3)

Focus on the five suggested activities/items for Q3. Ask: Which of these do you think will disappear soon? Elicit meaning of *become obsolete* (= no longer used as replaced by something newer / more effective), e.g. *I think plastic bags will become obsolete, as supermarkets will be forced to sell recyclable bags.*

In pairs, sts discuss the questions. Monitor, helping with vocabulary.

Invite sts to share their ideas with the class. Can the class agree an order in which they will disappear and on what will replace them?

Tip

When monitoring monolingual classes, and deciding when to intervene, try to judge sts on what wouldn't be easily comprehensible to an English speaker who didn't know your sts mother tongue. Teaching the same nationality for any length of time, it's all too easy to get used to understanding / letting go what others wouldn't get easily.

4 Grammar: Talking about the future (1)

A NB this lesson focuses more on the future perfect continuous vs. future perfect than distinguishing *going to* and *will* (since predictions can use both). *Going to* vs *will* is the focus of the next grammar lesson: 12.4.

Go through the example sentences in the grammar box. Check understanding of *TV set* and *driverless*. Elicit the negative forms, e.g. *TV sets won't / aren't going to be rare*.

Tip

Ask: *How would you say express these sentences in your language?* Mental translation is inevitable and the grammar of a second language is best understood through the "mother tongue grammar mirror." (Rinvolucri).

Sts match uses 1–3 to the examples. Paircheck, then classcheck. Then go through the text on the right-hand side.

As a class, find examples of uses 1 and 2 in the infographic. Each time, sts say which use it is, and how it would (have to) change if the other form were to be used. Encourage questions: this isn't easy and it's important sts express their doubts. Highlight that native speakers would find this difficult to explain, and usage has blurred over the years.

In the **Common mistake** check sts understand why the future simple form is incorrect. Emphasize the aspect of going to a point in the future, turning around and looking back, saying an action is finished then.

Answers

3 TV sets will / are going to become increasingly rare.
2 People will / are going to be riding driverless cars.
1 Bookstores will have disappeared by 2030.

1 *By 2020, printed newspapers and magazines will have disappeared*
2 *people are going to be driving ... , the combustion engine won't be going ... , By the end of the decade, we'll be using ...*

Refer students to the **Grammar expansion** on p.160.

Tip

Point out *probably* and *certainly* are common when predicting, depending on how strongly we believe something will happen e.g. *Check-in staff will probably become increasingly rare. Hardware stores will certainly have disappeared by 2025.*

B Ask: *How many of you wear glasses/contact lenses? How many of you have had laser eye surgery? What were the last three things you wrote by hand?*

Refer sts to the article title and elicit the meaning of *on their way out* (= becoming no longer desirable/needed).

Sts read the texts and correct the mistakes. Paircheck, then classcheck.

Answers

~~we'll have lived~~ > we'll be living
sunglasses ~~will still around~~ > will still be around
~~will be dropping~~ > will be dropped
~~you won't write~~ > you won't have written

Optional activity

Sts write a paragraph about an item from 3D for "Also on their way out." First, sts underline the future time phrases in 4B; *in the not-too-distant future, for a while, by the end of the decade, by the time you read this*. Elicit others, e.g. *in the near future, before long, in five years' time*. Tell them to use appropriate time phrases, and the texts in 4B as a model.

C Go through **Other ways to make predictions**. Check understanding by rephrasing the examples in the grammar box with *be bound to / likely to*. Explain these expressions are usually used in the present tense

In pairs, sts rephrase three sentences in B. Classcheck.

Answers

With laser eye surgery and contact lenses, we're likely to be living in a world free of glasses in the not-too-distant future. Sunglasses are bound to be around for a while, though. By the end of the decade, possibly before that, handwriting as an educational requirement is bound to have been dropped from the national curriculum. By the time you read this, it's likely that you won't have handwritten anything for ages.

D Make it personal Focus on the example, then elicit/give further examples for the different areas of our lives, e.g. *I think we'll be learning English at home via the Internet/Chinese instead of English./ I'm sure I won't still be learning English*. Ask: *Which of these areas do you think will change the most?*

In groups, sts discuss them all. Encourage use of both positive and negative forms, as in the stems in bubbles. Monitor and congratulate for correct tense use.

Classcheck, and ask: *Which group/student is the most optimistic/pessimistic?*

Workbook p.59.

4 Grammar: Talking about the future (1)

A Read the grammar box and write the correct numbers (1–3) next to the examples. Then find four more examples of 1 and 2 in the infographic.

Predictions with *going to*, *will*, future perfect, and future continuous

☐ TV sets **will / are going to become** increasingly rare.
☐ People **will / are going to be riding** driverless cars.
☐ Bookstores **will have disappeared** by 2030.

1 Actions completed before some point in the future.
2 Actions in progress at some point in the future.
3 Future predictions in general.

Will and *going to* are often interchangeable, but *going to* is more common when you are sure of your prediction because there is evidence:
*Watch out! You're **going to spill** coffee on your phone.*

Grammar expansion p.160

Common mistake

By the end of this lesson, you ~~will read~~ *will have read* 129 pages of *Identities 1*.

B More predictions! Correct four mistakes in the predictions below. There may be more than one answer.

ALSO ON THEIR WAY OUT

Prescription glasses

With laser eye surgery and contact lenses, it's possible that in the not-too-distant future we'll have lived in a world free of glasses. Sunglasses will still around for a while, though, for sure.

Writing by hand

By the end of the decade, possibly before that, handwriting as an educational requirement will be dropping from the national curriculum. By the time you read this, you won't write a letter by hand for ages.

C Read *Other ways to make predictions*. Rephrase three sentences in **B** using *be likely to* and *be bound to*.

Other ways to make predictions

You can use *be (un)likely to* and *be bound to* when making predictions. *Be bound to* is more definite:
Next year **is likely to be** better than this year. (I'm pretty sure it will be better.)
Climate change **is bound to get** worse. (I'm almost certain it will get worse.)

D Make it personal In groups, guess what life will be like in 2050. Who predicts the brightest future?

English | food | household chores | marriage | post offices | school tests | shopping

I think ... are going to ...

... are bound to ...

By ... I think ... will have ...

... will be ... -*ing*

What do you think the future has in store for us as far as household chores are concerned?

I'm sure people won't be spending their free time vacuuming or ironing.

5 Reading

A In groups, make a list of things you know about Mars in one minute. Which group has the longest list?

> Scientists have found water on Mars, right? But I'm not sure whether it's drinkable.

Common mistake

I don't believe there's intelligent life ~~in~~ on other planets.

B In pairs, discuss the photo. Ask *where, what, who, when, why*? Read paragraph 1 to check. Does the writer feel optimistic or pessimistic about the project?

C Read only the first sentence of paragraph 2 and guess why the writer feels this way. Then read to check. Do the same for paragraphs 3–5. Were you surprised?

Not the kind of place to raise your kids. Or is it?

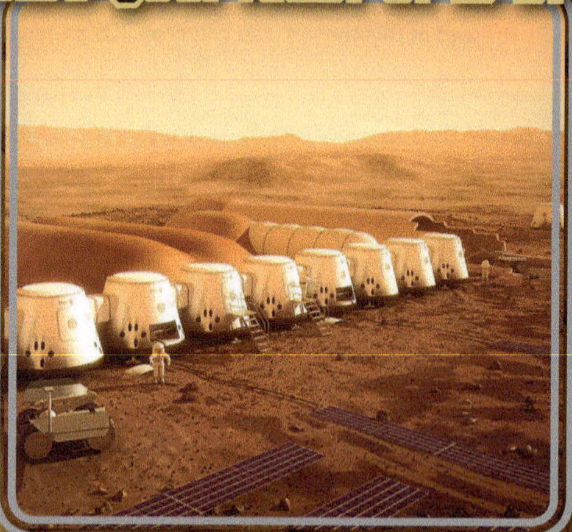

After the blockbuster movie *The Martian* in 2015, it seems we've been witnessing a new wave of enthusiasm for the idea that in the near future, some of us are going to be living on Mars. A Dutch nonprofit organization called Mars One, for example, is hoping to send four people on a one-way trip to Mars by 2026, as the beginning of a permanent human colony, which could in the long run ease overcrowding on Earth. To be honest, I still [1] **have my doubts** about whether this is a viable mission.

To begin with, getting there will be a nightmare. A trip to Mars will take up to nine months, which is a long time, especially when four people will be floating around in a tiny capsule, subjected to low gravity and insanely high levels of radiation. Then there are the inevitable equipment failures, which could [2] **pose a threat** to the whole mission. But that's just the beginning.

People seem to [3] **overlook the fact that** Mars is horribly inhospitable. The average temperature is minus 63 degrees Celsius, far too cold for it to rain, and people would need to [4] **figure out a way** to endure the year-long cold. Then there's breathing. The atmosphere is 96% carbon dioxide, so oxygen must be artificially synthesized, which will be [5] **hard to pull off**. And extremely dangerous, since peaks of oxygen may be potentially lethal, too.

Another key question is how the crew's health will be affected. Their bones and muscles evolved under Earth's gravity and on Mars they will weigh 30% of what they weigh on Earth. This means they're bound to lose a lot of muscle mass – and that includes the heart. Speaking of heart, their feelings of isolation and loneliness will probably be devastating, especially as time goes on. We don't [6] **have a clue** how this will affect their mental health.

And finally, the costs are going to be quite literally astronomical. At an estimated cost of $6 billion (!) for the first flight, the whole project begs the question: Is colonizing Mars worth the investment – and the risk? Wouldn't it be wiser to use this money to fix our own planet first?

D Read *How to know if a writer is certain*. Then re-read the article and write + (more certain) or – (less certain) for 1–5, according to the text. Underline the evidence.

1 There will be technical problems in the spacecraft.
2 Too much oxygen will kill them.
3 Their hearts will get weaker.
4 They will go crazy eventually.
5 The mission will cost $6 billion.

How to know if a writer is certain

	more certain	less certain
adverbs	The whole thing will **inevitably** fail.	It will cost $10 million, **possibly** $20 million.
adjectives	It's **bound** to go wrong.	There are a lot of **potential** problems.
expressions	It's off to a bad start, **without a doubt**.	**Who knows** what's in store for us.
modals	It'**ll** be a disaster.	It **might** backfire eventually.

Lesson Aims: Sts read about a project to send people to Mars, and discuss 21st-century innovations such as the driverless car

Skills	Language	Vocabulary
Reading a text about the problems of organizing a mission to Mars Discussing whether certain innovations are necessary are not	Using expressions for discussing innovation: *I have my doubts about life on Mars. I imagine a self-driving car wouldn't be hard to pull off.*	Expressions for discussing innovation: *(not) have a clue, figure out, have doubts, overlook, pose a threat, pull off* Phrases for expressing more or less certainty: *inevitably, possibly, be bound to ... , potential, without a doubt, who knows ...*

Warm-up

Ask: *What are the ten coldest places in the world?* In pairs, sts write a list, then compare it with other pairs.

Board the lesson title question and follow-up questions: *What's the coldest place you've ever been to? Did you wear any special clothes to keep warm? What problems did you have?* In pairs, sts discuss the questions. Class feedback for any interesting stories.

Background information

The ten coldest places in the world: 1 Antarctica 2 USA (Alaska) 3 Canada 4 Russia 5 Greenland 6 Finland 7 Kazakhstan 8 Iceland 9 Estonia 10 Mongolia

5 Reading

A Ask: *Can you name all the planets in our solar system?* In small groups, sts write them down as quickly as possible, and guess the stress/spelling in English. Hands up when they've finished. *Who was the quickest?*

In their groups, give sts a further minute to brainstorm and note down all they know about the planet Mars. Ask each group to share their information with the class. Other groups tick off each fact they too have written down as they hear it. Which groups had the longest list?

Focus on the example and **Common Mistake**. Elicit any rules they know for use of *on/in*, or get them to research them for homework.

Background information

The planets, in order of proximity to the sun are: Mercury, Venus, Earth, Mars, Jupiter, Saturn, Uranus, and Neptune. Mars is the fourth planet from the Sun, the smallest after Mercury and is often referred to as the "Red Planet" because of its reddish appearance. It's extremely cold because of its distance from the sun, about half the size of Earth, and like Earth, has seasons, polar ice caps, volcanoes, canyons, and weather.

Tip

This lesson is based around the KWL technique. Sts first brainstorm K (What I **K**now, then their questions (what I **W**ant to know) and then L (what I Learned by reading.)

B Quickly elicit and board the most interesting questions sts can ask about the photo using each question word, e.g. *Where is it? What's going on?, Who took the photo? When was the photo taken? Why are they there?*

In pairs, sts try to answer the questions, then read paragraph 1 to check.

Class feedback. Ask: *How does the writer feel about the project to send people to Mars?* (pessimistic). Ask: *Why do you think he feels like this?*

C Board the first sentence of paragraph 2: *To begin with, getting there will be a nightmare*. Elicit ideas why the writer says this. Then sts uncover and read paragraph 2 to check their guesses. In pairs, sts continue doing the same for the other paragraphs. Classcheck.

Answers

Paragraph 2 – getting there will be a nightmare
Paragraph 3 – Mars is inhospitable
Paragraph 4 – the crew's health may be affected

Optional activity

Sts write six comprehension questions about the text in 5C, e.g. *How long does it take to get to Mars?* In pairs, sts ask questions and answer their partner's questions.

D Go through **How to know if a writer is certain**. Read aloud sentence 1 and ask sts to find how the author expresses this idea in the text (*There are the inevitable equipment failures.*) *How certain is the author about this?* (Very certain). *How do you know?* (the writer uses *inevitable*).

Sts work individually through sentences 2–5 in the same way. Paircheck, then classcheck.

Answers

1 More certain – *Then there are the inevitable equipment failures*
2 Less certain – *peaks of oxygen may be potentially lethal*
3 More certain – *they're bound to lose a lot of muscle mass – and that includes the heart*
4 Less certain – *we don't have a clue how this will affect their mental health*
5 Less certain – *an estimated cost of $6 billion*

Song lyric: See Teacher's Book p.348 for notes about the song and an accompanying activity to do with the class.

E 12.8 In pairs, sts find and try to pronounce the underlined words in the text ending *-al* and *-able*. Classcheck their best guesses.

Sts listen, read and confirm pronunciation of these words, plus those in pink.

Sts write down the words marking the correct stress (VIable, inEVitable, inhosPItable, LEthal, astroNOmical), then practice saying them in pairs.

Elicit meaning and drill pronunciation of the pinked words as necessary too. Ask: *Is there anything else you struggled with? Did you enjoy the text? Were the activities useful?*

F Make it personal Go through the three questions, and example. In pairs, sts discuss the questions. Set a time limit of 5–6 minutes to give them a clear aim/end point.

Monitor to feed in as much help as you can. Whisper corrections as they speak, or write them on slips of paper, then jumble them up and give them out for sts to find and claim "their" mistake afterwards. They often claim all of them!

Class feedback. Ask: *How many of you would like to go on a mission to Mars? Were your answers to the other questions similar? What were the three most popular objects to take?*

Tip

If sts dry up during a discussion activity, they can move into groups of four with the pair next to them.

Optional activity

Class debate. Board: *Colonizing Mars is not worth the investment*. Divide into groups "For", and "Against." In their groups, sts brainstorm and note down ideas, then present them, justifying their points of view. The other group asks questions / challenge. Finally, sts vote for the most convincing group.

6 Vocabulary: Expressions for discussing innovation

A Go through the example with the class, highlighting that *doubts* = 1 feelings of uncertainty.

Sts match the bold words in the article with their meanings. Paircheck, then classcheck. Elicit and drill pronunciation of words / definitions as necessary.

Focus on the speech bubbles. In pairs, sts test each other. A says a highlighted expression, B gives an example sentence using it. Monitor for accuracy.

Answers

a 5 (pull off) b 3 (overlook) c 1 (doubts)
d 6 (clue) e 4 (figure out) f 2 (pose)

B Focus on the title and elicit the meaning of *blessing/ curse. Which is positive?*

In pairs, sts describe the picture and what it and the headline makes them think.

Class feedback. Ask: *Has anybody any experience of this sort of thing or seen them in movies? Would you buy an automated car if they were available? How would you pass the time while in the car?*

Give sts a maximum of two minutes to read and complete the forum entries with the highlighted expressions.

Paircheck, then classcheck. Ask: *Who's optimistic/ pessimistic about driverless cars? Which of the forum entries do you agree with? Any other such technologies you're looking forward to?*

Answers

1 overlook the fact that 2 have my doubts
3 hard to pull off 4 pose a threat 5 have a clue
6 figure out a way

Optional activity

Stronger classes: Thinking about exam practice, sts write a short paragraph about the advantages/ disadvantages of driverless cars. Allow time to search ideas online, and board suggested areas, e.g. road safety, advantages for the visually impaired or disabled, traffic congestion, environmental factors. Encourage use of expressions from 5D. Get them to swap texts to edit each other's work.

C Make it personal Go through the list of innovations with the class and elicit an idea or two about each of them, and add your own opinion to help broaden ideas. Be controversial, even if you don't believe it, e.g. *I can't wait for the end of physical classrooms as I'll never have to cross town through the traffic again!*

Highlight the scale, and example to show how it works. Individually, sts rank them 1–4.

In small groups, sts share, explain and justify ideas. Encourage use of **How to know** ... phrases in 5D.

Weaker classes: Board stems to help in their discussions:

We will inevitably see ...

Without a doubt, ... are not absolutely necessary.

... is desirable, but not very necessary.

... are bound to backfire.

If we introduce ... , it'll be a disaster.

Class feedback. Which was the most/least popular topic? And the most controversial?

Workbook p.60.

E 12.8 Read and listen. Notice the schwa /ə/ in the words ending in *-al* and *-able*.

F **Make it personal** In pairs, answer 1–3. Anything in common?

1 Why would anyone volunteer for a mission like that? Would you?
2 How would you answer the last question in paragraph 5? Give three reasons.
3 Imagine you're one of the astronauts. You can take three personal objects with you. What would you take and why? (Remember: No phones!)

I think I'd take a photo of my family.

You mean, so you could feel close to them, even if you couldn't see them?

6 Vocabulary: Expressions for discussing innovation

A Match the bold words 1–6 in the article in 5C with their meanings a–f. Then in pairs, test each other. Say the highlighted expression from memory and give an example sentence.

a ☐ achieve c [1] feelings of uncertainty e ☐ find
b ☐ ignore d ☐ relevant information f ☐ represent

Doubts ...

Have my doubts. I have my doubts about life on Mars.

B Complete the forum entries with the highlighted expressions 1–6 in 5C. Who do you agree with?

Cars that drive themselves: a blessing or a curse?

Aron4: The problem with the scientists behind this new driverless car is that they tend to [1] ________ a lot of people actually enjoy driving – at least I know I do. So I [2] ________ about whether self-driving cars will ever become popular.

Paula87: As far as the technology itself is concerned, I imagine a self-driving car wouldn't be [3] ________ . In fact, lots of prototypes already exist and have been tested on roads, with very few accidents, which means they probably won't [4] ________ to pedestrians and other drivers.

JJWilcox: Everyone's hyped up about driverless cars, but the truth is, we don't [5] ________ what our roads will be like with thousands of these. How safe and reliable are these cars, really?

Freerider©: Another car? Really? What the government should do is [6] ________ to persuade people to use their bikes or public transportation.

C **Make it personal** Rate each innovation below from 1 (unnecessary) to 4 (very necessary). In groups, share your ideas. Which innovation is most (least) popular?

Innovations we might see by 2025:

the end of physical classrooms   DNA mapping at birth to manage disease risk   pills to replace sleep
4D TVs   cosmetic face transplants   the end of baldness   music written by machines

I gave "music written by machines" a 2.

Me too. Machines are bound to be less creative than people!

⑦ Language in use

A In groups, make a list of excuses people usually make in situations 1–3. Which cartoon do you like best?

1   Leaving work early

2   Traffic violations

3   Being late

> When people want to leave work early, they often say, "I'm not feeling well."

B ▶ 12.9   Listen to Don's excuses and take notes. Who do you think believed him?

	2:00 p.m.	3:00 p.m.	4:00 p.m.
1 Who's he talking to?			
2 What's the excuse?			
3 Why did he make it?			

C ▶ 12.10   Complete the text with the words from the mind map. Listen to Don's conversation the next day to check.

The top ③ excuses
everybody is sick and tired of hearing

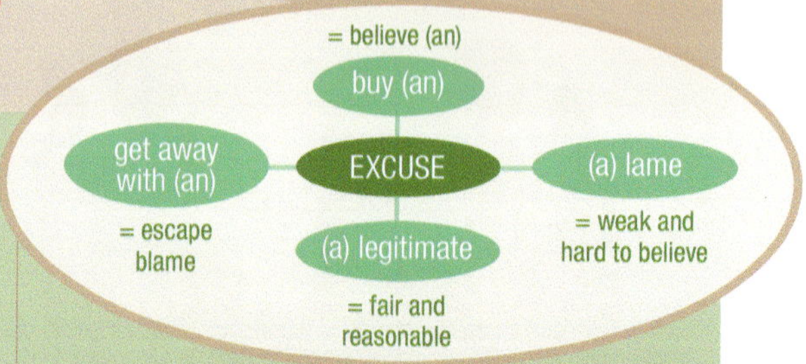

1   Heavy traffic can be a ¹_____ ☐ excuse if you live in a big city, but use your common sense. As soon as people realize you're overusing it, they won't ²_____ ☐ it anymore, even if you do get stuck. And be careful with "I think I'll be there in five minutes." You'll lose credibility if five minutes constantly becomes 15.

2   If you get pulled over by the police, it's unlikely you'll be able to ³_____ ☐ saying "There's an emergency you have to get to." The same goes for "My plane leaves in ten minutes." Honesty, on the other hand, might, in some cases, actually increase your chances of not getting a ticket: "Sorry. I was over the limit. It won't happen again."

3   At work, doctor's appointments can be pretty ⁴_____ ☐ excuses, unless it's an emergency or something you've been trying to schedule for a long time. "I'm taking my sister-in-law to the doctor in the morning" is no good either — pick a closer relative. Or, if it doesn't cost you your job, just be honest and say you're going to take the day off to run some errands.

D Make it personal In pairs, talk about the last lame excuse you or someone else made. Did you / the other person buy it?

> Last week my oldest friend forgot to call me on my birthday and said her phone was stolen. Of course I didn't buy it. I mean, she could have Skyped me.

> Pretty lame, huh? Or at least sent an e-card or message!

Lesson Aims: Sts read about common excuses people make in different situations, and discuss excuses they have made themselves.

Skills	Language	Grammar	Vocabulary
Listening to someone making excuses Reading about common excuses people make in different situations	Making excuses: *Sorry. I was over the speed limit, it won't happen again. I'm sorry, the traffic was awful.*	Talking about the future (2): expressing plans and intentions, decisions, and scheduled events; time clauses	Expressions with *excuse*: *get away with (an), buy (an), (a) legitimate, (a) lame* Time clause expressions: *as soon as, before, until*

Warm-up

Board *Excuses* and ask: *What excuses have you made this year for being late/leaving early/not doing homework/ forgetting books/missing tests? The best one was ...?*

In pairs, sts add as many "classics" as they can, e.g. *the dog ate my homework. My computer crashed and I hadn't saved it.* Classcheck ideas, and agree on the best.

Ask these questions, including the lesson title question: Ask: *Do you often make excuses? Are you good at it? What was the last excuse you made? Who did you make it to? Did the person believe it?* Have sts discuss in groups. Classcheck their best offerings.

7 Language in use

A Sts look at the cartoons and describe each location. (1 *in the office*, 2 *in a car / on the road*, 3 *at home*) Be careful with prepositions. Ask: *Who do you think they are?*
(1 *work colleagues*, 2 *driver and a police officer*, 3 *husband and wife*). *Which cartoon is the funniest / least funny?*

In groups, sts think of common excuses made in situations 1–3. Class feedback.

Possible answers

1 I have a doctor's appointment. / I'm not feeling well.
2 I was driving my friend to the hospital. It's an emergency. I left the cooker on.
3 The train was late. / The bus was full, so I had to wait for the next one. / I had a meeting at work.

B 12.9 Explain that sts are going to listen to Don in three different situations, making an excuse.

Sts listen and answer the three questions to complete the table.

Paircheck, then classcheck. Ask: *Who do you think believed him? Have you been in any of these situations (recently)?*

Answers

2:00 p.m. 1 His boss 2 He has a doctor's appointment. 3 He is going away for the weekend
3:00 p.m. 1 A police officer 2 His neighbor smells gas in his apartment. 3 He was driving badly.
4:00 p.m. 1 His girlfriend / a friend 2 The traffic was awful. 3 He was late to meet his girlfriend.
His boss believed him.

See Teacher's Book p.332 for Audio script 12.9.

C 12.10 Board the text title, and elicit the meaning of *sick and tired* (= fed up). Explain that this is a "binomial" (refer them back to p.33 if necessary), and that you cannot change the order of the words, i.e. ~~*tired and sick*~~ is incorrect. Go through the mind map, and check understanding. Sts might be surprised by *buy* as in *I don't buy it*.

Before reading, get sts to predict, from all the excuses so far in the lesson, which the top three might be. Give sts two minutes to read the text quickly to find out.

Sts re-read it more carefully to complete the missing words. They may need help with *pull over*. Paircheck.

Play the audio for students to listen to a conversation between Don and his girlfriend to check their answers.

Classcheck. Ask: *Does the text resonate? Would it be the same in our culture? If not, how might it be different?* e.g. The Anglophone world is obsessed with people being late, but here, we're a bit more relaxed.

Answers

Paragraph 1 – legitimate, buy Paragraph 2 – get away with
Paragraph 3 – lame

See Teacher's Book p.333 for Audio script 12.10.

Optional activity

Stronger classes: Sts write a similar text called *The top 3 excuses everybody is sick and tired of hearing about ...* and choose a topic relevant to their age group. Encourage use of the expressions from the mind map.

D Make it personal If necessary, refer sts back to the grammar sections in Unit 11 for reporting speech before they do this activity.

Go through the speech bubble example. Ask: *When did one of your friends or members of family make a lame excuse to you for something they did? When did you last make a lame excuse? Who was it to? Did they believe you?* Sts discuss in pairs.

Sts find the direct speech in 7C, and label each with the rules a–d. Quickly paircheck. Classcheck. Ask: *Any questions/doubts?* to allow sts to express their almost inevitable queries.

Weaker classes: Tell sts there's one quote in paragraphs 1 and 3, two in paragraph 2.

8 Grammar: Talking about the future (2)

A Go through the example sentences in the grammar table, and elicit what tense the verbs in bold are in, e.g. *leaves* = simple present. Ask: *What tenses would we use in our language?*

In pairs, sts match the tenses 1–4 with the uses a–d. Monitor to help. Classcheck.

Answers

a 4 b 1 c 4 d 2 or 3
"I think I'll be there in five minutes." – c
"My plane leaves in ten minutes." – b
"Sorry. I was over the limit. It won't happen again." – a
"I'm taking my sister-in-law to the doctor in the morning" – d

Refer students to the **Grammar expansion** on p.160.

Tip

The future in English is the hardest of the three tenses, as it has the least clear-cut rules. Reassure sts that uncertainty is normal. Non-teachers would find all this impossible to explain, and sts will virtually always be intelligible anyway when they interchange *going to* and *will*. The forthcoming practice will help.

Optional activity

Sts think up examples for rules a–d, e.g. *I'll try to get these sentences right. My English class starts at 9.30. I guess I'll probably practice English with local tourists in the holidays. I'm going to work hard this year.*

Song lyric: See Teacher's Book p.348 for notes about the song and an accompanying activity to do with the class.

B 12.11 Go through sentences 1–6. Check sts understand *to fire / fired* in 1 and 6 (= dismiss / lay off).

Have sts circle the correct answers, then play the audio for them to check.

Answers

1 'm going to fire 2 'll talk 3 'll give 4 'll probably be
5 'm taking 6 starts

C Go through **Time clauses**, and ask which tense is used after these time expressions in their language.

Focus on the **Common mistake**. Ask: *Why do you think this is a common mistake?* (Because in many other languages, you use the future form after *as soon as*.)

Sts complete the sentences with a suitable verb. Paircheck, then classcheck.

Answers

1 is 2 gives 3 wash 4 says

D Sts rewrite the sentences in C using the words in the box. Paircheck.

Classcheck, asking volunteers to board the sentences, all at once if possible, to save time. Ask the class to correct any if necessary. Ask: *Which sentences are true for you?* Ask for a show of hands for each one.

Answers

1 I'm going abroad as soon as my English is better.
2 I won't start saving money until my boss gives me a raise.
3 I'll wash the dishes and check my newsfeed before I get started.
4 I won't change my diet until my doctor says I'm in trouble.

E Make it personal Go through options 1–3 with the class. Illustrate each with an example yourself (e.g. 1 *I'm not going to stick to my diet. I'll pretend that I forgot I was on one*. 2 *I'm meeting my ex-girlfriend tomorrow, but I don't really want to. As soon as she starts to annoy me, I'll say I have to go back to work and leave.*) Encourage sts to ask you follow-up questions. One should be untrue, so bluff it imaginatively. Once sts have asked 1–3, say: *One of my stories wasn't true* for them to work out which.

Allow sts time to think of stories for 1–3. Feed in as much help as you can at this stage.

In pairs, sts share their stories, and guess which one is untrue. Monitor, praising correct use of time clauses and tenses.

Optional activity

In pairs, sts role play situation 2 in E. A plays the person being met, B calls to make an excuse. If necessary, board an example, for two sts to role play first.

A: *Hi Sally, it's me Josh.*

B: *Oh, hi Josh. Are you still OK to meet up on Wednesday?*

A: *Well, er ... actually, I'm not sure I can anymore.*

B: *Oh, no. Why's that?*

A: *Well, my cat's not very well, ... er she's not eating anything, and I have to take her to the vet. I'll give you a call as soon as she's better.*

B: *Hang on ... but you don't have a cat. You have a dog! ...*

If time, sts swap roles, and repeat it. Monitor, and note any good excuses.

Workbook p.61.

8 Grammar: Talking about the future (2)

A Study the examples and complete rules a–d with 1–4. Then write the correct rule (a–d) next to the quotes in 7C.

Expressing plans and intentions, decisions, and scheduled events

Listen, I have to go. The bus **leaves** at seven. My battery is almost dead. I'**ll give** you a call later!
I'**m going to join** a gym. I'**m signing up** today! I'm not sure, but maybe I'**ll take** a course this summer.

Use the ... 1 simple present 2 present continuous as future 3 future with *going to* 4 future with *will*

a ___ for a decision or promise you make at the moment you're speaking.
b ___ for events on a schedule or timetable, with verbs like *open*, *close*, *arrive*, and *start*.
c ___ for plans and intentions you're not sure of with expressions like *I guess*, *I think*, and *probably*.
d ___ or ___ for a fixed decision or plan you've already made.

Grammar expansion p.160

B 12.11 Don's boss, Miranda, is having a difficult day at the office. Circle the best answers 1–6. Listen to check.

1 I [**'ll fire** / **'m going to fire**] Sue Ann. She's been late every day for two weeks!
2 Please talk to her first. Or I [**'ll talk** / **'m talking**] to her for you.
3 OK, I [**give** / **'ll give**] her one more chance. But this is the last one!
4 Excuse me, Miranda, I [**'ll probably be** / **'m probably being**] late tomorrow.
5 I [**'m taking** / **'ll take**] my grandmother to the doctor.
6 Unacceptable! Our meeting [**starts** / **will start**] at 9:00 a.m.! One more excuse and you're fired!

C Read *Time clauses*. Then complete 1–4 with a suitable verb.

Time clauses

Always use the simple present in time clauses with words like *when*, *after*, *as soon as*, *before*, and *until*:
I'm going to buy a car **as soon as** I turn 18. (= immediately after)
I'm finishing the report **before** I leave.
I won't leave **until** the rain stops. (= up to the point that)

Common mistake

I think she'll get promoted as soon as she ~~will graduate~~ *graduates*.

1 Going abroad: "I'm not going abroad until my English ________ better."
2 Saving money: "I'm going to start saving money when my boss ________ me a raise."
3 Finishing an assignment: "I'll get started after I ________ the dishes and check my newsfeed."
4 Eating healthier food: "I'll change my diet when my doctor ________ I'm in trouble."

D Rewrite 1–4 in C using the words below. Which sentence is true for you?

1 as soon as 2 until 3 before 4 until

I'm going abroad as soon as my English is better.

E **Make it personal** In pairs, share stories about 1–3. Make one untrue. Can your partner guess which one?

1 Something you're not going to do even though you should. What's your excuse?
2 Someone you're meeting in the next few days even though you'd rather not. If you make an excuse, will he/she buy it?
3 Something old / useless you think you'll throw away soon. What's wrong with it?

I think I'll throw away all of my CDs this week. They take up a lot of space.

Me too. I'm getting rid of mine as soon as I can upload all of them.

9 Listening

A 12.12 Listen to Fred talking about a contest he entered. Answer 1–3.

1 What does Fred have to do?
2 What was the example he gave Tina?
3 How much older is Fred in photo 2?

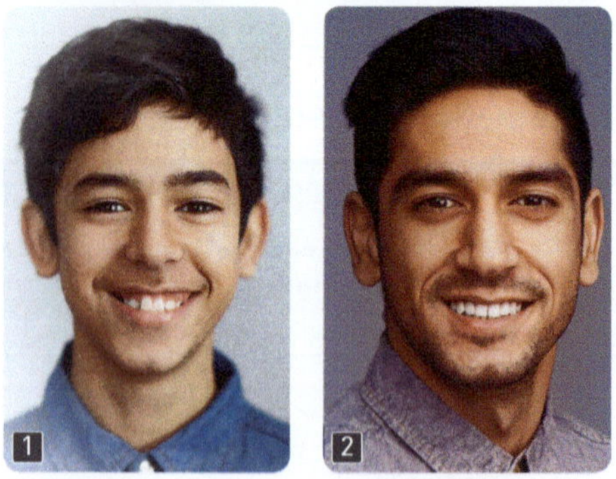

B 12.13 Listen to Fred 10 years later and complete sentences 1–4. One choice is used twice. Is Fred pleased with his decisions?

a expected to	b didn't expect to	c wondered if he'd

When Fred was younger, he ...

1 ______ look this old.
2 ______ become a teacher.
3 ______ have a girlfriend.
4 ______ live at home after graduation.

C 12.12 & 12.13 Complete 1–7 with the correct prepositions. Listen again to check. Did you understand all the highlighted expressions?

1 I'm taking part ______ a writing contest.
2 I could do ______ a little extra cash.
3 What ______ earth is that?
4 You could start with something ______ the lines of "Dear Tina ..."
5 Well, it's now a number of years ______ the road.
6 It may not satisfy me totally ______ a personal level.
7 That should be the least ______ your problems.

10 Keep talking

A Think ahead 10 years. What would you say now to your future self? Make notes on at least three topics.

career family life fitness and health friends looks love life money studies travel

I'm pretty sure you'll ...
I'm assuming ...
I'd love to ...
I hope you won't ...
I wonder ...

B In groups, compare ideas about your future selves. Any coincidences?

What do you think your life will be like in 10 years?
Well, I'm assuming I will have started my own business by then.
Really? What kind of business?

Common mistake
What
~~How~~ will your life be like in 10 years?

Lesson Aims: Sts listen to someone's letter to their future self, and write their own letter / email.

Skills	Language	Vocabulary
Listening to someone reading parts of a letter he wrote to his future self when he was a teenager Writing an email to your future self; using adverbs for emphasis	Making predictions about the future, e.g. *What will your life be like in 10 years' time? I'm assuming I'll have started a business by then.*	*assume, expect, wonder* Expressions with prepositions: *take part in, along the lines of, down the road, on a personal level, the least of your problems, (I) could do with* Adverbs: *certainly, eventually, hopefully, officially, probably*

Warm-up

In pairs, sts ask and answer random lesson title questions from earlier units. Monitor, celebrate quality and pick up on any slips, saying *Pardon me?* to see if they can self correct.

Lead up to the lesson title question. Board some questions for sts to discuss in pairs: *Do you worry about the future? What do you worry about most? What are you looking forward to in the future? What ambitions do you have? What will your life be like 10 years from now?*

9 Listening

A 12.12 Sts look at the photos of Fred. Ask: *How old do you think he is in each photo?*

Explain that sts are going to listen to Fred talking to his friend Tina about a competition he has entered.

Play the audio for sts to listen and answer the questions.

Classcheck. Ask: *How much does the winner get?* ($250)

Answers

1 He has to write a letter to his future self.
2 "Dear Tina, When you read this, you'll have been married for five years. Are you happy? Is married life everything you thought it would be?"
3 Ten years older.

See Teacher's Book p.333 for Audio script 12.12.

B 12.13 Explain that sts are now going to listen to Fred ten years later reading the letter that the younger Fred wrote for the competition. Ask: *What do you think he'll make of it?*

Sts uncover and read 1–4, and guess/try to work out logically which options are likeliest. This is good exam training as it can reduce the number of possible distractors.

Sts listen to complete the sentences with the phrases in the box. Paircheck.

Classcheck. Ask: *Do you think Fred's happy with his life decisions? Do you think his teacher's assignment was a good one? Did you do anything like this at school?*

Answers

1 b 2 a 3 c 4 a

See Teacher's Book p.333 for Audio script 12.13.

C 12.12 & 12.13 Sts fill in the missing prepositions from memory or intuition. Paircheck.

Play the audio for them to check their answers.

Sts listen to check. Get them to paraphrase meanings of the highlighted expressions (1 participating, 2 benefit from, 3 used to express surprise/confusion, 4 similar in type, 5 in the future, 6 used when talking about how something affects you, 7 for emphasizing that a particular problem is less important than other problems). Ask: *Which ones do you already use?*

Weaker classes: Alternatively, board the prepositions in random order to help them be more likely to get them correct.

Answers

1 in 2 with 3 on 4 along 5 down 6 on 7 of

10 Keep talking

A Board: *What would you say to your future self about your ...?*

Begin by sts asking you this question about all eight topics. Use and highlight your use of the speech bubble language in your answers, and encourage follow-up questions.

Give sts time to make notes about what they'd say to their future self. Monitor and prompt all you can. Encourage use of the bubble phrases, e.g. *I hope by now you'll (have a successful career). I wonder (what your family life will be like), and whether (you'll be married). I'm pretty sure (you'll be healthy, as you've always been sporty). I imagine you'll (have lots of friends because you're very sociable).*

B Go through the **Common mistake** and focus on the example, highlighting the use of *by then*. Elicit other questions sts can ask, e.g. *How many children do you think you'll have? What do you think you'll look like? What job will you be doing?* Push them to contract *will* whenever they can.

In groups, sts compare their ideas from A. Monitor for correct use of all future forms.

Finally, with the right class, ask an interesting summative question, like: *Do you think you'll like your future self? Would your grandparents be proud of you?*

Song lyric: See Teacher's Book p.348 for notes about the song and an accompanying activity to do with the class.

11 Writing: An email to your future self

A Begin with a discussion. Ask: *How do you envisage your future self? What would you most wish for yourself in ten year's time, apart from being alive and healthy?*

Have sts read the email quickly and find out if any of their ideas from 10A are mentioned. (She mentions: career, family life, love life, studies, travel.) Paircheck, then classcheck.

Optional activity

Sts underline all the predictions "Present Nina's email" makes about "Future Nina". Analyze which future tense is used in each. In pairs, they try to explain why.

You'll be celebrating (continuous), *You'll be surrounded by* (simple), *you'll end up taking* (simple), *you'll have graduated* (perfect), *You'll be able to* (simple), *You'll become* (simple), *you'll want* (simple), *You'll want* (simple), *You'll have done* (perfect), *You'll be* (simple), *It will have been* (perfect), *You'll have* (simple).

B Focus on the example speech bubbles. In pairs, sts re-read the email and note the purpose of each paragraph. Classcheck.

Weaker classes: Board the purpose of each paragraph in random order (see Answers) for sts to match to the paragraphs.

Answers

Paragraph 1 explains what the email is about
Paragraph 2 makes predictions about Nina's career
Paragraph 3 makes predictions about Nina's marriage and family, as well as travel plans
Paragraph 4 congratulates and encourages Nina in her English studies
Paragraph 5 wishes Future Nina well and promises to help

C Go through **Write it right!** with the class. Ask sts to underline the auxiliary verbs *be* and *have* in the examples (*my boss will have, I'll definitely be making*).

Have sts complete the rules. Paircheck, then classcheck.

Answers

1 after, before 2 before, after

D Sts add the adverbs to the correct place in the underlined phrases.

Paircheck, then classcheck. Elicit other adverbs they could use, which have similar meanings, e.g. *presumably, ultimately, finally, surely, totally, basically*.

Answers

1 You'll probably be celebrating
2 You'll have hopefully graduated
3 You'll eventually become
4 You'll have certainly done that
5 You'll officially be an advanced student

E Your turn! Go through the instructions and clarify the aim with the class, which is to write a similar e-mail to your future self.

Sts look back at 10A, circle the topics they wish to include and start making notes. Tell them to try and use all three future forms: *will*, future continuous, and future perfect.

Sts can begin writing in class, and finish for homework. Emphasize they should follow all the *While* and *After* steps, peerchecking before they post anything back to you or elsewhere.

Note that there are real websites which offer this service. Sts search online for "Future me" or "Send email to the future."

Classcheck by asking sts if they enjoyed the activity and if it was cathartic in any way. These emails have the potential to get quite personal so be careful either to look at them before you ask sts to share, or at least only ask volunteers to show them to others.

Congratulate sts on successfully completing iDentities. Celebrate with them!

Optional activity

Sts write an email to their Younger Self. They remember a difficult time, and give their Younger Self advice. Tell them that things will work out OK. Elicit/Board a few stems to help them:

I know you feel worried about the future and whether you'll ...

But try not to worry, you'll certainly ...

At the moment you aren't very happy / getting on very well with ...

Things will get better ... You will sorts thing out

Don't worry about ... (what other people think) ...

You'll find (friends who you can rely on)

11 Writing: An email to your future self

A Read Nina's email to her future self. Are any of your ideas from 10A mentioned?

From: **Present Nina**
Subject: **Future Me**
To: **Future Nina**

Dear Future Me,

I've just come across a website that allows someone to send an email to his or her "future self" 10 years from now. I thought, "What a cool idea!" And so, here it is: my first email to you, "Future Me." Today is August 30, 2016, so, when you read this, [1]you'll be celebrating your 27th birthday. I know you're not too crazy about birthday parties, so I hope you make it through this one! Well, at least you'll be surrounded by all the people you love, that's for sure.

Next year you're going off to college. Or maybe you'll end up taking a year off to travel around the world and do some volunteer work. Who knows? By 2022, [2]you'll have graduated and found a nice job in your field. Aren't you lucky that, unlike some of your classmates, you'll be able to build a career from your passion – looking after animals? Call me an optimist, but I'm sure [3]you'll become one of the best vets in the city!

As to marriage ... Well, I could be wrong, of course, but I have my doubts you'll want to settle down and have kids before you're in your thirties. You've always valued your freedom more than anything else and something tells me you'll want to enjoy your single life for as long as you can. Hmm ... What else? Oh, that trip to Cappadocia, Turkey, to go hot-air ballooning? When you read this email again, [4]you'll have done that – maybe more than once! Trust me!

Aren't you proud of yourself for writing this email in English? Wow! [5]You'll be an advanced student next year! Doesn't time fly? You may be a bit tired of studying English right now, but stick with it! I'm sure it will have been worthwhile in the end.

Future Nina, you'll have a bright future, wherever you are and whatever you may be doing. I'll do my best to help, I promise.

Love,
Present Nina

B In pairs, explain the purpose of each paragraph.

I think the first one explains what the email is about.

Yes, and it tells us something about Nina. It's an introduction.

C Read *Write it right!* Then complete rules 1–2 with *after* or *before*.

Write it right!

Use adverbs for emphasis and to show how certain you are of something:

I hope that, by the end of the year, my boss will have **finally** promoted me to assistant manager. I'll **definitely** be making more money, I know, but my workload will **inevitably** increase, too.

In sentences with *will*, adverbs usually go ...

1 ________ *will* and ________ the main verb.
2 ________ the auxiliary *be*, but ________ the auxiliary *have*.

D Add these adverbs to the underlined phrases in A (1–5).

1 (probably) *you'll probably be celebrating*
2 (hopefully) ________
3 (eventually) ________
4 (certainly) ________
5 (officially) ________

E **Your turn!** Write an email of 200–250 words to your future self.

Before
Choose three or four topics from *Keep talking* in 10A.

While
Refer to B and make sure each paragraph has a clear purpose. Re-read *Write it right!* and use a variety of adverbs in your predictions.

After
Post your writing, and if possible, set a delivery date to receive your own email.

Review 6

Units 11–12

1 Listening

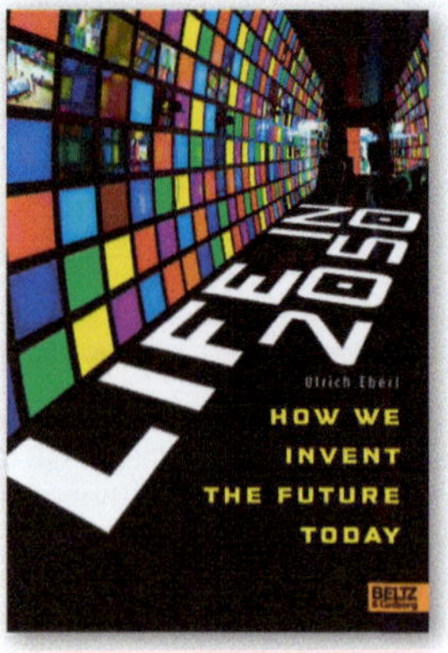

A R6.1 Listen to a conversation about Ulrich Eberl's book *Life in 2050*. Complete the sentences.

By 2050 ...

1 you'll be using a computer the size of a __________ .
2 a computer will be able to __________ a car.
3 there will be __________ farms in cities.
4 cars will be __________ to each other.
5 a "smart apartment" will recognize your __________ .
6 one in every six people will be over the age of __________ .

B **Make it personal** In groups, suggest as many innovations as you can for 2050 in two minutes. Which group has the most interesting ones?

I think food production will have doubled by 2050.

We'll be eating a lot more ...

2 Grammar

A Report the conversation using the words in parentheses.

GINA: I have something to tell you. (Gina told Len ...)

Gina told Len that she had something to tell him.

LEN: Really? Is it good news? (Len asked Gina ...)
GINA: Not really. (Gina admitted ...) I fell asleep during my interview last week. (She explained ...)
LEN: I don't believe it! (Len said ...)
GINA: It's true. (Gina assured Len ...) I don't think I got the job. (She added ...)
LEN: It's unlikely. (Len warned Gina ...) But some bosses have a kind heart! (But he reminded her ...)

B Report what happened next using the words in parentheses.

1 "Call your interviewer in the morning." (Len urged Gina ...)
2 "Please give me another chance." (Gina begged her interviewer ...)
3 "I'll go to bed early from now on." (She promised ...)
4 "I can't schedule another interview." (First, her interviewer refused ...)
5 "OK, I'll think it over and call you next week." (Then he agreed ...)

C Circle the correct future form for each of Gina's sentences.

1 [**I'm going to have / I'll have**] another interview tomorrow after all.
2 [**I'm getting / I get**] there early. That's for sure.
3 Maybe [**I'll go / I'm going**] to sleep at 9:00 p.m., too.
4 As soon as [**I'll get / I get**] home, I'll start preparing.

D **Make it personal** In pairs, role play one of these situations.

1 Report an embarrassing incident that happened to you or someone you know.
2 Apologize for something you've done and say what you've decided to do differently.

Warm-up

See page 61 of the Teacher's Book for warm-up ideas.

Tip

As this is the last lesson before any final test, use that "carrot" to encourage sts to really work hard here.

1 Listening

A R6.1 Focus on the book cover. Ask: *What do the images represent? What aspects of life in the future will be included? What do you think the author will say?*

Sts read the sentences, and guess the missing words. Play the audio for them to check. Classcheck.

Answers

1 pea 2 drive 3 vertical 4 talking 5 face 6 65

See Teacher's Book p.333 for Audio script R6.1.

B Make it personal Go through the example speech bubbles, and quickly review the future perfect and future continuous tenses. Refer sts to the Grammar section on p.129, if necessary.

In groups, sts think of as many innovations as they can. Monitor to help with vocabulary and future tenses, and look for good examples to share afterwards.

Have a volunteer from each group report back to the class. Ask: *Who thought of the most innovations?*

2 Grammar

A Invite two sts to read the dialog aloud. Check comprehension, e.g. *Why's Gina pessimistic?* (She fell asleep.) *What are her chances of being offered the job?* (Not good).

Set the activity up using the example. Individually sts report the rest of the conversation. Paircheck, then classcheck.

Answers

Gina told Len that she had something to tell him.
Len asked Gina if (whether) it was good news.
Gina admitted that it wasn't. She explained that she had fallen asleep in her interview last week.
Len said he didn't believe it.
Gina assured Len that it was true. She added that she didn't think she had gotten the job.
Len warned Gina that it was unlikely. But he reminded her that some bosses had a kind heart.

B Before starting, ask: *What do you think Gina should do now?* and brainstorm answers. Sts quickly read 1–5 to see if they guessed correctly.

Check sts understand the five reporting verbs and do the first item together as an example. You could do the rest of the exercise with the class, or individually, depending on time and how well sts know it.

Classcheck. Ask: *Do you think Gina will get the job?*

Answers

Len urged Gina to call her interviewer in the morning.
Gina begged her interviewer to give her another chance.
She promised she would go to bed early from now on.
First, her interviewer refused to schedule another interview.
Then he agreed to think it over and to call her next week.

C Sts re-read the grammar table on p.133, if necessary, or see the optional activity below.

Give sts 30 seconds to complete the exercise. Paircheck. Sts adjust their answers if convinced by their partner. Classcheck.

Answers

1 I'm going to have 2 I'm getting 3 I'll go 4 I get

Optional activity

Ask for volunteers to come to the front and play the role of teacher, explaining the future uses of 1) simple present 2) present continuous 3) *going to* and 4) *will*.

D Make it personal

Go through choices 1 and 2 in detail with the class. Elicit phrases sts can use while listening to keep the conversation flowing, e.g. *Really, what happened next? No way, that's so embarrassing. What did you do?*

1 In pairs, A reports an embarrassing incident while B listens, then swap roles. If necessary, brainstorm a few first. Encourage sts to use a variety of reporting verbs, e.g. *explain, ask, admit, wonder* and refer them to p.119 for more reporting verbs.

2 A tells B about something they've done, which they regret and wish to apologize for. Elicit and board an example role play, e.g.

A: *I'm really sorry I told Ana about seeing her boss with Sylvie.*
B: *Really? Why?*
A: *Well, Ana's such a gossip. She'll tell everyone!*
B: *I'm sure she won't.*
A: *Well, next time, I'm going to keep it to myself!*

In pairs, sts write their own role plays, at least in simple note form and then act them out. You could invite pairs to act out their role plays for the class.

3 Reading

A Board the text title and elicit the following: the year that will be, what the article might say, and what you and the sts might be doing then, e.g. *I'll be retired / long gone. And you?*

Read the rubric and three choices with the class. Ask: *Are you concerned about the environment? What do you do to help protect it? Do you belong to any environmental organizations?*

Give sts two minutes to read the text quickly, and choose the correct purpose. Paircheck, underlining the evidence in the text, then classcheck. Go through the meaning of any unfamiliar vocabulary.

Ask: *Did you learn anything from the text that you didn't know? Was it an easy read? How do you feel when you read texts like this? Would you be inclined to join? When will we ever learn and do something about these problems, do you think?*

Answer

The main purpose of the blog is to encourage people to join the organization and take action.

Optional activity

Sts re-read the text and write six comprehension questions, e.g. *How many people were displaced by natural disasters in a recent year?* Monitor.

In pairs, sts answer each other's questions.

Class feedback. Ask: *Did you find your partner's questions easy/difficult? Did you get them all right?*

B Elicit and board the questions the writer asks in the text:

What can you do to prevent global warming?

Do you know how to prevent overuse of fertilizers?

Do you know how to increase sustainable farming on dry land?

Do you recycle all you can?

Brainstorm what sts already know about these issues, and board anything sts find hard to express correctly.

Individuals choose one of the questions and research it further on the Internet. Monitor to weed out errors as soon as you can, e.g. simply by underlining anything that's 'wrong', for sts to try to self-correct.

Have a few sts present their answers to the rest of the class.

4 Self-test

To revise and consolidate the **Common mistakes**, sts do this individually then paircheck. Encourage sts to look back through Units 11 and 12 if they're unsure of how to correct the mistakes.

Classcheck by boarding the corrected sentences. If sts score less than 15 out of 20, suggest they look back over the grammar and vocabulary in Units 1 and 12, and re-do the exercise in a few days' time to see if they get a better score.

Answers

1. I try to keep up with the news, even though it's often biased.
2. My girlfriend told me she was sorry and admitted (or, admitted to me) ~~me~~ she was wrong.
3. I promised ~~her~~ to keep the secret, and I agreed ~~her~~ not to tell anyone.
4. I explained to my teacher I wasn't sure of the answer.
5. My mother persuaded me to apologize and she made me ~~to~~ call right away.
6. I'm definitely an optimist, so I'm keeping my fingers crossed about the future.
7. We're going there by bus, and as soon as we arrive, I'll be in touch.
8. By the time you read this, you will have almost finished *Identities*, and you will be likely to know a lot of English!
9. I'll give you a call later. Maybe I'll take a nap first.
10. I'm visiting Larry this weekend, so I won't see you until I get back.

Optional activity

Sts to write four of their own sentences (with errors) for the self-test exercise. Sts swap sentences with their partner, and see if they can spot the mistakes in their partner's sentences.

5 Point of view

See page 62 of the Teacher's Book for notes about this section.

Go through topics a–d with the class, and brainstorm a few ideas for each one.

Individually, sts choose one of them, and make some preparatory notes. Tell sts to make the notes they feel they need to be able to speak for about 80 seconds on the topic. You don't want full sentences or a script, just prompts from which they can talk naturally.

Weaker classes: Sts can write out their argument in full, ensuring they structure it logically. However, get them to rehearse so they don't just read it aloud.

If possible, sts record their opinion in class using a cell phone. Allow sts to re-record if they aren't happy. It's all good practice and everybody wants the best possible end product. Encourage sts to swap recordings with a partner and give each other feedback. You could play some of the answers to the whole class, and get class feedback. Ask: *Which argument did you think was most convincing?*

Optional activity

Hold a class debate on one of the topics in 5. See technique on Teacher's Book p.62.

3 Reading

A Read the blog about the future. The main purpose of the blog is to ...

- ☐ frighten people.
- ☐ encourage people to read about environmental problems.
- ☐ encourage people to join the organization and take action.

FIFTY YEARS FROM NOW ... by David Montalbán

When most people think about the future, they only think of positive developments: advances in medicine and technology, better living conditions, higher salaries. Concernedcitizens.id. is more realistic. The future is in our hands only if we are aware and responsible. Some of these facts may shock you!

- In a recent year, 22 million people, many of them poor, were displaced by natural disasters. People living in coastal areas will continue to suffer in the years ahead. Yet, despite enormous evidence to the contrary, some scientists still argue that computer models are "not sophisticated enough" to predict climate change. Is it that they don't want to spend money to control carbon monoxide emissions that raise the earth's temperature? What can you do to prevent global warming?
- By 2050, the Earth's population will have increased from 7 billion to 9.6 billion people. There will not be enough resources for so many people, especially if flooding and drought increase due to climate change. We will need more recycling and more solar energy. Farmers will need incentives to grow food in an environmentally sound way. But do you know how to prevent overuse of fertilizers or how to increase sustainable farming on dry land? And do you recycle all you can?

If these and other facts concern you, become involved! Contact us at concernedcitizens.id to see how you can get help. The future is now!

B In pairs, search on "global warming" or "preserving our resources." Then answer one of the writer's questions in a way you think he'd agree with.

4 Self-test

Correct the two mistakes in each sentence. Check your answers in Units 11 and 12. What's your score, 1–20?

1 I try to keep up the news, even though it's often bias.
2 My girlfriend said me she was sorry and admitted me she was wrong.
3 I promised her to keep the secret, and I agreed her not to tell anyone.
4 I explained my teacher I'm not sure of the answer.
5 My mother persuaded me apologize and she made me to call right away.
6 I'm definitely optimist, so I'm keeping my fingers cross about the future.
7 We're going there on bus, and as soon as we'll arrive, I'll be in touch.
8 By the time you read this, you will almost finish *Identities*, and you will likely to know a lot of English!
9 I'm giving you a call later. Maybe I'm taking a nap first.
10 I visit Larry this weekend, so I won't see you until I'll get back.

5 Point of view

Choose a topic. Then support your opinion in 100–150 words, and record your answer. Ask a partner for feedback. How can you be more convincing?

a You think gossip is part of human nature and no big deal. OR
You think gossip can be very dangerous and should be avoided at all cost.

b You think the economic situation is bad, and there's a lot to be pessimistic about. OR
You think there will always be jobs for people who are well qualified, and it's important to be optimistic.

1 *stop*, *remember*, *forget*, and *try* do after 1.2

I **stopped to buy** some meat for dinner. (= I stopped at the store in order to buy meat.) I **stopped buying** meat when I became a vegetarian. (= I no longer buy meat.)
I **remembered to call** Dad on his birthday. (= I didn't forget to call Dad.) I'm sure I talked to Dad last week, but I don't even **remember calling** him. (= I don't have a memory of the fact that I called Dad.)
I sometimes **forget to call** my parents to say I'll be late. (= I don't always remember to call my parents.) I'll **never forget calling** my parents to say I was getting married. They were so thrilled! (= I remember clearly calling my parents.)
I'm **trying to concentrate**. Please be quiet. (= I'm attempting to concentrate.) I **tried writing** down new words, but I still couldn't remember them. (= I experimented with writing down new words.)

More on *try* and *forget*

Only use *try* + *-ing* when the meaning is "to experiment with something." When the meaning is "to attempt," use an infinitive:

I've been **trying to be** nicer to my little sister.

Only use *forget* + *-ing* to remember the past. Otherwise, use the infinitive.

I sometimes **forget to set** the alarm, and then I'm late for school.

2 Using the infinitive with adjectives: More on negative sentences do after 1.4

Pay close attention to the position of the negative. Whether it goes with the verb or the adjective often depends on what's being emphasized.
It's important for you **not** to go. (= You shouldn't go.) It's **not** important for you to go. (= You don't have to go.)
It's critical for my daughter **not** to fail her exam. (= She must pass.) It's **not** critical for my daughter to pass her exam. (= It's OK if she fails.)

Sometimes if you move the negative, the sentence no longer makes sense. When in doubt, say the sentence aloud.
It's essential **not** to feel intimidated during an interview. (= Relax and don't feel intimidated.)
~~It's **not** essential to feel intimidated during an interview~~. (= Meaning is unclear.)

Sometimes both choices are possible and have a very similar meaning.	
It's **not** helpful to ... It's helpful **not** to ...	pressure your children. (= You shouldn't pressure them.)

1A Complete 1–8 with the infinitive or *-ing* form of the verbs.

1 I remember _________ (meet) Tim at a party last year. He was thinner then.
2 We stopped _________ (look) at the flowers. They were really beautiful.
3 I'm trying _________ (finish) as fast as I can! Be patient.
4 She stopped _________ (go) to dance class. She said it was really boring.
5 At the last minute, we remembered _________ (take) an umbrella. It's a good thing because it started pouring!
6 He forgot _________ (check) that the door was locked, and a robber walked in.
7 I tried _________ (take) French classes, but in the end, I realized I liked English better.
8 I just can't forget _________ (see) Tom again after all these years. I think I'm still in love!

1B **Make it personal** Write and share three facts about yourself. Use *remember*, *stop*, *try*, or *forget*.

2A Match the sentence beginnings with the most logical ending.

1 It's important not to — a ☐ agree with everything your teenager says.
2 It's not important to — b ☐ contradict your children in front of their friends. It could embarrass them.

3 It's not essential for you to — a ☐ understand your children at all times.
4 It's essential for you not to — b ☐ have rigid opinions.

5 It's not critical for older parents to — a ☐ be stuck in the past.
6 It's critical for older parents not to — b ☐ be up-to-date with technology.

2B Choose two sentences you agree with from A. Then give a reason for your opinion.

2C Circle the most logical options. When both seem possible, circle both.

[1][**It's important not to / It's not important to**] think all teenagers are alike. People mature at different rates, and [2][**it's useful not to / it's not useful to**] make comparisons. If you want to have a good relationship with your teen, [3][**it's essential not to / it's not essential to**] make unrealistic demands. In addition, things were very different when you were young, and it's [4][**critical not to / not critical to**] be closed-minded. Teens listen to their friends more than their parents, and it's [5][**helpful not to / not helpful to**] begin sentences with "When I was your age ... "

Bonus! Language in song

♫ It's been a hard day's night, and I've been working like a dog.

- What do you think the expression "a hard day's night" means?
- Give the singer from 1.3 on page 11 some advice beginning with "It's important (not) to ..."

1 Sentences with complements and conjunctions

do after 2.2

Sentences with complements can be followed by a conjunction and another sentence.			
Less formal	The most difficult thing about having children is it's expensive,	**and**	it's hard work, too.
	The advantage of working is I make money,	**so**	I'm looking for a job.
	The great thing about exercise is losing weight,	**but**	it's time-consuming.
More formal	The problem with teenagers is they don't think.	**Furthermore,**	they don't listen.
	The problem with English is pronunciation.	**Therefore,**	I need more practice.
	The great thing about technology is being connected all the time.	**However,**	it's expensive.

Common mistake

The problem with coffee is it keeps me ~~up so~~ *up, so* I never drink it at night.

The great thing about coffee is the ~~taste, however~~ *taste. However,* it keeps me up.

2 More on modals

do after 2.4

Using modals in negative sentences		
	Present	Past
Maybe it's true.	There might / may **not** be aliens.	It might / may **not** have visited us.
I'm pretty sure it's true.	It must **not** be a ghost.	You must **not** have seen him.
I really doubt it's true.	You can'**t** / could**n't** be serious!	It can'**t** / could**n't** have been an alien.

Common mistake

He ~~mustn't~~ *must not* have been home. He would have opened the door. I'm pretty sure.

Mustn't expresses prohibition in British English (American English = *can't*), but it cannot express probability.

Using modals in continuous sentences		
	Present	Past
Maybe it's true.	They **might / may (not) be watching** TV.	He **might / may (not) have been** robbing the house.
I'm pretty sure it's true.	It **must (not) be raining**.	You **must (not) have been paying attention**.
I really doubt it's true.	You **can't / couldn't be thinking** clearly!	We **can't / couldn't have been driving** that fast.

Common mistake

He ~~must have been~~ *was probably* being influenced by others.

Modal verbs are not used in the passive in continuous tenses.

1A Combine two advantages of fast food, or an advantage and a disadvantage, to give five opinions with conjunctions. Watch your punctuation!

Advantages	Disadvantages
it's ready made	it's not fresh
it tastes good	it usually has too much salt
it doesn't go bad	you don't know how old it is
it's not expensive	it's bad for you
you always enjoy your meal	children need healthy food
children love it	
they sell it everywhere	

The good thing about fast food is that it's ready made. However, you don't know how old it is.

1B Share in pairs. How many different combinations did you make in A?

2A Rewrite the underlined parts of the sentences with an affirmative or negative modal verb.

1 I really doubt there's life on other planets. We would have had some visitors by now.
2 I'm worried about Tim. He didn't answer his phone, but maybe he was sleeping.
3 I'm pretty sure Sheila didn't take her keys, and that's why she had to sleep in a hotel.
4 I'm pretty sure Amy wasn't paying attention. That's why she had an accident.
5 I really doubt a monkey was climbing in the window! You must have seen a shadow.
6 Roger didn't show up for his appointment because I'm pretty sure he didn't remember it.

2B Complete the story with past modal verbs in the continuous form, using the verbs in parentheses.

Ape costume or the real thing?

No one would believe this, but a gorilla [1]*might have been living* (maybe / live) in my neighborhood last year. It was filmed on video at about 1:00 a.m. one Saturday night. At that moment, a car [2]________ (probably / approach) because the headlights revealed a gorilla's face on a video the neighbors had installed to monitor coyotes. Then, suddenly, it disappeared.
It [3]________ (maybe / hide) behind some parked cars because no one could find it. I think the gorilla was frightened. It [4]________ (probably / not / expect) to see anyone.
When I told the story to my brother, though, he said the neighborhood [5]________ (probably / imagine) things. A gorilla [6]________ (very much doubt / walk) in the neighborhood. A person [7]________ (probably / wear) an ape costume. He or she [8]________ (maybe / come) home from a party.

2C **Make it personal** Using modals, share something surprising about your own neighborhood that you can't explain.

I think someone might be living on our roof. I found a shoe in the elevator!

Bonus! Language in song

♫ All day long I think of things, but nothing seems to satisfy. Think I'll lose my mind if I don't find something to pacify.

Rewrite this song lyric from 2.1, beginning with "The most difficult thing about my day is ... " Then combine the two sentences in the song with a conjunction.

1 Uses of the past perfect do after 3.2

The past perfect is used to avoid misunderstanding.

When my boyfriend **got** home,	he **texted** me. (= the actions occurred almost simultaneously)
	he **had already texted** me. (= he texted before he got home)
By the time my boyfriend got home,	he **had (already) texted** me. (= identical in meaning to above)

1 Always use the past perfect with *by the time*. Add *already* to avoid ambiguity.
2 We often avoid the past perfect when a misunderstanding is unlikely, even if one action clearly takes place before another.
- I **didn't get up** in time to have breakfast before I left for school.
- When the singer **walked** on stage, everyone **applauded**.

Common mistake

Oh hi, I ~~hadn't seen~~ *didn't see* you earlier. Sorry I didn't say "hello."

The past perfect is common with these expressions:
I was already working **by the time** I'd started college.
I didn't start studying English **until after** I'd finished high school.
I had studied English **before** / **previously**, but I didn't remember much.
I had **already** bought a house when I got married.
I hadn't bought a house **yet** when I had children.
I **still** hadn't saved much money when I turned 30.
Up until last year, I'd never met anyone from the U.S.

2 Past narration do after 3.4

Use *used to* and *would* to set the scene. Then use past tenses to show the order of events and whether they were continuous.

We **used to live** in an old house, and every so often we **would hear** noises. One day, I **was brushing** my teeth when I **heard** a strange, high-pitched sound. Before I could figure out where it **was coming** from, I **saw** glass on the floor. Someone or something **had broken** the window.

1A Complete the conversations with the correct form of the verbs in parentheses.

1 A: When I was a child, I really ________ (enjoy) playing alone.
B: Really? I never did.

2 A: When I arrived at the party, everyone ________ (leave).
B: You mean no one was there at all?

3 A: When Susanna arrived at the airport, her brother ________ (greet) her warmly.
B: I bet she was really happy to see him.

4 A: Hello, when I ________ (call) this morning for an appointment, no one ________ (answer) the phone.
B: Oh, we're so sorry. When would you like to come?

5 A: When Amy met George, she ________ (already / date) several other guys.
B: Yes, but he was "the one" for her from the second she saw him!

6 A: I was so worried about Tim when he disappeared on our hike.
B: Yes, when Sue and I finally saw him, we ________ (run) up and ________ (hug) him.

1B **Make it personal** Complete 1–6 so they are true for you. Use each verb only once. Share with a partner. Did you learn anything new?

be decide do go learn start

1 Up until last year, I ________________________________.
2 I __________ yet when I ________________________________.
3 Before I __________, I __________ never ________________________.
4 Until after __________, I ________________________________.
5 By the time I __________, I __________ already ________________________.
6 I still __________ when I ________________________________.

2A Circle the correct forms to complete the story.

I [1][**used to love** / **would love**] going to the beach, and I would go there whenever we could. One day I [2][**was** / **had been**] in the car with some friends when all of a sudden, I [3][**realized** / **had realized**] I had left my bathing suit at home. By the time I [4][**discovered** / **had discovered**] I didn't have it, we [5][**drove** / **had driven**] for over three hours. I still [6][**didn't go** / **hadn't gone**] swimming that summer, so I decided to make a bathing suit. First, I [7][**took** / **had taken**] my blouse, and I cut off the sleeves. Then I [8][**rolled** / **had rolled**] up the bottom and tied it to look like a bikini. I [9][**saw** / **had seen**] a friend do that previously, and it looked like a real bathing suit. Then I [10][**did** / **had done**] the same with my jeans. And here's the selfie I [11][**took** / **had taken**]! Only after I [12][**went** / **had gone**] swimming and everyone had complimented me on my new bathing suit, did I realize that I [13][**had** / **'d had**] no clothes to wear home!

2B **Make it personal** When was the last time you left something important at home? Complete the paragraph. Who has the best story?

One day I ________ when I realized I'd forgotten my ________. By the time I remembered, I ________. When I arrived at ________, I had to ________. To this day, I still ______________________.

Bonus! Language in song

♫ I **used to rule** the world, Seas **would rise** when I **gave** the word, Now in the morning I sleep alone, Sweep the streets I **used to own**.

Which verbs in **bold** can be replaced by a different past form?

1 Using conjunctions do after 4.2

Common conjunctions fall into several categories of meaning.		
Adding	**Comparing / Contrasting**	**Conceding**
besides	unlike	although
moreover	while	even though
what's more	whereas	though
	but	despite
	however	in spite of

Some can be followed by more parts of speech than others. Notice the position of *not* in negative statements.

Although **Even though** **While**	my phone's **not** expensive, (sentence)	it works great.
Despite **In spite of**	the fact that it's **not** expensive, (clause) **not** being expensive, (*-ing* form)	it has tons of features.
	the expense, (noun)	I buy a new phone every year.

2 More on reflexive pronouns do after 4.4

Some verbs are commonly used with reflexive pronouns.

Be careful! You'll **cut yourself**.
Melanie dived into the pool and **hurt herself**.
I really **enjoyed myself** last night at the party.
I met Sam at the concert when he came up and **introduced himself**.
Can you believe John and Louise **taught themselves** to speak Arabic?

Other verbs: *prepare, dry, help, imagine, express*

Other verbs, however, only use a reflexive pronoun for emphasis.

I forgot to **shave** today. I hope it's not obvious!
I forgot to **shave myself**. I was in a really big hurry this morning.

Other verbs: *feel, shower, get dressed, get up*

And some verbs, such as *concentrate* or *focus*, don't use reflexive pronouns.

I couldn't **concentrate** in class today. I was so tired!

1A Combine 1–7 in two different ways, using the conjunctions in parentheses.

1 I did a lot of research. I was taken in by the phone company's offer. (*despite* + *-ing*; *although*)
Despite doing a lot of research, I was taken in by the phone company's offer.
Although I did a lot of research, I was taken in by the phone company's offer.
2 I still failed my English test. I studied all night. (*in spite of* + clause; *even though*)
3 I'm able to work at my own pace. I'm not a fan of the flipped classroom. (*in spite of* + *-ing*; *although*)
4 My friends don't make much money. They still have nicer clothes than I do. (*despite* + clause; *while*)
5 Mountain climbing can be dangerous. I really enjoy it. (*despite* + noun; *while*)
6 I read lots of hotel reviews before I went to Berlin. I still paid too much. (*in spite of* + clause; *though*)
7 My brother is a genius. He's a nice person. (*besides* + *-ing*; *what's more*)

1B **Make it personal** Changing only the second part of the sentence in A, share four facts about yourself. Any surprises?

Although I did a lot of research, I still bought the wrong computer.

1C Find and correct Amanda's four mistakes. Then role play the conversation ending with "No, none at all!"

JIM: Your English has really improved in the last year.
AMANDA: You really think so? Despite study every day, grammar is still difficult.
JIM: But you have a really good accent.
AMANDA: Well, in spite of I might have a good accent, I still have a long way to go.
JIM: Maybe you could practice grammar by having a language exchange: you know, find someone who wants to learn Portuguese.
AMANDA: That's a good idea. I really try. However that my English will never be perfect. Conjunctions are so difficult!
JIM: Well, you just have to feel comfortable.
AMANDA: Yes, you're right. In spite of it's challenging, I should keep at it.
JIM: Yes, that's it.
AMANDA: How's my grammar today? Did I make any mistakes?
JIM: Well, just a few small ones!

2A Circle the correct options to complete the paragraph about Sayeed's visit to New York.

Every night I dreamed about my vacation. In my dream, I was staying [1][**myself** / **ø**] in an expensive hotel, right off Fifth Avenue with my cousin Laura. Every morning we got up [2][**ourselves** / **ø**] early to sightsee. Wherever we went, we dressed [3][**ourselves** / **ø**] fashionably. In fancy restaurants, I would often introduce [4][**myself** / **ø**] to famous actors. We taught [5][**ourselves** / **ø**] to think like celebrities, and in general, we felt great [6][**ourselves** / **ø**]! But, of course, it was all a dream, and at 7:00 every morning, I had to wake up [7][**myself** / **ø**], shower [8][**myself** / **ø**], and go to work.

2B Correct the mistakes.

1 I'm having trouble focusing myself in class. I'm always tired.
2 The students looked at them in the mirror and were pleasantly surprised by their appearance.
3 I went to a concert last night, and I really enjoyed.
4 When my daughter concentrates herself, she can succeed at anything.
5 My grandparents were immigrants, but they taught himself to speak perfect English.

Bonus! Language in song

♫ It took myself by surprise I must say. When I found out yesterday. Don't you know that I heard itself through the grapevine?

Are the reflexive pronouns correct? Correct the mistakes.

1 Imaginary situations: *hope, wish, if only,* and *supposing* do after 5.2

Future	I **hope you'll be** quiet during the performance. (= I don't know if you'll be quiet.)
Present	I **wish you'd be** quiet when I'm talking. (= You're not quiet, and it's annoying me.)
Past	I **hope** I **didn't fail** my test. (= I don't know if I failed.)
Past	I **wish** I **hadn't failed** my test. (= I failed, and I'm sorry I did.)
Future	**If only** I **could see** Sarah again. (= I don't think I'll ever see her again, and I miss her so much.)
Past	**If only** I **could have seen** Sarah again. (= I didn't see her and I'm sure we would have gotten back together.)
Future	**Supposing** Sarah **wanted** to go out with you again, would you say yes? (= It's unlikely Sarah will want to go out with you again.)
Past	**Supposing** Sarah **had wanted** to go out with you again, would you have said yes? (= She didn't want to go out with you again.)

Common mistake

hope
I ~~wish~~ I'll be able to go out tonight.

2 Shortening conditional sentences do after 5.4

Zero, first, second, third, and mixed conditionals can all be shortened when the information referred to is understood. The auxiliary cannot be contracted.		
Zero	My brother never **helps** me. If / When he **does** (help me),	I feel better.
First	I don't think my sister **is coming.** If she **is** (coming),	I'll be really happy.
Second	I **don't have** my parents' help. If I **did** (have my parents' help),	I'd go to college.
Third	I **didn't have** my parents' help. If I **had** (had my parents' help),	I would have gone to college.
Mixed	We **didn't make** any money. If we **had** (made money),	we wouldn't be living here any longer.

All conditionals can be contracted in a shorter way also.	
First	**With** my parents' help, I'll be able to go to college.
Third	**Without** my parents' help, I wouldn't have gone to college.

1A Complete the sentences with the correct form of *hope* or *wish* and the verb.

1 A: I ________ Ann ________ (call) me tomorrow. I really need to talk to her!
B: Oh, I'm sure she will.

2 A: I ________ my mother ________ (spend) more time with me when I was young.
B: I feel the same way. Mine was always working.

3 A: I really ________ I ________ (not fail) my final exams.
B: I'm sure you'll do well if you study!

4 A: I ________ I ________ (know) how to drive. It's such a useful skill.
B: Why don't you take lessons?

5 A: John ________ he ________ (not quit) school.
B: Yes, that wasn't too smart. You need a college education these days.

6 A: I ________ I ________ (not upset) my little brother when I yelled at him.
B: I don't think he's upset. Look, he's smiling!

1B Which is the full form? Write *had* or *would*.

1 Sue wishes she'**d** apologized sooner. *had*
2 Jim wishes I'**d** asked him to the party.
3 I wish they'**d** hurry up and finish.
4 We all wish they'**d** come to visit last year.
5 I wish they'**d** decide about this year.
6 I wish you'**d** sent the package yesterday.

1C Make it personal Share three hopes and three wishes that are true for you.

I really hope I ... , and I really wish I ...

2A Rewrite these short sentences using the word *if*.

1 With hard work, you can learn anything.
If you work hard, you can learn anything.
2 Without good grades, I never would have gotten into college.
3 With really good luck, maybe I'll win the lottery.
4 Without studying really hard, I wouldn't have passed the exam.
5 Without a lot of practice, you'll never learn to speak English.
6 Without the help of my parents, I wouldn't be living in this house today.

2B Shorten the underlined parts of each sentences, beginning with the word in parentheses.

When I was young, I didn't have many role models. [1]<u>If I'd had good role models</u> (with), I wouldn't have ended up in so much trouble. [2]<u>If I hadn't had the support of my neighbor Melanie</u> (without), I'd still be on the streets. She convinced me that I should go back to school. [3]<u>If I didn't go back to school</u> (if), she said, I'd be tempted to live a life of crime. [4]<u>But if I had a good education</u> (with), I'd have a satisfying career. I really listened to her. [5]<u>If I hadn't listened to her</u> (if), I might still be running around with those guys. I'll always be grateful to Melanie. [6]<u>If I didn't have her</u> (without), who knows where I'd be today.

2C Make it personal Write three sentences about your own role model. Be sure to use short conditional sentences. Choose from these topics or one of your own.

Someone who helped you ...
make friends   stay out of trouble   choose a career
understand your parents   learn a new skill
meet your boyfriend / girlfriend

I'll always remember the boy who sat next to me at my new school. Without him ...

Bonus! Language in song

♫ I can be your hero, baby, I can kiss away the pain.

Rewrite this song line beginning with *I hope*, *I wish*, or *If only*.

1 Questions in the passive do after 6.2

		Subject	*be*	Verb (+ *by*)
Simple present	Are	you	–	(ever) watched by your parents?
Present continuous	Are	you	being	bullied online?
Simple past	Were	you	–	(ever) spied on as a child?
Present perfect	Has	your profile	(ever) been	broken into?
Future	Will	teachers	be	replaced by computers?

The pattern is the same with question words.				
How often	has	your profile	been	accessed?

Causative sentences are always passive in meaning. The causative with *get* is a little more informal.

	Auxiliary	Subject	*have* or *get*	Object	Verb (+ *by*)
Present continuous	Are	you	having getting	your hair	cut by Ralph?
Simple past	Did	Amy	have get	her sentence	reduced?

Using the passive

The passive is very common in English and makes impersonal questions sound polite.
Can the phone **be exchanged** after 30 days?
Could I **have** my hard drive **checked**, please?

Common mistake

How many people ~~were~~ *was* your profile seen by?

Be careful with subject-verb agreement!

2 Uses of *whatever* do after 6.2

In spoken English, ***whatever*** often expresses strong advice or a warning:
- **Whatever** you do, don't talk about politics on Facebook®.

Whatever is also used to end conversations and avoid arguments:
- "You spend far too long online!" "Yeah, yeah, **whatever** (you say)."

Fixed expressions like ***whatever that means*** and ***whatever it's called*** can be used when you don't know, remember, or understand something:
- Mom says she's going to keep tabs on me "selectively," **whatever** that means.

1A Put the words in order to make questions. (Each has one extra word.)

1 to / by / ever / will / replaced / paper books / be / e-books / ?
2 does / why / still / is / considered / the iPad / a revolution in teaching / ?
3 being / students' / should / from the classroom / banned / be / native languages / ?
4 removed / be / from / always / photos / have / Facebook® / you / when friends ask you to / ?
5 privacy / can / your / be / how / you / violated by credit card companies / ?

1B **Make it personal** Ask and answer the questions. How many similar opinions?

1C Make conversations 1–4 more natural and polite. Replace the underlined sentences with sentences in the passive.

1 A: I 'd like you to check my computer, please.
B: OK, right this way.
2 A: Should you replace the battery?
B: Yes, that would be a good idea.
3 A: Will you repair this water damage by tomorrow?
B: We'll certainly try our best.
4 A: Have you fixed my phone yet?
B: We're very busy today, ma'am. I promise we'll get to it.

1D Trivia time! Complete 1–5 with questions in the passive. Then search on "fun trivia" and create two more questions.

1 Where ________________ ?
The Soccer World Cup? I think it was held in Brazil in 2014, wasn't it?
2 How many ________________ ?
The song *Imagine*? I'm sure it's been recorded well over 100 times. And translated, too!
3 Who ________________ ?
Everyone knows that! The Sistine Chapel was painted by Michelangelo.
4 Where ________________ ?
Ceviche? That's that dish with raw fish and citrus juices, isn't it? I think it's eaten throughout Latin America.
5 Where in the world ________________ ?
It's obvious you haven't been to Paris. The Mona Lisa can be seen at the Louvre!

2A Replace the underlined phrases with these expressions. There is one extra.

whatever you do   whatever the cost   whatever time   whatever   whatever that means

1 A: Oh no, why isn't the site loading?
B: It says here "bad gateway," but I'm not sure what that is. Let's try Bruno's iPad.
2 A: So you're moving on Sunday?
B: Yeah, and even if it's really expensive, I've decided to use a moving company.
3 A: But you said you wanted to go to the concert!
B: It doesn't matter. I've changed my mind.
4 A: I'm taking my first trip abroad next month.
B: Great, but don't let your credit cards out of your sight, under any circumstances.

2B **Make it personal** Start a conversation about home, school or leisure. How many ideas can you think of?

... and I mean it!

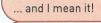

Yeah, yeah, whatever! That's the third time you've said the same thing in the last ten minutes.

Bonus! Language in song

♫ I always feel like somebody's watching me. And I have no privacy.

Make the first sentence in this song line passive.

1 More on *so* do after 7.2

So vs. *such* as intensifiers		
I'm	**so**	excited about the concert.
It's going to be		great!
I'm	**such**	a fan of Bruno Mars.
He's		a great singer.
There are	**so many**	people out there.
I've never heard	**so much**	noise.
Use *so* + adjective, but use *such* + (adjective +) noun. Use *so many* + count nouns, but *so much* + non-count nouns.		

Expressing purpose with *so as (not) to*		
I left an hour early	**so as to**	be on time for the interview.
I gave up my seat	**so as not to**	seem selfish.
So as (not) to means "in order (not) to," but is more formal. The negative *so as not to* is more common in conversation than the affirmative *so as to*.		

2 *because*, *because of*, and *for* do after 7.2

I couldn't go to the concert	**because of**	the expense. rain.
	because	it was expensive. I didn't have an umbrella.
John was fired	**for**	arguing with his boss.

More on *for*	
To express a reason	*For* meaning "because" or "as a result of" can replace *because of* in very few situations. Memorize phrases with *for* when you hear them. ▸ I canceled my trip **for (because of)** health reasons. ▸ John married Sue **for (because of)** her money.
	When in doubt, use *because of*. *For* to express a reason is often ungrammatical. ▸ I didn't buy a ticket ~~for~~ **because of** the expense. ▸ I felt sick on the plane ~~for~~ **because of** turbulence.
	Only use *for* to express a reason when an *-ing* form follows. ▸ She was arrested **for** arguing with a police officer. ▸ I yelled at my brother **for not** turning off the lights.
To express a purpose	*For* is often used, however, to express purpose. ▸ I went to the store **for** some bread. ▸ I sent in the paperwork **for** my application.

3 Other ways of specifying do after 7.4

Either ... or, both ... and, and *not only ... but also*
You choose the music. **Either** Adele **or** Shakira is fine. I really like **both** Taylor Swift **and** Katy Perry. I listen **not only** to rock **but also** to jazz.

1A Make sentences with *so, such, so much*, or *so many*. Then suggest a solution for each problem.

1 ... noise outside that I can't sleep.
2 .... people with cars that it's impossible to park.
3 ... good desserts, but I can't eat any because I'm on a diet.
4 ... exciting to travel to new places, but I don't have any money.
5 .... homework that I'll never finish it all before Monday.
6 ... nice person, but when we didn't agree, he refused to speak to me.

There's so much noise outside that I can't sleep!

Why don't you just shut the window?

1B Make five sentences using one item in each column.

A	B	C
1 I walk to school	so as not to in order not to	burn out.
2 I call my parents every day		forget any vocabulary.
3 I take at least one vacation a year		have to wait for the bus.
4 I hardly ever go to museums		pay the entrance fee.
5 I read three books in English a year		worry them.

1C **Make it personal** Change three sentences in B so they are true. Share them. Any surprises?

I walk to school in order not to take the bus with my brother.

2A Correct the errors (1–6) in the story.

I was so excited that I was going to see Shakira in concert, but when we got to the stadium, the concert had been canceled (1) for rain. (2) Because of it had just started, the organizers were totally unprepared. No one wanted to go home, and one woman was arrested (3) because jumping over a fence. (4) For the chaos, I was really scared someone might get hurt. (5) Because of there had been no warning, everyone was so upset. I just went home and went right to sleep (6) for my disappointment.

2B Complete the sentences using *for* and the correct form of these reasons.

not come home on time   leave the refrigerator open   speak English   talk back to my boss   write the best essay

1 I was fired ________ . She said I was totally rude.
2 My mother yelled at me ________ . All of the food spoiled.
3 I got an award ________ . I really worked hard at it.
4 I felt proud of myself ________ . I was a little self-conscious of my accent, though.
5 I was punished ________ . My parents were so worried.

3A Make sentences using *either ... or, both ... and*, or *not only ... but also*.

1 English / Chinese
2 Brazilian music / Latino music
3 the guitar / the piano
4 modern art / impressionism
5 novels / mysteries

3B **Make it personal** Guess whether your partner's sentences are true. If you think they're false, correct them.

I speak both English and Chinese.

That's false. You speak both English and Spanish, though!

Bonus! Language in song

♫ Music makes the people come together. Music mix the bourgeoisie and the rebel.

- Correct a grammatical mistake in this song line.
- Combine the two sentences starting with *since* or *because*.

1 More on expressing ability do after 8.2

Present	I	**can / 'm able to**	speak five languages.	1
		can	give him a call now.	2
Past	I	**could / was able to**	see the ocean in the distance.	3
		was able to	get in touch with my brother.	4
Future	I	**'ll be able to**	speak French a year from now.	5
Present perfect	I	**can / 'll be able to**	see you tomorrow.	6
		've been able to	swim since I was three.	7
Verb + verb	I'd love to	**be able to**	come to your wedding.	8

Use *be able to*, but not *can*:
- for specific past events. (sentence 4)
- for something you will learn little by little. (sentence 5)
- with perfect tenses. (sentence 7)
- after another verb. (sentence 8)

Use *can*, but not *be able to*, when you offer to do something. (sentence 2)

2 Uses of *be supposed to* do after 8.2

We	**were supposed to**	arrive in the morning, but there was a delay.
I	**had to**	wait hours because I missed my connection.
We	**weren't supposed to**	have any of these headaches. I expected an easy trip!
I	**didn't have to**	be understanding, but I decided to be nice about it.

Be supposed to is often used to express something that turned out differently than expected. *Have to* is often used to express something that was inevitable.

Common mistake

The bus ~~had to~~ *was supposed to* be here at 2:30. Where is it?

3 Obligation and advice in the past do after 8.4

Obligation	I **had to** get a visa to enter Russia.	I **didn't have** to get a visa to go to Bermuda. My passport was good enough.
Strong advice	You'**d better** have packed some warm clothes before you left! It's freezing here.	I know you packed quickly, but you'**d better not have** forgotten your coat!
Advice	You **should have** / **ought to have** visited Times Square. Too bad you didn't.	You **shouldn't have** missed it. Well, too late now!

Remember! *Must have* in the past expresses probability, not obligation.
I **must have left** my passport at home. (= I'm pretty sure I left it at home.)

1A Circle the most logical options.

1 Don't worry. I [**can** / **'m able to**] speak to your brother today and ask for help.
2 I was terrified when the rollercoaster started its descent, but I [**could** / **was able to**] hold on tight.
3 Even though I can't cook very well now, I'm taking lessons, and I'm sure I [**can** / **'ll be able to**] cook next year.
4 Don't worry. I [**can** / **'m able to**] call the travel agency and ask if there's another flight.
5 I [**'ve been able to** / **can**] save money to buy a house, and I'm moving next week.
6 I'd like to [**can** / **be able to**] fly, but my heart starts to race at the thought of getting on a plane.

1B In pairs, which rules from 1 helped you choose the correct answer?

The first one sounds like an offer, so you have to use *can*.

2A Complete the sentences with the correct form of *have to* or *be supposed to* and the verbs.

1 Our plane ________ (arrive) by 10 p.m., but it didn't come in until midnight, so we ________ (spend) the night in a hotel.
2 I know Barry is difficult! He ________ (be) away today, but he came to work unexpectedly, so I ________ (invite) him to the picnic with everyone else.
3 My Mom ________ (be) here! If she hadn't come home early, she wouldn't have caught us looking at her computer.
4 My boyfriend ________ (meet) me at the airport, but he always thinks of others. He didn't want me to take the bus.
5 There was no parking at all! I ________ (drive) around the neighborhood for at least a half hour.
6 We ________ (get) our test results last Friday, but we didn't, so I ________ (live) with my anxiety all last weekend. I'm glad I passed in the end!

2B Make it personal Thinking on your feet! Share three things that you didn't expect to happen, but did. What did you do?

Well, I wasn't supposed to fail math because I did my homework every day, but when I did, I had to find a tutor.

3A Are these conversations logical? Correct the mistakes in the underlined words.

1 A: Oh, no! I can't find our passports. But maybe they're in this bag.
B: You <u>should have brought</u> them, or they won't let us on the plane. I reminded you three times!
2 A: I loved the U.S. It's a shame I didn't have time to go to the Grand Canyon.
B: You<u>'d better have found</u> time to go there. Who knows when you'll be back in Arizona.
3 A: Look at that rain! You <u>didn't have to leave</u> the windows open. Our carpet will be ruined!
B: Don't worry so much! I'm pretty sure I closed them.
4 A: I found out my license had expired, and I <u>should have taken</u> another driving test.
B: That sounds awful! I'm sure it's not what you were expecting.

3B Make it personal Share three fears and regrets using *(didn't) have to*, *had better (not) have*, and *was(n't) supposed to have*. Your partner will cheer you up.

I'd better not have left my car unlocked! It might be gone!

Bonus! Language in song

♫ How am I supposed to live without you? How am I supposed to carry on? When all that I've been livin' for is gone.

Grammatically, *can* and *be able to* can both replace *be supposed to* in this song line. Sing the line to yourself. Which one do you think sounds better?

1 Common prepositions ending relative clauses do after 9.2

I gave the plants **to** a neighbor.	→	That's the neighbor (who / that) I gave the plants **to**.
We used to live **in** this house.		It's near the house (that) we used to live **in**.
I arrived **at** this airport.		Your flight leaves from the airport (that) you arrived **at**.
John talked **about** the movie.		It was the movie (that) John talked **about**.
The thief was jailed **for** the robbery.		The thief regrets the robbery (that) he was jailed **for**.
He was convicted **of** a crime.		It's a crime (that) he was convicted **of**.
I went on a trip **with** Amy.		Amy is the friend (who / that) I went on a trip **with**.

Common mistake

He's the guy ~~with who~~ *(who)* I went to the party ^ *with*.

She's the woman I was talking ^ *to*.

In conversation, the preposition goes at the end. In very formal English, you may use *whom:* "I'm afraid it's a company **with whom** we no longer have relations."

2 Using relative clauses: summary do after 9.4

Restrictive

I finished the book (**that**) I was reading.
My uncle is someone (**who** / **that**) I've always looked up **to**.
Our school makes rules (**that** / **which**) I don't agree with.

Marcia is a good friend **who** comes over often.
School is something **that** stresses me out.

Millenials are people **whose** values I really admire.
I bought a car **whose** brakes don't work.

That's the house **where** I was born.
It was a time **when** I was really happy.

Common mistake

He was late, ~~what~~ *which* upset me.
My dad, who is usually a sound sleeper, woke up when I came in.

You only have one dad. Remember to add the commas!

Restrictive, reduced

All those **standing** in the back, please exit through the rear door.

People **jogging** regularly may be prone to injuries.

Anyone **caught** entering will be arrested.

Non-restrictive

My grandfather, **who** is 70, bought his house in 1984.

People talk too loudly on their phones, **which** really annoys me.

We went to the theater last night, **where** we were surprised to see Martha.

More on relative pronouns

You can only delete a relative pronoun when the clause:

1. refers to the object of the sentence.
   I finished the book. I was reading it. → I finished the book (that) I was reading.
2. refers to the subject of the sentence, *be* is also deleted, or the verb changes to an *-ing* form.
   A person is speaking. The person is my son. → The person (who is) speaking is my son.

1A Circle the correct alternatives. Then complete the sentences.

1 Something I often worry [**about** / **for**] is ...
2 An issue I'm really interested [**about** / **in**] is ...
3 A time I got yelled [**at** / **to**] was when I ...
4 An event I'm really looking forward [**of** / **to**] is ...
5 Something really worth fighting [**to** / **for**] is ...
6 The hardest two things I've had to choose [**of** / **between**] are ...
7 The kind of person I'd like to get married [**to** / **with**] is ...
8 Something I've often wondered [**of** / **about**] is ...
9 A place I'd like to spend some time [**in** / **on**] is ...
10 A job I'm thinking of applying [**for** / **to**] is ...
11 Something I'm really hoping [**of** / **for**] next week is ...
12 Something I'm never really sure [**to** / **of**] is ...

1B **Make it personal** Share three sentences with a partner. Any surprises?

Something I often worry about is the future of our planet.

2A Add commas where necessary.

1 My only brother who's three years older than me wants to join the army.
2 Sally stepped on my foot three times which really made me mad!
3 We never think about the problems that we should worry about most.
4 My mother who's writing a novel always wanted to be a novelist.
5 Anyone who's caught cheating on this test will have to repeat the course. I mean it!
6 The man who I once almost married just got arrested.

2B Combine the two sentence with *who*, *that*, *which*, *whose*, *where*, or *when*, and true information.

1 I'm fascinated by a country. The country is ...
A country which I'm fascinated by is Japan.
2 I most enjoy spending time with a friend. The friend is ...
3 I take vacations somewhere. The place is ...
4 I really like the sense of humor of someone in this class. The classmate is ...
5 I love a musician's albums. The musician is ...
6 People never ... It really annoys me.

2C ~~Cross out~~ all optional relative pronouns (and any other optional words). Then complete the sentences.

1 The best place that I've ever been to is ...
2 The politicians who are running this country ...
3 A writer whose books I love is ...
4 The type of weather that makes me depressed is ...
5 ... is an activity which I'd really like to be good at.
6 The person in my family who I confide in most is ...
7 These days many people think ... , which is exactly the opposite of what I think.
8 People who are caught stealing sometimes ...

2D In groups, share four opinions from B and C. Who do you have most in common with?

A country that really fascinates me is Japan.

Really? Tell me why. It's a place I know very little about.

Bonus! Language in song

♫ I'm all lost in the supermarket. I can no longer shop happily. I came in here for that special offer. A guaranteed personality.

Combine two of the sentences in this song line with *which*. Do you need a comma before *which*?

1 Responding to indirect questions, negative questions, and tag questions do after 10.2

Answers to all three types of questions may not include the words "yes" or "no," but the meaning is clearly implied.		
Indirect question	**Do you know if** you're coming over?	Sure. I said I would, remember? (= Yes.) Not yet. I'll call you later. (= I don't know.)
Negative question	**Aren't you going** to school today?	I'm leaving right now. (= Yes.) Actually, I'm not feeling well, so I think I'll stay home. (= No.)
Tag question	You have a doctor's appointment today, **don't you?**	It's tomorrow. (= No.) I'll give them a call now. (= I'm not sure.)

Other types of indirect questions may not even sound like questions. They are statements and end with a period, not a question mark.	
Excuse me, **I'm wondering** which way the train station is.	Just turn right at the corner.
I can't understand why checkout is at 11 a.m.	We have other guests arriving and need to clean the rooms.
I'm curious to know whether this bag is leather.	Yes, of course. It's 100% natural leather.
My hesitation is if there's a better discount elsewhere, to be honest.	I can guarantee that our prices are the lowest around.

2 Questions with *be used to*, *get used to*, and *used to* do after 10.4

Questions follow the same patterns as other question forms in the appropriate tenses.	
Present continuous	I wonder if they**'re** slowly **getting used to** the spicy food in Seoul.
Past of *be*	You **weren't used to** the cold weather, **were** you?
Simple past	**Didn't** you **use to live** around here?
Present perfect	You**'ve gotten used to speaking** English by now, **haven't** you?
Modal verbs	**Shouldn't** you **be used to** your husband's snoring by now? You've been married 25 years!
Future with *will*	**Will** I ever **get used to living** abroad?

1A Complete the questions with the words in parentheses in the correct order and form. Then write N (negative question), I (indirect question), or T (tag question).

1 *Why isn't there* a room available today? I had a reservation. (be – neg / there / why) *N*
2 I'm curious to know ________________ the game last night. (win – past / we / whether)
3 Both you and Tom are going to the party tomorrow, ________________? (be – neg / you)
4 ________________ any smaller sizes? These are too big. (have – neg / you)
5 Do you have any idea ________________ to London? I'm totally confused. (go / train / this / if)
6 ________________ at this hotel before? He looks familiar. (stay – past, neg / that / guy)

1B Choose the most likely meaning for each response: *Yes*, *No*, or *I'm not sure*.

1 A: Isn't there a 20 percent discount on these pants?
B: Let me check with the manager.
2 A: Excuse me, could you tell me if there's a good restaurant on this street?
B: Actually, it's all residential down there.
3 A: We were in the same English class together last semester, weren't we?
B: You sure were a great student!
4 A: I can't understand why my car can't be fixed by tomorrow.
B: I'll take another look at our schedule.
5 A: I'd like to know whether these earrings are sterling silver.
B: For this price? But they're very attractive. I'm sure you'll enjoy them.
6 A: Hello, is this reception? I'm wondering if you can give me the WiFi password.
B: You're in Room 252? I'll call you in just a minute.

1C Choose three items and write three new sentences where B is a possible response.

2A Complete the sentences with a form of *be used to*, *get used to*, or *used to*.

1 A: I wonder if I ________ living here. It's so different from where I come from.
B: Give it time. I'm sure you will.
2 A: ________ work at Coffee Xpress, too? I'm positive I've seen you before.
B: No, but I was your next-door neighbor!
3 A: You ________ speaking English by now, haven't you? You've been in the U.S. for five years!
B: Not totally. I still wish I could speak French.
4 A: Your first winter in New York! ________ slowly ________ the cold weather and all the snow?
B: Little by little. But I'd still like to spend January on a beach in the Caribbean!
5 A: ________ travel more when you were younger?
B: No, I never traveled very much. I really didn't have the money.

2B Write three questions with *be used to*, *get used to*, or *used to* that you'd like to ask a classmate. Find the answers in your next class.

Bonus! Language in song

♫ Do you know where you're going to? Do you like the things that life is showing you? Where are you going to? Do you know?

Which song line is an indirect question? Which two lines can be rewritten as an indirect question?

1 More on reported speech do after 11.2

In some situations, the tense does not usually move back.
1 The statement is very recent. "I **want** to go to the movies tonight." → John said he **wants** to go to the movies tonight.
2 The statement is a universal truth. "The sun **rises** in the east and **sets** in the west." → My mother told me that the sun **rises** in the east and **sets** in the west.
3 The statement includes the modal verbs *might* and *should.* "I **might** go to Europe next summer." → Amy said she **might** go to Europe next summer. "We **should** call Mom more often." → They admitted they **should** call their mother more often.

Pronouns in reported sentences change to reflect the perspective of the speaker.

Direct sentence	Speaker	Reported sentence
"Why are **you** leaving?" Sarah's boss asked.	Sarah	My boss asked **me** why **I** was leaving.
	Sarah's friend	Sarah's boss asked **her** why **she** was leaving.

2 Reporting what people say do after 11.4

Notice the patterns possible for these verbs.

Verb	Correct	Incorrect	
I **said***	that I would call	~~her to call~~ ~~her that I would call~~	her parents.
I **told***	her that I would complain	~~to complain~~ ~~that I would complain~~	to her parents.
They **promised**	to keep that they would keep us that they would keep	~~us to keep~~	things secret.
They **agreed**	not to tell that they wouldn't tell	~~us not to tell~~ ~~wouldn't tell~~	anyone.
We **urged**	him to tell	~~to tell~~ ~~that he would tell~~ ~~him that he would tell~~	the truth.
He **threatened**	to call that he would call	~~her to call~~ ~~her that he would call~~	the police.
I **persuaded** We **begged**	them to tell	~~to tell~~ ~~that we would tell~~ ~~them that we would tell~~	their parents.

*Be careful! These sentences have different meanings. The second is a command.
"I'll call your parents." → I **said I would call** her parents.
"Call your parents." → I **said to call** her parents.
"I'll complain to your parents." → I **told her that I would complain** to her parents.
"Complain to your parents." → I **told her to complain** to her parents.

1A Change the sentences to reported speech. Pay careful attention to whether the tense moves back.

1 "You're going to get into trouble."
Sam warned Miles he ______________________.
2 "I'll be at the coffee shop in five minutes." (very recent statement)
Ellen said she ______________________.
3 "Stars only come out at night."
My teacher told us stars ______________________.
4 "I might be a little late tonight."
Phil reminded me he ______________________.
5 "I didn't tell anyone you and Ted broke up."
Melissa reassured me she ______________________.
6 "I didn't break the window!"
Eric denied he ______________________.

1B Report each sentence (a and b) using the correct pronouns.

1 "You can't take the day off, Sally."
a My boss told me ______________________.
b Sally told her parents ______________________.
2 "We're going to be moving, but we'll visit you often."
a My parents told me ______________________.
b My parents told their friends ______________________.
3 "What do you want?"
a The store owner asked us ______________________.
b The boys explained to the store owner ______________________.
4 "I don't have the rent money, so I can't pay you."
a My tenant Sue admitted to me ______________________.
b I told my landlady ______________________.

2A Correct the sentences so they are grammatical, paying attention to the underlined verbs. There may be more than one answer.

1 The guests noticed there had been a robbery, but they agreed me that they would stay calm.
The guests noticed there had been a robbery, but they agreed that they would stay (agreed to stay) calm.
2 Tim wasn't happy about lending me money, but I promised him to pay it back next week.
3 Lisa was very upset about failing her final exams, but I persuaded her that she wouldn't give up.
4 Bob had his credit cards stolen, but I urged him that he would keep his cool and call the bank to cancel them immediately.
5 Beth forgot all her lines during the play, and our director really lost it, but I begged him that he would give her a second chance.
6 Steve fell asleep in an important meeting, and his boss threatened him to fire him the next time it happened.
7 Our local TV station mispronounced my name, and I said them I wasn't happy at all about that.
8 Nancy's boyfriend is always asking her for money, and I told her stop seeing him.

2B Complete each sentence with the correct form of these verbs.

agree	beg	persuade	promise	threaten	urge

1 The way Larry __________ to call the police over a little loud music left me speechless. He shook his fist at us and started screaming!
2 Laura was caught looking through her boss's papers. I __________ her to apologize to him, but she just burst out laughing. (two answers)
3 George found a wallet on a bench. I urged him to try to find the owner, and eventually I __________ him to call the number inside.
4 Liz told me some juicy gossip, but I __________ not to tell a soul! So I really can't tell you, either. My lips are sealed. (two answers)

Bonus! Language in song

♫ You tell me that you're sorry. Didn't think I'd turn around and say that it's too late to apologize. It's too late.

Change the first sentence of this song line to reported speech beginning, "You told me that ... " and the second sentence (after "and") to reported speech beginning, "I said that ... "

1 More on predicting do after 12.2

Both facts and predictions use *going to* or *will*.	
Fact	My sister **is going to be** / **will be** 21 in August.
Prediction	Checks **are going to** / **will disappear** within five years.

When you use the future continuous, you emphasize the ongoing nature of a prediction, but you may also use the future with *will*.	
Future with *will*	People **will live** on the moon by 2030.
Future continuous with *will*	People **will be living** there in small huts.

When you use the future perfect, you emphasize the completion of a prediction by a certain time. This tense is often used with *by the time*.	
Future perfect	By the time you get here, we **will have finished** dinner. Before the end of the year, I **will have spent** all my savings.

If you use *going to*, you sound more certain. Predictions based on present evidence often use *going to*.	
Future with *going to*	Global warming **is going to get** worse.
Future continuous with *going to*	We're **going to be paying** much higher rents a year from now. That's for sure!

When you are less sure of your prediction, you can use *may* or *might*.	
Future continuous with *might*	We **might all be living** on the moon a few years from now.
Future perfect with *may*	By 2050, they **may have sent** people to other planets, too!

Common mistake

Do not use the simple present or present continuous for predictions:

're going to spend / going to be spending
We ~~spend / 're spending~~ more by the end of the year.

2 More on the present continuous as future, *going to*, and *will* do after 12.4

Use the present continuous as future or *going to* when your plan or decision is already made.
I'**m meeting** Pedro after class.
We'**re going to see** a movie.

However, if your plan is far in the future, use *going to:*
I'**m going to become** an engineer like my father.

Use the future with *will* when you're unsure about your plans:
I guess **we'll go** to the Rivoli for lunch.

Also use *will*, but not *going to* ...
1 when you make an offer or decide something as you're speaking:
- The phone's ringing. I'**ll get** it.

2 in stores and restaurants to express your intention:
- I'**ll take** the larger size.
- We'**ll** both **have** the fish.

3 to invite someone:
- **Will you join** us after class for coffee?

4 to make a promise:
- Officer, I promise **I won't speed** in the future!

1A Circle the best options.

1 A: Prices are through the roof! We [**'re going to be paying** / **'re paying**] even more by the end of the year.
B: That's for sure! We [**'ll be** / **'ll have been**] bankrupt soon.
2 A: Look how late we are! By the time we get to Bill and Marcy's, they [**will have left** / **will leave**] without us.
B: Stop worrying so much. I think they [**wait** / **'ll wait**] for us.
3 A: There [**are going to be** / **will be**] layoffs at our company. My boss told me!
B: Oh, no! We [**might be looking** / **might look**] for new jobs very soon!
4 A: By this time next year, we all [**will have graduated** / **will graduate**].
B: How can you be so sure? Maybe some of us [**will fail** / **will be failing**].

1B In pairs, answer these questions for each speaker in A. What other answers are possible?

- Is the event ongoing?
- Is it complete?
- Is the speaker sure?

In the first one, I think you can also say "We'll be paying ..." or even "We might be paying ... ." There's some evidence, but we can't be sure of the future.

2A Complete the conversations with a future form of the verbs in parentheses. There may be more than one answer.

1 A: ________ (you / come) to our party Saturday? We'd love to see you.
B: Oh, I wish I could, but I have some other plans.
2 A:I ________ (not do) it again! I promise.
B: That's what you said the last time! You ________ (not leave) home this weekend!
3 A: When I grow up, I ________ (study) architecture.
B: How can you be so sure? There are a lot of years between now and then.
4 A: What ________ (you / do) this weekend?
B: I ________ (go) camping. Helene invited me to go with her family.
5 A:Can I get you anything else?
B: No, I've decided. I ________ (take) the blue ones. Sorry to keep you waiting.
6 A: You failed your English exam? What happened?
B: I don't really know. I guess I ________ (talk) to my teacher on Monday and find out.

2B In pairs, try to explain the reasons for your choices in A before checking with your teacher.

In the first one, I chose will because it was an invitation: "Will you come to our party on Saturday?"

Oh, I decided the friend already knew about the party, so I chose "Are you coming to our party on Saturday?"

2C **Make it personal** Write three questions to ask a classmate about the future. How long can you continue the conversation?

What are you planning to do over the summer?

Bonus! Language in song

♪ I missed the last bus. I'll take the next train. I try but you see, it's hard to explain.

Rewrite the line "I'll take the next train" in two ways: (1) You've made a plan and have already bought your train ticket, and (2) You're not very sure what you'll do.

Grammar expansion answer key

Unit 1

1A

1 meeting 2 to look 3 to finish
4 going 5 to take 6 to check
7 taking 8 seeing

1B

Students' own answers

2A

1 b 2 a 3 a 4 b 5 b
6 a

2B

Students' own answers

2C

1 It's important not to
2 it's not useful to
3 it's essential not to
4 critical not to
5 not helpful to

Bonus! Language in song

- "A hard day's night" means it has been a long, difficult day.
- *Students' own answers*

Unit 2

1A

Examples:

It tastes good, but it usually ... salt in it.

It doesn't go bad, so/but ... old it is.

It's not expensive, but it's bad for you.

It's not fresh, but you always ... meal.

They sell it everywhere, but it's bad for you.

It's bad for you, but it tastes good.

It's not fresh, but they sell it everywhere.

Children love it, but children need healthy food.

2A

1 There can't be life on other planets.
2 but he may/might have been sleeping
3 Sheila can't/must not have taken her keys
4 Amy can't/must not have been paying attention.
5 A monkey can't have been climbing in the window!
6 he must not/can't have remembered it.

2B

2 must have approached
3 may/might have been hiding
4 must not/can't have been expecting
5 must have been imagining
6 can't/couldn't have been walking
7 must have been wearing
8 may/might have been coming

Bonus! Language in song

Example: *The most difficult thing about my day is that nothing seems to satisfy, and I think I'll lose my mind if I don't find something to pacify.*

Unit 3

1A

1 enjoyed
2 had left
3 greeted
4 called; answered
5 had already dated
6 ran; hugged

1B

Students' own answers

2A

1 used to love 2 was 3 realized
4 discovered 5 had driven
6 hadn't gone 7 took 8 rolled
9 had seen 10 did 11 took
12 had gone 13 had

2B

Students' own answers

Bonus! Language in song

'would rise' can be changed to 'rose'

Unit 4

1A

2 In spite of studying all night, I still failed my English test. / I still failed my English test, even though I studied all night.
3 In spite of not being a fan of the flipped classroom, I'm able to work at my own pace. / Although I'm not a fan of the flipped classroom, I'm able to work at my own pace.
4 Despite the fact that they don't make much money, my friends still have nicer clothes than I do. / While my friends don't make much money, they still have nicer clothes than I do.
5 Despite mountain climbing being dangerous, I really enjoy it. / While mountain climbing can be dangerous, I really enjoy it.
6 In spite of the fact that I read lots of hotel reviews before I went to Berlin, I still paid too much. / Though I read/had read lots of hotel reviews before I went to Berlin, I still paid too much.
7 Besides being a genius, my brother is a nice person. / My brother is a genius. What's more, he's a nice person.

1B

Students' own answers

1C

1 Despite ~~study~~ studying every day, grammar is still difficult.
2 Well, in spite of ~~I might have~~ having a good accent/even though I have a good accent, I still have a long way to go.
3 ~~I really try. However that~~ Even though I really try, my English will never be perfect.
4 ~~In spite of~~ While/Even though/Although it's challenging, I should keep at it.

2A

1 Ø 2 Ø 3 Ø
4 myself 5 ourselves 6 Ø
7 Ø 8 Ø

2B

1 I'm having trouble focusing ~~myself~~ in class. I'm always tired.
2 The students looked at ~~them~~ themselves in the mirror and were pleasantly surprised by their appearance.
3 I went to a concert last night, and I really enjoyed myself.
4 When my daughter concentrates ~~herself~~, she can succeed at anything.
5 My grandparents were immigrants, but they taught ~~himself~~ themselves to speak perfect English.

Bonus! Language in song

It took ~~myself~~ me by surprise I must say. When I found out yesterday. Don't you know that I heard ~~itself~~ it through the grapevine?

Unit 5

1A

1 I hope Ann calls me tomorrow. I really need to talk to her!
2 I wish my mother had spent more time with me when I was young.
3 I really hope I don't fail my final exams.
4 I wish I knew how to drive. It's such a useful skill.
5 John wishes he hadn't quit school.
6 I hope I didn't upset my little brother when I yelled at him.

1B

2 had 3 would 4 had 5 would
6 had

2A

2 If I hadn't had/hadn't gotten good grades, I never would have gotten into college.
3 If I have really good luck, maybe I'll win the lottery. / If I am really lucky, maybe I'll win the lottery.
4 If I hadn't studied really hard, I wouldn't have passed the exam.
5 If you don't practice a lot, you'll never learn to speak English.
6 If I hadn't had my parents' help, I wouldn't be living in this house today. / If my parents hadn't helped me, I wouldn't be living in this house today.

2B

1 With good role models,
2 Without the support of my neighbor Melanie,
3 If I didn't,
4 But with a good education,
5 If I hadn't,
6 Without her,

2C

Students' own answers

Bonus! Language in song

Example:

If only I were your hero, baby, I would kiss away the pain.

Unit 6

1A

1 Will paper books ever be replaced by e-books? (to)
2 Why is the iPad still considered a revolution in teaching? (does)
3 Should students' native languages be banned from the classroom? (being)
4 Have you always removed photos from Facebook® when friends ask you to? (be)
5 How can your privacy be violated by credit card companies? (you)

1C

1 I'd like my computer to be checked, please.
2 Should my battery be replaced?
3 Will this water damage be repaired by tomorrow?
4 Has my phone been fixed yet?

1D

1 Where was the Soccer World Cup held in 2014?
2 How many times has the song *Imagine* been recorded?
3 Who was the Sistine Chapel painted by?
4 Where is ceviche eaten?
5 Where in the world can the Mona Lisa be seen?

2A

1 whatever that means
2 whatever the cost
3 Whatever
4 whatever you do

Bonus! Language in song

I always feel like I'm being watched by somebody. And I have no privacy.

Unit 7

1A

1 There's so much noise outside that I can't sleep.
2 There are so many people with cars that it's impossible to park.
3 There are so many good desserts, but I can't eat any because I'm on a diet.
4 It's so exciting to travel to new places, but I don't have any money.
5 I have so much homework that I'll never finish it all before Monday.
6 He was such a nice person, but when we didn't agree, he refused to speak to me.

1B

Examples:

1 I walk to school so as not to have to wait for the bus.
2 I call my parents every day in order not to worry them.
3 I take at least one vacation a year so as not to burn out.
4 I hardly ever go to museums in order not to pay the entrance fee.
5 I read three books in English a year so as not to forget any vocabulary.

2A

1 because of 2 Because it 3 for
4 Because of 5 Because
6 because of

2B

1 I was fired for talking back to my boss.
2 My mother yelled at me for leaving the refrigerator open.
3 I got an award for writing the best essay.
4 I felt proud of myself for speaking English.
5 I was punished for not coming home on time.

3A

Examples:

1 She speaks both English and Chinese fluently.
2 The band are playing either Brazilian music or Latino music.
3 Not only does he play the guitar well, but he also plays the piano.
4 The exam included questions on both modern art and impressionism.
5 The books were either romantic novels or mysteries – I can't remember.

Bonus! Language in song

- *Music makes the people come together. Music ~~mix~~ mixes the bourgeoisie and the rebel.*
- Because music makes the people come together, it mixes the bourgeoisie and the rebel.

Unit 8

1A

1 can
2 was able to
3 'll be able to
4 can
5 've been able to
6 be able to

2A

1 was supposed to arrive; had to spend
2 was supposed to be; had to invite
3 wasn't supposed to be
4 didn't have to meet
5 had to drive
6 were supposed to get; had to live

3A

1 You'd better have brought
2 You should have found / You ought to have found
3 You'd better not have left
4 had to take

Unit 9

1A

1 about 2 in 3 at 4 to
5 for 6 between 7 to 8 about
9 in 10 for 11 for 12 of

2A

1 My only brother, who's three years older than me, wants to join the army.
2 Sally stepped on my foot three times, which really made me mad!
3 –
4 My mother, who's writing a novel, always wanted to be a novelist.
5 –
6 –

2B

2 The friend who I most enjoy spending time with is ...
3 The place where I take vacations is ...
4 The classmate whose sense of humour I really like is ...
5 The musician whose albums I love is ...
6 It really annoys me when/that people never ...

2C

1 The best place ~~that~~ I've ever been to is ...
2 The politicians ~~who are~~ running this country ...
3 A writer whose books I love is ...
4 The type of weather that makes me depressed is ...
5 ... is an activity ~~which~~ I'd really like to be good at.
6 The person in my family ~~who~~ I confide in most is ...
7 These days many people think ... , which is exactly the opposite of what I think.
8 People ~~who are~~ caught stealing sometimes ...

Bonus! Language in song

Examples:

I'm all lost in the supermarket, in which I can no longer shop happily.
I came in here for that special offer, which is a guaranteed personality.

Unit 10

1A

2 whether we won – I
3 aren't you – T
4 Don't you have – N
5 if this train goes – I
6 Hasn't that guy stayed – N

1B

1 I'm not sure
2 No
3 Yes
4 I'm not sure
5 No
6 I'm not sure

2A

1 will get used to
2 Didn't you use to
3 've gotten used to
4 Are you slowly getting used to
5 Did you use to

Bonus! Language in song

Do you know where you're going to? is an indirect question.
The last two lines can be rewritten as an indirect question: Do you know where you're going to?

Unit 11

1A

1 Sam warned Miles he was going to get into trouble.
2 Ellen said she will be at the coffee shop in five minutes.
3 My teacher told us stars only come out at night.
4 Phil reminded me he might be a little late tonight.
5 Melissa reassured me she hadn't told anyone Ted and I broke up.
6 Eric denied he had broken the window.

1B

1
a My boss told me I couldn't take the day off.
b Sally told her parents that she couldn't take the day off.

2
a My parents told me they were moving, but they'd visit me often.
b My parents told their friends they were moving, but they'd visit them often.

3
a The store owner asked us what we wanted.
b The boys explained to the store owner what they wanted.

4
a My tenant Sue admitted to me she didn't have the rent money, so she couldn't pay me.
b I told my landlady I didn't have the rent money, so I couldn't pay her.

2A

2 Tim wasn't happy about lending me money, but I promised to pay it/him back next week.
3 Lisa was very upset about failing her final exams, but I persuaded her not to give up.
4 Bob had his credit cards stolen, but I urged him to keep his cool and call the bank to cancel them immediately.
5 Beth forgot all her lines during the play, and our director really lost it, but I begged him to give her a second chance.
6 Steve fell asleep in an important meeting, and his boss threatened to fire him the next time it happened.
7 Our local TV station mispronounced my name, and I told them I wasn't happy at all about that.
8 Nancy's boyfriend is always asking her for money, and I told her to stop seeing him.

2B

1 threatened
2 urged/begged
3 persuaded
4 promised/agreed

Bonus! Language in song

You told me that you were sorry.
I said that it was too late to apologize.

Unit 12

1A

1 A: 're going to be paying B: 'll be
2 A: will have left B: 'll wait
3 A: are going to be B: might be looking
4 A: will have graduated B: will fail

2A

1 Will you come
2 won't do / 're not leaving
3 'm going to study
4 are you doing / 'm going
5 'll take
6 'll talk

Bonus! Language in song

I'm taking the next train. / I think I'll take the next train.

Audio scripts

Unit 1

1.1 *page 6 exercise 1B*

Gone are the days when most of us lived in traditional families – one mom and one dad. Today's families exist in many different shapes and sizes. Parents separate, remarry, and form new families, with stepmoms and dads, brothers, and sisters – united by love, rather than genetics. Uncles, aunts, grandparents, and even great grandparents sometimes become mother and father ... Single parent families, with only one mom or one dad, are also on the increase. The possibilities are endless! Welcome to ..., a state-by-state look at modern families in the U.S. In this episode, we're going to meet three very different families from New York.

1.2 *page 6 exercises 1D and E*

Marco

Until I was in 4th grade, I lived with my mom, my dad, and my older sister. Then my parents divorced, and my dad moved out. From then on, it was the three of us under the same roof. We used to live in a tiny one-bedroom apartment in Manhattan, which doesn't bring back the best of memories, to be honest. Anyway, Mom remarried a few years later, and we moved to my stepfather's house in Brooklyn. The whole thing took a little getting used to, you know. At first, Jeff and I didn't get along at all. I mean, you should have heard the fights – usually over stupid things. We always made up a few minutes later, of course, and became friends again – until the next fight. Anyway, eventually we learned how to trust each other ... and now we're the best of friends.

Karin

Well, our family owned a small record store downtown. But, you know, with digital music and everything, sure enough, it went out of business ... So Mom and Dad had to look for a job to put food on the table, which completely changed the dynamics of the family. Amanda and I no longer felt like siblings – I ... well ... I looked after her while Mom and Dad were at work. I kind of became her mom ... I used to take her to school every day and do all sorts of parental things ... In many ways, I still do. Even now. I think she really looks up to me – she says I'm her hero. I love her with all my heart, of course, but, you know, looking back, sometimes I wonder what things would have been like if I'd been allowed to be ... you know, just a teen, like most of my friends.

Josh

My parents died when I was a little boy, so I was brought up by my grandmother and my aunt ... Me and six cats! Six! Well, that kind of explains my allergy ... Anyway, we were extremely protective and caring of each other. The first years were tough, as you can imagine, but Grandma and Aunt Agatha were always there for me, no matter what. They always encouraged me to work hard at school. They, erm ... I guess they taught me ... they taught me how to deal with life's difficulties with courage and dignity, and I'll be forever grateful. They say my great-grandmother – Grandma's mother – was also a very strong woman ... So I guess it runs in the family!

1.3 *page 7 exercise 2A*

H = Helene, M = Marco, K = Karin, J = Josh

H: Hello! My name's Helene, and I'll be your cyber teacher in today's lesson. Let's look at 1 and 2.

M: Jeff and I didn't get along at all. I mean, you should have heard the fights – usually over stupid things. We always made up a few minutes later, of course, and became friends again – until the next fight.

H: "Get along" means "have a good relationship." "Make up" means "become friends again after an argument." Now let's look at 3 and 4.

K: I looked after her while Mom and Dad were at work. I kind of became her Mom ... I used to take her to school every day and do all sorts of parental things ... In many ways, I still do. Even now. I think she really looks up to me – she says I'm her hero.

H: "Look after" means "to take care of somebody or something." "Look up to" means "respect or admire." Now let's look at 5 and 6.

J: My parents died when I was a little boy, so I was brought up by my grandmother and my aunt ... They say my great-grandmother – Grandma's mother – was also a very strong woman ... So I guess it runs in the family!

H: "Bring up" means "care for a child and help him or her grow up." When something "runs in the family," it's a common family characteristic. Well, that's it for today, folks – six expressions you should now be able to use.

1.4 *page 8 exercise 3C*

P = Presenter, C = Carol

P: We spoke to Carol Zimmerman, the author of the popular, *In a nutshell* book review web page, about her latest review. What can you tell us about *Teenagers Explained*, Carol?

C: I learned so much from this book. I was doing it all wrong before!

P: What do you mean?

C: For example, I used to say things like, "I want you to feel I'm your friend, not just your mother."

P: That seems like a nice thing to say!

C: Well, actually, you need to give up trying to be one of them. They expect you to be their role model, someone they can look up to. "And, please, don't even try to be cool. You're not." That's what I learned from my son, Phil. Those were his exact words.

P: What else did he teach you?

C: Not to ask to meet his girlfriend! I remember saying, "So ... when are we going to meet your girlfriend? I'm getting impatient!" That was awful!

P: Why? Well, maybe the "impatient" part. But you're showing an interest in his life!

C: Well, you know, they feel self-conscious. In this case, pressuring teens will get you nowhere. You know what Phil said, "You'll meet her when the time is right. End of story."

P: Guess he felt strongly about that one. Go on ... this is fascinating.

C: And I used to be rude! I remember telling him, "I don't get it! I've been talking for hours, and all I get to hear from you is 'whatever'." As if it was all about me.

P: What did he say to that one?

C: Nothing. He just got up and left the room. I learned it's no use pushing your teenagers to talk. Just do your own thing, maybe in the same room. They'll start a conversation with you when they feel like it.

P: Wow! Maybe I need to read the book, too. Anything else?

C: Well, there's the classic, "Just because all your friends are doing it doesn't mean you should." Bet your mom said that one, too. I learned it from mine.

P: But it's an important piece of advice.

C: It doesn't work, though. Remember: teens have trouble dealing with rejection. They're building their identities and want to belong and to feel accepted. To them, if their friends are doing it, it *does* mean they should.

P: Guess it's been a long time since I've been a teenager. Thank you for joining us today, Carol ...

1.5 *page 9 exercise 4B*

C = Carol, P = Phil

1

C: Just toast for breakfast? How about some fruit?

P: Oh, Mom, not again. I don't really like fruit, especially in the morning.

C: Eating fruit every morning is good for you. Healthy habits start when you're young.

2

C: Phil, you've been working on that assignment for five straight hours!

P: So ...?

C: Take a break! Spending too much time in front of that computer will hurt your eyes. You know that.

3

P: Three hours, one paragraph! What's wrong with me?

C: Maybe it's the sort of stuff you read.

P: Oh, Mom, not again.

C: Reading good literature will help you write better. That's all I'm saying.

4

C: Phil, Phil, turn it down!

P: Oh, all right.

C: Listening to loud music can damage your ears. How many times do I have to tell you that?

5

C: Where are you off to?

P: The gym.

C: But you've just come back from soccer practice. Doing too much exercise isn't good for you, you know.

6

P: See you later, Mom.

C: Hey, hey, hey ... where do you think you're going?

P: It's, er ... it's Ron's birthday. Paul and Frank are going to be there, and ...

C: Hanging out with those guys will get you into trouble ... sooner or later. Mark my words.

1.6 *page 9 exercise 4C*

C = Carol, P = Phil

1

P: Mom, can I borrow the car?
C: You got two speeding tickets last month. Sorry.
P: I'll drive slowly, I promise.
C: Sorry, Phil. We've talked about it already. It's no use trying to convince me.

2

C: Hey, wanna watch *Modern Family*? Today is the season finale.
P: Hmm ... OK, whatever.
C: You don't sound very enthusiastic. Well, you know what ... Carry on doing what you were doing.
P: No! I do want to watch it.

3

C: Phil!
P: What?
C: Is everything all right? I can't help wondering why you've been so quiet lately.
P: I'm fine, I'm fine.
C: Well, I'm here if you need me.

4

C: Phil, can you help me with the dishes?
P: Mom, not now. I'm really tired.
C: Why? Are you having trouble sleeping?
P: Totally.
C: Too much homework, huh?
P: Yeah ...

5

C: Are you thinking about Lisa again, honey?
P: Yeah. I miss her.
C: I know. But, look, you're young and good-looking. You'll find someone new. It's not worth living in the past.
P: You're right, I guess.

1.9 *page 11 exercise 6C*

D = Donald, C = Claire

D: Oh, no, not again. Hey, give me back my iPad.
C: What are you reading?
D: Some study on dog people vs. cat people. Check it out: "A recent study found significant personality differences between those who self-identified as either dog people or cat people."
C: Oh, you've got to be kidding!
D: "Dog owners tend to be more extroverted, talkative, and approachable than cat owners. They also have greater self-discipline and tend to score higher on assertiveness. Dog people like to stick to plans and are not particularly adventurous."
C: Hmm ... interesting.
D: "Cat ownership is usually associated with openness to new ideas and different beliefs. Cat people are less predictable and more imaginative, and they value their personal freedom more than dog people."
C: That sounds a lot like you.
D: "Because cats require less maintenance than dogs, cat people are more likely to be busy individuals who work a lot and have less time for close relationships." Did you hear that? "Less maintenance." Claire, darling, can we please give Alex to your mom? Please?

1.10 *page 11 exercise 6D*

A: OK, so, erm ... I go first, OK?
B: Right.
A: Some people say they're a million times more talkative, more approachable ...
B: Hmm ... OK. More sociable you mean?
A: Yeah. Friendlier in general, I think.
B: What else?
A: They, erm ... I think they... I think their lives might ... I think they might lead more predictable lives sometimes ... You know, with fewer surprises ... but more security... more peace ...
B: You mean peace and quiet?
A: Yeah.
B: I think I know. ... Are you talking about small town people vs. big city people?
A: Yes, I am!

1.11 *page 12 exercises 7B and C*

S = Stacey Tisdale, M = Mary Bolster

S: I'm Stacey Tisdale for Howdini. OK, the sales clerk is snippy, your boss is grouchy, that irritating co-worker has done it again ... How do you react? It's an important question for your mental health. And for some answers, we're joined by Mary Bolster, Editor in Chief of Natural Health Magazine. Mary, good to have you with us. Now, someone that I might find annoying, you might not find annoying. How are you defining difficult people?
M: Well, you came up with some pretty good examples in the beginning there. And you know, it's like an indifferent sales person. You go in there, you're trying to find something and nobody will help you, and they seem to be willfully ignoring you. Strident, demanding bosses ... I think most people find them difficult. And then you mention this the co-worker ... the person that constantly gets you to do his or her work. That is so annoying. But it's really any kind of person who gets your blood pressure higher than it should be.
S: All of this reminds me of a difficult boss that I had and I always tried to clear the air and make things easy for us. But you say that we shouldn't necessarily try to find common ground with these people?
M: I would say that it is probably the wrong thing to do and it may encourage the rude person's difficult behavior. Umm, really what you want to do is remain neutral. You don't really want to create peaceful ground between yourself and the negative person. You want to protect your own ground. So you wanna ... you don't want to get your emotions higher than they should be. You really wanna to stay neutral. So, for instance, if you normally react with anger, you wanna kinda contain that anger, you wanna remind yourself that this person's difficult behavior is about them, not about you. You don't take it personally and you just state the facts. You're assertive without being aggressive, and you just ... that's how you get what you want from that person.
S: How should we handle our emotions when we're faced with these difficult situations?
M: There's a couple of ways that people typically respond to difficult people. One way is to get obsessed like "Oh my gosh, this person shouldn't be difficult and I'm going to change her". Well, hello, that is never going to happen. You just want to say ... you've got to let go of that. You've got to acknowledge that there are always going to be obnoxious, difficult people. There's two instances where you really want to kind of take stock. Another is if you act hurt when someone is difficult with you because difficult people take advantage of that kind of behavior – they think you want approval, and so they'll just be ... they'll really kind of milk that need for approval. So, you again, you wanna just visualize yourself being indifferent toward this person. That you're neither ... you don't need their approval, you don't need to get angry with them, you can just be neutral with them. And that's where you're more likely to get what you need from these people.
S: It sounds like the general message is that all that you can control is the way you react to these things – you can't control outside circumstances, you can't control the people.
M: That's right. Really, if you can change what's inside, the things on the outside won't have such a big effect on you.

1.12 *page 12 exercise 8A*

P = Presenter, A = Andrew

P: And now we're going to listen to some advice from Dr. Andrew Mulligan on dealing with difficult people.
A: Difficult people are everywhere: controlling family members, business associates, ex-friends fast becoming enemies, unreasonable teachers, inconsiderate neighbors ... The list goes on and on. Here are five easy ways to help you talk to them:
a) Pause and take a deep breath. Count to ten, if necessary. It's useful to give yourself time to think and assess the situation. The less you react, the better.
b) Think like them. It's important for you to put yourself in other people's positions so you can see the situation from another perspective. Listen carefully. If you were in their situation, what would it feel like?
c) Concede a little. Even if you agree with only one percent of what they are saying, let them know. Remember: It feels good to be heard and have your opinion valued.
d) Watch your body language. Look the other person in the eye, smile if you can, and don't cross your arms. These guidelines will make it easier for you to be understood. Remember: Successful communication is less than ten percent verbal.
e) Above all, be patient!

1.13 *page 13 exercise 9C*

T = Teacher, S = Students, B = Bruno, M = Maria, C = Carlos, L = Laura

T: Finished?
S: Yes.
T: Bruno, can you start?
B: Sure. I hope these tips will make it easier for you to handle some of the toxic people around you at home, school, or work.
T: Very good! Maria, would you like to continue?
M: OK. But keep in mind that it's important to choose your battles wisely ... Er ... Can I also say "It's important for you to choose your battles wisely?"

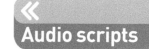

T: Yes, both are correct. Very good, María. Carlos ...
C: Excuse me?
T: Can you read the next sentence?
C: Oh, OK. There will be times when you will be successful and times when it will be very difficult for the other person ... Hmm ... very difficult for the other person to ... I don't know this one.
T: Passive voice, Carlos.
C: Got it. Very difficult for the other person to be persuaded.
T: Yes, exactly! Would anybody like to continue?
L: Me!
T: Thanks, Laura.
L: In those cases, it's no use trying. Oh, we learned this last week, didn't we? So ... it's no use trying. Remember: It's impossible to change someone ... or, erm ... It's impossible for you to change someone. Change comes from within.
T: Well done, Laura.
L: What does "from within" mean?
T: From inside you.
L: Oh, OK. Thanks.

1.14 *page 14 exercise 10A*

D = Dave, H = Host

D: ... and it's no good doing that, really. I mean, they're just kids.
H: If you've just tuned in, with me here in the studio tonight is Dave Jackson, renowned psychologist, family counselor, writer, and father of three, who's...
D: Four.
H: Wow! Really? Sorry!
D: Not a problem, as you may have guessed, I love kids. The more the merrier!
H: Right! We're talking about the challenges of raising kids in the digital age. Dave, during our break, you mentioned Steve Jobs.
D: Uh huh.
H: What about him?
D: A while ago I read a *New York Times* interview ... The, erm, the iPad had just been launched, and the journalist asked Jobs how his kids liked it. I remember the article said he limited how much technology his kids used at home.
H: No way!
D: It's true. And you know what? He was absolutely right. I mean, there ...

1.15 *page 14 exercises 10B and C*

D: ... I mean, there are a million reasons why parents should regulate their children's online activity. For one thing, I believe digital technology is making people crueler.
H: You're talking about online bullying?
D: Well, that's a serious issue, but not only that. Teens and kids are texting all kinds of things they should be saying out loud, face to face. For example, my daughter broke up with her boyfriend via text – a boy she'd been seeing for more than six months.
H: Wow.
D: And he replied with an icon – a broken heart or something. And that was it. Can you believe it? It seems to me that texting is taking away our ability to develop empathy and the ability to put ourselves in people's positions – and here I'm speaking specifically of children and teens. What's more, texting is making teens lazy. It's affecting their academic progress!
H: What do you mean?
D: I'm talking about text speak. Forgetting about capital letters and punctuation ... using lots of abbreviations ...
H: Oh, you mean things like writing the word *how* plus the letter *r* and then the letter *u* to mean, *How are you ...?*
D: Yes. And this is getting in the way of their writing skills – just ask any schoolteacher. The other day my daughter wrote LOL in a school essay! Not to mention the fact that we're unlearning how to communicate in the real world – and this doesn't apply to teens only. I mean, whenever you go out with a group of people for a night out, an event, a sports game, or something ... some people spend more time texting than they do talking to the "real world group," you know, the people they are physically with. Electronic devices are making us antisocial.
H: Yeah, I've heard of restaurants and coffee shops who stopped offering free WiFi to encourage people to interact with each other.
D: On top of that, our digital relationships are becoming too superficial. For example, an acquaintance decided she wanted to introduce me to her group of friends ... But instead of the old-fashioned way, she added me to their What's App® group.
H: So ...?
D: In a matter of hours, I started getting dozens of messages, day after day, sent by people I'd never met. Actually, I still don't know who they are. But I know what some of them had for lunch yesterday. I think it's really strange to chat with people you don't know. This just doesn't feel right.

Unit 2

2.1 *page 16 exercises 1A and B*

I = Interviewer

1
I: Hi, excuse me. We're doing a quick survey about different concerns people have. Can I ask you something? Just one question.
A: Yeah ... I guess.
I: What's most on your mind these days?
A: What do you mean?
I: What have you been thinking about lately – more than anything else?
A: Hmm ... can it be a person?
I: Sure.
A: I can't stop thinking about my dad. We, erm ... we had an argument a while ago and we've been ... well, things have been tense between us.
I: OK. So, that goes under ... hmm ... "family dynamics." Thank you.

2
I: ... yeah, it's one simple question: What's most on your mind these days?
B: Like ... things I can't stop thinking about?
I: Uh huh.
B: Hmm ... I'm considering going back to the gym ... You know, doctor's orders. Plus, I want to be able to wear my skinny jeans again.
I: OK, so that's physical appearance. Thank you and good luck.

3
I: ... And what's most on your mind these days?
C: I keep worrying about my fiancé.
I: Oh yeah?
C: He quit his job last year and, you know, it's a jungle out there ... He hasn't been very lucky lately, and he's running out of money.
I: Sorry to hear that. So "financial problems" then?
C: Yeah.

4
D: Hmm ... You mean, what's been worrying me?
I: Well, not necessarily. It could be anything – or anyone – that's really occupying your thoughts.
D: Well, I can't seem to focus on anything but the wedding.
I: Wow! Congratulations! So, there you go. "Romantic relationships."

5
I: ... yeah, exactly. What's most on your mind?
E: Well, my car's really old, and I need to buy a new one ... still choosing, though. Lots of good options! So, yeah, buying a car. I think about it night and day.
I: OK! "Material possessions" then.

6
F ... Wow, that's a tough one ... I guess ... well, I wish I was more popular in my class ...
I: Uh huh.
F That way I wouldn't have to do all sorts of stupid things, you know, just to prove that I belong. Like, look at my hairstyle. I hate it. But it kind of makes me look cool, so ...
I: OK. That would go under "peer pressure." Thank you.

2.2 *page 17 exercises 2B and C*

D = Dad, A = April

D: April, I'm worried about your schoolwork. Have you written that essay yet? You've been putting it off for weeks!
A: No, Dad. I told you, I'm going to do it later.
D: Hmm ... that's pretty typical, I guess.
A: Typical of what?
D: I was just reading an article about the adolescent brain and how it's not mature until the age of 25 or so.
A: And you believe all that stuff?
D: Well – it's science – you can't argue with scientific facts!
A: And what does this "science" say?
D: Well, first it says that young people are impulsive and ...
A: "... they make instant decisions they often regret." How predictable, Dad.
D: It also says that ... let me find it ... Look: "Young people find it hard to plan and organize behavior," which kind of explains why adolescents often seem to make bad decisions.
A: Do you think I make bad decisions?
D: Well ...
A: Dad, I had no idea at all you felt that way about me!
D: Honey you have to admit that last haircut wasn't such a good idea!
A: OK, you're right on that one! But that's the exception, not the rule ... Does it say why you want me to go to sleep when I'm not tired and wake up when I'm asleep?

D: Yes, it does, actually. Our sleep patterns, our body clocks, are different, apparently. It never occurred to me that the reason was our age.
A: That's what I always told you!
D: I know! But what can I do when you need to be in school by 8 a.m.?
A: Does it say anything else?
D: It says that lots of car crashes are caused by young drivers because they like to live dangerously.
A: Well, I do love roller coasters!
D: And that's partly because when you're under 25, you're much more vulnerable to peer pressure, much more so than children or adults.
A: So, you think my friends tell me to do dangerous stuff?
D: Definitely.
A: You've got to be kidding!
D: What about the time they told you to ride your skateboard down the steps and you fell off?
A: That was ONE time!
D: But it was peer pressure. The article suggests that young people should live with their parents until they're at least 25, and that sounds like a good idea to me.
A: Dad! It amazes me that you'd even suggest that. We'd just drive each other crazy if I did that – I think 18 is when you become an adult – some kids before that, and maybe a few after, but 18 is about right, I think.

2.4 *page 20 exercise 3A*

P = Presenter, C = Carmen, G = Greg, M = Marcella, D = Dieter, N = Nancy, B = Ben, J = Jackie

P: Please take a few minutes to fill in our OQS – yes, that's right, our Online Quick Survey. We have a few volunteers to show you how easy it is. ... And it's really quick. One simple question.
C: Sure. No problem.
P: Do you have a sweet tooth, Carmen?
C: Well, not exactly. But I usually have an energy drink every afternoon.
P: Oh yeah?
C: Uh huh. The best thing about it is that it wakes me up for my afternoon classes.
P: OK, this young man over here.
G: I'm Greg. Candy bars!! The biggest problem is weight gain if I have one every day.
P: And you're?
M: Marcella.
P: What would you say, Marcella?
M: Well, I love a big piece of cake for dessert in restaurants.
P: Sometimes it's too big!
M: Oh, no, not for me. The hardest thing is sharing it with other people!
P: Time for just a few more ...
D: I'm Dieter. I have two or three soft drinks a day. The good thing is the sugar, which gives me energy.
P: Why do you need energy? Young people always have energy. Wish I did!
D: Well, it keeps me going, and I really need it because I play a lot of sports.
P: OK, and let's see what this young woman thinks. What's your name?
N: I'm Nancy. Ice cream is my favorite! It's a family event.
P: How's that?
N: Going to our local ice cream parlor is a big deal for my family. The best part is all the different flavors, so it never gets boring!
P: Let's move to this young man. He's had his hand up.
B: Hi, I'm Ben. I think there's definitely an advantage to chocolate bars! I eat a lot of them to pick me up. However, the disadvantage is that they make you feel even more tired later, when the effect has worn off.
P: Last one ... how about you? And please let us know your name.
J: Great ... I'm Jackie. Well, in my family we don't have sweet stuff like ice cream and cookies, only fruit.
P: Wow! How did your parents manage that?
J: We just never got used to sweets. My mom says fruit has natural sugar.
P: We're out of time. Thank you very much, everyone, for participating in our Online Quick Survey! Now YOU try it ... the most original participant will receive a ...

2.5 *page 20 exercises 5A and B*

As we all know, traditionally, intelligence has been viewed as one single thing: Either you're smart or you're not. Psychologist Howard Gardner, however, disagrees, suggesting there are nine types of intelligence! Let's start from the first one: *Logical-mathematical* intelligence, which describes people who are good at analyzing and solving problems. These individuals tend to think conceptually about numbers, relationships, and patterns. The second type of intelligence is known as *verbal-linguistic*. People who are linguistically intelligent usually enjoy reading and writing. They find it easy to tell stories and explain new concepts ... you know, like teachers! They're also quite good at debates and speeches. Some people prefer to express themselves through music, of course, which brings us to Gardner's third type of intelligence: *musical* intelligence. Those of us with strong musical intelligence enjoy singing and playing musical instruments and are capable of remembering the lyrics to songs, and recognizing notes and tones. Another kind of self-expression, of course, has to do with the body, which brings us to our fourth kind of intelligence. People with a high *bodily-kinesthetic* intelligence – yeah, that's hard to pronounce, I know, *bo-di-ly-ki-nes-thet-ic* – usually have excellent physical coordination. These individuals usually enjoy building things and working with their hands, in general. They often have a gift for drawing and dancing ... some of them are quite good at sports, too. Here's the fifth type. People with strong *spatial* intelligence usually have a visual memory. They're adept at interpreting graphs and following maps and ... well, unlike me, they rarely get lost. Moving on, here's one of the most interesting types, I think: *interpersonal* intelligence. People with a high degree of interpersonal relationship are skilled at interacting with other people and identifying their emotions and intentions. You know, just generally being able to read faces and body language. Intrapersonal intelligence, on the other hand ... . OK, we'll carry on next class. Could you please Google *intrapersonal*, *naturalistic* and *existential* intelligences and read the article I sent you last week? It's called, "Fish and trees: Gardner's multiple intelligences revisited."

2.7 *page 22 exercises 7A and B*

T = Theo, R = Ruby, J = Judd

T: ... did you read this one? This woman says she found an alien in her backyard after a UFO sighting. Some small town in California.
R: What a weird story, Theo.
J: Here's what I don't get about the whole UFO thing. Why does it always happen in small towns?
R: Yeah, Judd. And why is it that everything "alien" needs flying objects? It's been the same old story since the 50s, maybe even before that. If aliens do exist, why do they need spaceships?
T: What do you mean "if"? There are billions and billions of galaxies out there. We can't be alone in the universe. We just can't!
R: Well, Theo, I think there might be life on other planets, though not necessarily intelligent life.
T: You mean like primitive creatures? Bacteria and ...?
R: Yeah. I mean it's not like we've ever made contact. So, how can we be sure that there are intelligent beings inhabiting other planets?
J: Exactly. We can't.
T: Or maybe ... Well, what if ... what if they have a completely different kind of intelligence? They could use a different form of communication that we haven't mastered yet. I mean, who guarantees they actually need to make sounds?
R: Makes sense, Theo, yeah.
T: Or, you know, take the pyramids, for example ...
R: What about them?
T: Lots of people say they were built for a reason ... Maybe they were trying to tell us something.
J: Wait, wait, wait. You don't mean the ... Oh, Theo, come on! The pyramids can't have been built by aliens. That's just crazy.
R: Yeah, I agree. The whole story seems unlikely.
T: That's going a little too far, I know, but a lot of people say that. Anyway, we can't ignore the fact that thousands and thousands of people from all over the world have reported seeing UFOs and aliens ... It's all documented.
R: True, but is it evidence you can trust? I'm not sure.
J: Of course not! It's all a bunch of lies.
R: Interestingly, most of the descriptions follow the same pattern, don't they? Two arms, two legs, big heads ... So ... if there are aliens out there, they must look a lot like us.
T: Definitely.
J: You guys are freaking me out.
T: Judd, the facts are clear. There are thousands of photos, reports, even secret documents ... We must have been visited by extra terrestrials. It's no use denying it ... Actually ...
R: What?
T: Oh, forget it.
J: What?
T: Well, OK, let me tell you something that happened to me a while ago.

2.8 *page 22 exercise 7C*

T: ... something that happened to me a while ago. It was so scary that I still remember it vividly. I was walking the dog one night ... It must have been, what, way past midnight ... Suddenly I started feeling very uneasy, so I thought, "There must be someone following me ... "

R: Walking the dog after midnight? You can't be serious!

T: It had been a busy day! So, anyway, I stopped and turned around and there was nobody there. Then I looked up ...

J: Oh, no, here it comes.

T: And I saw a relatively small object hovering ... flying above me ... similar in shape to an old vacuum cleaner. It was, erm, it was less than 10 feet away from me.

J: Oh, come on! It can't have been a vacuum cleaner.

T: It made a very low humming sound, like hmmmmmmmm, and there were small purple lights flashing around the top.

J: Oh, I bet it was a flying toy or something.

R: A toy? Yeah, that could explain the whole thing. You know, maybe the neighbors' kids were playing outside and ...

T: At that time of night?

J: Yeah, definitely ... I bet they were trying to scare you ... The whole thing must have been planned ...

T: You're saying it might have been a joke?

J: Definitely.

R: Possibly. What about the dog?

T: I haven't seen him since then.

J & R: What?!

2.10 *page 24 exercise 10A*

F = Flavio, C = Carol

F: OK Carol, ready? First question. Which number should come next in this series? Listen carefully. 25, 24, 22, 19, 15. I'll repeat. 25, 24, 22, 19, 15.

C: This one's easy. 10, correct?

F: Yeah. It decreases progressively: minus 1, minus 2, minus 3, and so on. Next one: Library is to book as book is to ... A – copy, B – page, C – cover, D – bookshop.

C: You said copy, page, cover, and ...

F: Bookshop.

C: Hmm ... Oh, OK. Page. You can find a book inside a library and a page inside a book.

F: Yeah. Bigger, smaller. How about this one? Mary, who is 16 years old, is four times as old as her brother. How old will Mary be when she is twice as old as her brother?

C: Oooh, I hate those word problems! Let's see ... If she's four times as old, he must be four. So a 12-year difference. I've got it: 24!

F: You're pretty good at this. The next one's a piece of cake. Look at these diagrams.

C: These?

F: Yeah. Which one is different?

C: Hmm ... They all look identical.

F: No, they don't! Take a close look.

C: I don't have the slightest idea.

F: Letter C.

C: I don't get it, Flavio. Why?

F: Well, it's the only one where the black squares move up diagonally from right to left.

C: What?

F: Look. The others move up left to right ...

2.11 *page 24 exercises 10B and C*

F: ... right here? Right, middle, left.

C: Oh, yeah! Well, I would have never seen the difference. Anyway, I didn't know you were into this sort of thing.

F: Oh, I love to take these quick Internet quizzes. Always have. IQ tests are fun!

C: Yeah, they're quite enjoyable, actually.

F: One of the best things about IQ tests is that ... You know, they exercise your brain ... It's like a quick workout. Another plus is that ...

C: True. But that's about it, isn't it?

F: What do you mean? Another plus is that ... that when you're in your late teens, a good IQ test might actually help you choose a career? For example, if you keep getting all the math questions wrong, then maybe engineering is not for you.

C: Well, I wouldn't be so sure. I think the trouble with these tests is that they tend to focus on very specific things, like logic, numbers, and ...

F: But those are signs of an intelligent mind, aren't they?

C: Yeah, but they don't tell the whole story. Take Philip, for example. We both think he's really smart, right?

F: Yeah. The guy's a genius.

C: Give him a piece of paper and ask him to draw a tree ... You'd think it was made by a two-year-old.

F: Point taken. I had a teacher who used to say you can't judge a fish by its ability ...

C: ... to climb a tree. Exactly. People are naturally good at different things.

F: Which explains why you found the last question so difficult.

C: Exactly. And you see, another problem with IQ tests is that they pay no attention, no attention at all, to your social skills. I mean, what's the point of getting a perfect score if you can't, say, carry on a conversation for more than a few seconds, look the other person in the eye, and ...

F: Yeah, that's one way to look at it, I guess.

C: And here's something that's just occurred to me: If you keep doing poorly in these tests – which in some cases are anything but scientific – you might convince yourself that you're not smart enough, which may have a negative effect on your self ... on your self-image, you know.

F: Absolutely, especially when you're young. But wouldn't you agree, though, that ...

Review 1 (Units 1–2)

R1.1 *page 26 exercise 1*

A = Amy, J = Joe

A: Did you grow up around here?

J: Well, no, we moved here when I was 16 so I could start over.

A: What do you mean?

J: You know how teenagers do some stupid things. They say our minds aren't fully developed until we're 25. I had some problems – peer pressure, that sort of thing.

A: And you had to leave town?

J: Well, that's one way to look at it. My friends weren't the best influence. The biggest problem was that they convinced me to take risks. Need I say more?

A: Oh! I guess not ...

J: And so my grandparents decided it was time to leave.

A: Your grandparents? Did they live with you?

J: Yes, I was raised by them. They were great. My grandfather was a movie actor, and my grandmother a novelist.

A: Wow! That must have been cool!

J: And how about you? What was your childhood like?

A: Well, I ...

Unit 3

3.1 *[audio icon 3.1] page 28 exercise 1A*

DJ = DJ, N = Narrator

DJ1: And now the moment you've all been waiting for! This week's "Don't you just hate it when ..."

DJ2: You voted all week and here are our top seven.

DJ1: Number 7. Don't you just hate it when you get into the wrong classroom and sit there for a long time before realizing you're not supposed to be there? Then you leave in the middle of the lesson while all the students stare at you.

DJ2: I sure do!

N: "Stare" is *b*.

DJ1: Number 6. A listener from Colombia says: "Don't you hate it when you push doors that you should pull and vice versa, especially in a crowded room. Twice, three, four times. I have a 50 / 50 chance, but, guess what, I always get it wrong."

N: "Push and pull" are *g*.

DJ1: Oh, yeah. Keeps happening to me all the time. Number 5. This one takes me back to my school days. Don't you hate it when you're in the middle of a boring lesson, and you're dying to break for coffee, so you yawn and glance at your watch – as discretely as possible. Trouble is, the teacher sees you. And again. And again.

N: "Yawn and glance" are *f*.

DJ2: Ouch! Number 4. This one comes all the way from São Paulo, Brazil! Amanda says, "Don't you hate it when you think a spider has landed on you, so you scream at the top of your lungs – in a public place. And, of course, the spider is just a fly."

N: "Scream" is *c*.

DJ1: Now we're getting closer to the top. Number 3. Gloria from Dallas says, "Don't you hate it when you're talking to a friend and whisper something to her so nobody can hear you – especially gossip! To your horror, she repeats what you said out loud, for the whole room to hear." Like you did yesterday!

N: "Whisper" is *a*.

DJ2: No, I didn't! What are you talking about? Number 2: Don't you hate it when you meet someone you don't know well, and neither one of you knows whether you should hug, shake hands, or kiss – one, two, three, or (if you're French) even four times. So you go for the hug, and the other person extends his or her arm, or tries to kiss you.

N: "Hug" is *d*.

DJ1: Oh, yes! That one's *really* really embarrassing. And now for this week's winner: Tomiko, from New York. Michael, drumroll, please.

DJ2: Don't you hate it when you're running on the treadmill ...

DJ1: Oh, no! Here it comes!

DJ2: ... when suddenly you trip on your shoelaces and fall? Tomiko says: "Trust me, it's painful on your body and on your ego."

DJ1: I know. Been there, done that.

DJ2: No way! Yeah, I still remember the day as if ...

N: "Trip" is e.

3.2 *page 29 exercise 2A*

A = Ana, L = Lucas, M = Marco

A: ... which, honestly, I'm never, ever going to do again.

L: OK, my turn. Don't you hate it when ...?

A: Yep. Keeps happening to me all the time, especially at work, where I have to deal with people from all over the world.

M: What do you mean?

A: Each culture has its own codes, so it's hard to know if you're being too formal or too casual. With Brazilian clients, for example, kissing is often acceptable, that sort of thing. OK, my turn. Don't you hate it when ...?

M: Yes, yes, yes, it happened last week, actually.

L: I didn't know you were working out.

M: I started last month.

A: Oh, Marco! Did you hurt yourself?

M: No, thank goodness. But it was really humiliating. You know, everybody staring at you, trying hard not to laugh. But that wasn't the worst part.

L: It wasn't?

M: No.

3.3 *page 29 exercise 2B and C*

M: But that wasn't the worst part.

L: It wasn't?

M: No. It had been a stressful day, lots of tests, lots of traffic, the treadmill ... and I wanted to relax before going back home, so I decided to catch a movie that night.

L: On your own?

M: Yeah. For a change, you know. I got there ten minutes before the movie started, got myself a soft drink, walked into the theater, sat down, and closed my eyes, as I waited for the lights to dim. I didn't even remember the name of the movie, you know ... I just wanted to relax for a while.

A: Were you still hurting from the fall?

M: A bit. So, anyway, I glance across the room, and I see someone who looks familiar. I mean, really familiar.

L: Uh huh.

M: But the theater was really dark, so I couldn't get a good look at her. Well, the lights go out, the movie starts, and the next thing I know the woman moves three rows back and sits right in front of me.

A: OK, go on.

M: I couldn't take my eyes off her ... I kept staring at her and, bingo, it was my sister-in-law – or at least that's what I thought.

A: That's what you thought?

L: Oh no!

M: I wanted to say hi ... So, I whispered something in her ear and gave her hair a little pull, you know. I was sure she'd be happy to see me there.

L: Oh boy. Here it comes.

A: You pulled the woman's hair?

M: Very, very lightly, just to get her attention.

L: And then what?

M: You won't believe what happens next.

3.4 *page 29 exercise 2D*

L: And then what?

M: You won't believe what happens next. The woman's hair comes off.

L: What? She was wearing a wig?

M: Yeah. It was totally false.

A: Oh, boy!

M: So she turns around and screams and ...

L: Oh no!

M: Before I know it, everybody's staring at us, telling us to be quiet, and ...

A: So what happens next?

M: I don't know. I just apologized, got up, and ran to the exit.

L: Oh, man.

M: I've never been so embarrassed in my entire life.

3.6 *page 30 exercise 3A*

Welcome to the March 2 episode of *Today in History*. Our story today takes place in Hollywood.

The year was 2014. TV celebrity Ellen DeGeneres had been hosting her own talk show for years when one day she received the biggest honor of her career: Host the 86th Academy Awards, to be held on March 2. Yes, the Oscars!

If you were watching the show, you'll recall that at one point, Ellen went into the audience to take a photo with a celebrity so she could post it on Twitter. She had initially wanted just a photo of herself and actress Meryl Streep. However, as Ellen was getting ready to take the picture, other stars quickly jumped in, including actor Bradley Cooper, who took the now world-famous selfie.

3.9 *page 32 exercise 5D*

Hi class. It's me, Helene, your cyber teacher back again.

1 When food is *crunchy*, it's firm and makes a loud noise when you bite it – like crunchy apples, crunchy potato chips, or crunchy crackers.

2 When you *slice* food, you cut it into thin flat pieces. You can slice bread, slice onions, or slice a cake.

3 Something *groundbreaking* is innovative and revolutionary. We can talk about groundbreaking discoveries, groundbreaking research, or a groundbreaking movie.

4 *Odd* means strange or weird. It can refer to people ("an odd couple"), to things ("an odd way to behave") or to places ("an odd house").

5 We use the adverb *widely* to describe something that affects a lot of people or happens in a lot of different places. For example, you can describe a method as "widely used" or a product as "widely available."

OK, that's all for today!

3.11 *page 33 exercises 6C and D*

S = Sue, A = Ann

S: So, Ann ... How did you two meet?

A: Well, I was doing a college assignment. It was nearly midnight, and I was **sick and tired** of studying. So I took a break and took the dog for a walk.

S: That late?

A: Yeah! Every **now and then** I do that. Anyway, then I saw this guy walking his dog, and he looked really familiar. Turns out it was Vince, an old boyfriend from high school! I'd seen him on Facebook, but I never thought we'd meet **face to face** again after all these years.

S: Wow! Did he recognize you?

A: Yeah. We met for coffee the very next day. Then time went by, and we started seeing each other nearly every day. Before we knew it, we were madly in love.

S: You seem very happy!

A: I am. Well, naturally, there have been problems along the way, and we've had our **ups and downs**. But we're crazy about each other, and I want him in my life **for better or worse**.

S: Wait a second! Are you talking marriage?

A: Sure. Maybe this year, maybe next year, maybe five years from now. But it's going to happen **sooner or later**. It's written in the stars.

S: Wow! To think how it all started ... Talk about serendipity!

A: Ser-en-dipity, yeah, love it! Definitely my favorite word in the English language.

3.12 *page 34 exercises 7A and B*

J = Joe, P = Pedro

J: I love these old fads. What a great site. Some of this stuff takes me back to my childhood, you know. So many great memories ... And so much wasted time!

P: What's a fad? Never heard this word.

J: It's kind of like ... It's, erm ... You know, when something's really big for a while and then it kind of disappears ...

P: You mean like the Macarena in the 90s?

J: The dance? Uh huh. That was a fad, for sure. I was crazy about [beep], you know. Actually, everyone in my class, boys and girls, used to love it.

P: Oh, yeah?

J: Uh huh. It was such an obsession. I used to sit in the back row so the teacher wouldn't see me. Then I'd get home from school, lock myself in my room, and start again, playing the same game over and over.

P: Sounds boring.

J: No, it was fun, actually, though a bit solitary. I'd spend hours and hours alone, trying to get rid of the pigs. I just kept playing the same game again and again.

P: How good were you?

J: I was OK, I guess. Well, eventually I began to use it less and less ... and then I just deleted the app from my phone.

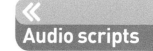

3.13 *page 34 exercise 7C*

See audio 3.12

3.15 *page 36 exercises 10A and B*

R = Reporter

Speaker 1

R: Hi, excuse me. I'm doing a survey for a program this evening ... What makes you happy?

A: What makes me happy?

R: Yeah. I know it's a hard question to answer.

A: Wow ... so many things. Hard to single out one in particular ... Let's see. Well, I'm majoring in literature, so it's, erm ... It might sound silly, but whenever I submit an assignment, it's great to get good feedback ...

R: On your writing?

A: Uh huh. I don't need to get an A or a B plus ... I couldn't care less about grades per se, but I want to be reassured that I'm on the right track, even if there's room for improvement here and there – which there always is, of course.

R: I see. That's an interesting way to look at it. Best of luck to you!

Speaker 2

R: Excuse me! I'm doing a survey for our evening program. What makes you happy?

B: Well, I have a little girl and she's my reason for living. That's her, right here! Emma ...

R: She's cute!

B: Thanks. So, what makes me really happy is being able to ... to spend time with her ... well, actually, to spend quality time with her, which, you know, is different from simply having your child within sight and ...

R: I see.

B: Unlike most single dads I know, I have a relatively flexible working schedule, which means I can play a very active role in Emma's upbringing. And that way I can be a *real* parent, not a weekend dad. So, really, that's all that matters to me.

R: Thanks very much.

Speaker 3

R: Excuse me ... I'm doing a survey for a program this evening. What makes you happy?

C: Hmm ... What makes me happy? You're probably thinking "kids and grandkids," right?

R: Well, no, not *really*.

C: Right now, *this* is what makes me happy.

R: You mean, your tablet?

C: Well, not the device itself, but the stuff you can do with it.

R: I see.

C: I've had it for a month and, honestly, I don't know how I ever managed to live without one. My, erm, my daughter-in-law is teaching me how to post on Twitter and Insta ... What's it called again?

R: Instagram.

C: Exactly.

R: So, learning how to use social media? That's what makes you happy right now?

C: Absolutely. Now I know why they call it social media. This feeling of being connected, you know, it's unlike anything I've ever experienced.

R: I see! Thanks very much!

Speaker 4

R: Excuse me ... can you participate in a survey for our evening program? What makes you happy?

D: Hmm ... lots of things ... my cats, my orchid collection ... the smell of freshly ground coffee every morning ... watching the seasons change ... hanging out with close friends Saturday night. There's so much to be thankful for.

R: You seem like a very positive person.

D: I've been through a lot.

R: Enjoying life's simple pleasures then is a good summary, isn't it?

D: Yes, if there's one thing life's taught me, it's that the stuff that makes you truly happy is the stuff money can't buy. It's, erm, it's the little things that count ...

R: Very good advice. I'll have to remember that myself!

Unit 4

4.1 *page 38 exercise 1B*

... and here are today's separable phrasal verbs. The first one is *give away*, which means "to reveal something that should be kept a secret"; for example, "I can't lie. My voice always gives me away." In other words, it shows what I'm really feeling. The next one is *take in* and it means "to fool or deceive somebody." You often use it in the passive voice, as in "I've never been taken in by a TV ad." Going down the list, we have *tell apart*, a phrasal verb that means "to recognize the difference between or distinguish two people or things," as in "The twins look so much alike that no one can tell them apart." The final separable phrasal verb for today is very, very common – *figure out* – and it means "to discover an answer or solution to something, to solve a problem." For example, imagine you buy a new washing machine, and it's really complicated to use. You can say, "It took me weeks to figure out how to use our new washing machine."

The next group consists of phrasal verbs that can't be separated. I'm sure you're familiar with *look out*, for example. The first one on our list today is *watch out for*, which actually means "to look out, be careful, and be on the alert for any problems"; for example, if you're buying a used car, you might ask a friend, "What problems should I watch out for when buying a used car?" The next phrasal verb on our list is *fall for*, which means "to be deceived by something, or to become a victim," as in "I can't believe you fell for that trick!" And finally, the last one for today is turn out, another very common phrasal verb. *Turn out* means "to prove to be the case in the end"; for example, "This jacket was cheap, but it turned out to be really warm."

4.3 *page 39 exercise 2A*

K = Kim, M = Mark, L = Linda

K: Cool phone. Is it new?

M: Yeah, Kim, I bought it on eBay. The one I had was still working, but who can resist a 40% discount.

L: Second hand?

M: No, it's brand new, apparently, except it came in a green box, not the white one I was expecting.

K: Hmm ...

M: What?

L: How do you know it's genuine?

M: What do you mean, Linda?

L: My brother just bought a phone from an online store for, like, half the price and it turned out to be a perfect, or almost perfect, imitation.

M: But how do I figure out if it's real? I mean, it's fully functional, but now that you're saying it ...

K: Let me take a look. ... Well, I can't tell them apart.

L: Let me try. ... Sorry, you've been taken in!

M: What?!

L: They're not identical. Look at the button right here!

M: Oh, no!

L: Sorry!

M: "Forty percent off!" – Yeah, it was too good to be true. Can't believe I fell for something like that. First time ever.

L: What are you going to do now?

M: I've got to figure out a way to get a refund.

L: Oh, you didn't read their ...

M: Return policy? Nope.

K: Oh, no!

4.4 *page 39 exercises 2B and C*

K: But do you have to return it?

M: Oh Kim! I can't keep this phone. It's just wrong. What do you think, Linda?

L: Yeah, absolutely.

K: Well, it's not a stolen phone. You bought it from a store, right?

M: Well, just because it's legal doesn't mean it's ethical.

L: I agree. The original company invested millions and millions of dollars to make this phone. It can't be, you know, just cloned like that. You're stealing their revenue! Their engineers spent ...

K: But ... Surely you'd agree that no one creates new stuff ... I mean, something entirely new ... You take an idea and you improve it and ...

M: You're missing the point, Kim. Let me put it another way. If you ran a company and if you knew you would lose millions and millions of dollars in revenue because of piracy, why would you bother to invest in new technologies?

K: Hmm ...

L: Look at it this way. Just imagine what it would be like to work from sunrise to sunset, with very short lunch breaks, extremely low wages, no benefits ... 'Cause that's how most fake goods are made.

K: Well, I hadn't thought of that.

M: Plus these people pay no taxes ... Think of all the money we're losing as a nation ... Money that could go to public health and education and ...

L: Yeah. And as if that weren't enough, you don't know how these phones are made, so there's a real chance that when they're thrown away, lots of toxic chemicals could be released into ...

K: Oh, all right, all right. Mark, get rid of it!

4.6 *page 40 exercise 3A*

I'm Aaron Sams and I teach science here at Woodland Park High School. My ultimate goal,

I guess, as a teacher is to help students become learners who can learn for themselves and by themselves. One of the problems that I was guilty of, even to prior to flipping my classroom around was the classroom was centered around me: I told them exactly what to learn, how to learn it, what assignments to do to "learn it," and when to learn it, and how to prove to me that that they learned it.

I don't do that anymore. We changed the place in which content is delivered. Instead of standing in front of a class and delivering "here's how you do this type of problem, here's how this works," I deliver that direct instruction now asynchronously at home through these videos that we make with Camtasia Studio.

The last step they were already whole numbers; we had 1, 1 and 4. Here we don't have a whole number, so here's a few little tricks when you need to multiply by whole numbers. If one of your numbers ends in 0.5, you're going to multiply by two.

Something point 5, times it by two. Write this down, guys.

Yes, so if something ends in 0.3, 0.33 or 0.66, you multiple by three.

When kids come to class, they don't show up to learn new stuff, they show up to apply the things that they learned at home and to ask me questions about the things they learned at home. So now they can have my lesson, if you will, without ... normally have stood up and lectured to them in class with some added features, they get that at home, and then what they're expected to do for homework is now what they do in my class.

4.8 *page 43 exercise 6A*

Conversation 1

W: Make a wish!

M: No, don't do that! You could kill somebody down there!

W: With a coin?

M: Yeah! We're on the 90th floor! Think of the speed this thing's gonna ...

W: Oh, you mean the Empire State story? The pedestrian that was killed by a falling coin?

M: Yeah! My cousin was there. He told me he saw the whole thing.

W: That's just an old urban legend.

M: What?

W: Yeah, it's an urban legend ... At first I wasn't sure whether the story was real ... But then my physics teacher said a falling coin couldn't kill anyone ... because of the air resistance or something.

M: Yes, of course! It's a law of physics! So I guess in the end Don was lying ... Again!

W: Who's Don?

M: My cousin. He's always making up stories, and we fight like cats and dogs over whether they're true.

Conversation 2

M: Hmm ... That was delicious!

W: Well, I'm glad you like my cooking.

M: You said the movie starts at 9:00? I just need to grab a quick shower first.

W: What? But you've just had a two-course meal!

M: So?

W: You know it's not good for you, right?

M: Says who?

W: Well, back in the day, people used to say that taking a shower after a meal could kill you, so my mother used to tell us to stay away from the shower. And she was never wrong about anything.

M: Hmm ... I eat and then shower from time to time – maybe once a month – and I'm still here.

W: Yeah, but you eat like a bird.

M: And you sound like a broken record. That's the fourth time this week you've told me that.

Conversation 3

M: Oh, no!

W: What happened?

M: Look who's died!

W: Oh, that can't be true. I'm on the *New York* Times site right now, and they haven't said anything.

M: Hmm ... try refreshing the page. Maybe it's out of date.

W: OK ... still no news. Oh, don't worry. At some point, we're going to find out that the rumors are false. You know, maybe her manager will release a statement or something.

M: The Internet's scary sometimes. You post something and, in no time, it's all over the web.

W: Yeah, it spreads like wildfire.

4.10 *page 43 exercise 4D*

1

W: Who's Don?

M: My cousin. He's always making up stories, and we **fight like cats and dogs** over whether they're true.

2

M: I eat and then shower from time to time – maybe once a month – and I'm still here.

W: Yeah, but you **eat like a bird**.

M: And you **sound like a broken record**. That's the fourth time this week you've told me that.

3

M: The Internet's scary sometimes. You post something and, in no time, it's all over the web.

W: Yeah, it **spreads like wildfire**.

4.11 *page 44 exercises 7A and B*

B = Bill, R = Rachel

B: And we're back with *Who's the real you?* – 'cause, remember, nothing is as obvious as it seems. Let me tell you about this three-minute video describing an experiment that a well-known company used in one of its advertising campaigns for a new brand of natural make-up.

R: Three minutes?

B: Yeah, but it's totally worth your time. You haven't seen it?

R: Hmm ... I might have, who knows?

B: Anyway, here's how it goes. They hired this artist and brought together a group of women of different ages and backgrounds ... He then asked each woman, one at a time, to describe the way she looked: facial structure, hair length, most prominent features, and so on.

R: So there was only one participant in the room at a time?

B: Yeah. And then he sketched each woman, based only on her self-description.

R: Oh, so you mean he couldn't see the women?

B: Exactly. They were separated by a curtain. Anyway, later on, participants were asked to spend some time in pairs getting to know each other ... you know, just chatting. Then the artist asked each woman to describe the other's face.

R: And he drew it?

B: Yeah. So each woman had two pictures, her own self-description and the one described by the other participant. At the end of the experiment, the artist met face to face with each one and revealed both sketches. Guess what happened.

4.13 *page 45 exercise 8C*

B: So ... One of our listeners, Paul, from New Mexico, tweets: "Why do I look good in the mirror and awful in photos? What do I *really* look like? Rachel, you're my favorite radio celebrity."

R: Oh, that's so sweet. But... Paul, I don't see myself as a celebrity at all.

B: Good question, Paul. This is something I've always been curious about myself, so I did a little research. So, folks, here's the deal: basically, you see yourselves in mirrors far more often than in photos, so your minds somehow internalize the mirror image as the "correct" one.

R: Interesting.

B: Also, because a mirror image is "live," if you see an ugly angle or facial expression, you can instantly correct it. I mean, subconsciously.

R: Right, plus the fact that we tend to stand closer to mirrors than to each other, so we see ourselves from the same height, too... Which doesn't seem to help, in my case.

B: Don't be so hard on yourself, Rachel! Anyway, I'd say photos are usually a little more accurate, though it depends on the camera, of course. But here's the thing ... People think they look ugly because when they see themselves in a photo, their imperfections are magnified, like, ten times. Plus, a photo is a paused, 2D representation of a moving, 3D person. Try pausing a video when someone is talking and you'll see what I mean!

R: Do you consider yourself photogenic?

B: Well, let's not go there. Anyway, long story short: We can't know what we really look like. On some level we will always be a mystery to ourselves.

R: But maybe not to others!

4.15 *page 46 exercise 10A*

R = Ryan, L = Liz

R: New glasses, Liz?

L: What? Oh, well, actually, Ryan ... yeah, in fact, they are. These are smart glasses.

R: Oh, are you wearing the X29 – those glasses everyone's talking about?

L: Yep.

R: I didn't know they were selling them in the U.S.

L: They're not. My husband bought them online, straight from a Japanese website.

R: Oh.

L: Not sure what made him think I wanted them, though, but they're kind of cool. I mean, they can help me with all sorts of tasks.

4.16 *page 46 exercise 10B and C*

R: You mean besides making phone calls, texting, searching the Internet ...
L: ... and social media. Oh, yeah. You know I went to Rio de Janeiro last month, right?
R: Yeah, you told me. I'm dying to go there!
L: This thing was a lifesaver, especially because of my Portuguese.
R: What do you mean?
L: The glasses translated all sorts of common street signs back into English and ...
R: No way!
L: Yeah. And it gets better. They can translate conversations, too – simultaneously. Just the simple stuff, of course, like shopping and asking for directions, but what else does a tourist need?
R: You mean the mic captures the sound and ...
L: ... it gets translated into English. Exactly.
R: Unbelievable.
L: But that's not all, Ryan. You know how I feel about public speaking, right?
R: Yeah ... remember that time your mind went blank?
L: Yeah, I remember. I nearly died of embarrassment. Well, now, whenever I give presentations, I can glance at my notes while I'm speaking.
R: You mean the text appears on the mini screen? Like a teleprompter?
L: Yeah. No more panic attacks! Well, the glasses monitor my heart rate and blood pressure, just in case.
R: Wow.
L: I wish they could also be my personal trainer, though.
R: So you could fire that awful Rick guy and save yourself a ton of money?
L: Yep. You got it!

4.17 *page 46 exercise 10D*

R: Pretty impressive.
L: Yeah. The kids love them to death. But I'm having second thoughts.
R: Oh yeah?
L: I'm not sure if they'll make life all that much easier ... I mean, the everyday stuff.
R: Like what?
L: For starters ... despite what they promised, the X29 is still a bit awkward to wear, so I find myself taking the glasses off from time to time. Here, try them on yourself.
R: Hmm ... but you wouldn't have them on all the time, would you? I mean, like while you're driving and ...
L: Oh, no! Or biking, or even crossing the street. It's hard to concentrate on the display and anything else at the same time. But then again, it's not like they didn't warn me, so ...
R: They look good, though, don't they? I mean, the glasses themselves.
L: Yeah, but some people still look at me as if I were a creature from another planet ... which is kind of annoying, though not unexpected, of course.
R: Not good for first dates then? Or job interviews?
L: Exactly. In fact, I find these glasses much more intrusive than I thought I would. It's like, it's like there's a wall between you and the person you're talking to. It's, erm, it's hard to explain. It's like you're trapped in your own virtual world.
R: Well, maybe, but I love them. I'd do anything to get my hands on a pair!
L: Hey, I can ask my husband how much ...

Review 2 (Units 3–4)

R2.1 *page 48 exercise 2*

S = Sally, R = Randy, C = Caller

S: On today's show, we're going to look at a problem that could happen to anyone. You send that email about your boss directly to him – or her! With us today is psychologist Randy Peters.
R: Thank you, Sally. You would *not* believe how common this is. Here's someone calling in right now.
C: I can sure relate. I'll never forget, I was having a really bad day. In fact, I'd just broken up with my boyfriend, and my boss was pressuring me to meet a deadline. So I type an email ... something you should never do from the office computer, and instead of sending it to a friend, I send it to her!
R: Uh, oh ... and what happened next?
C: Nothing right away. But as I was leaving for the day (finally!), I hear a familiar voice saying, "Can I see you for a moment before you go?"
R: Your boss?
C: That's right. And she hands me the email ... and waits.
R: So what did you do?
C: I wanted to disappear. I'd never felt so embarrassed in my life. I had no idea what to say. Just silence, 5, 10, 15 seconds. And finally, she says, "Is this really what you think of me?"
R: The crucial moment. What did you answer?
C: I had to think fast. And I have no idea where I got the courage, but I said "yes!"
R: You *did*?
C: I did. I told her the pressure was very stressful, and I was doing the best I could. And that she should try to imagine being me.
R: What happened next?
C: You know, life can be very unpredictable. She thanked me for my honesty! And ever since that day, she's been much more reasonable.
R: A story with a happy ending. And now let's hear from ...

Unit 5

5.2 *page 51 exercises 2A and B*

Speaker 1

Erm ... Hi! This is the first time I've ever recorded a home video, so, erm... Sorry about the quality. I'd like to nominate Tara Littlewood. She's a friend of mine – well, actually she's one of my closest friends. Tara is a single mom and she supported herself and her twins – yeah, twins – for years, with temporary jobs. Then a few years ago, when the economy collapsed, she had to drop out of college. She lost her home, so they, erm, they had to live with her parents for a while, which was a nightmare, she once told me, and it was really hard to earn a living and put food on the table. But Tara never gave up. You see, she'd always loved writing, so in the little free time that she had, she managed to write her first novel. Well, long story short, the book sold reasonably well, and she was able to finally go back to college to complete her BA in literature – at age 35. I, erm, I really admire her and, you know, her ability to pursue her dreams. Tara never let any obstacles stop her. She's inspired me to go back to college too, which I'm going to do next year, I hope.

Speaker 2

My name's Ricardo and I'd have to say that my hero is my grandfather, Fernando Gómez. In many ways, he's, erm, he's the father I never had, actually. When grandpa was in his early- to mid-fifties, he was diagnosed with a medical condition that was very serious. We were all shocked by the news – I mean, Grandpa sick? The two words just don't go together. His doctor – er, doctors – we went to at least five specialists – they told him that he might be too weak to walk and end up bedridden, but he ... but he never gave up. He quit his job, bought a house in the countryside, took up yoga ... you name it. He made many changes to have a healthier lifestyle and just kept going, no matter what. Today, he's ... he's turning 80 next week. He's such an inspiration. I wish I was a little – a lot – more like him. He's taught me that you can do just about anything you want to when you put your mind to it. He's inspired me to change my lifestyle too and, you know what, I've never felt better.

5.3 *page 52 exercises 3B and C*

C = Claire, A = Anthony

C: So ... how did it go?
A: What do you think?
C: Did you pass?
A: Of course not.
C: Oh, no!
A: Fourth one this year – and it's still June. I don't know what's wrong with me. I mean, I'm not stupid or anything, so how come I can't ...
C: But what went wrong? Were you nervous?
A: Yeah. I mean, the woman looked kind of scary ...
C: Don't they all?
A: At one point she said "turn right" and I ...
C: And you turned left?
A: Yep.
C: No, you didn't!
A: I did.
C: And then you freaked out?
A: Totally. And then it went downhill from there. I made a complete fool of myself.
C: Like what?
A: Hmm ...
C: What?
A: A tree appeared in the middle of the road!
C: Oh, no! Did you hit it?
A: What do you think?
C: Oh, no!
A: I wish I hadn't gotten out of bed today.

5.9 *page 56 exercises 7A and B*

K = Keith, L = Lorna

DJ: Welcome back to *Oops, wrong again*, your weekly radio show about unusual careers. Keith, your story reminded me of the Beatles back in 1962.

K: You mean when they got rejected by Decca records?

DJ: Exactly. Apparently Decca's executives wrote to them saying that guitar groups were on the way out, or something like that. Can you believe it?

K: I bet they wouldn't have sent that letter if they'd had a crystal ball at the time. The best-selling band in history!

L: Oops! But at least they signed the Rolling Stones soon afterwards. And what about J.K. Rowling? She got rejected by twelve different publishers.

K: Twelve?

L: Yeah. They thought the book was far too long for kids.

DJ: So what happened in the end?

L: Well, she found a publisher whose president gave it to his eight-year-old daughter. Guess what? She loved it. So they agreed to publish Harry Potter.

K: I really look up to Rowling. What a fighter she is. If she didn't have such willpower, she might have given up ...

DJ: That's so true, ... and she wouldn't be one of the wealthiest women in the world today.

K: Oops! Walt Disney had his ups and downs, too. He was fired from his job as a newspaper editor, wasn't he?

L: He sure was! In 1919. They said he lacked imagination and had no good ideas. Maybe if he hadn't had so much faith in himself, we wouldn't have Mickey Mouse today!

DJ: And that would be a real shame ... That sure is swell! See ya soon!

5.12 *page 58 exercise 10A*

See audio 5.13

5.13 *page 58 exercise 10B*

H = Holly, R = Ron

H: Did you see my message on your wall?

R: Yeah, thanks. Thought you were going to forget again.

H: So, did you go out to celebrate?

R: Uh huh. Lana Del Rey is on tour and Aimee bought two tickets. We just love her music.

H: Oh, you're still together? But, hadn't you broken up?

R: Yeah ... Well, life's full of surprises, though, huh? Anyway, that show had been on our wish list for, like, months. We couldn't wait to see her live. But the problem was, I had to leave work earlier so we could make it on time ... which my boss wasn't exactly thrilled about.

H: But did you tell him about the show?

R: Not exactly ... I, erm, I made up a lame excuse and apparently he bought it.

H: That is so wrong!

R: I know, I know. But, come on, give me a break ... It was my birthday.

H: Hmm ... Did you enjoy the show at least?

R: I wish I had. Aimee did, though. She even bought the T-shirt. But here's where the story gets weird. Barry texted me at 1:00 a.m. ...

H: Who's Barry?

R: My boss. He texted me at 1:00 a.m asking me about the show.

H: No way!

R: He did. Look.

H: "Hope you had a good time." But how did he find out you were there?

R: Well, there's only one explanation.

H: What? You mean somebody told him you were there? A coworker maybe?

R: Not likely.

H: Was he in the audience? Oh, come on! What are the odds of that happening?!

R: I doubt it. You see, there were lots of cameras in the place. We thought they were filming the show for a future recording or something. Turns out it was being broadcast live.

H: But how did he find out ... oh, no! You were caught on camera!

R: Yeah. And Barry must have been watching the show on TV.

H: Oh, come on! No one can be that unlucky! Well, serves you right! If you'd told the truth, none of this would have happened!

R: I was so embarrassed! Wouldn't wish it on my worst enemy. Anyway, he said he wants to see me on Monday. Wish me luck.

Unit 6

6.2 *page 61 exercises 2B and C*

Conversation 1

A: Rob, come to bed. It's ... It's 2 a.m. What are you doing?

B: Playing Diamond Dash. I'm winning, I'm winning!

A: Oh, the one on Facebook ... Mother was right, I married a fifteen-year-old.

B: This thing is pretty addictive. You should try it.

A: Yeah. Until the day those guys find out where we live, what our favorite food is, who ...

B: Don't worry. Diamond Dash is pretty safe.

A: Well, OK, whatever. Play it at your own risk. Good night. Oh, don't forget to ...

Conversation 2

A: Oh no!

B: What?

A: Just Googled myself.

B: So?

A: Check this out.

B: I-want-you-back-dot-com. Don, you asked for romantic advice online? Using your real name? What were you thinking?

A: I thought the whole thing was risk-free. How was I to know they'd use my real name? Oh, no ... What if Jerry finds out?

B: Jerry? Not sure he even knows how to use Google. Besides, he's too busy making sure we get our work done and ...

Conversation 3

A: Can I borrow your laptop?

B: Sure.

A: Thanks ... Erm ... Daniel, you, uh, you might want to clear your search history.

B: What? You mean on my browser?

A: Yeah. Take a look.

B: Oh, no! Cathy, this is like so embarrassing. Thank goodness it was you and not Gina. I don't want to risk losing her over a stupid Google search.

A: Miley Cyrus? Really? I mean, really?

Conversation 4

A: Oh, no.

B: What?

A: Forgot my twitter password. Again.

B: What do you mean your Twitter password? Do you have more than one?

A: Of course, Lynette! Don't you?

B: Only have one – my name spelled backwards. I use it on, like, 20 different sites.

A: You know you're at risk, right? I mean, using the same password.

B: Oh, yeah?

A: If a hacker steals your password, you ...

Conversation 5

A: Mom, can I borrow your credit card?

B: Erm ... Sure. What for?

A: Want to get a new phone. Goodphones has a sale and ...

B: Goodphones? Never been to this place.

A: It's not a place. Goodphones-dot-com! It's a brand new website. It's been ...

B: Sophie, so you're going to use my card on a site you've never heard of just to save a few bucks? I mean, isn't online shopping a bit risky?

A: Oh, don't worry. The site was rated ...

6.5 *page 63 exercise 4C*

A = Alison, W = Will, G = Grace

A: OK ... Here's what it says ... "Facebook should be treated like a social network, not a diary."

W: I couldn't agree more. I mean, who cares what you had for breakfast, what your dog has done to your ...

A: Hey, I like to post photos of my dog.

W: And that's why I've blocked you.

A: What?

W: I'm kidding, but, no, seriously ... People don't realize how insanely boring some of their posts are. The whole thing's just a huge waste of time.

G: Hmm ... I don't see it that way. I mean, I like it when my close friends talk about their day-to-day lives ... you know, the little things that . . .

A: Yeah, close friends, but not someone from high school you haven't seen in years – and that's who most of the stuff in your news feed comes from.

G: OK. point taken. But still ... look, here's the thing – dogs, cats, babies – that's all harmless stuff. What freaks me out is ... You know, when people write about very personal issues. ... The other day a friend of mine posted about her grandmother's funeral. I mean, you don't tell ...

W: Oh, that kind of diary. Yeah. Absolutely. There are certain things, certain things you just don't post on Facebook. Period. Alison, what's your take on it?

A: I think people should be free to post whatever they see fit. You see ...

6.8 *page 64 exercise 5E*

... but looking back, I think I've learned three lessons. The first one: None of the dangers I'd anticipated came true. There was no cyberbullying, no talk of drugs, no toxic relationships. They spent most of their time talking about girls, homework, the stress they were under because of school, and TV shows or books they liked. Second lesson: My spying showed me valuable things about my sons that I would never ever have learned otherwise. For example, Chris, the youngest one, had never shown any interest in writing when it came to school. As it turns out, he was spending hours every day writing and sharing some pretty impressive fiction online. Who would have thought it! So, thanks to my monitoring, I was

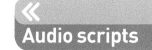

able to encourage him to pursue his passion. But here's the most important lesson: My husband didn't know about my spying, and he was really upset when he found out. So, from now on, no more secrets. It's important for couples to agree on important topics.

6.9 *page 65 exercise 6A*

Conversation 1

A: Dad, is that a ... a camera in my room? A surveillance camera?

B: Yes, Julia, it's a surveillance camera. Keith's house was broken into last week and ...

A: Oh, OK, for burglars. For a second, I thought you thought I was doing something illegal or something.

Conversation 2

A: Mom! What are you doing here? Spying on me? Again?

B: No, I was just ... watching you.

A: Secretly! So, yeah, you were spying on me.

Conversation 3

A: Dad, were you eavesdropping on me? Again?

B: No, of course not!

A: Listen, if you want to listen in on my private phone calls, I can put you on speaker! No need to eavesdrop!

Conversation 4

A: Mom, why is my browser history empty? Did you delete it? Are you keeping tabs on the sites I visit?

B: Yes, I am. As your mother, I need to keep myself informed about what you've been ...

A: Unbelievable! My own mother is keeping tabs on my Internet history.

Conversation 5

A: Jenny, listen, I don't like that Mark guy. I think he can be a little ... I think he's a threat to you.

B: A threat?

A: Yeah. That guy is dangerous. I don't want him anywhere near you.

6.11 *page 66 exercises 7B and C*

R = Reporter

1 James

R: Excuse me. Do you have a minute to spare?

J: Hmm, I'm on my lunch break.

R: It'll only take a minute.

J: Oh, all right.

R: Great, thanks. We're conducting a survey on social network sites. Take a look at this list, please ... Which of these apps do you think is the biggest threat to your privacy?

J: Hmm ... Facebook for sure.

R: And why's that?

J: Cause my parents seem totally obsessed with Facebook ... especially my dad ... He comments on whatever he sees on my newsfeed, which is, like, so uncool ...

R: Do you think this may be a trend? I mean, teenagers feeling too exposed on Facebook?

J: Yeah. I mean, the answer is always the same whoever you talk to. My friends all feel Facebook is a bit like big brother, you know. I actually ...

2 Audra

R: ... on how young people feel about social network sites. Can I ask you a quick question?

A: Sure.

R: From the sites on this list, which one poses the biggest threat to your privacy?

A: Hmm ... I'm not big on social networks – I think they're all awful – but ... Instagram maybe is the worst.

R: Instagram?

A: Yeah, I guess so ... I mean, people, like ... They stop and take a photo whenever they see something "interesting" – cars, trees, people – at the mall, on the street, at school. I mean, what's the point? Plus all your friends and classmates get to see your photos, which means they will find out where you've been and who you've been with. However you look at this Instagram craze, it's just pointless.

R: OK, but you know you can change your privacy settings, right?

A: I can?

R: Oh, yeah. You see ...

3 Tom

T: ... OK ... Hmm ... you mean my online privacy?

R: Yeah.

T: Foursquare. I have a love / hate relationship with Foursquare. You know how it works, right? Wherever you are, you just access the app and check in.

R: Uh huh.

T: I guess it's the idea of people keeping tabs on me that freaks me out. I mean, what if I want to miss school because "I'm sick," and then Ms. Roberts sees me at Starbucks?

R: Well, surely you don't have to log in when you ...

T: Yeah, but ... you know, whichever app I use, I always end up doing something wrong. I'm not good at these things, you know.

R: OK. What about your favorite app?

T: Well, I guess ...

6.15 *page 68 exercises 10B and C*

M = Mika, L = Larry

M: So ... how did it go?

L: Oh, you don't wanna know.

M: Why?

L: I was turned down. Again. The interview only lasted about five minutes.

M: Oh, Larry, I'm sorry, baby.

L: They said they needed someone with "more relevant experience," whatever that means.

M: I can't believe it. I mean you're so good. You've worked at lots of IT companies. You lived in Europe for a while ... You were actually ... You were offered a job at Apple, remember?

L: Yeah, I know. I still can't believe I refused it! Anyway, I think he liked me.

M: So, why didn't he give you the job for heaven's sake?

L: I don't know. I mean, I arrived on time, answered all the questions, talked about my experience ... Hmm ...

M: What?

L: At one point, he asked me about my Facebook profile.

M: Oh, no.

L: What do you mean, oh, no?

M: The birthday photo. The one you were tagged in.

L: Oh, no! You mean the one in the swimming pool in Tom's backyard?

M: Yep. That one.

L: Oh, no!

M: Listen, what's done is done. Don't let it get to you. We're in this together, whatever happens.

Unit 7

7.1 *page 72 exercise 1B*

T = Tim, N = Nina, V = Vicky

T: You're listening to XBIZ Chicago, and this is *Wait, I know this one!* – our daily music quiz where you have a chance to win a gift card from your favorite online music store. I'm Tim Oseary.

N: And I'm Nina Dunphy.

T: Now let's welcome our first contestant. Hello, you're on *Wait, I know this one*.

V: Hi, my name is Vicky Robinson and I'm calling from Seattle, Washington.

T: Hello, Vicky. Thanks for joining us. What do you do there in Seattle?

V: I'm an elementary school teacher.

N: Are you ready for our first question?

V: Yeah, I guess.

N: OK, here we go. Singer Sam Smith rose to fame in 2012 ...

V: Oh, I love Sam Smith.

N: What was his job before he became the high profile celebrity he is today? Option A, a taxi driver. Option B, a bartender. Option C, a pet groomer.

V: Oh, this one's easy. A bartender. He said it in an interview once.

T: Correct! Sam Smith used to work in a bar. Question 2. Erm ... Do you like Bob Marley?

V: Hmm. He's not my thing, no.

T: Well, but you know he's generally regarded as the king of reggae, correct?

V: Yeah.

T: Which of these statements about him is true? Option A, As a child, he could predict people's futures by reading their palms. Option B, He only released three albums in his lifetime. Option C, His biggest hit is *Don't worry, be happy*.

V: Oh, I know this song: Option C.

N: Are you sure?

V: Positive.

N: Actually, it was another Bob. It was Bobby McFerrin who sang that song, back in the 80s – not Bob Marley. Rumor has it that Bob Marley could predict people's futures, apparently.

T: Here's question 3. Adele's *21*, the best-selling album that came out in 2011, spent nearly six months at the top of the U.S. and UK charts. What does 21 in the title refer to? Option A, her lucky number. Option B, the number of songs on the CD. Option C, her age at the time.

V: Hmm ... You can't fit 21 songs on a single CD, so no. It could be A or C. I'll go with C.

T: Her age?

V: Yeah ... I'm not sure, though.

N: That is correct. Adele was only 21 when the album came out.

T: What a smash hit that album was! And speaking of hits ... Are you ready for our last question? You'll win a $200 gift card if you get this one right.

V: Bring it on!

T: The very first U.S. edition of the legendary *Rock in Rio* music festival took place in 2015 and featured the artist behind the smash hits *Uptown funk* and *Grenade*. Who are we talking about? Option A ...

V: I know, I know. Bruno Mars. I'm a huge fan!

N: Your answer is correct! *Uptown funk* spent seven weeks at number 1, both in the U.S. and the U.K., and was one of the biggest hits of 2015. Congratulations, Vicky!

T: Stay on the line so we can ...

V: Oh, I'm so happy!

7.2 *page 73 exercise 1C*

Hello! It's Helene again. OK, let's check. For number 1, we have a very common expression, "to rise to fame." For example, singer Sam Smith *rose to fame* in 2012, when he started to appear in other people's songs. *Rose to fame* means "suddenly became very famous."

Moving on to number 2, *high-profile* celebrities are people who are often seen in public or mentioned in newspapers because they're very prominent and well known. *High profile* doesn't only refer to celebrities, though. We can talk about a high-profile event, a high-profile politician, or even a high-profile company like Coca Cola or Apple.

Now notice number 3, *is regarded as*. *To be regarded as* means "to be considered."

The next expression, number 4: when we say that an album, movie, or book *came out*, it was officially released and became available. For example, even though Sam Smith rose to fame in 2012, his first album only *came out* two years later.

Finally, for the last one, number 5: *take place*. If something *took place*, it happened or occurred. We can say that a show, a meeting or, say, a game took place. For example, the first edition of *Rock in Rio* took place in the 1980s, and lots of high-profile artists were there, such as Guns n' Roses and Queen.

Well, that's it for today, folks. Five expressions you should now be able to use.

7.3 *age 72 exercises 2A and B*

T = Tim, N = Nina

T: Wow, that was painful.

N: What?

T: This whole music thing, Nina. Come on, a pop music quiz? Winning a prize? Really?

N: What do you mean?

T: I think I've had enough of this job.

N: Wow.

T: I know.

N: But you ... You have a background in music, right?

T: Yeah, my undergraduate degree. And I ... I used to be really fond of pop music. Like, I had this huge Coldplay poster in my bedroom and ...

N: Yeah... I was really into their music too. Still am.

T: And that's also why I got this job in the first place. I wanted to do something I really enjoyed. But after a while, I guess I ... I grew tired of playing the same old songs, listening to the same old melodies, day after day... And don't get me started about the lyrics. I mean, how many different ways of saying "Baby I miss you, come back to me" can there be?

N: Yeah, I know what you mean and I feel the same way sometimes, especially, you know, about having to look at the charts, predict the next smash hits, decide who's hot and who's not.

T: Exactly! Anyway, I've been listening to my dad's old CD collection a lot lately – for fun, really – and I think...Well, this may be hard to believe, but ...

N: What?

T: I'm getting hooked on jazz. Miles Davis, man, he was something else!

N: No way!

T: Yeah. Big time. I can't get enough of it. Which makes working at a station like this one even harder. I mean, I don't think our target audience is old enough to even know that jazz is not only a Honda car.

N: So, what are your plans?

T: Option 1 is to stick around till they decide they want to get rid of me. I mean, where else would I make 200 grand a year? Option 2 is to follow my heart, apply for a job at KW2 ...

N: ... which plays jazz 24/7, right?

T: Exactly! And maybe settle for a little less money.

N: Well, if I were you ... Oh, we're back on. You're listening to ...

7.5 *page 74 exercise 3A*

J = Josh, L = Liz

J: Still into Miley?

L: Uh huh. Can't get enough of her.

J: She puts on an amazing show.

L: Yeah, so I've heard. But ...

J: But you've seen her live, haven't you? I mean, during the Bangerz tour?

L: No. I ...

J: But I thought ...

L: Well, I was going to. I had to beg a colleague to fill in for me at work, paid someone to look after my parrot, spent a fortune on front-row tickets and ...

J: What?

L: She got really sick and the show was canceled.

J: Oh, no! Postponed or totally canceled?

7.6 *page 74 exercise 3B*

L: Canceled, at least at first. Yeah. They had to cancel at the last minute because she came down with a viral infection. Some ...

J: A viral infection? But was it serious enough to make them cancel the whole thing?

L: Well, apparently, it was. She took some really strong antibiotics and ended up in a local hospital because of an allergic reaction or something. I ...

J: Oh, yes, I remember. It was all over the news. The fans were furious!

L: You bet. There were people crying and screaming and ...

J: You too, I'm sure.

L: Right, well, in the end everybody just got a refund at the box office and went ...

J: Home! That must have been really frustrating!

L: It was. And to make things worse, they didn't know at the time whether the show...

J: Would be rescheduled?

L: Yeah. At least she tweeted a nice message to apologize to her fans. Poor thing. I mean, it's not her fault.

7.7 *page 74 exercise 3C*

J: But the show was rescheduled, right?

L: It was, eventually, but I couldn't miss work again. But in September, she was scheduled to play in Mexico City and ...

J: No! You ...

L: You know, since I was on vacation, I thought I'd give her a second chance. Plus, I have friends there, so finding a place to stay wouldn't be a problem. Besides, ...

J: Can't believe you went to Mexico! You lucky ...

L: I did! So, anyway, I borrowed money for the tickets and ...

J: I didn't know you were such a fan.

L: I am! Anyway, on the big day, I left home early so I'd have plenty of time to get to the airport.

J: Uh huh.

L: So I got on the plane and, guess what ...

J: Engine failure!

L: No! But something was wrong with the air-conditioning and, well, we nearly froze to death, so the plane was diverted back to ...

J: Kansas! No way!

L: Yep. I could have taken one the next day, but, you know, I was so fed up with the whole thing ... I just gave up. It wasn't meant to be, I guess.

J: But ...

L: In the end I downloaded the show just to have a taste ... of what I missed.

J: She'll go on another tour soon. Don't worry.

L: I hope so!

7.9 *page 76 exercise 5D*

Hi class. It's me, Helene, your cyber teacher back again. Just want to make sure you noticed a few things: *Hit* the noun and *hit* the verb have different meanings. The noun means "something that's very successful, such as a record, a book, or a play: a smash hit." The verb, in this case, means "to reach: to hit the market." *Work* and *work* have different meanings, too. The noun, in this case, means "something that results from an artistic effort." The verb, in this case, means "to function well." OK, that's all for today!

7.12 *page 78 exercise 8B*

P = Peter, R = Rick

P: I'm having some friends over tomorrow. Wanna join us?

R: No, thanks. I'm going on – are you ready for this – a date!

P: What? Really? Good for you! How long has it been, a year?

R: Well, not quite that long. About six months.

P: Do I know her?

R: No. Met her at a party last month.

P: What's she like?

R: She's amazing. Really good looking. And she seems funny and sweet and really, I mean, really smart. Harvard smart. And from what I can tell on the phone, she's into art and classical music and ... stuff.

P: Just like my ex.

R: Our first date will be at an art gallery or something. Can you believe it?

P: But you don't know the first thing about art!
R: I know! I can't tell a Picasso from a ... See, I can't even name another artist! Man, I'm freaking out. What if she thinks I'm stupid?
P: Hmm, what if you ...
R: What?
P: Never mind.
R: What?
P: Just Google it.
R: Google what?
P: How to pretend you're an art expert. I'm sure you'll find lots of tips.
R: Hmm.
P: Come on! Try it! What do you have to lose?

7.13 *page 78 exercise 8C*

You guessed it! It's Helene again. A few more words for you.

1 When you *frown*, you move your eyebrows together and lines appear on your forehead because you're unhappy, not pleased, or thinking hard.
2 To *rub* means to move something – such as your hand, a finger, or a cloth – back and forth, or in a circular motion – over a surface. For example: The first thing I do when I wake up is rub my eyes.
3 When you rub your skin with your nails, you *scratch* it, maybe because of an insect bite, for example, or you might scratch your head because you are thinking. *Scratch* can also mean to mark the surface of something with a sharp or pointed object.
4 To *squint* means to look at something with your eyes partly closed so you can see better. People who wear glasses often squint when they're not wearing them.
5 When you *nod*, you move your head up and down to show that you understand or agree with something. In other words, to nod is to say "yes" with your head.

7.14 *page 79 exercise 9B*

S = Sue, R = Rick

S: This one's nice. I like it better than the others.
R: Hmm ... Let me look at it another time. Yes, I agree. It really captures the essence of passion, conflict and ... and some other things. (Thinks: My cat could have painted this one.)
S: I guess. (Thinks: What's he talking about?)
R: And don't you just love his use of color? Experimental but structured. (Thinks: What have I just said?)
S: Err ... (Thinks: What?!)
R: Other artists may try, but nobody comes close to Picasso. (Thinks: Please, make this be a Picasso, make this be a Picasso.)
S: But that's a Kandinsky. (Thinks: Is he blind or something?)
R: Oh, yes, you're right. It's another metaperspective, isn't it? (Thinks: Hmm ... That sounded smart.)
S: What's that supposed to mean?

7.15 *page 80 exercise 10B*

A = Abby, J = Juan

A: Hey, look what I just bought.
J: Miles Davis? Who's that?
A: What do you mean, "Who's that?" He's the greatest jazz musician who ever lived! And *Kind of Blue* is one of the greatest jazz albums of all time!
J: Let me Google it ... *Kind of Blue* came out in 1959 ... Wow! That's old.
A: Not old. Timeless! It hasn't lost any of its appeal. This album changed everything in the jazz world.
J: You really seem to like it!
A: And so do all these famous people ... Let me play a little bit of this documentary for you. The DVD came with the album.
J: Hmm ... Herbie Hancock calls it "a cornerstone record." Erm ... Who's Herbie Hancock? And what do they mean by "a cornerstone record"?
A: Herbie Hancock is a famous pianist, and a cornerstone record means a very, very important one.
J: Oh, OK. Here's another one. Carlos Santana – the guitar player, right? The one who performed at Woodstock?
A: Yeah.
J: He says, "How do you go to the studio with minimum stuff and come out with eternity?" Eternity! Wow! I'm getting curious about this album.
A: I'm telling you, it's a gem! Look at how Dave Liebman sums it up ...
J: Wait, who's that?
A: He's a famous saxophonist. He says it captures the essence of jazz.
J: Hmm ... Is *True Blue* on Spotify?
A: *Kind of Blue*.
J: *Kind of Blue*, OK. Is it on Spotify?
A: Uh huh. Have a listen. If you like it, I'll lend you the DVD with the documentary.
J: Cool.

7.16 *page 80 exercise 10C*

J: Wow! Who would have thought I'd give jazz a try!
A: I told you! There's no one quite like Miles Davis. Did you watch the whole documentary?
J: No, just the first part. I had no idea jazz was so popular in the '50s. Like, it was everywhere. "Ubiquitous" I think they said.
A: Yes, exactly. "Jazz was ubiquitous in New York, and clubs were thriving across the city, from Greenwich Village to Harlem."
J: You've memorized the documentary?
A: Parts of it, yeah. I watched it like five times.
J: You really are a fan, aren't you?
A: Yes! How I wish I'd grown up in the '50s. Jazz was on TV, in the papers, in magazines ... my grandparents said the same thing – it was everywhere. You just couldn't escape it. Even teenagers listened to jazz in the '50s.
J: Really?
A: Yeah. Well, mostly R & B, you know, Rhythm and Blues, but their parents had older jazz musicians like Duke Ellington and Count Basie on the radio, so they came to appreciate jazz also. They were really eclectic back then.
J: Was Miles Davis born in New York?
A: Well, he grew up in St. Louis, Missouri, but after high school, he came to New York to study music at Juilliard. He was apparently charming, good looking ... on the DVD, Ed Bradley – he was a reporter – called him the "essence of hipness," because of the way he looked, dressed, and played.
J: Yeah, I remember that. I knew "hip," but I'd never heard the word "hipness" before.
A: He was so hip that eventually kids started copying the way he dressed! You know, the same olive green suits and white shirts. And everyone thought that was so cool.
J: Guess things have changed! I wouldn't be caught dead wearing an olive green suit!

Unit 8

8.1 *page 82 exercise 1A*

FEAR – F.E.A.R. It stands for False Evidence Appearing Real. Fear is everywhere! There are real fears (losing your job, getting ill, offending people), fears we love (scary movies, theme park rides, and fears that are exaggerated or even irrational (flying, heights, confined spaces, the dark). This last group can really make your life miserable.
Email a video to IQYP TV talking about your worst fear, and you could be invited to our groundbreaking show, Making F.E.A.R disappear!

8.2 *page 82 exercise 1B*

See audio 8.3

8.3 *page 82 exercises 1C and D*

Speaker 1

Hi, my name's Lucy, and I'm from Los Angeles. I've had this weird fear for the past ten years and it involves cars ... no, not driving ... I don't mind driving, but I – are you ready for this – I panic whenever I have to sit as a passenger in a vehicle, no matter if it's a car, a bus, or a taxi. When I'm in the passenger seat, I get really dizzy ... you know ... as if I was floating on a boat for hours and ... my... my heart starts to race ... like, really fast, as if I'd been running! As for planes ... well ... I avoid flying if I can... I get butterflies in my stomach, especially during takeoff – it's like I'm on a rollercoaster. But if I absolutely have to fly, fine. It's cars and buses and taxis that freak me out ... I've read a couple of self-help books and, quite honestly, they were a huge waste of time. So I hope you guys can help me.

Speaker 2

Erm ... I'm Rob. I'm a systems analyst at a multinational company. I'm married, and I have three kids. It may sound like a cliché, I know, and everybody's afraid of them to some degree ... but I'm ... I'm terrified of spiders – well, petrified, really. You see, I'm OK with other ugly creatures ... for example, I don't mind bats at all – I think they're kind of cute, actually. Cockroaches make me a bit uneasy, of course, but nothing out of the ordinary. But spiders ... they make me ... oh, man! I think it all started when I found a huge spider under my pillow once ... and, erm ... it's gotten worse over the years. I can't breathe whenever I see a picture of a spider ... and I start to sweat ... like it's a hundred degrees outside! Lucy – that's my wife – tries to keep bugs out of our house, which is nice of her, but my parents aren't exactly sympathetic. Dad keeps telling me they're more afraid of me than I am of them. Yeah, right.

Speaker 3
Hi, I'm Donna. I'm an undergraduate student at the University of Miami. I have a slightly unusual fear ... you may not believe this, but ... well ... clowns freak me out. Big time ... I've never set foot in a circus or anything, and ... dolls don't bother me – even Chuckie. I think my fear of clowns comes from TV. Whenever I see a clown on TV ... I burst into tears! Yeah, I'm serious. Someone has to hold my hand until I stop crying. Who knows what would happen if I ever came face to face with a clown. I think I would faint ... I mean, I almost pass out whenever I see a clown on TV! Except for Ronald McDonald. I like him. I think he's kind of cute, actually.

8.6 *page 84 exercises 3A and C*

D = Diego, L = Louise

D: So, in the end, did you go to Rita's party?
L: Yeah, Diego, but I wasn't able to get there until after 10, so I missed most of it.
D: How come?
L: Well, long story short there's a fence around our apartment complex, and I believe it or not, couldn't get out.
D: What?
L: Yeah. I'd lost my key to the gate and I couldn't find the spare one. So I couldn't get out onto the street!
D: That's so like you. But you were able to make it to the party ...
L: Well, I climbed the fence and ...
D: You what?
L: Yeah. My brother even took a photo. Look!
D: Why would he do that?
L: To embarrass me on Instagram, obviously. You know him, Diego ...

8.7 *page 84 exercises 3B and C*

D: But ... I don't get it. Why didn't you simply call your parents?
L: I did! But there was no coverage where they were!
D: No way!
L: I know! I mean, what are the odds of that happening?
D: But, but ... I thought you were afraid of heights.
L: Oh, no, on the contrary. Actually, in school, everyone used to call me spider girl, because, well ... I could climb just about anything.
D: So you're telling me you were able to climb the fence? All dressed up like that?
L: Yeah.
D: Wow! I'm impressed. Did you at least enjoy the party?
L: Not exactly. I ran into Zack and his new girlfriend.
D: Oh, no! Of all people!
L: Yeah. I still have feelings for him, you know, and I think he could see it in my eyes ... So that kind of spoiled the fun ...
D: Hmm ... it's been what since you broke up, a month or two?
L: Yeah. I still kind of miss him.

8.9 *page 88 exercise 7A*

See audio 8.10

8.10 *page 88 exercise 7A*

I = Interviewer, L = Laura

I: ... you mean Milan?
L: Yes. Milan, in northern Italy, is a very happy city. So much so that you're not allowed to frown unless you're at a funeral or at the hospital.
I: What?
L: Yes – smiling is required by law ... a pointless law, I know! Maybe they want to build the city's reputation as a happy, friendly place.
I: Besides the world's fashion capital?
L: Exactly. So, if you ever visit, you'd better forget about your troubles, or else you might have to pay a fine.
I: Did you?
L: Oh, no. I have no trouble smiling! But I did have to pay a fine in Rome.
I: What happened?
L: Well, in general, tourists are not supposed to eat and drink in museums – we all know that – but Rome has recently enforced a law banning eating and drinking at *all* historical sites. The fine? Up to $650!
I: Wow!
L: Yeah.
I: I'm actually off to Rome next week! I didn't know that.
L: So maybe you ought to eat an extra slice of bread before leaving the hotel ...
I: Well, but it's not a bad law. They probably want to protect the city's monuments.
L: Uh huh. And educate tourists, which makes sense, I think. Well, I sure learned my lesson.
I: Any other incidents?
L: Well, once I was stopped by the police while I was driving.
I: For speeding?
L: No. You see, in countries like Denmark and Sweden, driving with your headlights off is considered a violation of the law. You have to keep them on ...
I: Even during the day?
L: Even during the day. This may sound unnecessary, I know, but you've got to obey the local laws.
I: But is there a reason for that?
L: For driving with your headlights on?
I: Yeah.
L: Apparently, it seems that moving lights are relatively easy to notice, and this can reduce the number of accidents. There've actually been some studies that ...

8.11 *page 89 exercise 9A*

1 supposed to... sposta... Tourists are not sposta eat and drink.
2 ought to... oughta... Maybe you oughta eat an extra slice of bread.
3 have to... hafta... You hafta keep headlights on.
4 got to... gotta... You've gotta obey the laws.

8.13 *page 90 exercise 10A*

1 During tests, I feel very tense.
2 I wish examinations did not bother me so much.
3 I seem to defeat myself while working on important tests.
4 I feel very panicky when I take an important test.
5 During examinations, I get so nervous that I forget facts I really know.

8.14 *page 90 exercises 10B and D*

Hi, I'm Doctor Jennifer Price and I'm a Psychology professor here at Georgetown and one of the things I'm going to talk to you about today is the problem that many college students face and that's test anxiety. I'd like you to think for a minute about experiences you've had where you studied really hard for a test but then when you got it, you just blanked and forgot everything. If you've had that happen to you, you know exactly what I mean. Even if that hasn't happened, probably all of us have felt a little bit of anxiety when preparing for a test and so there are a lot of strategies that you can use to try to improve your performance. So I'm going to go over a few of those right now.
Before we do that though, it would be helpful for you to know exactly what your level of test anxiety is. So, I have a questionnaire for you to fill out – it's not a test, so don't be nervous! Let's start by giving that out and then we'll come back together and see how you did.
So, the survey you just took is called the test-anxiety index. The scores in this test range from 5 to 20, so if you scored a 5, or 6, even 7, that means you have relatively low test anxiety. If you have a score about 10, it means you have at least a moderate amount or even a high amount of test anxiety. So, if you are in the high level, I would really encourage you to pay special attention to the techniques I'm about to discuss. But even if your anxiety was low, these things can be helpful for you no matter what.

8.15 *page 90 exercises 10C and D*

One of the problems that test anxious people often face is that they don't do a lot of preparation for an exam because even just taking the time to study increases their anxiety because they don't want to think about the test they are about to take. But that strategy can really backfire because the more prepared you are, the less anxious you'll actually be when you go take the exam.
So, the first strategy is just to spend your time preparing way in advance, attending classes, taking notes, all the regular study skills that you've been learning about in freshman seminar and other areas this semester really will help ... yeah, really will help you when you're taking the test as well.
A few of the other strategies that are more specific to test anxiety have to do with studying in a distraction-free environment and engaging in something called distributed practice. You all know what a distraction-free environment is. You might think that you currently study in a distraction-free environment but if you study with music on or with people around, those really can be distractions. Even though it seems like it's more fun to study that way, a lot of times it can interfere with your ability to learn without even you realizing.
Study often, it really does not work to cram the night before a test. What research has shown is most helpful is to study over smaller periods of time in the days leading up to an exam, and just to practice, practice, practice – just like you've

learned your whole life on how to get better at something.
In terms of personal strategies, yeah, there are a few other things that you can do that will help you prepare and not be as anxious in the days leading up to an exam. One of those, it may sound a little silly but it really is helpful and that's engaging in self-talk. Self-talk is when you basically, in your mind, not out loud, talk to yourself about things that you can do to prepare and things that you can do to feel successful about your ability to prepare for the test.
You can also engage in relaxation exercises. Even if you're not feeling particularly anxious; if you practice relaxation on a daily basis, it lowers your overall anxiety so that when something does happen that makes you feel nervous, you don't get to that high anxiety, high panic so quickly. Related to that, you can also practice taking slow breaths. Many times people think that taking deep breaths is helpful, but especially when you're anxious, taking deep breaths means that you take in more oxygen which makes you more likely to hyperventilate, which we want to avoid. So the better strategy is to just slow down your breathing and focus on the exhale instead of taking in more air.

Unit 9

9.1 *page 94 exercises 1A and B*

M = Marco, A = Angela

M: Hey, Angela.
A: Oh, hi Marco.
M: That was a fun class! ... what's up? You look annoyed.
A: I'm just so sick of group work! Have you ever noticed people who talk the loudest always get their ideas accepted? The squeaky wheel gets the grease!
M: You mean Max?
A: Gee, how did you guess?!
M: Max is OK. He's just an extrovert!
A: Well, I'm tired of listening to him!
M: You have to admit group work is better than working alone which is deadly!
A: I like working alone! I'm an introvert!
M: Even introverts need to talk to people ...
A: All my good ideas happen when I think things over – on my own. Not in a group.
M: But great leaders come from groups.
A: Hmm ... most great leaders haven't been outgoing at all – look at Gandhi, Abraham Lincoln ... introverts change the world, too!
M: Well, if great leaders have been introverts, too, what's the problem?
A: There's too much pressure to be an extrovert, that's what! Introverts should be valued more!
M: I don't have anything against introverts. It's just that the people I work best with love talking.
A: Communication means listening, too. And, you know, what? It's good for extroverts to learn to sit quietly and just think ... without opening their mouths!
M: I don't think Max can sit quietly!
A: That's for sure!

9.2 *page 95 exercise 2B*

Some people really enjoy cocktail parties. They like to mingle, and they enjoy meeting people. They also really enjoy small talk. *Mingle* and *small talk* go under "socializing."
There are people who like to keep their feelings private – they don't reveal much about what they are thinking and feeling. Others prefer to open up, and share all their thoughts and feelings. They're the kind of people who in class are happy to suggest solutions so everyone can hear them. *Reveal* and *open up* go under "sharing".
Do you ever feel that you would rather keep quiet? If you have an idea, you'd rather keep it to yourself. I think every class has students who like to think up ideas, but when they come up with a good idea, they like to think it over. So three expressions, *keep quiet, think up, and think over*, all belong under "thinking."

9.3 *page 95 exercise 2C*

Number 1: "I don't mind revealing my phone number to people, but not my address." "Reveal" is like "explain." We reveal something to someone. And remember that "I don't mind" is followed by the *-ing* form of the verb.
Number 2: "I'm not really very good at thinking new ideas up. I guess I'm not very creative." "Think up" is a separable phrasal verb, but you can also say "I'm not really very good at thinking up new ideas."
Number 3: "Whenever I have things bothering me, I always open up to my friends." "Open up" is a good verb to know. We "open up *to*" someone.
Number 4: "I guess I'm more likely to keep things to myself." The reflexive pronoun goes at the end.
Number 5: "I tend to keep my opinions quiet. I hate disagreements." Remember, in English, the modifier goes at the end, so it's not correct to say, "I tend to keep quiet my opinions" – a very common mistake!

9.4 *page 96 exercises 3A and B*

Hi guys. Mark here with Woltersworld and we're in Beijing, China at the Black Bamboo Park. And what I thought I'd give you guys today is I've worked with a lot of Chinese business executives, a lot of Chinese students and I've found that there are certain things that you may do that may offend Chinese people when you do go to China so these are 10 ways you might offend Chinese people if you do come to China. I think it's important especially if you're gonna do business here to know that you want to show respect, you want to not offend people and things like that. So, here are 10 things you might not realize that you do that may offend people.
Now, the first thing is, if you're gonna do any kind of business thing, you've gotta have a gift or they're gonna give you gifts. The thing is, you do not open gifts in front of the people that gave them to you. Save the gift until later. Unless they tell you "No, no, open it now". Then it's OK, it's like a really big gift or something like that, you have to open, then it's OK, but in general, you do not open the gifts that people give you. You wait to open those until you go home. OK? Or back to your hotel, whatever.
The second thing is when you go to business lunches, you don't eat first. OK? The most senior executive goes first, or the oldest person at the table – they eat first. So you wait till they start, and then you get to eat. Now, they may say that since you're the guest that you can start, that's fine, just know that in general if no one says anything, it's best to wait until the most senior person starts eating. OK?
The third way you may offend people is it comes to business cards. You'll notice that when people give you a business card in China, they give it with two hands. Also gifts, they'll give things with two hands. Guys – you receive and accept gifts, and business cards, with two hands. That's the respectful way to do things. Also with business cards, think of a business card as an extension of that person so treat the business card with respect. Look at it, make sure you get the name right, all these kind of things, lay it in front of you in the meeting so it looks like you're looking at their titles, and stuff like that, because the business card is kind of treated as an extension of the person so make sure you treat it with respect. So, hold it with two hands, look at it, keep it – don't just stick it in your wallet right away 'cos that makes them think like you don't care about them. OK?
The fourth way you might offend people is goes with chopsticks. Guys, if you put chopsticks straight down into rice – you don't do that. Chopsticks always straight down into the rice; that's reserved for funerals, so don't do that. It can be a little bit offensive.
Number five on the list of things not to do that might offend people or make them feel uncomfortable is, guys, you won't see too much love and stuff like that here in China so when people, like westerners, we tend to give lots of kisses and hugs and stuff like that, you may make your Chinese friends uncomfortable if you are giving smooches to your wife – you know, PDA – not really an OK thing here so be ready for that. OK? So hold your hands, that's fine, you can give a little smooch, but hmmm, you want to stay away from that. OK?
Six – sixth thing that you might do that might offend people here is if you compare China and Japan. China and Japan have a really, really bad history together so what you really shouldn't do is just say "Oh, in Japan, they do this" or "I like stuff from Japan." They do not like those comparisons. So do not compare Japan and China to each other. They're not the same country, they're ... yeah ... very little in common with them, so do not compare the two. Alright 'cos you will offend people with that one.
Also, number seven, don't point. Guys, if you want someone to come, you don't do this. That's bad. What you do is, you do this; "Oh, come here", you do this. OK? 'Cos if you point at people or say "Come here", that's offensive to them, so don't do that.
Number eight on our list – this is one that I've seen a lot of professors here make the mistake is; if you invite someone out to eat, like "Hey, let's go have dinner, I'm inviting you out", that means you pay. The person that invites, they pay the bill. OK? So, if you have a translator, you have someone and then you say "Hey, will you come out to lunch with me?" and they say yes, they're expecting you to pay. And vice versa; someone invites you out to dinner, they pay for you. OK? So, just know that that's one thing I've seen a lot of westerners here – they've kind of upset their Chinese friends because ... "he invited me out to dinner, took me to this place, but he didn't pay". Here, you don't go Dutch in China. It's whoever invites, they do the paying. OK?
Oh, number nine on the list – this one I didn't really know about but ha ha, if you're gonna give gifts, you bring gifts from the US, your

company's colour is green – don't bring hats. A green hat means that your spouse is cheating on you, or you're unfaithful, so don't bring green hats. That's another way you might offend people. You may not realize it, but the Chinese people will, so be careful with that one. Alright? Number 10 – let's go back to those gift things. Gifts; you don't want to give people a clock. 'Cos if you give people a clock, it means I want you to die 'cos I'm counting down the time until your death – ha ha ha. So don't give – do not give – a clock for a gift.

And number 11 – if you're lucky enough to get invited to a Chinese person's house, it is a great honor and treat it like that. So you bring your gifts, but also, when you go into their home, you take off their ... you take off your shoes – and they'll have slippers for you and stuff like that. Put those on, even if they're not your size, you'll be OK, but you do not wear your shoes inside people's houses – that is very offensive. OK? So, those are 10, actually 11 little tips for you so you don't offend your Chinese friends when you come over here or your business colleagues. I hope this helps. If you want to learn more about traveling in China, a few Chinese words, five things you are going to love and hate about visiting Beijing, check us out on our website woltersworld.com, we're also on Twitter and Facebook and we really appreciate your subscriptions online so bye from Beijing, China.

9.7 *page 99 exercise 7A*

G = Gloria, A = Adam

G: ... we can pause the recording. Great interview, Adam. Thanks so much for taking the time to speak to us.
A: My pleasure. How long till it appears on the site?
G: About a week or so. I'll let you know, OK?
A: Sure... So, any typical screenagers in your family?
G: Yeah, I have a thirteen-year-old sister, but, erm... I wouldn't describe her as a typical Generation Z-er.
A: Oh yeah?
G: Uh huh. For example, she couldn't care less about what's going on in the world – far less than I ever did when I was her age, anyway. But at least she does take an interest in green issues and is not, you know, "eco-fatigued" like the rest of us.
A: Uh huh. I know what you mean.
G: And, unlike most of her friends, she prefers paper books to e-books and still buys CDs – I mean, the actual discs. I think the real screenager in the family is my grandmother, who – are you ready for this – has her own blog, listens to music through Spotify...
A: She *streams* her music?
G: Yeah! She's totally aware of all the latest technology and loves using it.
A: Wow!
G: I know, right? Which makes me wonder, is it about generation or personality? I mean, my young sister despises technology while my 70-year-old grandma loves it! Anyway, she's an amazing woman. Sometimes I'm under the impression that I have more in common with her than with Mom and Dad, despite the age difference.
A: Oh yeah?
G: My parents and I don't really see eye to eye on lots of things. My outlook on life is totally different from theirs.
A: In what ways?
G: Well, for one thing I don't value money and status as much as they do. Like, I don't make a lot of money as a journalist, but I love my job, you know. I, erm, I think I have a happy, carefree life and, at the end of the day, that's what matters to me. But mom keeps saying I should've gone to law school and stuff like that ... And she wants me to settle down and get married, which, honestly, is the last thing on my mind right now.
A: Tough, uh?
G: Yeah. I wish she was more tolerant of other people's lifestyles... and choices, which Grandma is... So, again, does generation matter at all, I wonder? Anyway, thanks again for ...

9.8 *page 99 exercise 7B*

1 My younger sister couldn't care less about what's going on in the world.
2 Grandma is aware of all the latest technology and enjoys using it.
3 Sometimes I'm under the impression that I have more in common with my grandma than with my parents.
4 My parents and I don't really see eye to eye on lots of things. My outlook on life is totally different from theirs.
5 I don't value money and status as much as my parents do.
6 I wish my mother was more tolerant of other people's lifestyles.

9.9 *page 100 exercise 8A*

R = Reporter, O = Officer

R: So you're trained to look for signs that a suspect is lying.
O: That's right, yes.
R: How do you do that?
O: Well, er, OK, so just recently, I questioned someone suspected of taking part in a robbery – a large amount of money was stolen from a store; no one was hurt, but one of the robbers had a gun, so ...
R: It was serious.
O: Most certainly. A guy claiming he was home watching TV with his mother was the key suspect. But he denied being involved.
R: Hmmm.
O: Now I didn't believe him from the start, so as he spoke, I was watching his body closely for signs of stress.
R: So what kind of things do you look for?

9.10 *page 100 exercises 8B and C*

O: Well the body's first reaction is, "This is a situation I want to run away from." And the first thing I noticed was, as soon as this guy started talking, he couldn't stop moving his feet, which was a sure sign he was lying.
R: That's the body trying to run!
O: Yes, that's what we do. And, I could see he wasn't telling the truth about being at his mother's house, because he scratched his nose – like this – whenever he mentioned that. This is a typical reaction, because more blood goes to the nose when we're emotional, and it ...
R: ... makes us want to scratch.
O: Exactly! So I showed him that night's TV schedules, and accused him of making his story up.
R: And what did he say?
O: Well ..., he only admitted to riding the motorcycle the robber got away on.
R: Oh sure!
O: It was so obvious he was lying. What gave him away the most was the direction he was looking in. When we have to think to answer a question, our eyes show which area of the brain we're using.
R: Oh really!
O: This guy just kept looking up and to the right all the time. And that is very often a sign it's a story you're making up.
R: Wow, that's amazing. So did he confess to the crime in the end?
O: Yes – I told him he'd been seen on the store's closed circuit TV climbing in through a window, and well, then, he owned up to robbing the store.
R: So I guess he's looking at a long time in prison.
O: Yes – he was a bad robber ...
R: ... and an even worse liar!

9.12 *page 102 exercise 10A*

L = Laura, A = Alfredo

L: ... so let me see if I got this right. We need to choose a problem facing society today, right?
A: Yeah, and think of possible solutions.
L: Hmm ... that's a tough question.
A: I guess I'd have to say consumerism.
L: Consumerism?
A: Uh-huh. Actually, I think it could very well be *the* defining issue of our time.
L: Really? You know, why people think it's a problem is beyond me. I mean, who doesn't love shopping and buying new things?
A: You're kind of missing the point here. Some people do, yes, myself included, but ... there's more to it than that. It's not black and white.
L: Yes, it is!

9.13 *page 102 exercise 10B*

A: Well, it kind of depends on what you buy and why – especially why. Some people go to the mall just to, you know, just to fill some kind of void, some kind of emptiness inside. To feel good for the moment.
L: Like, I hate my life, so let me get that brand new dress I don't really need and might not ever actually wear?
A: Exactly.
L: So?
A: Buying something new might make you feel happy for a little while, sure, but wouldn't you agree that it's just a quick fix?
L: No, it isn't! It's lasting! I'm still madly in love with the phone I bought last month. Seriously though, I know what you're getting at. But is it really such a big deal?
A: Yes, I think so. For one thing, if you're not careful, you might get into serious debt. Like this cousin of mine who had to sell his car to pay off his credit card bills.
L: Oh boy.
A: Well, some people don't have to go that far, but they end up working longer hours – or even getting another job – to be able to afford ... to,

you know, to sustain that kind of lifestyle, so they sleep less, exercise less, see less and less of their family and friends, and ...

L: Yeah, I've seen it happen to some friends of mine.

A: Surely you'd agree that it's just not worth it?

L: Hmm ... yeah.

A: Not to mention the fact that excessive, mindless shopping is destroying the environment.

L: You mean like more cars on the road, more pollution, that sort of thing?

A: Not only that ... for example, whenever you throw away ...

9.14 *page 102 exercise 10C*

L: ... never thought about it that way. You know what? You've kind of convinced me! So, anyway, what do you propose?

A: Oh, there are no easy fixes.

L: You mean it's a lost cause?

A: Let me put it another way ... I think what we need is a change in awareness and attitude, but these things take time, you know.

L: But you've got to start somewhere!

A: Well, I for one have been trying to shop less, to, you know, make sure that I only buy the stuff I really need.

L: Easier said than done ...

A: Well, why don't you start by getting rid of all the things you don't need – say, in your bedroom?

L: Like a detox?

A: Yeah, I guess you could say that.

L: Oh, I would need about a week – and I'm only talking about the closet!

9.15 *page 102 exercise 10D*

1

L: I mean, who doesn't love shopping and buying new things?

A: You're kind of missing the point here. Some people do, yes, myself included, but ...

2

L: But is it really such a big deal?

A: Yes, I think so. For one thing, if you're not careful, you might get into serious debt.

3

L: Yeah, I've seen it happen to some friends of mine.

A: Surely you'd agree that it's just not worth it?

L: Hmm... yeah.

4

L: You mean it's a lost cause?

A: Let me put it another way... I think what we need is a change in awareness and attitude, but these things take time, you know.

Unit 10

10.1 *page 104 exercise 1B*

A = Ana, J = Joel, I = Ian

Story 1

A: Travel nightmares ... Hmm ... I've sure had some of those!

J: Oh, I love this site. You know what, I think I'm gonna send them my story...

A: What story?

J: The London nightmare ... You see, a few years ago, I was working for IDealSolutions ...

A: The software company?

J: Yeah. I'd just flown in from Washington to attend a sales conference. So, erm ... I got to the hotel, checked in, and ... I was really looking forward to relaxing after a long flight. When I opened the door, to my surprise ...

A: What?

J: I saw a man in his forties in a robe ... sitting on the edge of the bed ...

A: You're kidding! Wrong room?

J: Well, it turned out the hotel had made a mistake and booked us into the same room. But here comes the worst part: I happened to know who the man was! His name was Barry ... Barry Sigsworth, and he was a sales rep for the competition!

Story 2

J: How about you, Ana? Do you have any travel nightmares?

A: Do I? I'm like a walking travel nightmare! Here's the latest one ... A few years ago I was flying from Santiago to Recife – up in the northeast of Brazil. It'd been a rough year and all I wanted to do was get away from it all and relax for few days and, you know, recharge my batteries.

J: Uh huh.

A: Well, my nightmare started in the check-in line. That's where I first saw them.

J: Who?

A: The twins ... Two five-year-olds running around, knocking over people's luggage, and screaming at the top of their lungs.

J: Oh, that can't be good.

A: When I got on the plane, it just so happened that the two boys were sitting there, right behind me!

J: Are you serious?

A: I sure am! Well, all I could do at that point was give them the benefit of the doubt and hope for the best.

Story 3

I: Well, if you think you had a rough time abroad, just wait until you hear my story. Let me get my phone.

J: You're gonna record it?

I: Yeah. That way I can send it to the site. ... My story has got to be the most movie-ready travel story ever ... I was on my way to Guwahati, India ... The train was waiting at the station, scheduled to depart in a few minutes. For whatever reason, the conductor stepped off the train and told the assistant conductor to start the engine, which he did. But ... Well, the poor man probably got mixed up and pulled the wrong switch ... and the train started to roll backwards. So, guess what, he gets scared and jumps off ... and the thing begins to pick up speed without the conductor or his assistant.

J: You're kidding!

10.2 *page 104 exercises 1C and D*

Story 1

J: I happened to know who the man was. His name was Barry... Barry Sigsworth and he was a sales rep for the competition!

A: Small world!

J: Yeah, and I'd heard lots of stories about him. People called him Mr. Evil. How about that? Anyway, erm, we called reception and, apparently, there were no other rooms available! None at all! So, instead of speaking to the manager or something, Mr. Evil suggested we share the room!

A: Why would he do that?

J: I knew what he wanted, of course: To pretend to be my friend and get as much information about our company as he could ...

A: No way! How did you manage to get through a whole week with him?"

J: Well ... In the end, strangely enough, it wasn't nearly as bad as I thought. We never even talked about work, and the guy turned out to be much nicer than people gave him credit for ...

A: Wow, who'd have thought ...

Story 2

A: Well, all I could do at that point was give them the benefit of the doubt and hope for the best. As it turns out, the twins were way worse than I thought and spent the whole flight kicking my seat, no matter how many times I asked them to stop.

J: No, they didn't! How aw ...

A: They did. I kept looking at their mother and frowning, but she couldn't be bothered.

J: Unbelievable!

A: When I finally asked her if she could *please* try to control her kids, the woman got really mad and we ended up arguing – loudly!

J: You? Arguing midflight? No way!

A: Yep. In a matter of minutes, the flight attendants showed up and threatened to call the local authorities as soon as the plane landed.

J: What?

A: They said they wouldn't tolerate "aggressive behavior," as they called it, on a flight. I've never been so embarrassed, I swear. It took me a couple of days to forget about the incident and begin to enjoy Recife.

Story 3

I: So, guess what, he gets scared and jumps off ... and the thing begins to pick up speed without the conductor and his assistant. When it finally dawned on passengers that they were in trouble, everyone started screaming "Help, help, somebody get me out of here! Runaway train!" It was my first experience of mass hysteria, I swear. It was a terrifying couple of kilometers. Well, eventually, the ticket inspector and a couple of very brave passengers got into the engine car and ... As luck would have it, they were able to stop the train before the worst happened. It may seem kind of funny now, but the whole thing could've been, well, a total tragedy.

10.5 *page 106 exercises 1C and D*

See audio 10.6

10.6 *page 106 exercise 3B*

Conversation 1

R = Receptionist, M = Marty

R: 6 a.m. to 10 a.m. Enjoy your stay, Mr. Falcon.

M: Thanks. Erm ... one more thing, I was wondering if I could get a late checkout on Wednesday.

R: I'm sorry, but you need to check out by noon.

M: Listen, my flight doesn't leave until 5:00 ... what am I supposed to do until then?
R: I'm really sorry, sir.
M: Can I speak to the manager, please?
R: Erm, she's on her lunch break.
M: Can you tell me what time she'll be back?
R: At around 2:00, sir.
M: Thank you.
R: My pleasure. Have a nice day!
M: Oh, by the way, I need a wake-up call tomorrow morning.
R: Of course. Just dial 00, set the time, and the system will wake you up.
M: You mean I have to use the phone in the room?
R: Yes, sir.
M: OK, thanks.

Conversation 2

S = Salesperson, M = Marty

S: ... the green ones over there.
M: Would you happen to know whether these are machine-washable?
S: Yes, I think they are, sir.
M: You mean they won't shrink?
S: Let me take a look at the label just in case. Erm ... it doesn't say anything. I'll check with the manager.
M: No need to, thanks. They're $19.99, aren't they, you said?
S: Erm ... No, $90.99.
M: How much?
S: $90.99.
M: Wow! Almost a hundred dollars?! That's a rip-off! Aren't these things supposed to cost about 20 bucks?
S: Actually, $90.99 is less than the suggested retail price, sir. They're 100 percent cotton.
M: Really? Wow! If you say so ... Well, OK, I'll take them.
S: Great! How would you like to pay?
M: Do you accept international credit cards? I'm living in London now.
S: Sure. Sir, I'm afraid your card didn't go through.
M: Really? That's weird. I use this card all the time.
S: Yeah.
M: Erm ... Can you try again, please?
S: Oh, of course. No, sorry. Don't you have another card?
M: Yeah. Do you ...

Conversation 3

F = Fiona, M = Marty

F: Spencer and White Rent a Car. Fiona speaking. How may I help you?
M: Erm ... My car broke down and I don't know what to do. I'm lost in the middle of nowhere.
F: OK. The fastest way to report a car breakdown is via our app. Do you know whether you have it installed on your phone? That way, we'll know exactly where you are and send someone over.
M: Yeah, but I don't have a login or a password. Can't you help me over the phone?
F: Erm, just a minute. Please hold. ... Yes, sir, I can now help you! Could I have your name, please?
M: Marty Falcon.
F: And your reservation number?
M: 8983F.
F: It says "invalid reservation number."
M: What do you mean? It's the number on the document.
F: Hmm ... It seems there's been a mix up. Hmm ... Let me see if I can correct it and fix things up. Hold the line, please. ...Thanks for holding. Mr. Falcon, do you remember if any warning lights came on?
M: Warning lights? You mean something that lights up red or is it blue? – like on the dashboard?
F: Yes.
M: Well, yeah, the "check engine" light was on, but, er, I figured it was nothing serious, so I just ...
F: I see. Do you know what your exact location is?
M: No, I don't! I'm completely lost and in the middle of nowhere.
F: OK. Hold the line, please.

10.11 *page 110 exercise 8A*

Welcome to Verpod, your weekly podcast with all the latest campus news. In this week's episode, we'll meet five of the many overseas students who joined us in August. They'll tell us what the first few months away from home have been like and how easy – or hard – it's been for them to adapt to college life here in Vermont.

10.12 *page 110 exercises 8B and C*

Mariana from Caracas, Venezuela

I love Vermont ... and the campus ... But, well, I was born and raised in Caracas, so I kind of miss the hustle and bustle of life there – you know, the noise, the crowds, even the traffic! I'm sure I'll get used to the peace and quiet eventually... Well, at least I hope so. The upside, though, is that life here is generally healthier ... plus, I'm no longer the couch potato I used to be, which is a good thing, of course.

Ignacio from Montevideo, Uruguay

I grew up in a big house, so my sisters and I had our own bedrooms ... So, erm, I'm not used to sharing a room with anyone – let alone someone I barely know. Besides, my roommate isn't very talkative, which doesn't exactly help. He's so quiet it's weird sometimes. I mean, it's been two months and we, erm, we hardly know each other. Not that I've tried too hard, to be honest, so I guess it's my fault as much as his. Mom says we'll get used to living together. I hope she's right.

Ines from Lisbon, Portugal

It's, erm, it's been tough. I'm fresh out of high school, where there was, you know, far more hand-holding and guidance. So, erm, I guess in many ways I'm not used to being treated as an adult. Also, at school our final grade was based mostly on exams. Here we have regular assignments, quizzes, projects, and exams, which can be a little overwhelming. I wonder if I'll ever get used to working this hard. Plus, you need a lot of self-discipline, which is definitely not my strong suit.

Diego from Bogota, Colombia

My father got transferred to Miami when I was little boy, and we lived there for, what, three years, so, erm, well, when I came here, I was used to life in the States ... I mean, there was less of a culture clash than I'd anticipated. But ... it took me a while to get used to the weather. It's freezing in Vermont in the winter! You have no idea, and it snows constantly. I was used to a mild climate. I even had to buy a whole new wardrobe!

Elena from Moscow, Russia

The first few weeks were kind of fun, but then I started to feel terribly homesick. I wasn't used to being away from my parents for more than a couple of days. I'm an only child, and we're a very close-knit family and, well, even though we Skype at least once a week and What'sApp constantly, it's not really the same. They try to act strong, but deep down I know they wish they could catch the first plane and take me back home.

10.14 *page 112 exercise 10A*

A = Announcer, S = Sonia

A: Welcome to WEID and our weekly travel quiz. For centuries, Istanbul, Turkey has been a favorite destination for tourists from every corner of the Earth! And here's your chance to learn some basic facts about this amazing city. Today Sonia Whitestone, in our audience, is going to help us. Welcome, Sonia.
S: Thank you.
A: If you're listening, that means you've taken our online quiz. So let's get started. Number 1: Istanbul is one of the five largest cities in the world. True or false?
S: Hmm ... I know it's pretty big. But is it in the top five? Gee, um, let's see. OK, true! Maybe it's number 5?
A: Well, actually, no: São Paulo, Mexico City, New York, Shanghai, Seoul, Delhi, Tokyo – all are bigger. Let's try number 2: Two-thirds of the city is located in Europe and one-third in Asia. True or false?
S: Now that has to be true. I read it was the only city in the world that sits on two continents.
A: And right you are! Number 3: Istanbul's subway is the oldest in the world. True or false?
S: How am I supposed to know that? Am I an engineer? Well, OK, a wild guess. False. I think the New York subway and the London Underground are both older.
A: Well, you're right about London, but not New York. The subway in Istanbul opened in 1875, twelve years after London. The New York subway didn't open until 1904. But a correct answer, nevertheless.
S: Not too bad, so far.
A: Now number 4: As the city is surrounded by water, it doesn't snow there. True or false?
S: Well, they say water has a moderating influence. I think that's true.
A: Sorry! It may not snow often, but when it does, it's really beautiful. Winter is a great time to visit. No crowds! Let's try one more: Over time, it has been the capital of three different empires.
S: That feels like it must be true. The Ottoman Empire ...
A: Yes, you got it! And don't forget the Byzantine and Roman Empires, which preceded the Ottoman Empire by 1,500 years. And now, the very last question: The Grand Bazaar is the world's most visited tourist attraction. True or false?
S: This sounds like the subway question. Am I a travel writer? Well, it must be important if it's on your questionnaire, so I say true.

A: Well, four out of six: very good, Sonia. It is the most visited tourist attraction. Over 90 million visitors a year! Wow! And we hope our listeners will download the video we've recommended, where you can see it, as well as many other scenes from this fascinating city. Thank you for listening ...

10.15 *page 112 exercise 10B*

G = Gail, B = Bill

G: First day in Istanbul! I can't believe we're here. And the weather's cool! I thought it would be hot here, even sort of tropical ... and that I'd have to get used to sweating.
B: Told you you'd like it! Wait 'til we get started. The food is out of this world, and you can't possibly get bored. It's affordable and pedestrian friendly, too.
G: I just feel blown away! The dream of a lifetime. I can't wait to explore the city over the next few days. Hey, what's going on over there?
B: Looks like people are fishing from the Galata bridge.
G: And what about over here? What's he selling?
B: I can't see ... Oh! It's a sesame-covered pretzel! They're very common here: just, you know, pretzels covered in sesame seeds. But they're good! We should definitely stock up on these for an afternoon snack or two.
G: Sounds good to me. So what do you want to do this morning?
B: How about a boat tour down the Bosphorus River? And then we can go for some Turkish ice cream. It's called "domdurma," which I heard means "freezing."
G: What's so unusual about that? Isn't all ice cream pretty cold?
B: Well, Turkish ice cream is supposed to be sticky, and it doesn't melt as easily.
G: Ice cream that sticks to the top of my mouth, and maybe my face! Not so sure about that. You'd better get a shave first!
B: Hey, what's wrong with my beard?
G: Nothing really, but I read you can get a really good, cheap shave here.
B: Do you know how much it costs?
G: I think just about five dollars.
B: I told you! Everything is affordable here.

10.16 *page 112 exercise 10C*

G: Strangely enough, I'm over jet lag already. Or at least I think I am. And the city doesn't feel overwhelming at all. I had expected to be bothered by the hustle and bustle.
B: Istanbul is love at first sight, isn't it? Everything is just so awe-inspiring. Today we have to check out the Grand Bazaar. It's one of the largest markets in the entire world.
G: And isn't it the oldest, too? Do you know how big it is?
B: One of the oldest, definitely. Yes, it has over 3,000 shops and takes up an estimated 61 streets. It might still be growing, in fact.
G: We could get lost in there.
B: Hey, it's fun to get lost! But some streets specialize. There might be an alley selling just leather, or silverware, or rugs, or jewelry, or even just slippers. So that way, you can remember more easily where you've been.
G: I was reading that despite the size and wealth, there haven't been many robberies. But one was famous. In 1591, 30,000 gold coins were stolen!
B: You're kidding. I didn't know that. Listen, we should get going. It's always less crowded in the morning.

Review 5 (Units 9–10)

R5.5 *page 114 exercise 2A*

E = Employee, D = Daisy

E: Hello, can I help you?
D: Yes, I rented this car at the airport the other day, and the GPS isn't working, which is really annoying.
E: What's wrong with it?
D: Well, for starters, when I put in my destination, it doesn't program the trip. There's no voice.
E: That's strange.
D: And when a voice does start speaking, it's all wrong. Three times I ended up back where I started!
E: Gee, I don't know much about these things. And, as luck would have it, our boss is away this week.
D: Can't you help me at all? I'm leaving the day after tomorrow!
E: Well, I wish I could, but it might be faster to drive to the airport where you got it.
D: I don't even know how to get there! The GPS isn't working, remember? Do you happen to know if there's another office near here?
E: I'm afraid there isn't.
D: Well, can I get my money back?
E: We don't handle refunds here. You'll have to file a claim on our website.
D: Hmm ... so can you at least tell me how I can drive to the airport to return the car? I'm staying at the Clairmont Hotel.
E: Sure. It's really easy. You just go straight. You don't even need the GPS!

Unit 11

11.1 *page 116 exercise 1A*

1 ... was spotted earlier this week with a very attractive man who some say could be her new boyfriend. Sources say that ...
2 ... has announced plans to develop a solar-powered family car, and it will cost less than you think. Geena Weiss has more.
3 ... sports news, we've just had word that soccer manager José Mourinho has left Chelsea Football Club. Stay tuned for the next move in Mourinho's remarkable career.
4 ... and here in the UK, at number 1 after his remarkable success at Glastonbury festival. Lionel Richie's *Definitive Collection* has put the singer back at the top of the charts after 23 years. Now that's what we call a comeback.
5 ... unemployment has dropped for the third consecutive month this year. At 6.4%, it's the lowest it's ever been since ...
6 ... where two lanes are blocked due to construction. So avoid Connecticut Avenue if you're heading downtown. Stay tuned for ...

11.2 *page 116 exercises 1B and C*

G = Geena, J = Jack

G: Hello. I'm Geena Weiss, and today we're looking at public opinion. Can I ask you a few questions?
J: Will it take long? I'm kind of in a hurry.
G: Five minutes at most, I promise. OK, take a look at this list, please ... What would you say your favorite news topic is?
J: Can I pick several topics or only one?
G: Just one topic.
J: OK. Hmm ... local news ... What does that include?
G: Traffic, weather, and stuff like that.
J: OK ... politics, business, and the economy – no way ... I already spend the whole day on my job talking about companies going bankrupt ... science and technology, hmm ... Well, I'm really into music, movies, and theater. That goes under "the arts," right?
G: Uh huh. "The arts" then?
J: Yes.
G: OK, how often do you follow the latest news on the arts?
J: Well, I try to keep up with what's going on. You know, learn about the latest releases ... read the latest reviews ... Some of my friends are really into movies and music, so I, erm, I don't want to seem stupid and make a fool of myself when we're hanging out ... You know, run out of things to talk about ... So, I'd have to say ... hmm ... at least once a day. I'm into sports, too, but I don't follow the news – well, not unless my team is playing.
G: Do you prefer to get the news in print, or on a computer or mobile device?
J: Hmm ... Whatever's available – my phone, tablet, or even my laptop. I don't have a TV at home, so...
G: You don't?
v No, but whenever I'm at my parents' or maybe at a restaurant and ... you know... if there's breaking news on TV, I might stop to watch – you know, those stories that make the room go really quiet. But that's about it.
G: I see. What's your favorite news source? Do you have one?
J: We're still talking about music, movies, etc., correct?
G: Yes.
J: Hmm ... well, lately I've been reading *Rolling Stone* more and more, especially because of their movie reviews, which are fantastic.
G: Rolling Stone.com?
J: Uh huh. It's been around forever, but I only stumbled upon it a while ago. It's great to have such an accurate source of information on the arts. I wish they'd post more behind-the-scenes stuff, though. Things like unofficial photos, gossip ...
G: OK. Do you trust the information you get from *Rolling Stone*?
J: Definitely. They're not biased in favor or against any particular artist, which is a good thing. Every artist – and every music genre – gets a fair treatment.
G: I see. Do you ever get news alerts sent to you?
J: Er, I used to subscribe to lots of sites. And, I'd sign up for nearly every news alert I could click on. But it was, it was kind of overwhelming, you know, and I usually ended

up with hundreds of links I never had time to access.

G: Uh huh.

J: So I'm done with news alerts, thank goodness. I, erm, these days I just check my newsfeed for interesting stuff.

G: Are you talking about Twitter or Facebook?

J: Both. I tend to skip most stories, you know – not all of them are worth my time. But if a headline catches my eye, I click on the link. But only if it makes me go "Hmm, that's interesting."

G: Right.

J: Otherwise, I keep scrolling down.

G: Thank you very much ... now let's see what this young woman thinks ...

11.3 *page 117 exercise 2A*

Hi, this is Helene again, your cyber teacher! Today we practice a very useful strategy for learning new words and expressions. You don't always have to look them up. Sometimes, by listening closely to what comes next, you can figure out the meaning from the context. Let's take a look at how.

1 I try to keep up with what's going on. Jack then adds, "You know, learn about the latest releases ... read the latest reviews ..." The meaning of *keep up with* is clearly "stay informed." The answer is A.

2 When talking about Rolling Stone.com, Jack comments, "It's great to have such an accurate source of information." Clearly *accurate* has a positive meaning. The answer is A.

3 I wish they'd post more behind-the-scenes stuff. Jack's next comment is, "Things like unofficial photos, gossip ..." Since "un" is a prefix meaning "not," we know the answer is B.

4 They're not biased in favor or against any particular artist. And then Jack adds, "which is a good thing. Every artist – and every music genre – gets a fair treatment." Remember how we learned that non-restricted clauses with *which* can be used to comment on an idea and give the speaker's opinion. Jack then adds that the treatment is fair. The answer is A.

5 I tend to skip most stories. And Jack's very next comment is, "Not all of them are worth my time." Therefore, logically, the answer is B.

6 If a headline catches my eye, I click on the link. Remember we asked you at the beginning of the lesson to tell us what recent news has caught your eye. What do you think this expression meant? If you weren't sure then, it's obvious when Jack adds, "But only if it makes me go "Hmm, that's interesting." Clearly the answer is A.

I hope you've found this useful. Listen carefully, and you may be able to leave your dictionary at home!

11.5 *page 117 exercise 3B*

1 What would you say your favorite news topic is?
2 How often do you follow the latest news?
3 Do you prefer to get the news on a computer or a mobile device?
4 What's your favorite news source?
5 Are you talking about Twitter or Facebook?

11.6 *page 118 exercises 4A and B*

A = Announcer

A1: Welcome back to *Behind the scenes*. Our focus today is "bloopers." Every day, professional news anchors and reporters report the day's events live to millions of viewers. Which means that when things go wrong, they go wrong before millions of viewers! YouTube is filled with videos of TV professionals falling off their seats, losing their scripts, bursting out laughing at the wrong time – you name it! Here are some of our favorite news bloopers ever – the ones that never get old. The first one. A few years ago, a reporter was doing a story on pets that act like humans, and he was holding a small dog who, well, gave him every warning sign that she didn't want to be held like a baby. At one point, the dog ... guess what ... attacked the reporter on live TV, for the whole country to see!

A2: Oh, boy.

A1: No one really knows why the dog lost it like that. The reporter himself claimed that everything had been going well behind the cameras. He kept his cool, though, and reassured viewers that he was fine.

A2: What a pro! ... And number 2 ...

A1: I bet this one is good.

A2: One of my favorites ... I know the evening news can put us to sleep sometimes, but a certain news anchor went too far. He, erm ... He fell asleep right in the middle of a news story before millions of viewers.

A1: Oh, no!

A2: The news anchor was woken up by his colleague, who stayed calm and reminded him he was on live TV! Now, here's the best part: He was able to keep it together and simply denied that he had fallen asleep. Then he admitted he was just kidding, of course – and said he was just getting ready for the next story or something. How about that?

A1: That's what I call class! ... Now, this is by far my favorite one. Number 3.

A2: You mean there are more?

A1: There sure are! A few years ago a well-known TV network tried to interview a woman who they thought was an economist. As it turned out ... well, she was a fashion student, but she had come for an interview for a summer job!

A2: A job interview?

A1: Yes, she had been waiting outside, and she was mistaken for the specialist. Apparently the two women looked pretty much alike!

A2: So they interviewed a job applicant instead of the next guest?

A1: Exactly! Anyway, the program began, and as soon as the poor woman realized what was going on, she warned them they'd made a mistake. But instead of freaking out, she just calmly got up and left the studio!

A2: An empty chair? Wow!

A1: Yes, maybe she was embarrassed. Wouldn't you be?

11.8 *page 118 exercise 7A*

H = Helene

Emotional baby This one will get you thinking, I'm sure. A ten-month-old baby gets teary-eyed as she watches her mother sing an old Rod Stewart song. This video moved me to tears when I first saw it, and it still gets to me whenever I play it again.

H: Hi, it's Helene again. Number 1 is the verb "get" and the expression is "to get someone thinking." "Get" here means "cause" – "to cause someone to start thinking." Hmm ... did that get you thinking? Number 2 is "moved," the past of "move." The expression "to move someone to tears" means "to make someone cry." Number 3 also uses the verb "get" and is the expression "to get to someone." "It gets to me" means "it affects me personally." In some contexts, it can also mean it "upsets me."

Sneezing baby panda A baby panda sneezes and the mother panda is caught by surprise. No big deal, right? Wrong. This clip is hilarious. When I first watched it, I burst out laughing so loud my family came running.

H: Number 4 is "caught," the past of "catch." The expression "to catch someone by surprise," as I'm sure you've figured out, means "to surprise someone suddenly." Booooh! Number 5 is an irregular past tense verb that doesn't change form: "burst." The expression "to burst out laughing" means "to start laughing suddenly." You can also use the verb "burst" if you start crying suddenly. You can say, "I burst into tears."

Friday by Rebecca Black *Friday* is about a girl who's bored Monday through Thursday, but cheers up, well, guess when. When the video took off, people either loved or hated the clip. Nobody said, "It does nothing for me." Did I like *Friday*? Well, let's just say it left me speechless.

H: Number 6 is "does" and the expression is "to do nothing for someone." When you say "It does nothing for me," it means "It has no impact on me." And finally, Number 7 is "left," the past of "leave." The expression "to leave someone speechless" means, "something is so surprising or shocking the person has no idea what to say."

11.9 *page 120 exercises 8B and C*

Conversation 1

M: Have you seen Lorrie's brand new Focus?

W: What?

M: Lorrie's new car.

W: Oh, yeah, it's nice.

M: Yeah... She's been in the company since, what, last year?

W: I guess.

M: I wonder if she got a raise or something.

W: Maybe.

M: What makes you say that?

W: Well, Truman seems to like her. He was very pleased with the way she handled the BW account.

M: Hmm... Do you know something I don't?

W: Look, all I know is that she's hardworking and smart and ...

M: Well, so am I, and I'm still driving a 2002 Civic.

W: Hmm ...

M: I asked Truman for a raise last week and he refused to even listen! By the way, this is between you and me, OK?

W: Of course. Don't worry. My lips are sealed. I won't tell a soul. Anyway, did you watch the game last ...?

Conversation 2

W: Some view, uh?
M: What? Oh, yeah, beautiful. Aren't we lucky we work on the thirtieth floor?
W: Too bad it won't last.
M: What do you mean?
W: Oh boy, me and my big mouth.
M: What?
W: Truman made me swear I'd keep it to myself, but, well ...
M: What?
W: The company, umm, we're ... all of us are relocating next month!
M: Get out of here!
W: Yeah, that's the idea.
M: Gee, where to?
W: Some building on North Street, apparently.
M: What? But that's like twenty miles away!
W: I know. What were they thinking? Promise you'll keep it between the two of us, please. If this leaks, Truman will kill me. Once he threatened to fire me because of my big mouth, remember?
M: Sure, don't worry.
W: Promise?
M: You have my word.

Conversation 3

W: You'll never guess who I ran into at the mall.
M: Who?
W: Truman and Lorrie.
M: Julia, keep it down! Ann's right over there. You know she can't keep a secret!
W: Oops.
M: So ...
W: So, they were having lunch together.
M: What's the big deal?
W: On the weekend! At the mall!
M: Oh ... You don't think they're ...
W: Seeing each other? Yeah, maybe.
M: Hmm ... I think we're both jumping to conclusions here. Just because they were having lunch doesn't mean they're dating.
W: Yeah. And even if they were, what's the big deal, they're both single, right?
M: Julia, look, this is none of our business. You haven't told anyone else, have you?
W: Besides you? Erm ... Ben, I think.
M: Ben? Of all people?
W: Not to worry. I asked him – well, I begged him not to spread it around and I'm sure he won't. Well, at least I expect him not to.
M: Hmm ...

11.12 *page 122 exercises 10A*

R = Rita, J = Jeb

R: This is unbelievable.
J: What?
R: Check this out.
J: TV star Rita ... What? Spotted with new boyfriend? I didn't know you and Ted had broken up.
R: We haven't! We're still very much in love!
J: So who's the guy in the photo?
R: My vocal coach!
J: Oh, that's right, you're taking singing lessons. Oh, well, what would you expect from a gossip site?
R: It's not exactly a gossip site! It's our reputable local newspaper I'm talking about!
J: Oh.
R: They even mention "movie plans" – which, by the way, I definitely don't have! I mean, who did these people interview?! Besides, why did they pick me? It's not like I'm a big time movie star or anything.
J: Well, not yet.
R: And, look, they got my age wrong. Do I look like I'm thirty two? I sure hope not! I'm not even in my mid 20s yet.

11.13 *page 122 exercises 10B and C*

J: Hmm ... At least you've made it to the home page of a well-known paper. I mean, it's your very first TV role, and you'll be the talk of the town for a day or two. And you know what they say, "Bad publicity is always better than no publicity."
R: Hmm ... I don't know about that.
J: Well, if you ask me, celebrity gossip is as newsworthy as other more "serious" topics. Look, they're just giving their audience what it wants. If the site is posting celebrity gossip, it's because people like it. Besides...
R: But what about my privacy?
J: Look, Rita, when you're a celebrity, there's no such thing as privacy. You're in the spotlight 24/7, and that's exactly the way it should be. Your whole career is based on people's interest in you – onscreen *and* offscreen.
R: OK, so what's next? Having the paparazzi camping on my front lawn? Not being able to do my grocery shopping without people trying to ...?
J: Maybe. And you'll have to learn how to live with it ... and be thankful that people even care about you.
R: But what about Ted? How will he react when he sees the photo and the headline? Oh, no! It's him! I can't talk to him right now. See? The whole thing's getting out of control ...
J: So what are you going to do about it?
R: Write to the site before the photo goes viral.
J: Good luck with *that*.
R: What? You don't think they'll remove the article?
J: Well, maybe, but they don't *have* to. I think newspapers are entitled to publish whatever they like.

Unit 12

12.1 *page 126 exercise 1A*

A = Announcer, C = Contestant

A: So ... are you an optimist or a pessimist? You're about to find out. But first, let's begin with some famous quotes on the subject. 1 "I used to be an optimist, but now I know nothing is going to turn out as I expect." Who do you think said that? Tom Cruise, Madonna, or Sandra Bullock? Yes, over there.
C1: Sandra Bullock? I think I read that somewhere.
A: And right you are! OK, 2. "A pessimist sees the difficulty in every opportunity; an optimist sees the opportunity in every difficulty." Who said that? Franklin D. Roosevelt, Winston Churchill, or Barrack Obama?
C2: Was it President Obama?
A: No.
C3: Winston Churchill! My mom used to say it all the time.
A: Yes! Just one more. 3. "The man who is a pessimist before 48 knows too much; if he is an optimist after it, he knows too little." Which writer said that? Was it William ... Oh, I see hands! OK, this young man over here.
C4: Mark Twain!
A: You got it! How did you know that?
C4: I'm an English literature major!
A: Amazing! Time for a station break. When we return, we'll be conducting a survey with some of our guests.

12.2 *page 126 exercise 1B*

A = Announcer, R= Rob, L = Lisa, M = Mike, T = Teresa

A: We're ready to survey our first guest over here on the right. And your name is ...
R: Rob.
A: OK, Rob, let's begin by talking about school tests. You said you're 19, so that means you're in college?
R: Uh huh, it's my second year.
A: How optimistic are you about your exams?
R: You mean my finals?
A: Yeah.
R: Hmm ... I haven't been putting a lot of effort into my work and it, it turns out I've had a couple of Fs ... I keep telling myself that it's not the end of the world if I fail an exam or two, but deep down, I know I'll be really upset.
A: So what are you going to do about it?
R: I guess I'd better start studying. Anyway, I'm keeping my fingers crossed.
A: So you're "unsure" about your exams?
R: You could say that again!
A: Let's try someone else. OK, in front. Your name?
L: Lisa.
A: Good. Let me ask you Lisa ... how optimistic are you about your career?
L: Well, I'm studying pharmacy, and right now I have a part-time job at ID drugs.
A: The drugstore chain?
L: Uh huh. It's great training. But they're going through a rough time right now, so who knows what the future has in store for me. If they have to let some people go, I'm pretty sure I'm at the top of the list. I mean, I've been there for less than a year, and I haven't even graduated from college yet.
A: Hmm ... So it doesn't look good?
L: Nope.
A: I'm sorry to hear that! What about your future in general?
L: All I can tell you is I'm feeling pretty down right now.
A: Let's try someone else. And you're ...
M: Mike.
A: OK, Mike. How optimistic are you about your team's chances of winning the championship?
M: You mean soccer?
A: Well, it could be any sport, soccer, football, baseb...
M: Hmm ... well, my soccer team hasn't been doing too well. We haven't won a single game.
A: You haven't?
M: No, but ... well, I know we've lost all the games so far this season, but now with this new coach, there might be a light at the end of the tunnel. I'm trying not to let it get me down.

A: Does that mean you're optimistic?
M: I just have no idea really, to be honest.
A: Time for just one more. You, over here. And your name?
T: Teresa.
A: OK, Teresa, how optimistic are you about the country's economy?
T: Well, it sort of depends on who you ask, doesn't it? If you watch the eight o'clock news, you get the impression that we're on the brink of chaos. I mean, the ... the media tends to blow things out of proportion but, on the whole, I think we're doing OK. Anyway, I try to keep my feet on the ground and save a little every month, you know, just in case. But I think we're definitely headed in the right direction.
A: Thank you. You're a lot more confident than I am!

12.4 *page 127 exercise 2A*

Conversation 1

W: Something happened. I can tell. What's up, Ed? Why the long face?
M: They let me go.
W: "Let go" as in fired?
M: Yeah.
W: Oh, no!
M: Yeah, looks like it finally happened. Wonder why it took this long.
W: Look, it's not the end of the world. Something better will come along, I'm sure.
M: Yeah, dream on.
W: What do you mean dream on? You're smart, you're qualified, you have people skills and ...
M: Sonia, who in their right mind would want to hire a man my age? I hate to think about what the future has in store for me!
W: Are you kidding? Ed, times have changed. Age is no longer an issue.
M: Well, even if something does come along, with this economy, I'm gonna make half of what I used to.
W: Not necessarily. Let's hope for the best! Listen, first things first: Is your LinkedIn profile updated?
M: I haven't logged in in years.
W: So that's a good place to start.

Conversation 2

M: Hey, Kate, looks like someone got a raise!
W: What?
M: Your new car!
W: What?
M: The red Cruze over there. It's yours, isn't it?
W: That's not my car!
M: But that's where you usually park.
W: Oh my gosh! Somebody took my car!
M: What? Oh, no!
W: I can't believe this is happening! I've got to call the police.
M: Hey, calm down! Erm ... How's your insurance?
W: Well, good, in fact. Full coverage for theft.
M: Hmm ... Hey, look on the bright side. You'll be able to get an even better model ...
W: I don't want a better model! I want my Fiesta back! I love that car! Plus it's the only one I can park easily. It's so nice and compact.
M: Look, it's been gone for, what, less than an hour. Maybe the police will find it.
W: No, I'm never gonna see it again.
M: Never say never! The police haven't even started looking for it. And remember, no news is good news!

Conversation 3

M: So, Linda ... you're off on Monday then?
W: Yep. Paris.
M: Three weeks?
W: That's wishful thinking! Just a week ... Still haven't started packing, though. Just the thought of it makes me exhausted.
M: Well, don't wait 'til the last minute. That way you won't forget anything.
W: Well, I always do. It doesn't matter whether I wait or not.
M: Cheer up, Linda! You're going to Paris!
W: Yeah, well, there's been talk of a general strike next week, you know. Trains, taxis, museums ...
M: Yeah, so I've heard. But often these strikes don't happen.
W: I just hope there's *something* for me to do there ... I mean, something I haven't done before.
M: Hmm ... If there's a strike, you can always enjoy walking and people watching!
W: I don't have to fly to Paris for that!
M: What time is your flight?
W: 8 a.m. Oh, Tom, how I hate these morning flights.
M: That's why you should pack in advance.
W: I have to leave home at four. You know what the traffic is like.
M: Yeah ... Better safe than sorry. But you can sleep on the plane. I'm sure you'll have a great trip!

12.6 *page 128 exercise 3A*

Welcome to *Here in the future*. Have you ever had conversations like these? I bet they'll sound familiar!

1

A: And I need two numbers where you can be reached, Mr. Sánchez.
B: 987 5999.
A: Is that your cell phone?
B: Yeah.
A: What about your landline?
B: Landline?
A: Yeah, your home number, in case we can't ...
B: But ... Does anyone still have landlines?

2

A: Two miles to empty. You'd better pull over.
B: You're sure? I think we can make it.
A: Better safe than sorry. Look, there's a gas station round the corner.
B: Hmm ... All the gas pumps are taken.
A: That one's open.
B: No, it says "gas pump out of service."
A: How many years till we can simply recharge our cars at home?

3

A: Rough day. Anyway, I'm on my way. Do you need anything? We're out of milk, right?
B: No, there's plenty. But could you get me the latest issue of *People*?
A: The magazine?
B: Yeah. There's a newsstand on the corner of Ocean and Fifth.
A: What happened to your virtual newsstand?
B: My iPad's dead. Remember? I dropped it in the pool last week by accident.
A: Oh, yeah. Wow. Paper. How twentieth century.

4

A: Watch out! Are you all right?
B: Yeah, yeah. Wow ... Third time this week. It seems that everything has a power cord attached to it!
A: Oh, no. My brand new printer! Smashed into pieces.
B: And the power cord is intact. How ironic. Why can't everything be wireless?!

12.9 *page 132 exercise 7B*

D = Don, M = Miranda, A = Announcer, O = Officer, G = Girlfriend

2.00 p.m.

D: Yes, we're going to spend the whole weekend there. We decided ages ago, remember? OK, I'll meet you at the station then. Love you. Bye. ... Excuse me ... Erm, Miranda, do you have a minute?
M: Hi, Don.
D: Hi, erm, I was wondering if I could leave work early today.
M: Hmm ... Not a good day, Don.
D: Oh.
M: You know we're meeting with the New York team next week, remember? I hope it's on your calendar.
D: Yeah, sure.
M: I really need everybody on top of all the ...
D: I know, I know, it's just that, well, I have a doctor's appointment at four and ...
M: Can't you reschedule?
D: The thing is, I've been on her waiting list for, like, months, and ...
M: Well, fine. Just be sure to go over the documents I sent you before you leave.
D: Yeah, sure, I'll get started on the ABC report right after lunch. Thanks, Miranda.

3:00 p.m.

A: ... IH-290 Eastbound closed due to construction from Main to Thompson.
D: Oh, no! I'm never gonna make it. Oh, come on!
O: License and registration, please. Mr ... Pendleton, do you know why I pulled you over?
D: Yes, I went through a red light a few blocks back and ...
O: ... and you did not come to a complete stop at the intersection of Jubilee and Bush Streets.
D: I know officer, but, you see, there's an emergency I'm trying to get to.
O: An emergency?
D: Yes, my next-door neighbor just texted me saying he smells gas in my apartment, so I...
O: You need to get there before the worst happens.
D: Yes!
O: I understand ... But I'm going to have to write you up anyway.
D: Oh, no!

4:00 p.m.

D: Wow, I never thought I'd make it.
G: What sort of time do you call this?
D: I'm sorry! The traffic was awful.
G: Again? Third time this month!

D: Yes, you're right, it won't happen again, I swear.
G: Well, what does it matter. We've missed the train.
D: What do you mean? The schedule says the train leaves at 4:30, right?
G: No. 3:30.
D: Oh, no! I'm so sorry!

12.10 *page 132 exercise 7C*

D: You're still mad about yesterday, aren't you?
G: You think?
D: Listen, how many times do I have to say I'm ...
G: Sorry? Twice a day for at least another week? Seriously though, listen to this article I've just read.
D: What's it about?
G: Excuses!
D: Oh, boy.
G: Let's see how many of them you recognize.
D: Maybe all of them.
G: OK, here's the first ... "Heavy traffic can be a legitimate excuse if you live in a big city ..."
D: See?
G: "But use your common sense. As soon as people realize you're overusing it, they won't buy it anymore, even if you do get stuck. And be careful with "I think I'll be there in five minutes." You'll lose credibility if five minutes constantly becomes 15."
D: OK, point taken.
G: Here's another: "If you get pulled over by the police, it's unlikely you'll be able to get away with saying there's an emergency you have to get to.
D: Oh!
G: "The same goes for "My plane leaves in 10 minutes." Honesty, on the other hand, might in some cases, actually increase your chances of not getting a ticket: "Sorry. I was over the limit. It won't happen again."
D: Erm... Actually, there's something I've been meaning to tell you ... I was late yesterday because I ... I also got a ticket.
G: You got stopped?
D: Uh huh. And I – don't laugh – I told him there was gas in my apartment.
G: Man, that was lame! I'm sure he's heard that one a million times. But wait, the article's not finished. One more: "At work, doctors' appointments can be pretty lame excuses, unless it's an emergency or something you've been trying to schedule for a long time. "I'm taking my sister-in-law to the doctor in the morning" is no good either – pick a closer relative.
D: Oops.
G: No!
D: I told Miranda I had a doctor's appointment ...
G: That is so unoriginal! Here's what they suggest: "Or, if it doesn't cost you your job, just be honest and say you're going to take the day off to run some errands."
D: Oh, I could never pull that one off with Miranda.

12.12 *page 134 exercise 9A and C*

F = Fred, T = Tina

F: Hey, check this out.
T: What's this?
F: I'm taking part in a writing contest.
T: "Write a letter to your future self and win two hundred and fifty dollars." Wow! Not bad.
F: Yeah, I could do with a little extra cash.
T: Hmm ... sounds interesting. But "your future self"? What on earth is that? What do you have to do exactly?
F: Well, basically, you have to send a letter to yourself, five, ten, twenty years from now – you choose.
T: Saying what?
F: Well, imagine you want to get married.
T: I do, actually.
F: Well, then you could start with something along the lines of "Dear Tina, when you read this, you'll have been married for five years. Are you happy? Is married life everything you thought it would be?"
T: Oh, OK, so it's kind of like a conversation with yourself. Now I get it!
F: Exactly. I'm writing to myself ten years from now.

12.13 *page 134 exercise 9B and C*

F = Fred, Y = Young Fred

F: Well, it's now a number of years down the road, and here I am, ten years later. I look a lot older, definitely not what I anticipated! But, hopefully, none the worse for wear! I think the braces helped! So let's look at what I wrote to my older self.
Dear Fred, Hey, how's it going? By the time you read this, you will have graduated long ago. And I sure hope that by now, you will have found a job as a teacher.
Well, when I graduated, the economy wasn't so great. I'm a schoolbus driver, believe it or not. It may not satisfy me totally on a personal level, but it's nice and steady.
Y: Really? You always did love to drive!
F: *And I hope your personal life is great. Do you think you'll have a steady girlfriend?*
F: It's even better than you imagined. I'm engaged! My fiancée is a wonderful person. And she loves me even if I look older than I am!
Y: That should be the least of your problems! I'm happy for you, Fred. I mean "me." It sounds as if your life has really come together.
F: Yes, I guess you could say that. Let's see what else I said to my older self.
And where will you be living? I imagine you'll stay at home until you graduate – and probably even well after.
Yes, I lived with Mom and Dad – by the way, they're fine – until recently, but now Amy – that is, my fiancée – and I are looking for a place. Our wedding is next week!
Y: Wow! I caught you at a busy time, didn't I? And an exciting one, too! All your hopes have been fulfilled!
F: Almost all of them. Remember, I wanted to be a teacher, not a bus driver! OK, back to the letter. We're almost done.
It's important to have realistic expectations. When you graduate, you may not find your dream job, especially if the economy is tight. But you're smart. I know you'll do well and have a satisfying life.
Sounds like my younger self was very mature! Wishing you all the very best. Fred.

Review 6 (Units 11–12)

R6.1 *page 136 exercise 1A*

L = Lee, D = Dan

L: Hey, Dan, ever read predictions about the future?
D: Sometimes. But do you really believe any of that stuff?
L: I do when they're based on scientific fact. I just finished Ulrich Eberl's book *Life in 2050*. Loved it!
D: What does he say? I assume it's a "he," right?
L: Yes, German, lives in Munich. He's one of the best science and technology journalists there is.
D: Well, I'm waiting ...
L: He says computer power will increase 1,000 times and all for the same price. Instead of a laptop for $500, you might get a small chip in your pocket that does the very same things. A computer will be the size of a pea.
D: No! Even better than the iWatch. But why do I need a computer in my pocket? I'm happy to leave mine at home, thank you.
L: You might change your mind if one could drive your car for you. You're always complaining about traffic. But by 2050, you'll be relaxing in the back seat with a book because according to Eberl, cars will be driving themselves.
D: Yeah, dream on. What else does he say?
L: Get this: By 2050, engineers will have designed skyscrapers to be energy-efficient farms. We might be looking at a vertical farm from our window.
D: What's wrong with the vegetable garden we have?
L: These farms will go up! They're vertical and won't take up any space. But here's my favorite: By 2050, traffic lights will have disappeared because cars will be talking to each other! That is, if you even need a car.
D: Cars that drive and talk. Maybe we won't need any people ...
L: Eberl says people will be telecommuting from smart apartments.
D: What's that?
L: An apartment that can recognize your face and even tell you what the weather is like!
D: Cars and apartments that are just like people!
L: Don't laugh. You'll probably live to see it. One in every six people will be over the age of 65!

Song activities

1.1

Song line: "Hey **Brother**. There's an endless road to rediscover. Hey **Sister**. Know the water's sweet but blood is thicker"

Song: ***Hey Brother***, released in 2013

Artist: Swedish DJ and producer **Avicii** (vocals sung by Dan Tyminski)

Lesson link: Family relationships

Note: The song has a country feel. The line comes from the saying *Blood is thicker than water*, which implies that family is more important than friends. The video shows two brothers growing up in wartime, with clips from the Vietnam War.

Before 1F, have sts try to sing the song line. Check if they know (and like) song. Get sts to highlight family words in the first verse and notice the schwa /ə/ rhymes (*broth***er**, *rediscov***er**, *sist***er**, *thick***er**). Focus on the second line, "Know the water's sweet but blood is thicker", and write on the board *Blood is thicker than water*. Sts discuss the meaning of this proverb in small groups. Classcheck.

1.2

Song line: "Tonight. We are **young**. So let's set the world on fire. We can burn brighter than the sun"

Song: ***Tonight***, released in 2011

Artist: American indie band **Fun**

Lesson link: Being young; teenage dreams and desires

Note: This is the song's powerful chorus. It's about young people having a bit of a wild night out. A worldwide hit after soundtracking Chevy Sonic's 2012 Super Bowl commercial, it won Song of the Year Grammy in 2013.

Refer to the song line before 3D to expand input on types of teenagers before the personalization. Elicit the melody of the song line from the class. Ask: *Do you know this song? Who recorded it?* Tell them *These lines show how empowered and free teenagers usually feel*. Ask sts: *Do you agree some teenagers feel they can do anything they want to?* Discuss possible reasons (e.g. enthusiasm of youth, inexperience, impulsiveness, rebellion, etc.).

1.3

Song line: "It's been a hard day's night, and I've been working **like a dog**"

Song: ***A Hard Day's Night***, released in 1964

Artist: British rock quartet **The Beatles**

Lesson link: Pets

Note: The song's odd name came when Ringo Starr emerged from a marathon studio session, still thinking it was day, and said, "It's been a hard day..." saw it was dark and said, "...night!" *A Hard Day's Night* is also one of the most influential music movies of all time.

Use at any time in the lesson, e.g., after 6C. Ask: *Do you know the Beatles? Any Beatles fans in your family?* Can you sing any lines from their songs? Sts read the line and infer meaning of the expression *work like a dog*. Classcheck. Ask: *Is there a similar expression in your language? / Any expressions with animal words in your language?* If time allows, write a few examples on the board and get sts to guess the meaning of: *have a cat nap, hold your horses, has the cat got your tongue?, to let the cat out of the bag, be in the dog house, dog days (of summer)*.

1.4

Song line: "I find it **hard to tell** you. I find it **hard to take**. When people run in circles it's a very, very, **Mad world, mad world**"

Song: ***Mad World***, released in 1982

Artist: British pop/rock band **Tears for Fears**

Lesson link: Adjective + infinitive; surviving in a crazy world

Note: An upbeat tune, it's actually about a depressed youth feeling out of place in this world, seeing life as empty and looking for ways to escape the pain. Gary Jules' slower, more emotive version, is equally well known and featured in the film *Donnie Darko*.

After 9B, have sts read the song line. Check if anybody knows the melody of the line, the song or artist(s), and identify which patterns (from the grammar box) are used in the first two verses. Classcheck.

Answer: adjective + infinitive

1.5

Song line: "**Waiting for your call**, Baby night and day. I'm fed up, I'm tired of waiting on you."

Song: ***Hung Up***, released in 2005

Artist: American "Queen of Pop" **Madonna**

Lesson link: Using the phone/waiting for a voice call

Note: The song samples Abba's *Gimme Gimme Gimme* (a Man After Midnight). In the video Madonna is in a dance gym. It became her best-selling single to date, shipping more than 8.7 million copies in only seven months.

As a follow-up to the question title (**warmer**), or before moving on to **12 Writing**, focus on the song line. Try to elicit the melody, song title and artist from sts. Ask: *What do you think this song is about?* (waiting for a phone call, relationships). Draw sts attention to the word waiting in 'I'm tired of waiting on you'. Ask: *Why is the -ing pattern used instead of to infinitive?* Sts discuss in pairs. Classcheck.

Write two sentences on the board for sts to compare: *I'm tired of cooking for you! and Sorry, but I'm too tired to cook you a meal now.*

Answers: preposition (*of*) + verb + *-ing* (collocation of adjective *tired of* and **not** *tired* + *to* + infinitive)

2.1

Song line: "All day long I think of things but nothing seems to satisfy. Think I'll **lose my mind** if I don't find something to pacify"

Song: ***Paranoid***, released in 1970

Artist: British heavy metal band **Black Sabbath**

Lesson link: Things on your mind; making mental choices

Note: The band's best-known song. Lead singer Ozzy Osbourne has been nicknamed, the "Godfather of Heavy Metal." The word *paranoid* is never actually mentioned in the song.

Get sts to read the song line. Check if they know the melody, song or artist. If time, show a video clip of it, or look at more verses from it on the Internet, e.g., "I need someone to show me the things in life that I can't find / I can't see the things that make true happiness, I must be blind."

In pairs, sts discuss which state(s) of mind can be implied from the song. Ask what might cause those feelings.

Possible answers: feelings of anxiety, hopelessness

2.2

Song line: "I can eat my dinner in **a fancy restaurant**. But nothing, I said nothing, can take away these blues"

Song: ***Nothing Compares 2 U***, released in 1990

Artist: Irish singer-songwriter **Sinead O'Connor**

Lesson link: Food/eating out; the silent /t/ in *eat* and *restaurant*

Note: A sad lament after a relationship break up, written and performed by singer Prince as an album track. O'Connor's re-release as a single, and stunning close-up video of her with shaved head, led to her being the first female MTV Video of the Year Award winner in 1990.

After 3A, sts find two examples of silent /t/ in the song line. If possible, show a 15-second snippet of the music video (00:54 to 01:10 on the official video on Youtube). Classcheck.

Elicit names of local "fancy" restaurants. Say: *According to the song, going to a fancy restaurant was supposed to have cheered her up, but it didn't work.* Ask: *Would it work for you?* Sts brainstorm pros and cons of the fancy restaurant experience (cost, dress code, food, service) and share their preferences. Classcheck opinions.

Answer: silent /t/ in eat restaurant

Tip: Avoid the temptation of playing the whole song/ video. The song lines are intended to be tackled mainly as a quotation with memorable pronunciation. Of course, time permitting, you can return later and use any full song for any teaching purpose.

2.3

Song line: "You live **you learn**, you love **you learn**. You cry **you learn**, you lose **you learn**"

Song: ***You Learn***, released in in 1995

Artist: Canadian singer-songwriter **Alanis Morissette**

Lesson link: Different ways to learn

Note: The song is about everything in life being a learning experience and is based on the saying *Live and learn*. A worldwide hit, the cast of *Glee* performed a version of it on the TV show in 2015.

Before 6A, get sts to read the song line and, elicit if they agree/disagree with it. With a more creative class, get them to invent additional options, e.g., *You breathe you learn, you sleep you learn*, etc.

Write the saying on the board: *Live and learn*, and highlight the use of the infinitive in English, rather than the gerund as, e.g., in Romance languages. *Is there an equivalent saying in their language?* Ask: *Do you believe experience makes people more intelligent? What is "intelligence"?* and move onto **6 Reading**.

2.4

Song line: "Well, I dreamed I saw the **silver space ships flying** in the yellow haze of the sun"

Song: ***After The Gold Rush*** released in 1970

Artist: Canadian singer-songwriter and musician **Neil Young**

Lesson link: Spaceships, aliens, life on another planet

Note: Re-recorded many times, it's become an environmentalist's anthem. The line suggests life on Earth will have to be rescued from human greed by flying Mother Nature to a new planet. The acoustic LP of the same name often appears in "Top 100 Albums of All Time" lists.

Focus sts' on the song line to see if anyone knows/can sing it. Use the content to provoke discussion. Ask: *Have you ever dreamed of flying saucers and/or aliens? How realistic are your dreams? Do you think humankind/the way we live would change if life on other planets were proven to exist? In what ways? Do you believe we can save Nature/ourselves by moving to another planet?*

2.5

Song line: "I'm **a science genius girl. I won the science fair**. I wear a white lab coat. DNA strands in my hair"

Song: **Science Genius Girl**, originally released in 2000

Artist: American "synthpop" band **Freezepop**

Lesson link: Having a high IQ; doing well at school

Note: Not a mainstream song, this is the first verse. It has a robotic sound that might not please all ears. Popular for its appearances as a playable song in several music video games, and as a downloadable song for the *Rock Band* video game series.

Use the song line to extend the discussion in exercise 11. Read it with the whole class and ask: *What do you think this song is about?* Write the word *geek* on the board and elicit meaning. Check if they know TV series such as *The Big Bang Theory*. If so, ask sts to explain what the characters are like. (They're a group of geeky scientists.) Ask: *Do you think schools/colleges should also teach students social skills? Why/Why not?*

3.1

Song line: "And every **glance** is killing me. Time to make one last appeal for the life I lead. Stop and **stare**, I think I'm moving but I go nowhere"

Song: ***Stop And Stare***, released in 2007

Artist: American pop-rock band **One Republic**

Lesson link: Ways of looking: *glance, stare, watch*

Note: A melancholic song about getting stuck in a rut and watching the life you wanted pass you by. The line suggests the singer is at a crossroads in life, wondering if he and his girlfriend are making the right choices. It has sold over 2 million digital copies worldwide.

After 1C, sts read the song line and underline the three verbs of vision. See if anyone knows the tune - the last two lines, which form the chorus, might well be familiar. Sts close their books to test each other in pairs, by quickly telling each other the difference between *glance* and *stare*. Books open. Check answers.

3.2

Song line: "I guess I **took a good selfie**. Let me **take a selfie**"

Song: ***Let Me Take A Selfie***, released in 2014

Artist: American/Slovakian DJ duo **The Chainsmokers**

Lesson link: Taking a selfie

Note: A disco-type song and never a great hit, it has a funny video of girls gossiping as they make themselves up, followed by a lot of amusing selfies. *Selfie* was the Oxford Dictionaries' 2013 Word of the Year, and this was the first song about the now worldwide phenomenon.

After 3C, read the song line with sts and have them guess the year the song was released (2014). Ask: *Do you remember your first selfie? Have you ever had/used a selfie stick? Have you ever asked a stranger to take a photo of you?* Move on to **3D Make it personal**.

3.3

Song line: "You could be my luck. Even in the hurricane of frowns, I know that we'll be **safe and sound**"

Song: ***Safe and Sound***, released in 2011

Artist: American electro-rock duo **Capital Cities**

Lesson link: The binomial

Note: Their debut single, it first became a hit in Peru, then spread to the world. Many people tend to think negatively about the times we're living in, and the message here is "think positive": we're better off now than ever before. The video shows a brief history of dance.

Use as an extension after **6C**. Sts find and circle the binomial in the song line. Classcheck.

Ask: *Have you ever seen that binomial before, in songs or films?* Elicit the meaning of *hurricane of frowns* too (a storm of negativity surround the couple, everything going wrong). See if anyone knows the tune/song/artist. Some students might be able to come up with binomials from songs they know, or you could set looking for one in songs they like as an interesting homework task.

Answer: safe and sound.

3.4

Song line: "I **used to rule** the world. Seas **would rise** when I gave the word. Now in the morning I sleep alone. Sweep the streets I **used to own**"

Song: ***Viva La Vida***, released in 2008

Artist: British rock band **Coldplay**

Lesson link: *used to* and *would* for past habits and states

Note: The title comes from Frieda Kahlo's painting by the same name, meaning "Long live life." It's a story about a king who lost his kingdom. The lyrics are complex and full of historical and religious imagery. It was the best selling album worldwide in 2008.

Do this after 8B as a lead-in to the pronunciation. Elicit the artist and see if anyone knows the melody. Get sts to underline used to and would in the song line, then, in pairs say whether each of them is a habit or a state. Classcheck.

Answers: *I used to rule* = a state; *Seas would rise* = a habit; *I used to own* = a state

If time, ask sts to mark the links in the lines; *I /juste/ rule, when I, now in, sleep alone, I /justew/ own*. Ideally, play the extract for them to listen and check.

3.5

Song line: "Clap along if you feel like a room with out a roof. Because ***I'm happy***! Clap along if you feel like ***happiness*** is the truth."

Song: ***Happy***, released in 2014

Artist: American singer, songwriter and producer **Pharrell Williams**

Lesson link: Being happy, happiness

Note: Written for the 3D computer-animated children's film *Despicable Me 2*. The title is repeated 56 times in the song and nearly two-thirds of the song is dedicated to the chorus. 2014's best-selling song, with a memorable video of people dancing along all over the world.

Use the song line as a **warmer**. Play the whole song or part of it if possible. Write the song line on the board and get sts to sing and clap to it. Check what they know about the artist/video, referring to the song facts above for more information. Elicit the meaning of the expression a room without a roof or have sts guess it in pairs (without limits). Classcheck.

4.1

Song line: "You **can't judge a sister by looking at her brother**. You **can't judge a book by looking at the cover**"

Song: ***You Can't Judge A Book By The Cover***, released in 1962

Artist: American R&B singer and rock 'n' roll pioneer **Bo Diddley** (1928 – 2008)

Lesson link: Not judging or being deceived by appearances

Note: Nicknamed "The Originator", because of his key role in the transition from the Blues to Rock 'n' Roll, Diddley influenced everybody from Elvis Presley to Jimi Hendrix. A catchy song with simple lyrics, it lists a series of metaphors for things you can't judge by their appearances.

After 1D, write on the board: *You can't judge a book by its cover*. Elicit meaning from sts and ask: *Is there a similar expression in your language? Do you agree with it?*

Sts read the song line. Check if they know either song or artist. With a more creative class, get them to invent additional options, e.g., *You can't judge an apartment by looking at the front door, a product by its price, a person by their job, a traveler by their suitcase, a person by looking into their sunglasses*, etc.

4.2

Song line: **"School's out for summer. School's out forever. School's been blown to pieces"**

Song: ***School's Out***, released in 1972

Artist: American singer, songwriter and musician **Alice Cooper**

Lesson link: The end of school

Note: Alice Cooper's biggest hit, a classic we can all relate to: being glad to be done with school! It's become an anthem for summer vacation. Featured in many TV shows and films such as *The Simpsons, Glee, Rock and Roll High School*, and *The Muppet Show*.

Use as a **follow-up to the question title warmer**. Ask class if they know the song and artist. Refer to song notes above for interesting facts, e.g., it was recorded in 1972, when technology posed no threat to teaching jobs. Encourage discussion by interpreting the lines, asking *What time of year is it? (end of summer semester), How does the singer feel about school? Why was school "blown to pieces"? How did you feel when you finished school?*, etc.

4.3

Song line: "It took me by surprise I must say. When **I found out** yesterday. Don't you know that **I heard it through the grapevine**"

Song: ***I Heard It Through The Grapevine***, released in 1968

Artist: American singer-songwriter and musician **Marvin Gaye**

Lesson link: Hearing/discovering gossip spread by rumors

Note: A classic about a man who finds out secondhand that his partner is cheating on him. First recorded by Gladys Knight and the Pips, this was Gaye's first number 1 hit, and made him a star.

If you have access to the music, try using as the **introduction** at the start of class, as this has a very catchy tune sts might know. Sts read the song line and try to sing it. Ask: *What do you think he heard through the grapevine?*

Some languages have colorful, equivalent expressions for how rumors spread, e.g., *The Arabic telephone* in French, *A little bird told me* in Brazilian Portuguese, as well as in English too, of course.

4.4

Song line: "One life. With **each other**, Sisters, Brothers, One life ... We get to **carry each other**"

Song: ***One***, released in 1991

Artist: Irish rock band **U2**

Lesson link: Reciprocal actions with each other

Note: A song about people struggling to be together, and how difficult it is to stay together, whatever relationship you're in. Released as a charity single, all the proceeds went to an AIDS charity. Often voted one of the best songs of all time.

After 8A, sts read the song line and try singing it. Check if they know/like the song or artist. Ask sts to interpret the line in pairs. Classcheck ideas.

Elicit the pronunciation of *other* and *brother* and raise sts' awareness that the letter o is commonly pronounced /ʌ/ as in the words *sun* and *run*. Elicit more words with the same pattern, e.g., *mother, another, love, come*, etc. Highlight that the verb *bother* is an exception.

4.5

Song line: "Don't tell me it's **not worth trying for**. You can't tell me ***it's not worth dying for***. Everything I do. I do it for you"

Song: ***(Everything I Do) I Do It For You***, released in 1991

Artist: Canadian singer-songwriter and guitarist **Bryan Adams**

Lesson link: Things being *(not) worth doing*, and the figurative expression *dying for* (their relationship)

Note: A memorable love song written specifically for the soundtrack to *Robin Hood: Prince of Thieves* starring Kevin Costner. One of the most successful singles of all time, it was number 1 for 16 weeks in the UK, seven weeks in the USA, and was nominated for an Oscar.

Before sts look at **Figurative expressions with die** in **10E**, focus on the song line. Check if anyone knows and can sing it. Ask: *Which old film was it the soundtrack to?*

Refer to the song notes above. Ask: *Is the singer in love? Would he die for his love?* (Yes). Explain the song has a literal – or dramatic! – meaning of dying for someone. In contrast, have sts interpret the sentence *I'm dying for a coffee*. Ask: *What does it mean? Is it literal or figurative? Do you say the same in your language?* Move on to 10E.

5.1

Song line: "I can **be your hero**, baby. I can **kiss away the pain**"

Song: ***Hero***, from 2011

Artist: Spanish singer, producer and actor **Enrique Iglesias**

Lesson link: Being someone's hero, helping someone overcome (pain)

Note: This sensitive ballad was a big hit after the September 11 terrorist attacks in New York City. The video follows Iglesias as a criminal on the run. It was remixed with real footage from the police, firefighters, and civilians at Ground Zero.

Focus on the song line and check if sts can sing it. Get them to interpret what he means (*he has the power to save her from her pain*).

Read the song notes above. Ask: *In your opinion, who are the everyday heroes? Who is/was your hero? Have you ever been a hero in somebody's life?* Invite sts to share their stories. Then, move on to **2 Listening**.

5.2

Song line: "I, **I wish you could swim** like the dolphins, like the dolphins can swim"

Song: ***Heroes***, from 1977

Artist: British singer, songwriter, actor and producer **David Bowie** (1947-2016)

Lesson link: *I wish* + past verb to imagine changing the present

Note: A beautiful song about a German couple who meet every day under a gun turret on The Berlin Wall. Bowie's performance of it in West Berlin on June 6, 1987 was said to have an influence in the bringing down of the Berlin wall two years later.

Before 4A, sts focus on this David Bowie song line to see if anyone knows and can sing it. Elicit the song title and what they know about the artist. Ask: *Can this person swim like a dolphin? Is it a possible or an imaginary wish?* To avoid confusion, explain that the figurative expression *swim like a fish* is not a wish, but an affirmation that one is a very skilled swimmer. If time allows, share more info about the song from the notes above.

5.3

Song line: "Beauty **school dropout**. No graduation day for you. Beauty school dropout. Missed your midterms and flunked shampoo"

Song: ***Beauty School Dropout***, released in 1978

Artist: American singer and actor **Frankie Avalon**

Lesson link: Pros and cons of studying hard, graduating from/flunking/dropping out of college, getting a job instead

Note: Featured in the hugely successful musical *Grease*. Avalon, one of the first teen idols of the 1950s, appears as the Teen Angel in a daydream sequence, encouraging failed beautician Frenchy (Didi Conn) to go back to high school. The cast of *Glee* also covered it in 2013.

After 5D, draw attention to the song line and check if sts know it. If possible, talk a bit about the musical *Grease* and share information from the song notes above.

Have sts act out a role-play in pairs. Say: *St A, you're planning to drop out of school or college. St B asks why and gives advice*. At the end, ask Sts A *What have you decided? Are you dropping out of school? Is (St B) a good adviser?*

5.4

Song line: "Why she had to go, I don't know, she wouldn't say. **I said something wrong, now I long for yesterday**"

Song: ***Yesterday***, released in 1965

Artist: British rock quartet **The Beatles**

Lesson link: Making and regretting a mistake and wishing to change it

Note: Melancholic ballad about a relationship break-up he caused by saying the wrong thing. He wishes he could change it and go back to how they were before. The most covered song in history, often voted greatest pop song ever. Paul McCartney wrote it and was the only Beatle to play on it.

Check if sts know and can sing the song line (and any other lines) from the Beatles' hit *Yesterday*. Elicit the meaning of to long for. Ask: *Does the singer wish he'd done something differently in the past? What do you think happened?*

Then, ask sts to find three rhyming words in each line. Paircheck, then classcheck and have the whole class chorally sing it together.

Answers: go-know / wrong-long / say-yesterday

5.5

Song line: "It ain't me, it ain't me. **I ain't no fortunate one...**"

Song: ***Fortunate Son***, from 1969

Artist: American rock band **Creedence Clearwater Revival** (often shortened to **Creedence**, or abbreviated to **CCR**)

Lesson link: Being or not being (born) lucky

Note: An anti-establishment song, both anti-Washington and against the Vietnam War. It's about blue-collar pride and the unfairness of class, and how the rich cause wars but the poor have to fight them. It's still used to protest against the military and elitism in the USA.

If possible, play the introduction of the song to check if sts know the tune. It's been featured in films such as *Forrest Gump* and *Die Hard*, adverts and TV shows. Ask: *Is the singer lucky? Is he rich?* Share more info from song notes above.

To start a discussion, ask: *Do you think most problems in the world are caused by the rich and powerful?*

6.1

Song line: "Let me be the one to **give you everything you want and need**. Baby good love and **protection**. Make me your selection."

Song: ***Let Me Love You***, released in 2004

Artist: American singer-songwriter, actor, dancer, model, and producer **Mario**

Lesson link: Protection; protecting someone from doing the wrong thing

Note: An RnB ballad about a guy urging a girl, who he thinks is in the wrong relationship, to become his girlfriend. This is the second half of the chorus. Written by fellow RnB singer, Ne-Yo, it was number 1 on the US Billboard chart for nine weeks in 2005 and is Mario's biggest hit.

At the **end** of the lesson, try to elicit the song line melody, title and artist. Ask: *What do you think the singer wants to protect the woman from?* Sts answer in pairs. Classcheck interpretations.

Use the line to expand the lesson topic. Brainstorm other forms of *protection* in society, e.g., emotional, parental, financial. Write this sentence starter on the board for sts to complete in as many ways as they can, giving an example:

(Parents) try to protect their (children) ...

from (growing up too quickly)

by (not allowing them access to adult themes and images.)

...

6.2

Song line: "Can call all you want but there's no one home, and **you're not going to reach my telephone**"

Song: ***Telephone***, from 2009

Artist: American singer, songwriter and actress **Lady Gaga**, ft. **Beyoncé**

Lesson link: Invasion of privacy via technology, and how to block it

Note: A song about being harassed by her lover on the phone when she's trying to dance in a club. It features Beyoncé, and the video is a 9-minute, entertaining (if controversial) homage to Quentin Tarantino. 2010's most played track on Spotify and Gaga's fourth UK number 1 single in a little over 14 months.

Sts guess song title and artist. Ask: *What's the link between this song line and the lesson? Why's it there?* (Determination to keep your privacy). Ask: *Why do you think she's refusing to take his calls? Do you like the song/artist?*

As a follow-up, ask: *How often do you ignore/delay responding to/immediately delete calls or messages? And how do people react to that?*

6.3

"I have no privacy"

Song: ***Somebody's Watching Me***, released in 1984

Artist: American singer and song writer **Rockwell** ft. **Michael Jackson**

Lesson link: Being watched/spied on, invasion of privacy

Note: It's about feeling you're constantly being watched. Rockwell's brother-in-law was Jermaine Jackson, and his megastar brother Michael agreed to sing on the chorus, ensuring a hit. People often mistake it for a Michael Jackson song. The scary music video is often associated with Halloween.

After 3B, ask if sts have ever heard the song *Somebody's Watching Me*, from 1984. Share the content from the song notes above. Then ask: *Have you ever been alone at home and felt the presence of somebody else in the room watching you?*

If time, find the lyrics online or play the video so sts see what the song is about.

6.4

Song line: "I'm free to be **whatever** I, **whatever** I choose. And I'll sing the blues if I want"

Song: ***Whatever***, from 1994

Artist: British rock band **Oasis** (led by Gallagher brothers, Noel and Liam)

Lesson link: Question words with *-ever*; *whatever*

Note: A song about non-conformity and freedom of choice. A reaction to how Noel's dad used to make him work on a construction site as a teenager, and wanted him to become a builder. Of course, he refused! Coca-Cola used it in their 2012 campaign to celebrate the drink's 125th birthday.

Before 9 Grammar, focus on the song line. Elicit the meaning of *whatever* (anything at all or anything I want). Try to elicit the melody, who recorded the song and what they know/feel about the band. They were famously anarchistic in their time, with an arrogant couldn't-care-less attitude, exactly as expressed in this line. If you can play it, see if sts can notice the close similarity to The Beatles (a common feature of many Oasis songs).

6.5

Song line: "Hey, hey, you, you. I know that you like me. I know that you like me. No way, no way. No, **it's not a secret**."

Song: ***Girlfriend***, from 2007

Artist: Canadian singer-songwriter and actress **Avril Lavigne**

Lesson link: (Not) Sharing secrets

Note: A girl sings about a boy she likes who already has a girlfriend. Her strategy is ultra-persistence in trying to convince him she's a better choice. The fun, massively popular video has Lavigne playing two different teenagers, competing for the same guy at high school.

Use the song to break up the lesson **before the writing**, or as a "reward" at the end of the unit. Invite sts who know the song to sing it to the rest of the class. Elicit the song title and artist. Ask: *Imagine the story behind the song and her choice of words?* Read the song notes above to check answers.

Ask: *Are you good at keeping secrets? Do you know anyone who isn't? Do you think it's harder these days for both individuals and institutions to keep a secret? Why (not)?*

7.1

Song line: "**Hello from the other side. I must've called a thousand times. To tell you ...**"

Song: ***Hello*** released in 2015

Artist: British singer and songwriter **Adele**

Lesson link: Adele sang the song and is in the quiz

Note: An apt lead single from album 25, as it marked Adele's return after a 3-year break. Epic ballad telling how sorry she is about breaking someone's heart. The video got 27.7 million views on Vevo in 24 hours, and over 50 million on YouTube in its first 48 hours. Adele plays the drums on it too.

After 1B, elicit the melody, song and artist. Ask: *Why was the line chosen to go with this lesson?* (She's question 3 in the quiz). Find out if they like/what they know about her and elicit any other lines they know from her songs.

Ask: *What's her third album called?* (25) *Why?* (Her age again). *How long do you think her album names will correspond to her age?*

7.2

Song: "**So I put my hands up. They're playing my song. The butterflies fly away. I'm nodding my head like yeah!**"

Song: ***Party In The USA***, released in 2009

Artist: American singer and former Hannah Montana actress **Miley Cyrus**

Lesson link: It's a well-known Miley Cyrus song and she's in the lesson

Note: The song details her arriving in Los Angeles as yet another wannabe superstar. Scared by what she finds alone in the huge new city, her nerves are allayed, she relaxes and starts to move whenever she hears her favorite song.

As a **warmer**, put sts in small groups to mime the song line together and enjoy the fun! After a minute, elicit a class mime to the line and see what they can tell you about the artist, rest of the song, video, etc. Check information about the song in the notes above. Ask: *Do you have a favorite Miley Cyrus song/anecdote?*

7.3

Song line: "Music, music. Music makes the people come together. Music makes the bourgeoisie and **the rebel**"

Song: ***Music***, released in 2000

Artist: **Madonna**

Lesson link: Pronunciation of the noun rebel /'rebl/

Note: An innovative dance-pop club anthem about the unitary power of music, with great hooks like *Hey Mr DJ* and *Do you like to boogie-woogie?* The video parodies rap, with Madonna cruising in a chauffeur-driven limo going to clubs and enjoying the trappings of success.

Before 7B, focus on the song line. If sts know it, ask them to sing it – and any other lines from the song as it has several good hook lines - and tell you what they know/feel about Madonna. Focus on the word rebel in the line. Ask: *Is it a noun or a verb?* Elicit the correct word stress.

Ask: *Do you agree with the message in the song line?* (that music is a great leveler). Then link this to Q3 in ex 7B when they do it.

7.4

Song line: "Hey, hey, my, my. Rock 'n' roll can never die. **There's more to the picture than meets the eye**"

Song: ***Hey, Hey, My, My***, released in 1978

Artist: Canadian singer, composer, and guitarist **Neil Young**

Lesson link: Pictures, and interpreting them

Note: A song about the fleeting nature of fame and difficulties of remaining relevant as an artist. Another line from it was quoted by Nirvana frontman Kurt Cobain in his suicide note in 1994. It read: "It's better to burn out than to fade away."

Do after 9C. Focus on the song line and check whether sts know it. Talk about who Neil Young is (see notes above). Sts in pairs interpret the meaning of *There's more to the picture than meets the eye*. Ask: *When might you say this?* Classcheck ideas. (It means things/pictures are more interesting or complicated than they first appear, and there's usually more below the surface/behind the image.)

If time, they could look back and try to apply this to the 3 paintings in 8A. Some sts might connect this to the song line from 4.1 You can't judge a book.

7.5

Song line: "I can see **clearly** now the rain is gone. I can see all obstacles in my way. Gone are the dark clouds that had me blind."

Song: ***I Can See Clearly Now***, released in 1972

Artist: American reggae singer-songwriter **Johnny Nash**

Lesson link: The adverb *clearly*; the lesson is all about music

Note: A song of hope and courage for those who've experienced adversity and overcome it. Jamaican artist Jimmy Cliff re-recorded it in 1993, and his hit version was soundtrack to the film *Cool Runnings* about the Jamaican bobsled team.

Before moving on to 12B, ask sts who know the line to sing it, or if no one knows it play a snippet of the music video. Share the info from the song notes above, adding that this was a forerunner to Bob Marley and the reggae boom of the mid-70's. Sts find the adverb in the line and notice its position. If time allows, elicit possible interpretations of the song.

8.1

Song line: "**You start to freeze**, as horror looks you right between the eyes. **You're paralysed. 'Cause this is thriller, thriller night!**"

Song: ***Thriller***, released in 1982

Artist: American singer, songwriter, producer, dancer, and actor **Michael Jackson** (1958-2009)

Lesson link: Symptoms (and thrills) of fear

Note: From *Thriller*, the biggest selling album ever, it's about terrifying creatures of the night – in this case, a werewolf. The Library of Congress chose it as *the* most famous music video. Its famous graveyard dance sequence began the trend for group dance scenes in pop videos.

After 2A, sts read the line and guess the name of the song and artist, adding anything they remember about him. Sts underline the words connected to fear (freeze, horror, paralyzed, thriller) and, for fun, mime all three lines.

Elicit the melody, and ask: *Do you know what this song is about? What's the music video like?* If time, brainstorm names of horror films and have the class discuss/choose the scariest movie/TV show they've seen.

8.2

Song line: "In my place, in my place, were lines **I couldn't change**. I was lost, oh yeah"

Song: ***In My Place***, released in 2002

Artist: British rock band **Coldplay**

Lesson link: Past ability: *couldn't* (meaning *was unable to*)

Note: A guy is in love with a girl who doesn't reciprocate, and seems to be waiting for someone else. He's telling her he'll always wait for her and feels "lost" because he's "crossed the line" with her. 2002 Grammy winner for Best Rock Performance by a Duo or Group with Vocal.

Address the song line after 4A. Elicit what you can about the line, melody, group, and any other lines they may know from the song. Include the song notes above. Ask: *What do you think he's talking about exactly in this line?* Then ask: *Can you replace couldn't by wasn't able to?* Elicit a third possible option, *was unable to*. Sts try singing the song line again with all three options and decide which fits the melody better.

8.3

Song line: "**I've been worrying that I'm losing the ones I hold dear**. I've been worrying that ***we all live our lives in the confines of fear***."

Song: ***The Fear***, released in 2011

Artist: British singer-songwriter **Ben Howard**

Lesson link: Being afraid of loss, the power of fear and fear-mongering

Note: The last lines in the song's chorus. He's worrying that he'll go through life, have nothing to show for it and die, without having achieved anything. He says that this fear of not becoming somebody, or amounting to anything, can both hold us back and ultimately consume us.

Before 5E, focus on the song line and elicit interpretation of *the ones I hold dear* (my closest friends/family), and *in the confines* (= limited by fear). Expand the topic of fear. Ask: *What can you infer about the singer's beliefs?* (e.g. a pessimist/worrier/realist?). *Do you agree we live in fear? What have you been worrying about recently?* Elicit what they know about Ben Howard. Some may know his better known songs *Keep Your Head Up* and *Only Love*.

8.4

Song line: "How a**m I supposed to live** without you? How **am I supposed to carry on**? When all that I've been living for is gone"

Song: ***How Am I Supposed To Live Without You***, released in 1989

Artist: American singer and songwriter **Michael Bolton**

Lesson link: *(be) supposed to* [phonetic font] /səpoustə/

Note: A soul ballad lamenting the loss of a lover. Laura Branigan recorded it first in 1983, but Bolton's later version of his own song won the 1989 Grammy for Best Male Pop Vocal Performance. Subsequently recorded by many artists worldwide, in several languages.

After **9A**, have sts read and interpret the song line: *What's happened?* (his partner has gone). Check if sts know and can sing it. Highlight *supposed* to and elicit the informal pronunciation. If possible, check pronunciation by playing a 20-second snippet of the official Michael Bolton music video on YouTube (01:05 to 01:25). Young sts may find the romantic style of the 1980s an amusing cultural experience!

8.5

8.5

Song line: "Head in the clouds, got no weight on my shoulders. **I should be wiser and realise that I've got one less problem**."

Song: ***Problem***, released in 2014

Artist: American singer and actress **Ariana Grande**

Lesson link: *should* (for advice), relaxing following her own advice

Note: She sings about her insecurities over renewing a relationship with an ex-boyfriend, who she knows isn't good for her. The song mentions the word *problem* 34 times! Grande has a very large social media following.

Check if sts recognize the song, hum the melody to help them, and have them sing the line if they do, hopefully completing the verse "One less problem without you." Elicit interpretations from sts. Expand, asking *Do you/ anyone you know often speak/give advice to yourself? Aloud or under your breath? On what matters? Does it work?*

9.1

Song line: "Everybody needs some time ... **on their own**. Don't you know you need some time ... **all alone**"

Song: ***November Rain***, released in 1992

Artist: American hard rock band **Guns N' Roses**

Lesson link: The phrase *on your own*; (the importance of) being alone
Note: Biographic song about lead singer-songwriter Axl Rose and his first wife, who broke up in November 1990. The video portrays their wedding, then her funeral. Originally 25-minutes long, edited down to 8.59, it's the longest ever Top 10 hit, and has the longest guitar solo in a Top 10 single.

Do before **Common Mistakes**. Books closed. Write the lines with common mistakes on the board for sts to correct: "Everybody need some time... on your own. Don't you know you need a time... all lonely." Tell sts it's by Guns N' Roses.

In pairs, they have to find and correct four mistakes. Open books to check answers. Then ask: *Do you agree with the song line? Imagine the context. Share content from the song notes above.* Ask: *What's the longest you can spend entirely on your own without any form of contact with the outside world?*

9.2

Song line: "Why you gotta **be so rude**? Don't you know I'm human too? Why you gotta be so rude? I'm going to marry her anyway."
Song: ***Rude***, released in 2013
Artist: Canadian reggae fusion band, **Magic**
Lesson link: The theme of rudeness
Note: Very catchy and lexically quite simple song for students, in which a would-be groom repeatedly asks his girlfriend's father for her hand in marriage, but keeps getting bluntly rejected. The inevitable outcome is in the chorus!

After 3C, invite the sts who know the song line to sing it. Elicit the story behind the song (see song notes above). If time allows, this would be an easy, fun video to do the full song in class. Ask: *What would happen in a situation like this in your country? Is it common in your culture to have to ask permission from the bride's father?*

9.3

Song line: "I've got so much love in my heart, no one can tear it apart, yeah, feel the love **generation**."
Song: ***Love Generation***, released in 2005
Artist: French producer and house music DJ, **Bob Sinclair**; vocals by Gary Pine, from Jamaican band The Wailers
Lesson link: The topic: different generations
Note: A huge hit all over Europe from a simple story with this great hook. Easy to do the whole song in class. The video is a schoolboy cycling to school but not stopping, instead visiting many places in the USA.

If possible, **start the lesson** by showing the first thirty seconds of the video and see if sts recognize the tune. You can also whistle the refrain to help sts guess the song line, or at least the chorus. Open books to read and confirm the line and chorus. Elicit or demonstrate the meaning of *tear it apart*, e.g., with a piece of paper. Ask: *Which do you think is the love generation? Why?*

9.4

Song line: "Can't we laugh about it (Ha Ha Ha), (Oh) It's not worth our time, (Oh) We can live without 'em, Just a beautiful **liar**"
Song: ***Beautiful Liar***, released in 2007
Artist: American singer **Beyoncé** and Colombian singer, **Shakira**
Lesson link: Liars, lying, spotting and reacting to lies
Note: Beyoncé and Shakira sing of how the same man lied to each of them about being 'the only one'. Rather than start a fight or take revenge, they decide he's not worth it, and just to ignore him. Latin-flavored with some Spanish lyrics.

After 7E, ask sts to read the song line to see if they recognize the melody, song, and singers, and their opinions of each of them. Elicit the meaning of *'em* (them), and who they might be (men). Share the information in the song notes above. Ask: *Who's the best liar you know?* And, with an older class, *Have you ever been lied to by a partner?*

9.5

Song line: "**I'm all lost in the supermarket. I can no longer shop happily. I came in here for that special offer. A guaranteed personality.**"
Song: ***Lost In The Supermarket***, released in 1979
Artist: British punk rock band, **The Clash**
Lesson link: The topic: how consumerism can consume us
Note: Originally punks, **The Clash** incorporated reggae, dub, funk, ska, and rockabilly into their songs. This one is about a disillusioned youth growing up in suburbia, attacking the increasing de-personalization, commercialization, and rampant consumerism in society.

Do the song line either as a **lead-in** to the lesson topic, ***or*** to **finish** the class on a high, once you've set up the writing activity for homework. Write these questions on the board: *Why's the singer lost? Do you think it's a man or a woman? Why? What do they mean by guaranteed personality?* In pairs, sts try to answer. Classcheck.

Ask: *Do you know/like the line, melody, song, artist?* Share the information in the song notes above. If appropriate, ask: *Do you know any other "political" songs in English?*

10.1

Song: "Hold me like you'll never let me go. 'Cause **I'm leaving on a jet plane. I don't know when I'll be back again**. Oh, babe. I hate to go"

Song: ***Leaving on a Jet Plane***, released in 1969

Artist: American singer-songwriter, actor, and activist **John Denver** (1943-1997)

Lesson link: The topic: traveling and transportation

Note: An emotional love song, Denver tells his girlfriend how he hates to leave her, intends to marry her, and apologizes for his behavior away on tour. American folk group Peter, Paul and Mary's biggest hit in 1968. If possible, show the clip of astronauts singing it in the film, *Armageddon*.

Do after 2B to get sts thinking about additional travel anecdotes before telling their own stories in 2C. Have sts read the line and, in pairs, imagine the context, singer, and the listener's response to these words. For fun they could mime or even roleplay it too. Classcheck answers.

Ask: *Have you heard the song? Who sang it?* Share the information in the song notes above, and suggest they watch the video or Google the best/worst version they can find for homework.

10.2

Song line: "**Do you know where you're going to?** Do you like the things that life is showing you? **Where are you going to?** Do you know?"

Song: ***Theme from Mahogany (Do You Know Where You're Going To)*** released in 1975

Artist: American singer, songwriter and actress, **Diana Ross**

Lesson link: Question types: indirect vs direct

Note: A song often requested at graduation ceremonies. From the film *Mahogany*, the lyrics look back at a relationship and forward with questions. With this song, Diana Ross was the first singer to perform at the Oscar ceremony live via satellite, from Amsterdam.

Do before exercise 5. Books closed. Write these two questions on the board and ask sts in pairs to correct the mistake in each and explain why.

To where are you going?

Do you know where are you going to?

Classcheck by reading or, if possible, playing the song chorus or part of the video. Ask: *Do you know/like the line, melody, song, artist, film? In general, do you prefer ballads and beautiful voices like hers, or faster, rockier songs/singing?*

10.3

Song line: "**Aaah, Home, Let me come home**. Home is wherever I'm with you."

Song: ***Home***, released in 2009

Artist: American indie folk band **Edward Sharpe and The Magnetic Zeros**

Lesson link: Being away, missing and wanting to come back "home."

Note: The song has a folksy feel, full of American imagery, and this is its catchy chorus. A 10-piece band whose image and sound evoke the hippie movement of the 1960s and 1970s, they run non-profit based projects to develop co-ops and land trusts in urban areas around the world.

Do either before or after 6F. Write the phrase *Home is ...* on the board and ask sts in pairs to complete it however they like. Look on Google Images for ideas, e.g., *Home is where the heart is/where your Wi-Fi connects automatically/ not a place, it's a feeling*. In pairs, sts read the song, interpret who might be singing to whom, and why. If your class is willing, get them to try to guess the melody too. Ideally, you'd be able to show a clip from the video to check their guesses as it's catchy and fun.

10.4

Song line: "**Can't get used to losing** you. No matter what I try to do. Gonna live my whole life through, Loving you."

Song: ***Can't Get Used To Losing You***, released in 1963

Artist: American singer **Andy Williams** (1927-2012)

Lesson link: The structure: *get used to + verb + -ing*

Note: An easy listening classic, popularized by Andy Williams, who recorded 44 albums in all and hosted his own TV variety show from 1962 to 1971. British band, The Beat, released a catchy reggae version in 1980.

After 9A, sts read the song line and interpret the situation the singer expresses. Ask: concept-check questions about "Can't get used to losing you": *Has he lost his girlfriend?* (Yes); *Has he got over it?* (No); *Is he trying to get accustomed to the situation?* (Yes); *Does he feel he will eventually recover from the loss?* (No).

If you're able to play the Andy Williams' version, highlight the rhymes you-do-through-you. Encourage reactions to this very 1960s genre. *Did their parents listen to music like this?*

10.5

Song line: "I can open your eyes... **A whole new world. A new fantastic point of view**"

Song: ***A Whole New World***, released in 1992

Artist: American singers **Peabo Bryson** and **Regina Belle**

Lesson link: Seeing fantastic new places/ perspectives; the (magic) carpet!

Note: The romantic theme to 1992 Disney's *Aladdin*, it's a love song between Aladdin and Princess Jasmine. In the scene we had in mind, Aladdin takes her on a magic carpet ride over a city resembling the souks and minarets of Istanbul. It won Oscar for Best Song From A Movie and Grammy for Song Of The Year.

Use the song line as a **lead-in** to the Istanbul quiz, especially if you're able to show a clip from the Disney video. If they don't recognize the line, establish it's being sung by Aladdin to his girlfriend Jasmine, as they ride on his magic carpet! Elicit what they remember about the Aladdin story.

Ask: *What's the best view you've ever seen? Where would you choose to go on a magic carpet ride? Imagine life if we all had a magic carpet!* Sts answer in pairs. Give your own example answers first to give them time to think. Classcheck.

11.1

Song line: "I thought I **heard** you laughing, I thought I **heard** you sing. I think I thought I saw you try."

Song: ***Losing My Religion***, released in 1991

Artist: Alternative American rock band, **R.E.M.**

Lesson link: Common errors between *listen to* vs *hear* (the news)

Note: A hit about obsessive, unrequited love, with an acclaimed video. It's on the Hall of Fame's list of 500 Songs that Shaped Rock and Roll. The phrase *losing my religion* comes from the US South. It means "losing one's temper or civility" or "being at the end of one's rope".

After 1C, focus on the song line. Elicit the melody, title, and artist. Ask if *heard* in the line could be replaced by *listened*. Why not? Take sts' answers but don't confirm yet. Write sentences 1-5 on to the board, telling sts only one is correct. In pairs, sts correct the four which are wrong.

1. *Have you listened to the news?* (Incorrect)
2. *Turn on the radio, please, we'd like to hear the news.* (Incorrect)
3. *Speak louder! I can't listen to you!* (Incorrect)
4. *We all listened carefully to the fire instructions.* (Correct)
5. *Do you hear the radio when you're driving?* (Incorrect)

Classcheck answers. Then, return to the song line and elicit why *heard* there can't be replaced by *listened*.

11.2

Song line: "And I **wonder**, When I sing along, If everything could ever feel this real forever. If anything could ever be this good again."

Song: ***Everlong***, released in 1997

Artist: American rock band **Foo Fighters**

Lesson link: Grammar: reported question using *wonder*

Note: A beautiful romantic song about loving someone so much you want it to last forever. The acoustic version is just as good too. In the video, the band's singer Dave Grohl is a kind of superhero with a giant hand to protect his girlfriend.

Before 5A, elicit information about the song and artist. Share more facts from the song notes above. Write this sentence on the board: *I wonder if everything could ever feel this real forever*. Ask: *What question is he asking himself?* Elicit the direct speech question from sts, get them to complete the prompt: *Could everything ... (ever feel this real forever)?* Sts compare the changes between the two sentences - reported speech with *I wonder* and direct speech *Could everything ever feel...?* E.g., use of *if*, inversion. Move on to the Grammar box.

11.3

Song line: "It's Friday, Friday, Gotta get down on Friday. Everybody's looking forward to the weekend, weekend."

Song: ***Friday***, released in 2011

Artist: American singer and Youtuber, **Rebecca Black**

Lesson link: The song is from the video in ex 7A.

Note: A song about hanging out with friends and having fun. *Get down* here is used informally, meaning "have a good time partying and dancing". The Friday music video has been watched more times than there are Fridays in recorded history!

Connect the song line to the third text in 7A. See if anyone can sing it before they search for the video in 7C. Share the information in the song notes above. Ask: *Which day of the week do you most look forward to? Do you know any other songs about days of the week?*

Or set a homework task to research songs about days of the week. There are a lot - the day with the most mentions being Sunday. See, e.g., http://www.vocativ.com/culture/music/days-of-the-week-songs/

11.4

Song line: "**You tell me that you're sorry**. Didn't think I'd turn around and say. That it's too late to **apologize**, It's too late."

Song: ***Apologize*** from 2007

Artist: American pop-rock band **One Republic**

Lesson link: The grammar: reporting what people say (the apology)

Note: A song about the pain of a relationship going wrong and the need to move on. A mixture of Britpop-influenced melodies and hip-hop, it was re-mixed and re-released by Timbaland in 2007. It became One Republic's breakout hit and first number 1.

Before 9A. Write the song line on the board with the suggested gaps: *You ________ me that you're sorry, didn't think I'd turn around and ____________, that it's too late to ___________, it's too late.*

Ask sts to guess the three missing verbs. Paircheck. Classcheck. (*tell, say, apologize*).

Check if sts know/like the melody, song, and artist. Elicit more reporting verbs from sts, e.g., *persuade*, *agree*, *threaten*, etc., and list their contributions on the board, for reference during the rest of the class.

11.5

Song line: "**Fame**, I'm gonna live forever, I'm gonna learn how to fly high, I feel it coming together, **People will see me and cry, Fame**"

Song: ***Fame***, released in 1980

Artist: American singer, songwriter and actress **Irene Cara**

Lesson link: Being famous

Note: *Fame* is a fictional movie about a real, NYC performing arts school. Irene Cara played the role of Coco Hernandez and sang this song, which captures the students' determination to be famous and have their names remembered.

Sts read the song line and guess the genre. Ask: *What type of music do you think this is?* (Disco) Share information from the song notes above. If possible, play a short snippet of the music video and check if sts have heard the song before. In pairs, sts interpret exactly how the song line relates to the topic of fame. Classcheck. If time, get them to brainstorm/Google other songs which relate to the topic of *fame*.

12.1

Song line: "And if you close your eyes, does it almost feel like you've been here before? **How am I gonna be an optimist about this**?"

Song: ***Pompeii***,released in 2013

Artist: British indie rock band **Bastille**

Lesson link: (The difficulty of always) Being an optimist

Note: The song is an imagined conversation between two corpses after Vesuvius erupted! A weird premise for a dance song with a catchy 'ayyyy ay-yo ayo' chant. Like *Paranoid* in Lesson 2.1, the title is never spoken. In the video, frontman Dan Smith runs through an odd LA and escapes to Palm Springs.

After Common Mistakes in 1A, sts focus on the song line. Elicit the song title (***Pompeii***) and ask: *What's the town of Pompeii famous for?* Help set the context of the song - the eruption of Mount Vesuvius in the year 79 AD, people frozen in lava, etc. Share information from the song notes above.

Highlight use of the article *an* + noun **optimist**.

Ask: *Have you ever been somewhere new but had the feeling you've been there before?*

12.2

Song line: "I can have another you by tomorrow, so don't you ever for a second get to thinking, you're **irreplaceable**"

Song: ***Irreplaceable***, released in 2006

Artist: American singer, songwriter, and actress **Beyoncé**

Lesson link: The topic: replacing one thing with another

Note: Written by Ne-Yo and sung by a woman addressing her lover, who's been cheating on her and taking her for granted. She's telling him that he can be easily replaced. The best selling US single of 2007.

Before 3D, check if sts recognize Beyonce's song line. Elicit the melody and get sts to sing this, plus any other lines they may know from the song. Do they like it/her?

Ask: *Do you think everyone is replaceable? Who is (ir) replaceable in your life?*

Then, write a few tech items on the board and ask: *What replaced these? Any other technologies that you miss?*

E.g.,

Calculators	*Candles*	*Cassette tapes*	*Horse and carriage*
Postcards	*Paper maps*	*Typewriters*	*Video cassettes*

12.3

Song line: "Where there is a flame, **someone's bound to get burned**, but just because it burns doesn't mean you're gonna die. **You gotta get up and try**"

Song: ***Try***, released in 2012

Artist: American singer, songwriter, dancer, and actress, **Pink**

Lesson link: Phrase: *(be) bound to*; theme: innovation - some failure is inevitable but you have to keep trying to succeed

Note: An anthem to not letting go of your dreams and aspirations, no matter what risk you have to take. Hand-clapping features strongly in the song. The impressive video features a paint-covered Pink and partner expressing themselves cleverly through dance.

After 5D, write a) and b) on the board; *a) Don't play with fire under any circumstances. b) You can't get anywhere in life without taking risks*. Have sts read the song lines and, in pairs, match its meaning to summary *a)* or *b)*. (answer *b*). Ask: *Do you agree?* Highlight the word *bound* in the line and ask: *According to the song, how likely are you to get burnt if there's a flame?*

12.4

Song line: "I missed the last bus, **I'll take** the next train. I try but **you see, it's hard to** explain

Song: ***Hard To Explain***, released in 2002

Artist: American rock band, **The Strokes**

Lesson link: *will* for a decision/promise you make at the moment of speaking; the topic: preparing someone for an excuse

Note: First single from their much acclaimed first album *Is this it?* A song about the importance of not trying to understand everything - some things just are the way they are, period, and you shouldn't worry about them.

After 8A, sts read the song line and imagine the context/ who might be saying it to whom. Brainstorm ideas, then elicit info about the song (from song notes above). Can anyone sing it? Focus on the grammar and get sts to match the use of *will* in *I'll take the next train* with one of the rules a-d in the **Grammar box**. Classcheck.

Answers: a (decision or promise made at the moment you're speaking).

12.5

Song line: "You may say I'm a dreamer, but I'm not the only one. **I hope someday you'll join us. And the world will live as one**"

Song: ***Imagine***, released in 1971

Artist: British singer and songwriter, **John Lennon**

Lesson link: *I hope; will*, the topic: imagining future life

Note: A strong political message softened by a beautiful melody. He asks us to imagine a much better place where things that divide us (religion, possessions, etc.) no longer exist. A unifying song loved and sung all over the world, and an uplifting note to finish the course on.

Books closed. Dictate the song line as below without giving away the melody, but saying gap to indicate each time they need to draw a blank line.

You may say ____ ____ ____ (i.e., "You may say gap, gap, gap")

But ____ not the ____ ____

I hope some ____ you'll ____ ____

And the ____ will ____ ____ one.

In pairs, whispering so they don't spoil it for others, get sts to try to complete it. Give more clues if they're too young to know the song. Classcheck.

Elicit name of artist and song, then sing it chorally. Explore what they think it's about (see song notes above). Focus on the pattern *I hope* + (*someday/one day*) + *will/ won't*, for sts to come up with similar sentences in pairs, e.g., *I hope one day I won't have to study English! I hope someday I'll be able to travel abroad*, etc. Classcheck a few sentences.

Phrasal verb list

Transitive phrasal verbs

Phrasal verb	Meaning
A	
ask someone **over**	invite someone
B	
block something **out**	prevent from passing through (light, noise)
blow something **out**	extinguish (a candle)
blow something **up**	explode; fill with air (a balloon); make larger (a photo)
bring something **about**	cause to happen
bring someone or something **back**	return
bring someone **down**	depress
bring something **out**	raise (a child)
bring someone **up**	introduce a new topic
bring something **up**	bring to someone's attention
build something **up**	increase
burn something **down**	burn completely
C	
call someone **back**	return a phone call
call someone **in**	ask for someone's presence
call something **off**	cancel
call someone **up**	contact by phone
carry something **out**	conduct an experiment / plan
cash in on something	profit
catch up on something	get recent information; do something there wasn't time for earlier
charge something **up**	charge with electricity
check someone / something **out**	examine closely
check up on someone	make sure a person is OK
cheer someone **up**	make happier
clean someone / something **up**	clean completely
clear something **up**	clarify
close something **down**	force (a business / store) to close
come away with something	learn something useful
come down to something	be the most important point
come down with something	get an illness
come up against someone / something	be faced with a difficult person / situation
come up with something	invent
count on someone / something	depend on
cover something **up**	cover completely; conceal to avoid responsibility
cross something **out**	draw a line through
cut something **down**	bring down (a tree); reduce
cut someone **off**	interrupt someone
cut something **off**	remove; stop the supply of
cut something **out**	remove; stop doing an action
cut something **up**	cut into small pieces
D	
do something **over**	do again
do someone / something **up**	make more beautiful
draw something **together**	unite
dream something **up**	invent
drink something **up**	drink completely
drop someone / something **off**	take someplace
drop out of something	quit

Phrasal verb	Meaning
E	
empty something **out**	empty completely
end up with something	have an unexpected result
F	
face up to something	accept something unpleasant
fall back on something	use an old idea
fall for someone	feel romantic love
fall for something	be tricked into believing
figure someone / something **out**	understand with thought
fill someone **in**	explain
fill something **in**	complete with information
fill something **out**	complete (a form)
fill something **up**	fill completely
find something **out**	learn information
fix something **up**	redecorate (a home); solve
follow something **through** / **follow through on** something	complete
G	
get something **across**	help someone understand
get around to something	finally do something
get away with something	avoid the consequences
get back at someone	retaliate, harm someone (for an offense or wrong act)
get off something	leave (a bus, train, plane)
get on something	board (a bus, train, plane)
get out of something	leave (a car); avoid doing something
get something **out of** something	benefit from
get through with something	finish
get to someone	upset someone
get to something	reach
get together with someone	meet
give something **away**	give something no longer needed or wanted
give something **back**	return
give something **out**	distribute
give something **up**	quit
give up on someone / something	stop hoping for change / trying to make something happen
go after someone / something	try to get / win
go along with something	agree
go over something	review
go through with something	finish / continue something difficult
grow out of something	stop doing (over time, as one becomes an adult)
H	
hand something **in**	submit
hand something **out**	distribute
hang something **up**	put on a hanger or hook
help someone **out**	assist
K	
keep someone or something **away**	cause to stay at a distance
keep something **on**	not remove (clothing / jewelry)
keep someone or something **out**	prevent from entering
keep up with someone	stay in touch
keep up with someone or something	go as fast as

Phrasal verb list

Phrasal verb	Meaning
L	
lay someone **off**	fire for economic reasons
lay something **out**	arrange
leave something **on**	not turn off (a light or appliance); not remove (clothing or jewelry)
leave something **out**	not include, omit
let someone **down**	disappoint
let someone / something **in**	allow to enter
let someone **off**	allow to leave (a bus, train); not punish
let someone / something **out**	allow to leave
light something **up**	illuminate
look after someone / something	take care of
look down on someone	think one is better, disparage
look into something	research
look out for someone	watch, protect
look someone / something **over**	examine
look someone / something **up**	try to find
look up to someone	admire, respect
M	
make something **up**	invent
make up for something	do something to apologize
miss out on something	lose the chance
move something **around**	change location
P	
pass something **out**	distribute
pass someone / something **up**	reject, not use
pay someone **back**	repay, return money
pay someone **off**	bribe
pay something **off**	pay a debt
pick someone / something **out**	identify, choose
pick someone **up**	give someone a ride
pick someone / something **up**	lift
pick something **up**	get / buy; learn something; answer the phone; get a disease
point someone / something **out**	indicate, show
put something **away**	return to its appropriate place
put something **back**	return to its original place
put someone **down**	treat with disrespect
put something **down**	stop holding
put something **off**	delay
put something **on**	get dressed / add jewelry (to the body)
put something **together**	assemble, build
put something **up**	build, erect
put up with someone / something	accept without complaining
R	
run into someone	meet
run out of something	not have enough
S	
see something **through**	complete
send something **back**	return
send something **out**	mail
set something **off**	cause to go off, explode
set something **up**	establish; prepare for use
settle on something	choose after consideration
show someone / something **off**	display the best qualities
shut something **off**	stop (a machine, light, supply)
sign someone **up**	register
stand up for someone / something	support
start something **over**	begin again
stick with / to someone / something	not quit, persevere
straighten something **up**	make neat
switch something **on**	start, turn on (a machine, light)

Phrasal verb	Meaning
T	
take something **away**	remove
take something **back**	return; accept an item; retract a statement
take something **down**	remove (a hanging item)
take something **in**	notice, remember; make a clothing item smaller
take something **off**	remove clothing, jewelry
take someone **on**	hire
take something **on**	agree to a task
take someone **out**	invite and pay for someone
take something **out**	borrow from the library
take something **up**	start a new activity (as a habit)
talk someone **into**	persuade
talk something **over**	discuss
team up with someone	start to work with, do a task together
tear something **down**	destroy, demolish
tear something **up**	tear into small pieces
think back on something	remember
think something **over**	consider
think something **up**	invent, think of a new idea
throw something **away / out**	discard, put in the garbage / trash
touch something **up**	improve with small changes
try something **on**	put on to see if it fits, is desirable (clothing, shoes)
try something **out**	use an item / do an activity to see if it's desirable
turn something **around**	turn so the front faces the back; cause to get better
turn someone / something **down**	reject
turn something **down**	lower the volume / heat
turn someone **in**	identify to the police (after a crime)
turn something **in**	submit
turn someone / something **into**	change from one type or form to another
turn someone **off**	cause to lose interest, feel negatively
turn something **off**	stop (a machine / light)
turn something **on**	start (a machine / light)
turn something **out**	make, manufacture
turn something **over**	turn so the bottom is on the top
turn something **up**	raise (the volume / heat)
U	
use something **up**	use completely, consume
W	
wake someone **up**	cause to stop sleeping
walk out on someone	leave a spouse / child / romantic relationship
watch out for someone	protect
wipe something **out**	remove, destroy
work something **out**	calculate mathematically; solve a problem
write something **down**	create a written record (on paper)
write something **up**	write in a finished form

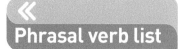

Intransitive phrasal verbs

Phrasal verb	Meaning
A	
act up	behave inappropriately
B	
blow up	explode; suddenly become angry
break down	stop functioning
break out	start suddenly (a war, fire, disease)
burn down	burn completely
C	
call back	return a phone call
carry on	continue doing something; behave in a silly / emotional way
catch on	become popular
check in	report arrival (at a hotel, airport)
check out	pay a bill and leave (a hotel)
cheer up	become happier
clear up	become better (a rash, infection; the weather)
close down	stop operating (a business)
come along	go with, accompany
come back	return
come down	become lower (a price)
come in	enter
come off	become unattached
come out	appear; be removed (a stain)
come up	arise (an issue)
D	
dress up	wear more formal clothes; a costume
drop in	visit unexpectedly
drop out	quit
E	
eat out	eat in a restaurant
empty out	empty completely
end up	do something unexpected; reach a final location / conclusion
F	
fall off	become unattached
fill out	become bigger
fill up	become completely full
find out	learn new information
follow through	finish, complete something
fool around	have fun (in a silly way)
G	
get ahead	make progress, succeed
get along	have a good relationship
get back	return
get by	survive
get off	leave (a bus, train)
get on	board (a bus, train)
get through	finish; survive
get together	meet
get up	get out of bed
give up	quit
go along	accompany; agree
go away	leave a place
go back	return
go down	decrease (a price, number)
go off	explode, detonate
go on	continue
go out	leave (a building / home); socialize
go over	succeed (an idea / speech)
go up	increase (a price, number); be built
grow up	become an adult

Phrasal verb	Meaning
H	
hang up	end a phone call
help out	do something helpful, useful
hold on	wait (often during a phone call)
K	
keep away	stay at a distance
keep on	continue
keep out	not enter
keep up	maintain speed / momentum
L	
lie down	recline (on a bed / floor / sofa)
light up	illuminate; look pleased, happy
look out	be careful
M	
make up	end an argument
miss out	lose the chance (for something good)
P	
pass out	become unconscious, faint
pay off	be worthwhile
pick up	improve
play around	have fun, not be serious
R	
run out	leave suddenly; not have enough (a supply)
S	
show up	appear
sign up	register
sit down	sit
slip up	make a mistake
stand up	rise (to one's feet)
start over	begin again
stay up	not go to bed
straighten up	make neat
T	
take off	leave, depart (a plane)
turn in	go to sleep
turn out	have a certain result
turn up	appear
W	
wake up	stop sleeping
watch out	be careful
work out	exercise; end successfully

Richmond
58 St Aldates
Oxford
OX1 1ST
United Kingdom

ISBN: 978-84-668-2084-4
DL: M-4706-2016
First Edition: February 2016

Publishing Director: Deborah Tricker

Editors: Laura Miranda, Shona Rodger

Proofreaders: Emma Clarke, Tania Pattison, Sophie Sherlock

Project and Cover Design: Lorna Heaslip

Layout: Oliver Hutton (H D Design), Dave Kuzmicki

Picture Researcher: Magdalena Mayo

Illustrators: Iker Ayestaran, Ricardo Bessa, Paul Boston, Ben Challenor, Dermot Flynn, Matt Latchford, María Díaz Perera, Nick Radford

Digital Content: Luke Baxter

Audio Recording: Motivation Sound Studios

Photos:
Prats i Camps; S. Enríquez; 123RF; 500PX MARKETPLACE/ Olya Mruwka; A. G. E. FOTOSTOCK; ALAMY/STOCKFOLIO, David Noton Photography, jeremy sutton-hibbert, C12, Blend Images, Zuma Press Inc., ZUMA Press, Inc., Darren Robb, Lasse Kristensen, OJO Images Ltd, Aleksandr Bryliaev, Jan Hanus, B Christopher, Chuck Nacke, Vanessa Miles, Chris Rout, Eyecandy Images, Trinity Mirror / Mirrorpix, PhotoAlto sas, Stock Experiment, AF archive, Pictorial Press Ltd, Malcro, ZUMA Press, Inc, dpa picture alliance, Glasshouse Images, Fine Art, Pictorial Press Ltd., Wavebreak Media ltd, Eddie Gerald, Oleksandr Prykhodko, Mint Images Limited, ClassicStock, Dmitri Maruta, Keystone Pictures USA, Heritage Image Partnership Ltd, GL Archive, Golden Pixels LLC, Daniel Kaesler, epa european pressphoto agency b.v., Anatolii Babii; BROOKSIDE MUSEUM/ Saratoga County Historical Society; CARTOONSTOCK/ Marty Bucella, Mike Flanagan; CORDON PRESS/Kevin Dodge; FOTONONSTOP; FOURSQUARE; GETTY IMAGES SALES SPAIN/ Sean Gallup, Planet Flem, PeskyMonkey, Wonwoo Lee, Timur Emek, Stockbyte, Anna Pena, filo, Thinkstock, Kevin Winter, E+, Paul Popper/Popperfoto, Hill Street Studios, Ulrich Baumgarten, franckreporter, FineCollection, Ullstein Bild, Steve Granitz, Peter Dazeley, Jupiterimages, Jamie Farrant, Photos.com Plus, Bernhard Lang, Steve Hansen, Sergei Kozak, PhotoAlto/Sigrid Olsson, Michael Tran; HIGHRES PRESS STOCK/AbleStock.com; INSTAGRAM; ISTOCKPHOTO/Daniel Rodríguez Quintana, Getty Images Sales Spain, Alina Solovyova-Vincent, YekoPhotoStudio, Peeter Viisimaa, digitalskillet, andresrimaging, worananphoto, Doug Bennett, Amanda Rohde, spinmysugar, shapecharge, caracterdesign, Yuri_Arcurs, damircudic, zlomari, andresr, Maridav, Nikada, rionm, DNY59; MAYANG MURNI ADNIN/www.mayang.com; PHOTODISC; REX SHUTTERSTOCK/Mars One/ Bryan Versteeg, Johnathan Hordle, Albanpix Ltd., Steve Meddle, Taipei Zoo, Sipa Press, Olycom SPA, MediaPunch, Startraks, Jim Smeal, Okauchi, ANL; VINE LABS, INC; Oliver Hutton; Doug Savage; Howdini.com/Touchstorm; Jennifer L. Price, PhD, Associate Professor of Psychology, Georgetown College; Mark Wolter www.woltersworld.com; Amanda Leroux; CREATIVE LABS; SERIDEC PHOTOIMAGENES CD; ARCHIVO SANTILLANA

Printed in Brazil by Forma Certa Gráfica Digital
Lote: 808113
Codigo: 290520844 / 2025